INTERNATIONAL MANAGEMENT
A Strategic Perspective

INTERNATIONAL MANAGEMENT
A Strategic Perspective

Rajib N. Sanyal

The College of New Jersey

UPPER SADDLE RIVER, NEW JERSEY

Library of Congress Cataloging-in-Publication Data

Sanyal, Rajib N.
    International management : a strategic perspective / Rajib N. Sanyal
      p. cm.
    Includes bibliographical references and index.
    ISBN 0-201-47153-1
    1. International business enterprises.   I. Title.

HD62.4.S265 2001
658′.049—dc21   00-062413

Editorial Director: James Boyd
Acquisitions Editor: Melissa Steffens
Managing Editor: John Sisson
Editorial Assistant: Samantha Steel
Assistant Editor: Jessica Sabloff
Media Project Manager: Michele Faranda
Executive Marketing Manager: Michael Campbell
Production/Manufacturing Manager: Gail Steier de Acevedo
Production Coordinator: Maureen Wilson
Senior Prepress/Manufacturing Manager: Vincent Scelta
Cover Design: Kiwi Design
Cover Art/Photo: Zoxox Digital/Stone
Composition: BookMasters, Inc.

10 9 8 7 6 5 4 3 2 1
ISBN 0-201-47153-1

To TheoRishi and Tracy, with love

CONTENTS

༄

PREFACE

❧

International Management: A Strategic Perspective is designed to be used as a textbook for a one-semester or one-quarter undergraduate course or as an introductory or background reading in graduate programs. The book consists of 12 chapters, but the coverage of topics is extensive with many student-centered exercises. These features provide the flexibility that an instructor needs to adapt the textbook content to fit the class schedule of either a semester or a quarter. Most students studying international management would have taken a prior course in management such as Principles of Management or Management of Organizational Behavior. This prerequisite is relevant as this textbook is written for the well-prepared student. The focus is on management and, even though it is acknowledged that in international business, finance and economics play critical roles, the treatment of these subjects is less detailed but nevertheless adequate for the reader to recognize and relate their relevance.

International Management: A Strategic Perspective is about how managers in firms, big or small, are affected by key environmental factors, such as politics and culture, and how they approach and resolve the differences and difficulties posed by international business opportunities and competition. The book presents a most up-to-date discussion of the contemporary managerial issues in international business and is firmly grounded in the twin dimensions of academic research and real-life business applications. Thus, the reader will find throughout the text a seamless transition between theory and practice with numerous current corporate examples drawn from countries, industries, and businesses around the world. These examples buttress scholarly findings while also illuminating successful or unsuccessful managerial practices. The writing is designed to keep the reader engaged in a dynamic subject, and a variety of end-of-chapter materials, including comprehensive case studies that have been extensively classroom tested, enable a deeper inquiry and analysis of the subject.

Scholars often debate the domains of international business and international management. International management is a subset of international business, the latter encompassing all aspects of doing business, which includes marketing, finance, accounting, and information systems, among others. In contrast, international management is much more focused, concentrating on the manager and the managerial functions of planning, organizing, controlling, and leading. Of course, the international firm and the manager do not function in a vacuum; the environment of international business in terms of laws, cultural mores, economic conditions, exchange rate changes, and so on affect the nature, scope, and consequences of managerial actions. Recognizing this distinctive nature of international management, this text takes the slant of how managers organize the firm to take advantage of various business opportunities at home and abroad, and what practices to adopt under what circumstances.

Many colleges and universities around the world are providing comprehensive educational programs that have a pronounced international thrust at both graduate and undergraduate levels to train people for positions in international firms, government agencies, nongovernmental organizations, and international institutions. In the United States, the main accreditation organization for business schools, American Assembly of Collegiate Schools of Business (AACSB), requires a strong component of international business in the curriculum. University programs have become more sophisticated and include such features as foreign language proficiency, study abroad, international guided travel, executives-in-residence, and internships in international firms, in addition to extensive coursework. More and more firms are placing fresh college/university recruits into tracks designed to build them into global managers. Overseas appointments, which at one time came much later in one's career, now often come at the outset of careers. This textbook provides a student with a comprehensive overview of the key managerial issues that a firm engaged in international business has to address and how they are being addressed.

ORGANIZATION OF THE BOOK

Throughout the book, the term *international firm* is used frequently. It is a generic and broad term used to describe any firm that is engaged in international business whether as exporters or importers, as licensors or licensees, as partners of strategic alliances or joint ventures, or as owners of businesses overseas. The reader will find the use of this term uncomplicated and effective in understanding the nature of management in the international arena. The term *multinational firm* is also used to refer to specific firms that are headquartered in one country and have operations in more than one country.

The 12 chapters in this book are presented in four parts. The following diagram presents the book's structure and the interrelationship among the topics. Both culture and politics constitute the external environment of international management and they affect the international firm and its sense of social and ethical responsibility. Internal to the firm is the main subject of strategy determination and formulation, which leads to selecting alternative or multiple methods of doing international business—trading (exporting and importing), licensing (and franchising), and equity/nonequity investments. Whatever form of business is selected, it gives rise to the attendant issues of organizing the firm in a way that the strategic goals are realized. Because management is also a matter of employing, motivating, and retaining employees to implement the work of the firm, the issues connected with both the managerial staff as well as the rank and file employees are discussed.

Part I discusses the environment of business today and the role of the manager in the international firm. The first three chapters set the stage for learning about specific firm behaviors.

Chapter 1 describes the place of the firm in today's international business environment, the growing importance of international management, and the characteristics of the successful manager. The material in the chapter serves as the foundation for learning about the managerial choices and skills required to make a firm function successfully in the international environment.

Chapters 2 and 3 expand on the environment of business by discussing the roles of national governments and national cultures. In Chapter 2, the focus is on the role of cul-

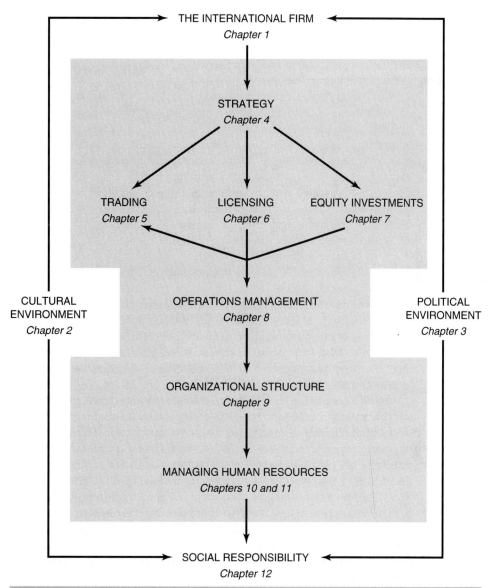

THE INTERNATIONAL FIRM
Chapter 1

STRATEGY
Chapter 4

TRADING
Chapter 5

LICENSING
Chapter 6

EQUITY INVESTMENTS
Chapter 7

CULTURAL
ENVIRONMENT
Chapter 2

OPERATIONS MANAGEMENT
Chapter 8

POLITICAL
ENVIRONMENT
Chapter 3

ORGANIZATIONAL STRUCTURE
Chapter 9

MANAGING HUMAN RESOURCES
Chapters 10 and 11

SOCIAL RESPONSIBILITY
Chapter 12

Diagram 1 Organization of the Book

ture in molding societies and business practices. Various paradigms on categorizing and understanding cultures are presented. In addition, the chapter illustrates how managers can adapt to specific cultural differences and successfully pursue the firm's strategic goals. Chapter 3 examines the demands that managers face from various sovereign governments with regard to running the business and the compromises they make. Because politics is a crucial factor in the environment of international business, the chapter looks at how managers anticipate, prepare for, and reduce, if not eliminate, the risk posed to their operations by a range of governmental activities.

Part II of the book focuses on the strategy formulation and foreign market entry choices. Four chapters examine these issues. The thrust of Chapter 4 is on how firms formulate their strategies to compete successfully. Two alternative strategies, one focusing on efficiency of the firm and the other on the firm responding to national differences, are examined in detail. The chapter also looks at some of the strategic issues faced by multinational firms such as developing and protecting core competencies of the firm.

Chapters 5, 6, and 7 study the management dimensions of various international business arrangements. The topic of Chapter 5 is exporting and importing with the latter including offshore sourcing. It also presents a discussion of trading companies. Chapter 6 examines licensing and franchising as international business activities and the managerial issues connected with them. In Chapter 7, the emphasis is on the management issues associated with ownership-related activities such as joint ventures and wholly owned subsidiaries. The chapter also discusses the strategic opportunities and the managerial challenges inherent in strategic alliances.

Part III looks at how the firm goes about organizing itself both in terms of creating its chain of value-adding activities as well as how it is set up in terms of departments, flow of authority, and locus of decision making. Chapter 8 examines the management of logistics issues, such as site selection for plant and facilities, the role of transportation, designing the operations process, and quality control. To run a business successfully and achieve its strategic goals, the firm has to be organized appropriately. Several alternative organizational structures are presented and evaluated in Chapter 9. The chapter also examines the issues of centralization and decentralization of decision making, the nature of the control system, and some of the mechanisms used by firms for enforcing control.

Part IV focuses on the subject of managing human resources in the international environment as well as on the issues of ethics and social responsibility. Chapters 10 and 11 deal with the human resource dimensions of international management. In Chapter 10, the emphasis is on recruiting, selecting, training, and compensating managers, especially those who are posted abroad. The chapter also looks at how firms deal with managers returning home after a period of duty abroad and the special circumstances of women managers. The material in Chapter 11 looks at the human resource aspects of the rank and file workers. An extensive discussion sorts out how the presence of labor unions among a work force complicates the managerial function. Labor unions in the home country historically have opposed overseas investment by firms seeing it as a threat to the continued employment of its members. Thus, managers have to deal with labor relations both in the home and the host country.

In the final chapter of this book, Chapter 12, the topic centers on the dilemmas posed by ethical choices in international operations and the exercise of social responsibility. The chapter also looks at how the international firm is affected by voluntary codes of conduct and how such firms try to influence host governments to avoid strict scrutiny of their practices.

ACKNOWLEDGMENTS

I would be remiss in my responsibilities if I did not acknowledge the value of the extensive comments and suggestions made by two teams of reviewers. Much of the improvement of this book can be credited to the following people.

Laurel Adams, Northwestern University; Trevor Bain, University of Alabama; John W. Clarry, Montclair State University; Andrew Delios, Hong Kong University of Science and Technology; Alan Ellstrand, California State University-Long Beach; David Flanagan, Western Michigan University; Maureen Flemming, University of Montana; Turgut Guvenli, Minnesota State University-Mankato; Erdener Kaynak, Pennsylvania State University; John Kilpatrick, Idaho State University; Hema Krishnan, Xavier University; Mike Lee, California State University; Douglas McCabe, Georgetown University; Ray Montagno, Ball State University; Leslie E. Palich, Baylor University; Carol Sanchez, Grand Valley State University; Manuel G. Serapio, University of Colorado at Denver; Nader H. Shooshtari, University of Montana; Bob Spagnola, Colorado State University; John Stanbury, Indiana University of Kokomo; Ken Tillery, Middle Tennessee State University; Fairlee Winfield, Northern Arizona University; Frederick M. Zimmerman, University of St. Thomas (MN).

I am especially indebted to the students at The College of New Jersey who have taken my international management course over the years. The classroom discussions, the case analyses, and their insightful comments provided me the encouragement and the ideas on what and how to present the material in the book. I am also grateful to Melissa Steffens at Prentice Hall for her constant encouragement and reassurance and for managing so competently the entire editing and publication process. Last but not least, the most important thanks go to my wife Tracy and son TheoRishi. This acknowledgment is more than a mere familial obligation. They suffered patiently through the years sacrificing much so that I could pursue and complete this project. To them, I dedicate this book.

1

THE INTERNATIONAL FIRM AND THE MANAGER

OPENING VIGNETTE

Philip Morris, a U.S. tobacco company facing costly lawsuits and tough regulations at home, began to look overseas for new markets and profits. Turkey provided an attractive market. Forty-three percent of its 63 million people smoked compared with 25 percent in the United States. More importantly, while smoking was declining in the United States, it was growing at an average annual rate of 4.75 percent in Turkey, making it one of the fastest growing markets in the world.

Turkish smokers got their first taste of Philip Morris brands such as Marlboro in the 1970s when smuggled, tax-free American cigarettes began appearing in Turkish cities. The exclusive right to sell tobacco in Turkey had long been in the hands of a state-owned monopoly organization, Tekel. Tekel's antiquated factories produced harsh cigarettes made from local tobacco. It did not deliver its products to wholesalers and retailers, which meant the distributors had to travel to Tekel's warehouses to pick up inventory. Furthermore, it did not advertise.

Philip Morris obtained the right to sell its cigarettes in Turkey in 1984 when the country's then-prime minister, as part of an ambitious effort to modernize the country, ordered Tekel to import and distribute foreign cigarettes. Tekel, however, retained the right to price as well as the right to distribute cigarettes—both domestic and foreign. That advantage proved useful to Tekel in 1988 when it launched Tekel 2000, a cigarette blended with American tobacco leaves designed to compete with Marlboro. Priced about 25 cents lower than a standard 20-cigarette pack of Marlboros at the time, Tekel 2000 quickly won a quarter of the market.

Arguing that it could not survive in Turkey unless it had the right to price and distribute its own products, Philip Morris lobbied the Turkish government to eliminate its control over tobacco prices and distribution. The company offered something the government badly wanted: millions of dollars to invest in the country in new factories. Philip Morris said it would not invest that money unless Tekel gave up control.

The company enlisted the help of Mr. Sakip Sabanci, one of Turkey's most powerful businessmen, to argue its case. Apart from being a scion of one of the wealthiest families in the world, he also enjoyed close ties with the prime minister, who once served as chief executive of the company.

All around us we find products and services, employers, suppliers, workers, and customers with a foreign dimension. The morning newspaper and the evening television program invariably carry news of international business transactions and of economic and political developments in far-off lands but with repercussions felt close to home. Indeed, today's business is international in scope. The world economy is increasingly integrated, and multinational firms are key business entities. Business activities are taking place on a global, not national basis. The growth of world trade in goods and services has gone hand-in-hand with investment by firms in overseas plants and facilities. New forms of business arrangements have emerged. Although large firms, usually from the developed countries, have come to dominate trade and investment, many other, often smaller, firms are now engaged in international business. It is difficult to find any firm or industry that is not affected, either directly or indirectly, by the internationalization of business activities.

The extension of business from a domestic to an international setting challenges the firm to work with and adjust to certain features of the international environment, such as multiple regulatory agencies, foreign currency rate changes, and cross-cultural differences. As trade and investment opportunities have opened up on a worldwide basis, the managers of traditionally domestic-focused firms have had to prepare and train themselves accordingly. Organizational structures, business strategies, production processes, and human resource practices have to be redesigned to enable the firm to compete successfully in this new business setting. This introductory chapter lays out the distinctive dimensions of international management, the process by which a firm internationalizes, the qualities and skills needed by international managers, and an overview of the managerial issues that arise while doing business across countries.

WHAT IS INTERNATIONAL MANAGEMENT?

International management involves planning, organizing, leading, and controlling the people working in an organization on a worldwide basis in order to achieve the organization's goals. The management of the organization takes place in a global context where the four managerial functions—planning, organizing, leading, and controlling—are performed in multiple, as opposed to single, political, cultural, and economic environments. The focus of much of the material in this book is on the strategic dimensions of international management, particulary the micro aspects. However, the macro dimensions of the subject—the overall political and cultural environment in which the firm operates—are covered in the introductory chapters to provide the reader with an understanding of the complex context in which the international manager functions.

Today, all business is international business. Few firms are not directly or indirectly engaged in international business or affected by international forces. Indeed, a business ignores the forces of global commerce at its own peril. Even the small fishing tackle shop beside a country lake in central Pennsylvania is not immune to the opportunities and threats of international business. Even though the shop may carry only locally made lures and baits and sell only to local fishermen, its business can be hurt severely should the local Kmart store decide to carry a line of cheaper, flashier, and equally effective lures made in Taiwan. Thus, the tackle shop manager, to retain customers, must do what is needed to keep the business competitive. In this way, even the smallest of business, without any apparent international business connections, is in fact, fully exposed to international competition.

At the other end of this spectrum are huge corporations such as Coca-Cola or Intel. These firms with billions of dollars in assets and sales all over the world compete in major world markets by designing and producing goods on a massive scale. Organizing and managing such firms pose formidable challenges to their managers. Table 1-1 lists the world's 15 largest firms in terms of revenue. While many of the largest firms are based in advanced industrial countries, successful international firms have begun to emerge from less developed and newly industrializing countries such as Mexico (e.g., Cemex) and Taiwan (e.g., Acer).

The integration of the world economy was demonstrated when an economic crisis engulfed East Asian countries in 1997 and soon spread to other parts of the world. The crisis led to the opening up of new sectors of the economy to foreign investments (such as banking in Thailand), the bankruptcy of several big industrial groups in Korea, political turmoil in Indonesia, the cancellation of orders for airplanes made by Boeing because of declining passenger traffic, lower earnings reported by foreign firms operating in the region, sustained rates of low inflation in the United States because of cheaper imports, cancellation of major business projects because of an uncertain future, the collapse of national currencies such as the Russian ruble, and volatility in exchange rates around the world. Big and small firms were affected by the economic meltdown through their interconnection with the global business network.

International management requires a thorough understanding of the influences of economic, political, cultural, and competitive pressures on business. It also requires that the firm be able to take advantage of the opportunities afforded by international businesses. Successfully managing businesses today require selecting new forms of strategies,

Table 1-1	The World's 15 Largest Firms by Total Sales 2000			
Company	*Business*	*Country*	*Revenue ($ millions)*	*Employees (in thousands)*
General Motors	Automobile	U.S.	178,558	392.0
Wal-Mart Stores	Retailing	U.S.	165,013	1,025.0
Ford Motor	Automobile	U.S.	162,558	364.6
ExxonMobil	Energy	U.S.	160,883	115.0
DaimlerChrysler	Automobile	Germany	151,632	463.6
Toyota Motor	Automobile	Japan	120,697	214.6
General Electric	Electric/Diversified	U.S.	111,630	316.5
Royal Dutch/Shell	Energy	Netherlands/U.K.	105,366	99.0
IBM	Computer Systems	U.S.	87,548	299.2
BPAmoco	Energy	United Kingdom	83,566	88.1
AXA Group	Insurance	France	83,068	92.0
Citigroup	Financial services	U.S.	82,005	173.5
TotalFina Elf	Energy	France	75,859	127.3
Siemens Group	Electric & electronics	Germany	72,074	440.2
Allianz Worldwide	Insurance	Germany	70,305	113.6

Source: The world super 50. *Forbes.* July 24, 2000, p. 289.

negotiating creative business arrangements, constructing flexible organizational structures, employing properly trained and culturally astute people, displaying political savvy, and recognizing and resolving ethical dilemmas.

DISTINCTIVE FEATURES OF INTERNATIONAL MANAGEMENT

How does managing a firm that is active internationally differ from managing a firm that is essentially rooted within the political borders of a single nation? Certainly, the environmental variables are more numerous and some of the managerial tasks much more complex. Managers have to work with different national governments (and thus legal systems) under widely disparate economic conditions, with people of diverse culture and values, and with clients and suppliers over vast geographical distances. These factors also make doing business much more expensive. The role of governments in creating the rules of business is a defining element of international management as was illustrated in the opening vignette and is discussed in following sections. Other distinctive characteristics include the need for understanding a variety of cultural attributes and to realize that the firm's competitive strategies may have to be developed differently. Management Focus 1-1 illustrates some of the challenges of managing international operations.

MULTIPLE GOVERNMENTS AND NATIONALISM

A distinguishing dimension of international management is the number of governments that regulate and define the environment and opportunities for international trade and investment. With 185 sovereign countries in the world, national governments have the legal right to create the rules and regulations of doing business within their geographical borders. Thus, any international business activity engages at least two governments—one home, where a firm is headquartered, and the other host, where a firm is doing business.

Governments reflect, to a greater extent in democratic countries than in autocratic states, the wishes and aspirations of the majority of the people living within its defined geographical territory. The national government is the guardian of the country's resources, an advocate of its people's best interests be they commercial or otherwise, and a defender of the culture and values of its citizens. The government, through public policy and enforcement of regulations, determines the priorities in the allocation of resources, the current economic structure, as well as the status of relations with the rest of the world. Government rules impose restraints on the unfettered activities of the firm. To the extent nationalistic passions are high, a mind set of "we" versus "them" tends to develop between the residents of a country and the foreign firm, seen as an extension or agent of a foreign government. Given this extensive and overarching ability of the government to define the rules of doing business, the international managers have the challenging task of understanding, influencing, and playing by the rules. They require a high level of expertise and sophistication in working with foreign governments while at the same time devising flexible strategies and structures to make the firm function efficiently in a world where multiple regulatory authorities wield supreme power. Indeed, as national governments strive to protect and advance the interests of their own people and businesses, they collide with the efforts of foreign firms to grow. Inevitably, com-

MANAGEMENT FOCUS 1-1

DOING BUSINESS IN THE UNITED ARAB EMIRATES

In 1984, as part of a global strategy to expand to markets outside Canada, McCain Foods Limited began exporting to the Middle East. Three years later, the company decided to set up a small marketing office in Jeddah on Saudi Arabia's Red Sea coast, then its only sizable market in the Middle East. Pierre Chammas, a Canadian working for McCain in Canada, was chosen to start and manage the operation in Jeddah. Besides being an excellent salesperson, Mr. Chammas spoke Arabic, the language of Saudi Arabia.

In 1993, based on Mr. Chammas's recommendation, McCain moved its regional office to Dubai in the United Arab Emirates (UAE). Dubai was more centrally located to McCain's target market and was easier to access. It had an excellent communications system, as well as minimal registration and licensing procedures for companies operating in the Jebel Ali Free Zone. Another factor was the lifestyle, which was more western-oriented and the quality of life superior to Jeddah—important consideration for foreign managers.

McCain marketed its products from Dubai to other Gulf countries, Jordan, Egypt, Syria, and Lebanon. After moving to the UAE, the operation was run more like its Canadian counterpart—the local operation did the marketing and appointed its own distributors. In Saudi Arabia, McCain had operated with one agent who decided what products to market and how to market them.

Sales in the region represented a small percentage of the company's overall sales, but were growing at 30 percent per year. They had sustained this growth rate over the last four years and ex-pected it to continue improving. In the UAE, McCain had achieved its greatest product success with its frozen french fries, even though they cost 35 to 40 percent more than competitor's brands. Customers recognized McCain's quality and were willing to pay a premium for it.

According to Mr. Chammas, three factors were key to successfully operating in the UAE:

1. Long-term planning was essential. Training and orientation programs were necessary before posting employees to the UAE. These programs helped to avoid dissatisfaction that could arise from being unprepared. Given the importance of establishing personal relationships prior to doing business, companies had to be prepared to show a commitment to the UAE over the long term.

2. Physical presence in the country was important. Personal contact played an extremely important role in the way business was conducted. Top managers were expected to entertain clients frequently which was time consuming and expensive.

3. Managers had to be aware of the many cultural differences. For example, it was not customary to invite local businessmen to functions with their wives, because wives were not seen in public. According to Mr. Chammas, "We have learned to adapt to local attitudes and requirements. You cannot change their attitudes or customs. You must change yours instead."

Source: O'Grady, Shawna and Yusef, Shalabi. 1996. The United Arab Emirates: A lucrative oasis for business. *Business Quarterly* Summer, pp. 85–92.

promises are necessary. The international firm has to balance its own quest for growth and efficiency with the objectives of individual governments to protect and advance the interests of its own citizenry.

The role and power of governments to influence international business activities was exemplified in 1997 when the European Union (EU) opposed the acquisition of

McDonnell-Douglas by Boeing in the United States. Although the transaction was approved by U.S. regulatory authorities, the EU threatened Boeing with fines and restricted access to customers in Europe unless it made certain concessions. Although some commentators suggested that the EU's actions were designed to protect the interests of the European airplane consortium, Airbus Industrie, nevertheless, Boeing made the necessary changes so as to preserve its opportunity to sell planes to European airliners. The incident revealed the growing cooperation among national governments to regulate and facilitate the global business environment. In 1991, the EU and the U.S. antitrust authorities entered into an agreement to work together to ensure that competition is not retarded by acqusitions or predatory behaviors.[1]

INTERNATIONAL FINANCIAL MANAGEMENT

A second key distinguishing dimension of international management is the difference in **exchange rates** between the currencies of the different countries of the world. The fact that countries have their own currencies is another manifestation of the political divisions in the world. The currency serves as a distinct identifiable moniker of a country. When a firm does business internationally it often has to complete transactions in foreign currencies. Currencies that are freely (that is, with no or minimum government restrictions) convertible into other currencies are referred to as "hard" currencies, and international firms prefer to conduct transactions in them. Examples of hard currencies are the U.S. dollar, Canadian dollar, Japanese yen, and Swiss franc. "Soft" currencies are those that are expected to drop in value relative to other currencies and as a consequence, free trading in them is often restricted by the monetary authorities of the issuing country. Currencies of Third World and highly regulated countries are considered to be soft.

The rate at which one currency is exchanged for another is always changing, depending on the supply of and demand for currencies. These changes affect a firm in numerous ways. They determine key business decisions, such as where to locate a plant or facility, which country to export to, how to reduce tax liability, and how to remain price competitive. Other issues such as how to manage working capital funds, where to raise funds for both capital and current expenses, and how they impact on the profit and loss statement are also critical from a currency perspective. When more and more of a firm's sales and profits come from outside its home country, the more it is exposed to changes in exchange rates.

Various techniques are available and used by firms in efforts to reduce the impact of exchange rate fluctuations on a firm's financial condition. For example, the Toronto Blue Jays, a baseball team, earns 80 percent of its revenues in Canadian dollars but 80 percent of its expenses are in U.S. dollars. These expenses included travel, lodging, and the club's roughly $50 million payroll. To protect itself from the decline of the Canadian dollar against the U.S. dollar in the late 1990s, the team tried to forecast its cash requirements and then relied on currency experts at banks and investment houses to lock in its position by buying U.S. dollars in advance.

---

[1]*International anti-trust cooperation: Wave of the future.* 1997, Fourth quarter. European Policy Analyst. London: The Economist Intelligence Unit.

International finance is a complex and important subject and it is beyond the scope and thrust of this book to discuss these issues in depth. Appendix 1-1 at the end of this chapter presents a brief overview of foreign exchange rates and their impact on business.

A key financial statistic is the **balance of payments statement** of a country. Governments maintain accounts that keep track of the economic transactions between its own citizens and firms with those in other countries. Data about a country's economy are published by the International Monetary Fund (IMF) through a document, International Financial Statistics, in a standardized and comparative format. Economic transactions include all purchases and sales of goods and services, capital inflows and outflows, gifts made and received, and changes in a country's international reserves. The balance of payments reflects these transactions in a summarized fashion. If during a period, the total amount of money coming into a country exceeds the total amount of money leaving a country, that nation is deemed to have a balance of payments surplus. When the outflows exceed inflows, the country has a balance of payments deficit.

A country's balance of payments statement is of great value to managers, investors, consumers, and government officials because it influences (and, in turn, is influenced by) other key macroeconomic indicators such as gross national product, unemployment rate, inflation rate, interest rate, and foreign exchange rate. It also indicates how the economy is faring especially with regard to foreign trade and the flow of funds in and out of the country. In addition, a government's fiscal and monetary policy is affected by the balance of payments.

A chronic or persistent balance of payments deficit would suggest that the government of that country may put restrictions on imports (as a way to balance outflows with inflows) and limit the amount of profits, dividends, and license and other fees that can be taken out of the country (to conserve precious and dwindling reserves). The exchange rate for the currency of such a country will depreciate as the demand for that currency to buy goods and services or to make investments in that country dry up.

An altogether different set of outcomes result when a country has persistent balance of payments surplus. The exchange rate for the currency tends to appreciate, which makes the country's products more expensive abroad. The economy signals an ample amount of money to buy imported goods and services. Often, political pressure is put on such countries to reduce their surpluses by increasing imports or making payments for all sorts of causes.

Countries with unstable economies sometimes link their currencies to the stable and more easily convertible currency of another country. Latin American countries such as Ecuador and Argentina, plagued by high inflation, falling currency values, and bad macroeconomic management, have tied their currencies to the U.S. dollar. This dollarization of the economy imparts stability to an economy and raises credibility with the international business community. International business managers do not have to worry about volatile exchange rate changes or convertibility.

On January 1, 1999, 11 member countries of the European Union replaced their individual currencies with a single new currency, the **euro.**[2] This move created a currency rivaling the U.S. dollar and the Japanese yen in clout and prestige and presented an

[2]Bray, Nicholas. 1998, August 26. Chase hopes to profit from new European currency. *The Wall Street Journal,* p. B4; Vogel, Thomas. 2000, January 31. Ecuador's dollarization faces hurdles. *The Wall Street Journal,* p. A22; Marsh, Peter. 2000, January 24. Komatsu investment in doubt over euro policy. *Financial Times,* p. 6.

enormous impact on companies doing business in the European Union countries. For instance, companies with production facilities in the United Kingdom, which had not joined the euro, found that a strengthening pound made their goods uncompetitive in European markets. Foreign investors such as BMW and Komatsu urged the British government to join the euro and thus eliminate the deleterious effect of exchange rate fluctuations.

CULTURAL DIFFERENCES

Even though differences in culture can be found in many countries, international managers have to contend with even greater differences in culture and customs the further they go from their home country. Thus, for a U.S. firm, the cultural distance to be bridged when doing business with Canada is relatively minimal. In contrast, the cultural differences with Saudi Arabia are more pronounced. Language differences impact communication and negotiation, attitudes toward work affect productivity, and leadership styles vary. The different ways of doing business require adjustment and understanding.

Culture also serves as a basis to unite people against perceived encroachment by foreign ideas and practices. Consequently, governments often put restrictions on the import of certain foreign products and services, such as movies and television programs. International firms need to be sensitive to cultural proclivities to avoid both cultural gaffes and political problems.

COMPETITIVE STRATEGY

Unlike the domestic-focused business, the manager of a firm engaged directly in international business may have to devise and implement competitive strategy on a much larger geographical scale. The domestic firm responds to competitive pressures in a single market; the international firm has to consider competitive pressures and counterpressures in multiple markets. An international firm may have to enter the home market of a rival foreign firm on a large scale just to reduce the pressure from foreign competitors on its sales in its own home country. In other cases, a firm may have to be present in a foreign market for potential profits far into the future; failure to enter early may mean that prize opportunties are lost to quick-moving competitors who gain what is called **first mover's advantage.** Thus, many firms have entered India and China, sometimes with small investments, to gain a foothold and to position themselves for the future when business opportunities may turn out to be highly lucrative. Amazon.com, the world's biggest Internet bookseller based in the United States, entered the European market by establishing two sites in the United Kingdom and Germany. The overseas expansion followed the entrance into the U.S. market by Bertelsmann, the German media group which owned the world's largest book publishing and book club businesses. Bertelsmann bought 50 percent of the Internet sales arm of Barnes & Noble, the U.S. book chain, and planned to use it to sell books in both the United States and Germany. Amazon's action was to preempt the launch by Bertelsmann and to provide books at a discount to European buyers from an European site thus reducing mailing costs and delivery times.[3]

---

[3]Rawsthorn, Alice. 1998, October 12. Amazon to open U.K. and German sites. *Financial Times,* p. 19.

GROWTH IN WORLD TRADE AND INVESTMENT

Since the end of World War II phenomenal growth has taken place in trade (selling and buying) between countries and in the level of investment by foreign firms in individual countries. More countries now trade more products in more quantities than ever before. Much trade is conducted by different units of the same firm—a testimony to the multinational nature of their operations. Annual world trade in 1998 was nearly $5.5 trillion compared to around $200 billion in the early 1960s. The growth in foreign direct investment is even more dramatic, from $68 billion in 1960 to more than $3.5 trillion in 1998.[4] Although these figures are enormous, they are not without precedent. The world economy had a previous globalization phase between 1870 and 1913. In fact, in real terms, the levels of world trade in modern times did not match the values of 1913 until 1986, and no country has yet reached the 9 percent of GDP capital outflow recorded by the United Kingdom in 1913.

The contemporary growth in international trade and investment has several distinguishing features. First, technological developments mean that business communication is much more extensive and wide-ranging than before, and consequently a greater variety of products and services can be delivered across national borders. Second, international business often takes the form of subsidiaries abroad, through which a firm exports products and provides services. By 1995, some 280,000 foreign subsidiaries generated $7 trillion in global sales, which exceeded global exports of goods and services by 20 percent. The subsidiary movement has brought with it a vast array of business types, inconceivable in previous eras.

Tables 1-2 and 1-3 list the top 12 exporting and importing nations in 1965 and 1999, respectively. The 1999 listings show the emergence of East Asian countries as major trading powers and the huge increase in volume of trade in 30 years. It is worth noting

Table 1-2	Leading Exporting Nations				
1965 Rank	*Country*	*Amount ($ billions)*	*1999 Rank*	*Country*	*Amount ($ billions)*
1	U.S.	26.699	1	U.S.	685.340
2	Germany	17.912	2	Germany	539.310
3	United Kingdom	13.810	3	Japan	403.690
4	France	10.053	4	France	298.150
5	Japan	8.451	5	United Kingdom	267.320
6	Canada	8.449	6	Canada	242.820
7	Netherlands	7.343	7	Italy	230.831
8	Italy	7.198	8	China	194.719
9	Belgium	6.388	9	Hong Kong	174.719
10	Sweden	3.971	10	Netherlands	167.994
11	Australia	3.005	11	Belgium	152.713
12	Switzerland	2.941	12	South Korea	144.745

Source: International Financial Statistics Yearbook 2000. International Monetary Fund. Washington, DC.

---

[4]*International financial statistics.* 1999. International Monetary Fund. Washington, DC.

Table 1-3	Leading Importing Nations				
1965 Rank	**Country**	**Amount ($ billions)**	**1999 Rank**	**Country**	**Amount ($ billions)**
1	U.S.	23.233	1	U.S.	1,030.160
2	Germany	17.612	2	Germany	469.800
3	United Kingdom	16.128	3	United Kingdom	310.390
4	France	10.342	4	Japan	280.370
5	Netherlands	8.925	5	France	278.080
6	Canada	8.597	6	Canada	220.064
7	Japan	8.169	7	Italy	210.445
8	Italy	7.378	8	Hong Kong	177.878
9	Belgium	6.458	9	China	158.509
10	Sweden	4.377	10	Netherlands	151.802
11	Australia	3.762	11	Belgium	145.227
12	Sweden	3.642	12	Spain	140.213

Source: International Financial Statistics Yearbook 2000. International Monetary Fund. Washington, DC.

that in 1965 China's total exports were valued at only $2.56 billion and that of Singapore just $981 million. South Korean exports during this same period leaped from only $173 million to more than $140 billion.

In 1965, South Korean imports totaled $463 million; in 1999, they reached more than $115 billion. The increases for other East Asian countries are similarly huge. The foreign market is so important for some firms that the bulk of their revenues come from abroad. Table 1-4 lists some of these companies. Table 1-5 identifies the leading U.S. firms with substantial sales and assets abroad. These overseas sales may occur through exporting or through manufacturing in overseas locations.

Table 1-4	Selected Firms With Large Overseas Sales		
Name of Company	**Product Line**	**Home Country**	**Foreign Sales (% of total)**
Roche Group	Pharmaceutical	Switzerland	98
Moore Group	Business forms	Canada	92
Volvo	Automobiles	Sweden	87
Nokia	Mobile telephones	Finland	85
Michelin	Tires	France	82
Pirelli	Tires	Italy	82
Aflac	Health insurance	U.S.	81
Manpower	Temporary staffing	U.S.	77
Sony	Electronics	Japan	73
Reed Elsevier	Publishing	U.K.	72
Coca Cola	Beverage	U.S.	61
Hyundai	Conglomerate	South Korea	60

Source: Hoover's Handbook of World Business 1995–96. 1995. Austin, TX: The Reference Press; The 100 largest U.S. multinationals. *Forbes.* July 24, 2000, pp. 335–338.

Table 1-5   U.S. Companies with the Largest Non-U.S. Sales

| Company | Product Line | Total Non-U.S. Sales | | Foreign Assets | |
		($ millions)	(as % of total sales)	($ millions)	(as % of total assets)
ExxonMobil	Energy	115,464	71.8	60,130	63.9
IBM	Computer systems	50,377	57.5	14,969	43.7
Ford Motor	Automobiles	50,138	30.8	22,014	44.2
General Motors	Automobiles	46,485	26.3	12,641	38.0
General Electric	Electric/diversified	35,350	31.7	19,447	47.4
Texaco	Energy	32,700	77.1	7,109	45.2
Citigroup	Financial services	28,749	35.1	239,889	41.0
Hewlett-Packard	Computer systems	23,398	55.2	2,231	51.5
Wal-Mart Stores	Retailing	22,728	13.8	25,330	36.0
Compaq Computer	Computer systems	21,174	55.0	917	28.2

Source: Forbes. July 24, 2000, pp. 335–338.

Between 1980 and 1997, trade in services grew at double the rate of trade in goods (8.7 percent versus 4.5 percent). In 1998, services accounted for one-quarter of all trade. This growth is not surprising—services have become the dominant component of the economies of the advanced industrial nations. An example of an export of service is that of launching communication and weather satellites for governments and telecommunication companies. Most satellites are launched by agencies of the French, U.S., and Chinese governments.[5] Arianespace, a partnership of 40 European aerospace companies led by Aerospatiale of France and the French space agency, now controls about 60 percent of the world's commercial launch market and takes in about $1 billion a year. The size of the commercial market is about 200 to 240 satellites in the next eight years. In the United States, the National Aeronautics and Space Administration (NASA) launches satellites for clients worldwide as does the Chinese space agency whose launch costs are lower but whose rockets' reliability is uncertain.

Other examples of internationally traded services include banking, insurance, shipping, airline, accountancy, consulting, tourism, and education. Services are distinct from manufactured products in that they are intangible—something that is not visible or physical, making value harder to assess. They also cannot be stored and thus are highly perishable. Services often require close interaction with customers and in many cases are provided in connection with the sale of a product (such as the servicing of airplanes sold by Boeing to Japan Air Lines). The world trade in services is restricted by governments through licensing or outright bans or regulations. For example, governments negotiate treaties with each other over airline flights—their number, destination, capacity, and sometimes fares. Table 1-6 shows the world's largest exporters and importers of services.

The United States, because of its large population, high income levels, capital, human and technical resources, and business-friendly operating environment, attracts investors from foreign countries. Table 1-7 provides a list of the largest foreign investors in the United States. U.S. firms are also among the largest investors in foreign countries. Companies such as Wal-Mart, which have been traditionally domestic-focused, have

---

[5]Costly failure: Space launch of Ariane 5 is aborted. *The New York Times,* 1996, June 5. pp. D1, D5.

Table 1-6	Trade in Services (in $billions)			
Country	1977 Exports	1977 Imports	1999 Exports	1999 Imports
United States	31.09	27.63	274.76	197.49
United Kingdom	20.28	14.62	103.46	84.78
France	22.86	17.72	83.34	64.26
Germany	19.51	24.81	83.07	134.34
Japan	11.77	17.68	61.00	115.16

Source: International Financial Statistics. 2000. International Monetary Fund. Washington, DC.

Table 1-7	Largest Foreign Investors in the United States			
Company	Country	U.S. Company	Percent of Ownership	2000 Sales ($ millions)
DaimlerChrysler	Germany	DaimlerChrysler Corp.	100	73,144
		Freightliner	100	10,469
		Mercedes-Benz U.S.	100	2,458
BPAmoco	United Kingdom	BPAmoco	100	38,786
		Atlantic Richfield	100	13,055
Royal Ahold	Netherlands	Ahold USA	100	19,344
		US Foodservice	100	6,198
Sony	Japan	Sony Music Entertainment	100	
		Sony Pictures	100	21,117
		Sony Electronics	100	
Royal Dutch/Shell	Netherlands/ United Kingdom	Shell Oil	100	18,438
Toyota Motor	Japan	Toyota Motor Mfg.	100	10,600
		New United Motor Mfg.	50	4,700
		Denso International America	100	2,563
Diageo	United Kingdom	Burger King	100	10,900
		Pillsbury	100	5,936
		United Distillers & Vintners	100	703
ING Group	Netherlands	ING North America Insurance	100	14,197
		ING Barings (U.S.)	100	800
Deutsche Bank	Germany	Deutsche Bank Americas	100	14,500
		DB Alex Brown	100	
Tyco International	Bermuda	Tyco International (U.S.)	100	14,409

Source: Forbes. July 24, 2000, pp. 342–348.

expanded overseas by opening stores in Latin America, Canada, Germany, and the United Kingdom. By 1999, foreign sales accounted for 13 percent of the company's total sales.[6]

WHY DO FIRMS TRADE AND INVEST ABROAD?

Various theories explain the international expansion of business. These theories provide useful insights into the motivation and behavior of firms expanding overseas. Four well-known theories explaining international trade are presented here.

Theory of Absolute Advantage   Advanced by Adam Smith in 1776, he suggested that a country will specialize in the production of that product for which it is uniquely suited, when more of the product could be produced for less than other countries who are not similarly endowed. The country would then trade its excess production with other countries who specialize in producing goods for which they are suited. Thus, given its climate, soil conditions, and labor supply, Sri Lanka can produce tea less expensively than most other countries. Similarly, New Zealand, given its climate, land supply, and technical skills, can produce mutton less expensively than most other countries. Sri Lanka and New Zealand have absolute advantage in the production of these two products respectively and by specializing, they can sell these products to each other. Firms in Sri Lanka are more likely to be in the tea business, and firms in New Zealand are more likely to be in the meat business.

Theory of Comparative Advantage   In 1819, David Ricardo extended Smith's ideas to suggest that a country should specialize in producing that good in which it has a comparative advantage over other countries, without regard to absolute advantage. For instance, New Zealand and Australia both raise millions of sheep and are thus big producers of wool and mutton. The sheep are either the wool variety or the mutton variety. Let us assume that the production functions for the two countries are as follows:

	New Zealand	*Australia*
Hours required to produce 1 kilogram of wool	4	6
Hours required to produce 1 kilogram of mutton	8	10

The production function clearly shows that New Zealand has an absolute advantage in producing both wool and mutton because it takes less time to produce a given amount of either product than in Australia. What should New Zealand do? Specialize in both wool and mutton production? Only wool? Only mutton? In New Zealand, the ratio of wool to mutton is 4:8 or 1:2 while in Australia the ratio is 6:10 or 1:1.67. Thus, Australia can exchange 1 unit of wool for 2 units of mutton by trading with New Zealand instead of getting only 1.67 of mutton in Australia itself. Thus, Australia has a comparative advantage in producing wool and New Zealand has the comparative advantage in producing mutton and hence, each country should specialize accordingly.

---

[6]Zajac, Brian. 1998, July 27. Yankee travelers. *Forbes,* p. 162; Edgecliffe-Johnson, Andrew. 2000, January 29. Does Wal-Mart have a surprise in store? *Financial Times,* p. 10.

Factor Proportions Theory   Developed by Eli Heckscher and Bertil Ohlin, the theory states the production of a good requires a combination of labor and capital as mediated by technology. Countries with relatively large resources of labor and small resources of capital would have lower labor costs and higher capital costs. Hence, a country such as China with its huge population should specialize in the production and export of labor-intensive products such as clothing. On the other hand, Sweden possesses relatively abundant capital but not labor and hence should specialize and export capital intensive goods such as luxury automobiles.

Overlapping Product Ranges Theory   Steffan Linder argued that trade in manufactured goods was dictated not by cost concerns but rather by the similarity in product demands across countries. Countries that would see the most trade are those with similar per capita income levels for consumers and would have similar tastes, sophistication, and resources. Thus, home-based businesses would know that people in another country with similar income levels would buy the same products and would export accordingly. This theory explains why trade is so intense between developed countries such as the United States and Canada and where the items exported by each other are similar.

Foreign investment has also been explained by various theories and two of them are presented here.

Product Life Cycle Theory   Raymond Vernon advanced a theory that focused on the product, and not country, as an explanation for the investment behavior of firms. According to Vernon the firm initially develops a new product in its home country. A plant is built to supply the new product to the home market. As the product matures and the production process becomes standardized, new competitors emerge, and the firm, to maintain sales and profits, increases exports. In the final stage, the product becomes completely standardized in its manufacture, profit margins are thin, and competition is fierce. The product is less profitable. To reduce costs, the firm looks for low-cost production sites, and moves its plant abroad. This theory explains why companies move their production operations, how export destinations change, and why firms change from export to investment.

Theory of Foreign Direct Investment   Firms are motivated to invest overseas for many reasons including obtaining access to key supplies (raw materials, knowledge, and labor), to seek new markets especially if the domestic market is small, and to reduce costs. Government policies around the world have created imperfections in the market place and international investment by firms is a way to exploit these market imperfections. According to John Dunning's eclectic theory, foreign direct investment as opposed to other market entry options such as exporting or licensing, occurs when three conditions are met: (1) location advantage, (2) ownership advantage, and (3) internalization advantage. Location advantage means that having business operations in a foreign location is more profitable for the firm. Direct investment enables the firm to retain ownership, and thus control, over proprietary information such as brand name, technology, and production processes. By controlling the operations in the foreign location, the firm avoids the risk of losing its core competencies and the unique knowledge of how to run its business. By producing on its own, the firm internalizes its capabilities without the need to share them with other firms.

A major reason to trade or invest abroad is the need for continued growth in sales and profits. Slowing sales in the domestic market is a strong motivator. Tupperware, a maker of plastic containers for household use, based in Orlando, Florida, earned 85 percent of its $1.36 billion sales in 1995 from overseas.[7] Tupperware, facing declining business in the United States, pushed aggressively abroad. More than 40 percent of its sales came from Europe, Africa, and the Middle East. In 1995, the company's representatives hosted about 13 million Tupperware parties in more than 100 countries. In 1996, it entered the two emerging giants of the global economy: India and China. Tupperware's domestic business in the United States fell as more women entered the workforce and were unable or unwilling to attend sales parties, and as stores such as Wal-Mart offered cheaper alternative products. Domestic sales had fallen in six of the last nine years, for a total decline of 37 percent.

Firms also go abroad to raise capital, as the role of brokerage firms, showcased in Management Focus 1-2, discusses. In many countries, capital markets are either small or undeveloped. For new companies, especially in high-technology where the product is unproven, getting capital for development and expansion is difficult. Brokerage houses provide help to such firms to raise capital.

The behavior of Spanish firms is an example of the forces and reasoning that underlie expansion and contraction in international business.[8] Following Spain's entry into the EU in 1986, the long-protected Spanish companies were exposed to new competition from firms elsewhere in Europe. Spanish companies tried to grow to face the new onslaught but found that they had little to offer other European companies in terms of management or technology, and they did not have the resources to acquire big companies in the other more advanced European countries. So they turned to Latin America, a region with which Spain has had close cultural ties for more than 500 years. Most countries in Latin America were suffering from high debt, stagnation, and inflation. Spanish firms found that in comparison, their technology was not outdated, the language and culture was similar, and they could afford to acquire big stakes in Latin American companies. This situation resulted in a spate of acquisitions by Spanish firms. For instance, since 1990 Telefonica, part-government owned phone company, acquired controlling stakes in the phone companies of Chile, Argentina, and Peru and a minority stake in Venezuela, and provides other phone services in Mexico and Puerto Rico. The company's overseas operations contributed more than one-fifth of Telefonica's annual profit.

Thus, the likelihood of bigger profits due to lower production costs or the ability to mark up prices, the presence of unique products or technology, exclusive knowledge of foreign consumers and markets, tax benefits and incentives, and economies of large-scale operations may all encourage a firm to internationalize. Similarly, competition from foreign firms, overproduction, limited resources to exploit a new technology, declining domestic sales, excess capacity, and nearness to foreign markets may all compel managers to look at international markets.

---

[7]Hilsenrath, Jon E. 1996, May 26. Is Tupperware dated? Not in the global market. *The New York Times,* p. F3.
[8]Looking for gold: Spanish firms discover Latin America business as new world of profit. *The Wall Street Journal,* 1996, May 23. pp. A1, A9.

A BROKERAGE FIRM GOES INTERNATIONAL

Cowen & Company, a New York–based brokerage house, provided the necessary services to foreign high-technology firms to make their initial public offering. As foreign firms have sought the U.S. financial markets to raise capital, the revenues of firms like Cowen & Company have doubled over the last three years, and the return on capital was now about 50 percent. In the year ending March 1996, the firm managed seven new public offerings for foreign high-technology and health care companies. As a result, Cowen had climbed up the list of firms that managed initial public offerings. It ranked 13th as a manager of initial public offerings in 1996, up from 18th the previous year, 34th in 1994, and 42nd in 1983, which still left it behind firms such as Robertson, Stephens & Company, and Morgan Stanley.

Among the European companies that Cowen helped bring to the NASDAQ stock market were Nera, a Norwegian firm that developed and made wireless telecommunications equipment; Xeikon, a Belgian company that developed and marketed digtal color printing technology; Lernout & Hauspie Speech Production, another Belgian firm that developed software for computers to recognize speech and turn written text into the spoken word; and Baan, a Dutch software developer.

Cowen's capital now totaled about $148 million, including $21 million of debt. Joseph Cohen, Cowen's chairman and chief executive, attributed the firm's success to "a well-thought-out strategy" and to perseverance. But he also sounded a note of caution: "Right now," he said, "the climate is a technology-driven climate; there's always an event that can change that."

The high-technology brokerage firms attributed much of their success with U.S. and foreign clients to their research analysts who could quickly add value in industries where technologies and companies were changing rapidly. "We started with research and we have stayed with our distinctive competence," said Terrence R. Connelly, Cowen's head of investment banking. Those areas, he said, were information technology, high technology, and health care.

Mr. Connelly contended that his firm's in-depth research was particularly useful for a client such as Xeikon. "Xeikon is covered by us by Stephen Weber, a managing director and an experienced and highly rated analyst who also covers Xerox as well as IBM," he said. "This all added to Xeikon's credibility."

Cowen was now trying to raise its profile overseas. In March 1996, it played host to a conference on emerging technologies in Cannes, France, where 60 client companies made presentations to investors. Of 400 executives attending, 150 were European portfolio managers.

Cohen says the trend would continue, with more European high-technology companies following the lead of Xeikon, Nera, and others. "The market wants quality companies, and the research base for understanding these companies is much stronger (here) than it is in Europe," said Adele M. Morrissette, a director in Cowen's investment banking department.

Jo A. Lernout and his partner, Pol Hauspie (of Lernout & Hauspie Speech Production), found the Brussels bourse too small. Turnover rarely approached five million shares a day, compared with hundreds of millions in the United States, and Belgians preferred to invest in established local companies. When a foreign company needs money to finance a high-tech company, it often looks to U.S. investment banking firms. Given its success, Cowen & Company became a target of acquisition by foreign firms. In early 1998, the privately held firm was bought by Societe Generale, a French bank.

Source: Truell, Peter. 1996, April 22. High technology, not huddled masses. *The New York Times,* pp. D1, D6; Rhoads, Christopher. 1998, February 17. Societe Generale expected to unveil Cowen purchase. *Wall Street Journal,* p. 8B.

ENVIRONMENT OF INTERNATIONAL BUSINESS

The international manager, at the start of the millenium, faces a world of unprecedented opportunities for trade and investment. Several factors are responsible, including the following.

1. *Political restructuring and changes in public policy.* During the late 1980s and early 1990s, the world saw the disintegration of the Soviet Union and its state-dominated economic system, which had in its orbit countries of Eastern Europe. Russia and the new countries that emerged out of the Soviet Union as well as the East European countries moved toward creating market-oriented economies. These changes meant that trade and investment with and from abroad were encouraged, laws protecting private property were enacted, state ownership in business was scaled down and state-owned enterprises were privatized. Other underdeveloped countries such as India liberalized their commercial policies and China actively encouraged an export-oriented, private sector–driven economic policy. Even in developed countries such as the United States and United Kingdom, many industries were deregulated allowing for increased competition and foreign participation. Thus, throughout the world, government policies have undergone a massive shift in favor of free enterprise, foreign capital, competition, privatization, and reduced intervention in the economy. These changes, not surprisingly, have provided new opportunities for trading and purchasing new business.

The pace of **privatization** has picked up since the 1980s. In its broadest sense, privatization means relying less on government to meet people's needs for goods and services, and more on private institutions such as the marketplace, the family, and voluntary organizations. Privatization takes many forms. The kind that tends to get the most attention is perhaps best described as "denationalization"—that is, when a government divests itself of a company it owns. Governments seek privatization to wring more efficiency out of the enterprises being privatized, and thus make the economy more productive. Another goal is to raise money, attract foreign capital, and invigorate the local capital market.

One of the major deregulated and privatized industries is telecommunications.[9] In 1996, the Mexican government ended the long-distance phone call monopoly enjoyed by Telefonos de Mexico, or Telmex. Under new deregulation rules, new companies could now provide long distance services to Mexican homes. U.S. companies teamed up in joint ventures with Mexican firms to build the systems to provide such service. A company called Avantel was formed by the alliance of MCI Communications of the United States and Mexico's largest banking group, Grupo Financiero Banamex-Accival, to provide telecommunication service. In 1990, Telmex was privatized and came to be owned by Mexican groups in partnership with France Telecom. International trade negotiations had led to liberalization of rules regarding ownership of telephone companies and telephone rates.

According to the International Finance Corporation, an affiliate of the World Bank, between 1988 and 1993, about 2,700 state-owned enterprises were transferred to private hands in more than 95 countries.[10] Latin American and the Caribbean countries accounted for more than half of the value of privatizations during this period. Privatization

---

[9]Preston, Julia. 1996, August 13. New era of phone competition in Mexico. *The New York Times,* p. D2.
[10]Sale of the century. World business supplement. *The Wall Street Journal,* 1995, October 2. pp. R1–R34.

provides opportunities for firms to enter a foreign market. For instance, when the Hungarian government privatized Tungsram, one of the largest electric lighting companies, G.E. of the United States acquired it.

2. *International trade agreements.* Successive rounds of negotiations under the General Agreement on Tariffs and Trade (GATT) greatly reduced **tariffs** on goods traded between nations from an average of 35 percent to under 4 percent. The most recent agreement, known as the Uruguay Round (because negotiations for it started in Punta del Este, a seaside resort in Uruguay), ended with the creation of the **World Trade Organization** (WTO), which is headquartered in Geneva, Switzerland and now serves as the nodal international authority to interpret and enforce the rules of international trade. The current emphasis of the WTO is to reduce **nontariff barriers** and to bring additional industries—especially services such as banking and insurance, and agriculture—within its fold. Under WTO rules, member countries agree to grant **most favored nation** (MFN) trading status to trading partners which means a country cannot discriminate among countries with regard to trading privileges.

At the same time, **free trade areas** are being created between countries. In a free trade area, goods produced in one country can be sold in a member country without paying tariffs. The **North American Free Trade Agreement** (NAFTA) unites Canada, Mexico, and the United States into a single market. The **European Union** (EU) is an attempt to integrate the nations of Europe into a single political and economic entity in which free trade among member nations is only one of the attributes. Another free trade area is **Mercosur** (the Spanish acronym for Southern Cone Common Market), comprised of Argentina, Bolivia, Brazil, Chile, Paraguay, and Uruguay. Mercosur includes South America's largest trading partners. For companies from smaller countries like Chile, the free trade bloc opens up new markets. In addition to reducing tariffs, Mercosur also has a "democracy guaranty clause" that would suspend commercial benefits to any country that strays from democratic principles.

Free trade areas have the effect of expanding the size of a domestic firm's market. Thus, Cemex, a Mexican cement manufacturer, under NAFTA can sell its product without restrictions throughout the United States and Canada.[11] NAFTA allows it to reap economies of scale and provides an unprecedented opportunity to expand, acquire new technologies, and raise monies at better rates than would have been possible in Mexico. Similarly, a U.S. manufacturer can relocate its manufacturing operations in Mexico to take advantage of lower production costs there and thus be able to supply the entire North American market with a competitively priced product. Mexican firms, which had been protected by tariff walls, were now exposed to competition from U.S. and Canadian firms.

Economic integration, such as NAFTA or EU, alters the entry behavior of foreign firms, their scale of operations, and the location of operations. Thus, because of the restrictive government regulations against countries not members of NAFTA, foreign firms may decide to invest in joint ventures or wholly owned subsidiaries in a member country rather than exporting and thus be treated on an equal footing as fellow NAFTA

---

[11]Millman, Joel. 1998, August 14. Asian firms plunge into Mexico on NAFTA's promise. *The Wall Street Journal,* p. 25; Bradsher, Keith. 1996. Navistar to cut jobs and move truck production. *The New York Times,* pp. D1, D17.

firms. Similarly, individual differences among nations would, in the past, force a firm to establish separate facilities in each country; the integration of the economies of the three member states means that operations can be consolidated at one or few locations. Many businesses that thrived because of protectionist policies find the advent of foreign competition overwhelming, potentially leading to bankruptcy, mergers, declining fortunes, or takeover by foreign firms.

Tijuana, a Mexican city on the U.S. border across from San Diego in California, has become a leading center of television manufacturing in the world.[12] NAFTA created a free market of nearly 400 million people, and companies like Samsung from South Korea built plants in Tijuana to produce color television sets for sale throughout Mexico, the United States, and Canada. Samsung moved its operations to Tijuana after closing its manufacturing plant in Ridgefield Park, New Jersey, in the United States. Assembly line jobs, often held by young women, in Tijuana pay about $50 a week, compared with the $9 an hour in the United States. Navistar International, America's largest producer of trucks and school buses, downsized its operations in Springfield, Ohio, and moved its heavy truck production to Mexico in 1999. This move followed the setting up of a heavy truck factory in Mexico by Paccar, Navistar's main rival. Paccar moved to Mexico after closing down a plant in Canada following a strike by workers. Under NAFTA, the United States will phase out over 10 years the 25 percent tariff on truck imports from Mexico.

3. *Revolution in communication.* The fantastic advancements in communication technology as evidenced by wireless telephone, facsimile transmissions, television, electronic mail, teleconferencing, and communications satellites have led to improved and increased collection and dissemination of information on a worldwide basis. Current technologies allow managers to conduct businesses and monitor developments at distant locations, and enable people around the world to share common experiences, such as the Olympic games, and lead to a convergence of consumer tastes and lifestyles. Indeed, coupled with government deregulation of the telecommunications industry in many countries, the changes afforded by technical developments have created new and growing businesses. For example, the News Corporation, a global media company based in Sydney, Australia, and controlled by Rupert Murdoch, owned the Fox Broadcasting Company in the United States, operated a 24-hour news network, and had a 40 percent share in the European satellite broadcaster B Sky B, in addition to newspapers and educational books in many countries.[13] Trade and investment are being encouraged by the wealth of information now available to the manager and the investor. On-line computer linkups with stock markets, for example, allow analysts, traders, investors, and managers to research and obtain information quickly on products and markets and evaluate performance of firms.

4. *Improvements in transportation.* Technological advancements in transportation in the form of airplanes, ships, trucks, and railways, as well as packaging materials, handling facilities, and containerization, now make it possible for managers, employees, raw materials, and finished goods to travel vast distances quickly and relatively cheaply. Indeed,

---

[12]DePalma, Anthony. 1996, May 23. Economics lesson in a border town. *The New York Times,* pp. D1, D5.
[13]Landler, Mark. 1996, May 6. Cellular spinoff finds success overseas. *The New York Times,* p. D3.

trade in certain products has opened up primarily because of lower transportation costs and improvements in storage technology. It has now become common for fresh food to be shipped across vast distances and made available to customers with a minimum of time lapse. For instance, in Britain, food snobs seek out grouse on August 12, traditionally the first day of the hunting season there. Three thousand miles away in New York City, Americans are able to do the same. The dead birds travel from the Scottish Highlands to be cooked and served in New York restaurants less than 24 hours later. Grouse shot at 3 A.M. are trucked to London, packed onto a British Airways Concorde flight, and rushed to Manhattan just before a $75-dollar-a-plate dinner celebrating their demise.[14] Indeed, the menu at many restaurants and the bins of supermarkets in the United States reveal a wide range of foods—fish, meat, fruits, vegetables, dairy products, and grains—that are grown, raised, or harvested abroad. The managerial challenge usually is to ensure that the transportation logistics works smoothly to deliver the products in a timely manner.

5. *Size of the world's capital pool.* It is now being recognized that the world's pool of capital is much deeper than originally believed. Huge amounts of money are available for investment as is evidenced by the steadiness in interest rates despite increased demands for capital in newly industrializing economies. Government relaxation of rules on foreign investment, privatization, and the heightened awareness of business opportunities in foreign countries have encouraged domestic investors, banks, individual savers, and fund (e.g., pension) managers to finance international business projects. In 1994, the Bank of International Settlements reported that worldwide foreign direct investment rose to nearly $240 billion, more than seven times the levels of the late 1970s and four and a half times the levels of the early 1980s. Foreign equity portfolio investment has risen nearly tenfold to a yearly average of nearly $100 billion in the early 1990s from about $10 billion in the early 1980s.[15]

6. *Rapid economic growth.* The centers of international economic activity long concentrated in what is referred to as the Triad—United States, Western Europe, and Japan—have now expanded to include countries of Eastern Asia. The growth rates in these newly industrial countries have been high, and with increasing affluence, the opportunities for trade and investment have flourished. The vaulting of some of these countries into the top rungs of trading nations as noted previously in Tables 1-3 and 1-4 is a result of this economic growth. Economic growth has created large amounts of wealth in hitherto impoverished countries. A substantial middle class has emerged who demand increasing amounts of consumer goods. Although average per capita incomes may remain low, they often mask vast disparities in a country. For example, India has a per capita income of less than $500 annually; however, it has a burgeoning middle class estimated to be 200 million strong.

RESISTANCE TO TRADE AND INVESTMENT

At the same time though, barriers and resistance to open international trade and foreign firms and products persist in many parts of the world and in many different ways. The manager needs to be especially sensitive to these factors; a failure to recognize and work

---

[14]Mathews, Anna. 1998, July 2. Modern menus star flown-in fish, game. *The Wall Street Journal,* pp. B1, B14.
[15]*International Financial Statistics.* 1996. Washington, DC: International Monetary Fund.

with these forces of localization may hurt the international firm. One of the biggest barriers to trade and investment is the continuing existence of nontariff barriers. Harder to dismantle, they work against "outsiders" to the system. Cultural differences in the form of language, religion, social customs, habits, and traditions force the international manager to make major adjustments that may not be perceived, at least initially, as worth the time and cost. As discussed in the section on politics earlier, **nationalism** remains a potent force around the world. A powerful emotional expression, nationalism is evidenced in the determination of governments to protect "national interests" from foreign encroachment. Nationalism encourages isolationism and protectionism and thus deters world trade and investment by keeping foreign products and firms out. For instance, in the United States, which has experienced persistent balance of trade deficits and a belief that good-paying jobs are being lost due to international business, some politicians have been quick to capitalize on the latent anxiety of certain segments of the American population. In 1996, during the U.S. presidential campaign, candidate Patrick Buchanan criticized the WTO as infringing on U.S. sovereignty. The following is taken from the *New York Times:*

> *Under the trade organization (WTO), he (Buchanan) said, "The greatest nation on earth gets one vote—the same as Bangladesh and Burundi." He derided the director-general of WTO, Renato Ruggiero, as "an Italian bureaucrat." He said Mr. Ruggiero had ordered the United States to change its environmental laws.*
>
> *"He's giving America orders!" Mr. Buchanan said. "Can you imagine what would happen if Mr. Ruggiero picked up that phone in Geneva, and he called the President of the United States, and I picked up that phone at the other line?"*
>
> *Mr. Buchanan said he would say, "Mr. Ruggiero, you're out of a job, boy, because we're leaving the World Trade Organization!"[16]*

A coalition of advocacy groups, referred to as **nongovernmental organizations** (NGOs), has emerged as a strong force against the unfettered growth of international business generally, and in particular, against multinational firms. Composed of human rights activists, environmentalists, and labor unions, these NGOs were successful in stopping negotiations in late 1999 on a new world trade treaty. The NGOs believe that the current system of trade exploits workers in poor countries, pays scant attention to environmental protection, jeopardizes living standards in developed countries, and gives too much power to large international firms at the expense of local and national governments. Faced with protests and opposition from NGOs around the world, international business managers have begun to address some of their concerns. National governments have also recognized that public support for a liberal trade and investment regime would erode if the issues raised by the NGOs are not satisfactorily addressed.

FORMS OF INTERNATIONAL BUSINESS

Firms engage in international business in a variety of ways. The selection of one or more of these strategic options over another is contingent on factors such as the nature of the firm's product line, resources, and strengths and weaknesses; a firm's historical

---

[16]Bennett, James. 1996, February 9. A gleeful Buchanan takes message to Iowa. *The New York Times,* p. A10.

experience and current objectives; the competitive environment and market conditions, both domestic and foreign; the extent of governmental regulations and political risks; and the availability of opportunities. A brief description of the most common forms of international business activities follow. Every one of these choices presents managers with a whole different set of managerial decisions and issues that require a unique set of analyses.

1. **Exporting** occurs when the firm sells its output to foreign customers. Some of the managerial issues include the decision to export, selecting the foreign market, and choosing the distribution channel and the sales outlet, adapting and pricing the product, and organizing the export department. Exports may include both goods and services. A type of export is a management contract in which one firm manages the operations for another entity, in effect selling managerial expertise.

2. In **importing,** considered the reverse of exporting, the firm buys its inputs or its supplies from firms in a foreign country. The managerial issues here include the decision to make or buy, factors to consider when selecting overseas suppliers, quality control, and organizing the import department. Imports may include both goods and services.

3. In **countertrade,** a sale is paid for not entirely in cash, but an in-kind trade takes place. Countertrade poses unique managerial challenges including the selling of the products received in kind, the organizing of the countertrade transaction, and determining prices. Each of the many types of countertrade operations has special requirements. Trading firms usually specialize in countertrade operations.

4. **Licensing** and **franchising** are both popular methods for international business. One firm allows another to use a technology, brand name, or a way of doing business for a fee. Selecting the licensee or franchisee is a key managerial decision as is negotiating the contents of the licensing/franchising agreement, monitoring performance of the licensee/franchisee, and exercising control.

5. **Joint ventures** exist when a firm cooperates with another to own and run a business. For such ventures to succeed, managers have to determine the rationale for such a partnership; carefully choose the partner firm; delineate each partner's role; and nurture the relationship carefully. Strategic alliances, which are usually joint ventures without equity investments, also require managerial astuteness to ensure that the firm benefits from the venture and does not lose key resources or capabilities to the other party. Thus, issues of organizational goals, control, organizational structure, and staffing assume key importance.

6. **Wholly owned subsidiaries** are overseas businesses owned entirely by the firm. These wholly owned subsidiaries have a distinct legal status, independent of the parent firm. The managerial issues concern the reasons for seeking complete ownership as opposed to a joint venture; where to locate facilities; how to organize, integrate, and control the subsidiary in relation to the parent; staffing the foreign operations; and working with the various governmental rules and regulations. The issue of whether to buy an existing business or to build a brand new one must also be addressed.

EMERGENCE OF E-COMMERCE

One of the most innovative developments in the late 1990s has been the emergence of **e-commerce,** where firms use the Internet to transact business with suppliers, customers, and other units of the same organization. E-commerce is rapidly altering the traditional ways in which firms buy and sell and organize themselves. It is creating global on-line economic entities that are not constrained by traditional barriers such as distance, time, or language. For example, about half of the 1999 revenues of Intel, the chip maker, came through e-commerce, compared to 20 percent just the previous year. The experience of Ducati, an Italian manufacturer of high-performance motorcycles, illustrates the potential of e-commerce.[17] The company decided to develop a super sports bike and sell it only on-line. In 31 minutes, a year's production of the new $14,850 MH900 model was sold, on January 1, 2000. *"Our original plan was to produce 500 bikes this year,"* explained a company spokesperson. Thirty-six percent went to Japan, another 30 percent to North America, and a further 30 percent went to Europe. The rest were bought by enthusiasts in Australia and New Zealand. Following the remarkable response, the company decided to increase production of the model to 2,000 units in 2000. At the end of January, it had already sold 1,500 of the machines.

Ducati's website (*www.ducati.it*) received an average of 150,000 hits a day. The company also launched a number of other sites, including Desmobid, which auctioned bike components and other gadgets to fans after a championship race. It also launched a business-to-business network to connect the company with its dealers throughout the world. It is worth noting that Ducati designed the MH900 exclusively for the net to avoid cannibalizing its dealer network and its existing range. It was aimed at the global market—more particularly the "global village of Ducati fans" as the company's spokesperson put it.

The success of e-commerce depends on an efficient and modern telecommunications system. Technical developments are leading to a covergence of hitherto separate industries such as broadcasting, news media, electronic entertainment, and mobile telephony. Consequently, new industries are emerging, existing firms are branching into new businesses, and new products are being developed. Political and cultural boundaries appear to be less relevant to e-business. The Internet is ensuring that huge amounts of information—data and images—are available quickly and inexpensively at either fixed computer terminals or on mobile machines through wireless applications.

The so-called dot-com companies that grew initially in the United States have begun to sprout in Western Europe and Japan. Many U.S. companies have aggressively expanded into Europe and Canada to be near their customers or provide e-mail services. It is safe to say that a whole swath of business from banking to travel to retailing will be affected in important ways by the World Wide Web. One impact will be on how these firms are organized. Because the need to be nimble and fast is important, hierarchical and rule-bound organizations are likely to be left behind. Access to venture capital becomes important and so does the willingness to take risks.

INTERNATIONALIZATION OF THE FIRM

A simple model can be used to explain how a firm internationalizes over time to become a multinational corporation. A firm typically starts by being local or national in focus. Its goal is to make products/services for the immediate geographical market. In time, the

---

[17]The *Web@Work/Intel* Corp. *The Wall Street Journal.* 2000, January 31. p. B8; Betts, Paul. 2000, February 1. Bike sales at full throttle. *Financial Times,* p. 9.

firm receives and fills unsolicited small orders from overseas buyers. As foreign orders continue to grow, the firm reorganizes itself and establishes a foreign division to actively seek and support sales overseas and to handle the special demands of exporting such as exchange rates, customs rules, packaging, and transportation. With growing export sales, the firm may decide to license producers in the foreign market to sell the product in those overseas markets. At the next stage, with foreign sales growing, the firm may enter into a joint venture with the foreign licensee to manufacture the products in the foreign market. With increasing expertise in manufacturing abroad, the firm moves to acquire complete ownership over its overseas facilities. At every stage, the firm's degree of control over its operations changes as the amount of financial exposure changes. Thus, with wholly owned subsidiaries, control is high, but so is financial exposure. The reverse occurs with licensing where both control and financial exposure are low.

Of course, not all firms progress from being a domestic firm to a multinational enterprise as described. For every stage, several other options may be available. Some firms may skip a step and move to a later stage. A firm may also move in the reverse direction of this sequence if it decides to divest an overseas investment. However, this **stages model** posits that as firms acquire international experience, they expand their overseas links and activities. Moving through the stages brings about greater complexities in managing the enterprise. Issues such as selecting managers to work overseas, negotiating with labor unions abroad, organizing and coordinating the firm's divisions, developing effective control mechanisms, moving goods and services around, formulating business strategies, maintaining relationships with licensees and joint venture partners, and understanding and working with multiple governments come to the fore.

The gradual expansion of activities into the international arena can be illustrated through the actions of a commercial bank. Let us assume a bank is located in Rome, Italy. As its clients in Italy begin exporting to buyers in the United States, the bank enters into a correspondent relationship with U.S. banks in New York and Chicago. Correspondent services include accepting drafts, honoring letters of credit, and furnishing credit information—all in connection with export and import transactions. With growing business in the United States, the Italian bank establishes a representative office in New York. The representative office, usually small and staffed by a few officers, provides information, advice, and local contacts for the parent (Rome) bank's business clients and provides a location where business persons from either country can initiate inquiries about the parent bank's services. In the third stage, the bank opens a branch in the United States. The branch is a legal and operational part of the parent bank, with the full resources of the parent behind the local office. The branch bank provides a full range of banking services. Finally, the Italian bank may create a banking subsidiary in the United States. A subsidiary is a separately incorporated bank, owned wholly or in part by a foreign parent, which conducts general banking business. The subsidiary operates within the laws of the host country (in this case the United States). To Americans, the foreign banking subsidiary would be akin to a local American bank. These various forms of banking activity suggest that the management and organizational issues grow complex, and more regulations and more personnel and control issues require attention as the bank moves from a purely domestic operation to owning a foreign subsidiary.

The **multinational firm** is the most recognized entity through which international business takes place. Today, nearly all firms of any significant size are multinational enterprises, which are firms that own and operate production or service facilities in two or more countries. An estimated 36,000 multinational enterprises operate in the world, most of them based in developed countries. With the fast economic growth in several developing countries, more and more firms from developing nations are entering the ranks of multinational enterprises. These firms have invited intense attention because of their large influence on world trade and investment activity and the management of these organizations provide managers with complex demands and organizational challenges. Management Focus 1-3 discusses how General Motors gradually built up its parts operations in Mexico and the interrelationship of those operations with U.S. operations.

However, as the stages model outline suggests, a firm does not have to be a multinational enterprise to be engaged in international business. Thousands of smaller firms, including small sole proprietorships and partnerships, are engaged in international activities in various ways.

OUTWARD VERSUS INWARD PERSPECTIVE

When a firm internationalizes, it does so through adopting an **outward-looking perspective** or an **inward-looking perspective.** In many cases, a firm internationalizes by having elements of both the outward and the inward activities. In some ways, the outward- and inward-looking activities are mirror images of each other.

What is an outward-looking perspective? It is the firm that, aware of business opportunities and competition abroad, decides to export its product or service, license its technology to a foreign firm, establish joint ventures abroad with foreign firms as partners, build or buy wholly owned operations in a foreign country, and forge strategic alliances with foreign firms to access new markets or exploit new technologies. The thrust of this firm is to internationalize by going abroad. An example is Renault, a French automobile company, which acquired a controlling interest in Nissan of Japan to gain access to the Japanese market and Nissan's technical know-how.

In contrast, the inward-oriented firm also internationalizes, but by being the entity through which foreign products and foreign firms enter the home market. Here too, the managers are acutely aware of the nature and strength of foreign competition, firms, and products. They tap into these opportunities by importing or sourcing products or components, by being a licensee for the technology of a foreign firm, by being a joint venture partner with a foreign firm in the home country, by being a wholly owned subsidiary of a foreign firm, or by being sought after by a foreign firm to be a strategic alliance partner. An example of an inward perspective would be an automobile dealership in the United States carrying a line of luxury imported cars to complement its offerings of domestically made mid-priced vehicles.

The inward-oriented firm is no less internationalized than the outward-oriented firm. The difference is that with outward orientation, the firm is actively looking to foreign countries for new markets and new investments. In inward orientation, the firm taps overseas opportunities and resources to strengthen its performance and profits in the home market. Thus, for example, Sears, a leading retail store chain in the United States, buys from foreign suppliers the refrigerators, dishwashers, and washing machines and dryers it sells, instead of placing orders with firms in the country. The advantages to Sears of this offshore sourcing are in cost, quality, and delivery schedules. Many large

MANAGEMENT FOCUS 1-3

THE MEXICAN CONNECTION

Since 1978, General Motors (GM) had built more than 50 parts factories in Mexico. By 1998 it employed 72,000 workers there in its parts subsidiary. As a result, the subsidiary, Delphi Automotive Services, emerged as Mexico's largest private employer.

GM said that transferring production south had enabled it to cut costs in labor intensive assembly production, compete more effectively against Ford, Chrysler, and Japanese automakers, and keep engineering and other operations in the United States. With NAFTA, the financial advantages of producing in Mexico had only increased. Many plants had no union, and those that did were represented by the Conferderation of Mexican Workers, which was controlled by Mexico's then ruling Institutional Revolutionary Party and worked with the government to avoid strikes. The union had kept its American counterpart, the United Auto Workers (UAW), at arm's length.

Mexico's minimum wage was $3.40 a day but experienced workers earned several times that. GM opened its first factory in Mexico in 1935, assembling trucks in the capital from parts imported from the United States. After a 1962 Mexican law required foreign automakers to increase the local content of their vehicles, GM built three engine and vehicle plants in the 1960s and 1970s. The new plants assembled vehicles for the Mexican market.

In the late 1970s, in response to a 1965 law that allowed foreign manufacturers who produced goods in Mexico to export them tax-free, GM changed its strategy. It began to see Mexico as a supplier for its U.S. vehicle assembly plants and in the 1980s built an entire parts industry. The Mexican plants now produced parts that used to be made by UAW workers in U.S. plants.

According to Michael Hissam, a spokesperson at Delphi's Mexican headquarters in Juarez, "What is now Delphi Automotive had run into unprecedented competition. We embarked on a plan to reduce costs by focusing final assembly in Mexico while keeping our more captial-intensive engineering, tooling, and prototyping activities in the U.S. Did we come to Mexico for lower labor costs? Yes. But we also found something else—excellent Mexican management and a dedicated Mexican workforce."

A strike by the company's workers in the United States in the summer of 1998 led to the closure of the Mexican plants because the parts they produced could not be used to make vehicles in the United States. Managers at the Mexican plants told the workers that the union in the United States was demanding that GM close its Mexican plants and return its parts production to the United States. "Most of our workers understand that they are doing work that used to be done in United States' factories because managers explain that to them on the plant floor," said Juan Villafuerte Morales, a union officer representing workers at Delphi's Matamoros factories. "And let me tell you, the jobs are very welcome here."

Source: Dillon, Sam. 1998, June 24. A 20-year GM parts migration to Mexico. *The New York Times,* pp. D1, D4.

firms combine elements of both inward and outward perspectives as the example of General Motors in Management Focus 1-3 showed. IBM imports components for its personal computers from abroad (inward focus) while also exporting these machines to foreign countries (outward focus). Table 1-8 shows these twin orientations.

Both the inward and outward perspectives and the managerial calculations behind them are discussed throughout the book, because a firm could be totally immersed in international business without selling or manufacturing anything in a foreign country. As the inward perspective showed, this firm, focusing entirely on the domestic market, could be an importer of foreign products, or a licensee, or even be a subsidiary of a foreign firm.

Table 1-8	Inward and Outward Business Orientations
Inward Orientation	***Outward Orientation***
Importing	Exporting
Licensee/Franchisee	Licensor/Franchiser
Become a strategic alliance partner of a foreign firm	Set up a strategic alliance with a firm in a foreign county
Become a joint venture partner of a foreign firm	Acquire a joint venture partner abroad
Become a wholly owned subsidiary of a foreign firm	Create a wholly owned subsidiary abroad

THE INTERNATIONAL BUSINESS MANAGER

A manager is someone responsible for the work performance of one or more other persons in an organization. Effective managers utilize organizational resources in ways that result in both realization of the organization's goals and high levels of satisfaction among people doing the required work. The manager in the international firm has to perform the managerial functions of planning, organizing, leading, and controlling in a global setting while being cognizant of the complex issues of doing business internationally.

The success of a firm in the global arena depends to a great extent on the caliber of the managers, both line and staff, to recognize the competitive environment and develop appropriate strategies, to select and appoint properly trained people to key positions at the head office and abroad, to fathom government policies and devise ways to minimize political risks, to evaluate alternative forms of business relationships, to negotiate with government officials and potential joint venture partners, and to organize the activities of the firm in a way that allows goals to be achieved, both in terms of efficiency and effectiveness. The manager has the task of integrating diverse and far flung business enterprises into a coherent, functional organization; evaluating performance under differing operating circumstances; building and operating an international logistics network; and balancing the competing demands to integrate worldwide operations while responding to local and regional needs.

All these tasks suggest that the international business manager has to be able to understand and evaluate multiple realities and relationships simultaneously and be able to make and implement decisions in a highly skillful manner. Thus, managers of a German plant in Canada manufacturing automobile air conditioning units have to be concerned about a whole host of issues other than producing efficiently. They will have to negotiate contracts to supply the air conditioners to automakers in the United States and have to compete with other plants in the company to retain the mandate to make air conditioners. To meet prices demanded by the customers, they may have to subcontract some of the work to firms in Brazil and South Korea and in turn build a reliable transportation system to ensure timely delivery and hire quality control inspectors to check on product specifications. They also have to maintain close links with the firm's research and development center in Germany to learn about and adopt any technical innovations that engineers and scientists there may have come up with. All these transactions occur in an environment of constantly changing foreign exchange rates, of multiple governmental and regulatory agencies, and of cultural differences in the form of language, business practices, and workplace habits.

Although the activities of a firm may have expanded beyond the frontiers of the **home country** where the firm has its headquarters, many managers remain focused on home country customers and the organizational units that serve them. They retain a "headquarters mentality" in their foreign operations. Here, the home country manager takes policies and practices from the home country and attempts to graft them on to the operations in the **host country,** the foreign country where the firm has operations. However, effective international operations require managers to adopt a genuine equidistance of perspective. Maintaining this perspective, though, is often easier said than done. For example, Honda has manufacturing divisions in Japan, North America, and Europe but its managers do not think or act as if the company were divided between Japanese and overseas operations. On the contrary, Honda sees itself as equidistant from all its major customers.

As firms expand internationally, they require highly specialized yet closely linked groups of product or global business managers, country or regional managers, and worldwide functional managers. In addition, of course, managers at headquarters coordinate the complex interactions between these three groups, as well as identify and develop executives with the knowledge, skills, and panache to move up to leadership roles.

The role of the global **product manager** is to further the company's global efficiency and competitiveness. This task requires not only the perspective to recognize opportunities and risks across national and functional boundaries but also the skill to coordinate activities and link capabilities across these barriers. The product manager's job is to serve as the strategist for the firm, as the architect of its worldwide resource usage, and to coordinate the various international transactions for the good or service the company creates.

The **country manager** has the task of responding to the needs of local customers, meeting the requirements of host country governmental agencies, and defending the firm's market share. The need to be responsive to local customers means that conflict with the product manager is likely. Effective country managers keep their ear to the ground to pick up early local market trends, opportunities, and threats. The intelligence gathered has to be passed on to managers higher up in the firm, implying the need for good communication networks. Often a particular geographical market may serve as the test ground for a new technology or product; success here may signal success in other markets.

Functional managers, many of them in staff departments, focus on transferring knowledge across the organization and bringing resources and capabilities together. These managers scan the world for specialized and up-to-date information such as marketing trends or technical innovations. They also identify best industrywide practices and advocate the adoption of programs and innovations that appear to have promise in the firm's many international markets. The expertise and perspective of functional managers enable them to integrate disparate bits of information into useful and complete pictures and communicate them throughout the firm.

What about the managers at headquarters? They integrate the firm's diverse operations, provide leadership, identify and develop new executives, and negotiate and balance the relationship between the product, regional, and functional manager. For example, the top management at Unilever, the Anglo-Dutch consumer products company, has made the recruitment, training, and development of new executives a high-priority focus. The company has a policy of rotating managers through various jobs around the world, usually early in their career. It is an important task because many international firms have a paucity of skilled, globally oriented managers.

Not all managers, though, need to be globally oriented. For instance, Percy Barnevik, a former president and chief executive officer of Asea Brown Boveri (ABB), a Zurich-based Swiss-Swedish electrical products company, felt that he needed about 500 of his 15,000 managers to be global managers. These managers were needed in the higher rungs of the firm: on the executive committees, on the teams running the business areas, and other key positions. He realized that most people cannot forget their nationalities and in many cases, it indeed helped to have a person with a parochial outlook. For a company selling products and services in, say, Ghana, it made sense to have a Ghanaian as a manager.

How are internationally minded managers different? They have exceptionally open minds. They understand and respect how things are done in different countries. But they are also pushy—testing the limits of the foreign culture by trying new ideas and policies. These managers are also patient and can handle the difficulties inherent when people of many linguistic groups try to communicate. In ABB, all managers with a global role had to be fluent in English and those with regional general management responsibilities had to be competent in English.

Finding such managers is not easy. The international firm is often required to look at foreign countries where it operates for potential managers. The careers of promising managers have to be tracked carefully before determining their suitability for senior-level appointments. To develop their managerial talent means giving them suitable and challenging assignments. ABB stresses the use of teams in its management ranks. Managers are encouraged to work in mixed-nationality teams, which forces the formation of personal ties across borders. As Percy Barnevik observed: *"If you have 50 business areas and five managers on each BA team, that's 250 people from different parts of the world—people who meet regularly in different places, bring their national perspectives to bear on tough problems, and begin to understand how things are done elsewhere."* Management Focus 1-4 describes the rise of a manager in the international banking world.

The need for managers who can perform effectively in the complex world of international business has never been greater. Table 1-9 compares the qualities that managers today need to have with those in the past. Even domestically focused firms now need internationally focused managers to prepare them for the globally competitive environment in which they function. A worldwide shortage of executive talent has come about because of the huge demand for managers from the Internet sector, together with demographic factors (such as fewer people in the 35–44 age group). Although top managers have often not paid much attention to developing capable executives, they are recognizing the need to rectify this situation.[18]

---

[18]Sanghera, Santham. 2000, February 1. Shortage of executives starts "war on talent." *Financial Times,* p. 7.

THE MAKING OF A MANAGER

In 1998, Standard Chartered, a British banking group with roots embedded deep in British colonial history, appointed an Indian national to be its chief executive officer. Rana Talwar, 49 years old, who had joined the group from Citibank the previous year, became the first Indian to take the helm of a leading British bank and brought an international perspective to a boardroom dominated by graduates of Eton, Oxford, and Cambridge. Describing his appointment as a "matter of pride," he noted that "I have always been a believer in ability over labels."

Mr. Talwar began his banking career with Citibank in India after graduating from St. Stephens College in Delhi in 1969. In his younger days, he was at a boarding school in the mountains, one of the legacies of British rule in India. "Cold water baths when it was snowing outside, and tea at 6 A.M.," he recalled. He went on to become country treasurer in Saudi Arabia and chief of staff in Hong Kong. He spent a long spell in Singapore, where he took Citibank into credit cards and other areas of consumer banking. He later become responsible for all of Citibank's consumer businesses in North America and Europe and for the Diners Club charge card globally. In 1991, he was appointed an executive vice president of the company's banking group.

Mr. Talwar took over Standard Chartered at a time when the bank was heavily exposed to Asia's economic downturn. Talwar was confident of "riding" the economic cycle and given the low prices, planned to pick up some strategic acquisitions in that region. "There are long-term buying opportunities, but only at the right price. After that my aim is to take this respected and recognized name and build on it. I am not the world's best cutter, but I am a builder." That was a curious metaphor, for in Hindi, *talwar* is a sabre.

Empire building may leave little time for Mr. Talwar to pursue three of his leisure interests—bridge, golf, and tennis. Of the fourth, travel, there would be plenty. He was married and lived in London, United Kingdom, with his two sons and daughter.

He had wanted the job at Standard Chartered. Through headhunters he had been introduced to Mr. Patrick Gillam, the bank's chairman, in the mid-1990s, and the two talked for over two years. Talwar recalled, "I said to him, 'I'll come if I have a crack at the top job.'" Barely 14 months after giving up his senior position at Citibank where he was tipped as a potential successor to the incumbent CEO, Talwar's calculated gamble had paid off.

Source: The Times (London). 1998, June 13. Talwar wins Standard Chartered job, p. 30.

Table 1-9	Managerial Traits: Past and Future
Past	*Future*
All knowing	Leader as learner
Domestic vision	Global vision
Predicts future from past	Intuits the future
Caring for individuals	Caring for institutions and individuals
Owns the vision	Facilitates the vision of others
Uses power	Uses power and facilitation
Dictates goals and methods	Specifies processes
Alone at the top	Part of an executive team
Values order	Accepts paradox of order amidst chaos
Monolingual	Multicultural
Inspires the trust of boards, shareholders	Inspires the trust of owners, customers, and employees

Source: Galagan, Patricia. 1990, June. Executive development in a changing world. *Training and Development Journal*, pp. 23–41.

CONCLUSIONS

This introductory chapter sets out the dynamic global business environment in which businesses exist. While a variety of forces have worked to open up business opportunities, countervailing forces have tried simultaneously to limit such opportunities. Too often, the firm is caught in the middle. Firms have an extensive menu of how to be involved in the promise that doing business across countries offer. These options range from exporting and importing to owning business ventures abroad. Each option presents a different set of managerial concerns. Similarly, firms can be proactive and have an outward orientation or alternately reap the opportunties of international business through an inward stance. In either case, the firm needs to have capable managers who understand the environment, the competition, and the business. The global environment requires an extra set of skills on the part of managers so that they can fashion the strategies that will enable the firm to succeed over the long haul.

Throughout the text, the emphasis is on a strategic approach to managing international operations. The goal is to provide the reader with a comprehensive perspective of the key managerial issues connected with different types of international business activities and the business environment in which the international manager has to operate. Every chapter is followed by an extensive set of learning activities including a comprehensive case study. The cases allow the reader to apply concepts learned in the chapter to real-world analytical and decision-making settings.

OPENING VIGNETTE EPILOGUE

After initially refusing to give up control over pricing and distribution, Tekel eventually relented. In May 1991, Philip Morris got the right to market, price, and distribute its own cigarettes, conditioned on a number of factors, including building its own plant. Months later, it announced a joint venture with Mr. Sabanci's company and invested $100 million in a new plant. Subsequently, another $120 million was put into the state-of-the-art facility with a capacity to make 12,000 cigarettes a minute.

The company embarked on a massive advertising campaign. The Marlboro chevron could be seen everywhere. It carefully engineered its cigarettes to appeal to Turkish taste buds, but with a stronger kick than the local products. It sent salepersons to 130,000 stores across the country to distribute its products. In the process, Philip Morris saw its share of the cigarette market in Turkey rise to 23 percent in 1997 from less than 2 percent in 1984. Tekel's market share had fallen to 70 percent.[19]

[19]Hwang, Suein. 1998, September 11. How Philip Morris got Turkey hooked on American tobacco. *The Wall Street Journal,* pp. A1, A8.

Key Terms

- international management
- exchange rates
- balance of payments statement
- euro
- first mover's advantage
- privatization
- tariffs
- nontariff barriers
- World Trade Organization (WTO)

- most favored nation
- free trade area
- North American Free Trade Agreement (NAFTA)
- European Union (EU)
- Mercosur (Southern Cone Common Market)
- nationalism
- nongovernmental organizations (NGOs)

- exporting
- importing
- countertrade
- licensing
- franchising
- joint venture
- wholly owned subsidiary
- e-commerce
- stages model
- multinational firm

- outward-looking perspective
- inward-looking perspective
- home country
- host country
- product manager
- country manager
- functional manager

Discussion Questions

1. Consider the stages theory of the internationalization of a firm and explain it in terms of a firm that has an inward perspective.

2. How will international business be affected as countries replace their own currencies and link them to dominant currencies such as the U.S. dollar, the euro, and the Japanese yen?

3. Examine the managerial issues faced by a Mexican firm after NAFTA. How are these issues different from those experienced by U.S. firms?

4. How is international management different from management of a purely domestic firm? What are the characteristics of managers needed by multinational firms?

5. Explain how e-commerce opportunities are changing international business and impacting the management of such firms. Use examples to illustrate your answer.

6. Given the challenges and risks of doing business outside one's home country, why should managers of a domestic firm consider internationalizing their activities?

Writing Assignment

Your employer sells chocolates through a chain of retail stores in the United States. The company is considering carrying several lines of Belgian chocolates in addition to the American products it currently sells. You have been asked to investigate and prepare a report identifying the major business and management issues that will arise if the company decides to import chocolates from Belgium. The company has no previous experience with international business.

Internet Exercise

Select a company that has a significant portion of its revenues coming from foreign markets. Use the Internet to track the exchange rate of the company's home country currency in relation to the currency rates of its major markets. Visit the company's Web site and the archives to trace the impact of the exchange rate changes over the past five years on the firm's performance and strategic behavior.

Internet Resources

The Internet has emerged as an excellent source of information about international trade and investment, economic policies and developments in individual countries, the activities of international organizations, corporate plans, and financial conditions. In fact, the Internet has opened up vast and varied sources of information that are easy and quick to access relatively inexpensively. In addition, such information is much more current than data typically obtained from printed documents.

Many organizations post information about their activities as well as data on their Web page. Web addresses of organizations can be easily obtained by using a search engine. Some of the more effective search engines and their universal resource locators (URL) are: About.com (*about.com*), AltaVista (*av.com*), Direct Hit (*directhit.com*), Google (*google.com*), Goto.com (*goto.com*), and SavvySearch (*savvysearch.com*). Note that hot links enable the browser to check out related and distant Web sites. In effect, a single address may well open the door to many others.

Many daily newspapers and business magazines that are superb sources of information about international management issues and financial data are also available on-line. Some addresses worth checking out are: *Financial Times,* London (*www.ft. com*), *The Wall Street Journal* (*http://wsj.com*), *The New York Times* (*www.nytimes. com*), *The Economist,* London (*www.economist.com*), *Business Week* (*www.business-week.com*), *Forbes* (*www.forbes.com*), Reuters (*www.reuters.com*), Bloomberg News Service (*www.bloomberg.com*), Knight-Ridder Financial News (*www.cnnfn.com/ news/knight_ridder/*), and Asian Business Watch (*www.webcom.com/darrel/com*). For information on currency exchange rates, check out *www.xe.net/ucc.*

U.S. government agencies, the European Union, the United Nations (and its specialized agencies), and many nongovernmental organizations provide information on-line. For instance, data on trade and investment in the United States and by American firms can be obtained from the Department of Commerce (*www.doc.gov*) and the Bureau of Economic Analysis (*www.bea.doc.gov*). The U.S. Federal Reserve Bank and its branches have Web pages too. The Federal Reserve Bulletin can be accessed through *www.bog.frb.fed.us.* The Bank of England maintains a site at *www.coi.gov.uk.* The Web site address of the European Union is *http://Europa.eu.int*, and for the United Nations it is *www.un.org/.* Two directories about international firms that are useful are Hoover's Handbook of World Business (*www.hoovers.com*) and Directory of Corporate Affiliations (*www.gale.com*).

Note that many firms have their own Web sites that provide a wide range of information. These Web sites also have e-mail addresses so that the user can pose and seek answers to specific questions.

❧

Case 1–1   MICHAEL HILL INTERNATIONAL LIMITED

With the loss-making shoe division now behind it, Michael Hill International Limited (MHIL) was refocussing its attention to its core business activity—jewelry retailing and manufacturing. Even as it pursued expansion plans in Queensland and New South Wales in Australia, the company was also concerned about consolidating its gains.

THE COMPANY

Michael Hill International Limited (MHIL) was a New Zealand–based jewelry retailer, which opened its first store in 1979 in Whangerei, a small town north of Auckland. In 1987, with 10 retail outlets around the country, the company listed on the New Zealand Stock Exchange. That very year, it expanded into

Australia. By 1994, the company had 55 jewelry stores (29 in New Zealand and 26 in the eastern Australian states of New South Wales and Queensland, and the territory of Canberra). With 640 employees, the company had manufacturing operations in both countries.

In 1991, the firm diversified into retailing shoes. After three successive years of loss and the failure to integrate shoes with jewelry, the firm closed down its shoe division. The company decided that jewelry retailing and manufacturing would be the sole business activity of the firm in the future. Its goal was to establish 100 stores throughout Australia and 35 stores in New Zealand by the year 2000. Management had no intention of raising further equity capital in the immediate future to fund this growth; financing would be by bank borrowings and through retained earnings.

MICHAEL HILL, THE ENTREPRENEUR

The founder of MHIL, Michael Hill, was the chairman of the board and joint managing director and held a little more than half of the company's shares. As a youngster, Mr. Hill was a talented violinist, who after failing to be selected for the National Youth Orchestra was sent to be a watchmaker's apprentice. Disliking the job and at the urgings of his parents, he entered the family jewelry business owned by his grandparents in Whangerei, now run by his uncle. Reluctantly, he started working there. In 1969, success came in the form of an international prize—he received top honors in a window dressing competition run by a European watchmaker. The prize was a trip to Switzerland to a watch fair where he took notes on the innovation and creative flair of European jewelers.

He returned to New Zealand to work for another eight years for his uncle. As he and his artist wife, Christine, were putting the last touches to their newly built home, a fire destroyed the building. It was a turning point in his life. He decided he was either going to buy out the family business, or start his own. The family did not want to sell out, so Michael and Christine started the Michael Hill jewelry chain. He was 40 years old.

THE JEWELRY STORES

Hill opened his first shop opposite his family's shop. It immediately attracted attention because of its decor, gloss, and sparkle. Believing that jewelry shops intimidated shoppers, Michael and Christine designed their shops with a look that set them apart from the traditional jewelry stores. Each store was a virtual "Aladdin's cave"—the black, silver, and gray decor provided a quiet backdrop for the extensive range of jewelry that filled the shop. Store fronts were wide and the counters U-shaped so the public could see clearly what was inside. Also, the Hills standardized the design and display throughout each store, giving them an instantly recognizable look. Although most MHIL shops were small—from 600 to 1000 square feet—they followed an open plan design and arrangement with all stock on display; their stores had no drawers under the counters. To Michael Hill, appearance was vital. He felt that overall shop presentation in New Zealand needed improvement: "Frontages are poor, their signs are dull. They don't have the zing to pull you in. The shops look dowdy. New Zealand retailers need to be more colorful," he observed.

A new jewelry outlet cost about NZ$100,000 to set up and a further $400,000 to stock it. MHIL shops were sited in prime locations such as shopping malls or busy main streets where pedestrian flows were high. Although rents were higher at these sites, the higher cost was outweighed by the need to access customers and present a high visibility profile. The following table shows how the jewelry chain had expanded since its inception.

Number of Jewelry Stores						
Year	*1989*	*1990*	*1991*	*1992*	*1993*	*1994*
Stores	20	28	34	38	45	55

PRODUCT LINE

MHIL concentrated on fast-moving, high-margin lines of gold, silver, and diamond jewelry. The stores sold conventional jewelry products such as rings, chains, bracelets, watches, and other common accessories. The products were of average to high quality and provided customers with good value for the money. The company philosophy was "offering the best made product at the lowest possible price with the most friendly service." Between 80 and 85 percent of the products were manufactured by MHIL in its workshops in Brisbane, Australia, and at Whangerei. The rest of the merchandise was purchased in bulk from overseas manufacturers. The company also owned an antique and estate jewelry outlet in Auckland and regularly held antique fairs around New Zealand. MHIL sold identical products in its two geographical markets.

JEWELRY RETAILING INDUSTRY

Jewelry retailing is an industry with standardized products, distinctive styling, competitive pricing, and intense competition. Industry sales in New Zealand in 1993 were estimated at NZ$124 million, compared to NZ$588 million in Australia. In general, the market in both countries had been expanding. New Zealand had about 660 jewelry outlets. MHIL held more than one-third of the market with only 3 percent of the shops. Competition in New Zealand came from another retail chain, Pascoes with 21 stores, and numerous independent jewelers, many of them specializing in antique and estate jewelry. Another firm that had tried to copy the MHIL model of fine shops, in-house manufacturing, prime locations, and aggressive advertising was the Jewelry Company based in the Auckland area (home to half the country's population). Competition was also emerging in the form of a franchise chain owned by Kleins, based in Melbourne, Australia.

In the Australian market, a number of prominent retail jewelry chains included names such as Angus & Coote and Hookers. These competitors were equal in size and power and sold relatively undifferentiated products and were MHIL's biggest competitors in Australia.

OVERSEAS EXPANSION

Australia was often the first country of choice for foreign direct investment and foreign trade for New Zealand firms. The two countries were bound by a free trade agreement known as Closer Economic Relations (CER) in addition to sharing common language, laws, and business practices. Tourists from both countries visited each other in large numbers and a significant number of retired New Zealanders lived in Queensland. Australia had a population six times larger than New Zealand, and its per capita income was also higher.

Finance for the move into Australia came from proceeds from its first public issue of shares. Although Australia was familiar to New Zealand firms, entering that market was not easy for MHIL. As Mr. Hill said, "Even after opening the first shop in Queensland, it was like starting from scratch again." The firm was repeatedly advised that Queensland was "over-jewelered" and competition was sophisticated. Doubts were raised about the ability of a firm from Whangarei to success-

fully operate in Australia. However, within 18 months of opening, MHIL was the number one jewelry retailer in Brisbane in terms of sales.

One of the major difficulties encountered by MHIL was the reluctance of shopping malls in Brisbane to offer a rental lease for another jewelry shop. Also competition came not only from other jewelers but also from other retailers offering a wide variety of sophisticated products. In 1992, MHIL entered the lucrative, competitive Sydney market. Additional advertising was needed to build market awareness for the chain, shop opening costs were higher, and staff training expenses were larger. It was nearly two years before size economies began to take effect. With a dozen shops in the metropolitan area by 1994, the required core size needed to experience substantial sales and increasing profits had been achieved.

The Australian market provided 46 percent of total MHIL sales, the balance came from New Zealand (see following table). In 1994–1995, the company planned to open an additional 12 stores—all in New South Wales and Queensland. It was expected that by 1995, Australia would eclipse New Zealand as the larger market for MHIL. In 1993, the Australian manufacturing division was relocated to larger premises. Expanded capacity was expected to be able to supply up to 50 shops.

Turnover (in thousands of New Zealand dollars)		
	1994	*1993*
Total	87,858	72,827
New Zealand	47,280	42,655
Jewelry	40,294	36,837
Shoes	6,986	6,268
Australia	40,578	29,722

Note: One New Zealand dollar equaled about 60 U.S. cents.

PRODUCT DIVERSIFICATION

In 1991, the company entered the retail women's fashion shoe industry by acquiring three retail outlets of John Craig Shoes Ltd. of Christchurch, New Zealand, for NZ$700,000. Muriel Newman, public relations manager of MHIL said, "Diversification into shoes was very much a 'dip the toe in the water' exercise. Shoes and jewelry were complementary in that they were both fashion items." Over the next two years, the number of shoe outlets expanded to nine around the country. Wherever possible, the new stores were located next to the jewelry stores, a strategy designed to pull in customers as well as make the organization of management easier. Nearly 60 percent of the shoes were New Zealand–made and specially designed for MHIL.

However, the retailing formula that worked well for jewelry did not work for shoes. A policy of discounting across the line, which was common for jewelry, did not transfer to shoes. Customers perceived "cheap" shoes to equal poor quality. Revenue targets and profit expectations were not met. Although sales rose they were not enough to cover overhead expenses and reduce oversized inventories. It was felt that MHIL did not have enough outlets to generate the necessary volume. Not enough senior management time was made available to the new division. In 1993, Mr. Hill made the decision to close down the shoe division. It took more than a year to sell off the stores and the loss incurred affected the 1994 financial results.

OPERATIONS MANAGEMENT

A "Michael Hill" style of jewelry, usually designed by Christine Hill, had evolved and had gained popularity. In less than two years, the output in Australia had doubled as the chain grew. All shops were connected through a centralized computer network allowing prices, sales, and inventories to be continually monitored at headquarters. Such instant reporting allowed the firm to adjust in-house manufacturing to real demand, drop slow-moving models, and increase production of fast-moving items. The firm was also able to reap economies of scale in its bulk purchase of raw materials and, because it produced much of what it sold, to capture the profits that would otherwise have gone to wholesalers and intermediaries. Manufacturing its jewelry gave the firm a significant edge over competitors in the areas of quality control, styling, and exclusivity of design. The growing number of stores had enabled the further spreading of the fixed administration and advertising overheads. MHIL's goal was to provide jewelry for its customers for prices lower than competitors. It constantly searched to reduce costs in all areas. Finally, the firm strove to keep overhead costs as low as possible. For example, the company had fewer than a dozen employees at its head office.

However, as might be expected, the company had a large promotional budget and spent a considerable sum advertising, especially as it expanded in Australia, where distances were vast and MHIL was not as well known. Mr. Hill himself appeared in television commercials and the company used special sales and dis-

counts to convert customer inquiries into sales. The marketing strategy emphasized the Michael Hill name in advertising on television, radio, newspapers, and magazines.

ORGANIZATION

Apart from Michael Hill, the rest of the company's shares were held by firms and individuals throughout New Zealand. Less than 2 percent of the shares were owned by foreign investors.

The company had a geographical structure reflecting its two markets—New Zealand and Australia. Between 1992 and 1994, the New Zealand division comprised a jewelry and a shoes line. Each of the two country divisions had its own separate functional departments such as marketing, distribution, manufacturing, and finance. Michael Hill, commenting on the organization structure, said, "The open-plan nature of shops is echoed in the structure of the company, which has minimal hierarchy to ensure unimpeded information flow and a high degree of autonomy." However, elements such as product design and store design were centralized. To better address the needs of the growing Australian market, a separate human resource unit was established in Australia primarily to recruit and train staff.

Believing that only a satisfied worker would treat a customer well, a supremely important factor in a business such as retailing, MHIL strove to create a pleasant working atmosphere. Communication channels were open and a simple organizational structure allowed information to flow freely. Top managers frequently interacted with lower-level employees who were also encouraged to take initiative and develop their skills. As Mr. Hill said, "Managers should employ someone better than themselves, show them how the job is done, and leave them to get on with it. There's a fear that if you hire someone better, they will put your job in jeopardy but in fact they strengthen you. You want the best possible team you can get."

The success of the firm was very much a team affair. Although Mr. Hill had received much of the accolade and attention, many members of the executive team had been with the company since its inception. For instance, Howard Bretherton, the joint managing director, joined the company in 1981, and had extensive retail business management experience both in New Zealand and Australia. Employee turnover remained low, and a great deal of effort was put into fostering the "family" spirit. An open-door policy existed. As Mr. Hill puts it, "We like an open philosophy where everybody can see everybody and anyone can communicate. There is no hierarchy hidden away in separate offices. Anybody can come along and tell me off."

Shop managers regularly got together in their regions to brainstorm ideas for marketing, merchandising, or advertising. They visited and critiqued each other's shops as well as discussed upcoming promotions and forwarded their suggestions for advertising copy to the head office. Stores were operated as individual business units, and each manager was evaluated and rewarded on store performance. With a profit sharing system in place, managers had an incentive to enhance sales. Consequently, some shop managers received compensation approaching $100,000.

Competition and flat profits in the early 1990s forced MHIL to initiate a series of cutbacks. Top management and head office staff took pay cuts of 10 percent but front-line store managers were spared.

FINANCIAL RESULTS

The 1994 results included all costs and losses associated with selling off the shoe division, which Mr. Hill said, "in hindsight, the decision to enter the shoe industry was a mistake. However, the lessons learned have been invaluable, and the group is now much stronger as a result of this somewhat painful experience." In 1994 the company achieved a record turnover, up 21 percent on the previous year. However, because of the losses incurred in the shoe division, the overall profit was down 17 percent (see following tables).

Sales and Profits (in thousands of New Zealand dollars)		
Year	*Total Sales*	*Net Profit (before tax)*
1994	87,858	3,770
1993	72,827	4,314
1992	63,041	5,301
1991	53,256	4,168
1990	49,875	4,043
1989	37,221	3,279

Net Profit Retained (in thousands of New Zealand dollars)						
Year	*1994*	*1993*	*1992*	*1991*	*1990*	*1989*
Sum	1,136	1,655	2,078	1,652	1,576	1,094

PROSPECTS

Although the company's objective was to establish 100 stores throughout Australia and 35 stores in New Zealand by the year 2000, it was becoming clear that MHIL had matured in its home market. Increases in sales were coming from new stores as existing stores were reporting only stagnant or marginally improved sales on a year-to-year basis.

Medium-term plans were to expand only in Queensland and New South Wales, where the company had now established itself. Expansion to other states in Australia would require large investments in leasing property, advertising and promotion, training personnel, inventory, and expansion of in-house production of jewelry. The average cost of opening a store in the Sydney area was over $600,000. As the Australian market became more important for MHIL, the economic condition of Australia and the attendant ex-

change rate would assume importance. In recent years, the Australian economy had grown slowly and the declining Australian dollar, for instance, led to a loss of about $550,000 over 1993 and 1994 in exchange rate translations. Jewelry sales were largely dependent on discretionary income and with a slower economy, discretionary expenses tended to suffer.

Mr. Hill had long-term ambitions of setting up stores in Europe, principally Great Britain. He also felt he needed to consolidate in Australasia. Expanding to these overseas markets would put strain on the organizational structure, management, and coordination of the firm. The profit margins, both operating and net, had been declining over the years (see following table), partly because of the slower economic conditions and partly because of intense competition. Despite efforts to improve inventory management, the ratio of net working capital to inventory remained high.

Consolidated Balance Sheet			
	1994 **(in '000)**	**1993** **(in '000)**	**1992** **(in '000)**
SHAREHOLDERS' FUND			
Issued and Paid-Up Capital	6,994	6,994	6,347
Reserves	1,223	1,300	2,369
Retained Earnings	10,077	8,941	7,286
Total Shareholders' Funds	18,294	17,235	16,002
Convertible Notes	2,667	2,667	2,684
Total Capital Funds	20,961	19,902	18,686
Deferred Taxation	1,109	1,024	773
Term Liabilities			
Bank Term Loans (Secured)	12,950	12,155	9,690
	$35,020	$33,081	$29,149
Fixed Assets	9,435	9,585	7,745
Expenses Carried Forward	534	806	1,336
Goodwill	928	1,000	1,071
CURRENT ASSETS			
Cash on Hand	586	581	424
Trade Debtors	3,104	2,909	2,487
Other Debtors and Prepayments	498	1,172	623
Inventories	26,617	24,352	21,218
	$30,805	29,014	24,752
CURRENT LIABILITIES			
Bank Overdraft (Secured)	209	1,796	583
Creditors and Accruals	4,816	3,742	3,688
Short-Term Liabilities	279	798	210
Taxes Payable	679	289	463
Proposed Dividend	699	699	811
	6,682	7,324	5,755
WORKING CAPITAL	24,123	21,690	18,997
	$35,020	$33,081	$29,149

Note: All amounts are in New Zealand dollars. Transactions in foreign currencies are converted to New Zealand dollars at the rates of exchange prevailing on the dates of the transactions. Amounts receivable and payable in foreign currencies are translated to New Zealand dollars at the rates of exchange prevailing at balance date, or when forward exchange cover has been obtained, at the settlement rate. Realized and unrealized gains and losses arising from exchange rate fluctuations in foreign currencies are included in the Income Statement.

QUESTIONS

1. Discuss the challenges facing Michael Hill as the company expands into Australia.
2. As the firm expands, will Mr. Hill be able to maintain his intense hands-on management of the business? Explain.
3. Explain the choice of Australia as the first foreign country for the firm's expansion. Which country would you advise the company to move into next?
4. What managerial changes—both in terms of thinking and action—do you believe the company went through as it expanded beyond its Whangarei origins?

References

Bartlett, Christopher, and Sumantra Ghoshal. 1992. What is a global manager? *Harvard Business Review.* September–October, pp. 124–132.

Landler, Mark. 1996, May 6. Cellular spin-off finds success overseas. *The New York Times,* p. D3.

Ohmae, Kenichi. 1989. Managing in a borderless world. *Harvard Business Review.* May–June.

Taylor, William. 1991. The logic of global business: An interview with ABB's Percy Barnevik. *Harvard Business Review.* March–April.

Vernon, Raymond. 1966. International investment and international trade in the product cycle. *Quarterly Journal of Economics* 80, pp. 190–207.

APPENDIX 1-1   ❧
FOREIGN EXCHANGE RATES AND BALANCE OF PAYMENTS

EXCHANGE RATES

Foreign exchange rate changes affect the value of transactions, the amount of profits, the cost of an investment and the consequent effects on sales, investment choices, market share, production costs, and profitability. The following example illustrates how a change in the exchange rate affects an international buyer and seller.

When a Dutch firm exports tulips to a florist in New York, the Dutch firm is paid in U.S. dollars. The Dutch firm converts the dollars into guilders, the currency of the Netherlands, through a bank, so that it can use the money in the Netherlands to buy goods and services it needs. The rate of exchange between the U.S. dollar and the Dutch guilder is however not fixed. Depending on the demand for and supply of these two currencies and other economic and political developments around the world, the exchange rates change. Currencies are traded in foreign exchange markets around the world around the clock. Thus, on May 1, 2000, at 4 P.M. (Eastern Time) the exchange rate at New York was 1 U.S. dollar equal to 2.4066 Dutch guilder. If, for instance, the New York florist had contracted to buy tulips worth U.S. $10,000, the Dutch exporter would receive 24,066 guilders. Let us assume that payment can be made within 30 days of delivery of the flowers. If payment is made on say, May 31 and the exchange rate should change to 1 U.S. dollar equals 2.39 guilder, the Dutch importer would receive 23,900 guilders—166 guilders less than originally planned.

Let us look at this transaction from another perspective. The Dutch exporter quotes a price of 24,066 guilders for a consignment of tulips. With the exchange rate at 1 U.S. dollar equal to 2.4066 guilder, the New York florist will have to pay the equivalent of $10,000.

If payment is made 30 days from delivery, and the exchange rate has changed to 2.39 guilders, the American florist will have to pay $10,649.46—$69.46 more than originally planned.

The decline in the value of a currency against a foreign currency is known as depreciation (or devaluation), whereas the increase in the value is referred to as appreciation (or revaluation). Over the past 20 years, the value of the Japanese yen has tended to appreciate in relation to the U.S. dollar. Therefore, more U.S. dollars are needed to buy one unit of the Japanese currency, the yen or alternatively, for the same amount of U.S. dollars, one receives fewer units of yen.

Although currencies are bought and sold in the foreign exchange markets at the spot rate (where the delivery and payment of the currencies take place normally by the next business day), several alternatives are available to the international firm to reduce the risk that emanates from exchange rate changes. In addition, many firms, and not just financial firms, try to profit from foreign exchange rate changes and differences in the various markets by buying and selling currencies.

A common method of protection against exchange rate changes used by many international firms is the forward transaction, which establishes the rate of exchange at the time of the agreement, but payment and delivery are made at a future date—usually one, two, three, six, or twelve months. In the previous example, the American florist may protect itself by buying guilders in the forward market, which on May 1 may be quoted at the 30-day forward rate of 2.35 for 1 U.S. dollar. What this transaction does is remove the uncertainty for the florist as to how much it would have to pay when the payment for the flowers is due. Irrespective of what the rate is on the date of payment, the buyer will pay at the forward rate negotiated 30 days earlier.

Another alternative is the foreign currency option, which is a contract that gives the option to the buyer the right, but not the obligation, to buy a given amount of foreign money at a fixed price per unit for a specified time period. Thus, with our example, the American florist would

have the right to buy guilders at the rate of 2.38 for every dollar but would not be obligated to do so. This alternative helps the florist if the rate should go lower than 2.38.

In addition to these techniques, many other complex arrangements are available to hedge against adverse exchange rate changes. Management Focus 1-5 discusses how some firms address the issue of fluctuating

MANAGEMENT FOCUS 1-5

PERILS OF HEDGING

A company such as Minnesota Mining & Manufacturing (also known as 3M), which gets more than half of its sales and profits in foreign currencies and is thus very much exposed to exchange rate changes, does not use hedging. 3M is not alone; many big firms such as Eastman Kodak, Deere, and Exxon, choose to hedge very little or not at all. A study of 400 companies by the University of Pennsylvania's Wharton School and the Canadian Imperial Bank of Commerce found that only one-third of them engage in foreign currency hedging.

Many firms believe that currency fluctuations help profits as often as they hurt them and that hedging simply does not pay. Because over the long run currencies both appreciate and depreciate, the net effect on the firm's operations evens out. Because hedging is not always effective, and is also costly, these firms believe that it is not worth the effort. Moreover, a firm's own strategies may change during the period and so may the underlying business conditions.

The argument for hedging, of course, is increased stability. When effective, hedging decreases the volatility of a firm's cash flow making it easier to plan spending. Lower volatility also reassures lenders and investors and makes forecasting income and expenses easier.

The U.S. pharmaceutical company, Merck & Co., hedges somes of its foreign cash flows using one- to five-year options to sell the currencies for dollars at fixed rates. Merck believes that it can protect against adverse currency moves by exercising its options, or enjoy favorable moves by not exercising them. Either way, the firm aims to guarantee

that cash flow from foreign sales remains stable so that it can sustain research spending in years when a strong dollar reduces foreign earnings. Coca-Cola's managers claim that by using options they can limit the negative impact of unfavorable currency movements on earnings to 3 percent annually over the long term. However, in 1998, the company announced that currency changes would reduce its expected profits for the year by much as 10 percent.

The cost of hedging is, however, not inexpensive. It eats into the profits of the firm. A simple forward contract that locks in an exchange rate costs half a percentage point per year of the revenue being hedged. Other techniques such as options are even more costly. And the empirical evidence is that it may not be worth it. Using 10 years of earnings statements from 198 large U.S. firms, a study found that only one could have reduced its annual volatility by more than 20 percent through hedging. Because it can be hard to get hedging right, many companies have decided to stop using it altogether. Eastman Kodak, for instance, abandoned its aggressive hedging strategy in 1993.

Given the mixed record of much hedging, why do firms engage in it? Firms may do so to simplify corporate budgeting or to please investors. It may improve the ability to forecast currency volatility over the short term. In fact, some firms that hedge claim short-term planning is the driving determinant. Although over the long haul the ups and downs of the dollar eventually net out, as the director of global capital structure at Honeywell noted, "But we have never had a CFO (chief financial officer) or chairman that had a 20-year tenure."

Source: Perils of the hedge highwire. *Business Week.* 1998, October 26, pp. 74–76.

exchange rates. One solution to changing exchange rates is to have both expenses and revenues in the same currency. Although foreign sales, assets, and profits have to be converted into the home currency for accounting purposes, by using revenues earned in host countries to fund investment expenses in those countries, the firm reduces the hit to earnings that comes from exporting products from a strong currency country to one with a weak currency country. IBM locates facilities in countries where it does a lot of business. Coca-Cola, rather than repatriate profits in devalued foreign currencies, reinvests in local bottling operations.

EXCHANGE RATE CHANGES AS THEY IMPACT A FIRM

When the currency depreciates, the product becomes less expensive abroad. This situation would, as per the law of demand, stimulate sales. However, imported products become more expensive, and presumably their sales would decline. Purchasing businesses in foreign countries or investing otherwise abroad becomes costlier. In contrast, domestic businesses look cheaper to foreign investors and foreign investment in the country rises. The reverse is true when the currency appreciates.

A good example of how exchange rate changes affect individual firms is seen in the reaction of the Japanese automobile companies in the light of a strengthening yen. In 1965, one U.S. dollar was equal to 360.9 Japanese yen. In May 2000, the dollar had depreciated to about ¥108. As the Japanese yen appreciated, cars made in Japan became more expensive in the U.S. market, which triggered increased consumer resistance. To maintain their former profitable presence in the huge U.S. market, Japanese managers were forced to change their strategies. They reduced the cost of production by introducing efficient production methods, cutting waste, and turning over the supply of components and parts to outside contractors. They worked to reduce the margin of profit and absorb some of the increased cost. Moving production to plants in the United States meant incurring both costs and revenues in U.S. dollars. A change in the product line to a more luxurious, high-price end allowed higher prices to be charged to the extent the market would bear. Withdrawing from particular product segments eliminated less profitable areas. Because an appreciating yen also meant a depreciating dollar, it was no surprise that many U.S. firms found that their sales in Japan had increased as U.S. products became comparatively cheaper there.

As interest rates differ from country to country, so does the rate of return on investment. Managers in international firms closely monitor the exchange rate and its implications for cash flow and firm profitability. Specialized personnel in the finance department scout exchange rate changes and interest rates on a continuous basis and are in a position to raise capital at the lowest cost or avoid losses on currency fluctuations. In fact, they often make profits through speculation on the foreign exchange market. In addition to banks and independent consultants, some large international firms have their own in-house exchange rate forecasting capabilities.

2

CULTURAL VARIABLES

᷇

OPENING VIGNETTE

Immediately after acquiring the French medical equipment maker, Cie. Generale de Radiologie (CGR), General Electric Co. (GE), the giant American conglomerate, started introducing its way of doing business. It began by organizing a training seminar to boost the morale of its new French employees. In the hotel rooms of the French managers, GE left colorful T-shirts emblazoned with the GE slogan "Go for One." A note urged the managers to wear the T-shirts "to show that you are members of the team." The French wore them reluctantly to the seminar, one manager commenting, "It was like Hitler was back, forcing us to wear uniforms. It was humiliating."

The T-shirt gaffe was the first of many clashes between the two companies. CGR, formerly state owned and run like a government department, was now in the hands of an aggressive, profit-oriented U.S. multinational firm. At CGR, employees were accustomed to government subsidies and guaranteed purchases by state hospitals and had little competitive market experience at home or abroad. And GE wanted to change the status quo.

As part of the strategy to integrate CGR into its way of doing business, GE managers put up English language posters everywhere, flew GE flags and otherwise made GE's culture ubiquitous. "They came in here bragging, 'We are GE, we're the best and we've got the methods,'" said a CGR labor union official. "The more they said, the worse it got." GE's culture was an extension of the strong personality of its combative leader, John F. Welch, Jr., who preached a philosophy of self-reliance, hard work, and big profits. At company meetings in Paris, gung-ho Americans would chant his credo—"speed, simplicity, and self-confidence" to skeptical French managers.

GE executives acknowledged that the company had underestimated the cultural problems it would encounter. "We've tried to avoid the impression of imposing a victorious culture on a vanquished culture," said a senior GE manager. "But nobody has discovered the perfect formula for cultural integration."

Together with politics, culture creates the environment in which the international manager operates. Cultural practices vary across and within countries. Managers need to recognize, understand, and adjust to the unique culture of a society if they are to avoid major mistakes when negotiating a business arrangement, in conducting business overseas, or in dealing with employees and customers abroad. Culture imbues every society with distinctive practices, values, and outlooks that immutably mold how businesses are organized and operated. It impacts implicitly and explicitly on the firm itself by influencing its corporate culture and on various areas of the management function. This chapter examines the different dimensions of national culture as they affect international management and how managers prepare themselves to work effectively in a multicultural world. The effects of culture on communication, negotiations, motivation, and leadership are examined.

DEFINING CULTURE

Culture can be defined as the norm, values, and beliefs shared by a group. Common beliefs and value systems influence members of a society to behave and act in predictable ways, and structure their perception of the world. Geert Hofstede, a noted Dutch cultural expert, described culture as the collective programming of the mind, which distinguishes the members of one group from another.[1] Although culture is learned by individuals and passed down from generation to generation, it is not permanent or fixed. Cultures change over time.

Some broad characterizations can be made about culture:

1. It is a shared system of meanings. People in a particular cultural group have values, symbols, and behavioral patterns that everyone in the group understands and anticipates.
2. It is a relative concept in that no standard culture exists. Every culture is different from one another to a greater or lesser extent without one being superior or inferior, right or wrong.
3. It is learned by human beings, as they are reared, from their social environment. It is not a trait people are born with, nor is it inherited.
4. It applies to groups of people; however individual values and behaviors vary widely within each culture.

Largely because of historical evolution, most political nation-states today encompass distinctive cultures. Thus, the country of France is essentially composed of people who are "French"—people with a distinctive culture. However, because of events such as conquests, colonialism, and transmigration, many countries are bicultural or even multicultural. The migration of Africans, Arabs, and Indo-Chinese from France's former colonies has created distinctive subcultures in France. Given the myriad strands of human experience and history, the distinction between a culture and the political nation-state may or may not be informative. Thus, when speaking of Finnish culture, one can relate it to the nation of Finland; it requires considerable probing to determine what is American culture because the United States is a diverse society of immigrants or their descendants from virtually every society of the world. Although substantial subcultures exist in the United States, assimilation among the various groups has created some common values and practices. One perspective on the major attributes of American culture is presented in Management Focus 2-1.

---

[1]Hofstede, Geert. 1980. *Culture's consequences: International differences in work-related values.* Beverly Hills, CA: Sage Publications.

THE AMERICAN CULTURE

Most Americans have a difficult time telling a foreigner the values Americans live by, largely because they may not have given the matter much thought. Even if they pondered the question, a definitive answer might not be forthcoming. The reason for this ambiguity is itself indicative of American values—an entrenched belief that every individual is so unique that the same list of values could not be applied to all citizens. Despite this sense of individualism, a foreigner, observing the behavior and actions of an American, would be able to develop a profile of American culture—a profile that would aptly describe most, if not all, Americans. The following 13 characteristics of Americans provide a helpful framework to understand American culture.

1. *Personal control over the environment and personal responsibility.* Americans rarely believe in the power of fate and they look at people who do so as being backward, primitive, and hopelessly naïve. People consider it normal and right that humans should control Nature, rather than the other way around. The problems of one's life are not considered as the result of bad luck as much as having come from one's laziness in pursuing a better life.

2. *Change seen as natural and positive.* To an American, change is unquestionably good; it is inextricably linked to progress, growth, and well-being. Older societies, in contrast, see change as disruptive, destructive, and to be avoided. These older societies value stability, continuity, tradition, and a rich heritage—values that do not appeal strongly to many Americans.

3. *Time and its control.* Time is money to Americans, and as such it is a valuable resource. Schedules are planned and followed in detail. Indeed, the language of Americans is filled with references to time—it is something to be on, to be kept, filled, saved, used, spent, wasted, lost, gained, planned, given, made the most of, even killed. Being on time to meetings is expected; being late is considered rude.

4. *Equality and fairness.* The notion of equality is ingrained among Americans, beginning with the U.S. Constitution, which says that all men are created equal. This idea of equality translates into equal opportunities for all to succeed irrespective of their station in life, their physical status, or intelligence. In this respect, the United States is different from most societies in the world. Elsewhere, great stress is given to rank, status, and authority. In the United States, Americans are averse to treating people in high positions with deference and conversely treat lower class people as if they were very important.

5. *Individualism and independence.* The idea of individualism—each human being is considered unique and precious—is most pronounced among Americans. Privacy is considered a positive condition and is zealously guarded. Individualism is reflected in the wide range of opinions and the unfettered right to express them. The major political parties, though only two in number, encompass the broadest spectrum of views.

6. *Self-help and initiative.* Americans celebrate rags-to-riches stories, which are numerous. The social system enables Americans to easily move up the social ladder. Credit is given for individual accomplishments, initiative, and enterprise.

7. *Competitive spirit.* Americans believe that competition brings out the best in human beings, forcing them to put all their efforts in the enterprise. Competition is present in all aspects of society from education to sports to the business environment where free market concepts rule virtually unchallenged.

8. *Future orientation.* Americans are forward looking; the past does not weigh heavily on them. All efforts and energies are directed towards betterment in the future. This future orientation in outlook and behavior is consistent with an earlier stated characteristic of being able to control Nature.

(continued)

(continued)

9. *Action/work orientation.* The life of an American is an active one. Everything, including leisure, is planned. It is considered sinful and a personal failure if somebody is slothful. This attitude that life should be full of action and accomplishments has turned many people into workaholics who think constantly about their jobs, even on vacations. People are ready and willing to work, including hard physical labor.

10. *Informality.* Informality informs the behavior of Americans. In dress, manners, and greetings, Americans are much more casual than people in most other societies. People, even superiors by their subordinates, are often referred to by their first names.

11. *Directness, openness, honesty.* Unlike many other societies where unpleasant topics, if discussed at all, are presented in subtle and indirect ways, Americans adopt a much more direct approach. Negative performance evaluations are provided bluntly and quickly. Numerous assertiveness training programs encourage the docile to express their thoughts without inhibition. In contrast, Americans

consider those who do not level with them or who are not frank to be dishonest, insincere, manipulative, and untrustworthy.

12. *Practicality and efficiency.* Americans are a realistic, practical, and efficient people. The philosophy that Americans may be said to embrace wholeheartedly is one of pragmatism. Dogma and theory rarely guide their actions. Every situation is judged on its own merit, and subjectiveness is eschewed as much as possible. A problem-solving approach to difficulties enables them to experiment with various alternatives.

13. *Materialism and acquisitiveness.* A popular bumper sticker says: He who dies with the most toys wins. Americans possess vast amounts of material goods. Indeed, the acquisition of material goods is seen as the reward for hard work, initiative, and seriousness of purpose, which also means that Americans give a high priority to acquiring, maintaining, and securing their material possessions. Because they embrace change unquestioningly, they frequently change or replace their material possessions.

Source: Kohls, Robert. 1996. Intercultural training seminar. Piscataway, NJ: Lucent Technologies.

IMPORTANCE OF CULTURE

The study of culture is important for the international business manager because it explains and determines many aspects of human behavior. Individuals and groups are influenced by the cultural milieu in which they have been brought up and live in. Hence, when managing operations abroad, foreign managers need to understand the cultural values and habits of the employees they are supervising. Cultural peculiarities of the foreign country may determine what motivates the employees, what leadership styles may work best, the way to communicate effectively, the extent of adjustments that the foreign manager may have to make, and the factors to consider when making decisions. Because people and governments feel strongly about protecting their cultural institutions, icons, and practices, foreign firms have to adjust to the cultural environment of the host country. The opening vignette illustrates the difficulties firms encounter when they try to do business abroad without respecting local sensibilities.

The growth in international trade and investment has meant that managers must interact more and more with individuals (be they customers, suppliers, employees, or competitors) from other cultures. Managers who cannot work effectively with members of other cultures will find fewer opportunities for career advancement. They are more likely to succeed if they go through a **cross-cultural training** program. Cross-cultural training means learning to work with people from different cultures, recognizing and understanding differences, and respecting the views and values of others.

Difference in culture among countries is illustrated by the following quote made by a manager of the Japanese automobile firm, Toyota, assigned to its American joint venture with General Motors, New United Motor Manufacturing Industry (NUMMI):

> Here in America, the competition is among individuals, but the Japanese compete as a group. If you look at how many gold medals Americans got from the Olympic games, you can easily see just how capable and skillful each American is. In contrast, Japanese individuals cannot compete with Americans at all.
>
> The most important thing is the extent to which each individual joins his or her effort in the company. Each Japanese individual is far less strong than each American, but when they join their efforts, they are stronger. American individualism is not bad if you look at it from the perspective of an individual. However, it is big trouble for a company or for industry.[2]

This view suggests a difference between Japanese and American workers—one group-oriented, the other much more individualistic. Thus, when the NUMMI joint venture began, the Japanese managers would lead the American workers, to background music, in warm-up exercises to loosen their muscles and enhance group spirit. Over time, interest in the exercises died, though the music still played. One worker who quit the exercises said, *"They just went too far. I mean we're Americans. We're not robots!"*

This example suggests that to achieve organizational goals, managers must ensure that employees behave in a certain way. To accomplish that goal, managers need to recognize that culture plays a role in human behavior, and an understanding of the cultural dimensions makes for a more effective manager. A critical challenge for all international managers is how to work effectively with people from a variety of cultures.

COMPONENTS OF CULTURE

What separates one culture from another? Variables such as religion, language, race, social systems, ideology, and mindsets do. As noted in Chapter 1, these elements of culture are among the most potent manifestations of localization. They are deeply embedded in human societies, and appear to be strengthening in the face of the forces of globalization. Based on the degree of cultural diversity, one can broadly distinguish between countries that are culturally homogeneous and those that are culturally heterogeneous. In a society with homogeneous culture, little variation can be found in beliefs and shared meanings among its population. In such societies, the degree of consensus is high. Examples of such societies are Japan, Saudi Arabia, and Finland. In a heterogeneous society, multiple population groups have a specific identity and distinct values. A dominant culture may exist side by side with multiple secondary cultures. Examples of heterogeneous nations are India, Switzerland, and South Africa.

---

[2]Wilms, Wellford, Alan Hardcastle, and Deone Zell. 1994. Cultural transformation at NUMMI. *Sloan Management Review.* Fall, pp. 99–113.

Religion   As the faith people have in God, a creator, or the supernatural and reflected in service, devotion, and worship, religion determines many aspects of life including dietary habits, holidays and work schedules, relationship between genders, motivation and work ethic, and its meaning. The extent to which business practices are affected by religion depends on the depth of religious fervor and the support of the government for it. In Israel, for instance, because of demands from Orthodox Jews, the state-owned El Al Israel Airlines was not permitted to fly on the Jewish Sabbath—Friday evening to Saturday night—which cost the company some $36 million annually in potential net earnings. The weekend traffic out of Tel-Aviv was thus controlled by foreign airlines, which offered more than 80 scheduled flights on Saturday alone. This Sabbath restriction also made it harder for the government to privatize the airline.[3] In multireligious societies, violent conflict among the faithful is not uncommon, interrupting normal business operations. In Northern Ireland, hostility and tensions have marked the relationship between the majority Protestant community and the minority Roman Catholic community. Evidence of the disparity can also be found in discriminatory workplace practices where Protestants dominate the upper echelons of management.

Language   Many societies have their own distinct language. The differences in languages affect the interactions among societies. Language also gives rise to other differences such as distinctive expressions (idioms, phrases, and slang), literature and the arts, and the descriptions of concepts and emotions unique to a society. Like religion, language too can be a cause of conflict. The secessionist movement in the Canadian province of Quebec is fuelled by fears of the French-speaking Quebecois that their language and culture are hard to safeguard in a majority English-speaking country. Because of colonialism, many countries of the world now have a language of commerce and government that is the language of the former colonial ruler. This language often supplants the native tongues of the people of the country. For example, the official language of Nigeria is English, thanks to more than 100 years of British rule, though the people in the country speak many different local languages.

Race   In the United States, immigration has led to a racially diverse society. In some countries, separation among the races is stricter. To a business, the race issue assumes importance when societies are multi- or biracial and a foreign firm must be sensitive to it. Managers from primarily uniracial societies (such as Japan) may lack the experience of working with people of other cultures or hold stereotypical views about others. Multiracial societies sometimes experience racial tensions when one race appears to dominate the economic and political structures of the society.

Social Systems   Every society's social system is characterized by rules and practices that govern the behavior and customs of people over matters such as courtship and marriage, entertainment, communication styles, living patterns, and attitudes toward wealth, authority, and outsiders. A social system develops in response to unique environmental and historical circumstances and with its own logic and justification. To the international manager, understanding and accepting a society's unique social systems

---

[3]Orme, Jr., William A. 1999, March 5. El Al at a turning point. *New York Times,* pp. C1, 17.

ease the demands of doing business successfully. Violation of local mores and customs invariably draws censure and unfavorable attention to the foreign firm.

Rites, ceremonies, and symbols also characterize the social system. In Japan, the ceremonial exchange of business cards reflects the importance of social status and a person's relative position in a social or work group. When meeting for the first time, Japanese businesspeople exchange carefully prepared cards that specify their position in their respective firms. Those who discover from the card exchange that they are lower in the hierarchy are appropriately respectful to those higher up. Business cards indicate a person's place in a group. Without a card, a manager has no status; thus, business travelers to Japan are advised to take along a supply of cards, preferably with a translation in Japanese on the reverse side.

These elements of culture, together with economic, political, and demographic factors, influence the nature of government in a country. The type of laws it enacts and how they are enforced are affected in turn. The quality and attitude of its workforce, attitudes towards foreign investment, and the vigor of its institutions also reflect the culture. International managers need to study and understand how doing business in a country would be impacted by cultural and related factors.

Although many behaviors may appear to be cultural, a deeper analysis often reveals some less obvious economic reasons. A proper set of economic incentives and signals can change supposedly culturally determined behaviors. For instance, the high rate of tardiness and absenteeism among Mexican workers is not a reflection on the absence of an industrial work ethic; it is due to a paucity of adequate day care facilities that often force parents to stay at home with a sick child. Similarly, the much-acclaimed lifetime employment system in Japan has been attributed to cultural factors. However, with the protracted economic stagnation throughout the 1990s in Japan, many Japanese firms, to remain competitive, downsized and laid off thousands of workers.[4]

FRAMEWORKS TO CATEGORIZE NATIONAL CULTURES

Several researchers have studied the cultures of different nations and have, on the basis of similarities and dissimilarities on various dimensions, categorized them. These studies are helpful to managers because they distill the complexity of a culture into simple, easy-to-relate frameworks that aid in understanding the extent to which a foreign culture may differ from that of their own. However, the broad generalizations made about a culture by these studies should alert managers to the likelihood that, in a foreign society, they would encounter values, behaviors, and attitudes at variance with the supposed norm for that society. Four models or frameworks are described here.

HOFSTEDE'S VALUE SURVEY MODEL

The seminal work on national culture was done by Geert Hofstede.[5] Between 1967 and 1973, he surveyed 116,000 employees (managerial and nonmanagerial) in the branches and subsidiaries of International Business Machines (IBM). These employees represented

---

[4]WuDunn, Sheryl. 1996, June 12. When lifetime jobs die prematurely. *New York Times,* pp. D1, D8.
[5]Hofstede, Geert. 1980. *Culture's consequences: International differences in work-related values.* Beverly Hills, CA: Sage Publications.

extremely well-matched subjects of each country's population, because they did the same jobs with the same technology in the same firm, had the same education levels, and could be matched by age and gender. Hofstede collected data from 50 countries and three geographic regions for a total of 53 "national" cultures. The study revealed that the 53 countries differed along four cultural dimensions: power distance, individualism-collectivism, masculinity-femininity, and uncertainty avoidance.

- **Power distance.** This dimension measured the extent to which inequality in a society is accepted by its members. Where the power distance is low, the society believes that inequality should be minimized. Conversely, a high power distance means an acceptance of a hierarchy in the society.
- **Individualism-collectivism.** This dimension is measured along a continuum with individualism and collectivism being at the polar ends. Individualism describes the degree to which individual members look out for themselves and status derives from individual accomplishments. In individualistic societies, ties among individuals are loose; all are expected to take care of themselves and their immediate family. In contrast, collectivism refers to people bound into strong, integrated, cohesive groups where extended families protect members in exchange for unquestioning loyalty.
- **Masculinity-femininity.** On this continuum, the masculine end describes a culture where men are assertive, sex roles are clearly differentiated, and wealth and material possessions are important. Femininity, at the opposite end, describes a society where men assume nurturing roles, suggesting greater equality between the genders, and greater emphasis is placed on human relationships and quality of life issues.
- **Uncertainty avoidance.** This dimension measures the extent to which a society accepts and prepares itself for uncertainties and the future. People in high uncertainty avoidance countries are uncomfortable in unstructured situations and try to prevent such situations by having strict laws and rules on safety and security. In uncertainty accepting cultures, people are more likely to take risks, are less resistant to change, and have fewer rules and regulations.

Table 2-1 shows the scores calculated on the four dimensions for the various countries in the study.

Given the scores it is possible to create country clusters, or groups of countries that are more or less similar to each other on one or more of these dimensions. Thus, the Anglo-Saxon cluster comprises countries such as Australia, Canada, Great Britain, Ireland, New Zealand, and the United States. Brazil, India, Israel, and Japan could not be placed in any of the country clusters and are thus in a separate group by themselves without any significant commonness among them. Table 2-2 presents the country clusters.

RELEVANCE OF HOFSTEDE'S FINDINGS

Hofstede's study has had a major impact on cross-cultural studies. It has been replicated and adapted in many other disciplines including psychology, sociology, accounting, business ethics, political science, development economics, and finance. Validation studies have tended to broadly support Hofstede's contention about national differences in culture.

Table 2-1	Country Scores on Hofstede's Value Survey Model			
Country and Region	*Power Distance*	*Individualism*	*Masculinity*	*Uncertainty Avoidance*
Argentina	49	46	56	86
Australia	36	90	61	51
Austria	11	55	79	70
Belgium	65	75	54	94
Brazil	69	38	49	76
Canada	39	80	52	48
Chile	63	23	28	86
Colombia	67	13	64	80
Costa Rica	35	15	21	86
Denmark	18	74	16	23
Ecuador	78	8	63	67
Finland	33	63	26	59
France	68	71	43	86
Germany (West)	35	67	66	35
Great Britain	35	89	66	35
Greece	60	35	57	112
Guatemala	95	6	37	101
Hong Kong	68	25	57	29
Indonesia	78	14	46	48
India	77	48	56	40
Iran	58	41	43	59
Ireland	28	70	68	35
Israel	13	54	47	81
Italy	50	76	70	75
Jamaica	45	39	68	13
Japan	54	46	95	92
Korea (South)	60	18	39	35
Malaysia	104	26	50	36
Mexico	81	30	69	82
Netherlands	38	80	14	53
Norway	31	69	8	50
New Zealand	22	79	58	49
Pakistan	55	14	50	70
Panama	95	11	44	86
Peru	64	16	42	37
Philippines	94	32	64	44
Portugal	63	27	31	104
South Africa	49	65	63	49
Salvador	66	19	40	94
Singapore	74	20	48	8
Spain	57	51	42	36
Sweden	31	71	5	29
Switzerland	34	68	70	58

Table 2-1 (*Continued*)

Country and Region	Power Distance	Individualism	Masculinity	Uncertainty Avoidance
Taiwan	58	17	45	69
Thailand	64	20	34	64
Turkey	66	37	45	35
Uruguay	61	36	38	100
United States	40	91	62	46
Venezuela	81	12	73	76
Yugoslavia	76	27	21	88
Regions:				
East Africa	64	27	41	52
West Africa	77	20	46	54
Arab Countries	80	38	53	68

Source: Hofstede, Geert. 1980. *Culture's consequences: International differences in work-related values.* Beverly Hills, CA: Sage Publications.

Hofstede's findings provide a guide to managers on what to expect when interacting with people in a foreign country. In countries with high individualism, performance appraisal systems would work best if directed toward rewarding individual, rather than group behavior. The technique of **management by objectives** where superiors set goals for the subordinate in consultation would work well. In contrast, in societies with low individualism (or collectivism), reward systems that are group-oriented would be appropriate. Participative styles of management may be easily accepted in these societies.

Where uncertainty avoidance is high, the emphasis is best placed on long-term planning, of preparing for contingencies, and providing employees with a variety of benefits and job protections. In low uncertainty societies, planning tends to be short-term and flexible. Job security is less of an issue, and individuals have greater control over their lives.

Table 2-2 Country Clusters Based on Hofstede's Value Survey Model

Country Cluster	Countries
Anglo	Australia, Canada, Great Britain, Ireland, New Zealand, South Africa, United States
Germanic	Austria, Germany, Switzerland
Latin European	Belgium, France, Italy, Portugal, Spain
Nordic	Denmark, Finland, Norway, Sweden
Latin American	Argentina, Chile, Colombia, Costa Rica, Guatemala, Mexico, Peru, Venezuela
Far Eastern	Hong Kong, Korea, Malaysia, Philippines, Singapore, Taiwan, Thailand
Near Eastern	Greece, Iran, Pakistan, Turkey
Independent	Brazil, India, Israel, Japan

Source: Adapted from Punnett, Betty. 1994. *Experiencing international business and management.* 2d edition. Belmont, CA: Wadsworth, p. 15.

In countries with high power distance, decisions tend to be centralized and organizational mobility is low. Firms tend to have tall structures and participants prefer direction from superiors. Where low power distance exists, organizations tend to be flatter, decision making is participative, and mobility within the organization is feasible and accepted.

In a country with a high score for masculinity, a firm's goals tend to focus largely on profit making and raising market share. Men are likely to predominate in the upper echelons of management and the focus is usually on task accomplishment. In societies where femininity is more characteristic, issues of quality of work life, environmental protection, notions of equity and fairness, and corporate social responsibility are important. Less overt differences separate men's and women's work roles.

Hofstede's study has been faulted on several grounds. His sample was drawn from one organization in a high-tech industry. The findings cannot be generalized to all workers in all industries. Also the assumption of cultural homogeneity in a country was made. Several countries in this study (e.g., India, South Africa, Switzerland) are home to many cultural groups. The study considers all Indians, South Africans, and Swiss to be a homogeneous group of people when they are not. Hofstede also could not gather information on several key countries such as China and Russia. It has also been suggested that many of the concepts have different meanings in different societies. For instance, collectivism in Chile is not the same as collectivism in Japan. Finally, from a research perspective, it should be noted that the study itself is highly culture bound—conducted by a European in an American firm. Many of the questions asked and the analysis performed reflect Western training, sensibilities, and interests. Despite these drawbacks, Hofstede's study provides managers with a valuable framework to guide them in their cross-cultural analysis and preparation.

Hofstede himself has responded to the criticisms made of his work.[6] He has admitted that surveys are not necessarily the best way to collect data about culture and recommends that multiple methods be used. He also agreed that, while nations are not always the proper unit of culture because cultural groups often tend to spill over national boundaries, they however remain the best available source of data. Regarding the charge that his findings are IBM specific, Hofstede has noted that the company prided itself on the uniformity of its corporate culture and precisely because it operated in many countries, it made sense to compare whether workers in different countries had different values especially when all did similar work under similar organizational conditions. He has emphasized that he was not measuring culture; he was measuring differences between cultures.

In a subsequent study, Hofstede teamed with Michael Bond to create a fifth cultural dimension, called **Confucian dynamism,** based on the basic values of the Chinese people.[7] Based on surveys of respondents from 22 countries, this dimension had a positive and negative side. On the positive side were values such as perseverance, ordering relationships by status and observing this order, thrift, and having a sense of shame. On the negative side were personal steadiness and stability, protecting one's face, respect for tradition, and reciprocation of greetings, favors, and gifts. In some countries, the values

---

[6]Hofstede, Geert. 1998, August 10. *Talk at the Academy of Management annual meeting.* San Diego, CA.
[7]Hofstede, Geert, and Michael Bond. 1988. The Confucius connection: From cultural roots to economic growth. *Organizational Dynamics* 16(4), pp. 4–21.

on the positive side are more important; in others, those on the negative side are emphasized. All these values are associated with the teachings of Confucius, dating from 500 B.C. The values of the positive side are more oriented toward the future while the values of the negative side are oriented toward the past and present. Countries that have long-term orientation are China, Hong Kong, and Taiwan. In contrast, Canada, the United Kingdom, and the United States score low on this dimension. India, Netherlands, Singapore, and Sweden fall in the middle.

CULTURAL ORIENTATIONS FRAMEWORK

Florence Kluckhohn and Frederick Strodtbeck offered a model to analyze cultures based on how members of a society view different aspects of life and the world.[8] Their model identified six different orientations and the possible range of attitudes toward each of them. Table 2-3 summarizes the managerial implications of the Kluckhohn-Strodtbeck model.

Applying this model to the dominant cultural group in the United States, one could conclude that Americans are a mixture of good and evil, whose relationship with nature has been one of control and domination. Individualism is a cornerstone of American society where instant gratification and constant change are readily accepted. Americans value privacy and protect it zealously.

As summarized in Table 2-3, it can be said that where the assumption about a people is good, managers may find the application of Theory Y principles appropriate; in contrast where the assumption is evil, Theory X ideas may be more suitable. In countries where the relationship with nature is one of subjugation, people are less likely to bring about change—a sense of fatalism prevails. In hierarchical societies, attention is given to the opinions of superiors and decisions tend to flow down from the top. Performance is valued and rewarded in "doing" societies; in "being" societies, status is derived from birth and is dependent on age, gender, and family connections. Where the focus is on the past, the culture gives greater respect to those who are senior in the organization and emphasize precedence. Public conception of space breeds suspicion of activities conducted in secret just as private space suggests respect for personal ownership, privacy rights, and a distinction between personal and private life.

Kluckhohn and Strodtbeck did not develop their model with management and business in mind and hence its applicability to international managers has to be drawn out. The interpretations of the orientations can be subjective, and it is always possible to find the entire range of variations in any large and diverse society. Nonetheless, this model offers a vehicle to compare cultures on a set of dimensions and should allow managers to be better prepared when interacting with individuals in another society.

TROMPENAARS'S CULTURAL PARAMETERS

Based on a 10-year study that involved questioning more than 15,000 managers from 28 countries, Fons Trompenaars developed a set of parameters for analyzing cultural differences. Each parameter is presented in Table 2-4.[9]

---

[8]Kluckhohn, Florence R. and Frederick L. Strodtbeck. 1961. *Variations in value orientations.* Westport, CT: Greenwood.
[9]Trompenaars, Fons. 1993. *Riding the waves of culture.* Chicago: Irwin.

Table 2-3	Cultural Orientations	
Orientations	**Range of Attitudes**	**Implications for Managers**
Nature of People	Good	Theory Y orientation; participation encouraged; direct communication valued; trusting; optimistic about people
	Evil	Pessimistic; Theory X orientation; secretive; suspicious of peers and subordinates
	Mixed	Use of intermediaries and consultants; a discrepancy between optimistic attitudes and behaviors
Relationship to Nature	Dominant	Imposing one's will on the natural environment and the business environment
	Harmony	Coexistence; search for common ground; respect for diversity
	Subjugation	Fatalistic; ready acceptance of external control; aversion to independent planning
Relationship to Others	Lineal (hierarchical)	Respect for authority and seniority; tall organizations; communication on a hierarchical basis
	Collateral (collectivist)	Relationships within the group influence attitudes toward work, superiors, other groups; members of other groups viewed with suspicion
	Individualist	People perceive themselves as individuals rather than as members of groups; competition encouraged
Modality of Human Activity	Doing	Performance valued; practical orientation; work central to the individual's life
	Being	Status derived from birth, age, sex, family connections more than by achievement; feeling valued; short-term planning
	Containing	Focus on self-control; striving for balance between feeling and doing; self-inquiring
Temporal Focus of Human Activity	Future	Future planning prioritized; past less important; concept of change valued
	Present	Immediate realities prioritized, and used as the basis of planning; long-term plans liable to modification
	Past	Past used as the model; respect for precedence; respect paid to age
Conception of Space	Private	Respect for personal ownership; what is private is valued; social distance
	Public	Suspicion of activities conducted in secret; public meetings valued
	Mixed	Private and public activities distinguished

Source: Adapted from Mead, Richard. 1998. *International management.* pp. 26–27. Oxford, UK: Blackwell.

Table 2-4	Cultural Parameters	
• Universalism vs. Particularism	Social vs. Personal Obligations
• Collectivism vs. Individualism	Group vs. Personal Goals
• Neutral vs. Emotional Relationships	Showing Emotion in Business Relationships
• Specific vs. Diffuse Relationships	Degree of Involvement in Personal Relationships Between Subordinates and Superiors
• Achievement vs. Ascription	The Basis for Determining Status
• Sequential vs. Synchronic	Attitude Toward Time
• Inner-directed vs. Outer-directed	Control over Destiny

Source: Riding the waves of culture, by Fons Trompenaars, © 1993. Irwin. Reprinted with permission of The McGraw-Hill Companies.

Trompenaars's parameters offer useful guidelines for international managers. For instance, in universal cultures, more focus is placed on rules than on relationships; in particularism cultures, it is the opposite. In collectivism cultures, the emphasis is on "we" rather than "I" or "me." Group rewards and holidays involving families are emphasized rather than the individual. In neutral relationship cultures, showing anger, delight, or intensity in the workplace is thought of as unprofessional; conversely, affective cultures openly express their emotions. Cultures that are characterized as specific relationships separate the world of business from the world of private life. Not so in diffuse relationship cultures where work and private life are closely linked. In achievement-oriented cultures, managers are evaluated on how well they perform on the job. In contrast, in ascription-oriented cultures, power and status are given to those who are admired or are loyal or are senior and experienced—it has less to do with performance on a particular task. Sequential cultures follow a specific plan of action whereas synchronic societies do several things at the same time.

COUNTRY CLUSTERS

Simcha Ronen and Oded Shenkar categorized countries of the world into nine clusters based on an analysis of studies that examined variables in four categories: (1) importance of work goals, (2) need deficiency, fulfillment, and job satisfaction, (3) managerial and organizational variables, and (4) work role and interpersonal orientation.[10] These clusters are Anglo, Germanic, Latin European, Nordic, Latin American, Near Eastern, Far Eastern, Arab, and Independent (to capture those countries that did not fall into the eight clusters).

These clusters, similar to those of Hofstede's, suggest that individual countries within a cluster are more or less similar. Thus, in the Latin American cluster, a foreign manager would find the cultural differences between Argentina and Chile minor as opposed to the differences between Chile and a country from the Nordic cluster, say Finland. A Chilean manager in Argentina would have to make relatively smaller adjustments to be able to work with the Argentine workforce, which would differ little from Chilean workers. Clustering helps a manager reduce the large number of countries into smaller, easily identifiable sets.

With ever-increasing interaction between peoples and the flow of information among societies, cultures across countries are changing and affecting communication, motivation, lifestyles and consumption, and ways of doing business. International business operations function as critical change agents themselves, altering the nature of and attitude toward work. The international aspect of business is frequently the impetus for introducing new concepts and for validating effective and efficient ways of doing things. The changing role of the Chinese business community around the world is described in Management Focus 2-2.

ORGANIZATIONAL CULTURE

Sometimes referred to as corporate culture, **organizational culture** is the system of shared beliefs and values that develops within a firm and guides the behavior of its employees. It is the glue that holds the organization together. It is formed from individuals' beliefs,

---

[10]Ronen, Simcha, and Oded Shenkar. 1985. Clustering countries on attitudinal dimensions: A review and synthesis. *Academy of Management Review* 10(3), pp. 435–454.

MANAGEMENT FOCUS 2-2

THE WORLDWIDE WEB OF CHINESE BUSINESS

Although much of today's global economy centers on the Triad region of North America, Western Europe, and Japan, it overlooks Chinese businesses—many of which are located outside China itself—which makes up the world's fourth economic power. The Chinese encompass an array of political and economic systems that are bound together by a shared culture, not geography.

For many generations, emigrant Chinese entrepreneurs have been operating comfortably in a network of family and clan, laying the foundations for stronger links among businesses across national borders. Chinese-owned businesses in East Asia, the United States, Canada, and even further afield are increasingly becoming part of what may be called the "Chinese Commonwealth." This commonwealth is primarily a network of entrepreneurial relationships. From restaurants to real estate to plastic-sandal makers to semiconductor manufacturing—from a staff of five or six family members to a plant floor of thousands—the Chinese commonwealth consists of many individual enterprises that nonetheless share a common culture.

For more than 2,000 years, the Chinese culture has stressed the importance of social order. Given China's long history of political upheavals, natural disasters, and economic scarcities, well-defined relationships have often helped keep social chaos at bay. A survivor mentality and the Confucian tradition of patriarchal authority inform the values of the typical Chinese entrepreneur. Characterized by thrift, a high level of savings, and hard work, these entrepreneurs typically rely on family members as opposed to outsiders and base their business links on kinship. They also tend to invest in tangible goods, like real estate and gold, and exhibit a readiness to move if circumstances so warrant.

As Chinese communities around the world—in Hong Kong, Taiwan, Singapore, Malaysia, Indo-nesia, Canada, the United States, and elsewhere—have flourished, the commonwealth has expanded and changed. The children of first-generation entrepreneurs have assimilated to a greater extent with the host community. They are multicultural, having lived and been educated in a manner different from their parents. The community has shifted into other types of businesses such as computers. The new entrepreneurs have moved away from a survivor mentality to a focus on self-actualization. Chinese-owned businesses are major foreign investors and a source of capital.

The abundance of capital in the Chinese communities has inevitably lead to greater flexibility and mobility. Chinese entrepreneurs now find themselves in an expanding social network, trafficking in capital. Because of their worldwide presence, they have been able to exploit fully the financial anomalies in the various Chinese markets. The Chinese businessperson is well positioned to take advantage of another market difference—knowledge. Given differences in product market, technology development, and consumer trends, the Chinese commonwealth can tap its resources to raise money in one country, buy technology in another, produce in a third country, and sell in a fourth.

Unlike the Japanese, with their closed networks, the Chinese commonwealth represents access to local resources like information, business connections, raw materials, low labor costs, and different business practices in a variety of environments. It is an interconnected yet potentially open system and provides a new mechanism for conducting global business. By participating in such a pervasive economic network, potential partners of Chinese entrepreneurs can obtain not only greater access to Chinese-based markets at much lower costs but also access to world markets in general.

Source: Kao, John. 1993, March–April. The worldwide web of Chinese business. *Harvard Business Review*, pp. 24–36.

values, and unconscious assumptions. Its invisible quality also renders it elusive and difficult to change. Organizational culture is also difficult to map, but its qualities tend to surface during times of crisis. Because firms are composed of people, the organizational culture is greatly determined by the national or subnational culture of the employees. In most countries, organizational cultures vary dramatically from industry to industry and from firm to firm.

To what extent is a firm's culture influenced by the culture of its home country? Is the difference between Bridgestone's (a Japanese tire company) emphasis on groups and Goodyear's (an American tire company) emphasis on individual achievement due to the Japanese tendency toward collectivism and the American proclivity toward individualism? When the firm employs people from the country where it is located, it brings into the organization the cultural values of the society as held by these employees. In that case, organizational culture and national culture cannot be meaningfully distinguished. As the firm establishes offices or factories in another country, the company carries with it abroad its corporate culture, which has been molded by the culture of the home country. Managers need to be alert to the possibility that the corporate culture, which works so well at home, can be difficult to implant in the foreign setting, especially when the employees are not from the home country. GE faced this experience when it acquired the French medical technologies firm as detailed in the opening vignette. At the same time, individuals who move from firm to firm during their working life acquire and abandon a series of organizational cultures. However, these individuals do not shed their national culture. It is, therefore, reasonable to assume the following:

1. The organizational culture in a firm reflects to some extent the national culture.
2. Employees of a firm would resist the imposition of a corporate culture that is at variance with the attributes of the national culture.
3. Differences between corporate and national culture would cause conflict between the employees and upper level managers (who usually craft, implement, and reinforce the various elements of the organizational culture).

Whether a firm is able to introduce its organizational culture in its foreign facilities is affected by the manner in which the foreign operations come into being—as an acquisition or as a startup. The relationship between the parent and the subsidiary and the nature of control exerted by the parent would also be influential factors. When a completely new facility is built, the firm has the greatest freedom to hire employees and institute rules that create a culture compatible with that of the parent. An entity that has been acquired offers the hardest resistance to headquarters' efforts to integrate the subsidiary into the same cultural mold as the opening vignette illustrated. Management Focus 2-3 illustrates how a distinct organizational culture was built in a joint venture enterprise. A study of 176 work units of a multinational firm located in 18 European and Asian countries found that when a firm's management practices are congruent with national culture, work unit performance is higher, implying that management practices should adapt to the local culture to be most effective.[11]

---

[11]Newman, Karen L., and Stanley D. Nollen. 1996. Culture and congruence: The fit between management practices and national culture. *Journal of International Business Studies* 27(4), pp. 753–780.

MANAGEMENT FOCUS 2-3

CULTURAL TRANSFORMATION AT NUMMI

NUMMI, a joint venture between Toyota and General Motors was located in Fremont, California, in the shell of a huge GM assembly plant that had closed in 1982. NUMMI opened two years later. The joint venture demonstrated how the introduction of a new production system and a foreign culture transformed one of the worst GM plants into a world-class assembly operation in a unionized environment.

The success of the company stemmed largely from its ability to create a new "third" culture, a hybrid of the best of its American and Japanese parentage. Toyota and GM had not intentionally set out to develop a new culture. They aimed to build a new organization designed around the Toyota production system that rested on a radically different set of assumptions than did mass production. The new assumptions placed different demands on U.S. production workers and union leaders, most of whom came from the old GM plant. Likewise, members of the management team, who were hired from Ford, Chrysler, and other GM plants, also had to learn new ways of working.

Toyota wanted the joint venture to obtain a foothold in the U.S. auto market and to learn whether its production system could be successfully implemented in the United States. GM wanted to add a new small car to its line and also hoped to learn Toyota's production system. At the negotiation stage, GM involved the union in its plans. The union agreed to accept Toyota's demand for flexible work rules, and Toyota, in turn, agreed to the joint venture hiring unionized workers and recognizing the union.

Ten years after production began, NUMMI's cars received favorable publicity, industrial relations were cordial, and productivity and quality were high. Most employees were proud of their job and equally proud of the plant's diverse workforce. A union official commented, "This place is a blend. We have Mexicans, blacks, whites, Japanese, men, and women. And we all think a little differently. That's good." What accounts for NUMMI's success?

The company constructed its organizational culture around four principles.

1. Both management and the union recognized that their futures were interdependent, committing them to a mutual vision.

2. Employees felt secure and trusted assurances that they would be treated fairly, enabling them to become contributors.

3. The production system formed interdependent relationships throughout the plant, helping to create a healthy work environment.

4. The production system was managed to transform the stress and conflict of everyday life into trust and mutual respect.

Also, by concentrating on areas where Japanese and American culture naturally converged, while openly acknowledging their differences, NUMMI was able to establish a common ground on which to create a new culture. The points of convergence included employment security, consensual decision making with employee participation, and discipline in the workplace. The main area of difference was American individualism versus Japanese collectivism. NUMMI had avoided the problems that this difference could have caused by focusing on critical issues where the Japanese and Americans could find agreement.

Source: Wilms, Wellford, Alan Hardcastle, and Deone Zell. 1994. Cultural transformation at NUMMI. *Sloan Management Review.* Fall, pp. 99–113.

The human resource manager in the firm plays a key role in developing, protecting, and communicating the organizational culture. Managing the organizational culture occurs through every step of the process from developing policies that can be embraced by all members of the organization to communicating corporate values at the recruiting and hiring stages, as well as training and performance management that maintains consistent corporate messages. The task is to blend the various values of the worldwide workforce into a single system that embodies the firm's vision. In short, the human resource manager is the guardian of the organization's culture.[12]

MANAGERIAL PHILOSOPHY TOWARD INTERNATIONAL OPERATIONS

Howard Perlmutter has presented a well-known method of categorizing organization culture and how it impacts international management practice.[13] International business firms may be described as **ethnocentric** (home country oriented), **polycentric** (host country oriented), or **geocentric** (world oriented) in their philosophical outlook.

The firm with the ethnocentric attitude believes that its homegrown management styles, home country business culture, and home country managers are more able and trustworthy than those elsewhere. In this firm, the performance criteria for employees and products are determined by the standards used at headquarters as the following quote illustrates. *"We have found that a salesman should make twelve calls per day in Hoboken, New Jersey (the headquarters location), and therefore we apply these criteria everywhere in the world. The salesman in Brazzaville is naturally lazy, unmotivated. He shows little drive because he makes only two calls per day (despite the Congolese salesman's explanation that it takes time to reach customers by boat)."* Policies are determined by the head office and communicated to the subsidiaries. Key people overseas are from the parent firm. The overseas entities of the firm are controlled from headquarters.

Polycentric firms assume that host country cultures are different and that the ways of the foreigners are different from those at home and may be difficult to understand. Because local host country employees presumably know what is best for them, it follows that the overseas branches or subsidiaries of the firm have a local identity and employ local managers and employees. The prevailing philosophy is summed up by the adage, "When in Rome, do as the Romans do." It also means limited promotion opportunities into headquarters on the part of host country nationals and little input by the subsidiary into the parent's strategies and activities. Considerable autonomy is given to the overseas entities of the firm.

Firms with the geocentric philosophy do not equate nationality with superior performance. They seek the best employees anywhere and adopt the best practices, regardless of nationality, in running the firm's operations anywhere in the world. The geocentric firm adopts a worldwide approach in both headquarters and subsidiaries, where the subsidiaries are neither satellites (as in ethnocentrism) nor autonomous (as

---

[12]Schell, Michael S., and Charlene M. Solomon. 1997. *Capitalizing on the global workforce: A strategic guide for expatriate management.* New York: McGraw-Hill.
[13]Perlmutter, Howard V. 1969. The tortuous evolution of the multinational corporation. *Columbia Journal of World Business.* January–February.

in polycentrism). This attitude requires a collaborative effort with two-way communication between the headquarters and the subsidiaries and among the subsidiaries to establish universal standards and permissible local variations, and to make key decisions concerning products, operations, and managers.

Many large firms are moving toward geocentrism largely because of globalization pressures. The parent firm desires to make optimum use of material and human resources. The decline in morale and performance caused by an ethnocentric attitude and the high level of duplication and redundancy caused by a polycentric attitude are two more factors in the trend toward geocentrism. Also, the increased availability of technology—communication and transportation—has made global operations increasingly feasible. Table 2-5 shows how the three philosophies affect the design of a firm and its processes.

CONVERGENCE VERSUS DIVERGENCE

Are firms around the world becoming more similar (**convergence**) or are they maintaining culture-inspired differences (**divergence**)? It may be argued that as a result of "common industrial logic"—usually technology—institutional structures and patterns and managerial practices across nations are converging. Managers of a steel manufacturing

Table 2-5	Parent Company Philosophical Orientation Toward Subsidiaries		
Organizational Design	*Ethnocentric*	*Polycentric*	*Geocentric*
Complexity of Organizations	Complex at home; simple in subsidiaries	Varied and independent	Increasingly complex and interdependent
Authority and Decision Making	High in headquarters	Relatively low in headquarters	Collaboration between headquarters and subsidiaries
Evaluation and Control	Home standards applied	Determined locally	Find standards that are universal and local
Incentives: Rewards and Punishments	High in headquarters; low in subsidiaries	Wide variation; can be high or low rewards for subsidiary performance	All executives rewarded for reaching local and worldwide objectives
Communication and Information Flow	High volume to subsidiaries: orders, commands, advice	Little to and from headquarters; little between	Both ways and between subsidiaries; part of management team
Identification	Nationality of owner	Nationality of host country	Truly international company but identifying with national interests
Perpetuation: Recruiting, Staffing, and Development	Recruit and develop people of home country for key positions worldwide	Develop people of local nationality for key positions in their own country	Develop best people worldwide for key positions throughout organization

Source: Reprinted from *Columbia Journal of World Business,* January-February, 1969, Perlmutter et al, "The tortuous evolution of the multinational corporation." © 1969, with permission from Elsevier Science.

plant in Canada and a similar plant in South Korea both have to work with the issues such as technology, large-scale production, and competition, which transcend any cultural peculiarities that characterizes these two countries. A study of 20 different organizations in Denmark and Holland found that organizational culture was determined by elements such as organizational structures and control systems, rather than national cultural traits.[14]

At the same time it has been suggested that firms are and remain tied to the culture of the country in which they are established. The value systems of those in the workforce remain largely unchanged and individuals retain their diverse, culturally determined values regardless of economic ideology and institutional requirements. Sony Corporation, the Japanese electronics giant, is still a Japanese firm though it has operations in and employees from all over the world. It has its headquarters in Tokyo and is registered under Japanese law. Most of its shareholders and top managers are Japanese, and Japanese cultural icons and practices imbue the organization.

More convergence can be found at the industry and organization levels, while divergence persists on the individual and informal levels. Thus, steel plants in Canada and South Korea operate under similar conditions requiring managers to organize the business and establish the processes as dictated by the need to manufacture steel, but individual employees in both countries may exhibit differences in values, beliefs, and attitudes. These differences are more pronounced at the informal level rather than in the formal organization.

What about national cultures? Are they converging? The forces of globalization have tended to create a certain homogeneity among cultures. This trend has made business easier as people in different countries, while remaining culturally distinct, now share a common bond and outlook with regard to lifestyles, product use, and economic goals. Exposure to industrialization, new technologies, and capitalist ways of doing business may shape and change in various ways the value systems of a society, creating a unique and distinct culture that is neither home culture nor host culture oriented, an outcome referred to as **crossvergence.**

Samuel Huntington, a political scientist, has argued that a universal culture is unlikely to develop because individual civilizations were determined to protect their culture.[15] Although trade and investments may provide a veneer of universalism throughout the world, in reality the underlying culture of the recipient society has not changed. In the 1990s, Europe saw the creation of many new countries (e.g., Croatia, Estonia, Latvia, Slovakia, and Slovenia) on the basis of ethnic identity. National governments remain alert to protecting their cultural industries from foreign domination and influence. On the surface the movement may be toward convergence, but cultural differences among peoples persist. Thus, although Americans consume millions of Japanese cars, television sets, cameras, and electronic gadgets, they have not become Japanized. Similarly, just because non-Westerners sip Coca Cola, chomp Big Macs, and don Levi jeans, they do not suddenly become Westerners or Americanized. Consequently, when it comes to doing

---

[14]Hofstede, Geert, Bram Neuijen, Denise Daval Ohayv, and Geert Sanders. 1990. Measuring organizational cultures: A qualitative and quantitative study across twenty organizations. *Administrative Science Quarterly* 35, pp. 286–316.
[15]Huntington, Samuel. 1996. *The clash of civilizations and the remaking of the world order.* New York: Simon & Schuster.

business internationally, managers need to recognize and adapt to the deeply embedded cultures in the countries in which they operate. Academic research finds evidence for both convergence and divergence. A cross-national study of 567 managers from 12 countries found that managerial values were becoming increasingly homogeneous across nations even as value differences continue to persist across cultures.[16] Managers for each of the 12 nationalities ranked four sets of value dimensions in the same order of importance. At the same time, for instance, while the value dimension of being cheerful, forgiving, helpful, and loving was ranked the least important of the four value dimensions, Japanese managers ranked this dimension as significantly more important than did any of the other nationalities. However, another study of the impact of national culture and economic ideology on managerial work values among managers in the United States, Russia, Japan, and China found less support for either the convergence or the divergence perspective.[17] A study based on a survey of 326 managers from the United States, China, and Hong Kong found that the values of Hong Kong managers neither converged or diverged from United States and Chinese values; instead, they were a mixture of both.[18] It appears that some aspects of culture change, while others do not. Some values may change more rapidly than others. Other unique values may evolve from a combination of influences. The evidence suggests a concurrent possibility of convergence, divergence, and also crossvergence.

COMMUNICATION

Communication refers to the process of transferring meanings from the sender to the receiver. This process becomes complicated when the two parties belong to different cultures and different linguistic groups, because the manner in which people communicate differs from society to society.

International management requires communication to take place on a continuous basis between peoples of different cultures—between a firm's head office and its overseas branches and subsidiaries and with outside entities such as customers, suppliers, government agencies, and other interest groups. In the same organization, communication often occurs between individuals of different cultures. Take, for instance, the situation of an American firm with offices in Malaysia. When communication occurs between the head office and the foreign office in Kuala Lumpur, who is communicating with whom? Is it an American with a Malaysian or an American with an American or an American with an American-trained Malaysian, or any of a countless number of other possibilities? The cultural background, experience, and training of the parties in the communication relationship affect the quality of the communication. Headquarters sometimes overlook the need to have managers who understand the environment of managing and decision making in the foreign country.

---

[16]Bigoness, William J., and Gerald Blakely. 1996. A cross-national study of managerial values. *Journal of International Business Studies* 27(4), pp. 739–752.

[17]Ralston, David A., David H. Holt, Robert Terpstra, and Yu Kai-Cheng. 1997. The impact of national culture and economic ideology on managerial work values: A study of the United States, Russia, Japan, and China. *Journal of International Business Studies* 28(1), pp. 177–207.

[18]Ralston, David A., David J. Gustafson, Fanny M. Cheung, and Robert H. Terpstra. 1993. Differences in managerial values: A study of U.S., Hong Kong, and PRC managers. *Journal of International Business Studies* 24(2), pp. 249–276.

Edward Hall has pointed out that the nature of communication differs between high-context and low-context cultures.[19] In a **high-context culture,** the external environment, the overall situation, and nonverbal behaviors create the setting in which communication occurs and is interpreted. In such a culture, members rely on cues and clues and instead of being direct, convey and understand the meaning in a more subtle fashion. The dominant cultures of Japan, China, and Saudi Arabia are examples of high-context.

A **low-context culture,** in contrast, relies more on a direct and matter-of-fact manner of communicating with little or no attention given to the contextual environment. The language used is explicit and thus the words are carefully chosen to convey the exact meaning to avoid any misunderstanding. The North American (United States and Canada) and Germanic (Germany and Austria) societies are examples of low-context cultures. The characteristics of these two cultures as they affect communication are contrasted in Table 2-6.

Table 2-6 Communication in High-Context and Low-Context Cultures

High-Context Culture	*Low-Context Culture*
Context	
The meaning lies in the environment of the context, relationship, status, protocol	The meaning is explicit and often written down
Nonverbal cues are important	No ambiguity
"Yes" may be ambiguous	Nonverbal supports verbal expression
Space	
Greater group emphasis	Individual space
Smaller physical distance	Large physical distance
Time	
Polychronic	Monochronic
Involved with many things at once	Do one thing at a time, concentrate on the task
Easily interrupted and allow distractions	Take deadlines and schedules seriously
Priority for people and relationships	Accustomed to short-term relationships
Verbal/Nonverbal	
Greater use of nonverbal cues	Mostly verbal communication
Hands and face expressions	Hands support speech
Silence could be communication	Low tolerance for silence
Language	
Circular use of language, subtleties	Linear, mean what they say
Indirect and more comprehensive thought	Direct and linear thinking process
Use of intuitive and inner knowledge	Others orientation
More emphasis on inner orientation	
Agreements	
Emphasis on someone's word	Emphasis on written contract
Indirectness is considerate and honest	Directness is honesty
Laws are flexible and situational	Laws are rigid and universal
Contracts are symbolic of a relationship	Contracts are binding

Source: From *Hidden Differences* by Edward T. Hall and Mildred Reed Hall, © 1987 by Edward T. Hall and Mildred Reed Hall. Used by permission of Doubleday, a division of Random House, Inc.

---

[19]Hall, Edward T. 1976. *Beyond culture.* New York: Anchor Press-Doubleday.

THE COMMUNICATION MODEL

The process of communication has several consequential segments:

- The sender
- Determining the contents of the message
- Encoding the message (in words and symbols)
- Choosing the message medium (such as face-to-face, telephone, written memorandum, e-mail)
- The receipt of the message
- Decoding of the message by the recipient
- Providing feedback to the sender

The smooth flow of this process, however, is affected by cross-cultural interference or noise of all sorts, which distorts communication and makes it ineffective. Communication is effective when recipients understand what the sender intended in the message. This model is described in Figure 2-1.

Each of these segments requires careful attention. For instance, the rank and status of the sender becomes relevant, especially in relation to whom the message is being sent. It is important to go beyond job titles, which vary from firm to firm and from country to country, and instead focus on the authority and seniority of the individuals. In a bureaucratic culture, such as France's, all upward communication must flow through the formal line of command even if the communication is to a peer in another department. It is also common sense to know how to address one's counterpart. In Japan, managers are called by their last name plus "san" such as Mr. Nakasone-san. The use of business cards is common in East Asia and often done in a highly formal manner. Business cards are received with due seriousness and read carefully before being put away. In certain languages such as Hindi and Spanish, people can be addressed in two ways—the familiar, informal way and the more polite and formal way. The formal manner is used in initial communication, with someone with seniority or higher status.

The content of the message should be relevant to be persuasive. In high-context cultures, the tendency, at initial stages at least, is to convey in generalities, whereas in low-context cultures the sender comes to the substance of the matter quickly and directly. Another issue with regard to content is the amount of information provided, without overloading the receiver. West European and Anglo-Saxon societies often rely on objective

FIGURE 2-1 The Communication Process

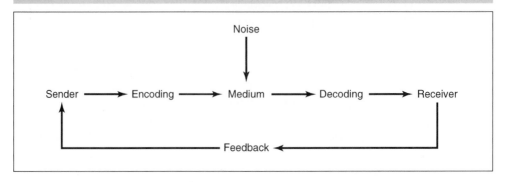

data and information, something that may not be easily recognized and understood by the other party.

The medium of communication is critical too. While English is the international language of commerce, competency as well as differences in its usage vary across countries. Even though technology—Internet, e-mail, telephone, facsimile, video conferencing—now affords easy, cheap, and frequent communication, face-to-face meetings are essential in some situations. Use of interpreters becomes necessary when the parties use different languages and contracts drawn up must be translated in the languages of both parties. A firm can use in-house translators or hire external contractors. To ensure that the documents are similar in both languages, **backtranslation** is recommended. Here, a document in, say Russian, is translated into English, which then is retranslated back into Russian. Ideally, the latter Russian version should exactly match the original Russian version. A question that is often posed is whether the international manager should know a foreign language. Although such knowledge is useful and should be encouraged, it is not essential. The use of competent interpreters is common and quite effective. The advantage of knowing the local language is it allows the manager to gain insights into the local culture and become more sensitive to nonverbal aspects of communication, about the importance of cultural or religious symbols, celebrations, and holidays, and such other aspects of the foreign society. Because of these advantages, more and more universities require learning foreign languages as part of the coursework.[20]

Proper interpretation becomes essential for languages such as Chinese, because many business terms have no official equivalents in that language. Thus, companies bringing unfamiliar products and technology into China must decide exactly what these products should be called. Company names that are simply transliterated phonetically may cause problems. Written Chinese is made up of single characters that represent both a syllable and a meaning (unlike English where words can be created by using compounds or adding a prefix or suffix). Thus, many characters have discrete meanings, and companies must make sure that they are not associating something negative with their name. Also, many European words and names are quite unpronounceable in Chinese.

Other factors that affect communication are the place and time surrounding it. While in Anglo-Saxon cultures punctuality is expected and valued, in many Latin societies the appointment time is often only an approximation; one is not expected to arrive at a meeting at the precise time. In addition, cultures differ with regard to the amount of time spent on informal interactions or nonbusiness issues. When it comes to communicating on a face-to-face basis in Japan and Korea, business-related interaction often extends to after-hours and in social settings such as nightclubs and restaurants.

Communication also occurs through the nonverbal medium, which usually accompanies the verbal. Nonverbal signals have different meanings in different societies and can easily be misinterpreted. Some nonverbal signals include the physical distance maintained between individuals, physical contact or touch (or its absence), eye contact, volume and pitch of the voice, kinesics (body movements such as facial expressions, gestures with one's hands and fingers, posture, and stance), and the use of silence. In high-context cultures, where nonverbal symbols carry great weight, managers should be conscious of the signals they are sending out and be extra sensitive to pick up on the nonverbal signals being conveyed to them.

---

[20]Bradshaw, Della. 1999, March 22. Mastering the word. *Financial Times,* p. 9.

The communication process can be improved by providing cross-cultural training to help managers to understand the nature of the foreign society more thoroughly and to avoid common gaffes. In addition, the feedback system, which checks on whether the communication sent out has been received and understood as intended, must be of a high caliber. One way to ensure accurate interpretation is to seek frequent reports so that misunderstandings are immediately corrected. Another way is to have frequent face-to-face meetings, which can help to build up personal relationships and enable the parties to clarify the issues.

NEGOTIATIONS

The importance of good communication becomes apparent when firms negotiate with other entities such as suppliers and customers. Negotiation is the process by which managers attempt to settle what each shall give and take or perform and receive in a transaction between them. While all business negotiations require careful preparations, cross-cultural negotiations require greater awareness about potential problems because people from different cultures use different negotiation approaches. They do so because of differences in their perceptions that are conditioned by the characteristics of the national culture to which they belong. Therefore, managers from collectivist cultures bring to the bargaining situation a different set of attitudes and values than do people from individualistic cultures. While negotiations between two parties could be complicated in itself, it is much more so in the case of multilateral negotiations.[21] Multilateral negotiations have become more common, as evidenced by the creation of strategic alliances among various firms in the airline industry (the Star Alliance includes airlines from the United States, Germany, Brazil, Thailand, and Scandinavia), by consortiums such as the Airbus Industrie, by international trade treaties (e.g., NAFTA, EU, WTO), and by global projects (the international space station).

Cultural differences may contribute to four potentially problematic aspects of international negotiations: language, nonverbal behaviors, values, and decision-making process. A common complaint heard from American managers regards foreign negotiators' practice of breaking into side conversations in their native languages. Americans hate it. At best, they think it is impolite and are likely to suspect sinister content in the foreign conversation—they are plotting or telling secrets. This interpretation is usually wrong. Videotaping and translation of such conversations show that their usual purpose is to clarify a translation problem or reflects a disagreement among the foreign team. By not knowing the foreign language, Americans fail to appreciate the reasons why the other team is speaking in its own language.[22]

Studies show that most non-U.S. negotiators tend to adapt their styles more than Americans to the other party, increasing their attractiveness.[23] Managers may not extend the negotiating style they use with their domestic counterparts to their foreign partners. One approach may be to appear similar to the other party with the hope of enhancing

[21]Money, R. Bruce. 1998. International multilateral negotiations and social networks. *Journal of International Business Studies* 29(4), pp. 695–710.

[22]Graham, John. 1996. Vis-à-vis: International business negotiations. In Pervez N. Ghauri and Jean-Claude Usunier, eds. *International business negotiations* (pp. 69–90). Tarrytown, NY: Pergamon.

[23]Graham, John L., Alma T. Mintu, and Rodgers Waymond. 1994. Explorations of negotiation behaviors in ten foreign cultures using a model developed in the United States. *Management Science* 40(1), pp. 72–95.

the bargaining outcomes. Managers may also approach every set of foreign negotiators differently. Thus, when managers of an Italian company negotiate with other Italian suppliers, the negotiating style is not the same as the one adopted when dealing with U.S. suppliers. The style adopted with Americans also differs from the approach used with, say French suppliers. Some cultures pay more deference (and profits) to the buyer, particularly in Japan—where the customer is apparently more highly regarded than in other cultures.[24] Communications of managers from high-context cultures, where face-saving, innuendo, and between-the-line communication are important, are often misunderstood by their counterparts from low-context cultures.[25] Hall's perspective suggests that in high-context cultures, considerable time and effort need to be expended to build up a trusting and reliable relationship before a business transaction can be consummated. In contrast, in low-context cultures, negotiations are more direct, matter-of-fact, with the personal characteristics and relationships only marginal to the business at hand.

A study of inter- and intracultural negotiations between U.S. and Japanese managers found that in intercultural negotiations (between the U.S. and Japan), the joint gains were lower when compared to intracultural negotiations (that is among the Americans themselves or the Japanese themselves). The difference is attributed to the distinctive cultural values of the two societies and that members of a society know and understand negotiating partners from their own country as compared to those from another country.[26] A study of negotiating strategies of Canadian and Chinese managers found that home culture orientation was a significant determinant.[27] In Chinese society, where collectivism and group harmony are emphasized, managers prefer to avoid conflicts in advance of their occurrence. When they have to deal with conflicts, Chinese managers are more inclined to use more negative strategies, such as halting or even withdrawing from negotiations, when compared to their Canadian counterparts.

Results from a negotiation simulation in the United States and Hong Kong indicated that U.S. negotiators were more likely to subscribe to a negotiating strategy designed to maximize their own gain and to promote an integrative outcome.[28] Hong Kong negotiators were more likely to adopt a strategy aimed at distributing the outcomes equally between the two parties. The differences lie in the respective cultural profiles of the two countries. American culture values individualism, which encourages self-interested negotiating norms. The culture is also more open to change and creative solutions to problems. In contrast, Hong Kong Chinese culture is more collectivist and conservative with emphasis on seeking more equal outcomes when resolving workplace conflict. Another study found that Chinese managers tend to avoid conflict in negotiations while U.S. managers had an assertive style focusing on high self-concern.[29]

[24]Graham, John L., and Yoshihiro Sano. 1989. *Smart bargaining: Doing business with the Japanese.* New York: Harper & Row.

[25]Usunier, Jean-Claude. 1996. Cultural aspects of international business negotiations. In Pervez N. Ghauri and Jean-Claude Usunier, eds. *International business negotiations* (pp. 69–90). Tarrytown, NY: Pergamon.

[26]Brett, Jean M., and Tetsushi Okumura. 1998. Inter- and intracultural negotiation: U.S. and Japanese negotiators. *The Academy of Management Journal* 41(5), pp. 495–510.

[27]Tse, David K., June Francis, and Jan Walls. 1994. Cultural differences in conducting intra- and inter-cultural negotiations: A Sino-Canadian comparison. *Journal of International Business Studies* 25(4), pp. 537–555.

[28]Tinsley, Catherine H., and Madan M. Pillutla. 1998. Negotiating in the United States and Hong Kong. *Journal of International Business Studies* 29(4), pp. 711–728.

[29]Morris, Michael W., et al. 1998. Conflict management style: Accounting for cross-national differences. *Journal of International Business Studies* 29(4), pp. 729–748.

When U.S. managers negotiated with counterparts from more "distant" cultures, they were likely to use hard tactics such as threats, demands, and sanctions.[30] No differences were noted in the tactics U.S. managers used with Japanese and Western European managers, largely because they were familiar with these cultures due to extensive and long interactions.

PREPARING FOR INTERNATIONAL NEGOTIATIONS

Recognizing that cultural factors affect international business negotiations, managers should bear in mind the following sets of issues:

1. *Know the culture of the opposing side.* The team that has studied the culture of the other side and has incorporated that knowledge in its negotiating strategy is better placed to strike a deal than the team that has not. Cultural variables should not be over-generalized. Thus, while most Mexicans do not discuss business over lunch, a Mexican negotiator who has studied the U.S. culture and has a degree in international business from New York University, may not be averse to talking shop at lunchtime.

2. *When to negotiate?* This issue requires knowledge of national and religious holidays, anniversaries, climatic conditions, the financial calendar, and regular working hours of the foreign country.

3. *How much time to devote to negotiations?* In many countries, it takes longer to negotiate because negotiators do not have the authority to make major compromises and offers or sign a contract. Constant reference to individuals higher up in the hierarchy often causes delays. In high-context cultures, considerable time is initially spent in "feeling" out the other party. Much socializing and general conversations take place but no substantive discussions. In low-context cultures, negotiations move fast—time is money, and managers are task-oriented at the meetings. Consequently, they are punctual, and meetings have goals. High-context cultures place great importance on personal relationships, which take time to build. The need for building trust in one's counterpart is particularly strong in countries where the legal system cannot be relied upon to adjudicate disputes fairly and expeditiously.

4. *How to greet and address?* The first meetings usually are heralded through mutual greetings. Even though a (right) handshake is common, others use an embrace, or a kiss, or a slapping and grabbing of the hands, or even no touch at all. The Japanese greeting is in the form of bows whereas in India, Nepal, Thailand, and Sri Lanka, among others, people greet by placing the palms of their hands together at the level of their eyes. The initial meetings are also used in some countries to exchange business cards. The ways individuals are referred to also differ from culture to culture.

5. *Gift giving and entertainment.* Gifts are expected in certain cultures, such as the Japanese, while in others it may be considered improper, almost a bribe, as in the United Kingdom. International negotiators often find themselves sharing food and drink with their hosts at after-hours get-togethers. Sometimes formal meals are elaborate feasts, as in much of Asia. In some countries, certain foods may be uncommon and

---

[30]Rao, Asha, and Stuart M. Schmidt. 1998. A behavioral perspective on negotiating international alliances. *Journal of International Business Studies* 29(4), pp. 665–694.

foreign managers would embarrass their hosts if they insist on not having these foods. Although a certain degree of adjustment to the host country is expected, ideally, hosts should not subject their guests to food and entertainment that would make the guests uncomfortable.

6. *Composition of the negotiating team.* Costs often prohibit sending a large team abroad. However, the team sent can expect to meet a large delegation from the company in the host country. American teams often include a lawyer to nail down the legal aspects of a contract. Teams should have members familiar with the language of the other party. Asian countries, which give great weight to age, often select older managers to lead their teams. It is important to be aware of the rank and status of one's counterpart at the negotiations so that the meetings are conducted between individuals of similar stature and authority. Although practice and law prohibit U.S. and Canadian firms from excluding women or racial minorities in negotiating teams, in many countries, the negotiators are likely to be males.

7. *Preparing for the negotiations.* At the outset the parties should determine that the negotiations are feasible and show promise. Before starting, each side should define what they want from a contract. They should research the facts, especially culture-specific information and business style. In assembling the team, the parties should carefully include capable, knowledgeable, and authoritative people. Where necessary, an interpreter should be part of the team and thus avoid relying on the one brought by the other party. Ample time should be allocated for the negotiations without revealing the timetable.

8. *Beginning the negotiations.* It is essential that the parties know the place where they are meeting, the arrangement of the room(s), and are familiar with the agenda, which should have been established in advance. In many Ibero-American countries, formal negotiations are preceded by elaborate social interactions during which time personal relationships with their opposite numbers are forged.

9. *Bargaining.* Some bargaining tips to keep in mind include the following:
  • Control the amount of information provided to the other party
  • Be aware of and carefully use idioms, slang, and verbal and nonverbal communication
  • Put oneself in the shoes of one's counterpart as a way to understand the opposite member's thought process and reasoning
  • Adjust to the way of life in the host culture (such as eating, gift giving, and entertaining)
  • Strive to save everyone's face
  • Refuse a bad deal and be ready to walk away
  • Sign the agreement before the parties leave after making sure the agreement is understood by all parties
  • Be flexible in interpreting what a contract is.

10. *Post-contract.* While contracts should include clauses that spell out how to resolve disputes, initial efforts should be made to discuss the differences and come to a resolution without seeking legal recourse. Legal intervention should be reserved for when all else fails. Successful relationships are characterized by open communication and frequent exchanges of personnel and information among the parties. In many cases, contracts are for long terms with the possibility of continuous extensions, hence the need to maintain amity in the relationship.

11. *The negotiating partners.* The parties should know the identity of the individuals with whom they are negotiating. Having contacts in a foreign country can help a firm by creating the proper groundwork for formal negotiations to occur. Many international firms set up representative offices to understand the local environment and culture and cultivate key business and government relationships before initiating any formal business ventures. In China, for instance, businesses can benefit from having connections or **guanxi,** as is illustrated in Management Focus 2-4.

By using the preceding guidelines, planning properly, and treating people as individuals rather than stereotyping them, one will have made a good start to becoming a successful cross-cultural negotiator. It is important for the negotiators to hold a high degree of personal respect for one another. The best approach is to learn to understand and respect cultural differences while retaining one's own.

MOTIVATION

What is the role of culture in motivating individuals and groups to perform? Most studies on motivation have come from the United States and Europe and are based on the behavior and goals of individuals and groups in these countries. Thus, managers in Western firms trained in concepts such as Theory X and Y, Maslow's hierarchy of needs, McClelland's achievement-motivation theory, Herzberg's motivator-hygiene theory, Vroom's expectancy theory, and equity theory may not be able to apply them with similar results with a foreign workforce or in a foreign country. To test the validity of these theories elsewhere, research instruments have to be prepared in local languages, and it is not easy to find word equivalents for many Western concepts such as self-actualization. Also, because managers in a foreign country may use different concepts of motivation, foreign workers may not understand the Western ideas as being similar.

Some studies have been done to check for the validity of Western motivation theories in other countries and the results are inconclusive.[31] For instance, the hierarchy of needs suggested by Maslow exists in many societies but not always in the specific sequence of physiological, safety, social, esteem, and self-actualization needs. For instance, Arab managers identify esteem and social needs as more important than self-actualization. McClelland found that if motivation is developed as a trait in early childhood, adult people in other countries can be taught to become motivated for high achievement.

To what extent do work and its various dimensions differ in their importance across national cultures? A survey of employees in Belgium, Germany, Israel, Japan, Netherlands, the United Kingdom, and the United States found that interesting work and pay ranked among the highest work goals while opportunities for promotion and working conditions were ranked low across all these countries.[32] Other work dimensions such as job security, job variety, or interpersonal relationships were rated differently by the various country respondents. Another study asked employees in China, Russia, Taiwan, and

---

[31]Hofstede, Geert. 1980. Motivation, leadership, and organization: Do American theories apply abroad? *Organizational Dynamics.* Summer, pp. 42–63; McClelland, David C. 1965. Achievement motivation can be developed. *Harvard Business Review,* November–December; Deresky, Helen. 1997. *International management.* 2d ed. Reading, MA: Addison-Wesley.

[32]Harpaz, Itzhak. 1990. The importance of work goals: An international perspective. *Journal of International Business Studies* 21(1), pp. 75–93.

MANAGEMENT FOCUS 2-4

GUANXI AS A SOURCE OF COMPETITIVE ADVANTAGE

There is a saying in China: "China is a land of *guanxi*. . . . Nothing can be done without *guanxi*." Chinese businesspersons and executives believe that once good guanxi is established, business ventures can operate smoothly, business opportunities open up, and information about government policies and government approvals of permits become easier to obtain.

What is guanxi? Guanxi (pronounced gwan-see) means relationship or connection, and without it, a foreign firm may have a hard time doing business in China. More than a pure interpersonal relationship, guanxi is a sense of reciprocal obligation to respond to requests for assistance. It exists at both the personal level as well as the organizational level. Guanxi in Chinese society is ubiquitous and plays a crucial role in daily life.

Guanxi between individuals can be formed on the basis of blood ties (e.g., family members, relatives, and members of the same clan) or through social interactions (e.g., same hometown, schooling, and place of work). Given the importance of the family in Chinese society, blood guanxi takes primacy over social guanxi.

An important dimension of both types of guanxi is the degree of emotional closeness between the individuals, which is determined by *ganqing* (pronounced gahnt-chin), or affection. It is possible for individuals to have guanxi but not ganqing. Ganqing is created through shared experiences brought about by living, working, or studying together and through its conscious cultivation.

The underlying dimensions of guanxi are trust and credibility, and they tend to supplant legal contracts among Chinese businessmen. Maintenance of guanxi requires that the individuals in the relationship put a "face"—a public image, created by performing expected social roles. Someone with a large guanxi network has a bigger face just as a certain amount of face is needed to create a viable network. Time, money, and effort are required for creating and maintaining social guanxi.

Because guanxi is a system of reciprocal favors, it means that a favor received has to be returned some day; otherwise the system cannot be sustained. The reciprocity is morally binding and linked to the dimensions of trust and credibility. The value of the guanxi depends on the status of the individuals in the relationship. If the individual loses power, guanxi with him becomes useless.

How can foreign firms develop guanxi in China? One common technique is as follows: If person A wants something from B with whom he does not have any guanxi, he may seek out a member of his own network, say C, who has guanxi with B. By asking C to introduce B to him, a guanxi base between A and B is established. Avon, the cosmetics manufacturer, initially failed to win the approval of the Chinese government to sell its products through the direct marketing method. Avon obtained the assistance of David Li, the head of Hong Kong's Bank of East Asia. Li was well known for his guanxi with the Chinese government. He successfully introduced Avon to the appropriate Chinese ministry. An arrangement was worked out in which Li became a partner with 5 percent equity because of the services that he rendered.

It should be recognized that a quality social guanxi takes considerable time to develop, and quality is a key component of guanxi. Thus, foreign companies that have been in China for a long time are likely to enjoy an edge over their newer competitors. In addition, the guanxi needs nurturing to develop ganqing, which requires time, money and effort on the part of the foreign firm. It is another reason long-established relationships are harder to break into or replace. It is useful for foreign firms to have many employees develop guanxi instead of relying on one or two employees in order to protect the firm if an employee should leave the firm taking away guanxi connections. For Western expatriate managers though, joining the Chinese guanxi is not easy; the cultural and language barriers are often difficult to surmount. Hence joint ventures or using Chinese nationals is the preferred way of doing business in China.

Source: Tsang, Eric W. K. 1998. Can *guanxi* be a source of sustained competitive advantage for doing business in China? *The Academy of Management Executive* 12(2), pp. 64–73.

the United States to rank their preferences for what they want in a job.[33] The results showed considerable variation among the four groups with regard to which attributes of the job were more important and which ones were less important. While good wages and good working conditions were ranked highest by the Chinese, to the Russians, the top two items were "promotion and growth in one's skills within the organization" and "a feeling of being in on things; being well informed and involved." High job security, followed by good wages, was ranked top by Taiwanese respondents. To the Americans, full appreciation of the work done and interesting work were the most important dimensions of the job. These variations make it hard to generalize about motivation and workplace expectations across countries.

An individual's needs are determined by many factors, including age, education, economic status, experience, and organizational culture, in addition to national culture. In general, the deeper the level of poverty, the greater is the importance attached to the resources needed to sustain life. For example, a breakdown of compensation packages of Mexican and U.S. general managers reveals important value differences: U.S. managers are motivated by long-term incentives, whereas Mexicans prefer a more dependable base pay. In introducing American corporate culture in say, Mexico, it is best to proceed slowly. Mexican business and cultural practices collide with more "Americanized" programs such as total quality management and participative management. Generally, such practices have to be adapted to the conditions of the host country. Practices that have been in effect for many years, if changed overnight, especially unilaterally, arouse anxiety and opposition.[34]

Hofstede's Value Survey Model offers some insights into what may serve as effective motivators in different cultures. Opportunities for individual promotion and growth would be important in individualistic cultures, whereas opportunities to belong to a social group would be highly valued in a collectivist society. Autonomy would be important in an individualistic society. Job security and extensive benefits programs would be important to workers in a society where uncertainty avoidance is high. Conversely, job variety would appeal to members of a low uncertainty avoidance culture. Where power distances are greater, employees need greater direction and rely on mentors and patrons. In low power distance cultures, interaction with peers, autonomy, and fewer rules are expected. Finally, in feminine cultures, a flexible work schedule would be attractive.

LEADERSHIP AND DECISION MAKING

Managerial leadership centers on the relationship between the manager and the subordinates. The manner of relating to the subordinates, the style of projecting and using power and the method of dealing with conflict and crisis set the context for leadership.

Just as with the study of motivation, most contemporary theories of leadership have originated in the United States. The basic thrust of most theories is that participative

---

[33]Fisher, Cynthia, and Anne Yuan. 1998. What motivates employees? A comparison of U.S. and Chinese responses. *The International Journal of Human Resource Management* 9(3), pp. 516–528.
[34]Harris, Philip, R., and Robert T. Moran. 1996. *Managing cultural differences,* 4th ed. Houston, TX: Gulf Publishing Company.

styles are preferable to authoritarian styles. Other theories such as Fiedler's contingency theory and Vroom-Yetton's model suggest that certain situations require a participative style while others require an authoritarian style. Many of these theories have been tested on managers in foreign countries and the conclusions are ambiguous. For instance, a survey of managers from Australia, Canada, South Africa, the United States, and Middle East countries found that when it came to actual behavior on the job, managers preferred a task-oriented rather than a relationship-oriented approach.[35]

In the United Kingdom, where class distinctions are severe, firms tend to be more hierarchical. Managers are often drawn from the upper crust of society, reflecting education in prestigious schools, connections, and good breeding. Class conflict is more common as evidenced by the size and power of labor unions and in the number of strikes. In contrast, in Germany, where many managers are by training engineers, the bureaucratic model is the norm. Managers define tasks, create job descriptions for the tasks, and establish behavioral and performance standards for the job. In this rational system, managers work and motivate workers to meet corporate goals. Legally mandated participation of workers in decision making tempers the task-oriented style of German managers and forces them to accept input from subordinates.

In France, the development of managers does not take place in formal company training programs but begins long before employment at prestigious colleges called *grande ecoles*. Management is considered a "state of mind" rather than a set of techniques.[36] There, it is a profession with its own entry requirements and regulations. *Cadre* (the French term for manager) status is attained through educational credentials or through loyalty to a particular company. Unlike the Anglo-Saxon view of management, French managers have a bias for intellect, rather than for action. People who run big enterprises must above all else be clever; that is, they should be able to grasp complex issues, analyze problems, and evaluate solutions. When hiring executives, companies do not look for drive or initiative in the recruits; instead, they look for qualities such as analytical skills, independence, and an ability to synthesize information. Communication or interpersonal skills are less important.

French managers maintain close links with each other as alumni of the prestigious colleges. They are also less likely to trust their intuition, are more likely to centralize decision making and create hierarchies. In Japan, in contrast, even though managers are often top graduates of highly regarded schools, the leadership style appears to be participative. Subordinates tend to be involved in the decision-making process, often through the ***ringi*** system, which is described in Management Focus 2-5.

A study of leadership in Arab societies noted that Arab leaders tend to centralize power and authority and adopt an authoritarian style.[37] Often, efficiency goals are subordinated to the needs of the lower-level employees and personal friendships. Nepotism

[35]Bhagat, R. S. 1990. Cross-cultural issues in organizational psychology: Emergent trends and directions for research in the 1990s. In C. L. Cooper and I. Robertson, eds. *International Review of Industrial and Organizational Psychology.* New York: Wiley and Sons.
[36]Barsoux, Jean-Louis, and Peter Lawrence. 1991. The making of a French manager. *Harvard Business Review* July–August, pp. 58–67.
[37]Ali, A. 1990. Management theory in a transitional society: The Arab's experience. *International Studies of Management and Organization* 21(30), pp. 38–61; Al-Jafary, Abdulrahman, and A. T. Hollingsworth. 1983. An exploratory study of management practices in the Arabian Gulf region. *Journal of International Business Studies* Fall, pp. 143–152.

MANAGEMENT FOCUS 2-5

DECISION MAKING IN JAPANESE FIRMS

Ringi is the system of circulating an intra-office memorandum (*ringhisho*) to obtain approval for a proposed course of action and literally means "circle of discussions." Ringi's primary function is a referral and clearance system that, in effect, embodies the consensus of all prior processes and negotiations. Once the document has been circulated and approved with the personal seals of all the participants, it is passed on to higher levels for information purposes or, if necessary, for further approval. The achievement of consensus as represented by the ringhisho document can be a long and slow process; once reached, implementation is rapid because no visible opposition exists. Indeed, the ringi system, which is quite formal, is in many cases preceded by more informal discussion and negotiations, sometimes over drinks and entertainment at after-hour parties or at sporting events. A typology of this type of decision making follows.

> Stage 1. *Chotto ippai* (little drink) refers to simply getting together after work at off-business premises to exchange information and opinions. This concept of a "little drink" can take place in a local pub, at a restaurant, a sporting event, coffee shop, or over tea. Regardless of the physical setting, the context of chotto ippai is principally an informal get-together where issues or ideas can be discussed without any further recourse or as a testing ground for discussions at work. Ideas

that find little support here go no further than the few individuals privy to them.

Stage 2. *Hanashiai* (talk and fit together) usually involves a few members of a work group who meet informally at work for exploratory talks without any clear agenda in order to feel out the thoughts of other interested or affected parties. Notions receiving general support and agreement from these informal talks lead to involving others in the issue at the kaigi stage.

Stage 3. *Kaigi* (department group meeting) is a meeting or conference held to discuss problems and issues and eventually reach a consensus. The Western equivalent of this setting would be a staff or department meeting. Kaigi is also often an informal consultation prior to formalizing a decision statement requiring approval.

Stage 4. *Ringi* is the system of circulating an intra-office memorandum to obtain approval for a proposed course of action. It has the virtue of engaging a large number of subordinates in providing input to the issue before the manager makes a decision. In general, managers are concerned with saving face, thus overt conflict is rare and sincere efforts are made to maintain harmony. Therefore, most Japanese managers have less authority and appear to be less decisive than their Western counterparts.

Source: Hayoshi, S. 1988. *Culture and management in Japan.* Tokyo: University of Tokyo Press; Pascal, Richard T. 1978. Communication and decision-making across cultures: Japanese and American comparisons. *Administrative Science Quarterly* 23(1), pp. 91–110.

is, therefore, quite common. Even though many firms in Arab countries are organized and influenced by Western practices, in many cases, the organizational structures and the rules and regulations are often facades of modernity while in effect the traditional practices endure.

In recent years, the formal study of management has become exceedingly popular around the world and the model adopted by universities everywhere has been the one used in the United States. At the same time, more and more students from all over the world go to United States institutions of higher learning for a management education. As a consequence, American leadership and management concepts have become familiar to managers everywhere. Managers around the world often make a conscious effort to adopt and apply many of the leadership ideas espoused in the United States.

Should the international firm strive to have a uniform managerial style across its global offices and facilities? Managerial styles can be presented as a continuum with autocratic at one end and participative at the other, or traditional (where the patriarch exercises authority) to modern (participative). Variations between these two styles are numerous. Participation may be restricted to top management levels or may be extended throughout the firm. The degree of employee participation in decision making is determined by many factors including the manager's personal attributes, organizational structure and culture, the business environment, the nature of the task, as well as the culture of the society. The number and complexity of these and other variables would strongly suggest that no managerial style is universally valid. Thus, it is quite possible for a managerial style, effective in the United States, to not work in a foreign setting, and vice versa. For instance, in the United States, managers are trained to use statistics and numbers to make decisions in addition to relying on intuition. South American managers are more likely to make decisions on subjective behavioral dimensions. In conclusion therefore, it would appear that the best leadership approach is one that embodies a strong contingency element. Depending on a particular setting and the particular issue, the manager will have to fashion a leadership style. Therefore, a successful global leader should be able to

- Function successfully in multiple cultural environments
- Communicate proficiently across cultures
- Understand the impact of cultural influences on human behavior
- Adjust to different cultural environments
- Understand national cultures and the limitations of transferring management ideas across cultures
- Motivate and evaluate subordinates from different countries
- Consider the impact of cultural differences on standard business practices
- Seek out synergy by working with diverse cultural groups
- Relate national culture to an individual's work ethic
- Promote and use the various vehicles of international culture such as the media and travel

PREPARING FOR CROSS-CULTURAL MANAGEMENT

With the accelerating pace of demographic change in the United States and Canada since the 1980s, valuing and managing a diverse workforce has become a compelling managerial preoccupation and a matter of public policy. Managers of North American firms going abroad must now frame and implement their organization's diversity goals on a worldwide basis. The question then is how do the North American notions of diversity—race, religion, gender, sexual orientation, age, and disability—apply in homogeneous South Korea or stratified India, or bicultural Belgium? How do Americans of non-European descent perform in international firms abroad and how are they perceived in foreign countries?

Colgate-Palmolive, an American multinational consumer products company with a majority of its sales from abroad, frames its perspective on global diversity by focusing on respect for all its workers.[38] Through a program called "Valuing Colgate People" in which all managers participate, the company seeks to help employees recognize that people of all backgrounds are able to work productively together.

Through a combination of individual and team exercises, role-playing, and other educational material, employees study a variety of diversity issues that lead to valuing differences because they contribute to organizational goals. The first day of the program is the global section. It focuses on themes and values of Colgate: caring, global teamwork, and continuous improvement. These values are corporate-wide and give Colgate employees shared goals. The second day focuses on issues within a particular country. In the United States, the focus is on race, gender, age, sexual harassment, and disability status. Other countries focus on the key issues that prevent their people from treating each other with respect, such as gender bias and discrimination based on class or religion. One country in each region—Latin American, Europe, and Asia—develops specific curricula for this segment. The next issue is to ensure that all the facets tie in with the underlying premise of respect. Colgate's performance evaluation system, for example, appraises how well managers exemplify and reinforce respect. Managers are trained first because they set the tone for their work sites and reinforce values. Then, the company trains its nonmanagers.

Instead of exporting the American approach, the company examines what kind of training is needed in each country. It attempts to blend the two cultures. For instance, Colgate ran a survey in Brazil, which was sent out in translation. One of the questions was, "Do you feel you receive equal opportunity in the organization?" The term *equal opportunity* was unfamiliar to people in Brazil. Colgate rewrote the question as "Do you feel you are treated fairly?"

Other companies too have developed programs to prepare their managers to function effectively in the foreign cultural milieu.[39] AT&T trains its American managers on the nuances of conducting business meetings in Mexico. British Airways has a training program called Kaleidoscope to increase its flight attendants' sensitivity to other cultures. The flight attendants—men, women, white, Asian, blacks, British, Europeans—are reminded that 60 percent of the airline's passengers come from outside the United Kingdom. Encyclopedia Britannica sends managers overseas who have strong ties to the foreign country. Typically they are Americans who have already lived in or studied in the foreign country or are hyphenated Americans, i.e., Japanese-Americans, Mexican-Americans, or Chinese-Americans. Such people are often familiar with the language, customs, and values of the foreign culture and thus are able to adapt easily and quickly.

However, sending managers to foreign countries just because their cultural background relates to the foreign culture does not always guarantee success, as the following story illustrates.[40] A person may look and talk Japanese, but socially and psychologically the person is American.

[38]Solomon, Charlene M. 1994. Global operations demand that HR rethink diversity. *Personnel Journal* July, pp. 40–46.
[39]Skapinker, Michael. 1999, June 21. Variety is taken on board to meet customers' needs. *Financial Times,* p. 10.
[40]Lublin, Joann S. 1996, June 3. Is transfer to native land a passport to trouble? *The Wall Street Journal,* pp. B1, B6.

Seiji Sanda, a 47-year-old Japanese executive who worked in the United States for 22 years, was hired as president of Apple Computer's Japanese unit in 1994. He resigned a year later. His egalitarian American style dismayed his Japanese colleagues. He recalled that Apple Japan's personnel director chastised him for greeting a cleaning lady, noting that "Japanese presidents don't talk to janitors." "If you ask the Americans, I was too Japanese," Mr. Sanda observed. "If you asked the Japanese, I was too American."

Generally, the cross-cultural issues that come into play in business have to do with different styles of managing, communicating, and negotiating. Hence, more and more firms are putting their employees through cross-cultural training programs. Even English-speaking countries such as the United Kingdom seem different to Americans. The British appear to the Americans as reserved, shy, and formal. To the British, the Americans appear to be open, friendly, and eager to share their life history. British companies have realized that everyone, including Americans, needs assistance as they adjust to work in the United Kingdom.

Where can managers obtain information about foreign cultures? Many reliable and useful sources are available. Managers can tap into the experience and knowledge among the employees in the organization itself, especially employees who have served abroad. Managers can gain first-hand experience from traveling and staying abroad and by learning the language of the foreign country. Study about a country or culture in school or college, or interaction with people from the foreign country can also be valuable. The media—magazines, newspapers, television, and radio—offer a wide range of global information. Managers can also conduct scholarly research, participate in specially created cross-cultural training programs, and accept short- and long-term assignments to foreign locations.

Cultural fluency refers to the ability to conduct business effectively in a diverse, global environment. This ability is best developed when it is an integral part of a firm's overall plan. Firms planning to expand internationally, send employees abroad, or bring in employees from abroad should focus on developing global careers by preparing managers from an early date. Such a program would greatly benefit from integrating the diverse value systems inherent in an international firm in order to create a universal organizational culture.

CONCLUSIONS

Culture plays an important role in how international business is conducted, how governments act, how employees, suppliers, and customers behave and communicate, and how decisions are made. Although many factors have contributed to a convergence of managerial ideas and practices the world over, cultural differences persist and shape business relationships. Successful managers must know the cultural environment in which they operate. This knowledge will determine the most effective ways to communicate, motivate, and lead. Understanding the underlying dimensions of culture and categorizing societies help the international manager to avoid cultural mistakes and commercial losses. More and more culturally fluent managers are being created thanks to increased international exposure, foreign language proficiency, global travel, and formal educational programs that focus on cultural enrichment.

OPENING VIGNETTE EPILOGUE

Two years into the takeover, GE-CGR was still posting losses. The workforce had been reduced from 6,500 to about 5,000 and many French managers and engineers had quit. The chief executive officer GE had brought in two years earlier from the United States was replaced. Morale was low, and it was hard to recruit new employees. Of the 12 vice presidents, only five were French. Most key business functions—finance, marketing, and personnel—were run by Americans. GE had closed down several product lines. Contrary to the original plan that called for CGR to be the world center for making sophisticated ultrasound machines and devices, which many French employees had accepted, GE moved that product line and development to Japan, triggering further layoffs.

   GE's difficulties illustrate how a big, experienced company renowned for its management skills can falter when entering a different business environment. "Integrating cultures is one of the major challenges of business today; it's an acute problem," noted Martin Waldenstrom, president of Booz-Allen Acquisition Services. "It's humiliating enough for a company to be acquired. If you add to that a very different style of management, chances are that both sides are going to have problems."[41]

[41]Nelson, Mark M., and E. S. Browning. 1990, July 31. GE's culture turns sour at French unit. *The Wall Street Journal,* p. A10.

Key Terms

- culture
- cross-cultural training
- power distance
- individualism-collectivism
- masculinity-femininity
- uncertainty avoidance
- management by objectives

- Confucian dynamism
- organizational culture
- ethnocentric
- polycentric
- geocentric
- convergence
- divergence

- crossvergence
- high-context culture
- low-context culture
- backtranslation
- *guanxi*
- *ringi*
- cultural fluency

Discussion Questions

1. Explain clearly Hofstede's four dimensions of culture. How do the United States, Germany, and Japan differ on these four dimensions? What sort of cultural adjustments would an American manager have to make when doing business in Germany?

2. Distinguish between national culture and organizational culture. How does national culture affect an organization's culture?

3. Explain the concepts of ethnocentrism, polycentrism, and geocentrism. Under what international business conditions would it be appropriate for a firm to apply each of these concepts to its operations abroad?

4. It is not unusual for a foreign firm to find that the motivation and leadership techniques it uses at home do not work as effectively in the host country. Why? What should the home country manager do to be effective in the host country?

5. Explain the principal barriers to effective communication in the international context. How can managers overcome these barriers?

6. The manager of a Japanese company is in the United States to negotiate a contract with a large department store to supply it with sunglasses. Identify the cultural elements in the United States that the Japanese manager would find different when compared to Japan. How should the Japanese manager prepare for his negotiations with the U.S. firm?

Written Assignment

The president of your American company, accompanied by a team of senior officials, will be visiting Vietnam shortly to negotiate with the Vietnamese government the right to build and operate a toll highway. Several other foreign firms are also competing for this project. In preparation for the trip, you have been asked to prepare a list of "Cultural Do's and Don'ts in Vietnam." This document will serve to prepare your company's team for the negotiations with the Vietnamese. Prepare a five-page document that focuses on the cultural dimensions of negotiating a business transaction with the Vietnamese government.

(*Note:* The instructor may assign another country.)

Internet Exercise

Use the Internet to access statistical information about the ethnic, religious, and linguistic composition of the population of the following countries: Brazil, Canada, India, Portugal, South Africa, and Turkey. Based on the information, determine the degree of diversity in these countries.

Internet Resources

A good source of information about the culture of a country is Culturgrams. They are four-page briefings about a nation's background and society, and highlight the people's daily living patterns, customs, courtesies, and lifestyles. For more information about obtaining Culturgrams, access *www.culturgram.com.* Berlitz International Inc. is a leading firm in the area of language training and provision of cross-cultural services. Their Web site is at *www.berlitz.com.*

Experiential Exercise

Upside Down—A Cross-Cultural Exercise

Aim: This exercise prepares participants to confront, understand, and effectively overcome culture shock and cultural differences. It is designed to sensitize participants to cultural issues when groups with different backgrounds and values interact. This exercise is played in groups and specific group goals have to be achieved.

Format of the Exercise: The participants are divided into two groups to represent two different cultures. In a large room, the two groups congregate in two separate corners, learn the key traits of their assigned culture, and then are sent to interact with the other group to accomplish a defined mission. On a sheet of paper, the facilitator assigns members of each group a set of unique behavioral characteristics, which define their culture. In order to differentiate the members of the two groups, identifying tags can be used. These tags should not display the names of the players or any information other than the group they belong to.

Play of the Exercise: Specific instructions are provided to each of the two groups. In the first phase, group members interact among themselves to internalize their assigned patterns of conduct. This phase takes 10 to 15 minutes. After convening the groups separately, the facilitator provides instructions and a specific mission (to each group) for playing the second phase. Both groups interact with each other to achieve their assigned goals. The effectiveness of the two groups is heavily influenced by the cultural traits of each group and the extent to which one group is able to understand the culture of the other group. The second phase lasts about 15 minutes. Debriefing follows.

Time: One hour.

Preparation: Copies of the instructions should be made in advance for distribution to the participants of both groups.
(*Note:* The instructor will provide additional information to play this exercise.)

Case 2–1   ORGANIZATIONAL TRANSFORMATION AT SKODA
(prepared by Diane Cyr)

Skoda had a century-long history of motor vehicle manufacturing in a small town in the Czech Republic, about 40 miles from the capital, Prague. Despite many early achievements, the firm had fallen on hard times during the latter years of Communist rule. With transition of the country to a market economy in the early 1990s, the firm's fortune appeared to revive when German auto manufacturer Volkswagen (VW) acquired, in 1991, a 30 percent ownership of the equity, since increased to 70 percent. At the senior-most decision-making level was a five-person board of directors, composed of two Czechs (the chairman and vice president of human resources) and three Germans, on assignment from VW's headquarters.

In the joint venture's annual report in 1996, the vast changes in the company's products and activities were noted. Quality of cars had been raised to international standards, and new models had been introduced. Local suppliers were now providing quality parts and components at relatively low cost. With a modernization of the factory, production, sales, and wage rates had increased. The number of workers had

been reduced, and those employed had been trained in advanced manufacturing methods. For the first time after years of losses, the joint venture produced breakeven financial results. Skoda was chosen as the Best Company of the Year in the country in 1996. With all these laudable results, the question that worried many Czech managers was whether the company was Czech any more or was it a German company.

THE TANDEM SYSTEM

From the outset, a goal of the venture was to transfer knowledge and expertise to the Czechs from the German managers who were at Skoda on temporary assignment. German and Czech managers were paired as part of a "tandem system" for the purpose of exchanging know-how. As the then-German vice president of human resources noted, "Integration, not domination" of locals was the goal.

In the early stages of the venture, the tandem concept was both necessary and useful because the factory and its managers needed to be pulled into the world of modern automobile manufacturing. Over the years, as Czechs gained experience and confidence, they started taking primary control over their tasks. For instance, the top position of the human resource function had now shifted to a Czech. In contrast, a German in the department now assisted Czech managers in a support capacity, worked on special projects, and maintained a link to the parent firm in Germany. However, as a Czech manager noted, "The number of foreign managers is declining and by 1999 there should only be a few of them here. They will be focused on strategic issues. As VW has the majority of the shares, they will maintain decision-making power. The tandem system has been replaced with Czech managers now taking responsibility."

Sharing responsibility in the tandem system did not come easily. Instead of sharing, one person tended to take the lead. A German manager said: "In my view, I think the tandem concept normally always needs one leader. You can't share the leadership. That's a problem with the tandem concept. But you can have a leader, and you can have a deputy. For example, you can say the foreign manager is the boss for two years, and maybe during the last year that would change and the national managers would take over the responsibility, so that in the last year the foreign manager is like a consultant."

Both Czechs and Germans agreed that the effectiveness of the tandem system was related to the personalities of individual managers, and to the level of expertise possessed by the German. A German manager remarked, "If the human chemistry worked, then everything was O.K. There were cases where cooperation had not been the best. But generally we are abandoning the system, so Czech managers have responsibility of individual posts." On the other hand, a Czech manager said, "Not all experts coming from Bremen were the best. Sometimes VW's interests prevailed over the interests of Skoda. For some of the foreign managers, they were at a mid-point in their career when here and they didn't have the motivation to do their best."

CZECH SENSIBILITIES

In the initial stages of the venture, the Czech managers felt that they had much to offer, considering their long history in automobile manufacturing. However, the opinions of Czech managers were rarely solicited. One Czech manager lamented, "They [Germans] come and they go, and change everything. They don't ask 'What was here before? How do you do things? What did you do well? What can we im-

prove?' And if they come and change everything, it's like saying it was done bad or wrong, and I am here to do it right. And after awhile people say it was already here. You should have asked!" Czech managers noted that the early batches of German managers did not try to understand the legal system, history, and culture of the Czech Republic. Subsequent waves of German managers, though, were more sensitive and better informed, which led to greater cultural understanding.

One of the biggest problems initially was the difficulty of the two sides understanding each other. It was not just the language, but also what the other party expected. A Czech manager said, "For example, the Czech party wanted to do something but the Germans didn't understand what it was. In the national character, the Czechs are more action-oriented and less theoretical, whereas the Germans are more concept-oriented and prepare things systematically. The initial problems were to make sure there are different ways to reach the same target."

In addition to culture, the Czech workers felt that they needed to better understand the concept of competitiveness. Over four decades of Communism, the Czechs had forgotten what working "hard" meant. A Czech manager continued, "The point is to motivate people at work. The Czechs are a bit skeptical, as many things were presented in the last 30 years—and they think they are right. So the point is how to motivate the people?"

The Germans, on the other hand, emphasized efficiency and organization. They emphasized training of the workers, higher wages, work clothes and equipment, discipline on the shop floor, and cleanliness and orderliness in the factory. These factors had an impact on the Czech managers as the following comment by a Czech manager suggested: "We had to learn how important it was to behave the Western way. And, of course, the bilingual environment brought some initial problems because not always could the interpreter be present. But continuously, we reached some mutual understanding. The coming of the foreign colleagues changed the behavior of the Czech colleagues."

Not all changes were perceived positively however. Some Czechs felt the focus was on materialism. One Czech manager regretted that workers had lost an innate sense of loyalty to Skoda, and instead now only "adored money." He continued, "The pride of being a Skoda member has been lost."

COMMUNICATION

Although communication between the German managers and their Czech counterparts had improved over the years, problems remained. The departure of the Germans at the end of their term left gaps in the information flow. The absence of a common language meant hurdles to easy communication. A German manager observed, "If you would like a career in the group, then you should learn German." The Czechs would prefer the company use English as the common language. The language barrier prevented them from always expressing themselves, which was perceived by the Germans as a lack of opinion or participation on a topic.

Communication between the parent and the subsidiary took place through e-mail, Intranet, and the company newsletter. Two or three special events held each year for managers were designed to help everyone get to know each other better. Over the years, more and more information about how to do their jobs and enough information about company policies was provided to the workers.

DEVELOPING LOCAL MANAGERS

In the initial years of the joint venture, managers who already had a position in the plant were allowed to remain provided they adapted to the new procedures and circumstances. Many were replaced in 1994–1995 and only those who were successful remained at Skoda. New Czech managers were generally selected from young (usually under 35), top university graduates. They were subjected to an extensive battery of selection tests and put in a management development program that combined formal coaching with job rotation to various posts to gain practical experience. The program lasted one year during which the trainee held at least three positions. "High potential" candidates took specialized seminars on management topics and completed a project on a topic of interest. Opportunities were offered to young and aspiring Czech managers to train and work in VW worldwide operations. Other managers were hired on the basis of recommendations or through the services of headhunter agencies. This system paralleled the one in place at VW.

Participants in this development program had to be proficient in either German or English. The absence of Czech language skills on the part of the German managers rankled many Czechs. "An obligatory part of training for Germans should be to learn the Czech language," said a Czech manager. "When proving he or she is able to learn Czech, this is appreciated a lot and this [German] person is immediately accepted by this community. Line workers appreciate a lot when a top manager is able to speak in the mother tongue."

William Bockel, a German who headed the research and design department at Skoda said, "The training we do here is quite different from the training we do in Portugal (where VW also had a subsidiary). Skoda was world-class to the end of the 1930s. Even in the Communist era they came up with original solutions, because they had a good deal of technical freedom until the mid-1950s." He went on to say that VW would not have invested in Skoda if the industrial culture had not been present. "It's a town that has been dedicated to manufacturing cars for nearly 100 years. You can't just create this technical memory. It is where your grandfather and great-grandfather worked at making cars."

THE FUTURE

Both sides agreed that the joint venture had been successful and had brought about many changes, particularly in the mindset and outlook of Czech managers and workers. They now looked at the company in strategic and competitive terms. A German expatriate commented, "Today there is a mixture between the two worlds (Communist and post-Communist). So there are some parts of the old system that are still alive. People are afraid to take responsibility. What is missing is self-confidence. The people need to be given the chance to grow in their own way. In five years, the average young Czech in management will be between 35 or 40, and they will be able to run the company. The most important question is: Will we give these young people the responsibility?" A young Czech manager observed, "There is a tradition in the people here. And the manager needs to work creatively. From the German side there is good organization. It is their mentality. And if we give each other room to work then we can compete with the world."

QUESTIONS

1. What does it mean to be a "Czech company"? Why are many managers at the company concerned at the loss of the Czech corporate culture?

2. If the Germans start the joint venture again, what changes would you suggest to their strategy of modernizing the workings of the company?

3. Identify and explain the ways in which the German company has sought to change the organization culture of the Czech company.

4. What language should be used in a multinational firm? Justify your answer based on the experience in Skoda.

5. How easy or difficult is it to instill a foreign culture in a business in another country?

References

Adler, Nancy J., and Robert Doktor. 1986. From the Atlantic to the Pacific century: Cross-cultural management reviewed. *Journal of Management* 12(1), pp. 295–318.

Ferraro, Gary P. 1998. *The cultural dimensions of international business,* 3rd ed. Upper Saddle River, NJ: Prentice-Hall.

Hoecklin, Lisa. 1995. *Managing cultural differences.* Workingham, England, UK: Addison-Wesley Publishing.

Marschan, Rebecca, Denice Welch, and Lawrence Welch. 1997. Language: The forgotten factor in multinational management. *European Management Journal* 15(5), pp. 591–597.

Mead, Richard. 1998. *International management.* Oxford, UK: Blackwell.

Paik, Yongsum, and Derick J. H. Sohn. 1998. Confucius in Mexico: Korean MNCs and the maquiladoras. *Business Horizons* 41(6), pp. 25–33.

Prahlad, C. K., and Yves Doz. 1987. *The multinational mission: Balancing local demands and global vision.* New York: The Free Press.

Xing, Fan. 1995. The Chinese cultural system: Implications for cross-cultural management. *SAM Advanced Management Journal* 60(1), pp. 14–20.

3
MANAGEMENT OF POLITICAL RISK

OPENING VIGNETTE

In 1995, Christoph Meilli, age 27, a night guard at a bank in Switzerland, stumbled upon documents that were to be shredded. Realizing that the papers were about bank accounts from the Holocaust era of the Second World War, Mr. Meilli turned them over to Jewish groups. He was fired from his job and interrogated by the police for stealing documents.

That incident became an international event as Jewish groups around the world supported by politicians in the United States demanded that Swiss banks pay the survivors of Holocaust victims the money now in their dormant accounts. As negotiations progressed on how much money was in the accounts, the banks appeared to balk at the demands made of them. While the U.S. government opposed any sanctions against Switzerland or Swiss banks, individual states were not deterred. A U.S. senator from New York threatened to start Congressional hearings that would reopen the 1946 Washington Accords, which determined the amount that the Swiss government agreed to turn over to the Allies to compensate for stolen assets.

The two big Swiss banks in the dispute, Credit Suisse and UBS, offered $600 million, which was rejected. Various states announced that they would impose sanctions against the two banks that would greatly limit their operations in the United States. These sanctions, to come into effect in September 1998, would prohibit state and local governments from keeping money in Swiss banks. State and city pension funds would not be handled by Swiss banks and trading through Swiss banks would be prohibited. Existing fund management contracts would be cancelled, Swiss companies would be barred from bidding on city and state contracts, and pension funds would sell off all their Swiss stock holdings. In effect, the two banks would suffer enormous losses as would other Swiss businesses. The Swiss government protested what it saw as blackmail of a small country by the United States, but the government refused to help out the private banks. As the September deadline for sanctions on the banks neared, they felt great pressure to reach a settlement.

As discussed in Chapter 1, a distinguishing feature of international business is the existence of multiple political entities in the operating environment. Governments and businesses often have competing goals, which result in an uncertain relationship between them. The divergence of interests stem from the outward international views of the firm and the essentially domestic, national perspective of governments. While the international firm pursues gains worldwide for its shareholders, governments usually concern themselves with the well-being of its national population. Governments, as guardians of national well-being, have the sovereign right to create and alter the rules of trade and investment. International firms are always exposed to changes in government policies and their enforcement and the political environment. Understanding these risks and determining ways to reconcile corporate interests with governmental goals are critical tasks for international managers. This chapter examines the source and nature of risk that arises from political changes, how firms assess such risk, and the different types of strategies that managers adopt to minimize it.

THE INTERACTION BETWEEN POLITICS AND BUSINESS

Politics and business are closely intertwined. Political forces, both domestic and international, influence economic policies of individual countries. Similarly, political decisions by national or local governments affect economic activities and corporate behavior. For instance, when Greece entered the European Union in 1981, Greek firms not only gained access to economic opportunities and financial assistance, it also strengthened the democratic institutions and practices in that country. By being integrated with the liberal democracies of Western Europe, Greece was able to shed its recent history of military dictatorships. In contrast, when a new Indian government, for national security reasons, tested nuclear bombs in 1998, the action led to worldwide condemnation. Foreign governments imposed various restrictions against doing business in India and with Indian firms. The Indian rupee depreciated markedly and foreign investors withdrew or delayed their investments. Political disturbances in a country may also vitiate the economic environment to an extent that normal business activities are no longer possible. In the late 1990s, civil wars, border disputes, and religious fundamentalism in the countries of Central Asia stopped Western oil companies from proceeding with the building of pipelines to export the huge petroleum deposits in that region.[1]

A government has the sovereign right to create and enforce policies that it believes are in the best interests of its citizens. Such policies constrain unfettered business activities. Host governments tend to favor domestic firms (its own citizens and constituents) over foreign investors; the latter are sometimes suspected of not having the best interests of the country in mind. However, international firms create economic growth in the form of jobs and income, and governments want economic development and better opportunities for their citizens. International investors want satisfactory returns on

---

[1]Borchardt, Klaus-Dieter. 1996. European unification: The origins and growth of the European Community. In Costin, Harry, ed. *Managing in the global economy: The European Union.* Fort Worth, TX: The Dryden Press; Why India's ruling party is flirting with disaster. *Business Week.* 1998, August 10, p. 42; Szulc, Tad. 1998, July 19. Will we run out of gas? *Parade Magazine,* pp. 4–6.

investment and a stable, operating environment. Consequently, government policies have to balance national political goals and national economic interests with the needs of the foreign investors. The inevitable tension between the two sides arises as governments set limits and businesses test the limits. In recent years, multilateral and bilateral agreements have required national governments to treat domestic and foreign firms even-handedly.

DEFINING POLITICAL RISK

Because government policies, or government themselves, can change, they present the likelihood that the rules of business may become less favorable. **Political risk** is the possibility that political decisions, events, or conditions in a country or geographical region of the world will affect the business environment adversely. Investors may lose money, have a reduced profit margin, or have their personal well-being threatened. Political risk is one of the oldest areas of political analysis and has been faced by firms and managers for centuries. It exists for both domestic and foreign firms alike, and many of the techniques used to assess such risk and to prepare for it are the same for both sets of firms.

A definition of political risk offered by Stefan Robock noted that risk in international business exists when (a) discontinuities occur in the business environment, (b) they are difficult to anticipate, and (c) they result from political change.[2] To constitute a "risk," these discontinuities in the business environment must have the potential for significantly affecting the profit or other goals of a particular enterprise. Events that are either expected or easy to anticipate do not constitute political risk. Changes in government policies and intergovernmental relationships bring about political risk in the form of uncertainties, dangers, and sometimes, outright hostility, in the business environment.

Managers want stability in the political environment because it ensures predictability and continuity in economic policies. Stability allows the firm to take a long-term perspective with regard to planning and investment decisions. Interruptions in operations affect sales and profits as well as business confidence. Managers understandably prefer countries where assets are protected. They desire returns on investments that are determined by competitive and business factors rather than by national or international politics. The assurance of personal safety and a judicial system to resolve disputes fairly and independently also promote stability. Management Focus 3-1 discusses how political uncertainty can affect business activities.

Figure 3-1 provides a road map of the sources and forms of political risk and the corporate strategies used to reduce or minimize such risks.

SOURCES OF RISK

The political risk a firm faces can emanate from the home country, the host country, and third countries. Political actions in any or all of these three areas can lead to changes in the business environment.

---

[2]Robock, Stefan. 1971. Political risk: Identification and assessment. *Columbia Journal of World Business.* 6(July–August), pp. 6–20.

SEPARATIST SENTIMENTS IN QUEBEC

In the fall of 1995, in a referendum on secession, the separatists in the Canadian province of Quebec failed to realize their goal by the slenderest of margin. It was the second defeat for the separatists, having been rejected decisively in another referendum in 1980. Although the defeat temporarily ensured the continued association of Quebec with Canada, businesses around the province began to take anxious stock of the situation.

The installation of Lucien Bouchard as head of the ruling Parti Quebecois who advocated independence for the largely French-speaking province and opinion polls showing a strong support for independence fueled pessimism among businesspersons. Expansion plans were put on hold. Jack Kivenko of the Montreal-based Spratt Manufacturing Inc., a garment maker of jeans, observed, "There's so much political uncertainty that I can't imagine anyone investing long-term dollars." The housing industry ground to a virtual standstill as companies began relocating offices and operations out of the province. Surveys showed that only a third of Quebec executives felt economic conditions were "good or very good," down from 63 percent the previous year.

Companies began to draw up contingency plans in case Quebec became an independent country, which could come should the separatists triumph in another referendum. Canadian Pacific Ltd. announced plans to move the headquarters of its CP Rail System unit from Montreal to Calgary. The Bank of Montreal also warned that it would move its head office out of the province should it split with Canada. Other companies such as Air Canada and telecommunications giant BCE Inc. could follow. "You name me a company with pan-Canadian or North American interests now headquartered in Montreal," said Gordon Ritchie, chief executive of Ottawa-based trade consultants, Strategico, Inc. "and you've named a company looking at moving out."

Companies such as General Motors, which produced its Chevrolet Camaros and Pontiac Firebirds at its plant in Quebec, were concerned about the application of the North American Free Trade Agreement should Quebec secede. "It would complicate our lives tremendously if we didn't have the free trade agreement to ship duty-free into the United States and Mexico," said GM of Canada president, Maureen Darkes. Although Mr. Bouchard planned to improve business confidence by reducing the budget deficit, bringing down the size of the large public sector, and cutting the debt burden, his determination to make Quebec a sovereign country had forced many firms to hedge their bets.

In the election campaign for the provincial elections in the fall of 1998, Quebec's business leaders, who were staunchly pro-Canada, were nonetheless unwilling, for several reasons, to be seen as vigorously supporting candidates opposed to Parti Quebecois. With the provincial government accounting for more than half of Quebec's economic activity, companies simply could not afford to antagonize the government. "The day after the elections we have to knock on the door of Mr. Lucien Bouchard and Mr. Bernard Landry (the finance minister) and continue to do business," said Ghislain Dufour, a consultant with a Montreal public relations firm. Second, despite Quebec's high tax levels and heavy regulation, most businesses had been satisfied with Mr. Bouchard's efforts to stimulate the economy. Finally, the opposition candidates did not have a powerful message except to say that no more destabilizing referendums should be considered.

The Parti Quebecois won the election and set the stage for another referendum. However, the party won fewer seats and the margin of victory was smaller than they believed was necessary to launch a winnable third referendum over the next few years to take Quebec out of Canada.

Source: DePalma, Anthony. 1998, December 1. Separatist premier keeps control in Quebec's provincial election. *The New York Times,* pp. A1, A3; Alden, Edward. 1998, November 30. Business fails to stem Quebec's separatist tide. *Financial Times,* p. 4; Symonds, William. 1996, February 5. Business in Quebec is voting with its feet. *Business Week,* p. 60.

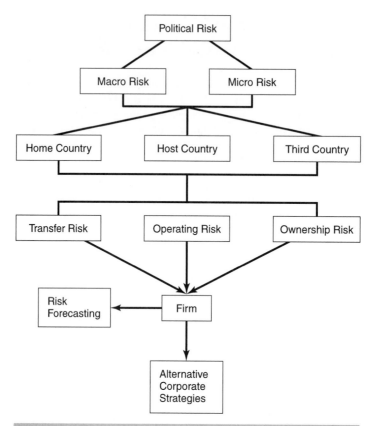

FIGURE 3-1   Political Risk and the International Firm

HOME COUNTRY

Political instability and unpredictability in the home country of the firm affects its international business activities in several ways. The home country may institutionalize changes in public policy that adversely affect international trade and investment. Institutions, politicians, and interest groups may propound protectionist philosophies, which although not coded in law, may compel a firm to moderate its international activities. The victory of particular political parties in the elections may be perceived as detrimental to business interests and indeed, may preface alterations in public policy.

The U.S. government, for national security and foreign policy reasons, often imposes economic sanctions and embargoes on different countries. **Sanctions** refer to specific restrictions on the conduct of business with a particular country. The opening vignette and Management Focus 3-2 are examples of sanctions. **Embargoes** refer to the complete ban on commercial ties with a particular country. Following the defeat of Iraq in the Gulf War in 1991, the United Nations (UN) imposed an embargo on trade with that country. The embargo forbade member countries of the UN to conduct any commercial transaction with Iraq. In effect, sanctions and embargoes bar specific foreign countries from being markets for American products or recipients of American investment, or alternatively, as sources of imports or for investments.

EXPORTERS DECRY SANCTIONS

Fearful of drug lords, spies, and terrorists communicating with each other over the Internet, the U.S. government banned the export of advanced encryption software to customers abroad. This decision evoked considerable unhappiness among American exporters who lost lucrative foreign sales opportunities to overseas manufacturers.

Encryption software uses mathematical formulas to scramble data and thus protect information sent or stored by computers. The minimum safe level of encryption was thought to be a 128-bit technology. It meant that users needed to correctly employ 128 binary numbers, or bits, to produce the "key" to decode information. U.S. firms who developed the 128-bit software were allowed to sell it domestically to anyone but only to banks overseas under an export license from the government. Less sophisticated encryption software, using say 40- or 56-bit technology, could be exported, but buyers obviously wanted the more secure versions.

American exporters lamented the loss of export opportunities. Said Jim Bidzos, chief executive of RSA Data Security, a leading U.S. encryption software firm, "It's so frustrating to stand by and watch the market you created get handed on a silver platter to the rest of the world." He said he had to turn down deals from such well-known foreign firms as Lloyds, Siemens, and Machines Bull, to name a few. Microsoft said that it lost "hundreds of thousands" of potential users of its software. Consensus Development, which licensed encryption to firms such as International Business Machines, said it lost about 40 percent of new business leads because they turned out to be foreign clients. One survey predicted that the U.S. technology industry overall would give up 200,000 jobs and $60 billion in revenue over the next four years because of export controls.

This restriction on exports gave a boost to the European encryption industry. In 1996, the German insurance giant, Allianz, was looking for software to protect its Internet site. Because it was not allowed to buy the desired software from U.S. companies,

Allianz turned to Brokat Informationssysteme, a Stuttgart-Germany firm whose products did not face any such restrictions. "It would have been like importing a tank without a cannon," said Michael Schmidt, an Internet consultant for Allianz. "We couldn't risk it. We had to use a European company." Added Stefan Roever, a managing partner of fast-growing Brokat, "The U.S. really shot itself in the foot on this one." Brokat's workforce increased tenfold by 1998 to 230 employees since it was founded in 1994. The company counted more than 1,400 customers including names such as Germany's Deutsche Bank and America Online's European subsidiary, in addition to Allianz.

Another company that benefited from the absence of American competition was Baltimore Technologies, a small Irish company that started marketing encryption software at the end of 1996. Siemens, the German electrical giant, had installed Baltimore's products at more than 500 corporate sites around Europe. Analysts estimated that more than 500 non-U.S. encryption products were on the market, up from just a handful five years ago.

American companies lobbied to have the restrictions lifted. The ban had affected more than just the niche market for encryption software, because encryption products were sold as part of a complete package of computer software and hardware. Brokat, for example, always introduced potential clients to its showcase product—an entire software platform that was the equivalent of a Microsoft Windows for the financial world. Most clients went for the whole package, and as a result only about 10 percent of Brokat's revenue came from encryption software.

Unfortunately for American companies though, even if the ban was removed, most of the damage had already been done. European companies had gained precious time and the financial incentive to catch up technologically with the Americans. Recognizing this, the U.S. government began to relax the export restrictions in September 1998.

Source: Strassel, Kimberly. 1998, July 7. U.S. rules boost Europe's encryption. *The Wall Street Journal*, p. B6; Simons, John. 1998, October 19. U.S. to allow coalition of companies to export new encryption technology. *The Wall Street Journal*, p. B5.

Business groups, hurt by policy changes, first try to prevent such policies from coming into effect. If they fail to do so, they work to have the rules watered down or even eliminated. They pressure legislators, engage in advocacy advertising, and form coalitions with other groups to mount a credible offensive. Throughout the 1990s, critics of China's poor record on human rights, trading in nuclear material, and the use of penal labor, lobbied the U.S. Congress to stop granting that country most favored nation trading status. U.S. companies opposed this move drawing attention to the growing size of the Chinese economy and the lucrative business opportunities that it afforded. The companies argued that curtailing economic links with China would only help European and Japanese firms who would win the contracts that might have otherwise gone to the Americans and that economic engagement was the best way to induce changes in China's political society.[3]

Some firms, however, benefit from changes in government policy. They, in fact, may push for such changes. In the early 1980s, as Japanese automobile sales in the United States soared, and the United States experienced sizeable trade deficits, American automobile companies pleaded with the U.S. government to limit the number of Japanese cars imported into the U.S. market. The United States persuaded Japan to adopt a "voluntary restraint program" whereby Japanese firms agreed to limit the number of vehicles they shipped to the United States. In justifying this quota on imports, the U.S. firms argued that American jobs would be saved and the trade deficit would decline. However, it also ensured that with less competition, the profits made by the U.S. automakers would rise, and Japanese cars would become expensive in the United States.

HOST COUNTRY

The major source of risk is usually unwelcome changes in the host country or in countries where a foreign firm is planning a business venture. The host government may make changes in its rules governing foreign trade and investment in response to domestic or international economic, political, and social pressures. Sometimes, the general business climate changes due to both internal and external factors, making a country or region less attractive to international investors. The economic and political crisis—in the form of the collapse of its currency, the abdication of the president, the flight of the Chinese entrepreneurial class, and widespread civil unrest—that befell Indonesia in 1998 put a damper on new foreign investment and led to the closure of many foreign operations.[4] Facing a huge budget deficit and massive foreign debt, the Romanian government suspended, in early 1999, the incentives it offered to foreign investors. These included customs duty and value added tax exemptions on imported capital goods and the offset of advertising expenditure against tax. Foreign firms who had invested more than $2.5 billion criticized the government's action, calling it a "serious breach of faith" and warned that it would have a "serious impact on Romania's credibility with existing investors, and future investors will have to very, very careful."[5]

[3]Bradsher, Keith. 1996, May 21. G.M. wants China's trade to be favored permanently. *The New York Times*, p. D2; Stevenson, Richard. 1996, May 11. Tread carefully with China, business leaders urge U.S. *The New York Times*, p. 5.
[4]Sapsford, Jathon. 1998, May 20. Japanese firms face music in Indonesia. *The Wall Street Journal*, p. A11; McDermott, Darren. 1998, May 17. Indonesia's troubles again threaten Asia. *The Wall Street Journal*, p. A19.
[5]Cook, Joe. 1999, February 12. Investors hit out at Bucharest. *Financial Times*, p. 3.

THIRD COUNTRIES

Risk to a firm's operations may also come from third countries, which are neither the home country where the firm has its headquarters nor the host countries in which the firm has business operations. Third countries have the power to affect a firm's activities because the firm has some sales or presence in the third country or because the third country has the political and economic muscle to extend its laws outside of its borders. In 1996, following an incident with Cuba, the United States passed the Cuban Liberty and Democratic Solidarity (Libertad) Act, popularly known as the Helms-Burton law. The law sought to punish any firm doing business in Cuba that involved the use of properties seized by that country from Americans during the Cuban revolution in 1959. The U.S. government warned Mexican, Canadian, and Italian firms who were considering major investments in Cuba that their senior executives, major shareholders, and their immediate families would be prevented from entering the United States if their businesses involved the use of seized American property. In addition, the law allowed American citizens to sue these companies in U.S. courts. The law led to strong protests from foreign governments charging that the United States had no right to impose sanctions against companies not based in the United States and challenged this notion of **extraterritoriality**—extending one country's laws to firms and lands outside its own borders. Bowing to international pressure, the U.S. president waived the application of parts of the law. The law would have adversely affected companies like Grupo Domos, a Mexican firm that had bought half of the Cuban telephone company in 1994 for $750 million. The phone operations were housed in property owned by Americans before they were seized by Cuba.[6]

WHY DOES POLITICAL RISK ARISE?

As Management Focus 3-1 illustrated, political risks increase because of uncertainties in the political environment, which in turn affects the conditions for conducting business. These uncertainties arise for a variety of reasons, several of which are listed in Table 3-1. Political differences among various constituencies within a country regarding the most appropriate ways to develop the society may spook business confidence. In some countries, the political processes and institutions may be undeveloped or unable to handle the challenges that appear. This breakdown in the political system, as evidenced in Eastern Europe and the former Soviet Union following the collapse of communism, creates instability, arbitrary changes in policies, and sometimes violence and riots. Governments also attempt to achieve foreign policy goals by using economic clout to restrict trade and bar investments. The result is that economic relations with some countries are encouraged and discouraged with others. It is not uncommon for governments, faced with intractable economic difficulties, to adopt political and economic steps that are detrimental to foreign firms. Risk also results from clashes between

---

[6]French threaten to kill U.S.–E.U. sanctions pact. *The Wall Street Journal.* 1998, May 20, pp. A9, A11; Myers, Steven Lee. 1996, October 23. Clinton troubleshooter discovers big trouble from allies on Cuba. *The New York Times,* pp. A1, A14; Farnsworth, Clyde. 1996, June 18. Canada warns U.S. on law penalizing Cuba commerce. *The New York Times,* p. D6; DePalma, Anthony. 1996, June 13. Canada and Mexico join to oppose U.S. law on Cuba. *The New York Times,* p. A3.

Table 3-1	Reasons for Changes in Government Policies

- Conflict between nations over ideology and differences in perceptions (which may strain political and economic ties and may even lead to wars)

  For example: U.S. policy of not permitting American companies to trade and invest in Cuba
- Protection of national interests, including military security, home-based firms, and industries, and access to resources

  For example: U.S. policy of restricting the export of dual use technology or products (those that can be used for both civilian and military purposes) to China
- Absence of stable or mature political, governance, and judicial structures in the country

  For example: The situation in Afghanistan and Somalia in the late 1990s
- Economic nationalism (an inward-looking ideology that favors home-country firms)

  For example: Chinese restrictions on the activities of foreign telecom companies, such as Sprint and Siemens, to allow domestic companies more time to reap profits and cement control over the industry
- Failure of the political system to handle competing claims in the national politics leading to breakdown and instability

  For example: The rise of Parti Quebecois and separatism in the Canadian province of Quebec
- Economic problems that force governments to impose restrictions on businesses

  For example: Restrictions on foreign exchange convertibility in Malaysia following a massive depreciation of the local currency, the ringgit, in 1998
- Historical experiences and events

  For example: Settlement of Holocaust-era claims by Swiss banks as precondition for continued business activities in the United States.

foreign firms and domestic firms, rather than between foreign firms and governments. As local and international firms compete for economic opportunities, powerful local firms use their political influence with their national government to gain advantages over the foreign firm. Political influence leads to actions on the part of government that discriminates against the foreign investor in favor of the local firm. For example, British Airways, which had a dominant position at London's Heathrow airport, had long and successfully argued with the British government to limit the number of U.S. carriers allowed to fly there.[7]

MACRO AND MICRO RISKS

When political changes affect all businesses and not just the foreign firms, it is referred to as **macro risk** or country-specific risk. In most cases, the conflicts and changes have little, if anything, to do with the foreign firm. However, by simply being present in such a country, the foreign firm's operations get hurt. For example, civil war in Yugoslavia during the 1990s and consequent imposition of sanctions on doing business there by the UN led to the closure of businesses, both Yugoslav and foreign.[8] The state-owned

---

[7]Done, Kevin, and Mark Odell. 2000, January 27. BA seeks protection from competitors on transatlantic flights. *Financial Times*, p. 5.

[8]King, Neil, Jr. 1998, June 16. To understand Yugoslavia's state, visit the Yugo plant. *The Wall Street Journal*, p. A12; Done, Kevin. 1998, October 21. Returning on a shoestring budget. *Financial Times*, p. 4.

Zastava Automobili division, which produced the Yugo car, was idled and so was Volkswagen's joint venture plant in Sarajevo.

In contrast, **micro risk** affects a specific industry, firm, or project usually because of targeted action against it by governments and/or political forces. Thus, a foreign firm may be singled out for discriminatory treatment, or alternately, the foreign firm may suffer because it is in an industry that is affected by political changes. The Canadian government, for instance, to protect the country's culture from American influence and imports, placed limits on American music programming on radio stations, American entertainment shows on television, and American editorial content and advertisements in magazines sold in Canada. Canadian publishing companies—primarily MaClean-Hunter and Telemedia—lobbied their government to keep the Americans out of the magazine business. In 1998, Canada began a campaign for an international cultural agreement that would help countries curb growing U.S. entertainment industry exports.[9]

Although a macro level analysis is a useful first step, the international manager is usually keen to determine how changes in the political environment would affect his/her own specific firm. Because different firms, even in the same industry, have different levels of risk, it is quite possible for a country to appear highly risky and at the same time pose little risk for a particular firm.

IMPACT OF POLITICAL RISK ON THE FIRM

Changes in national and international politics can impact three areas of a firm: (1) transfer of resources, (2) operations, and (3) ownership.

TRANSFER RISKS

Transfer risks occur when government policies limit the movement of capital, equipment, materials, and personnel in and out of the country. These restrictive policies can emanate from the home, host, and even third countries. An international firm brings to the host country a whole range of inputs—construction and production equipment, technical knowledge, managerial talent, raw materials, components and parts, and capital and operating funds. The firm also takes out of the country semifinished or finished products, licensing and technical fees, royalties, interest payments, profits and dividends, and managerial and technical experts. The firm would prefer unfettered transfer of inputs and outputs across national borders but governments regulate such transfers. The regulations may take many forms and affect the firm in numerous ways. For instance, controls on capital movements by the central bank of the country may limit the amount of local currency that can be converted into the foreign currency desired by the firm. This limitation makes import of raw materials and components difficult and reduces the amount of profits or fees that can be taken out of the country. Similarly, the government may impose tariffs or quotas on imported goods. They may also reduce the number and type of work visas available to foreign workers or restrict the export of certain technologies (usually those that are high-tech or military-oriented).

---

[9]Alden, Edward. 1999, January 19. Canada faces $4 bn sanctions threat as US opens new front in fight to make WTO judgments stick. *Financial Times,* p. 10; Tamburri, Rosanna. 1998, June 29. Canada to promote pact to curb U.S.'s cultural exports. *The Wall Street Journal,* p. B6.

The removal of restrictions, in contrast, may also affect a firm adversely especially if it had been established and had prospered because of protective regulations. To develop an indigenous industry, the Canadian government had established high tariffs, which forced many U.S. firms to establish facilities in that country. With the enactment of the Canada–U.S. Free Trade Agreement in 1989, the tariff walls came down, and businesses in Canada were fully exposed to competition from U.S.–based firms.

OPERATIONAL RISKS

Operational risks arise when government policies adversely impact the actual activities of the firm in the foreign location. Examples of such risks include increasing the local content proportion of the goods produced, putting ceilings on what prices can be charged, imposing new pollution control requirements, or mandating that workers be provided an annual bonus. These restrictive policies can emanate from the host, home, and third countries.

Because a firm sets up its operations under a particular set of understandings, requirements, and conditions, the subsequent changes in rules are usually unwelcome. With the altered operating conditions, purchase of components and raw materials would have to be changed (to meet new local content requirements), additional capital investments would be required (for instance, to install antipolluting devices), labor costs would increase (should bonuses be made mandatory), and profit margins would be pared (should price controls be imposed). As a consequence, the entire competitive position of the enterprise may be weakened. Table 3-2 provides a list of government actions that can negatively change the operating conditions of a business.

OWNERSHIP RISKS

Ownership risks occur when government policies require foreign firms to reduce or end their ownership of the business. These policies usually emanate from the host country.

Table 3-2	Examples of Government Rules That Adversely Affect a Firm's Operations

- Require senior management positions to be held only by host country nationals
- Provide employer-sponsored housing, medical care, and other social services to employees
- Export a certain portion of the production
- Limit exports of certain products and/or to certain countries
- Regulate the availability of foreign exchange
- Impose special taxes or fees on foreign-owned firms
- Change working hours, wage rates, and benefits
- Permit labor union activity including striking
- Require adherence to national employment goals
- Increase the percentage of local components in the final product
- Alter tax rules and the basis of taxation
- Deny expansion into certain product lines or markets
- Remove preferential tariffs and overseas market access
- Make foreign policy changes that strain political relations between host country and home and third countries

Changes in ownership requirements have a direct impact on the firm's finances, organizational structure and control, and the integration with the parent firm. The freedom of the foreign investor is seriously circumscribed. Where wholly owned subsidiaries are required to acquire local partners, and thus in effect, change the organization into a joint venture, the entire culture of doing business in the firm may undergo a change. The foreign firm loses its formerly unchallenged control over the operations, which could be problematic if the local owners' agenda and goals for the business are at variance with that of the foreign owners. The process by which ownership in the foreign firm by host country investors is increased is referred to as **domestication.**

The most extreme form of ownership risk is **confiscation.** Here, the host government acquires the physical assets of the foreign firm without paying any compensation. When compensation is paid it is known as **expropriation.** The new owners may be the host government itself or host country private firms.

The legal right of a government to acquire and control a business operating in its jurisdiction is not disputed. However, the exercise of this right is usually bad news to the foreign firm. While compensation is some consolation for the loss of assets, in many cases, the payment is usually not adequate or prompt or in the currency desired. Problems often arise in assessing the value of the seized assets. Should they be based on historical costs, replacement costs, current book value, or the tax base?

Confiscation and expropriation are less frequent today. National governments have recognized that such measures tend to discourage other foreign investors, which adversely affects economic development, angers foreign governments, and leads to other negative fallout. However, they still occur as is illustrated by the following examples.[10]

In early 1999, Transworld Group, a London and Geneva-based metals and commodities trading company, said its assets in Kazakhstan had been expropriated following a ruling by the Kazakh Supreme Court. The court transferred the 30 percent ownership of Transworld in a Kazakh power plant and three metallurgical plants to its local joint venture partner following charges of mismanagement by Transworld of the plants. About the same time, the Yugoslav government unilaterally acquired a majority stake in ICN Yugoslavia, a U.S.-owned pharmaceuticals company in Belgrade and the biggest foreign-owned firm in the country. The government justified its seizure by saying that the chairman of the parent company had broken an agreement to invest $270 million when he took a 75 percent stake in the company in 1991.

RISK-PRONE FIRMS

The risk faced by a firm is dependent on several factors. These factors include the characteristics of the firm itself and the conditions in the home, host, and third countries. Because these variables interact, a particular firm may be quite successful in a risky country while another firm may not be. Because conditions vary from country to country, this section describes in broad terms some of the characteristics and behaviors of foreign firms that make them more prone to government intervention.

---

[10]Robinson, Anthony. 1999, February 14. Kazakhs 'seized company assets.' *Financial Times,* p. 4. Dinmore, Guy. 1999, February 10. Executives flee police in Belgrade. *Financial Times,* p. 2.

When foreign firms were expropriated in the 1960s and 1970s by host governments, mining, petroleum, agriculture-based businesses, public utilities, and banks were most commonly targeted. These industries were considered to be crucial for the development of the country and were therefore suitable for public or national ownership. Firms in such industries typically did not require any unique managerial or technical skills that would have required continued foreign ownership. These firms were often highly visible symbols of foreign presence and influence to the host population. Large-scale foreign operations were more noticeable and appealed to the government both as a scapegoat for domestic economic and political problems as well as being a potential source of revenue.

In recent years, the restrictions on foreign firms have been less drastic. For example, when a foreign firm is a large net consumer of foreign exchange and consumes foreign exchange in a way that renders host country currency controls ineffective, the firm could invite new government regulations. If the firm is perceived to be indifferent to the overall economic goals of the country or does not explicitly describe its net contribution to the host country, it might also become a target for government restrictions.

The nationality of the parent firm and the degree of foreign ownership in the subsidiary are also relevant factors.[11] If the parent of the foreign firm is clearly identified with a country that has an unpopular image or is a country with which the host government has poor or no political ties, intervention can be expected. As investors, Canadians are probably more acceptable than the Chinese in the United States. American investors are probably more welcome than the Japanese in South Korea. It is not uncommon to find these attitudes transformed into political action. One hundred percent foreign ownership tends to attract government intervention and hence joint ventures or contractual relationships (e.g., licensing) are alternative ways to ensure that part of the profits and resources are controlled locally. Firms that commit to earning foreign exchange through exports are treated more favorably than those who do not. Another factor to consider is whether the risk applies to the entire country or to a geographical region. Conditions may be attractive for locating in one region and not another. In the 1990s, while the southern state of Chiapas in Mexico was wracked by a guerilla war mounted by the indigenous Indian population against the Mexican government, the northern and central parts of the country remained a haven for foreign investment. Finally, it can be predicted that some kinds of foreign investments (such as in manufacturing) may be more welcomed than say, farming in a country.

The type of products a company makes is a factor too.[12] A firm that makes **dual-purpose products** (goods and technology that can be used for both military and civilian purposes) is more likely to find strict government regulations on a company's exporting or licensing. In 1999, the U.S. government forbade Hughes Electronics from exporting a communications satellite to China believing that such sale would enhance the technological ability of the Chinese military.

Globally integrated firms and those that are in high-tech industries are less vulnerable to government interventions. Little is gained by interfering with the local opera-

---

[11]Howell, Llewellyn, and Brad Chaddick. 1994. Models of political risk for foreign investment and trade: An assessment of three approaches. *Columbia Journal of World Business*. Fall, pp. 70–91.
[12]Washington tries to reassure exporters over China trade. *Financial Times*. 1999, February 24, p. 1; Takeover curbs on foreigners. *The New York Times*. 1988, March 29, p. D2.

tions of a global firm, because the benefits of control would only accrue if the entire firm is taken over. Firms in the pharmaceutical, electronics, and chemical industries may be too sophisticated for local managers to run and may rely for their growth and value on new products and processes developed in research centers abroad. Especially where local firms or competent host country personnel are absent, the government is likely to acquiesce to its existence.

RISK-PRONE COUNTRIES

Are some countries politically more risky than others? Political climate is rarely stable all the time in all countries. Countries that are stable may experience sudden political convulsions. Indonesia, a stable country for more than 30 years, experienced riots, political change, and economic collapse in 1998. Countries known for instability can transform themselves into comparative calm and predictability. Peru, wracked by guerilla war and political mismanagement through the 1980s, was turned into a stable, business-friendly place in the 1990s by its new president, Alberto Fujimori.[13]

Sometimes, a gap between perceptions and reality about a country may discourage foreign investment. Take, for example, Turkey, where foreign investment flows averaged only about $1 billion a year and most of that was actually reinvestment of profits earned by foreign companies in their Turkish operations.[14] Foreign investors kept away because of the country's high inflation, political instability, and bad relations with neighboring countries. However, as Christoph Urban, executive vice president of the Turkish subsidiary of Siemens, a German electrical goods manufacturer, observed, *"People ask me when is the right time to invest. Turkey's image is so bad and the government is unreliable, but you just have to take the decision to invest regardless."* He noted though that Siemens earned a return of 10 percent on its investments in Turkey and had not lost a single penny in the 40 years since it opened its first factory there, even though *"every 10 years there has been a crisis."*

Similarly, Paul Albisser, who headed the Turkish operations of Nestle's, a Swiss food company, observed, *"Turkey has a bad image in Europe, but I have never seen such a gap between image and reality as far as business is concerned."* He said that demand for processed food was growing by as much as 20 percent a year, five times faster than the growth market in developed countries.

Firms with extensive international experience are more likely to accept and cope with a higher level of risk than companies new to the international field. Colgate-Palmolive, an American consumer goods firm, when faced with hyperinflation in Brazil, changed to dealing strictly in cash, payable on delivery, and priced each shipment as it left the warehouse.[15] Large firms tend to have the resources to stay for the long haul. They can offer tangible benefits to the host country, and at the same time are able to influence home, host, and third country policies. Savvy, experienced, and well-connected managers are able to find creative solutions and stave off government interventions, which their less-experienced counterparts are unable to do. Management Focus 3-3 looks at how foreign

---

[13]Ratliff, William. 1996, August 23. Fujimori makes enemies, but look at his results. *The Wall Street Journal,* p. A11.
[14]Barham, John. 1998, June 23. Handicaps and hurdles. *Financial Times,* p. 12.
[15]King, Neil, Jr. 1994, June 6. On guard against a storm of goatherds. *Industry Week,* pp. 57–58.

MANAGEMENT FOCUS 3-3

RISK? WHAT RISK?

In 1998, the ruble was devalued and Russia defaulted on its foreign debts. Violent crime was rampant and the political situation was highly unstable. Stock prices around the world fell in response to the news. Such a recipe would be frightening enough to scare away foreign investors, but not necessarily so. Although many foreign companies withdrew from Russia or postponed expansion plans or reduced their presence, others continued to expand.

Fiat, an Italian automobile group, which was a partner with a Russian company, pressed ahead with building an automobile factory in Russia. "Obviously you monitor what's going on, but from a strategic point of view, decisions that were made two years ago are going ahead," said a spokesperson for the company.

The spokesperson of Campofrio, a Spanish meat producer, who was going ahead with its plans to build a third factory in Russia pointed out that, "This isn't much different from other difficult years. We've already been through several very similar situations in Russia." The comment on behalf of Bayer, a German pharmaceuticals firm, was similar. "If we were to change direction because of the whims of the stock market there would be chaos. In this business, strategic plans have to be set 5 to 10 years in advance."

Wobbly though Russia might look, many firms may not have much choice but to embrace it. For Fiat, emerging markets offer the opportunity to expand sales. Demand for vehicles outside the Triad countries was expected to grow 50 percent during the next 10 years, as opposed to just 1 percent in Western Europe and 6 percent in North America. "If you want to grow, those are the markets where you have to be," said the Fiat spokesperson. Simi-

larly, General Motors said that it was doubtful it would abandon plans to build plants in Russia despite all the uncertainties. What was likely to happen was that the pace of expansion might slow. As the spokesperson of a Spanish oil company, Repsol, observed, "Our investments are for the long term. We know that no matter how severe the crisis is, our investments will pay off in the long run."

This long-run approach was also echoed in China where foreign firms found that business conditions had become tougher and the Chinese government had begun to actively favor domestic companies. Foreign exchange controls had been instituted and the government was helping Chinese companies win control of the market in certain industries such as telecommunications. Ernst Behrens, the president of Siemens in China, said that long-term investors like his company came to China with their eyes open. "We all believe in the future of this market," he said, "and as much as we would like certain different conditions in operations and profitability, we are all aware of the importance of this market and we make the necessary investment in terms of manpower and capital."

Siemens was one of the leading European investors in China and had 45 joint ventures in the country, most of which were profitable. Mr. Behrens said, "We will not put up another 40 joint ventures in the next 10 years. Basically all the technologies that we want to bring in we have here. Now it is all set up and we come into the second phase of operation in China . . . we have to look into profitability and success. . . . We are not deterred in any way, first, by the Asian crisis and, second, by the somewhat difficult internal conditions within the Chinese economy. We will just go ahead."

Source: Mitchener, Brandon. 1998, September 8. Moscow's financial problems don't frighten everyone. *The Wall Street Journal,* p. B9A; Harding, James. 1998, December 29. Siemens optimistic on China despite difficulties ahead for foreign investors. *Financial Times,* p. 4; China: What's going wrong. *Business Week.* 1999, February 22, pp. 48–50.

firms perceive political uncertainties in China and Russia, two countries that are making a transition to market economies from socialism. Political changes can come suddenly or slowly, predictably or unpredictably. However, change is a fact of international business. Being prepared for a healthy dose of political instability while keeping a long-term perspective is an approach taken by many experienced international firms.

FORECASTING RISK

Many international managers try to forecast the extent and nature of political risk so that they can adapt their business activities and decisions accordingly. A firm can obtain information about current and future risk in a country from external agencies that specialize in political risk forecasting or through its own in-house research and analysis.

EXTERNAL AGENCIES

Specialized consulting firms, big investment banks, law firms, insurance companies, and accounting firms create country-by-country reports that provide a generalized analysis of risk conditions by examining political and economic trends. They also prepare specific studies to meet the particular needs of a firm. Table 3-3 presents a ranking of nations on the basis of their riskiness as determined by a financial news magazine,

Table 3-3	Country Risk Ranking, 1998	
Rank	*Country*	*Total Score*
1	Luxembourg	98.9
2	United States	97.85
3	Germany	97.06
4	Netherlands	96.92
5	Austria	96.79
6	Switzerland	96.43
7	France	95.87
8	Norway	95.83
9	United Kingdom	95.01
10	Ireland	94.87
. . . .		
171	Antigua & Barbuda	16.2
172	Liberia	15.82
173	Somalia	15.68
174	Djibouti	15.02
175	Cuba	14.76
176	Sao Tome & Principe	14.22
177	New Caledonia	10.26
178	Iraq	6.85
179	North Korea	2.25
180	Afghanistan	2.01

Note: Score of 100 is least risky and 0 is most risky.

Source: Euromoney, 1998, December, pp. 105–109.

Euromoney. In calculating the overall country risk score, *Euromoney* evaluates a country in nine categories: politics, economic performance, debt, defaulted debt, credit ratings, access to bank finance, access to short-term finance, access to capital markets, and discount on forfeiting. Note that the countries deemed to be least risky—the ones with the high scores—are advanced industrial democratic nations with well-established and transparent rules and regulations for business. In contrast, the 10 riskiest nations are underdeveloped countries that have seen in recent years wars, civil disturbances, absence of governmental authority, and political instability.

Government agencies, particularly those concerned with defense and foreign affairs, study political situations in foreign countries on a continuous basis and attempt to reach informed conclusions about likely political changes there. Such information, obtained through diplomatic missions abroad and contacts with foreign decision makers, are sometimes available to the firms of that country.

IN-HOUSE ANALYSIS

Large multinational firms sometimes perform in-house risk analysis in their strategic planning, legal, and/or public affairs departments at headquarters. These studies focus on political risk as it affects the firm's own business plans and activities in the foreign country. They rely not only on published information but also on reports received from their foreign offices and home government advisories and through interpersonal contacts with officials.

FORECASTING TECHNIQUES

A wide variety of techniques are used to perform risk analysis and to forecast the risk of doing business in a particular country.[16] The techniques can be broadly categorized as qualitative and quantitative. Given the complicated nature of the task of forecasting, a combination of techniques is used.

Qualitative Techniques   Among the most widely used qualitative methods are the grand tour, Delphi technique, and opinions of experts. The **grand tour** requires that a team of people, usually executives from headquarters, develop a report based on their impressions obtained through travel to a foreign country and meeting key political and economic leaders. Under the **Delphi technique,** a group of experts is questioned and surveyed repeatedly about a particular country on an individual basis until a consensus emerges. Another method is to consult individuals who are familiar with or are experts about a particular country and region. These individuals may be academic, political, diplomatic, or economic experts. For instance, Kissinger and Associates, formed by Henry Kissinger, a former U.S. Secretary of State, provided risk analysis, troubleshooting advice, and access to key government officials and politicians in the host country to its clients.

Ciba-Geigy (China), a Swiss pharmaceutical firm with operations in China, engaged in an activity known as scenario building to prepare for likely political changes in China in the aftermath of the pending handover of Hong Kong in 1997. The company established a task force to describe three possible situations: optimistic, pessimistic, and in-between, over the next four years. The scenarios were based on analyses of the poli-

---

[16]Banker, Pravin. 1983. You're the best judge of foreign risks. *Harvard Business Review.* March–April, pp. 157–165.

tics, economy, science and technology, and society of China. Each scenario was given an overall probability rating by each member of the task force. Given the closeness of the ratings, a fourth scenario was created that was based on the most likely future development described in the first three scenarios.[17]

Quantitative Techniques   Quantitative approaches tend to use computer modeling and simulation to forecast risk. Economic, financial, political, social, and cultural information are quantified and the consequent data subjected to statistical analysis. One such method is known as **probability analysis.** It uses a decision tree to predict the probability of advantageous and disadvantageous events occurring. **Regression models** are used to calculate risk based on the interaction of a set of independent variables such as political ideology of the government, strength of democratic institutions, state of the economy, and level of economic development.

An organization called Political Risk Services publishes the International Country Risk Guide (ICRG), which provides explicit monthly measures of political risk for more than 130 countries by examining a whole range of political variables. Some of the factors that ICRG incorporates are included in Table 3-4.

Table 3-4   Determinants of Risk

Economic Expectations vs. Reality
  Perceived gap between popular aspirations for higher living standards and the ability or willingness of the government to deliver improvements in income and welfare

Economic Planning Failures
  Businesses' support for the current government and the ability of the government to adopt a suitable and successful economic strategy

Political Leadership
  Viability of the current government based on the degree of stability of the regime and its leader

Political Continuity
  Probability of the effective survival of the government and the continuation of its policies if the current leader dies or is replaced

External Conflict
  Presence of border threats and geopolitical disputes, and the probability of external invasion or full-scale war

Corruption in Government
  Assessment of how long a government has been in continuous power, whether a larger number of officials are appointed or elected, and the frequency of bribe demands

Role of the Military
  Degree of military control over government and government policies and the likelihood of a military takeover of the government

State of Law and Order
  Degree to which citizens of a country are willing to accept the established institutions to make and implement laws, the strength and independence of the judicial processes, and provisions for orderly change of power

Racial and Ethnic Issues
  Number of racial and ethnic groups within a country and the nature of the relationships among them

Organized Religion
  Role and influence of organized religion on politics

Threat of Terrorism
  Extent of dissidence that is expressed through political terrorism such as guerilla activities and assassinations

Civil War Risks
  Likelihood that opposition to government or its policies will turn into a violent internal political conflict

Political Party Development
  Broad-based political participation in the determination of changes in government and in formulating policies

Quality of Bureaucracy
  Ability of government officials to govern without interruptions and interference from politicians

---

[17]Turpin, Dominique. 1996. *Ciba in China* (case study). Lausanne, Switzerland: International Institute of Management Development.

The need for firm-specific analysis of political risk has led to the creation of customized studies by in-house specialists or consulting firms. These "micro" analyses relate the macro risk attributes of specific countries to the particular characteristics and vulnerabilities of their own or client firms. The framework of such analyses depends on variables such as the ratio of a firm's foreign to domestic investments, the size of the firm, the product line, and the political sensitivity of the particular industry.

An example of how such a risk assessment works is outlined here. Take the hypothetical case of a medium-sized U.S. firm planning to build a small factory in Hungary. First come the obvious questions: Is there a market for the product? By how much is the purchasing power of Hungarians likely to grow in the coming years? The list lengthens as questions focus on labor unions, production costs, and transportation systems. The questions then dwell on the stability of the government, the tax rates, and the stability and convertibility of the local currency. All these questions lead up to the final one: How long will it be before the firm can expect a profit on the venture? The adage is, The higher the risk, the faster the return. This process of risk analysis is often time consuming, taking up to 18 months in some cases.

RELIABILITY AND USEFULNESS OF FORECASTING TECHNIQUES

Predicting political risk is an unreliable exercise. The ratings are usually determined by analyzing historical trends, and an attempt is made to discern the future by looking at current happenings. The variables that affect risk are often too many and too complicated to be fully captured and integrated in any meaningful analyses or predictive model. As the opening vignette illustrated, it is simply impossible to determine where and what the source of risk will be or its nature. Furthermore, the information and data used in the analysis may not always be legitimate or accurate leading to a model that is based on faulty premises.

The track record of accurately forecasting political risk is spotty at best. It is rare for the analyst to anticipate a cataclysmic or sudden change in direction, which is precisely the sort of forecast that managers want to have so they can be prepared for adverse consequences. For example, no prediction alerted anyone to Iraq's invasion and capture of Kuwait in 1990.

In 1997, as an economic crisis engulfed East Asian countries, rating agencies were criticized for failing to anticipate it. The two leading rating agencies in the world, Standard & Poor's and Moody's Investor Service, had as late as September 1997, rated bonds issued by an agency of the South Korean government as A+/A1—in other words, a safe credit. Two months later, the bonds were downgraded to junk status. Although the two agencies were highly regarded in the United States, they were recent arrivals in non-Japan Asia and were using methods common in the United States. Most Asian countries are often subject to a lack of transparency with respect to corporate and government activities. Consequently, the rating agencies relied on public information data from people who were interested in providing a positive spin, such as managers of firms being rated or government officials. Furthermore, these two agencies had not yet developed strong local sources of knowledge and thus were unable to verify the information being provided to them.[18]

---

[18]Caught with their pants down? *Euromoney.* 1998, January, pp. 51–53; Luce, Edward. 1998, January 14. Credit agency accepts criticisms over Asia. *Financial Times,* p. 15.

Based on a comparison of three well-established risk assessment models—produced by *The Economist* news magazine, Political Risk Services (PRS), and Business Environment Risk Intelligence (BERI)—researchers reported that while forecasting of macro political risk can work, the existing models exhibited variation in their ability to do so accurately. They found that the PRS predictors were the most reliable, and that the projections by BERI were superior to those provided by *The Economist*.[19]

In the 1980s, the use of political risk assessments by firms declined. Among the reasons cited for this decline were (1) a failure in many firms to incorporate the results of political risk analysis into corporate decision making because many executives viewed it as an ivory tower exercise; (2) the increased level of risk in the 1970s and early 1980s led to reduced international activity on the part of smaller firms, which reduced the need for such assessments; (3) the profit squeeze experienced by many firms trimmed political risk assessment functions along with other activities deemed less essential; (4) resistance from managers to include risk analysis into the decision and evaluation process, primarily because reward systems are usually constructed to induce managers to make profitable decisions; and (5) reliability and credibility issues in the assessments and reports.[20]

CORPORATE STRATEGIES TO AVOID AND REDUCE RISK

Risks can be reduced or avoided if they can be anticipated and managers take appropriate precautionary measures. A variety of strategies are used by firms to ensure that losses from political risk are minimized. These strategies are discussed below in the following sections.

TIMING THE INVESTMENT

A firm planning an investment in a country that is politically unstable at a given time may consider deferring it until the political environment becomes more predictable. The Dutch brewer, Heineken, decided against buying a stake in South African Breweries because of political and economic uncertainties in South Africa. Uncertainties included the stability of the currency, the rand, and the empowerment drive to widen shareholding to include members of the country's black majority. The chairman of Heineken said, *"I have to ask myself whether I would as an individual invest 20–30 percent of my savings in that company. I can imagine safer investments in safer areas."*[21]

The Democratic Republic of Congo (formerly Zaire) has vast mineral deposits but the country suffered from civil war, corruption, and lack of transparency in government decisions. Foreign mining companies, willing to invest to exploit the copper, diamond, and gold reserves held back, not sure whether the current government would survive and whether any contracts made would be honored by any successor government.[22]

[19]Howell, Llewellyn, and Brad Chaddick. 1994. Models of political risk for foreign investment and trade: An assessment of three approaches. *Columbia Journal of World Business.* Fall, pp. 70–91.
[20]Wells, Louis, Jr. 1998. Multinationals and the developing countries. *Journal of International Business Studies* 29(1), pp. 101–114.
[21]William, John, and Gordon Cramb. 1999, January 18. Brewing group rules outbid for 29 percent stake in SAB. *Financial Times,* p. 15.
[22]Turner, Mark. 1998, November 25. Rebellion casts shadow over nation's riches. *Financial Times Survey,* p. III.

NEGOTIATING A FAVORABLE ENVIRONMENT

Should the firm decide to go ahead and invest, it can negotiate a set of agreements with the governments concerned. The firm tries to obtain guarantees about the continuity and stability of governmental regulations, tax codes and financial incentives, and repatriation of profits for a set number of years. Such investment agreements may deter the government from making changes capriciously. However, not all firms can obtain such guarantees. Firms making large investments or in the areas in which the host government lacks resources may be better able to obtain assurances than other firms. Where the international firm is large (in terms of total assets and sales) and is a source of advanced technology (especially to less-developed countries), new products, and markets, its bargaining power is greater. Because international firms and national governments each control resources necessary for the success of both entities (profits and sales for the firm, economic development for the government), their relationship may be described as interdependent.

Of course, having a signed agreement that assures the firm of certain continuities is no guarantee that a new government would honor it. The agreements may be abrogated because political, social, and economic conditions had changed drastically since they were signed. In Indonesia, during the long presidency of Mr. Suharto, foreign firms such as Freeport McMoRan, a U.S. mining company, obtained favorable mining rights to gold and copper deposits in the country. With the overthrow of the government, the company became the target of a public backlash against investors associated with the former president. In 1999, the new government demanded that Freeport McMoRan renegotiate the mining terms and royalty rates, though the company had only in 1991 negotiated a 30-year lease.[23]

To the extent some long-term ground rules are established prior to committing to the investment in the foreign country, the firm may be confident that the government, or its successors, would either hesitate or at least consult with the firm before tearing up the agreement. In some cases, the firm may be able to apply diplomatic pressure through its own home government on the host government. Once the investment has been made, the firm, though, has less leeway to change its operations. While the firm may cancel new investments because the rules are changed, it may not be able to divest itself of its operations in the foreign country. In that sense, the company may be "stuck" in the foreign country. Raymond Vernon wrote that *"almost from the moment that the signatures have dried on the document, powerful forces go to work that quickly render the agreements obsolete in the eyes of the government."*[24] Once a firm has made the necessary investments to begin operations in a country, and then proven that the operation has the potential to be successful, the government has far less motivation to follow through on any concessions or incentives that it had offered at the time of the original deal.

However, it is quite possible, that even with the restrictive business conditions, the firm may still find it profitable to continue operations. The firm may believe that the restrictions are short-term and that the long-term prospects of the foreign market are sufficiently attractive to warrant a continued presence. The firm may calculate that if it withdraws completely from the foreign market, it may find it difficult to reenter in the future when conditions may have changed for the better.

---

[23]Thoenes, Sander. 1999, February 2. Freeport McMoRan in royalties struggle. *Financial Times,* p. 30.
[24]Vernon, Raymond. 1971. *Sovereignty at bay.* New York: Basic Books, p. 47.

An investment agreement spells out specific rights and responsibilities of both the foreign firm and host government. The typical issues covered in an investment agreement are presented in Table 3-5.

Risk Insurance   International firms can reduce political risk by buying **risk insurance** policies. Many countries have programs designed to compensate their firms who lose investments abroad, especially in developing countries, due to political problems. Political risk insurance is a thriving business, worth around $400 million in premiums covering risks worldwide of about $40 billion.[25] Some of the types of political risks covered by insurance are presented in Table 3-6.

Insurers are either government-run agencies or big private companies. The largest of the government agencies are the Export Credit Guarantee Department in the United Kingdom and the Overseas Private Investment Corporation (OPIC) in the United States. The largest private insurers are Lloyds of London, Trade Indemnity and Pan Financial in London, and AIG and CITI (subsidiary of Citibank) in New York. In Russia, the government established the State Investment Corporation in early 1993 to sell political risk coverage for foreign firms operating in the country. Designed to insure the investments of foreigners, the corporation had resources to sell $1 billion worth of coverage every year. The World Bank has a political risk insurance division, the Multinational Investment Guarantee Agency (MIGA), which focuses on protecting investments in developing countries.

The usefulness of buying risk insurance is illustrated by the following example.[26] The Ohio-based Nord Resource Corporation entered into a joint venture with Consolidated Rutile Limited of Australia to mine gold and copper in Sierra Leone. Antigovernment rebels captured the mines and the project had to be abandoned. Fortunately for Nord, it had purchased insurance that covered about one year's loss of revenues. Nord had

Table 3-5	Typical Issues in an Investment Agreement

- Tax rates
- Access to foreign exchange to import supplies and equipment and to repatriate profits, dividends, and fees
- Basis on which fees, loan repayments, and dividends will be calculated
- Proportion of output that the firm is expected to export
- Proportion of locally made materials incorporated in the production of the goods
- Social obligations, such as building roads, operating townships, and providing training programs
- Customs duties on imported raw materials and machinery
- Extent of equity ownership
- Price controls on sales in the host country
- Access to the host country's capital markets
- Method of resolving disputes, which may include international arbitration
- Method by which investment can be divested
- Provision of security services to protect installations, materials, and personnel

---

[25]Kielmas, Maria. 1995, November 13. Political risk market steady. *Business Insurance,* p. 1.
[26]Tilley, Kate, and Michael Schachner. 1995, May 15. Seizure in Sierra Leone. *Business Insurance,* p. 17.

Table 3-6	Types of Political Risk Covered by Insurance

- Inconvertibility
  The investor is unable to convert profits, dividends, fees, royalties, the original capital invested, and other income from the foreign currency into U.S. dollars or home currency.
- Expropriation
  The investor is unable to effectively operate and control its overseas operations for one year because of the policies of the host government.

- War, Revolution, Civil Strife
  The investor suffers losses due to damage to physical property or is unable to repay a loan because of these reasons.
- Business Income
  The policy can cover loss of business income that occurs due to political violence that directly damages the assets of the foreign operation.

$23 million of combined war and expropriation coverage through OPIC and $8 million through a private American insurer. The Sierra Leone venture accounted for about $30 million of Nord Resource's $70 million sales in 1994. Not so lucky was Consolidated Rutile. Its claim was rejected by the Australian equivalent of OPIC, the Export Finance & Insurance Corporation, because the agency specialized in projects in Asia. The firm's request was also rejected by the World Bank's agency, MIGA, because Australia was not a signatory to the Bank's agreement that allowed companies access to the agency's insurance arrangements. Consolidated Rutile's share in the ill-fated Sierra Leone project was $62 million.

DEFENSIVE STRATEGY

A **defensive risk management strategy** is designed to protect the foreign firm by ensuring that only minimal ties are established with the operations in the host country. The objective is to minimize the impact of political changes in the host country on the firm's overall activities. With this strategy, the firm organizes its key functions of operations and logistics, finance, management, and marketing in such a way that government interventions are either ineffective or extremely costly.

Defensive Operational and Logistical Techniques   Deciding what the operations in a foreign country will produce can reduce the firm's vulnerability to restrictions by the host government. The firm can locate a key segment of its operations' process outside a particular host country. Thus, the foreign operations are dependent on critical components from elsewhere in the firm. Similarly, the firm may establish several units in different countries producing the same item. In case of stoppages or restrictions in operations in one country, overall supplies are not affected because the firm is not dependent on a single source. The firm may also carry out research and development activities in the home country. In industries where innovation and inventions are important for continued success, the subsidiaries are dependent on the parent for new products and processes. Control of key patents and processes is a viable way to keep government interventions at bay, especially if the host country does not have the skilled workforce needed to run the operations or to keep up with changing technology.

Control of transportation by the firm is another means to reducing political risk. Control of oil pipelines that cross national frontiers, oil tankers, ore carriers, refrigerated ships, and railroads can reduce the ability of the host government to either obtain inputs or export outputs.

Defensive Financial Techniques   The international firm can select from several alternative techniques to finance its foreign activities. It may choose a high debt-to-equity ratio where the burden of risk is shifted to banks (even local banks) and other financial institutions. The firm may seek funds from multiple sources including both home and host governments, local and foreign banks, international lending agencies, and local suppliers and customers. By increasing the number of parties in the investment, the firm calculates that the host government would be hesitant to interfere in the operations because so many other parties would be antagonized.

The firm can also consider joint ventures with local or foreign parties. A local partner removes the image in the host country that the firm is totally foreign-owned and may serve to inoculate the foreign operations against various government interventions. Similarly, having joint venture partners from other countries may bring to the operations a different set of foreign government influences that the host government may be wary of challenging.

Another set of financial techniques focuses on handling earnings. The firm can reduce the amount of earnings retained in the host country by repatriating as much of it as possible through payments for dividends, interests, consulting services, and appropriate **transfer pricing** for components and parts supplied to the foreign operations. Transfer pricing refers to the price that a firm charges its subsidiaries or other units for the goods and services provided to them. Firms price intracompany transactions in such a way that it will maximize the firm's overall profits and reduce taxes. Thus, a company that wishes to take out the profits from its subsidiary in country A may charge that subsidiary a high fee for technical service it receives from another subsidiary in country B. Indeed, transfer pricing may lead to the country A subsidiary showing red ink in its accounting books and thus avoid paying local taxes that are probably higher than in country B. By transferring money out of country A to country B the company is able to reduce its tax liability. Transfer pricing arrangements are closely scrutinized by national tax collecting authorities, such as the Internal Revenue Service in the United States, that worry that the specific transfer prices are designed to avoid paying taxes.

Defensive Marketing Techniques   Marketing techniques focus on controlling the firm's products, brand names, and trademarks. By controlling access to markets, the firm makes it harder for the host government to take over operations because they would not know where and how to sell the products. This technique is especially effective if the product made in the foreign operations is sold only to the parent firm which is sometimes the case with components and parts. Similarly, well-established brand names and trademarks give a firm its marketing edge over competitors. Ability to produce and sell under a recognizable name is valuable for a firm, and the parent firm may prevent the subsidiary from using it should the host government interfere.

Defensive Organizational Techniques   These techniques focus on how the firm's overseas operation is organized. Common methods to reduce political risk include using exporting, management contract, licensing, joint venture or strategic alliance instead of a wholly owned enterprise. Another organization issue is where to locate a firm's regional headquarters. Many U.S. and European firms have established the headquarters of their Latin American operations in Miami or southern Florida. The many advantages to this site include a well-serviced international airport, state-of-the-art communication links, and the working environment of a developed country, including political stability. By locating in Florida, the regional headquarters does not become a hostage to local politics. If the situation in a country deteriorates, the firm can hold back on local operations or pull out with a minimum of disruption to other Latin American operations.

INTEGRATIVE STRATEGY

In contrast to the defensive approach, the **integrative risk management strategy** focuses on tightly binding the operations in the host country with the rest of the firm's worldwide activities. The focus is on making the foreign operations as local as possible and thus reduce the liability of foreignness. By presenting itself as a local organization, the firm aims to remove any threat that foreignness might otherwise present and in turn obtain nondiscriminatory treatment from the host government. Several integrative techniques are available to the firm and in many ways, they are the opposite of the techniques used to pursue a defensive strategy.

Integrative Operational Techniques   The firm locates the entire range of its production sequence in the host country. Instead of setting up screwdriver assembly plants where all components are imported and merely assembled in the host country, the firm establishes facilities that add substantial local value to the production. The firm would consider sourcing as much of its inputs as possible within the country, setting up research and development centers that focus on local needs and ingredients, and relying on local firms for office supplies, subcontracting, professional services, transportation, and marketing. In these ways, the firm is considerably more integrated into the local economy with many firms and jobs linked to and dependent on the foreign firm. Government intervention against the foreign firm, if any, will end up affecting many local businesses. In addition, the firm works to develop satisfactory working relationships with local labor unions.

Integrative Financial Techniques   One option that firms adopt is to sell shares in the firm's local operations to the residents—individuals and institutional investors—of the host country. By doing so, the firm ensures that should the host government intervene, its own citizens would be hurt.

Transfer pricing is a source of much friction between governments and international firms. To erase the suspicion about the true financial performance of its overseas operations, the firm can ensure fair interfirm transfer pricing by using objective and arm's length practices. Transparent reporting systems where accounts and financial statements are available for inspection can show the foreign firm in a positive light.

Integrative Government Relations Techniques   The foreign firm develops and maintains close ties with the government in the host country. The purpose is to both influence host country policies and to receive advance intelligence about the government's plans so that the firm can be prepared. The firm approaches its relationship with the host government with the attitude and goal of sharing its latest technology, investing its profits in the host country, creating jobs, and earning foreign exchange. Chemical companies such as Dupont and Rhone Poulenc have been successful in China partly because they embraced the Chinese government's five-year plans that focused on using agro-chemicals to boost the production of agricultural crops.[27] The firms built modern

---

[27]Turpin, Dominique. 1996. *Ciba in China* (case study). Lausanne, Switzerland: International Institute of Management Development.

plants and introduced new products even though China had no laws protecting intellectual property rights, and political relationships with the home countries were highly strained. Where the foreign firm is seen as performing in a manner that contributes to the country's economic and political goals, it is perceived to be a partner and resident of the host country, and not an outsider.

Integrative Management Techniques   When it comes to staffing its operations in the host country, the foreign firm would rely on host country nationals. Where host country employees are not available, the firm would train and develop such employees to take over in due course. Host governments and the citizens of the host country see employment opportunities as one of the benefits of foreign investment. Thus, when foreign firms employ local residents and promote them to the higher echelons, the expectation of the host government is met, charges of a glass ceiling are allayed, and morale is fostered among the workforce. In contrast, in a defensive strategy, the foreign firm would consciously keep host country nationals out of key positions so that the company's strategies, business plans, and production processes are kept secret and to prevent their being leaked should the host country manager quit.

PROTECTING THE SUBSIDIARY

Generally it is the overseas branch or subsidiary, rather than the parent, that is vulnerable to political changes in the host country. Because foreign firms are more likely to face discriminatory policies and a more vigorous enforcement of laws and regulations than domestic firms, managers have to increase their bargaining power with the host government by building up a subsidiary whose product line and performance are valued by the host government. Building value can be achieved in a number of ways, including larger investments in the subsidiary and creation of high-skilled and high-paying jobs. A firm can also introduce advanced technology, reinvest earnings in the host country, and produce new and advanced products. In various ways, staying ahead of the capabilities of either domestic producers or other potential foreign rivals adds competitive value. To the extent the foreign subsidiary is able to maintain a lead, it wields that much power over the host government and would be able to discourage and fend off any encroachment on the freedom of its operations.

The likelihood of intervention increases when the foreign subsidiary is no longer seen to be contributing anything unique and substantial to the host country, especially where domestic firms have acquired the capabilities to produce similar products. The ability of the foreign subsidiary to maintain a lead over actual or potential competitors is closely tied to the strategic goals and support of the parent firm. When the subsidiary is included as a key element in the firm's overall strategy through the provision of important technical, managerial, and financial resources, it is in a stronger position to maintain its advantages. As access to technology and knowledge becomes easier, domestic firms in many countries are rapidly acquiring advanced competencies. Other foreign firms are eager to enter new countries promising to invest in state-of-the-art facilities and introduce cutting-edge products. Against this backdrop, it becomes imperative on the part of the subsidiary to maintain a continuous program of upgrading and modernizing of the production and operations systems in order to introduce a steady stream of value-added products, which in turn bring in foreign exchange earnings through exports.

The power of the foreign subsidiary is diminished when the host country's market is deemed very attractive. Foreign firms are eager to gain access to large, affluent or growing markets. It also means that the host government is in a stronger bargaining position, able to demand certain levels and types of investment as well as particular standards of performance. These governments also have many foreign firms to choose from, which also reduces the bargaining power of a single firm. To successfully carry out this strategy of staying ahead of local competition and potential foreign competition, the parent firm needs to have a keen sense of the timing as to when to upgrade the capabilities of its subsidiary and to successfully install the upgrade. When to upgrade is dependent on the lead that the subsidiary has over its competitors and how quickly it is narrowing. Because the usefulness of the subsidiary will disappear if competitors catch up with it in terms of its capabilities and contributions, upgrading and enhancements must take place before the equalization occurs. This strategy is shown diagrammatically in Figure 3-2.

COALITION BUILDING

To counter negative political changes in the business environment, international firms need to create a large and friendly constituency. The focus of this strategy is on enlisting the support of and negating the opposition of nonmarket players in home, host, and third countries. This function is normally handled by a firm's public affairs department or the legal department.

As a first step, the firm must identify the major players in each country. Table 3-7 provides a list of such players. The firm needs to understand their influence and how they function so that it is able to influence them and convey its views. All the players do not act in unison and indeed often have competing and conflicting interests. However, they have important and large memberships over which they have considerable influence.

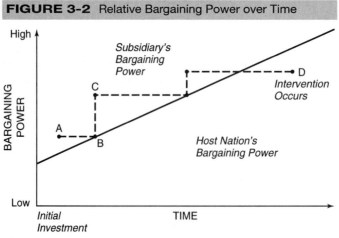

FIGURE 3-2 Relative Bargaining Power over Time

Source: From *International Management-Text and Cases,* by Paul Beamish, Allen Morrison and Philip Rosenzweig, p. 204, © 1997. Irwin. Reprinted with permission of The McGraw-Hill Companies.

Table 3-7	Key Nonbusiness Players in a Country

- The government, legislators, and the bureaucracy
- Special individuals and institutions, such as the monarchy or influential nonpolitical leaders
- Various advocacy groups, such as labor unions, environmentalists, and professional (legal and accounting) and other nongovernmental organizations
- Academicians and the intelligentsia including scientists, authors, philosophers, and artists
- Religious leaders
- Newspaper editors, television commentators, radio call-in show hosts, movie and television stars
- The firm's own employees and stockholders
- The general public

The firm may choose either a high-profile or a low-key approach toward these various constituencies. Foreign firms are liable to be charged with meddling in the ways of the host society if they are perceived to be too uppity in their efforts to influence various stakeholders, especially if they are easily identifiable as "foreign." In contrast, a foreign firm that has blended well into the business environment of the host country or is from a culturally similar country is more likely to adopt a high-profile posture. On some issues, firms may be reluctant to adopt a public posture, preferring to remain neutral. Typically, a high-profile strategy is effective only when the firm has high credibility with the target audience or is the only one affected by a potential change.

Another decision the firm needs to take is whether it should pursue its strategy of building support in the community on its own or align itself with other firms (domestic and/or foreign) or other institutions such as universities or professional associations. A firm may join with others if it lacks credibility on its own; if it is the only one with a problem; if it lacks resources to mount its own public relations campaign; and if its own corporate culture discourages independence of action. It may also align with others if by doing so its foreignness is diluted and thus not draw attention to itself. Forming an alliance with other firms may help to develop uniform standards for the industry or deter the government from imposing one. If standards are imposed and the firm is not part of an alliance it may soon be out of business.

To get a sense of prevailing sentiments, the firm may participate in and sponsor surveys or fund research projects that are designed to show the costs and benefits of specific public policy proposals. It can also collaborate on projects with universities and research centers. Engaging in advocacy advertising and lending corporate talent to public institutions are also powerful ways to build community support. Providing open and transparent reports about the firm's practices as well as maintaining close contact with senior government officials and elected legislators also help to strengthen the flow of communication.

The ability to build coalitions depends on how well the firm can scan the environment to identify the issues that affects it. The firm needs an extensive information gathering system. With such a system, it is better able to perform cost-benefit analyses of proposed policies. A high level of communication or public relations skills and a capacity to effectively negotiate with public authorities are also critical in identifying and dealing with issues that affects its operations in the host country.

EXIT STRATEGY

In some situations, the political conditions may become such that conducting business in a certain country or in certain products or industries is no longer viable. Consequently, the firm should prepare an **exit strategy** for leaving that country, business, or industry. In the mid-1970s, the Indian government demanded that the wholly owned Indian subsidiaries of foreign companies dilute their foreign ownership to less than 50 percent. Companies like Coca-Cola and IBM refused and withdrew from the Indian market. Other companies such as Philips and Dunlop adjusted, becoming minority partners by selling the majority of the shares to Indian investors—individuals and institutions. Should a firm decide to sell off its business, it needs to be able to ensure that the buyer is able to pay the price asked for and that the seller can take the proceeds out of the country without foreign exchange restrictions. It may not be able to find a buyer for its operations or, if it did, receive only a fraction of what it invested. Alternately, it may change its relationship from manufacturing to licensing to a local firm. In anticipation of exiting, the firm may begin cutting down on new investments, repairs and maintenance, hiring personnel, and reducing production.

International firms usually use a combination of the various strategies just discussed. Elements of all are appropriate under certain conditions. No one strategy is appropriate for all firms and much depends on the size of the firm, its strategic goals, the industry it is in, the country in which it operates, and its historical experience.

Generally, the firm would focus on protecting its vital assets, which may be its manufacturing process or its brand name or its product line. On these issues, the firm may adopt a more defensive approach, while being integrative in all other aspects of its business. In a large and growing market, a firm may constantly upgrade its product lines to stay ahead of the competition and to maintain a favorable relationship with the host government. In a country such as the United States where advocacy groups are well organized and forums for expressing views are plentiful and sophisticated, companies are more likely to consider coalition building to protect and expound their views. In countries that are politically stable, where the changes in the rules of the business game can be anticipated, and where the firm has considerable operating experience, an integrative approach is more likely to be embraced. If a company establishes operations abroad as part of a centralized approach, the defensive strategy would be more appropriate. In establishing large projects, as in mining or infrastructure, it is useful to negotiate in advance the terms with the host governments.

CRISIS MANAGEMENT

International firms should be prepared for events in the foreign country that affect its physical presence and the well-being of its personnel. **Crisis management** is concerned with planning ahead for a crisis in order to minimize physical and human losses and to rebound to normal operations as soon as possible. Crisis management represents a strategy to handle particular types of operational risks.

The importance of crisis management was highlighted in 1990 when Iraq militarily annexed Kuwait. Although some international managers were able to escape to Saudi Arabia many others could not and were held as hostages by the Iraqi authorities for several weeks before being released. Many properties were either destroyed or damaged.

Foreign firms had to turn to their home governments to intervene on behalf of their employees and investments.

The plan for crisis management consists of four main parts: (1) conducting a crisis audit, (2) developing a plan of action, (3) establishing a crisis management team, and (4) rehearsing the action plan.

A systematic **crisis audit** can identify the potential sources, nature, and impact of crises. Managers create disaster scenarios and examine how various aspects of the firm's operations—plant and equipment, employer safety, key documents and files—are affected. Continuous monitoring of developments in the host, home, and third countries alert managers to potential crises. Many times, though, crises assume huge and debilitating proportions because managers ignore early warning signals and deny the existence of a problem when it occurs.

The second phase of a crisis management plan is to draw up plans to implement when the crisis occurs. These plans may include the evacuation of expatriates from the country, safekeeping important documents, preventing the destruction of the physical facilities, or activating alternative sources of supply. Contingency plans should be detailed and readily implementable. Both crisis audits and action plans need to be periodically updated.

When a crisis strikes, the firm should be able to immediately activate a crisis management team. The team, drawn from managers at headquarters and regional offices, would work to handle the crisis and to ensure organizational continuity. They would also communicate with the media as well as contact senior officials in the home country, and through them the host government. The team would be responsible for establishing links with its managers in the foreign location and with other organizations such as industry associations, other firms who may be similarly affected, and NGOs such as the Red Cross.

The final phase of planning is to rehearse the plans to ensure that they will actually work should the crisis occur. Rehearsing means simulations. Mock exercises and drills can help to iron out glitches, build up teamwork, and ensure that communication systems work. Familiarity with the operation of the plans can cut down response time. Most of all, rehearsal allows the team to assess whether the plans will be effective. The firm would be able to provide all necessary information to the parties that require it (such as the home government or families of managers abroad). The phone numbers of government officials who would be contacted in such emergencies would be correct and current. Frequent practice ensures that the crisis can be handled in an expeditious and effective manner.

KIDNAPPING

A manifestation of political instability and the need for crisis management is kidnapping of foreign managers. Kidnappings affect morale, remove vital workers from a project, disrupt business, tarnish corporate image, lead to potential litigation from employees or their families, and force international managers to assume a low profile and a reduced presence. Sometimes a general breakdown in law and order in a country may account for kidnappings that may not single out foreign managers; in other situations though, foreign managers are the specific targets of kidnappers. The goals may vary from plain criminal intent (to obtain a sizeable ransom) to achieving a particular political agenda (such as discouraging foreign investment to undermine the economy and the government). Management Focus 3-4 describes how general lawlessness and political instability affect international managers.

The number of kidnappings rose dramatically in the late 1990s. More than half the worldwide total was reported from Colombia where poor people often use ransom to raise capital in order to enter the lucrative drug business. In Chechnya, as discussed in Management Focus 3-4, the kidnappings were politically motivated. In countries marked by economic turmoil and political instability, the government is often powerless to stop kidnappings.[28]

Most firms try to protect their employees, but few do enough. As Andre Pienaar, a director at Kroll-O'Gara, a firm specializing in corporate security, noted: *"There are large international companies flying into difficult parts with very little idea of the country's peculiarities and problems. They become too deal-focused and are not aware of the grey issues below the surface."*[29] The cost of not doing the homework can be enormous. The average ransom for westerners kidnapped in the northern Caucasus was $1 million.

The profile of the business traveler had changed in recent years. Younger employees found that their first job with a company takes them abroad, and smaller companies were entering international business without the contacts to ensure due diligence. Sometimes, the foreign contract was the only big contract the company had and thus the success of the contract became an overriding objective. Consequently, the physical risk to its managers may not get the attention that it deserved until it was too late.

Crisis management plans should prepare a firm to anticipate and handle such problems as kidnappings. Some firms train their managers in how to survive should they be kidnapped. The simplest training is based on "common sense" and includes advice on how to reduce the chance of being kidnapped: avoid wandering alone at night, take alternative driving routes to work, change the routine of activities frequently, don't show off wealth. Specialized training may focus on how to drive evasively, in evaluating signs that may trigger a dangerous situation, and in installing surveillance systems. Finally, training is also directed at preparing the manager to endure the kidnapping trauma. The focus is on mental exercises to guard against intimidation, developing communication codes with would-be rescuers and other hostages, and how to negotiate with the hostage takers.

Companies usually turn to specialized risk management and security firms for advice on how to handle crisis situations. Among some well-known companies are Magallanes Associates International, Kroll-O'Gara, and Control Risks. These agencies provide an extensive range of services including training programs, surveillance, risk analysis, security systems, and post-incident stress management.

The increase in kidnappings has given rise to insurance policies that cover ransom costs.[30] Firms buy insurance to reduce the financial burden of a kidnapping and to pay ransoms, if necessary. Hiscox, a London insurer, specializes in kidnap and ransom insurance and provides a wide range of consulting services on security and risks. Among the losses covered by kidnapping insurance are ransom/extortion monies, disappearance or

---

[28]Timmins, Nicholas. 1998, October 9. Kidnappings reach record levels worldwide. *Financial Times,* p. 8.
[29]Maitland, Alison. 1998, October 8. Rewards that risk human loss. *Financial Times,* p. 24.
[30]Morrison, Scott, and Adam Thomson. 1999, January 15. Colombian settlement will turn on ending the guerillas' income from kidnappings. *Financial Times,* p. 4.

MANAGEMENT FOCUS 3-4

PERSONAL INSECURITY

Even as Mexico liberalized its economy and foreign investment poured in, civil unrest and high crime rates persisted in many parts of the country. Crime rose sharply following the collapse of the economy after the peso was devalued in 1994. Personal security was often under threat. On average, Mexico experienced between 300 and 500 kidnappings a year.

In 1996, Sanyo Electric Company paid $2 million ransom to kidnappers holding one of its executives in Mexico. The executive, Mamory Konnu, president of Video Component Corporation U.S.A., the company's subsidiary that assembled parts for television sets made in Mexico, was abducted by armed gunmen on an afternoon at a city park in Tijuana, Mexico, where he had gone to attend an employee baseball game. A large number of foreign firms had established plants in the Tijuana area just across the California border from San Diego, and many foreign executives, like Mr. Konnu, lived in San Diego and commuted across the border to the Mexican city to work. Though most kidnappings were of local wealthy Mexicans, the distinction in the nationality of the victims was less important to the criminals as the foreign presence in the border industrial regions became larger. In some cases, kidnappers were in league with the local police, which made reliance on the public safety system chancy. In addition, the judicial system was often weak.

U.S. officials and foreign firms had warned the Mexican government that worsening law and order conditions were tarnishing its image and would adversely affect foreign investment. Although crime statistics were somewhat unreliable, no one doubted the increase in physical assaults, robberies, kidnappings, and even murder. "Forget the statistics," said Carlos Zagal, director of Sears Roebuck de Mexico, the Mexican subsidiary of the U.S. retail chain, who had strengthened security measures. "There isn't one person here who hasn't experienced or doesn't know someone who has been robbed."

In response, foreign firms stepped up their spending on security, ran security checks on the homes of executives, and enrolled spouses and family members in personal security courses. The business in personal security for large companies had soared in Mexico.

Of course, Mexico was not alone as a country where personal safety was under threat. In 1998, four foreigners working in Chechnya for Granger Telecom, a British telecommunications company, were kidnapped and executed by rebels fighting for Chechen independence from Russia. In 1997, more than 1,000 kidnappings were reported in the Russian Federation, the vast majority of which were in Chechnya where at one time about 100 foreigners were held hostage.

Granger Telecom said that it knew of the dangers but believed the telephone installation contract, worth about $300 million, justified the risks—and that its employees' safety was guaranteed by the Chechen government and Chechen Telecom.

According to security experts, kidnappings and hostility to foreigners was likely to rise as economic conditions worsened and disillusionment with free markets set in. "We're picking up vibes like this in a number of emerging markets," said a director of Kroll Associates, a personal security firm.

Source: Torres, Craig. 1996, October 29. Mexico City crime alarms multinationals. *The Wall Street Journal,* p. A18; Millman, Joel. 1996, August 14. Sanyo electric offers $2 million ransom to kidnappers holding aide in Mexico. *The Wall Street Journal,* p. A7; Maitland, Alison, 1998, October 8. Rewards that risk human loss. *Financial Times,* p. 24.

wrongful appropriation of ransom monies while being delivered, expenses relating to rewards for informants, medical costs, increased costs of security, legal costs, and deaths and dismemberment coverage.

Crisis management extends beyond kidnappings, ransoms, and extortions. Managers have to be prepared for events such as terrorism, military coups, accidents, and employee misconduct. The focus is initially on ensuring the physical safety of the managers and their families and their evacuation out of the country if necessary. Then the focus shifts to minimizing damage to plant and equipment, damage control, and safeguarding the firm's proprietary information and secrets.

CONCLUSIONS

Domestic and international politics are a constant in the environment of international business. With more than 185 independent countries in the world—each with its own sovereign government—international managers operate under an umbrella of rulemakers and rules. The challenge for managers is to understand the sources, types, and nature of political risk so that appropriate management policies and actions can be taken. Gathering information in a timely manner about political developments in the host, home, and third countries, analyzing such information, and integrating it into the firm's business strategy is at the core of political risk management. Changes in the political environment are often sudden and can be detrimental to the firm. Consequently, the focus of decision making is to continue to pursue economic goals effectively while adapting to political changes. Firms have a wide choice of strategies available to them to minimize the adverse impact of political changes on their operations. Depending on circumstances, some strategies may be more effective than others.

OPENING VIGNETTE EPILOGUE

On August 13, 1998, it was announced that Credit Suisse and UBS had reached an agreement to pay $1.25 billion over three years to Holocaust survivors in an out-of-court settlement. All threatened sanctions against the two banks and Swiss businesses were withdrawn. At a news conference in New York City to announce the agreement was Mr. Meille, now a U.S. citizen living in New Jersey and working as a guard at an office building in Manhattan.

The Swiss bank accounts episode triggered enquiries into the activities of other European banks, insurance companies, and large industrial firms during World War II. Taking the lead, the U.S. government pressured foreign governments and companies to settle claims from that era. Failure to settle would be met with restrictions on doing business in the United States. Government approval of the takeover of Bankers Trust investment bank by Deutsche Bank of Germany was delayed until all claims against Deutsche on Holocaust-related issues were resolved. Other companies voluntarily began reviewing their conduct during the war and making reparations to the survivors of victims.[31]

[31]Moore, Stephen. 1998, August 14. Choices few to Swiss banks on war claim. *The Wall Street Journal,* pp. A12, A13; Swiss banks: The noose tightens. *Business Week.* 1998, July 27, p. 66; Waldman, Amy. 1998, August 14. Holocaust accord ends plan for sanction. *The New York Times,* p. A8; Authers, John, and Tracy Corrigan. 1998, December 8. Blow for Deutsche-Bankers Trust deal. *Financial Times,* p. 1; They've decided it's better to tell the whole truth now. *Business Week.* 1999, February 22, p. 56.

Key Terms

- political risk
- sanctions
- embargoes
- extraterritoriality
- macro risk
- micro risk
- transfer risks
- operational risks
- ownership risks

- domestication
- confiscation
- expropriation
- dual-purpose products
- grand tour
- Delphi technique
- probability analysis
- regression models
- risk insurance

- defensive risk management strategy
- transfer pricing
- integrative risk management strategy
- exit strategy
- crisis management
- crisis audit

Discussion Questions

1. The possibility exists that in the near future the province of Quebec may secede from Canada and become an independent nation. How should U.S. firms with operations in Quebec evaluate this possibility and prepare for it? What would it mean for the firms if Quebec indeed became a separate country?

2. Evaluate the various elements of the defensive strategy to reduce political risk. What factors are necessary for the strategy to succeed?

3. Evaluate the various elements of the integrative strategy to reduce political risk. What factors are necessary for the strategy to succeed?

4. Identify a set of developments that would indicate a possible government intervention in the economy in the near future. How can a firm gather information about such developments and use it to protect itself from adverse government actions?

5. What actions can a firm take to protect itself from political risk that emanates from third and home governments? Are Mexican firms in the United States more vulnerable to political risk than firms from Japan? Explain.

6. The politics of a country always changes. Sometimes it is favorable to international business, other times it is not. Consequently, over the long run, the positive and negative effects will neutralize each other. Therefore, a firm with a long-term perspective does not have to be concerned with political risk. Do you agree with this premise? Justify your answer.

Writing Assignment

Identify a multinational firm and a foreign country where it has had operations for at least 10 years. Visit your library (and contact the firm, if necessary) and write a four-page report from the perspective of the international firm, describing the political situation in the country today and comparing it to the situation of 10 years ago.

Internet Assignment

Access the U.S. Department of State Web site and check out the advisory it issues to travelers planning a visit to Colombia, Mexico, and Russia. Prepare a report comparing the risk to personal safety in each of these three countries for a visitor from the United States.

Internet Resources

Information on political risk is available on the Internet from a variety of sources. The U.S. government's Department of State is a good source of official information about U.S. foreign policy, U.S. diplomatic missions abroad, foreign diplomatic missions in the United States, and travel advisories. The address is *www.state.gov*. Financial statistics can be obtained from the World Bank at *www.worldbank.org*. The daily newspapers carry extensive information on political developments around the world. Two business papers worth checking out are the *Financial Times* (London) at *www.ft.com* and *The Wall Street Journal*'s interactive edition at *http://interactive.wsj.com*. Other useful sites include the U.S. Department of Commerce (*www.stat-usa.gov*), Global Risk Assessments (*www.grai.com*), and Magallanes Associates International Inc. (*www.mai-assoc.com*). For information about the Pinkerton security firm, visit *www.pinkertons.com*.

Case 3–1   ENRON IN INDIA

On August 3, 1995, Rebecca Mark, chairperson and chief executive officer of Enron Development Corporation (EDC) received the news at her Houston, Texas, office that the government of the state of Maharashtra in India had formally cancelled a contract for the company to construct and operate an electricity generating plant in Dabhol, 180 miles south of Bombay. The news was not entirely unexpected. The state government, which had come to power in March, had opposed the project in the election campaign, and had set up a committee to reassess the project. The committee had recommended the cancellation of the project. Ms. Mark, who had negotiated the contract with the previous state government, prepared to fly to India and find out what could be done, if anything, to save the project. EDC was expected to generate $180 million in pretax profits in 1995, 16.5 percent of Enron's total. It would be difficult for Enron to meet its financial targets if the project in India was abandoned.

ENRON

Enron was an energy company based in Houston. It was North America's number one buyer and seller of natural gas and also built and managed natural gas transportation, power generation, liquids, and clean fuels facilities. Enron had taken advantage of the worldwide deregulation of the electricity industry to expand abroad. It had operations in many countries including Brazil, China, Philippines, Argentina, and Chile, in addition to the United Kingdom and continental Europe. The company ranked 54 on *Fortune*'s list of 500 largest companies. In 1994, its revenue was close to $9 billion.

EDC was one of Enron's five operating divisions and had responsibility for the development of international energy infrastructure projects such as power plants, pipelines, fuel transportation, and natural gas processing plants. The division had actively sought projects and was now engaged in numerous countries around the world.

With the liberalization of the Indian economy and the opening up of the power sector to private and foreign investment, Enron saw an opportunity to enter a potentially huge market. Demand for power in India was expected to rise to 230,000 megawatts by the year 2005, with current installed capacity at about 80,000 megawatts. Rebecca Mark, who had earlier made a name for herself by establishing a power project in the United Kingdom for Enron, visited India and proposed building a power plant in Dabhol.

REBECCA MARK

Ms. Mark had almost single-handedly pushed Enron into becoming an international energy firm. At age 41, she had risen fast in the corporate world and had been rated by *Fortune* magazine as one of America's most powerful businesswomen. She had not planned it that way. "Opportunities and challenges define your career," she said. "You have to follow your instincts. Do what excites you. And you don't see the path until you get there."

Her path began on the family farm in northeast Missouri. After finishing high school, she put herself through two years at William Jewell College before transferring to Baylor University where she graduated with a degree in psychology. Initially, she wanted to be a clinical psychologist but then realized that working with juvenile delinquents was "personally depressing . . . the antithesis of everything I learned growing up: that you can control your own destiny." Instead, in 1978 she entered a training program at First City National Bank of Houston and soon was lending money to energy companies for big, risky development projects. In 1982, she joined Continental Resources, a natural gas company, which later became a part of Enron.

At Enron, working for John Wing, Ms. Mark developed even more self-confidence and a tougher attitude. Mr. Wing, a West Point graduate, Vietnam veteran, and former manager at General Electric, frequently yelled at Ms. Mark in meetings and called her a failure. Sometimes, he fired her for a few hours or a few days. It was his way with many people, but Ms. Mark endured it. She recalled, "John gave me my fearlessness. He taught me not to be afraid to make decisions in intense, difficult, and emotionally charged situations."

In 1990, she moved to Boston for graduate study in international management at Harvard Business School. There she earned the nickname "Mark the Shark" for her ferocious ambition. As one classmate recalled, she would come dashing into classes late, overstuffed brief case in hand. "She could read a case study and boil it down quickly. We learned a whole lot from her." She continued to work for Enron on a part-time basis and won a deal for Enron to own 50 percent of a power plant in England. After completing her MBA she returned to Houston, ready to take off.

Her career was boosted when Mr. Wing, who had made many enemies at Enron, left the company; she was promoted to his position as chief of power plant development. Soon, Ms. Mark persuaded Ken Lay, the CEO of Enron, to create a separate firm to build power projects in less-developed countries. In 1991, she became CEO of Enron Development Corporation. With 25 managers under her, Ms. Mark traveled around the world looking for opportunities to build power plants and supply infrastructure, and negotiating with government officials, bankers, and equipment suppliers. Ms. Mark recalled, "In the early days, I'd meet with almost anyone who might have a good idea." One consultant, impressed, noted, "She has some unfathomable source of energy that allows her to crisscross time zones and operate with acuity and focus."

Ms. Mark was divorced with twins. She ran 15 miles a week as exercise and went horse riding and skiing with her children. When asked if she was eyeing the top job at Enron, she replied, "As I said, I don't plan my career. Maybe I'm going to run the World Bank, or CARE. I think of my job as one step in a life's work. It'll lead to bigger and different things."

ECONOMIC SITUATION IN INDIA

Since independence from British rule in 1947, India had followed a socialistic policy of economic development, which reserved most infrastructure projects to public sector or state-owned enterprises. Foreign investment was discouraged, and foreign direct investment inflow into the country was miniscule. By the late 1980s, it became clear that the economic policy was failing to deliver higher standards of living and fast economic growth. In 1991, as foreign exchange reserves declined precipitously and the country came close to defaulting on its foreign debt, the government began to deregulate the economy, opening up sectors to foreign investments. It cut down on government bureaucracy and reduced state involvement in the production of goods and services.

THE POWER SECTOR

A principal bottleneck to rapid economic development was the insufficient capacity in the country's infrastructure—roads, seaports, telecommunications, railroads, airports, and electric power supply. Power outages were common, and many parts of the country did not have continuous supply of electricity. Barring a few producers in some cities, almost all the power generated in the country came from state-owned enterprises, called state electricity boards.

The state electricity boards were known for their inefficiency, financial problems, and operational difficulties. Capacity utilization was often 50 percent or less; collection of revenues was tardy; and theft of electricity was high. Political interference in the industry was rampant, and political leaders would often demand and get concessional tariffs for key constituencies, such as farmers. The state electricity boards did not have the resources or the ability to develop and manage an expanding power industry.

Given the huge amounts needed to build power plants and the growing gap between the demand for electricity and its supply, the government was compelled to make a policy change and invite private, both foreign and domestic, investors. To increase power generation, the government approved eight proposals from foreign investors. These proposals were referred to as "fast track" projects because they were approved without going through the time-consuming bureaucratic process for obtaining various permissions.

EFFECTS OF THE REFORMS

The economic reforms had several positive effects, including a dramatic improvement in the country's balance of payments, increased entrepreneurial activity, and greater show of interest by foreign firms. However, across much of Indian society, people expressed opposition to the reforms. The concern was that opening up the economy to foreign investors would enable multinational firms to dominate the country and destroy the public sector. Critics noted that nearly four years after the reforms began in right earnest, the inflation rate remained high, growth rates were still low, and more than 40 percent of the population—390 million Indians—continued to live below the poverty line as defined in bare survival terms as the consumption of 2,200 calories a day. As the government cut subsidies, food prices, especially of food distributed through the public distribution system to the poor, rose. Under the new economic policy, a small but highly prosperous layer of managers and executives emerged, who earned first world salaries, while the average daily wage for unskilled workers was about $1. A group of highly respected Indian economists called for remedial measures, including better macroeconomic stabilization, greater public investment in infrastructure and an end to the policy of privatization of the public sector, considerably greater spending on health, education, social security, and employment programs, and heightened food security.

POLITICAL SITUATION IN INDIA

The Indian constitution prescribed a federalist system with power shared between a relatively strong central government based in Delhi and the various provincial or state governments. According to the constitution, responsibilities for specific social and economic functions were either reserved exclusively for the central government or the states or shared between the two. The electricity industry was on the concurrent list, which meant that both the central and the state governments had a say in the development and functioning of that industry.

Since 1947, the Congress Party, which was at the vanguard of the freedom movement, had been the dominant political force in India. It had ruled at the national level for all but 5 of the country's 50 years since independence. In the late 1980s, the Congress Party began to decay and splinter, and its performance in the elections eroded. The main beneficiary of the decline was the Bharatiya Janata Party (Indian People's Party), commonly referred by its initials BJP. The BJP saw its share of seats increase with every election. Although the Congress was a broad-based national party with a left-leaning stance, the BJP was a right-wing party, committed to strong economic nationalism, with a predominant base among the Hindus in India's North and West. The BJP's thrust had been to emphasize and celebrate Hindu culture and traditions, to help domestic businesses, and restrict foreign investment. In 1991, the Congress formed a coalition government at the national level with a tenuous majority. It was this government that had been spearheading the economic reforms in the country.

At the state level too, the national parties competed for power. In addition, there were, in many states, regional or state-specific political parties who had narrow agendas or represented particular constituencies. The Congress Party had lost power in many of the states.

NEGOTIATING THE CONTRACT

EDC began negotiating with the state government of Maharashtra for a project to build and operate a power plant with a capacity of 2,015 megawatts (mw) at a cost of $2.8 billion. Maharashtra was one of India's most affluent states with a rapidly growing manufacturing base. In 1995, the power capacity in the state was 11,582 mw while demand was 7,900 mw. The state estimated that it would need 13,147 mw by 2000. For this supply, the installed capacity would have to be 20,500 mw. The Maharashtra government was controlled by the Congress Party. Negotiations continued over nearly four years in secrecy, and an agreement was reached to build a gas-fired power plant at Dabhol.

THE DABHOL POWER PROJECT

The project would be India's single largest power plant and was one of the eight "fast track" projects cleared by the central government in Delhi. Enron set up a joint venture, Dabhol Power Company (DPC), a 100 percent foreign-owned, private, limited-liability company. Enron held 80 percent of the shares of DPC, while Bechtel and GE each held 10 percent. Bechtel was a U.S. construction company and would do the construction work for the project. GE was a U.S. conglomerate that would provide the gas turbines to generate electricity. The three partners controlled DPC through a chain of companies based in Mauritius.

Enron sought and got several guarantees as part of the agreement to build the power plant. These guarantees included the following:

- All power generated by DPC would be purchased by the Maharashtra State Electricity Board (MSEB). Thus, the responsibility of distributing the power to final consumers rested with MSEB. However, MSEB would pay DPC for the power. This payment was guaranteed by the state government as well as the national government in Delhi.

- The payment for the power would be in U.S. dollars. The contract was finalized using the current rate of 36 Indian rupees per U.S. dollar. The payment in dollars was guaranteed by the national government in Delhi.

- DPC had a license to operate the plant for 20 years. During this period, the plant would not be nationalized by either the state or central government.

- MSEB promised to buy 90 percent of the power produced by DPC, regardless of demand, and even if cheaper power was available from its own generating plants.

- DPC was assured a posttax return of 16 percent on capital investment, with no limit on the capital expenditure Enron could make.

- In case of disputes over the contract, settlement would be through arbitration under English law in England, United Kingdom.

It was decided to build the project in two phases. Phase I would be a 695 MW plant using distillate fuel instead of natural gas. The second phase would be a 1,320 MW plant using liquefied natural gas (LPG). The capital cost would be $920 million for phase I and $1.9 billion for the second phase. The breaking up of the project into two phases followed Enron's inability to finalize long-term gas supplies and because the government had become concerned about criticism of the project. The shift to distillate fuel was made because it could be sourced from Indian refineries. India was a net importer of oil, which imposed a heavy burden on foreign exchange reserves. Using distillate would reduce the amount of imported fuel and eliminate the need to build a port near Dabhol for phase I.

EDC, in addition to the development, construction, financing, and operation of the power plant would also implement a liquefied natural gas (LNG) unloading port terminal. The project would have a storage and vaporization facility for providing natural gas to the power plant. A deep-water harbor, fuel oil unloading and storage facility would also be constructed. Construction work began on March 1, 1995. The phase I cost of the project also included infrastructure costs such as land development, roads, and pipelines and was expected to be completed by early 1998.

OPPOSITION TO THE CONTRACT

The Dabhol power plant was opposed by a wide range of groups and for a variety of reasons. Foremost was concern at how the negotiations had proceeded between the company and the government—in secrecy. Being a "fast-track" project, no bids were solicited from other companies. In addition, the contract was complex and difficult to follow, making it hard for third parties to raise questions. The spending of $20 million by Enron for educating the various constituencies about the project and for project development was seen by some as bribe money paid to members of the ruling party in the state.

After work began at Dabhol, hundreds of villagers stormed the project site and injured many of the 1,500 construction workers, including three of the 60 foreign advisers on the project. The villagers complained that effluent from the power plant would destroy their fisheries and kill the coconut and mango trees that had traditionally grown there. "There were election promises that the project would be stopped," said Mahmood Ibrahim Mastan, the headman of a local village. "The (news)papers started talking about pollution in the area. And people heard they would have to leave their homes. They said, 'Why not remove them before they remove us?'" No environmental assessment study of the project had been done.

Economists associated with Prayas, a nongovernmental organization, charged that "Enron, in collusion with certain business interests, tried to pull off quite an unfair business deal, if not outright plunder." They said that the World Bank had rejected requests to fund the Enron project because it was too expensive. Prayas had calculated that Enron would receive an after-tax rate of return of 32 percent on the project, which was roughly three times the average rate in the United States. It was noted that a similar-sized plant had been completed by Enron in the United Kingdom for less than half the price it had quoted for the Dabhol plant.

Enron's deal locked the MSEB into buying power from DPC at 7.4 cents a kilowatt hour. (In the United

States, prices ranged from 4 to 15 cents.) The cost would rise further for the MSEB to distribute that power to the consumer. The problem was that domestic consumers in the state paid about 4 cents. The negotiated price was too high, according to an economist with a research institute. He said that the operating cost to generate power from a coal plant was only 2 cents. "As a consumer, I shouldn't bother about the cost of the plant but the price that I'm being charged." Enron's decision to use a LNG plant design rather than a coal model because of environmental concerns and worries about assured coal supply also raised the costs. LNG plants, although cheaper to build, were costlier to operate.

STATE ELECTION IN MAHARASHTRA

Elections to the Maharashtra state assembly were held in February 1995. The Dabhol power plant project featured heavily in the election campaign. The opposition parties in Maharashtra state, the BJP and its local ally, the Shiva Sena (Shiva's Army), had opposed the negotiations with Enron arguing that the contract was against the interests of the state and the country. During the election campaign the two allies threatened to cancel the deal and complained about its high price tag. It alleged corrupt behavior on the part of the ruling Congress Party, especially because the contract had been awarded without an open tendering process. During election rallies, the BJP candidate, Gopinath Munde, claimed that the Enron project could easily be built by Indian companies. But the Enron deal, he said, would send abroad huge profits made off "the backs of India's poor." The BJP-Shiva Sena candidates promised to "bundle Enron into the sea."

The Congress Party was defeated in the elections and the BJP-Shiva Sena alliance assumed office. Following up on its election pledges and in response to the criticisms from various quarters, the state government commissioned an enquiry into the Dabhol project headed by Mr. Munde, now the deputy head of the government. A BJP spokesperson said, "We are for foreign investment in the infrastructure sectors, but we want everything to be transparent and above board. We feel that the way the project was negotiated was not in the interests of the state."

REACTION TO THE REVIEW

"I'm in grief," said Ms. Mark when told that the state had ordered the review. She went to Bombay to meet the new leaders and persuade the government not to cancel the deal.

The national government in Delhi was also unhappy with the actions of the newly elected Maharashtra government. The Dabhol project was the single largest foreign project in the country and was seen as a litmus test of the country's commitment to economic liberalization. It was afraid that the other fast-track electricity projects would be derailed as foreign investors, looking at the Enron events, decide to abandon their commitments.

The review also sparked angry comments from the U.S. government, which had helped Enron negotiate the deal. "Failure to honor the agreements between the project partners and the various Indian governments will jeopardize not only the Dabhol project but also most, if not all, of the other private power projects being proposed for international financing," said a statement issued by the office of the secretary of the U.S. Department of Energy. Other foreign governments whose firms were involved in other Indian power projects chimed in. The British chancellor of the exchequer warned India that pulling out of the Enron deal could have repercussions for Indian investment.

These foreign government statements angered many Indians, who regarded them as another example of imperialist arm-twisting. Newspaper editorials weighed in. "It is time the West realized that India is not a banana republic which has to dance to the tune of multinationals," said the *Hindustan Times* of Delhi. Calcutta's *Business Standard* wrote: "A necessary condition for newlyweds to work out a long-term *modus vivendi* is that the bride's father stays out of the relationship." Even the Indian government felt compelled to object to the U.S. statement. Describing it as unwarranted, the national power minister said, "The Indian government is not going to act under any pressure from the U.S. government." To cool the rising passions, Frank Wisner, the U.S. ambassador to India, took a conciliatory approach. He opined, "I can see no reason . . . why this review cannot reach a conclusion that will satisfy the needs of all parties, the state, its citizens, its need for power, and Enron's desire to create a long-term and productive relationship with India."

Despite the review, Ms. Mark vowed that EDC would not stop work on the project until it had been formally notified of the cancellation by the Maharashtra government. "We don't have anything to do with politics," she said. "We came here to get our work done. The project will continue to be built regardless, until the day the Maharashtra State Electricity Board serves us a termination notice revoking the contract and says we no longer want you in the country."

Sharad Pawar, the leader (chief minister) of the outgoing state government that had negotiated the Dabhol contract warned his successor that the state would have to pay severe penalties of up to $286 million if it violated its contractual guarantees by scrapping the deal. He also said that cancelling would reduce the flow of foreign investments into India. Enron indicated, however, that the state's cost would be much lower, closer to $100 million. Defending the project he had negotiated, Mr. Pawar said, "Without participation of foreign capital and technology, growth in this most crucial section of the economy will slow down and the ill-effects will spill over to all other sectors of the economy." Other supporters pointed out that any failure to complete the project would hamper plans for India to add 150,000 mw of power capacity over the next 10 years.

Prayas's economists claimed that conservation measures, establishment of cogeneration plants (which generate electricity from the excess heat given off in other industrial processes), and smaller hydro-electric plants could add enough power supply to match the proposed Dabhol project's capacity. The group claimed that all these projects could be built and the fines for expelling Enron paid at a significant saving over the current price tag for the project.

The villagers around Dabhol said that even if the state government approved the project after review, it would continue its agitation. The resolve of the villagers could not be easily dismissed. In early 1995, Dupont, a multinational chemicals company, had to abandon the building of a plant in the southwestern state of Goa after public protests made construction work impossible.

ENRON'S RESPONSE

According to an independent attorney, the Dabhol project should not have been independently bid. "That was the opportunity cost of getting a company to come and create an industry. When I first went to India, nobody would ever dream of coming over if negotiated deals weren't offered." Ms. Mark insisted that the DPC was competitively priced relative to other "fast-track" projects. The company also vigorously denied all allegations of bribery.

THE REVIEW DECISION

In late July, the final review of the project was handed over to the chief minister, Manohar Joshi. He announced in the state assembly on August 3 that he had accepted the recommendations of the review committee to cancel the project. Excerpts from the chief minister's statement are provided here:

The Enron project in the form conceived and contracted for is not in the best interests of the state. Being conscious of the deception and distortion in the Enron-MSEB deal which have caused grave losses, the subcommittee is clear that the project must not be allowed to proceed. The subcommittee wholeheartedly recommends that the Enron-MSEB contract should be canceled forthwith. . . . Considering the grave issues involved in the matter and the disturbing facts and circumstances that have emerged pointing to extracommercial considerations and probable corruption and illegal motives at work in the whole affair, immediate action must be initiated under the penal and anti-corruption laws by police.

The wrong choice of LNG as fuel and huge inflation in capital costs, along with unprecedented favors shown to Enron in different ways, including the fuel procurement [all resulted in an] unreasonable fuel cost to the consumers. . . . The documentary evidence obtained by the committee shows beyond any reasonable doubt that the capital cost of Enron Plant was inflated and jacked up by a huge margin. The committee believes that the extent of the inflation may be as high as $700 million. . . . Being gas-based, this project should have been cheaper than coal-based ones but in reality, it turns out to be the other way about.

. . . This contract is anti-Maharashtra. It is devoid of any self-respect; it is one that mortgages the brains of the state which, if accepted, would be a betrayal of the people. This contract is no contract at all and if by repudiating it, there is some financial burden, the state will accept it to preserve the well-being of Maharashtra.

Ms. Mark left for India to salvage the project. She was determined to do whatever was necessary. True to her style and grit, she noted, "I enjoy being a world-class problem solver. I am constantly asking, 'How far can I go? How much can I do?'" The Dabhol project was crucial to Enron because it would open the door to many more opportunities in India. In addition, the company had already spent $200 million on construction work alone. More than four years of negotiations had preceded the signing of the contract, negotiations in which Ms. Mark had been closely involved. The contract contained both provisions for taking any disputes to international arbitration in London, and guarantees from the state and central governments. Ms. Mark, however, hoped for a settlement. "While we can say that we are extremely content with our legal position, we are absolutely willing to negotiate."

QUESTIONS

1. What are the choices available to Ms. Mark? Discuss them. Recommend the course of action that Ms. Mark should take. Justify your answer.
2. Evaluate the bargaining power of Enron. What is the bargaining power of the Maharashtra government?
3. Who are the allies that Enron can count upon as it squares off with the state government?
4. What political miscalculations did Enron make when it negotiated the Dabhol power project with Indian and state government officials?
5. Despite the negative implications for business, foreign investment, economic development, and power generation, why might politicians cancel an agreed contract?

References

Boddewyn, Jean. 1988. Political aspects of MNE theory. *Journal of International Business Studies* 19(3), pp. 341–363.

Caves, Richard. 1996. *Multinational enterprise and economic analysis,* 2d ed. Cambridge: Cambridge University.

Kobrin, Stephen. 1987. Testing the bargaining hypothesis in the manufacturing sector in developing countries. *International Organization* 41(4), pp. 609–638.

Lecraw, Donald. 1984. Bargaining power, ownership, and profitability of transnational corporations in developing countries. *Journal of International Business Studies* 15(2), pp. 27–43.

Poynter, Thomas. 1985. *Multinational enterprises and government intervention.* New York: St. Martin's Press.

Ring, Peter, Stefanie Lenway, and Michele Govekar. 1990. Management of the political imperative in international business. *Strategic Management Journal* 11, pp. 141–151.

4

STRATEGY FORMULATION AND IMPLEMENTATION

❧

OPENING VIGNETTE

Driving to the outskirts of Sao Paulo, Brazil, or Buenos Aires, Argentina, one is likely to come across a new foreign-operated supermarket. Hampered by saturated markets and planning controls in their home countries, some of the world's leading retailers expanded into Latin America, attracted by the continent's new economic stability and a growing middle class. With the onslaught of this foreign invasion, many local retailers, lacking sufficient capital or modern technology, had been acquired or had cut back on operations.

In most Latin American countries, retailing has historically been much less protected than manufacturing. Hence, it has been easier for foreign firms to set up shop. Nearly half of the increase in supermarket retail floorspace in Latin America in the 1990s was accounted for by foreign firms. For example, Carrefour, a French hypermarket operator, set up in Argentina and Brazil in the 1970s; by 1997, it had sales of $7 billion in that region. Wal-Mart, America's and the world's largest retailer, moved aggressively into Mexico where it acquired a controlling interest in Cifra, a local supermarket chain, and had since 1995, opened stores in Brazil and Argentina. The chief advantage of Carrefour and Wal-Mart was size. Latin America's family-owned corner shops and small supermarkets found it hard to match the low unit-costs of the foreign giants and the bargaining power they wielded over suppliers. Carrefour's Brazilian operation extracted net-profit margins of close to 4 percent, compared with only about 1 percent in France.

The competition from the foreign supermarkets hurt the domestic companies in Latin America. In Brazil, owners of four of the top dozen supermarket chains got out of the business. Pao de Azucar, Brazil's second largest retailer, extended its stores all over Brazil, even in towns in the Amazon, which had to be supplied at great cost from its base in Sao Paulo. With competition from foreign-owned supermarkets, Pao de Azucar cut back its distant stores to concentrate in Sao Paulo state. Together with other Latin American supermarket chains such as Disco and Santa Isable, Pao de Azucar required new ways to retain its market presence as its foreign rivals opened more and more stores. They needed to find ways to match the foreigners and fight back.

The principal goal of a business is to make a profit or, in contemporary parlance, increase shareholder value. To achieve this goal, a firm has to produce a good or service desired by customers and sell it at a price greater than the cost. To maintain or widen the profit margin, firms can reduce their production costs and/or increase the selling price by adding value to the product or service in the form of added features, customer service, and better quality. In a business setting where firms from around the world are competing in multiple markets, the successful firm has to engage in activities that distinguish it from competitors. Thus, a firm's strategy is to ensure that the actions it takes reduce costs, add value, and present a distinctive face to the customer. This chapter discusses various issues connected with formulating and implementing business strategy and presents various strategy alternatives that international firms use. Strategy formulation includes the need for a thorough understanding of the business environment in which the firm operates and of the firm's internal capabilities. Implementing a strategy requires the involvement of the entire firm and its various functions, and addressing issues such as how the firm is organized, the location and nature of activities, corporate goals, foreign entry and ownership choices, and identifying sources of competitive advantage.

WHAT IS STRATEGY?

Strategy is basically about deciding where the firm should go and how should it go there. Thus strategy refers to the plans of top-level managers to achieve outcomes that are consistent with the firm's mission and goals. Michael Porter, a professor at Harvard University, explains strategy as finding the position in the market place that best suits a firm's skills. An alternative view is provided by Gary Hamel, a professor at London Business School. He suggests that strategy means deciding what a future market would look like and then stretching a firm's skills so that it could take advantage of the market. Hamel's view focuses on the firm constantly reinventing itself and developing a capacity to anticipate the future and be prepared for it. Porter takes a more static view of the firm suggesting that its strategy is determined by its resources and abilities.

In developing the firm's strategy, managers evaluate the external environment, particularly the threats and opportunities that might exist for their particular organization, and critically analyze the firm's own capabilities and shortcomings. Based on such extensive reviews, managers formulate strategies—for the overall firm, for each of the business units (in multi-unit firms), and for the functional areas—that fit with both the external environment and the internal resources of the firm, and then take steps to implement them. Such a diagnostic process provides a direction to the firm's activities, creates the basis for organizing itself, and serves as a gauge to measure performance. Deciding which target group of customers and needs the firm should serve is essential to developing a strategy. But so is deciding not to serve other customers or needs and not to offer certain features or services. Thus, strategy requires a clear focus and a full understanding of the business situation.

ROLE OF MANAGEMENT

Strategy making and implementation are usually the domain of top management. While the chief executive officer is ultimately responsible for the firm's strategy and its management, that person is assisted and guided by a team of senior managers, the board of directors, and staff specialists. Large firms such as IBM and Philips have planning divisions at headquarters whose task is to engage in analysis, strategic planning, and providing advice to top management. Usually, information is gathered from various sources (such as country managers overseas, scientists in the research and development (R&D) department or salespersons in the field) and then collated and analyzed to create the reports on which strategic decisions are finally made by the top-level managers. Thus, strategic management requires the involvement of the entire organization. It also take time to develop and even more time to implement and for the results to be discernible. Consequently, strategy is a future-oriented activity with long-term implications for the firm.

The task of formulating a clear strategy is heavily dependent on the firm's leadership. The core of general management is strategy: defining and communicating the company's unique position, making trade-offs, and forging a fit among the firm's multifaceted activities. The leadership must provide the discipline to decide how to respond to industry changes and customer needs, and to maintain the company's distinctiveness while avoiding organizational distractions. Managers at lower levels lack the perspective, experience, and confidence to develop the overall strategy. One of the leader's jobs is to teach others in the organization about strategy and keep the firm on the path it has charted out. Management Focus 4-1 discusses the character and track record of a strategic manager.

STRATEGY IN INTERNATIONAL BUSINESS

Various ideas have been advanced about the nature of strategy issues in international business. The earliest view offered a marketing perspective: strategy required that the firm develop a standardized product that would be produced and sold the same way throughout the world. Another view was that an international firm by virtue of its size could exploit economies of scale, engage in quick and large investments, and manage interdependently to achieve synergies across different activities. A third view was that a successful international business strategy required the firm to make and sell a variety of products (instead of a single standardized product) so that investments in technologies and distribution channels could be shared and cross-subsidized. Yet another perspective was that the international firm was able to succeed by being flexible and taking advantage of differences among markets through multiple sourcing of inputs, shifting production sites to benefit from changing cost structures and exchange rate fluctuations, and exploiting imperfections in information and financial markets. More recently, as competition becomes more international and intense, the prevalent thinking emphasizes continuous innovation and distinctive positioning in the market place as the means to stay ahead of one's rivals.

These ideas highlight the complexity of the strategic issues that managers in international firms face. To ensure that a firm is able to compete successfully over the long haul, it needs to achieve three strategic goals:

1. Produce goods and services efficiently
2. Be flexible enough to exploit worldwide opportunities and manage global risks
3. Learn from the various experiences that accrue through doing business in a highly diverse international environment.

MANAGEMENT FOCUS 4-1

VOLKSWAGEN'S LEAD DRIVER: FERDINAND PIECH

Since Ferdinand Piech succeeded to the post of chief executive officer of Volkswagen (VW) in 1993 at the age of 56, he has pursued with obsessive zeal the goal of molding Europe's leading auto mass-marketer into one of the world's mightiest, most respected automakers. He intended to shed the company's plebian image and move the VW brand upmarket.

After consolidating power by replacing dozens of top managers who did not follow his lead, he embarked on a series of actions designed to achieve that goal. When Mr. Piech took over, the company was so inefficient that it had lost $1.1 billion. But he turned it around. He lured the cost-cutting maven Jose Ignacio Lopez from General Motors to streamline VW's raw materials and parts purchasing. He launched a range of new cars from the $10,500 Lupo minicar and the $21,700 Passat family sedan in Europe to the $16,500 New Beetle in the United States. The concept of the New Beetle had been strongly opposed by the company's R&D chief, but Mr. Piech, whose grandfather had conceived the original Beetle at Hitler's behest, pushed for the new car, equipped it with modern automotive technology, and drove it to wide public acclaim. The car drew enthusiastic shoppers into VW's showrooms in the United States where the company experienced in 1998 its highest sales since 1984. In just five years, he revived the moribund SEAT and Skoda brands, raised the company's market share in Europe, and strengthened its position in the emerging markets of Central Europe and Latin America. In 1998, the company made a net income of $1.3 billion.

Mr. Piech also embarked on a high-stakes acquisition binge. In just three months in the summer of 1998, he bought the prestigious Rolls-Royce Motor Cars of the United Kingdom; Lamborghini, the Italian producer of ultra high-priced sports cars;

Cosworth, a British manufacturer of specialty engines; and Bugatti, a bankrupt Italian sports car maker.

Born in Vienna, Austria, to Anton and Louise Piech, the daughter of Ferdinand Porsche, the younger Ferdinand otained an engineering degree from Zurich's Technical Institute and landed his first job testing engines at sports car maker Porsche. His success was attributed to his engineering skills, a passion for automobiles, and the enormous wealth of his family. He was described as a combative yet insecure man driven by a deep desire to match his grandfather's mythical stature. Others considered him unpredictable, even potentially dangerous.

Because he silenced any opposition, he brooked hardly any debate over his actions, which in turn raised the risk of major blunders. For example, the purchase of Rolls-Royce from Vickers of the United Kingdom went awry when it was found that the rights to the Rolls-Royce name and trademark belonged not to Vickers but to Rolls-Royce, the aerospace company, which had no connection to the luxury car maker. The name was eventually bought by archrival BMW.

Mr. Piech had many critics about his autocratic management style. After all the purges, he was now surrounded by "yes men." The concern was that should he die or leave the company suddenly, a giant power vacuum would ensue. His iron grip on the company meant few checks and balances on his decisions. Mr. Piech had shrunk VW's management board to just five members, from nine before he took the top job. He held personal responsibility for R&D, production, purchasing, and VW—areas typically assigned to individual directors. The supervisory board would like to spread the workload more evenly among a team of managers. With his successful track record, it was unlikely that Mr. Piech would yield any ground unless a serious mistake cast doubt on his skills.

Source: Business Week. 1998, October 5. Hard-driving boss. pp. 82–89.

STRATEGY FORMULATION

THE DYNAMIC EXTERNAL ENVIRONMENT

As was discussed in Chapter 1, the global environment, never stable, has been particularly volatile in recent years. Table 4-1 presents some of the important variables in the international environment that impact on strategy formulation. An assessment of the environment allows managers to identify threats and opportunities to the firm.

ASSESSING A FIRM'S CAPABILITIES

In addition to evaluating the business environment, a firm needs to identify its internal strengths to take advantage of the opportunities and avoid dangers that may exist. One way is to examine closely the firm's resources and capabilities and identify the resource gaps that need to be filled and weaknesses that need to be addressed. To sustain a competitive advantage, resources and capabilities must have the following characteristics:

1. *Durability.* Durability refers to the rate at which a firm's underlying resources and capabilities depreciate or become obsolete. Patents on pharmaceuticals provide a time-bound protection of a key resource. Where durability is missing, the firm has to constantly come out with new products or innovations and reduce the time to make the transition from the laboratory or drawing board to the market.

2. *Transparency.* Transparency is the speed with which rival firms can understand the relationship between resources and capabilities that undergird a successful strategy. Complex patterns of various resources are harder to comprehend than a capability based on a single key resource. The success of Honda, a Japanese auto company, is not based merely on good designs, but also on a sophisticated and integrated set of activities ranging from R&D to production techniques to workers' training and dealer service.[1] Joint ventures and strategic alliances with other firms are potential ways of understanding how a successful system works.

Table 4-1   Selected Variables in the International Environment

Economic	*Technological*	*Political-Legal*	*Social-Cultural*
Economic development	Regulations on technology transfer	Form of government	Customs, norms, values
Per capita income	Energy availability/cost	Political ideology	Language
Climate	Natural resource availability	Stability of government	Demographics
GDP trends	Transportation network	Policy toward foreign investment	Life expectancies
Monetary and fiscal policies	Skill level of workforce	Strength of opposition groups/terrorism	Social institutions
Unemployment level	Patent/trademark protection	Trade regulations	Lifestyle
Currency convertibility	Information-flow infrastructure	Foreign policy	Religious beliefs
Wage levels		Legal system	Attitude toward foreigners
Membership in economic groups			Literacy level

Source: Wheelen, Thomas L., and Hunger, J. David. *Strategic management and business policy.* © 1995, Addison Wesley Longman, Inc. Reprinted by permission of Addison Wesley Longman.

---

[1] Honda. *Business Week.* 1997, September 8, pp. 100–108.

3. *Transferability.* Transferability refers to the ability of competitors to obtain the resources necessary to mount a competitive challenge. Successful brand names, such as Gucci, which promotes exclusivity and quality, discourage imitators.[2]

4. *Replicability.* Replicability is the ability of rivals to duplicate a successful strategy. A company's culture, history, philosophy, and structures may militate against an easy replication of a formula that has worked well with another company. Philips, the Dutch electronic giant, has tired to emulate Sony, the Japanese consumer electronics firm, but with little success.[3]

An analysis of the firm's capabilities requires posing questions such as:

- Does the company have a strong position in the countries and in the product categories in which it operates?
- Does the company have a technological advantage?
- How reputable is its brand name and image abroad?
- How capable are its managers in handling overseas assignments?
- How successful has the company been in introducing new products?
- How well has the company been able to work with political authorities abroad?
- Are new markets opening up to foreign investment or trade?
- Are state-owned enterprises available for privatization?
- What is the potential and actual growth rate in the industry?
- What is the intensity of competition in the industry?

The result of such an analysis would be to identify a variety of strategies that the firm might pursue.

VARIOUS STRATEGIC CHOICES

Scholars and practitioners have identified several sets of strategic choices that international firms have. Selecting one over another is contingent upon a whole host of factors including the firm's resources, product lines, leadership, history, nature of the industry, and business environment. Some of these choices are discussed in this section.

EVOLUTIONARY APPROACH

Christopher Bartlett and Sumantra Ghoshal, two academics who have written extensively about multinational firms, have described four different strategies that firms in international business may adopt.[4] This **evolutionary strategy** approach reflects increasing levels of international activities on the part of the firm.

1. *International strategy.* Firms adopting this approach create and apply on a worldwide basis the innovations they develop in its home country. Consis-

---

[2]Barrett, Amy. 1997, August 26. Gucci's big makeover is turning heads. *The Wall Street Journal,* p. A12.
[3]Ultimatum at Philips. *Business Week.* 1997, November 17, pp. 134–135.
[4]Ghoshal, Sumantra. 1987. Global strategy: An organizing framework. *Strategic Management Journal 8,* pp. 425–440.

tent with the life cycle theory, the firm develops products, processes, strategies, and organizations for the home market and then transfers them to foreign markets. This strategy is more suitable in the early stages of internationalization of the firm.

2. *Multinational strategy.* Under this approach, strategies are designed for each of the unique countries in which the firm has operations. This approach focuses on recognizing national differences and adapting products, processes, and organizational forms to each country. Consequently, the firm's foreign operations are given considerable autonomy. Although responsive to individual markets, this approach is inefficient and makes it difficult for the firm to fully absorb the knowledge and experience it gained at different locations.

3. *Global strategy.* This strategy emphasizes efficiency by centralizing global operations, often in the home country. Firms pursue a single strategy across national markets, usually ignoring national differences. It relies heavily on exporting from centralized facilities and presents an inability to exploit country-specific knowledge and capabilities.

4. *Transnational strategy.* The firm with the transnational strategy encompasses the three strategic goals identified earlier—produce goods and services efficiently, be flexible enough to exploit worldwide opportunities and manage global risks, and learn from the various experiences that accrue through doing business in a highly diverse international environment. Thus, the transnational approach focuses on both responding to national differences while ensuring that the overall firm is run efficiently.

LOW COST AND DIFFERENTIATION

Another approach to strategy focuses on low cost and differentiation. **Low-cost strategy** refers to the ability of the firm to design, produce, and deliver a comparable product cheaper than its competitors. **Differentiation strategy** is the ability of the firm to distinguish its products from those of its competitors through superior quality and service, augmented features, brand image, technology, or dealer network, among others. Note that the multinational strategy described by Bartlett and Ghoshal is based on differentiation of national markets. Both the global and international strategies have an efficiency or low-cost dimension to them. The transnational strategy tries to combine both low cost and differentiation.

Each of these strategies has its risks. For example, the low-cost strategy may not be sustainable if competitors are able to reduce their own costs. Technological changes can cut costs, and other sources of cost advantage may erode over time. Footwear makers such as Nike and Reebok have migrated their offshore production sources from South Korea to Taiwan to Indonesia to Vietnam in a bid to find low-cost sites as existing locations become more expensive to operate. The differentiation strategy too may not be sustainable because competitors can mimic all the distinctive features and when all products carry similar features, no differentiation is achieved in the mind of the customer. The strategy of focusing on niche markets may be unstable because the segment is too small to be economically viable. It may invite new entrants because it may require less resources or the customers may be more open to alternatives, or the differences with the differentiated strategy may become blurred.

Although firms can choose between one of these strategies, in reality, many firms compete in a variety of segments. However, this segment success is usually feasible for only a short period. Japanese automobile firms entered the U.S. market with small, fuel-efficient, less expensive cars. Over time, their product line expanded to include full-size sedans and, later on, luxury models and van-like vehicles. Such a wide range catered to all market segments. Maintaining both low cost and differentiation, though, became unviable over the long run, and most of the Japanese companies, as they moved upscale in their product offerings began to deemphasize their low-priced line of vehicles.

GLOBAL STRATEGY

We will expand on the global strategy mentioned earlier and examine its many facets in greater detail. The global strategy is also contrasted with the multinational strategy.

When a firm pursues a **global strategy,** it chooses to compete on a worldwide rather than on a country-by-country basis in all major international markets (typically the Triad consisting of North America, Western Europe, and Japan), produces standardized products for all markets, sites and integrates its production facilities in locations where the costs in relation to technology and quality are the least, and has a uniform marketing approach around the world. Such firms, therefore, develop and design products for the world market, which can be sold in various countries with minimum changes or alterations. These components of global strategy are elaborated here.

- *Global Market Participation.* Firms select and invest in countries on the basis of global strategic importance as well as the attractiveness of the opportunity in an individual country. Such a decision may include entering a market that by itself may not be attractive, but has global strategic importance, such as the home country of a competitor. The firm could also build up share in a limited number of key markets.
- *Global Products and Services.* The firm designs and makes products for the international consumer everywhere rather than for customers in a particular country. This approach does not imply a complete standardization; the emphasis is on designing for maximum worldwide acceptance.
- *Global Location of Activities.* Global strategy calls for firms to create an international network of activities by selecting a few, best locations where cost, quality, and technology can be optimally combined. By locating key activities in a few centers, the firm achieves scale economies, cuts duplication, and provides focus.
- *Global Marketing.* The firm uses its brand name, advertising copy, and other marketing elements without significant modification around the world.
- *Competitive Moves.* The firm integrates actions against its rivals on a worldwide basis rather than fighting separate country battles.

Global Products and Industries   Certain industries or products are more suitable than others for a global strategy. Examples of such products or industries are aircraft manufacturing, watches, computers, consumer electronics, computers, and chocolates. These products are bought by consumers in many countries and can be produced in a few chosen locations on a large scale. Trade barriers and transportation costs are also low, and the product can be advertised and marketed in a uniform manner. Companies making these products compete with each other across the world in multiple markets. In general, it appears that the global strategy is becoming feasible for more and more products and industries.

However, many other industries or products exhibit some dimensions that make them amenable to globalization but other dimensions may prevent their globalization from happening. For example, automobiles would appear to be a global industry. They are a standardized product made in large numbers in huge factories in low-cost locations and are sold throughout the world under well-established brand names through auto dealerships. Automobile companies vie for customers everywhere. In many markets though, automobiles may have to be redesigned (say, for poorer roads or humid and dusty tropical settings), priced lower (in recognition of lower purchasing power in particular countries), and equipped with fewer features (such as antilock brakes). They also face a variety of tariff and nontariff barriers in many countries, and individual governments may favor domestic producers against imported products.

Hence, some automobile companies have tried to build a "world car" that would appeal to low-income buyers in countries everywhere. The Honda Motor company's City model car is an example of this effort. It was designed for Asia's emerging middle class as well as their poor state of roads. Although similar to the Civic (which was sold in the West), the City differed in important respects as Table 4-2 shows.

Determinants of Global Strategy   To determine the suitability of an industry or product for a globalization strategy, managers have to recognize whether various key conditions (or levers) exist. They are as follows:

- Market Drivers
  - Homogeneous customer needs
  - Global customers (such as a multinational firm or a country's armed forces who may scout the world for suppliers)
  - Existence of global channels
  - Transferability across countries of brand names, marketing strategies, and advertising campaigns

Table 4-2 The Honda Civic and the Honda City	
Features	*Differences*
Road Clearance	The City's clearance is 6.8 inches, about an inch more than the Civic, because of Asia's bumpier roads.
Engine Computer	The City's engine control computer is positioned higher than the Civic's to protect it from flooding.
Engine Size	Poor road quality and congestion means lower speeds, so the City is built with a smaller engine.
Suspension	The City's strut system is simpler than the Civic's wishbone system, which can handle higher speeds.
Turning Radius	The City's tighter turning radius can better negotiate the narrow, twisting Asian roads.
Comfort/Safety Features	The City is smaller than the Civic, has no airbags, antilock breaks, heaters, and rear window defrosters, but has an extra air conditioner because of Asia's torrid climate.

Source: Pollack, Andrew. 1996, June 6, pp. D1, D7. "4 Doors and Air, But No Heat". *The New York Times.*

- Cost Drivers
  - Ability to reap economies of scale and scope
  - Ability to continually climb the experience curve
  - Ability to source materials and inputs from low-cost suppliers
  - Lower transportation costs
  - Ability to locate in low-cost production sites
  - Avoid duplication in product development programs and facilities
- Governmental Drivers
  - Favorable policies toward international trade
  - Compatibility of worldwide technical standards
  - Commonality of marketing rules and regulations across countries
- Competitive Drivers
  - Interdependence of countries (opportunity to participate in several markets)
  - Globalized competitors (compete with rival firms in several markets including one's own home market)

Table 4-3 presents a matrix showing how these four sets of competitive drivers interact with the five components of a globalization strategy.

In determining whether a firm has the necessary characteristics to compete on a global basis, its managers often look at potential economies of scale. **Economies of scale** refers to reduction in unit cost achieved by producing in large volumes. Unit cost can be reduced because the fixed costs (such as the cost of building a plant or developing a new product) can be spread over the large volume. Worldwide volume is also big enough to support high levels of investment in research and development activities, which are necessary for industries such as pharmaceuticals and aerospace. Advantages to producing or dealing in large volume not only comes from large capacity plants or distribution centers but also from efficient logistics networks. The opening vignette illustrates the advantage foreign retailers had in relation to the home-based firms in Latin America. Transportation costs is another key determinant of globalization. Some products, such as bricks, are simply too expensive to ship worldwide, but not, say, sunglasses.

Combined with the experience curve, large-scale production contributes to lower unit costs of production and thus lower prices. The cost advantage of large-scale production is well illustrated by the action of Matsushita, a Japanese conglomerate. After securing as the industry format the video home system (VHS) over Sony's Betamax, the company expanded the production of video cassette recorders more than thirtyfold from about 200,000 units in 1977 to nearly 7 million units in 1984, all at a single plant in Japan. The company was able to reap the benefits accruing from this large-scale production and was constantly able to reduce prices. By the early 1980s, Matsushita's video cassette recorders under brand names such as Panasonic and National were runaway market leaders.

Benefits of a Global Strategy Companies that are able to pursue a global strategy can expect the following benefits:

1. *Reductions in cost.* As already noted, by producing in one or few plants for the global market, the firm can benefit from economies of scale. By locating facilities and activities in low-cost locations, the firm takes advantage of

Table 4-3 Effects of Industry Globalization Drivers on the Potential Use of Global Strategy Levers

Industry Drivers	Strategy Levers				
	Major Market Participation	*Product Standardization*	*Activity Concentration*	*Uniform Marketing*	*Integrated Competitive Moves*
Market					
Homogeneous needs	Fewer varieties needed to serve many markets	Standardized product is more acceptable			Allows sequenced invasion of markets
Global customers			Marketing process has to be coordinated	Marketing content needs to be uniform	
Global channels			Marketing process has to be coordinated	Marketing content needs to be uniform	
Transferable marketing	Easier to expand internationally			Allows use of global brands advertising, etc.	
Cost					
Economies of scale and scope	Multiple markets needed to reach economic scale	Standardization needed to reach economic scale	Concentration helps reach economic scale	Uniform marketing cuts program development and production costs	Country interdependence affects overall scale economies
Learning and experience	Multiple markets accelerate learning	Standardization accelerates learning	Concentration accelerates learning		
Sourcing efficiencies			Centralized purchasing exploits efficiencies		
Favorable logistics	Easier to expand internationally		Allows concentrated production		Allows export competition
Differences in country costs and skills			Exploited by activity concentration		Increase vulnerability of high-cost countries
Product development costs	Multiple markets needed to pay back investment	Standardization reduces development needs	Concentration cuts cost of development		

Table 4-3 (Continued)

Industry Drivers	Strategy Levers				
	Major Market Participation	Product Standardization	Activity Concentration	Uniform Marketing	Integrated Competitive Moves
Government					
Favorable trade policies	Affects nature and extent of participation	May require or prevent product features	Local content rules affect extent of concentration possible		Integration needed to deal with competitive effects of tariffs/subsidies
Compatible technical standards	Affects markets that can be entered	Affects standardization possible			
Common marketing regulations				Affects approaches possible	
Competitive					
Interdependence of countries	More participation leverages benefits	Accept trade-offs to get best global product	Locate key activities in lead countries	Use lead country to develop programs	Integration needed to exploit benefits
Competitors globalized or might globalize	Expand to match or preempt	Match or preempt	Match or preempt	Match or preempt	Integration needed to exploit benefits

Source: From Global Strategy . . . In a world of Nations? In *Transnational Management*, 2E by Christopher Bartlett and Sumantra Ghosal, p. 362, © 1995. Irwin. Reprinted with permission of The McGraw-Hill Companies.

lower factor costs. The strategy also allows the firm to be flexible by being able to move production, at short notice, from one location to another. This ability tends to enhance the firm's bargaining power (e.g., with national or local labor unions). In addition, gains may accrue from advertising and promotion on a global scale.

2. *Higher quality of products.* By focusing on a smaller number of products usually based on a common platform and a narrow research stream, the company is able to devote attention to improved quality of its products and processes. Because the firm is catering to the world market, it must be sensitive to standards of product reliability, technology, and quality.

3. *Customer satisfaction.* Customers can obtain the product and have it serviced in more than one country. The brand is recognizable worldwide and thus conveys an assurance of quality, standards, and certainty, which in turn reinforces customer use and satisfaction with the product.

4. *Increased competitive power.* A global strategy allows a firm to compete with its rivals in myriad ways in a variety of markets. Such an approach often overawes rivals and forces the latter to defend their own turf instead of expanding.

Not all companies can or should adopt a global strategy. Even though the rewards of competing globally are great, so are the risks. Major policy and operating changes are required. Competing globally may require unconventional approaches to managing the firm in the form of the following:

- Major investment projects with zero or even negative return on investment
- Financial performance targets that vary widely among foreign subsidiaries
- Product lines deliberately overdesigned or underpriced in some markets
- A view of country-by-country market positions as interdependent and not as independent elements of a worldwide portfolio to be increased or decreased depending on profitability
- Construction of production facilities in both high- and low-cost countries.

Global Strategy in Service Industries   Can the global strategy be applied to service firms? In many cases, the answer is yes. Services differ from goods in several ways—intangibility, heterogeneity (variability), perishability of output, and simultaneity of production and consumption.

In many manufacturing operations, supplementary elements are categorized as services. For instance, Canon not only makes and sells photocopiers, they also engage in service activities such as leasing and providing credit, repairs and servicing, market research and surveys, and staff functions such as those connected with human resources (e.g., payroll, record maintenance, and human resource information systems). Many service functions can be divided into front office activities (such as a bank branch office) and back office operations (such as data processing). While the former involves interacting with customers, the latter are self-contained and can be located elsewhere. The attractiveness of a product can be augmented by surrounding it with a plethora of other services such as personalized attention to customers, easy credit terms, extended warranties, convenient hours, and so on.

Whether a service firm can effectively globalize can be determined by examining the application of the various globalization levers.

- *Commonality of customer needs across countries.* To the extent that a service has a universal acceptance, the more easily can a service firm globalize its activities. Thus, an international bank providing deposit, lending, and other financial services can expand into different countries, the main constraint usually being host country restrictive policies. Citibank, for example, through its branches in India, not only provides the usual panoply of banking services, but also offers specialized deposit programs for people of Indian origin who live outside India.
- *Global activities of customers.* As firms have expanded overseas, the service providers have tended to follow suit. The entry of Japanese manufacturing firms into the United States has been followed by the companies that provide them with banking, insurance, and advertising services back in Japan. Firms expect a certain level and familiarity of service when abroad and for cost reasons too prefer to limit the number of service providers they have to deal with. It also allows service firms to adopt a worldwide approach to their product offerings and capabilities.
- *Channels of distribution.* Unlike manufacturing industries that usually have to rely on long, and often slow, distribution networks, most services require a short distribution channel. Advances in computer-linked communication systems, for example, have shortened the distribution channel and made possible the elimination of intermediaries. The Internet and the worldwide Web afford firms opportunities to reach every corner of the world. Overnight letter and package delivery companies have flourished as long-haul jet planes are used and landing slots at airports become available. Thus, the presence in a country of a good infrastructure in the form of telecommunication systems, computer support, technically oriented populace, and a liberal government policy on information flows, all contribute to globalization of service activities.
- *Global economies of scale.* Some service businesses might be better situated to secure economies of scale by operating on a worldwide basis. International banks would be an example. Fast food companies or hotel chains, given the vast number of locations, differences in capacity, and the need to be highly interactive with customers, however, may find that only some aspects of their operations are capable of benefiting from scale economies. Individual hotels in a chain, for instance, gain from having access to a central reservations computer system, but usually not when it comes to purchasing food and beverages.
- *Favorable logistics.* For many service firms, being close to customers is essential. In other cases, the customers can come to where the service company is located. Thus, many U.S. universities offer programs of study in cities outside the United States. For possession-processing services such as transporting freight, a good transportation system assumes some importance whereas for information-based services, modern telecommunication facilities are a key requirement.
- *Information technology.* Technology has made it possible in some cases to centralize certain activities and reap scale economies. For instance, the Chase Bank has established its data processing center in Ireland to take

advantage of the latter's educated and cheaper workforce. Excellent communication links between the New York head office and Ireland and the time difference also allows the bank's computers to be used when they are not busy.

- *Government policies and regulations.* Despite deregulation of several service industries such as banking, insurance, and telecommunications, many restrictions on service firms continue to exist worldwide. These restrictions include outright exclusion of foreign companies (sometimes even private domestic firms) from a particular industry (e.g., insurance), differences in technical standards (as in television signals), nonreciprocity with regard to professional qualifications (such as refusal by one country to accept the accounting qualifications from another country), requirements that local nationals be employed, policies that favor host country firms, and government social policies (such as free or subsidized universal health care for its population).
- *Ability to transfer best practices.* A firm that has gained a competitive advantage in one country may not necessarily be able to maintain it as it expands abroad. Thus, for instance, despite the enormous appeal and success of the Disney theme parks in the United States, the company faced numerous difficulties with its Eurodisney park near Paris, France. The ingredients of success in the United States could not be readily replicated in France.

These determinants of globalization of service firms understandably impact different industries in unique ways. Some determinants are more important for some industries and not for others. For example, the ability of U.S. airline companies to fly to overseas destinations is dependent on what aviation agreement the U.S. government can wring out in negotiations with foreign governments.[5] In contrast, McDonald's ability to support a worldwide chain of franchises is dependent on how well it can transfer its competitive advantage to other physical settings. In 1998, following an economic crisis in East Asia and Russia, many European banks revisited their global strategies. Banks such as ING Group and ABN-Amro Holding of the Netherlands, Banco Santander of Spain, and the Swiss banks, Credit Suisse Group and UBS, experienced sharp losses in their businesses in the emerging economies and as a consequence sharply curtailed their overseas operations and laid off workers.[6]

MULTINATIONAL OR MULTIDOMESTIC STRATEGY

As noted in Chapter 1, the pressure to globalize has been accompanied by a set of countervailing forces of localization. Before the forces of globalization became critical determinants in the international business environment, the usual strategy of international firms was to pursue a multinational or **multidomestic strategy.** Under this strategy, the firm established miniature replicas of the parent in the various overseas countries in which it operated. Products were first developed in the home country to meet home market demands and were then offered to the various overseas affiliates to be

---

[5]Goldsmith, Charles. 1997, September 24. Open-skies pacts lift U.S., European carriers. *The Wall Street Journal,* p. A15.
[6]Rhoads, Christopher. 1998, October 5. European banks rethink globalization. *The Wall Street Journal,* p. A23.

made and/or sold for their respective markets. Usually, the overseas affiliate would adapt the product to meet local needs or in some cases, not offer it at all, if it was deemed unsuitable for that market. In many cases, the overseas affiliate functioned largely to supply the individual overseas market, occasionally tapping into the parent's product lines, technology, and experience. Consequently, an enormous amount of duplication of functions occurred under the multidomestic strategy. Table 4-4 compares the multidomestic and global strategies.

The multidomestic strategy flourished when global trade was constrained by high tariff walls. They forced firms to establish operations in foreign countries because exporting to them was not a viable alternative. The dismantling of trade barriers in some cases have removed the reason for maintaining overseas affiliates. As we have noted earlier, Canada tried to encourage manufacturing investment in the country by constructing a tariff wall. With the enactment of the NAFTA, tariffs had come down and many of these firms were no longer viable in the face of cheaper exports from the rest of North America.

Many businesses are localized and are likely to remain so, competing on a domestic market-by-domestic market basis. Typically these businesses have products that differ greatly among country markets and have high transportation costs (for example, bricks), or they lack sufficient scale economies to yield a significant edge, or they have distinct culturally based customer preferences (such as packaged foods), or are heavily regulated by governments (food and agricultural products, among others). Nestle, the world's largest food products company, uses the multidomestic strategy largely because many food items are country-specific. The type of cereal and the way it is eaten in the United States are different from the way it is eaten in France. A multidomestic strategy allows Nestle to cater to each individual market more effectively.

Standardized products, the hallmark of the globalization strategy, may not please huge sections of customers in many countries, and thus businesses have a compelling reason to adapt the product. Indeed, McDonald's for the first time anywhere, did not offer its famous Big Mac sandwich in its Indian restaurants in recognition of Hindus' cultural averseness to eating beef; instead the company sells a mutton burger named the Maharaja sandwich. Similarly, Coca-Cola in India has, in contrast to its actions elsewhere, retained and supported a local brand Thums Up, which it acquired from an Indian bottler. Thums Up outsold Coca-Cola in many Indian markets by a 4-to-1 margin.[7]

Table 4-4   Comparing Multidomestic and Global Strategies

Firm Activities	Multidomestic	Global
Market participation	No particular pattern	In globally strategic countries
Products and services	Customized in each country	Standardized core
Location of value-adding activities	All activities in each country	Concentrated—One activity in each different country
Marketing	Local	Uniform worldwide
Competitive moves	Stand alone by country	Integrated across countries

Source: Yip, George S., and Coundouriotis, George A. 1991. "Diagnosing global strategy potential: The world chocolate confectionery industry." *Planning Review.* January–February, pp. 4–14.

---

[7]Deogun, Nikhil, and Jonathan Karp. 1998, April 29. For Coke in India, Thums Up is the real thing. *The Wall Street Journal,* p. B1.

Also, the likelihood is that a globally standardized product, designed for the global market, may fail to meet the needs of different types of users or perform under the conditions prevalent in different markets. Product size, maintenance needs, labeling requirements, market price, packaging, supporting systems (electricity, air conditioning, trained personnel, and others) do differ, requiring considerable adaptation to individual markets. Uniform marketing may reduce adapting to local sensitivities and may in fact distance the firm from its diverse customers. Politically, a firm that decides to supply a market through imports rather than local manufacturing, may incur host country prejudice and hostility. The host government, indirectly or directly, may favor firms with direct investment in the country. Finally, the multidomestic approach allows the firm to tend to individual markets without regard to the competitive environment in other country settings. Under a global strategy, one country subsidiary may be called upon to do battle with a rival for no local reason but to advance the corporate headquarters global strategy.

TRANSITION FROM MULTIDOMESTIC TO GLOBAL STRATEGY

The multidomestic strategy is heavily reliant on the work of host country nationals and country managers. For a firm to shift to a global strategy requires country managers to make a big change in their perspective, which can be difficult, especially for host country nationals who are country managers. To overcome this issue, the parent firm may have to appoint nonnationals to head up the foreign affiliates. A program of job rotation as part of an executive development schedule to develop a cadre of global managers, or sending country managers to headquarters on assignments are two other approaches to developing a globally focused management. Many top-level managers assume that because consumers differ from location to location, their businesses cannot operate effectively as a unified entity. As a result, they see their industry as a mosaic of specialized businesses, each with its own unique constraints and its own finite opportunities. In fact, companies rarely engage in a self-scrutiny. One reason is that they are successful, profitable, and reasonably secure in a domestic market. Whirlpool, the white goods manufacturer, found that, although it had lowered costs and improved product quality, profit margins in North America continued to decline because every firm in its industry was pursuing the same types of activities in a mature market. The company studied its options—financial restructuring with large payouts to shareholders, diversification of the business, horizontal and vertical expansions. In doing so, the managers realized that the basics of managing their business and its process and product technologies were the same in Europe, North America, Asia, and Latin America. It then dawned that the firm needed to enter appliance markets in other countries and learn how to satisfy different kinds of customers. Once this need was recognized, the firm began looking to acquire businesses abroad.[8]

A multidomestic strategy, by definition, delegates considerable autonomy to the affiliate. Country managers have specific mandates and control over the firm's activities

---

[8]Maruca, Reginald F. 1994. The right way to go global: An interview with Whirlpool CEO David Whitwam. *Harvard Business Review.* March–April, pp. 135–145.

within a particular country or region. Evaluation of their performance is thus relatively easy in terms of meeting sales targets, market share, rates of return, and pace of growth. But with a globalization strategy, decisions are centralized at headquarters. The performance evaluation of individual managers becomes difficult and complicated to determine. Headquarters subsidize prices in one country to gain market share in another. They set transfer prices on goods shipped among the firm's affiliates and production mandates are determined by global strategy. In such cases, a variety of influences may distort how well or how poorly an individual manager is performing.

Obviously, in most cases the successful strategy finds a balance between overglobalizing and overlocalizing. Much depends on the nature of the product and the industry. Environmental forces present key determinants too. Take the airline and telecommunications industry, for example. Until recently, both were highly regulated by home governments and, in case of the latter, was characterized by multiplicity of technical standards and equipment. However, deregulation, privatization, bilateral and multilateral trade agreements, and changes in technology, created conditions for many firms (e.g., AT&T and British Airways) in these two industries to pursue global strategies.

ELEMENTS OF SUCCESSFUL STRATEGIES

REVOLUTIONARY THINKING

Any industry has three kinds of companies.

1. *The rule makers:* firms that built the industry, such as Coca-Cola and IBM
2. *The rule takers:* firms that follow the lead of the rule makers and strive to catch up with them (e.g., Fujitsu, Hyundai)
3. *The rule breakers:* firms that are changing the rules of the industry, such as Swatch and the Body Shop

Rule makers and rule takers run the constant danger of being eclipsed by the revolutionary attitudes of the rule breakers. To avoid such a plight, companies could adopt strategies that allow them to constantly redefine the nature of the industry. Table 4-5 presents a list of ten principles that can guide a firm into adopting a radical approach to creating strategy.

How does a firm become a rule breaker? It can do so by looking for ways to redefine its products and services, redefine the marketing, and change the boundaries of the industry.

1. *Redefining the product or service.* This process has three aspects. One, the firm should strive to vastly improve—not by 10 percent or 20 percent but by say, 500 percent or 1,000 percent—the price-to-performance ratio of the product or service. Such an improvement radically redefines the product or service. Second, the firm can try to separate the benefits (function) of the product or service from the ways in which the benefits are presently embodied in a product or service. For instance, while credit cards are accepted by merchants, rising fraud may lead to the cardholders' identity to be encrypted in the card itself. The rule breaker firm would jump at this technological possibility. Third, the product or services should be fun to use, informative, and whimsical, representing the lifestyle of contemporary times.

Table 4-5	Principles to Revolutionize Corporate Strategy

1. Move the company's planning process to be more inquisitive, expansive, prescient, inventing, inclusive, and demanding. Most firms have a planning process that is a calendar-driven ritual, based on simple rules and heuristics, based on the past and present, set within the parameters of the industry's current conventions, conceived by a small group of managers, and easy.

2. Challenge existing ideas and conventions by examining the firm's own practices and be willing to abandon them.

3. Recognize that top managers with their privilege and experience are the biggest obstacle to the generation of revolutionary ideas.

4. Offer the constituents for change, who exist in every organization, the opportunities and means to advocate and express their emotional and intellectual ideas.

5. Give all employees the responsibility for bringing about change by providing them control over their destinies. The object is not merely to get them to support change.

6. Involve all segments of the organization in creating strategy, not just top managers. Three traditionally underrepresented constituencies that should be tapped are young employees, employees in the firm's distant locations, and those who have joined the firm recently.

7. Recognize that strategy activists exist throughout the organization, not just among top managers. These activists are not to be likened to anarchists but rather to patriots who hold dear the long-term interests of the organization.

8. Look at the organization and the industry from a new perspective based on a thorough understanding of the functioning and core competencies of the firm, conventions of the industry, and the existence of discontinuities in technology, lifestyles, working habits, or geopolitics.

9. Avoid making the strategy creating process either a top-down or a bottom-up exercise. Instead it must involve a deep diagonal slice of the organization, which can ensure both diversity of perspectives as well as a unity of purpose.

10. Encourage an open-ended strategy making process in which managers should be prepared for unanticipated results.

Source: Gary Hamel, "Strategy as Revolution." *Harvard Business Review* (July/August, 1996), pp. 70–71 and 74–82.

2. *Redefining marketing.* The rule breaker expands the size of the market by making the product affordable and attractive to segments of the population who in the past were not considered the natural target for the product. For example, disposable cameras have vastly expanded the types of people who now use cameras and the occasions when they are used. Also, products/services could be customized for individual needs and tastes—a departure from mass-produced products. Finally, access by customers to the products could be made easier by, for example, establishing Web sites and allowing e-commerce transactions.

3. *Changing the boundaries of the industry.* Altering boundaries can be achieved in three ways. First, the size of operations can be expanded to reap the obvious scale economies or alternately, a firm can be scaled down to serve niche markets. Secondly, firms can eliminate intermediaries such as wholesalers or transportation companies. Thirdly, businesses do not have to be constrained by the specific industry they are in; they can expand to related industries, effectively blurring any boundaries that may have existed between them. This expansion process is illustrated by the changing profile of Nokia, the Finnish company that was the world's largest supplier of mobile phones. Its

president, Pekka Ala-Pietila said, *"We have been addressing information technology, telecommunications, and media as three separate industries. But that is no longer a realistic view. We now regard it as one industry and it looks that way from head-on, but from the side the volume of the combined business is much bigger."*[9] Nokia calls it the "info-media" sector, and this strategy marked the latest phase in Nokia's transformation into a dedicated telecom equipment and software company.

The success of revolutionary thinking is best illustrated by the success of the Swiss watch, Swatch. Management Focus 4-2 presents how Swatch emerged in response to the decline of the Swiss watch industry in the face of Japanese competition, especially in the form of digital watches.

INNOVATION

The underlying thrust of many successful strategies is the continuous ability of the firm to innovate, as the Swatch example explained. Innovation includes the application of new technologies and better ways of doing things. These changes come through design, development, and marketing; through discovering new applications for products; and in creative use of human resources and information. Innovation is often incremental, occurring in small doses rather than in giant leaps. Over time, though, these minute changes add up and result in a major transformation. By being first, whether in introducing a new product or entering a new market or building a product in a cost efficient way, the firm pulls away from its competitors and is able to reap the advantages—larger profit margins, establishment of standards and distribution networks, and creation of brand recognition, among others—that accrue to pioneers or first movers.

Even though a firm may become successful because of its innovativeness, to remain ahead of existing and potential competitors, it has to keep on innovating. If it does not innovate, rivals will soon imitate the successful strategy and overtake the firm that rests on its laurels.

Facing the entry of Shima Seiki, a Japanese manufacturer of knitting machines, into its market, Stoll, Germany's biggest maker of flat knitting machines, had to move quickly to retain its edge. To reduce high costs, Stoll consulted experts from the Technical University of Munich to conduct an audit of its factory near Stuttgart. The company looked at all aspects of the production process and evaluated new and efficient ways of making the machines. It asked questions such as: Could we make something from one part rather than two? Could we glue components instead of using screws? By modernizing production methods, cutting staff, and reducing inventory, the company increased its cash flow, enhanced the quality of its products, and held on to its market share.[10] The opening vignette illustrates how domestic retailers in Latin America attempted to compete with the larger and more resourceful foreign companies.

Management Focus 4-3 illustrates how Procter & Gamble, a U.S. consumer products company, crafted a strategy for entering Poland, the former Czechoslovakia, Hungary, and Russia that was different from the way it approached Western Europe. In the early 1990s, the company decided to enter these Eastern European countries almost simultaneously with five to seven product categories based on the goal of rapid entry

---

[9]Burt, Tim. 1999, June 18. Nokia: Running at the head of the pack. *Financial Times Survey*, p. 3.
[10]Marsh, Peter. 1999, July 12. Changing the pattern. *Financial Times*, p. 8.

MANAGEMENT FOCUS 4-2

KEEPING UP WITH THE TIMES

Today, the idea of an inexpensive fashion watch is common, with hundreds of brand names on the market. But in the late 1970s and early 1980s, Swatch was the first quality watch that was also a fashion accessory.

In the mid 1970s, the Swiss watch industry was in a crisis with market share having slid from 43 percent to 15 percent in less than 10 years. A group of Swiss watch engineers and marketing people realized that to compete with the Japanese watches they had to come out with a product that would be inexpensive, of fine quality, and could be produced quickly. Under the direction of Nicholas Hayek and Ernst Tomnke, the watch engineers reduced the number of working parts in their experimental watch from 91 to 51 and housed them in a case that robots could produce entirely. The patents that Swatch holds today are on the robotics, not on the actual watches.

In 1983, Mr. Hayek, president and CEO, formed SMH, Swiss Watches & Microelectronics Ltd., and launched Swatch in Switzerland as a quartz-powered analog watch at a price never before seen in Switzerland—about 60 Swiss francs ($40). Fifteen years later, SMH was the largest finished watch-making company in the world, with brands such as Omega, Longine, Rado, Tissot, Hamilton, Blanc-Pain, and Flik Flak children's watches, in addition to Swatch.

The initial launch was led by an upbeat, irreverent advertising campaign that helped get the Swatch to the target market of primarily young, fashion-conscious people. The idea was to develop a brand that could cross international boundaries and command the immediate recognition that brands such as Coca-Cola or Levi could claim. Despite initial resistance from watch sellers who thought a cheap, plastic watch produced in Switzerland would harm the entire industry, persistent attention to quality won them over. Within a few years, shipments went from about 6,000 pieces to one million, and by 1996, more than 200 million Swatch watches had been produced and sold in 67 different countries. Swatch was not only the leader in watch fashion, it had created a new category of watches with prices that had stayed virtually unchanged over 10 years.

What accounted for the success of Swatch? One explanation was the firm's ability to present its watches as lifestyle symbols by quickly adapting to any emerging style or trend. To do that, the firm kept its design team "flexible," both in terms of who was on the team and what they were allowed to create. The watches were designed at two design labs, one in Milan, Italy, and the other in New York City. In addition, Swatch worked closely with a variety of artists to come up with new designs. Fresh ideas were imperative for the brand's continued success. Watches shaped like cucumbers and bacon, watches that were black with black hands, black numbers on black dial, watches that gave the general time in hours only, watches that were covered in fake fur that had to be blown away to see the time, and watches that didn't tell the time at all, were just a few of the many incredible designs for Swatch watches. The mandate of the designers was always the same: "There are no limitations on what you can do."

Maintaining Swatch's success required that the firm remained innovative, which meant looking beyond the time-keeping function of the product to other possible applications. For example, the firm entered into a joint venture with SkiData, an Austrian computer company that specialized in access control technology. Together they developed Swatch Access, a new type of access control that would revolutionize procedures for getting skiers and snowboards through the control gates at base stations in winter sports resorts. Swatch had developed a watch with two ingenious electronic features: a chip for storing details of the wearer's ski pass and a "sensor ring"—a kind of antenna—that emitted an impulse to open lift and cable car gates. The wearer simply pointed his or her arm with the Swatch Access watch towards the gate, and the gate automatically opened. Another innovative product, introduced in 1998, was the Swatch Smart Car,

(continued)

Management Focus 4-2 (*continued*)

a two-seater, environmentally friendly city car, built in cooperation with Daimler-Benz.

The company had also sought to create a global image. All markets used the strong corporate identity. A Swatch point-of-sale piece looked the same in Singapore as it did in Stockholm. Creating a global, highly recognized brand required this uniformity. But even this overall identity had to be adapted to certain markets. For example, in the Middle East, the Swiss cross could not be used in the Swatch logo even though it was an integral part of the company's image; instead "Swiss Made" was used with the same colors as the usual logo.

The company was always looking for new, innovative ways to market products by encouraging diversity, creativity, and fun in the Swatch culture. Although the firm did not sponsor traditional sporting events, it had always promoted an offbeat lifestyle in commercials, marketing strategies, and events. For instance, Swatch had rock climbers climb the tallest buildings in Frankfurt and Madrid. They built a 50-foot, 13-ton working watch and hung it in the biggest bank building in Tokyo. In 1992, in Zermatt, Switzerland, Swatch celebrated the production of 100 million watches with a three-day party attended by 25,000 people.

In a company that produces more than 250 fashion watch styles a year, flexibility is critical in keeping it ahead of the next trend. Thus, the firm requires a lean organization, readily adaptable to change. Without layers of middle management to work through, if a crucial decision was needed, the CEO could be reached directly by phone anytime, as could any of Swatch's top managers. Mr. Hayek subscribes to a total hands-on approach and an open-door policy to any of the 17,000 SMH employees worldwide. Managers are expected to get out of the office and into the marketplace to find out what is happening, be it new trends or changes in consumer tastes, and to pass this information on to headquarters in Biel, Switzerland. At Swatch, infrastructure largely resides in ideas as opposed to organization, and ideas are acted upon quickly. In essence, it is a good example of a global product—a transnational system or idea that can be delivered locally. Swatch clearly believes that being innovative is key to maintaining success in the global marketplace.

Source: Abson, Michael. 1996. Keeping up with the times. *Business Quarterly.* Autumn, pp. 65–69; Mitchener, Brandon. 1998, October 2. Can Daimler's tiny "Swatchmobile" sweep Europe? *The Wall Street Journal,* pp. B1, B4.

and the need for critical mass. In Western Europe, the company entered one category in one country at a time. It took decades—a luxury it knew it did not have in Eastern Europe.

What are the characteristics of truly innovative companies?

- They tend to pursue a multiplicity of smaller initiatives rather than putting all of their innovation eggs into one or two large baskets.
- They favor early and frequent "reality testing" of new products, services, and ideas, and are eager to incorporate the resulting feedback into new and improved iterations.
- They consciously structure their incentive and reward systems to encourage successful innovations and to celebrate and broadcast them.
- They set exacting expectations. For instance, 3M has a policy that 30 percent of annual revenue must come from products less than four years old.
- They make a fetish out of consciously linking innovation with organizational learning.

LEADING THE CHANGE IN EASTERN EUROPE

The collapse of communism opened up the Eastern European countries and Russia to western products and investment. With more than 400 million consumers—50 percent larger than Western Europe—these emerging economies beckoned to Procter & Gamble (P&G), which already earned more than half its revenues from outside the United States. After visiting these countries in 1990, John E. Pepper, chairman of the board and chief executive of the company's international division, decided to enter these countries despite problems of currency inconvertibility, poorly developed infrastructure, shaky governments, and low living conditions. He developed the following four key strategies.

1. *Conduct in-depth research.* Knowing that success would depend on building strong leadership brands, the company started by doing what it had done in every other market it had entered: conducting in-depth research into the needs and behaviors of consumers. The company tested its products to ensure they would be preferred. More than 50,000 consumer interviews were conducted and the findings were instructive. As Mr. Pepper noted, "Our researchers were surprised at how small living quarters are. The average home or apartment houses four people in living space of 50 square feet per person. That compares to an average of 660 square feet per person in the United States. Living in a limited space can be stressful. Even the smallest chores, such as laundry, can become very difficult. Laundry is generally done in a tiny, cramped bathroom of about 20 square feet. And to make matters worse, the only detergent available required hours of presoaking and filled the entire apartment with a rancid, chemical odor that hung around even after the wash was finished. We had known there was a need for better cleaning products, but we had not understood until then that fragrance would be nearly as important as cleaning power to these consumers."

2. *Achieve lowest-cost/best-quality sourcing.* The second strategy was to achieve lowest-cost/best-quality sourcing for their products. The company had to deliver western quality at a price Eastern Europeans could afford. This goal would require regional production capacity. Given the need to start up fast and without too much capital exposure, however, the company could not build new plants, at least not right away. The logical option was to pursue acquisitions or joint ventures but the company was not sure this plan would work given that plants were overstaffed and productivity was low. For these reasons, an acquisition would require too much upgrading and training to be cost effective. But the company was wrong on this count. Mr. Pepper observed, "We have found that with a lot of hard work, well-selected joint ventures and acquisitions have proven to be a winning strategy. A good example is the detergent plant we acquired in what is now the Czech Republic."

The Czech plant was operated by Rakona, a state-owned enterprise and the largest single maker of laundry and dishwashing detergents in the country. The equipment was antiquated and product quality poor, yet it was the best facility in East Central Europe. While negotiations were undertaken to acquire it, P&G engineers were sent to work with the Czech employees. The objective was to do a test run to see whether the plant could produce P&G's Ariel brand (the European equivalent of Tide) laundry detergent at a level of quality equal to the company's German-made products and do it in three months. Within six weeks, the country manager was presented with two bags of detergent—one contained German Ariel and the other contained Czech Ariel. They were identical in quality and performance. P&G had achieved this result without any major upgrades to the equipment or other physical

(continued)

Management Focus 4-3 (*continued*)

changes to the plant. It was the cooperation and eager-to-learn attitude of the employees at that plant that made the high-quality output possible. By 1995, the Rakona plant was one of the lowest-cost producers of all P&G plants in the world.

3. *Achieve superior distribution.* Mr. Pepper found that the distribution infrastructures in Eastern Europe and Russia were poor. In the United States a case of detergent could be sent to almost any location in 24 hours; in Russia, in the best of circumstances, it took three weeks to get a case from its plant in Novomoskovsk to reach Vladivostok. The company, therefore, began to create a distribution network from scratch. P&G's products were among the first western goods ever available in some of the cities. New marketing territories were opened up by local managers, usually young Russian men and women, often 23 and 24 years old, right out of school.

4. *People, partnership, and values.* The final strategy involved people, partnerships, and values. To get started fast and well in Eastern Europe, P&G drew on experienced P&G employees from outside the region and also hired capable local people from Czech, Polish, Russian, and Hungarian universities. The company was fortunate, as Mr. Pepper put it,

"in the number of P&G people who had been born in Eastern Europe and held up their hand to return."

The values that had served the company well were its commitment to serve the consumer through its brands, leadership in all it did, doing the right thing for the long term, and emphasizing the importance of its employees and promoting from within. Mr. Pepper went on to say, "I have found that what we try to stand for as a company is very attractive to the men and women we want to hire, as well as to government officials and potential joint venture partners. In an environment where there is still suspicion of the motives of western companies, I have found that a commitment to the long term, to consumers and to employees in a country is attractive."

Did this four-point strategy work? In just over four years of operation, P&G built a half-billion-dollar business in Eastern Europe. It was the largest consumer goods company in that region with more than 25 brands on the market. Virtually all of them were among the top two or three in their categories. The business became profitable after four years; in contrast, it took about eight years on average to reach profitability in each country in Western Europe.

Source: Pepper, John E. 1995. Leading the change in Eastern Europe. *Business Quarterly.* Autumn, pp. 27–33.

Michael Porter has advanced a framework of national competitive advantage to explain why certain firms from certain countries are able to succeed through continuous innovation. He has shown that four aspects of a nation individually and as a system create a business environment in which businesses are formed and operate. These four aspects are (1) factor conditions, (2) demand conditions, (3) related and supporting industries, and (4) firm strategy, structure, and rivalry. Factor conditions refer to the elements of production such as labor, land, natural resources, capital, and infrastructure. Availability of these factors and the ability to create such factors provide the platform for businesses to emerge and grow. Demand conditions refer to the characteristics of the home market. Demanding consumers pressure firms to innovate. The presence of internationally competitive related and supporting industries ensures cost-effective quality inputs in a timely manner. Individual businesses also work closely with a firm to upgrade products. The conditions in a country also influence how firms are created, organized, and managed and the nature of interfirm rivalry. The ability to compete successfully is helped by the convergence of management practices and organizational forms. These four aspects of national competitive advantage are presented in Figure 4-1, and the nature of the diagram has led it to be called a diamond.

Porter says that each of these four aspects interact with the others, reinforcing the system. Weakness in any one aspect hurts an industry's ability to innovate just as its strength facilitates the need and ability to innovate.

CORE COMPETENCE

Some scholars have argued that successful firms focus on their **core competencies**—activities at which they are especially good and that provide a base on which the various products of the firm are built. Core competencies are the collective learning in the firm, especially how to coordinate diverse production skills and integrate multiple streams of technologies. In the short run, a firm focuses on the price and performance of their current products. Over time, as best practices are copied, convergence occurs in the product cost and quality of the successful firms. In the long run, strategy needs to focus on building at lower cost and more speedily than competitors and to tend to the core competencies that spawn unanticipated products.

The strategy built around the firm's distinct core of uniqueness can be established by asking the following sorts of questions:[11]

- Which of our products or services are the most distinctive?
- Which of our products or services are the most profitable?
- Which of our customers are the most satisfied?
- Which customers, channels, or purchase occasions are the most profitable?
- Which of our activities are the most distinct and effective?

FIGURE 4-1 Porter's Determinants of National Competitive Advantage

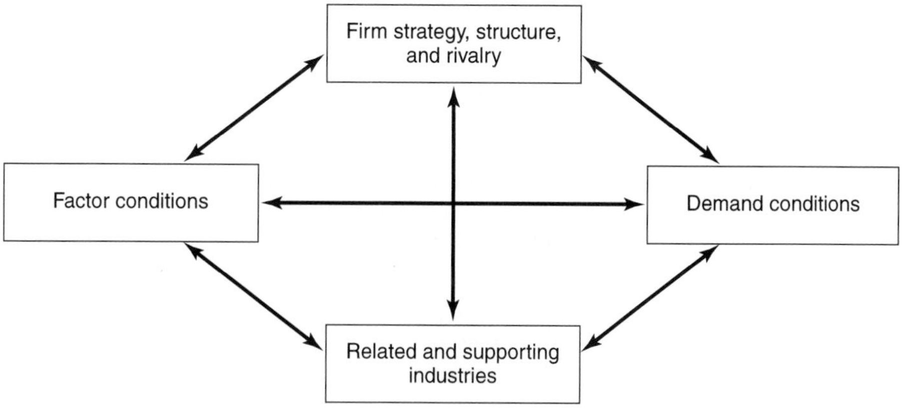

Source: Reprinted by permission of *Harvard Business Review.* Figure from The Competitive Advantage of Nations by Michael E. Porter, March–April, 1990. Copyright © 2001 by the President and Fellows of Harvard College; all rights reserved.

---

[11]Prahalad, C. K., and Gary Hamel. 1990. The core competence of the corporation. *Harvard Business Review.* May–June, pp. 79–91.

How can core competencies in a firm be identified? Three tests can be used to answer that question. First, a core competency should be able to provide potential access to a wide variety of markets. Second, a core competency should make a significant contribution to the value the customer perceives in the finished product. Third, a core competency should be difficult for competitors to copy.

Core competencies translate into core products. A good example is Canon's core competencies in precision mechanics, fine optics, and microelectronics. Because of the company's ability to unite research, design, development, and production across its many divisions, it has been able to create numerous products that spring from one or more of these core competencies. The result is the development of a low-cost disposable drum for minicopiers and the addition of microelectronics and electronic imaging to its arsenal of core competencies. Canon then went on to capitalize the market for small personal copiers, a market niche previously unrecognized or undervalued by its competitors. Canon continued to leverage its diverse core competencies into new products and markets. In a single decade, it doubled its revenues and dominated the world market in low-end copiers, color copiers, and laser printer engines.

What did Canon do to achieve this market domination? To finance its R&D, it licensed some of its best established technologies to foreign companies, including its chief rival, Xerox. It gave up its lifetime employment system and demanded creativity from its employees: scientists were expected to apply for three or four patents a year. The company also restructured its management into three separate systems for development, production, and marketing. The reasoning was that the mindset and skills needed to develop new products were essentially the same regardless of the specific product under consideration. By grouping these skills together in the same unit, specialized experience and insights could be effectively consolidated and leveraged to the benefit of the entire range of Canon's products.

The emphasis on core competencies has led many firms to sell off their peripheral activities. For example, Nokia was once a conglomerate, producing paper, rubber goods, power and phone cables, television sets, and telecommunication equipment. Since 1985, the company had focused on its core competency in cellular phones, and by 1995, cellular phones and supporting infrastructure technology contributed to 85 percent of its total sales from only 17 percent 10 years earlier. This was much higher than its two main rivals, Ericsson of Sweden and Motorola of the United States. Nokia got out of its other businesses and focused exclusively on innovations and new usages for mobile phones.[12]

Likening a business to tending a garden, Niall FitzGerald, the co-chair of Unilever, the Anglo-Dutch consumer goods giant, said, *"It occasionally needs weeding. If businesses aren't creating value we shouldn't be in them. It's like having a nice garden which gets weeds. You have to clean it up, so the light and air get to the blooms which are likely to grow the best."* Over 100 years, the company, with $50 billion in annual revenue, has grown to include 57 businesses ranging from heavy equipment to olive oil. It includes brand names such as Lipton teas and Calvin Klein perfume.[13]

Mr. FitzGerald culled a slew of smaller underperforming brands and companies outside the company's priority categories of ice cream, margarine, tea, detergents, skin-

---

[12]Nokia. *Business Week*. 1998, August 10, pp. 54–60.
[13]Parker-Pope, Tara. 1996, September 3. Unilever plans a long-overdue pruning. *The Wall Street Journal*, p. A13.

care products, and prestige cosmetics and fragrances. Units that were sold included the company's fish businesses in the United Kingdom and Germany, the British franchiser of Caterpillar heavy equipment, animal feed businesses, as well as some oil-processing operations. In 1996, Unilever sold its mass-market cosmetics business and other poor performers. In recent years, aggressive pricing by archrival Procter & Gamble had affected Unilever's bottom line. At the same time, a consumer recession in Europe and the onslaught of powerful store brands, together with the declining market for margarine and other fats (which represented about 20 percent of total sales) in Europe and North America had affected its performance. Profits had been seesawing, increasing in 1992, falling in 1993, back up again in 1994, only to drop the next year.

As managers in many Western countries move toward dismantling conglomerates, diversified groups such as keiretsu in Japan, chaebol in Korea, grupos in Mexico, and business houses in India too have come under pressure. In developing countries where many of the elements of the institutional framework necessary for firms to function are inadequate or absent, the conglomerate firm provides to its member organizations these necessary elements. These institutional elements that exist in advanced Western countries include availability of full information about buyers and sellers, well-developed labor markets, predictable enforcement of commercial contracts, unobtrusive government regulations, and strong product liability laws. Diversified companies in developing countries provide these elements to firms in the group and thus make up for the deficiencies in the institutional context. Table 4-6 discusses how institutional context drives strategy.

Take for example, the house of Tata, India's largest conglomerate in terms of sales and assets.[14] The Tata house employs about 300,000 workers in 90 companies of which more than 40 are publicly traded. The companies are united by the Tata name and by interlocking investments and directorates.

The Tata companies were in a variety of businesses and provided much of the institutional context that a developing economy such as India lacked. One such company was a venture capital vehicle that drew its pool of investment funds from the member companies. This venture capital company provided the resources for the Tatas to set up new businesses in information technology, computers, oil field services, and advanced materials, among others.

The various new Tata companies were able to tap into the reservoir of skilled managers from Tata's existing businesses. Since 1956, the house had run an extensive in-house training program to create a cadre of general managers. Entry into Tata Administrative Services was highly competitive and the training program was rigorous. Fully half of the trainees of the program stayed with the Tatas over the long run. These managers were moved about among the member companies as and where their talents and capabilities could be used.

These activities enabled the Tata companies to grow and be successful. The Tata group provided services and advantages to its member companies that were not easily available in the developing Indian economy—services such as venture capital and capable managers.

---

[14]Khanna, Tarun, and Krishan Palepu. 1997. Why focused strategies may be wrong for emerging markets. *Harvard Business Review.* July–August, pp. 41–51.

Table 4-6	Institutional Context and Choice of Strategy		
Institutional Factor	*United States*	*Japan*	*India*
Capital market	Equity-focused; transparent disclosure rules	Bank-focused; monitoring by interlocking investments and directors	Underdeveloped; illiquid equity markets; monitoring by bureaucrats
Labor market	Many business schools	Few business schools; in-house training	Few business schools; scarce management talent
Product market	Reliable enforcement of liability laws; activist consumer consumer groups	Reliable enforcement of liability laws; some consumer groups	Limited enforcement of liability laws; few consumer groups
Government regulation	Limited; relatively low corruption	Moderate; relatively low corruption	Extensive; high levels of corruption
Contract enforcement	Predictable	Predictable	Unpredictable
Result	Diversified groups have many disadvantages	Diversified groups have some advantages	Diversifed groups have many advantages

Source: Adapted from Khanna, Tarun, and Krishna Palepu. 1997. Why focused strategies may be wrong for emerging markets. *Harvard Business Review.* July–August, p. 44.

INFORMATION TECHNOLOGY

The 1990s experienced a revolutionary change in the use of information technologies to conduct businesses. Different types of electronic products facilitated near instantaneous communication between points across the world and enabled the fast dissemination of data. A system of satellites, fiber-optic telephone lines with wide bands, and wireless applications provide a worldwide network that enables firms and individuals to talk and to exchange data and images worldwide. Supported by companies such as Motorola, Hughes, and Alcatel, the systems play two main roles in telecommunications: creation of the next generation of mobile telephones that will work almost anywhere on the planet and worldwide access to high-speed data, voice, and video networks. These information technologies are altering in significant ways not only the telecommunication companies but also other firms who are finding that these technologies can be a source of competitive advantage. The strategy of a publishing company is illustrated in Management Focus 4-4.

IMPLEMENTATION OF STRATEGY

Large firms often pursue several strategies simultaneously, each determined by the peculiarities of the market and the characteristics of the firm. Thus, while the production function of a firm may be organized on a global basis, its marketing may be designed to meet the needs of local customers—the multidomestic approach.

The proper execution of a carefully designed strategy requires addressing several issues. First, it includes locating facilities—production, distribution, research, sales, and

---

A PUBLISHING COMPANY GOES ON-LINE

Long considered a stodgy giant of the publishing industry, the Anglo-Dutch company of Reed Elsevier rapidly moved into the digital age with a goal of becoming a world leader in electronic information. The company set its eyes on the United States, where on-line publishing and electronic data had exploded, and allocated a war chest of $1.7 billion for acquisitions. In addition, the company opened a technology center in Cambridge, near Boston, and loaded hundreds of its journals on compact disks and Internet sites, and formed an alliance with Microsoft.

For Reed Elsevier, shifting to electronics was more than a growth strategy—it was a matter of survival. Rivals had gone on-line. On-line bulletin boards were challenging its trade magazines and academic journals; Knight-Ridder and Reuters and other firms were taking on Reed's LEXIS NEXIS Internet business; and hotels and airlines were bypassing Reed's travel information business and going directly to consumers.

"We want to lead the migration rather than follow," said Nigel Stapleton, the company's co-chair. "It can be rather expensive to try to follow it." And it was proving to be expensive—the company's share price had fallen, profit increases had been slight; and the costs of developing new technologies had been heavy. In six months in 1997, the company spent more on acquisitions than it did the whole of 1996. Building on LEXIS NEXIS—the huge U.S. database that it purchased in 1994 and built into its core electronic business—it bought the Chilton Business Group trade magazines and the MDL Information Systems, a California software provider.

Reinventing itself was a big job for the company. Jointly owned by London-based Reed International and Amsterdam-based Elsevier, Reed Elsevier was the largest publisher of academic and trade journals in the world, with more than 1,800 titles. It had two headquarters and two chairpersons who shared the top decision making—Mr. Stapleton in London and Hermann Burggink in Amsterdam.

By 1995, the company was spread out over consumer magazines, books, newspapers, and trade journals in hopes of becoming a media conglomerate like Time-Warner and Rupert Murdoch's News Corp. But as competition toughened, it changed its focus. Instead of providing what Mr. Stapleton called "nice-to-have information"—newspapers, magazines, television—it concentrated on "must have information" through business-to-business information, trade journals, and other publications that people needed to do their jobs. The company sold its newspapers and much of its books unit. While not as glamorous, the "must-have" business carried higher profit margins and steadier growth. 'We simply didn't have the management resources to try to compete against the Murdochs of the world," admitted Mr. Stapleton.

The company was forced to react to on-line publishing. As the world's largest publisher of scientific journals with more than 1,200 titles, Reed Elsevier found that scientists were now looking for cheaper alternatives such as posting on a community bulletin board on the Internet or planning to create their own journals and information "communities." In response, Reed Elsevier launched 80 to 100 of its journals on-line and planned to have all 1,200 of them on-line by the end of 1998. More crucially, the company used its dominance in certain fields—cardiology and chemistry, for example—to extend its reach in cyberspace. Thus, a cardiologist browsing through the *Journal of American College of Cardiology* would discover a paper he wanted to buy from the company's *European Journal of Cardio-thoracic Surgery*. It meant revenue from the original subscription and the related articles.

The company aimed to create the same critical mass in other professions: law, engineering, and real estate. It created a mega-site, called Manufacturing Marketplace, which encompassed 13 magazines in manufacturing and engineering, where an engineer could search out articles on, say, computer-aided design. "The idea is to go beyond just an electronic magazine rack," said Michael Cole, executive vice president of electronic media at Reed Elsevier's business-information unit. "We want to use our strength in hard copy and combine it with the Internet to make us even stronger."

Source: Frank, Robert. 1997, August 11. A stodgy publisher is turning electronic. *The Wall Street Journal*, p. A10.

administration—at sites around the world that contribute to the realization of the firm's goals. Locational issues are discussed in Chapter 8. Another key issue is the method of entering the foreign market and the extent of ownership in overseas facilities. As discussed in Chapter 1, a firm has the choice of exporting (or importing), licensing, direct investment, management contracts, and strategic alliances. Each of these choices has advantages and disadvantages and is appropriate under certain circumstances and to achieve certain strategic goals. Chapters 5, 6, and 7 discuss these entry and ownership strategies and the management issues surrounding them. Management Focus 4-5 describes how a Japanese pharmaceutical company, planning an overseas expansion, considered alternative entry strategies.

STRATEGIC TASKS

The competitive challenges faced by a firm require responses that vary from firm to firm. Firms that dominate the industry focus on protecting their position by reinforcing their existing assets and capabilities, modernizing facilities, and using advanced production processes. For smaller firms aspiring to be bigger players on the world stage the task is to build the resources and capabilities to challenge the industry leaders through acquiring other firms, cutting costs, developing a competitive position in niche markets, and using information technology to offer new products or new ways of doing business. Domestically focused firms need to protect their domestic turf from foreign competition, which they do in a variety of ways: acquiring domestic firms to bolster their size and resources, tying up distribution channels, influencing customer preferences, lobbying host governments for protection, subsidy, or other forms of support, and even forming strategic alliances with other firms, which would allow the firm to access some of the advantages of going international.

ORGANIZATIONAL STRUCTURE

The role of the firm's structure in strategy implementation is discussed in Chapter 9. The major problems arise when a company moves from a multidomestic strategy to a global strategy because, among other reasons, country managers are unprepared and unwilling to give up their control over their subsidiaries. Tensions arise between headquarters' desire to exercise control and subsidiaries efforts to retain autonomy. The danger of relegating subsidiaries to the role of local implementers of global directives is that the capabilities, resources, and experiences of the company's worldwide assets are sorely underutilized. Also, expanding headquarters control may deprive country managers of outlets for their skills and creative energy, leading to low morale and high turnover. Decentralization of decision making is sometimes helpful to achieve strategic goals if too much centralization impairs the company's ability to meet the needs of users in key markets.

Strategy can be pursued through **global subsidiary mandates.** Such a mandate exists when the local subsidiary of a multinational corporation has worldwide (or regional) responsibility for a product or product line. An example of such a mandate is Siemens Japan, which, in partnership with Asahi Medical, has a mandate to produce and market compact magnetic resonance image (MRI) machines for the world market. Thus, the implementation of global strategy does not have to reside with the firm's head-

WHICH PATH TO TAKE?

The world's second largest pharmaceutical market, Japan, had been stagnant for much of the mid-1990s. Because drugs constitute a high proportion of the total cost of health care, the Japanese government implemented a series of aggressive price cuts. Faced with this situation at home, Fujisawa, a mid-sized Japanese drug company wanted to expand its international reach. This goal contrasted sharply with securing market share inside Japan, which characterized the behavior of many Japanese pharmaceutical companies.

The new president of the company, Hatsuo Aoki, fluent in English and with extensive experience in the United States, felt the Japanese pharmaceutical industry, a minnow by U.S. and European standards, could not survive without expanding abroad. His goal was to increase the share of revenues from outside Japan to 50 percent by 2004. Mr. Aoki felt that further price cuts would follow and the stagnation in the domestic market would persist for another five years while demand in the United States and Europe was expected to grow strongly.

Mr. Aoki adopted a twin-track strategy. The first track was to defend Fujisawa's domestic position. The group cut costs by reducing the number of medical sales staff from 1,300 to 1,000—one of the smallest forces among big Japanese pharmaceutical companies. At the same time, it looked to bolster its product development efforts by licensing in compounds from foreign firms. "We have two options. One is to strengthen the development of in-house products and the other is to seek alliances with outside partners. Since we have inadequate in-house products, we are eagerly looking for drugs from other companies," he explained. He had just completed negotiations with AstraZeneca, the Anglo-Swedish company, to market a treatment for schizophrenia in Japan.

The second track was to replicate the international product development skills of its foreign rivals so that it could simultaneously apply for regulatory approval of its drugs in Japan, Europe, and the United States. Seven of the eight drugs Fujisawa was currently working on were being developed for foreign markets.

Mr. Aoki admitted that Fujisawa's international marketing reach was limited. The aim was to develop drugs for the hospital market, rather than doctors, so that fewer sales staff would be required. For instance, Prograf, the company's immunosuppressant drug used to prevent transplant patients from rejecting new organs, was targeted at hospitals. "That means the target market is small and we don't have to build up a huge sales force," he explained. However, for a drug to treat diabetes, which the company was developing, "... we can either increase the number of overseas medical representatives dramatically or form a marketing alliance with a foreign partner. To be honest I prefer the latter option. I don't want to build up the huge fixed costs associated with a big infrastructure. That would prove difficult to sustain." He thought that progress in genomics (the study of the relationship between genes, the environment, and diseases) and other technologies meant opportunities to create a network of virtual companies and partners, allowing Fujisawa to buy in expertise in particular areas. "It would be better to have a network of two or three companies, rather than having one headquarters that dictates everything from overseas."

Source: Abrahams, Paul. 1999, July 15. Outward-looking ambitions. *Financial Times Survey,* p. II.

quarters, but can be maintained by individual subsidiaries. The global subsidiary mandate allows the subsidiary to maintain a degree of autonomy through responsibility over its mandated product line. The subsidiary is able to continue to develop competencies, not only with respect to product and process expertise but also in understanding the industry worldwide.

INTEGRATING OPERATIONS

Another aspect of effective strategy is the ability to combine the firm's various activities by enabling each activity to fit with and reinforce the others. A good fit creates a strong chain that makes it harder for competitors to imitate. David Whitwam, the chief executive officer of Whirlpool Corporation, has discussed how in seven years the company transformed itself from being primarily a North American company to a manufacturer in 11 countries with sales in 120 locations.[15] He maintained that, *"The only way to gain lasting competitive advantage is to leverage your capabilities around the world so that the company as a whole is greater than the sum of its parts. . . . Our vision at Whirlpool is to integrate our geographical businesses wherever possible, so that our most advanced expertise in any given area—whether it is refrigeration technology, financial reporting systems, or distribution strategy—isn't confined to one location or one division. We want to be able to take the best capabilities we have and leverage them in all of our operations worldwide."*

A look at how small and medium-sized German companies have come to dominate their markets worldwide is instructive. Known as the *Mittelstand,* they are less well-known compared to such famous German firms as Siemens, Daimler-Benz, Bayer, and Volkswagen, primarily because the products they make—such as labeling machines for beverages, bookbinding textiles, tropical fish foods, cigarette machines—are used in the manufacturing process or subsumed by the end product and also because they relish their obscurity and shy away from publicity. What practices do these firms engage in that makes them so successful?

They combine strategic focus with geographic diversity. In doing so they emphasize factors such as customer value, and blend technology with closeness to customers. They rely on their own technical competence, and create mutual interdependence between the company and its employees. These companies demonstrate that global leadership depends less on great technical breakthroughs than on vigilant attention to improvement, a commitment to serving foreign markets, and persistence.[16]

Although these strategies have led to success, to keep flourishing the firms may have to pay greater attention to professional marketing plans and conducting formal market research and planning. With rising R&D budgets, increased costs, heightened competition, and unfavorable exchange rates, these companies may have to consider outsourcing some of their functions. Similarly, their corporate culture may prevent talented outsiders from entering or rising up in the hierarchy. Despite these potential difficulties, they offer much for other companies to learn. Decentralization, small units with high autonomy, being close to customers, integration of technology with marketing, and employee identification are all characteristics that can be emulated by other firms.

STRATEGY-MAKING PROCESS

The strategy-making process in the firm itself is a key determinant of effective strategy implementation. When deciding whether or to what extent strategies should be carried out, managers throughout the firm accord great importance to the way in which those

---

[15]Maruca, Reginald F. 1994. The right way to go global: An interview with Whirlpool CEO David Whitwam. *Harvard Business Review.* March–April, pp. 135–145.
[16]Simon, Hermann. 1992. Lessons from Germany's midsize giants. *Harvard Business Review.* March–April, pp. 115–123.

strategies are generated. Their chief concern: Is due process exercised in the strategy-making process? Such due process means (1) that headquarters is familiar with a firm's overseas situation, (2) that two-way communication between headquarters and foreign operations exists in the strategy-making process, (3) that the head office is relatively consistent in making decisions across the firm's various operations, (4) that managers abroad can legitimately challenge the strategic views and decisions of headquarters, and (5) that foreign operations are provided with an explanation for the strategic choices made by headquarters. In the absence of these elements of the due process in strategic decision making, managers at the firm's subsidiary are less likely to be favorably disposed to implementing the firm's strategy. In contrast, when these elements are present, subsidiary managers are favorably disposed to implementing the strategy even if those strategic decisions are not in line with the interests of a particular subsidiary. The due process in strategic decision making is presented diagramatically in Figure 4-2.

CONCLUSIONS

The fast pace of change in the business environment has compelled international firms to decide where and how they should compete. Managers realize that to remain competitive, they must go into foreign countries both to market products and to source inputs. Companies are faced with choosing from a wide assortment of strategy options as to how best to compete and maintain a sustainable advantage over their rivals. No obvious formula makes a strategy successful. Constant innovation is often needed to keep ahead of one's competitors. At the same time, firms need to be able to respond effectively to their diverse customers located in different countries. Operating internationally requires flexibility on the part of the firm so that it can meet the challenges and at the same time take advantage of the knowledge, experience, and insights that become available. Strategy formulation and implementation are key managerial tasks that determine how successful a firm will be. Strategy is about seeking new advantages in the marketplace while slowing the erosion of present advantages. Effective strategy is

FIGURE 4-2 Due Process in Strategic Decision Making

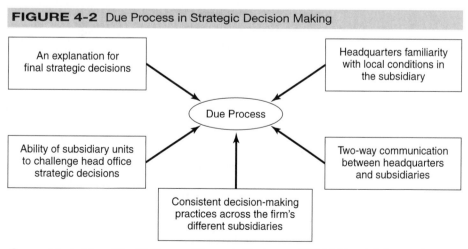

Source: Adapted from Kim, W. Chan, and Renee A. Mauborgne. 1993. Making global strategies work. *Sloan Management Review.* Spring, p. 12.

grounded in insightful monitoring of the competitive environment, coupled with the firm's own strength and resources. Various foreign market entry and ownership choices are available to international business managers, and the next three chapters discuss the characteristics and appropriateness of these choices.

OPENING VIGNETTE EPILOGUE

The local supermarket chains used their knowledge of their home markets to thwart the foreign competitors. They were also helped by a sharp decline in the cost of retailing technology that allowed them to install the inventory-control and logistics computers that had contributed so much to the efficiency of the likes of Carrefour and Wal-Mart.

Pao de Acuzar now spends only half of its annual investment budget on new stores. The rest is aimed at increasing the productivity of the existing shops, which means investing in information technology and in doubling the size of its central warehouse in Sao Paulo. Sales per employee continue to increase, helped partly by new incentive bonuses and flexible working practices. But the highest return on investment, according to Luiz Antonio Viana, Pao de Azucar's chief executive officer, comes from refurbishing the firm's old-fashioned neighborhood supermarkets that occupied prime locations—an advantage foreign firms could not match.

Pao de Azucar also draws on a more traditional Brazilian habit. In a country that loves to buy on credit, the firm accepts post-dated checks—on which it charges interest. Such financial income accounts for 58 percent of its net profits. This practice might look risky, but Mr. Viana said that his company knows its customers well: less than 1 percent of these checks bounces.

The Argentine firm, Disco, on the other hand, decided not to imitate the hypermarkets. Its 59 small neighborhood supermarkets in the richer parts of Buenos Aires and Argentina's provincial cities emphasizes quality, freshness (half of sales are of perishables) and services, such as home delivery, telephone ordering, and Argentina's first customer-loyalty card, which attracted 750,000 members in its first year. Disco's store managers have autonomy to adapt their product range and prices to local tastes. Beef, for example, is cut in a different way in Tucuman in Argentina's interior, from how it is cut in Buenos Aires.

Eduardo Orteu, Disco's boss, admits that foreigners still have some advantages (such as Wal-Mart's cost of capital, which was much lower than Disco's), but he stresses his firm's local knowledge and its sensitivity to customer needs. Disco also acquired a smaller chain of supermarkets and through ownership in Santa Isabel, Chile's second biggest food retailer, gained bargaining strength with suppliers and vendors. Prime locations and superior knowledge of local tastes afford these Latin American stores protection as well as the realization that they need to improve their supply chains and control costs to successfully match the foreign hypermarkets.[17]

[17]Retailing in South America—Survival skills. *The Economist.* 1997, July 12, pp. 57–58.

Key Terms

- strategy
- evolutionary strategy
- low-cost strategy
- differentiation strategy
- global strategy
- economies of scale
- multidomestic strategy
- core competency
- global subsidiary mandate

Discussion Questions

1. For each of the following products, explain why the global strategy can or cannot be successfully adopted:
   - electricity generating plants
   - cut flowers
   - international long-distance phone service
   - Barbie doll toy
   - beer
   - computer chips
   - legal services
2. Clearly distinguish between international, multinational, global, and transnational strategies. Why would a firm choose one strategy over another?
3. Can the global strategy be used for service industries? Explain using examples.
4. Distinguish between cost and differentiation strategies.
5. What is the role of innovation in ensuring international competitiveness? What can a firm do to ensure a high level of innovativeness?
6. To what extent does the personality and experience of the chief executive officer of a firm determine and drive a firm's strategy? Explain.

Writing Assignment

Select two international firms in any industry, obtain their mission statements, and prepare a report comparing the two. Identify the key characteristics of the mission statements and evaluate them in terms of the firm's current financial and market peformance.

Note: The mission statements and other information may be available in a library or may have to be obtained from the firms themselves.

Internet Exercise

Use the Internet to access Web sites of three international firms in any particular industry. Obtain sales information of the three companies for the Triad (North America, Western Europe, and Japan) for the past three years. Comment on the trends, similarities, and dissimilarities of the three companies. (*Hint:* Airline companies may include United Airlines, JAL, and British Airways; telecommunications firms may include Ericsson, Motorola, and Nokia; automobile firms may include General Motors, Toyota, and Volkswagen).

Internet Resources

Most companies today have a Web site and visiting them can give the surfer information about their strategies and activities. Articles on business strategies are covered in national business newspapers, which too can be visited on the Web, e.g., *The Financial*

Times at *www.ft.com*. Technology companies have transformed the industrial landscape and one of the largest such firms is Cisco Systems at *www.cisco.com*. Corporate Web sites also carry company mission/vision statements, such as the Japanese cosmetics company, Shiseido, at *www.shiseido.com.jp/e/*. Some of the companies mentioned in this chapter—Carrefour, Philips, Unilever, Honda, and Delta Air Lines—have Web sites. Their addresses are *www.carrefour.fr, www.philips.com, www.unilever.com, www.honda.com,* and *www.delta-air.com*. The consulting firm of Booz, Allen, and Hamilton carries some articles and references on business strategy at its Web site at *www.strategy.business.com*. As always, a search engine such as Yahoo! can be used to search for a particular firm or topic. Click on *www.yahoo.com/Business_and_Economy/ Companies* to find the firm of your choice.

Case 4–1   THE DECLINE OF MITSUBISHI

It was the summer of 1999. Although some indicators suggested that the Japanese economy was looking up, many Japanese companies continued to report unprecedented losses, sell off assets, lay off workers, and cut back expansion plans. At Mitsubishi, one of the world's largest keiretsu, negative financial and performance news continued to be reported from across its vast and diverse businesses. In common with similar situations faced by other Japanese keiretsu, the senior management at Mitsubishi (the "Group") was now confronted with the need to take difficult and unprecedented decisions to ensure its continued existence.

KEIRETSU

A key feature of the industrial structure in Japan had been the intercorporate group alliances known as *keiretsu*. A keiretsu was defined as a group of interrelated organizations that had cross-ownership, joint shareholdings, common trademarks, commodity transactions, and bank loans between themselves. Although member companies were independent entities, they were also bound together by both informal and formal ties including cross-ownership of equity. Belonging to a keiretsu influenced the flow of transactions between member firms and created a thick and complex skein of relations not matched in any other industrial country.

The Mitsubishi Group was the biggest keiretsu in Japan. It included banks, insurance companies, automobile and auto component firms, electronic factories, research laboratories, shipping lines, breweries, steel, real estate, and aerospace plants, among others. These individual firms owned shares in each other and bought goods and services from each other at preferred prices.

They conducted joint research and development on new products and processes, and coordinated their activities against other groups and foreign firms. They jointly relied on central banking service for financial needs and maintained links with several layers of suppliers and subcontractors. Thus, the Mitsubishi Group, like other keiretsu, was a huge family of related and unrelated businesses.

The nature of the keiretsu was best illustrated by the business practices at Mitsubishi Motors, one of the Group's leading companies. The company was Japan's fourth largest automobile maker. Members of the Group bought a third of the company's trucks and buses. A third of the Group's employees owned Mitsubishi cars. Group companies also bought 30 percent of their own fleets from Mitsubishi Motors. Cheap financing for expansion was provided by the Group's bank, Bank of Japan-Mitsubishi.

GENESIS OF THE PROBLEM

Throughout the 1990s, Japan had been mired in recession. Despite numerous public policy steps that included massive public works projects and severe cuts in interest rates (to 0 percent) to stimulate consumption, the economy showed little sign of recovery. Consumption stagnated and real estate prices plummeted. The situation was aggravated by a huge financial crises that began in Thailand in 1997 and soon spread throughout much of East Asia. The crisis led to a shrinkage in the size of national economies, high unemployment, and diminished levels of economic activities. Japanese exports to these countries fell sharply and so did related economic activities (e.g., banking, production, and travel) conducted by Japanese firms. The country suffered from an excess capacity of most manufactured goods. Japan had 11 vehicle manufactureres, 5 integrated steel makers, 10 semiconductor companies, and 17 money center banks. Sales were declining; borrowers were unable to repay loans; indebtedness grew. Thus, many Japanese companies found themselves both at home and abroad in a difficult economic situation.

REPERCUSSIONS AT MITSUBISHI

In February 1999, the head of Mitsubishi Motors, one of the leading members of the Group, conceded that mounting losses and falling market share was forcing it to consider an alliance with another, and in all likelihood, foreign, automaker. Earlier in the year, one of Japan's largest automobile companies, Nissan, had sold a controlling stake to the French automaker, Renault, following record losses and mounting debts. Rising losses at Mazda and Suzuki had persuaded Ford and General Motors, respectively, who held small equity stakes in those two Japanese companies, to increase ownership to controlling levels. Another member of the Group, Mitsubishi Electric, projected a massive loss of $330 million. The chemicals and materials companies too expected large losses. The Bank of Tokyo-Mitsubishi, the firm that bankrolled the activities of the Group, was saddled with huge bad debts and was forced to raise $2 billion worth of capital from other firms in the Group. The Kirin Brewery was in danger of losing its top place in the Japanese beer market.

In less than 10 years, Mitsubishi had seen its fortunes swerve from success to failure. In 1989, it created much angst among Americans when it bought a majority share in an American icon, New York City's Rockefeller Center. Around that time, Mitsubishi Motors was experiencing huge surges in sales in the United States. Mitsubishi Electric, a pioneer in many electrical and electronic gadgets, had acquired a lock on big-screen television sets. The Mitsubishi bank expanded rapidly in California and cheap loans financed the Group's worldwide expansion. The Mitsubishi keiretsu appeared to be godzilla-like, unstoppable. Much of the success of Mitsubishi was attributed to the strengths of the keiretsu system.

With rising profits, the Group diversified even more and expanded rapidly overseas. Without shareholder activism, senior managers focused on higher market share rather than on higher returns on equity. The main Mitsubishi companies averaged a return on equity of 4 percent; some member companies had nega-

tive returns. In contrast, in the United States, returns less than 15 percent were considered poor. Even in Europe, expected returns were set at 10 percent or better.

As the domestic economy slowed, poor returns and the heavy obligations of the various member companies led international rating companies to downgrade the credit of 13 members of the Group including Mitsubishi Heavy Industries and Bank of Tokyo-Mitsubishi. Mitsubishi Rayon, Japan's largest acrylic-fiber manufacturer, saw its shares downgraded to junk status. Once the first choice of graduates of the country's finest universities, Mitsubishi cut down on new hires. At the same time, the famed organizational loyalty credo eroded; turnover rose.

A TRAPPED PRESIDENT

When Minoru Makihara was appointed president of the keiretsu in 1992, many thought far-reaching changes would occur at Mitsubishi. He had risen to the top of Japan's in-bred, conservative business elite with a different background. He was born in England, went to private schools there, and graduated from Harvard University. Thus, he had a cosmopolitan background.

As early as 1990, Mr. Makihara had admitted that Mitsubishi needed to change in light of the changing business environment. But even after becoming president he found instituting meaningful change extremely difficult. A disconnect appeared between Mr. Makihara's goals and his ability to achieve.

This disconnect was not restricted to Mitsubishi. Many senior managers at many of Japan's big companies were considered to be among the best in the world in terms of their intelligence, insights, experience, and track records. But, unlike their western counterparts, they found it difficult to introduce change in the Japanese context where wholesale restructuring that might cost jobs and shut down businesses were not generally considered socially responsible. Drastic restructuring, common in North America and Western Europe, was generally shunned in Japan where great emphasis was placed on building consensus and saving face. Thus, senior executives were often unable to impose their strategic views on the firms they supposedly ran.

Because radical restructuring was not feasible, Mr. Makihara had to introduce incremental changes, which meant letting go a small percentage of workers, withdrawing from certain markets, closing down an office, discontinuing a product line, or holding back on expansion. This drip-by-drip restructuring was time consuming with few immediate results.

DECISION MAKING

The difficulty of introducing and administering changes at Mitsubishi Group was worsened by the fact that the Group did not have a centralized chief executive officer. Mr. Makihara came closest to that role simply by being the chairperson for the Group's flagship trading company.

The chairpersons and presidents of the 28 Group companies met regularly to consider new projects, investments, and policies. These Friday Club meetings, however, suffered from slow and indecisive decision making. Decisions normally had to be taken by consensus. Mr. Makihara admitted, "I'm sorry to say that there has been no meaningful discussion. Twenty years ago, there were powerful leaders in the group. People are now more concerned with their own problems." Besides, the Friday Club members did not believe in embarrassing members whose companies were doing poorly. As the president of Kirin Breweries observed, "We never raise topics related to the management of the individual companies."

Because of the emphasis on consensual decision making, Mr. Makihara found it almost impossible to impose his views. When difficulties arose in the past, the leaders of the four most powerful companies in the Group—Mitsubishi Trading, Mitsubishi Heavy Industries, Mitsubishi Electric, and Bank of Tokyo-Mitsubishi—would meet to chalk out a new strategy. In 1984, for instance, the Group bought Mitsubishi Oil Company stock to defend it from a raid by Getty Oil. But now, in 1999, the pressures were too intense for Group members to stick together. As one analyst observed, "The reality is that Mitsubishi presidents aren't really talking to each other. The companies just happen to have the same name."

The boards of directors at the member companies were packed with insiders who were usually too timid to kill a bad idea or push a promising one further. In the United States, where independent boards comprised by outsiders were often the norm, board members were more likely to act decisively when problems loomed.

RECENT DEVELOPMENTS

As member companies reeled from losses and setbacks, they sought alliances on their own with firms outside the Group. In 1998, Nikko Securities, the Group's primary investment banker of which 20 percent was owned by Bank of Tokyo-Mitsubishi, sold 25 percent of its equity to a U.S. firm. With rising losses, Nikko Securities needed the cash from the sale as well as the marketing skills the foreign presence brought in. This act of Nikko was, however, seen negatively by the Group, especially because it was never discussed with the Group. It was a telling sign that the interlocking ties among the member companies were fraying.

Following Nikko Securities, Mitsubishi Oil, which too had been losing money, merged with another out-of-the-Group firm, Nippon Oil. Mitsubishi Motors began talks with Fiat of Italy and Ford of the United States for both equity sale and technology collaborations. Both Mitsubishi Chemicals and Mitsubishi Trust & Banking Corporations also were looking for equity tie-ups with members of other keiretsu. These sorts of behaviors by individual Group members would have been unthinkable in the past.

DIFFICULTIES IN MAKING CHANGES

Top executives at Mitsubishi were beginning to question the viability of the keiretsu. They argued that unless Group companies raised their efficiency, profitability, and business practices to global levels, they were doomed and even outside alliances may not suffice. However, severing old ties was not easy. Group companies continued to reach out to each other for subsidies, loans, and bailouts. Weaker members raided the Group's declining capital resources. For example, Optec Dai-Ichi Denko Co., a manufacturer of electronics wire, sought a $150 million loan from Mitsubishi Electric. Mitsubishi Trust and Bank of Tokyo-Mitsubishi both agreed to write off $46 million loans made to each other.

Despite the heavy reliance of Mitsubishi Motors on Group members to lift substantial portions of its car and truck production, Mitsubishi Motor's share of the domestic market was only about 10 percent. The company suffered from a lack of attractive new models, problems of sexual harassment at its plant in the United States, and the collapse of the Thai and Malaysian automobile markets in which the company had invested billions of dollars. Similarly, Mitsubishi Electric, which relied on Group companies to sell its computers, was taken by surprise when Compaq Computer of the United States entered the Japanese market in a big way. Its easy access to cheap capital from the Group's bank led to generous borrowing to finance expanded production of high-end computer chips. But a global chip glut led to a crash in prices and a huge loss for Mitsubishi Electric. Now the company was thinking of focusing on a few businesses. However, as an analyst noted, "It is hard for a big company like Mitsubishi Motors to switch gears, but that is precisely what it needs to do."

CONCLUSION

With financial results suggesting the need for radical change, Mr. Makihara continued to believe in the staying power of the Mitsubishi Group. He commented, "There is still tremendous value in this Group." However, changes in how the Group was set up and run were imminent and radical. All around Japan, actions, once unthinkable, were taking place. Foreign companies were acquiring beleaguered Japanese firms, plants were being closed down, bankruptcies were at an all-time high and so was the unemployment rate, the government was deregulating the economy, opening it up to more domestic and foreign competition, and the stock prices continued to languish. Mr. Makihara was now being compelled to take decisive actions to ensure the survival of the Mitsubishi Group. He was now seeking an 8 percent return on equity, requiring greater disclosure of financial performance, and approving alliances with other companies. The challenge remained—that of creating a broad strategic plan for the Group.

QUESTIONS

1. What factors explain the change in the fortunes of this formerly successful keiretsu?
2. What steps should Minoru Makihara take to ensure profitability and growth of Mitsubishi Corporation?
3. Identify the difficulties Mr. Makihara may face implementing the proposals suggested in the previous question.
4. Explain the concept of core competencies as it applies to Mitsubishi Group.

References

Bartlett, Christopher A., and Sumantra Ghoshal. 1986. Tap your subsidiaries for global reach. *Harvard Business Review.* November–December.

Bartlett, Christopher A., and Sumantra Ghoshal. 1995. *Transnational management.* Chicago: Irwin.

Caves, Richard, and Mariko Uekusa. 1976. *Industrial organization in Japan.* Washington, DC: The Brookings Institution.

Gerlach, Michael L. 1992. Twilight of the keiretsu? A critical assessment. *Journal of Japanese Studies* 18, pp. 79–118.

Grant, R. M. 1991. The resource-based theory of competitive advantage: Implications for strategy formulation. *California Management Review* 33(3).

Hamel, Gary. 1996. Strategy as revolution. *Harvard Business Review.* July–August, pp. 69–82.

Hout, Thomas, Michael Porter, and Eileen Rudden. 1982. How global companies win out. *Harvard Business Review.* January–February, pp. 98–108.

Kiernan, Matthew J. 1996. Get innovative or get dead. *Business Quarterly* 61(1), pp. 51–58.

Kim, W. Chan, and Renee Mauborgne. 1993. Making global strategies work. *Sloan Management Review.* Spring, pp. 11–27.

Levitt, Theodore. 1983. The globalization of markets. *Harvard Business Review.* May–June.

Lindell, Martin, and Necmi Karagozoglu. 1997. Global strategies of U.S. and Scandinavian R&D-intensive small- and medium-sized companies. *European Management Journal* 15(1), pp. 92–199.

Lovelock, Christopher H., and George S. Yip. 1996. Developing global strategies for service businesses. *California Management Review* 38(2), pp. 64–86.

Porter, Michael E. 1990. The competitive advantage of nations. *Harvard Business Review.* March–April, pp. 73–93.

Porter, Michael E. 1996. What is strategy? *Harvard Business Review.* November–December, pp. 61–78.

Prahalad, C. K., and Yves Doz. 1988. *The multinational mission.* New York: Free Press.

Segal-Horn, Susan, David Asch, and Vivek Suneja. 1998. The globalization of the European white goods industry. *European Management Journal* 16(1), pp. 101–108.

Yip, George S. 1995. Global strategy . . . In a world of nations? In Christopher A. Bartlett and Sumantra Ghoshal, eds. *Transnational management,* 2d ed. (pp. 353–367). Chicago: Irwin.

5
EXPORTING AND IMPORTING

❧

OPENING VIGNETTE

Rusty Thompson, a farmer in Kentucky, became almost emotional when he talked about the fertilizer spread on his tobacco farm. "It's 20 percent more expensive than traditional fertilizer, but it's worth it," he said. "The roots just grab at it, and the plant greens up real well."

These words were music to the ears of Patricio Contesse, the 46-year-old chief executive officer of Sociedad Quimica y Minera de Chile S.A. (SQM), a Santiago-based manufacturer of specialty fertilizers and chemicals. Buoyed by a growth in exports, SQM enjoyed a net margin of more than 14 percent in 1996—its closest U.S. competitor netted only 2.5 percent.

The company had access to mining rights to the world's largest known deposits of nitrates and iodine in northern Chile. The desert terrain yielded a mineral rich ore called *caliche*. From it came the nitrates used in SQM's fertilizers and chemicals. The company claimed that its extraction process was cheaper than synthesizing nitrates, as its competitors did. Low production costs and high selling prices were every company's dream and SQM had found that farmers like Mr. Thompson were willing to pay a premium to obtain higher crop yields.

In Mr. Contesse, the company had an indefatigable champion. He spent half his time on the road, drumming up business for his company's products. In 1990, he took over as chief executive after the former state-owned enterprise was privatized in the mid-1980s. An ambitious forest engineer who had turned around a state-owned coal operation, his main challenge at SQM was to rid the employees of their state-owned mentality. "People were making political decisions rather than economic ones," he recalled. He encouraged employees to become shareholders by offering them low-interest loans. "Today we have one-third the people we had in 1988, and we're five times as productive," he reported.

SQM's other advantage was its innovative marketing. A decade ago—when exports of $48 million were only 20 percent of revenues—Mr. Contesse realized that growth lay outside Chile's small domestic market. The big question though was how could a small company in a remote country enter world markets on a small budget.

As the stages model of internationalization theorizes, exporting and importing represent the first acts of international business activity in a firm's evolution toward becoming a multinational enterprise. Unlike transactions in the domestic market, international trading requires that the firm deal with issues such as foreign exchange rates and trade regulations, international politics and business practices, and new competitors. A strategy for sustained and successful exporting and importing requires international business managers to take a proactive interest in foreign buyers and suppliers. Such a strategy invariably requires that the firm hire specialized staff and reorganize departments. It also means the development of new products and services as well as new pricing policies. For an international strategy to work, a firm must understand government regulations, negotiate access to distribution channels or create new channels, and look for ways to reduce exchange risks. This chapter examines the key managerial issues that surround the international trading activities of firms. We first look at the global trading environment and examine the reasons why firms engage in international trading. Among the managerial issues discussed are choice of countries, product adaptation, choice of channels, and pricing strategies. In addition, we review export of services such as management contracts, the role of trading companies, countertrade arrangements, and the financial issues that surround international trade.

THE GLOBAL TRADING ENVIRONMENT

International trade in the form of exporting and importing goods and services takes place under a global system of rules and regulations agreed upon and enforced by national governments and international organizations. The international manager, as a first step, must be familiar with the environmental realities of international trading. As discussed in Chapter 1, globalization forces have vastly increased opportunities for exporting and importing.

The emergence of trading blocs has increased the size of national markets by eliminating trade barriers among member countries. Some blocs, such as the European Union, aim to integrate the member countries into an economic and political entity with common governance institutions as well as coordinated economic policies, including a single currency. The creation of a single large market with minimal restrictions on movement of goods and people has had a major effect on the export operations of many European firms who have had to restructure their operations. Many firms—in Europe and abroad—now consider Europe as one large market and not 15 separate markets.

The creation of trading blocs affects firms in member and nonmember countries in different ways. For some firms, the home market, in effect, expands to include the population of the member countries. This expansion means simplified paperwork that accompanies international transactions, increased economies of scale, and uniformity of procedures and rules. It also means increased imports from firms located in the member countries. Thus, under NAFTA, Mexican companies have been able to export, without hindrance, many items, in which they have a locational advantage, to the United States and Canada. In other cases, U.S. firms have relocated their operations in Mexico and now supply the U.S. market through exports.

While free trade areas remove trading barriers to firms located in the member countries, barriers may continue to exist for products coming in from firms based in nonmember countries. Thus, free trade agreements may keep out firms from nonmember countries. These nonmember firms, unable to export to member countries because of trade walls, set up production facilities in one of the member states and supply those markets from this unit.

The levels of economic integration vary among countries. At the lowest level is an agreement to reduce trade barriers among member nations, creating a free trade area. Under a customs union, member countries agree on a uniform tariff and quota system for imports entering into the member countries. The common market goes further and allows movement of all factors of production among the member countries. The next level of integration takes place in the form of an economic union where member countries integrate their economic policies. At the highest level of integration, member countries replace their individual governance systems and institutions with supranational organizations. Table 5-1 shows the different levels of integration that can take place among countries.

E-COMMERCE

The Internet has rapidly become a medium for international trade. By offering to sell products on-line through a Web site, a company in effect enters into international trade that allows anyone anywhere in the world to place an order and pay by a credit card. Many domestic and foreign companies in India produce software that is exported through high-speed telecommunication links.[1] The United Nations Center for the Facilitation of Administration, Commerce, and Transport (UNCefact), in collaboration with Oasis, an industry group, has begun to develop international standards for paperless trading and devise standard Web-based electronic business procedures for international trade. Currently 99 percent of all global trade transactions use paper documents. It is estimated that the cost of producing a single invoice is $75, compared with an on-line transaction cost of about 50 cents.[2]

Table 5-1   Forms of Economic Integration

Characteristics	*Free Trade Area*	*Customs Union*	*Common Market*	*Economic Union*	*Political Union*
Removal of Internal Tariffs	X	X	X	X	X
Common External Tariffs		X	X	X	X
Free Flow of Labor/Capital			X	X	X
Common Economic Policy				X	X
Integration of Governments					X

Degree of Integration ⟶

Source: Albaum, Gerald, Strandskov, Jesper and Duerr, Edwin, *International Marketing and Export Management, 3/E.* © Addison Wesley Longman Ltd. 1998.

---

[1]Taylor, Paul. 1998, December 2. Big names drawn by high skills and low cost levels. *Financial Times Survey,* p. III.
[2]Williams, Francis, 1999, November 30. Web standards promise boost for commerce. *Financial Times,* p. 5.

A Swedish white goods company, Electrolux, used its Web site (*www.electrolux. com*) to conduct a variety of transactions with its suppliers and customers. For instance, the company's sea distribution division conducted all its business through the Internet. If its suppliers were not on-line, they could not do business with the division. The Web site was also used to promote the company's brand names and solicit customer inquiries. The contact with customers enabled the company to get to know them, to find out what they liked and what their problems were. It was the customers who now drove product development, and the company changed in response to demand from customers for information, services, support, and eventually products themselves. The Internet was also used to forge closer ties with retailers, to widen access to information on Electrolux products, to sell spare parts, and to post manuals for appliances. However, direct purchase on-line by customers was still a distant prospect primarily because of the key role played by retailers and by the preference of customers to view and discuss the products.[3]

LIMITATIONS TO TRADE

As noted in Chapter 1, localization forces remain strong, and tariffs, quotas, and nontariff barriers still present obstacles to trade. The biggest proponent of trading restrictions are firms who are unprepared to face the discipline of foreign competition as well as employee groups who fear losing their livelihood to cheaper imports. Governments, for domestic political purpose, national security reasons, and to pursue foreign policy goals, impose restrictions on exports and imports. For instance, the United States bars trade with Cuba because of the political character of Cuba's government. Not infrequently, policies of two countries can be at cross-purposes, leaving a firm's managers on the horns of a dilemma. An example of this dilemma is presented in Management Focus 5-1.

As discussed in Chapter 3, political instability in the form of wars, rebellions, and frequent changes in government policies discourages and interrupts the normal flow of commerce. Exporters worry about receiving payments for their goods, insurance premiums rise, transportation services may not be reliable. Other problems include imposition of tariffs, devaluation of currencies, destruction of goods, and threat to the personal well-being of a firm's employees.

Foreign exchange rates have a major impact on the profitability of international trade transactions. Two issues of concern are volatility in the rates and the inconvertibility of currencies. Changes in exchange rates may reduce the profitability of a transaction or conversely, make prices much more competitive. Countries with persistent balance of payments problems often impose restrictions on imports and on payments to outside suppliers. Exporters, therefore, need to be familiar with the importing country's foreign trade regime and foreign exchange rates and payment rules.

STRATEGIC PURPOSES FOR EXPORTING AND IMPORTING

Trade, in the form of selling goods and services to customers in a foreign country and buying goods and services from suppliers in a foreign country, is the most common form of international business. For many firms, it is also the easiest way to go international

---

[3]Price, Christopher. 1999, February 3. Electrolux sees e-commerce light. *Financial Times,* p. 12.

MANAGEMENT FOCUS 5-1

PAJAMAS: MADE IN CUBA?

For more than 30 years, the United States has maintained a trade embargo against Cuba, forbidding U.S. firms from doing business with the communist government of Fidel Castro. In 1995, following the shooting down of two small airplanes by the Cuban air force off the Florida coast, the U.S. Congress passed the Helms-Burton law, which sought to force other nations to join the U.S. effort to isolate the Cuban regime. Not all countries share America's passion for anticommunism and certainly not its largest trading partner, Canada. And it put Wal-Mart, America's largest retailer, in a bind.

Wal-Mart Canada, a subsidiary of Wal-Mart Stores, sold $8 Cuban-made pajamas in its Canadian stores. A store manager in Winnipeg, Manitoba, fearing that selling them would find the company violating U.S. law against trading in Cuban goods, pulled the Cuban pajamas off the shelves. When his action was reported in the newspapers, the Canadian government reacted by announcing an investigation into whether Wal-Mart's action violated a Canadian law that expressly prohibited Canadian companies from complying with U.S. policy toward Cuba by joining the U.S. embargo. Penalties for violators could exceed $1 million.

After studying the issue for a week, Wal-Mart Canada announced that it had decided the Canadian government was right. In a news release, it said that following "a comprehensive review and con-

sultation" that included discussions with Canadian officials, it would start selling the pajamas again. The company said that its actions reflected "our commitment to meet the expectation of the Canadian marketplace."

Unfortunately for Wal-Mart Canada, it did not meet the expectations of its parent in the United States. The parent said that "Wal-Mart Canada made this decision in direct contradiction of directives it received from Wal-Mart Stores, Inc.

"We told them to comply with U.S. law and regulations, including the Cuban assets control regulations," a company spokesperson said. The Canadian subsidiary refused to explain why it was defying its parent. It was possible that the split between the parent and its subsidiary is for show: It enabled the Canadian subsidiary to maintain that it was complying with Canadian law, and it enabled the U.S. company to maintain that it had taken a position consistent with the U.S. law.

Some participants in the case also suggest that marketing considerations were at work here. Wal-Mart Canada feared that if it was seen to be bending to the U.S. statute, consumers in Canada could react angrily. As it was, Canada was enormously sensitive to what it viewed as an imperialistic attempt by the United States to enforce U.S. law beyond its borders.

Source: Sanger, David. 1997, March 14. Wal-Mart Canada is putting Cuban pajamas back on shelf. *The New York Times,* p. D4.

because the risks are relatively minor, the financial requirements are relatively small, and the commitment to the foreign market or supplier does not have to be deep at the outset. By basing production facilities at one location and supplying all markets from it, the firm is in a position to reap economies of scale.

Exporting represents the outward-looking orientation of internationalization, while importing represents the inward orientation. An export invariably leads to an import because a necessary component is the buyer for the good or service that is exported. Firms may engage in direct exporting (or importing) where the sales take place between the company and distributors (or final customers) in the foreign country. In indirect exporting (or importing), the firm sells (or buys) through one or more intermediaries in the home country.

A large part of international trade today takes place between different units of multinational firms who have production and sales facilities in different countries. This level of trade is not surprising because an estimated 40,000 multinational firms in the world have approximately 270,000 foreign affiliates. It is estimated that 38 percent of total country exports in the case of Sweden and 24 percent for Japan are between parent firms and their affiliates. Intrafirm imports as percentage of total country imports is 14 for Japan and 43 for the United States.[4] As international firms, in part because of their global strategy, locate their value-adding activities in countries where costs are low and the necessary resources are available, more and more goods are moving across borders between different addresses of the same firm.

Exports and imports take place in every conceivable product and service, and for some firms foreign markets are crucial. Boeing, the world's largest airplane manufacturer, obtains two-thirds of its revenues from abroad and so does Caterpillar, a maker of earth-moving equipment. In recent years, trade in services has increased dramatically. Some commonly traded services are tourism, accounting, banking, insurance, education, transportation, and advertising.

ANALYSIS OF OPPORTUNITIES

Many firms stumble into international trade because of chance happenings such as an unsolicited order from abroad. Other firms consciously seek to export or import as part of a strategic plan. Successful exporters and importers find that international trading requires a systematic analysis of opportunities abroad and changing all phases of its business activities, especially production, marketing, and staffing. A strategic approach requires managers to address issues such as the purpose of exporting (or importing), which countries to export to (or import from), what products to sell (or buy), how to distribute and price the products, and the implications of trading on the organization and management of the firm. Firms generally start off in international trading on a small scale, after having been primarily focused on the domestic market. Over time and with positive experience, the volume and value of the transactions grow as does the variety and sophistication of products; support services in the form of information, repairs, and servicing; and the nature of the relationship between the export and import firms.

The commitment of a firm to exporting or importing may vary greatly. It may be content to merely fill unsolicited orders or it may decide to specifically design and make products for new markets abroad. The various levels of export commitment are presented in Table 5-2. Level four exporting represents a significant commitment of financial and managerial resources to foreign markets and a recognition that the export market is vital.

With regard to importing, a firm occasionally may carry an item from abroad or it may have most of its product line imported. For example, Pier 1 Imports is the preeminent U.S. retail importer of home furnishings, sold through its 688 stores. More than 5,000 products, made to U.S. standards, are imported from 44 countries. The company maintains competitive retail prices while using an extensive system to buy and move the products across national borders. The company invests in both hardware (in the form

[4]*World Investment Report 1996—Investment, trade and international policy arrangements.* 1996. New York: United Nations.

Table 5-2	Levels of Exporting	
Level One	Export of surplus	Firm exports occasionally and usually when it has excess supply
Level Two	Export marketing	Firm actively solicits overseas sales of existing products and is willing to make slight changes to the products and marketing procedures to accommodate the needs of the buyers
Level Three	Foreign market development	Firm makes major modifications in products for export and in marketing procedures in order to reach overseas buyers
Level Four	Technology development	Firm develops new products for existing or new markets

Source: Albaum, Gerald, Strandskov, Jesper and Duerr, Edwin, *International Marketing and Export Management, 3/E.* © Addison Wesley Longman Ltd. 1998.

of computerized inventory and cash register systems) and software (in the form of person-to-person and long-term relationship building).[5]

The primary reason a firm engages in international trade is because it is profitable to do so. In addition to this basic goal, a firm may have specific strategic reasons. These reasons can be classified as internal or external to the firm. Among the internal reasons are an international orientation on the part of top management and the desire to reduce risk by diversifying into different markets. Opportunities to secure economies of scale and the need to access cost-competitive and quality inputs or finished products are other often-cited reasons. Firms also seek specialized knowledge about particular markets and particular expertise in certain products or services, and a desire to obtain first mover advantages. External reasons would include declining or stagnant sales in a mature home market or a small home market. Lucrative opportunities in foreign markets and the availability of more suitable alternatives for products or components abroad are definite incentives for focusing internationally. Firms may also respond to the removal or lowering of barriers to trade, changes in foreign currency exchange rates, and the need to react to a competitor's action. The opening vignette illustrates some of the reasons for exporting and what it takes to be successful.

The search for foreign markets and winning foreign contracts can be intensely competitive. For example, the two major civilian aircraft manufacturers in the world—the Seattle-based Boeing and the European consortium, Airbus Industrie—were engaged in a massive campaign to win a major share of the estimated 13,500 to 16,160 aircraft, valued at $1.1 trillion, that were expected to be sold over the next twenty years, most of them outside the United States and the home countries of Airbus. Because a plane costs from $38 million to $174 million, depending on size and model, and buyers usually ordered several pieces, the competition between the two aircraft manufacturers to win orders was intense. Both companies made determined efforts to sell their planes to airline companies, often painting the other's planes in a poor light. They also developed new products for their customers. One example was Airbus's proposal to build a double-decker plane that could hold more than 550 passengers, but had an $8 billion price tag

---

[5]Jones, Arthur. 1997. Imports: It's more than just bamboo furniture. *World Trade.* June, pp. 36–37.

for its development. In recent years, Boeing's strategy was to commit the airline companies to long-term exclusive deals. Not only did such a move assure Boeing of multibillion dollar sales, it also reduced the likelihood that the airlines would switch to Airbus planes—mixing fleet types sharply increased training and other costs.[6]

MANAGEMENT CONTRACT

Management contract is a form of export of services in which a firm uses its own personnel, procedures, and systems to operate a facility owned by another firm. In return, the exporter is paid a fee. Successful companies often sell their management expertise and access to support systems to other firms in related industries. For example, Jamaica's Super Clubs, a leading owner of holiday resorts, manages hotels on a day-to-day basis in Cuba for the Cuban government.[7]

Management contracts are used in a variety of service businesses such as hotels, restaurants and catering services, hospitals, data processing, repairs, and servicing (such as aircraft). Increasingly, operations of electrical companies, pipelines, water companies, and even a government's customs department are being contracted out to companies with the requisite managerial and technical skills. Note that ownership does not change. What the exporter provides is superior management skills and techniques that the current owners do not have but need to either remain competitive or to improve performance and productivity. The exporter, therefore, needs to be both experienced and competent in managing run-down operations. When Speedwing, the consulting arm of British Airways, won a contract from the Greek government in 1999 to manage its ailing airline, Olympic Airways, it faced opposition from Greek labor unions who feared loss of jobs and who were opposed to foreign managers taking charge. Speedwing also had to fathom the depth of Olympic's financial problems because, for the previous two years, it had not published accounts that were in accordance with internationally accepted standards.[8]

The export of management skills is particularly evident in the construction industry. Teams of home country managers use equipment and imported or host country workers to build bridges, roads, houses, water supply and sewage systems, and pipelines, among other projects, around the world. Such infrastructure projects are usually built under three types of arrangements: turnkey, build-operate-transfer (BOT), and build-operate-own (BOO). Under a **turnkey** arrangement, the firm builds the project, say, an electricity-generating plant and hands it over to the owners ready for operation (with the turn of the "key"). Among the issues that have to be addressed in negotiating turnkey arrangements are the price, including clauses for cost overruns and stages of payment; design specifications; sources of equipment and labor; schedules and performance standards; and the support systems provided by the importer (or buyer).

BOT and BOO are extensions of the turnkey arrangements. Under **build-operate-transfer,** the exporter not only builds the project but also is required to manage it for a certain period of time, at the conclusion of which the management is turned over to the buyer. From the buyer's view, BOT ensures that the exporter addresses any teething

[6]Bryant, Adam. 1997, March 23. The $1 trillion dogfight. *The New York Times,* pp. 1, 14, 15.
[7]Fletcher, Pascal. 1998, June 17. World's hotel groups seek to put their men in Havana. *Financial Times,* p. 3.
[8]Hope, Kerin. 1999, July 27. Speedwing sees profitability as Olympic ideal. *Financial Times,* p. 16.

troubles that often accompany new projects. By the time the buyer takes over, the functional viability of the project is fully established. In addition, this intervening time period is usually used to train local personnel in the technical and managerial aspects of operating the project. From the exporter's point of view, BOT arrangements impose additional responsibilities for which it may not have the capabilities. A company that builds a sewage system does not always have the experience, resources, or even the inclination to manage such a system for, say, five years. Thus, where BOT arrangements are involved, the exporter may be reluctant to get involved or if it does, it may enter into arrangements with other firms to run the completed project.

Under **build-operate-own,** the seller is expected to buy the project it has built, after a certain time period. Thus what started as an export, over time turns into a foreign direct investment. The exporter, again, may find these long-term arrangements unattractive unless it is a firm that is highly integrated and provides export services, management services, as well as owns and controls infrastructure projects.

Contracts for large projects tend to be awarded on the basis of competitive bidding. Bids are made under sealed covers and opened by the buyer on a specified date. Great care has to be taken in putting in the bid not only in terms of following the guidelines but also with respect to the quoted price. To reduce the number of sellers, the importer usually prescreens many of the bidders and makes a short list of companies that have the experience, resources, and reputation that are deemed necessary. Large projects in developing countries are often funded by international financial organizations such as the Inter-American Development Bank and the Asian Development Bank. Firms keep track of loans made by these organizations and follow announcements for tenders by the buying organization, which is often a government. Even after bids are accepted, it is not uncommon for the buyer and the exporter to negotiate specific terms and in some cases, the buyer may play off one bidder against another to obtain even more favorable terms.

Under these three arrangements, in addition to negotiating the contract, management issues focus on the logistics of bringing together materials, equipment, and personnel to work on the project. The contract itself is a complex legal document and unique for every case. Because these projects are one-of-a-kind, not all problems that could arise can be foreseen. Hence, the contract should be clear on how disputes should be settled.

In carrying out these contracts, a project manager would be assigned who would draw resources (specialists, equipment, engineering designs) from the rest of the firm and from outside vendors. In many such projects, especially in less-developed countries, managers have to negotiate with the officials of the host government to ensure that supplies are allowed to be imported without interference and that the firm has access to vital support services, such as roads, work visas for technicians, and labor dispute mediation. In addition, continuous contact with the buyer is needed to ensure that guidelines and specifications are being met to the mutual satisfaction of both sides, that host country personnel are being properly trained (where so agreed upon), and that problems are quickly and effectively resolved.

From the buyer's point of view, the key managerial issues include evaluating bids, selecting suppliers, and negotiating the contract; monitoring performance, payment schedule, and performance guarantees; training of personnel; access to designs and other specifications; and post-contract matters such as repairs, servicing, obtaining parts and components, and technical expertise.

CHARACTERISTICS OF THE FIRM

Many studies have looked at the relationship between the size of a firm (in terms of number of employees and/or the monetary value of total sales) and its level of export performance.[9] Smaller firms may lack the resources to enter into exporting when compared to larger firms. The management of smaller firms may be more risk averse with regard to going abroad, conscious that a failure may impact the firm greatly. Smaller firms are also at that stage in their life cycle when they tend to focus mainly on their domestic market. However, little consistency was reported in the results. Some studies found a positive relationship between firm size and export activity. Others have found that size exerts little or no influence. Still others have found that size does influence export activity, but only for certain size ranges.

A study of the export behavior of 14,072 Canadian manufacturers—both large and small—found that larger firms were more likely to export and to export to a wider range of countries. They were also more likely to have been exporting for a longer period of time. However, smaller firms, while possessing fewer resources than larger firms, nevertheless may have appropriate resources to be involved in international activities.[10]

MANAGERIAL ISSUES IN EXPORTING AND IMPORTING

When a firm engages in exporting or importing, it assumes a whole new set of responsibilities and challenges. Usually, the firm's marketing department handles the export function, but they may lack the knowledge of export markets and export procedures to do a particularly fine job. The importing function tends to be handled by the purchasing department. Different firms organize their trading activities differently depending on many factors including the size and importance of international operations to the firm. Generally speaking, a firm takes a proactive stance toward foreign markets or foreign suppliers when upper-level managers push for it. Of the many facets of international marketing—and it is beyond the scope of this textbook to address them all—several key issues, such as selecting overseas markets, product adaptation, choosing distribution channels, and setting prices, are discussed here. The issues that managers need to understand and follow when it comes to exporting are presented in a sequential manner in Table 5-3. Because most issues pertaining to exports and imports are similar, the presentation of the material takes the perspective of exporting, though it applies equally to importing. Other issues of importing, sometimes referred to as sourcing, are discussed in Chapter 8.

SELECTING COUNTRIES

Although many firms export in reaction to overseas inquiries, proactive firms tend to first explore markets "closer" to home. Importers too, first consider suppliers in countries closer to home before venturing afar. Closeness is measured by the physical or geographical distance, the economic distance (in terms of convergence of living standards),

---

[9]Bonaccorsi, Andrea. 1992. On the relationship between firm size and export intensity. *Journal of International Business Studies* 23(4), pp. 605–636.
[10]Calof, Jonathan. 1994. The relationship between firm size and export behavior revisited. *Journal of International Business Studies* 25(2), pp. 367–387.

Table 5-3	Steps in the Exporting Process

- Assess the needs of the potential market and identify potential customers.
- Assess one's own capability to meet those needs.
- Identify the tools—technology, finance, and regulatory expertise—needed.
- Match specific capabilities of the firm to the specific needs of the customer.
- Prepare for and arrange to meet the foreign client or importer.
- Meet the importer.
- Assess the results of the meeting with particular attention to cultural issues and differences.
- Meet the importer again to discuss specific business relationships.
- Implement the sales agreement.
- Periodically reevaluate the relationship and the arrangements.

and cultural or psychic distance (in terms of similarity). Thus, historically, when Irish firms considered exporting or importing, they would first think of the United Kingdom. Many Spanish firms are heavily engaged in trade with South American countries because of the historical and cultural ties that bind them. Relatively little adjustment to the product, negotiating strategies, pricing, or to other aspects of doing business are necessary when exporting and importing countries are close. Business practices among "near" countries tend to be similar, and thus, transaction costs are lower.

However, with more than 185 countries in the world, many opportunities may be lost without a systematic examination of the various markets. Managers can readily access macroeconomic data from numerous sources about individual countries, which can form the basis to determine their viability as export markets. Some of the variables that are considered are population size, gross national product, per capita income, distribution of income among the population, living costs (usually determined by purchasing power parity calculations), life expectancy, level of urbanization, and literacy rates. Such information forms the basis of creating market segments to determine the viability of a market for the firm's products in a particular country.

A sense of certainty accompanies the decision to first enter countries that are similar to the host country. By first exporting to a "close" country, the exporter acquires experience and is also better placed to handle problems that may arise. These markets present less likelihood of major adjustments to the product or to marketing procedures because the foreign market closely resembles the home market. Having gained experience and confidence, the firm may target another market slightly less "close." Such a deliberate pace also allows the firm to make the necessary changes to its product, managerial staff, marketing procedures, as well as production capacities, so as to be fully prepared for the new market. The downside is missing out on market opportunities in countries that to the firm are currently "distant."

Managers may consider many models for evaluating the potential of a foreign market. One such model is described here. The manager may consider looking at a foreign market in terms of six successive levels leading to an understanding of what the actual sales might well be. At level one, the attempt is to identify the *potential need* for a product that is physically determined (e.g., size of population, life expectancy, climate, and natural resources). In level two, the *felt need* is identified as determined by the culture of the society in terms of class structure, literacy rates, and lifestyle. The third level focuses on *potential demand,* which is determined by economic factors such as per capita income, income distribution, consumption patterns, and the like. In the fourth level, the analysis is on calculating the *effective demand,* which is determined by political factors such as foreign exchange restrictions, import tariffs, nontariff barriers, tax rates, and trademark protection. At the penultimate level, the manager tries to establish the *market demand* for the product. The market demand is affected by commercial factors such as transportation costs, the existence of warehousing facilities, costs of advertising, existence of and access to channel intermediaries, availability of credit, and insurance. Finally, at the sixth level, the analysis focuses on identifying the *specific demand* or the sales potential as determined by the presence of competitors, the appropriateness of the firm's own product for that market, price, delivery schedule, and after-sales service, among other factors. This model, presented in Figure 5-1, can be viewed as a filter that, with every level, narrows the potential market until the sixth stage identifies the actual potential sales. To complete the analysis at each level, the manager needs access to a whole set of information.

Note that aggregate national figures may mask vast regional differences. For instance, since China opened its economy for development, much of the growth has occurred in the Southeast (around Hong Kong) and the East (Shanghai and to its south in Fujian province). The rest of the country had not benefited as much because the special economic zone designation was given only to specific regions. Consequently, vast disparities exist in economic and social status among the different regions and in distribution of income among the population. For instance, the poorest 20 percent of the population in Brazil earn only about a tenth of what the average Brazilian earns whereas in Japan the income disparities are much less severe.[11]

After having established the viability of a market in the foreign country, the export managers should consider the following important issues.

FIGURE 5-1 Market Research Filter

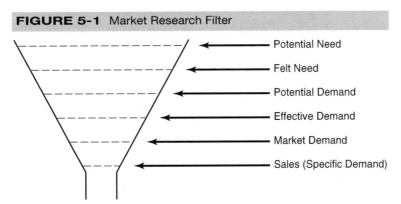

Source: Robinson, Richard. 1980. *International Business Management, 2/E.* Hinsdale, Illinois: The Dryden Press. With permission of the author.

---

[11]*Human Development Report.* 1999. United Nations Development Program. New York: Oxford University Press.

- *Entry barriers.* Barriers include the likely reaction of domestic and existing suppliers in the foreign market and import restrictions. A firm may also need to supply minimum amounts or overcome the unavailability of distribution channels. Freedom to use brand names, and the protection of relevant trademarks, copyrights, and patents can be critical issues, as can the legal framework in which business is conducted. For instance, Anzai Medical Company, a small Japanese manufacturer of high-tech health care devices, sells its products in Germany, Italy, Poland, and the United Kingdom, but not in the United States. The barrier that the company fears—that of lawsuits, should the product fail—is a business hazard that is common in the United States but not in Japan.[12]
- *Exit barriers.* These barriers include the ability to receive payment for exported goods and services in a timely fashion in the desired currency, protection of the goods shipped, and safety of the exporter's sales personnel. In 1997, following the sharp decline of its currency, the ringitt, the Malaysian government imposed restrictions on foreign exchange transactions, which made it difficult for exporters to receive payments from their importers.
- *Competitive barriers.* Costs of shipping, advertising, and opening stores are major barriers to competing effectively. Consider also the costs of making promotional visits, including airfare, hotels, and entertaining. These factors, along with the freedom to determine pricing and price margins and the certainty of the legal framework for conducting business are not small considerations. Many foreign firms, for instance, consider Japan to be an expensive and difficult market to enter; it holds the perception that the rules of the game are tilted in favor of the home companies.
- *Customer boycotts.* The use of boycotts as a coercive marketplace tactic has increased in recent years. Consumer and allied groups, to protest particular products or the behavior of the firm making and selling it, mount boycotts. A class of boycotts is fueled by international animosity, where consumers avoid a particular country's products because of the current or past behavior of its government. The World War II U.S. veteran who refuses to buy a Toyota car does so because he remembers Pearl Harbor, not because he dislikes Toyota's business practices. A 1998 study of consumers, ages 18 to 92, in the Chinese city of Nanjing—a site of massacre of Chinese civilians by the Japanese military during December 1937 and January 1938—found that animosity towards Japan was a powerful predictor of a refusal to buy Japanese products. Thus, consumer animosity led buyers in Nanjing to participate in an indirect, expressive boycott.[13]

The best strategic response that a foreign firm can adopt in response to consumer animosity is to decouple the product from its country of origin in markets where animosity is high. It can be done by downplaying the "Made in . . ." aspect of the product

---

[12]Warner, Susan. 1998, April 27. A small company explores world markets. *The Philadelphia Inquirer,* pp. D1, D16.
[13]Klein, Jill, Richard Ettenson, and Andrew John. Undated. How should companies respond to boycotts? Mastering Marketing, Part 10: International Marketing. *Financial Times,* pp. 6–7

or by developing hybrid products. Animosity can also be addressed directly by attempting to improve perceptions of the country and to address the sources of international tension. Firms may also find it worthwhile to put pressure on their home governments or the firm may try to disassociate itself from the offending act and could even take a public position against its government's behavior. Another alternative is to capitulate to the boycott acknowledging that the public is correct—perhaps the act to which it objects is indeed, unethical, inappropriate, or unwise. If so, managers should look beyond the bottom line and even if the boycott is deemed unfair, it may be easier and more profitable to give up.

Decision Techniques   Given the depth and variety of data available, managers are able to analyze them to determine which markets and which market segments are more appropriate for immediate entry and which are not by using a variety of analytical tools. This section briefly discusses several commonly used techniques.

1. **Demand pattern analysis.** Industrial growth patterns provide a perspective into potential market demand in a country. Production amounts also imply consumption trends, which point to potential market opportunities. For example, a country in the early stages of industrial development is likely to have low per capita income levels and manufacturing centered around necessities such as food, beverages, textiles, and light manufacturing. However, as incomes grow, other, more sophisticated industries gain in importance. To the exporter eyeing such a market, analyzing the patterns of industrial growth would enable it to determine the extent of demand for new products.

2. **Income elasticity measurements.** Income elasticity is defined as the relationship between the demand for a product and changes in the income. If a 5-percent increase in income leads to a 10-percent increase in the sale of cosmetics, the income elasticity coefficient is 2.0. On the other hand, if a 10-percent increase in income leads to a 5-percent decline in demand for black and white television sets, the income elasticity coefficient is 0.5. Elasticity studies show that as income rises, smaller amounts are spent on necessities of life such as food and clothing. Instead, demand grows for consumer durables such as refrigerators, television sets, bicycles, and services such as travel. Elasticity explains why growth in income in China has triggered a huge increase in consumption and many foreign firms are eager to export to that country.

3. **Estimation by analogy.** This method is used when complete data are not available for a company. Researchers try to determine a factor that correlates to demand for a particular product in one country. They then apply it to another country to get a rough estimate for the potential size of the market there. For example, it may be that in Country A, the sales of television sets were correlated to the number of movie theaters. Using that information, researchers can determine the potential size of the market for television sets in country B by counting the number of movie theaters there.

Another version of this technique focuses on time as the variable and is known as the **lead-lag analysis.** For instance, based on an analysis of factors associated with demand for a certain product, it could be assumed that 2001 Vietnam is similar to what Malaysia was in 1971. If demand for automobiles in Malaysia was a certain amount, one can infer what the demand for automobiles in Vietnam would be in 2001.

Although estimation by analogy is a popular technique, managers using it should bear in mind certain factors.

- Are the two countries used as the basis of the analogy comparable either in cross-section or time-displaced terms? Determining this comparability requires a thorough understanding of the two countries' culture as well as the nature of the products.
- Some societies are advancing so rapidly that they are skipping the transitional phases that other societies went through. When sequences vary, the estimations may not hold. For instance, the growth of the South Korean economy since the 1950s represent the fastest escape from poverty for an entire people in recorded history.
- A big difference may separate potential demand for a product based on underlying factors and actual sales as determined by factors such as price and quality, among others. The extent to which potential was translated into actual sales in one country may not occur in another country.

4. **Comparative analysis.** This type of analysis refers to analyzing intracompany and intercompany data across countries as well as national data to determine comparative sales performance and potential. For example, the Japanese market is about half the size of the U.S. market and comparable in per capita income. Consequently, sales of cars and cameras would be expected to be similar. Companies can look at their sales performance, budgets, and resources, and determine where they are effective and where they are not.

5. **Cluster analysis.** A statistical tool, cluster analysis groups variables into clusters that maximize within-group similarities and between-group differences. This method allows managers to distinguish markets and consumers on the basis of their similarities and dissimilarities. Market potential in one of the cluster countries enables a prediction of the market potential in another country in the cluster.

6. **Multiple factor indexes.** A multiple factor index measures potential demand indirectly by using as proxies variables that either intuition or statistical analysis suggests can be closely correlated with the potential demand for the product under review. Macroeconomic indicators such as gross national product and total population are considered but so are more specific factors such as number of urban households and television stations to determine the potential market for television sets.

7. **Regression analysis.** This well-established statistical technique is used for predicting demand. Various predictors are used to determine the dependent variable (usually the size of the market). To use this technique, managers need to obtain or estimate figures for many of the variables.

Sources of Information   Information about markets is available from numerous sources. A firm may find knowledge in its own sales records and in the experience and insights of its employees. Personal visits to foreign countries are a common way to understand potential markets or suppliers and develop one-on-one relationships with distributors. In most other cases, the firm looks outside for information. Such information may be obtained from primary or secondary sources. **Primary sources** refer to the collection of information about the market and suppliers through interviews, surveys, and observations. **Secondary sources** include newspapers, trade journals, chambers of commerce, trade shows, foreign government trade offices, and consulting firms. Many governments provide a full range of information about export and import regulations in their countries. They also identify products or services that are suitable for import or export from their respective countries. For instance, a publication of the Polish Embassy in the United States identified products such as pharmaceuticals, computer hardware and software, telecommunication equipment, and the construction of toll highways as opportunities for U.S. exporters.[14] In recent years, the Internet has become a quick, inexpensive, and comprehensive source of information. Government and private organizations post much information on their Web sites, which can be accessed either through subscription or through unrestricted access. Many firms that specialize in providing trading services, such as banks, distributors, and transport companies, are also valuable sources of information. Advancements in information technology and an explosion in information means that an efficient information system to collect and analyze vast amounts of data needs to be in place. Such a system can be expensive and overwhelming for firms with limited financial, human, and managerial resources. Consulting firms, for a fee, provide customized information to exporters and importers.

PRODUCT ADAPTATION

One of the management issues that firms face is whether to adapt its product for the markets it wants to serve or make products that can be sold across various markets with no or few changes. The standardized product approach is consistent with the global strategy; adapting products to different markets reflects the multidomestic strategy.

Firms that are primarily oriented towards the domestic market do not usually design products for the foreign markets. Those firms that cater primarily to homogeneous markets are also less likely to have an awareness of the advantage of adapting products for overseas markets. In contrast, firms that sell to a heterogeneous market at home are more apt to recognize the value of and indeed make the necessary changes to meet customer approval. Of course, firms producing a "global" product, by definition, have little need to alter it for foreign customers. As discussed in Chapter 4, some products are more suitable for standardization while others need to be adapted.

Firms in countries with smaller populations and in countries with liberal trade regimes have tended to grow by exporting. The domestic market is simply too small. Examples of such countries are Switzerland and the Netherlands. U.S. firms, in contrast, historically have paid little attention to foreign markets no doubt because of the large size, high income levels, and the sophistication of the domestic market. The generally lower income levels abroad and the relative isolation of the U.S. market from other major developed markets also contribute to the lack of U.S. participation in foreign markets. An insufficient understanding of the cultural characteristics of consumers in many foreign countries provided another obstacle. This situation has markedly changed in recent years, though, as the domestic U.S. market has matured and foreign markets have blossomed. The potential for export earnings increases where the product is designed keeping in mind the needs of the consumer. Exporters are often disappointed when a product, a hit at home, generates only lukewarm interest abroad. Table 5-4 offers a list of the sorts of changes that a firm may need to make to its products for them to be accepted abroad. In the service sector, Endemol Entertainment, a Dutch company, has been able to successfully adapt television shows for different markets in Europe. A show in which teams of male and female celebrities take part in a karaoke competition can be watched in France as "La Fureur," in the United Kingdom as "Night Fever," and

---

[14]*Business opportunities in Poland: A guide for American investors.* 1996. Embassy of the Republic of Poland.

Table 5-4	Product Adaptation
Foreign Market Characteristics	*Changes in Product*
Lower level of technical skills	Simplify the product; increase product tolerance levels; increase reliability; train local technicians
Lower level of literacy	Use symbols and pictures instead of text
Different language	Provide instruction and labeling in new language
Lower income levels	Lower price; eliminate features; reduce size; reduce quality; arrange for financing
High interest rates	Lower price; provide financing
Different climate	Redesign the product; change packaging
Isolated customers	Increase reliability; simplify product
Different measurement standards	Recalibrate product components; change size and/or capacity
Erratic or insufficient power supply	Increase tolerance levels; provide alternate energy source
Absence of repair facilities	Increase reliability; use standard and fewer components; arrange for after-sales service

Source: Robinson, Richard. 1980. *International Business Management, 2/E.* Hinsdale, Illinois: The Dryden Press. With permission of the author.

under other names in Belgium, Italy, and Germany. John de Mol, one of the owners of the company said, *"There are hardly any borders in television. A successful format in Holland works in 95 percent of cases, if you can adjust for local culture. . . . We have the advantage of being Dutch. We operate from a small country, so the outside world is so large that we are used to adjusting to local tastes, rather than saying our way is best."*[15]

Adapting products for a foreign market can be expensive and time consuming with no assurance that an "adapted" product will be successful. A firm's willingness, capacity, and resources to adapt its products are factors that should be considered. Especially where potential export orders hinge on making samples that conform to the importer's specific requirements, the exporter runs the risk of having locked a large portion of its resources into a project that may ultimately prove futile. As the exporter invests more and more to create a product that matches the importer's exacting specifications, the exporter becomes more and more beholden to the importer's demands and needs. To the extent a particular market is deemed important for strategic reasons, the firm should spend the resources and the time to adapt its products to ensure a credible presence in that market. General Motors' Saturn division, for example, changed its cars by installing right-hand drive steering wheel and other features such as folding side mirrors (useful in Japan's narrow streets) in an effort to sell them in Japan.[16] Failure to adapt a product may lead to a firm being locked out of a market altogether. However, some products have appeal abroad precisely because they are seen as different or unique to a country (e.g., movies made in Hollywood).[17] Standardization saves money and allows the firm to capture the gains that accrue from economies of scale. Management Focus 5-2 dis-

---

[15]Gapper, John. 1999, January 15. Selling soap to Europe's viewers. *Financial Times,* p. 20.
[16]Shuchman, Lisa. 1998, August 25. How does GM's Saturn sell cars in Japan? Very slowly. *The Wall Street Journal,* pp. B1, B4.
[17]Barth, Steve. 1998, March. Exporting fantasy. *World Trade,* pp. 40–45.

MANAGEMENT FOCUS 5-2

THE U.S. WAY CATCHES ON IN EUROPE

Less than nine years after it opened its first store in the United Kingdom in 1987, Gap, a U.S. clothing retail chain, had 71 stores in three European countries. The casual clothes had been a big hit with younger Europeans who had grown up watching Gap advertisements on MTV or U.S. fashions on favorite rock and movie stars.

For Gap and other U.S. retailers, the main reason for expanding into Europe was stagnating sales in the home market. For European merchants, though, the arrival of the U.S. stores threw their business into turmoil. In the last 10 years, the share of women's clothing sold through independent retailers in Italy had dropped to two-thirds from three-quarters, and in France from half to one-third. U.S. firms were exporting not just a fashion sensibility but ways of doing business that were transforming retailing in Europe.

Of course, it had not been easy for the Americans. Because malls were still rare, chains like the Gap had to bid for high-rent sites on city streets. In some countries, such as Germany and the Netherlands, store operating hours were restricted. In the United States, the Gap opened 59 of its Old Navy stores in the first year of that venture; in the United Kingdom, it took 10 years to open that many Gap stores.

U.S. retailers often began in the United Kingdom because, after deregulation in the 1980s, bureaucratic hurdles and costs became lower than in other European countries. With weaker unions and lower social security tax payments, labor costs in U.K. could be 50 to 60 percent cheaper than in Germany.

Did Gap change its formula for success at home when in Europe? No. To assure low prices, Gap contracted for deliveries of clothing from manufacturers in low-wage countries like Spain and Portugal. To stay in touch with changing fashions, the company fed new designs and colors into its stores every four to six weeks, compared with four or five times a year for other European retailers. Moreover, wherever the practice was legal, Gap continually cleared inventory by lowering prices on slow-moving items, rather than relying on seasonal sales.

Companies such as Gap were accustomed to these activities from their operations in the United States where the environment is highly competitive and the market huge. Gap executives had no doubt that all their products were marketable in Europe. "We feel that each of our corporate brands—Gap, Gap Kids, Baby Gap, Banana Republic, and Old Navy Clothing Company—can be successful overseas," said William Fisher, the president of Gap International.

Source: Tagliabue, John. 1996, April 24. Enticing Europe's shoppers. *The New York Times,* pp. D1, D20.

---

cusses how a U.S. clothing chain succeeded in Western Europe aided by a fascination with popular American culture and a competitive aggressiveness shaped at home.

CHOICE OF CHANNELS

A key question for management is whether the firm should undertake the tasks necessary to move the products from the home country to the overseas customer by itself or whether it should employ an external specialized agency (e.g., wholesaler, export houses, or agents). In making this decision, the firm has to consider several factors such as its own experience and capabilities with exporting (or importing), and the desirability of establishing direct links with the overseas market (or supplier). The nature of the product and the size of the transactions and potential profits also figure prominently in any decision. A firm must assess its long-term goals on how to cater to the foreign market as well as developing in-house competency, and then consider the abilities, experience, and fees of the external agency in light of those goals.

A firm has numerous choices when it comes to choosing a **channel** for exporting (or importing). It can sell its products directly to the final consumer in the foreign country using the postal service, overnight delivery courier services, or shipping firms. Dell Computer Company sold computers in China over the Internet.[18] A firm can also ship its products to an overseas location and then distribute them to final customers through the postal system using a catalog to describe the wares as is done by L.L. Bean, a U.S. outdoors clothing company, in Japan. Or it can sell the products to an export house that sells them to an import house in the foreign country who then provides them to wholesalers, who in turn distributes through retailers to the final consumer. A group of Italian companies in machine tools and related technologies industries created an Italian Technology Association in New Jersey. This joint marketing effort was set up as a way to reduce the costs of launching exports to the United States. The association had about 20 employees handling sales and service activities on behalf of its 15 members.[19]

The emergence of Web sites and e-commerce has resulted in disintermediation, or cutting out intermediaries. By enabling exporters and final importers to communicate directly, wholesalers and retailers are being bypassed. In Japan, where distribution channels are complex and multilayered and often served as a barrier to foreign exporters, e-commerce offers a unique opportunity to overcome this barrier. However, the growth of e-commerce in Japan can be constrained by high telecom charges, low penetration of personal computers, overall economic conditions, and lack of Japanese-language Internet applications.[20] Table 5-5 presents some of the many channel alternatives that exist. International channels of distribution usually tend to be longer, more expensive, and more numerous than in the domestic market. Selecting the correct channel often assures success in the overseas market.

Using agents, wholesalers, import houses overseas, or other intermediaries is usually necessary to avoid the huge costs that reaching the final customer on one's own may

Table 5-5	Alternative Channels
Exporting Country	*Importing Country*
Exporter sells to/through ⟶	Final buyer directly
↦Web site/Internet ⟶	Franchises——Final buyer
↦Export house ⟶	Sales branch——Final buyer
↦Resident foreign buyer ⟶	Sales branch——Distributors——Final buyer
↦Export association ⟶	Import house——Distributors——Final buyer
↳Trading company ⟶	Distributors——Final buyer
⟶	Sales subsidiary——Final buyer
⟶	Sales subsidiary——Distributors——Final buyer

---

[18]Lee, Linda. 1998, April 27. U.S. theme can make a film a tough sell abroad. *The New York Times,* p. C8.
[19]Einhorn, Bruce. 1999, February 15. Foreign rivals vs. the Chinese: If you can't beat 'em. *Business Week,* p. 78.
[20]Nusbaum, Alexandra. 2000, January 5. Web cuts out an entire order of middlemen. *Financial Times,* p. 14.

entail. Sometimes, a small exporter may piggyback on larger, well-established players, especially if the product is seen as complementary. For instance, Amstel beer (from Netherlands) was distributed in the United States through Budweiser's trucking system and distributorship. In contrast, BMW, the German automaker, entered the Japanese market by investing in a network of its own distributors. In the 1990s, BMW was the number one imported car in number of units sold in Japan. BMW's action was contrary to what was generally recommended for accessing the Japanese market: seek an alliance with a local Japanese firm. This advice is usually true for smaller exporters and those with a less well-known product or brand name. Setting up one's own channels of distribution is not only expensive, it is also time consuming and requires hiring and training proper personnel, renting warehouses and other facilities with the necessary infrastructure, and arranging for imports through customs, all requiring managerial attention that the firm may be hard pressed to provide, especially if it has not been marketing oriented. The attention of managers, therefore, in such cases is to identify potential distributors in the foreign country who would be willing to carry the exporter's line. The role of the distributor has to be clearly established especially with regard to title of the goods, exclusivity of dealership, customer service, and payment terms.

Choosing the right distributor can have strategic advantages. In the long run, the distributor, should the relationship succeed, may become a licensee or a joint venture partner if the exporter decides to expand its involvement in the foreign country. The distributor is a potentially invaluable source of information about the foreign market. Where the exporter is dependent on the overseas distributor for market intelligence in addition to sales, the bargaining power clearly is tilted toward the distributor. In the case of certain products, particularly industrial products, the exporter may need to place trained personnel in the export market to provide after-sales service or to repair breakdowns. Alternately, employees of distributors would be trained to provide such services. Management Focus 5-3 illustrates the key role played by distributors in ensuring the successful marketing of a product.

Accessing distribution channels is obviously important to the exporter. Inability to access a channel will prevent the firm from establishing itself in the foreign market, especially when a firm is a latecomer to a market. When it does come, it finds that other competing firms have exploited the first mover advantages by having signed exclusive deals with existing distributors. Distributors seek special incentives to carry the exporters' product line, which obviously increases costs.

The first step in establishing an overseas sales network is determining whether to select a foreign **agent** or **distributor.** An agent uses the firm's product literature and samples to present the product to potential buyers. Agents usually work on a commission basis, assume no risk or responsibilities, and are under contract for a definite period of time. Agents give the exporter the advantages of greater control over performance, resale, and pricing factors. A foreign distributor is a merchant who purchases goods from U.S. exporters, often at a discount, and resells them at a profit. The distributor will normally handle noncompetitive but complementary product lines. Generally, the distributor carries an inventory of products and a sufficient supply of spare parts at facilities staffed by trained personnel to provide normal servicing. Payment terms and length of association, as with the agent, are established by contract.

Many firms that are new to exporting prefer distributors who allow them to minimize their economic and management involvement. A distributor provides the exporter

SUCCESS OF CORONA BEER

In 1998, Corona soared past Heineken to become the leading imported beer in the United States and the tenth best-selling beer in the country. In less than a decade, Corona's manufacturer, Grupo Modelo S.A., had transformed an obscure Mexican beer into an internationally recognized global brand. The key to Modelo's success lay in appealing to Mexicans living in the United States while at the same time giving it a special cachet among U.S. college students.

In the late 1970s, Antonino Fernandez Rodriguez, then Modelo's chief executive, decided to export Corona to the United States in direct competition against Heineken, Beck's, and other European beers that dominated the imported niche of the U.S. beer market. Corona's sales in the United States were sluggish until the mid-1980s when one of Modelo's U.S. distributors—Barton Beers Ltd. of Chicago—came up with a clever marketing strategy: selling Corona to young American beer drinkers, many of whom had spent spring break at Cancun or Cabo San Lucas. Barton created television spots featuring attractive young people in tropical surroundings, under palm trees on sun-drenched beaches.

Separately, another of Corona's U.S. importers, the Gambrinus Company of San Antonio, targeted another growing market: the millions of Mexicans living in the United States. It advertised the beer using Spanish language advertisements with music instantly recognizable to Mexicans and with images of Mexico's pastel-colored colonial cities and pre-Columbian ruins flashing across the television screen.

Modelo set Corona's U.S. prices above domestic beers but slightly lower than Heineken and many other imports, which added to Corona's appeal. The beer benefited from the rise of a group of more selective drinkers. As Bill Hackett, president of Barton Beers observed, "People figure that if they drink less, they may as well drink better."

As sales in the United States took off, so did the company's share price, even during the severe recession in the mid-1990s when the Mexican Stock Exchange performed poorly. While still focused on the American market, company officials turned to push Corona in Europe, Israel, and Japan.

Source: Wills, Rick. 1999, May 28. The king of imported beers. *The New York Times*, pp. C1, C2.

with a local sales force and office, the ability to import into the distributor's country, and knowledge of local customs and business practices. The exporter reduces its risk because the distributor will buy on its account and resell.

Locating Candidates   To build a distributor or agent network, an exporter needs to locate candidates, select and appoint a firm, and train and work with the foreign representative selected. The selection of a representative should be approached carefully: many countries have laws that make termination of relations difficult. Agents in particular enjoy extensive legal protection emphasizing statutory notice periods and termination compensation covering goodwill, agent expenditure on behalf of the principal, and reimbursement to the agent for employee severance costs. Not every representative appointed will perform as expected and the exporter must be prepared for termination of the relationship.

The best place to locate representatives and foreign buyers is at trade fairs, both at home and abroad. In the United States, lists of prospective agents or distributors can be obtained from state and federal government agencies, exporters of related but noncompetitive products or services, the international departments of U.S. banks, freight forwarders and carriers, port authorities, chambers of commerce, foreign consulates, and trade promotion offices in the U.S.

In selecting a distributor, the following guidelines should be kept in mind:

- The distributor should be organized to import products and have the physical facilities, and financial and organization strength to import, warehouse, market, extend credit, and collect payments.
- The distributor should have a good working relationship with customs and other governmental agencies.
- The distributor should be willing to consider new methods of marketing and new products.
- The distributor should have the financial capability to develop the exporter's business to its ultimate potential in the country concerned.
- The distributor should relate well to the exporting firm's product and markets.
- The exporter should have a high degree of confidence in the trustworthiness and business reputation of a distributor.
- The exporter should be able to communicate easily with the distributor verbally, through writing, and electronically.
- The distributor should be able to service the exporter's products and train its personnel and customers on product maintenance and use.

The last criterion is particularly important because of the distance between the exporter and distributor. Once the best candidate is selected, an agreement has to be negotiated. An initial question to resolve is exclusive versus nonexclusive representation. The best candidates, particularly in small countries, often are interested only in an exclusive rights relationship, which can pose risks for the exporter. One option is to use a "trial" period with the preferred candidate prior to awarding an exclusive rights appointment.

In addition, the exporter should investigate and review the financial records of the distributor. A check of business and credit references is also a must, using such sources as bank references, U.S. Department of Commerce, credit reference manuals, and interviews with the distributor's other suppliers. Before signing any agreement with a distributor, the exporter should study the host country laws with regard to terminating distributor and agent relationships.

It is always wise to secure a legally binding contract with the distributor to govern the relationship. The final draft should be negotiated in person preferably with the help of legal counsel. Topics such agreements would cover include the geographical scope of sales, definition of products, right to carry the products of competitors, distributor's responsibilities for maintaining inventory and providing market information, the size of consignments, credit and shipping terms, pricing, rights to modify or discontinue products by the exporter, limitations on product warranties, and termination conditions.

Successful relationships depend on the mutual trust and understanding between the parties. Once appointed, distributors or agents should be provided with as much information and contact as the exporter's domestic distributors. Distributors should be provided with updates on new products, new techniques, and new applications. Where contracts have to be terminated, the best means is through mutual agreement and by obtaining a letter of withdrawal from the relationship from the representative. Arbitration is often the recommended way to resolve disputes.

Many U.S. retail companies such as the Gap, Blockbuster Video, Foot Locker, Toys R Us, and Espirit De Corp sell their products through their own stores abroad. In contrast, Benetton, an Italian clothing manufacturer, expanded in the United States by granting franchises to independent operators to open retail stores. Franchising as a foreign market entry method is discussed in the next chapter. In other cases, a firm opens a representative office in a major commercial city in the foreign country where it expects to win substantial export orders.[21] Such offices enable potential and current exporters to have a formal presence in the foreign market, be closer to their customers, gather market intelligence, liaise with host government officials, and appear to be committed to the market. These offices can also serve as the focal point for any deeper involvement in that market should the firm decide to do so in the future. However, setting up such offices and staffing and operating them can be quite costly. The average annual cost for a full-time representative office in Beijing, China, including salary and accommodations for a foreigner as chief representative, is approximately $700,000.

Foreign trade also requires special attention and additional resources to deal with matters such as meeting home and foreign country regulations, customs, transportation, and packing rules, and exchanging currencies and exchange rate changes. In this context, many firms resort to using the services of specialist organizations that provide every conceivable type of assistance needed to successfully complete an export or import transaction.[22] For instance, importers benefit from using customs brokers (licensed by the U.S. Customs Service in the United States) who provide such services as determining the proper classification under the U.S. Import Tariff rules, dealing with shipping documents and customs clearance, and arranging for storage and necessary bonds as well as delivery to inland destinations.

Many governments offer tax incentives, subsidies, and other forms of assistance to encourage exports. In the United States, an exporter can obtain a 15-percent tax exclusion on earnings from international sales if it uses a **foreign sales corporation** (FSC). An FSC is an offshore subsidiary of U.S. exporters, which acts as an agent for export sales. Boeing Company, the biggest user of this tax opportunity, saved $130 million in U.S. income taxes in 1998, 12 percent of its earnings that year.[23] FSCs have been deemed illegal by the WTO and their future is therefore uncertain. Federal and state agencies, such as the New Jersey Department of Commerce, also provide information about foreign markets and trade fairs and sponsor trade missions. For example, the International Trade Administration of the U.S. Department of Commerce has trade specialists who provide individualized export counseling; identify potential agents and distributors for specific products in foreign countries; develop reports that evaluate potential trading partners, including background information, standing in local community, creditworthiness, and overall reliability and suitability; and collect and disseminate trade statistics and data both through print and electronically.

Often small and medium-sized manufacturers, to avoid the complications that foreign trade appears to pose, use Export Management Companies (EMCs) and Export Trading Companies (ETCs) to serve as their export departments. The main distinction between

---

[21]Rothstein, Jay. 1996. Easing your way into China. *The China Business Review.* January–February, pp. 30–32.
[22]*Trade Link.* New Jersey's international business magazine. 1995.
[23]Magnusson, Paul. 1999, August 16. U.S. exporters get the word: Guilty. *Business Week*, p. 42.

the two is that ETCs can purchase a firm's products domestically and sell them abroad using established facilities and overseas contacts. Both contract with manufacturers to solicit and transact business for a commission, salary, or retainer plus commission.

Most EMCs and ETCs provide a multitude of services that include marketing research, appointing overseas distributors or commission representatives, exhibiting a client's product at international trade shows, and handling financing, advertising, shipping, and documentation. All the U.S. manufacturer has to do is fill the order.

Japanese Trading Companies   Although international trading companies can be found in several countries, those in Japan are among the best known and successful of export and import intermediaries. Known as *sogoshosha,* their growth has been linked with the development of Japan's modern industries. Some of the leading sogoshosha are Mitsui, Mitsubishi, C. Itoh, Marubeni, Nissho-Iwai, and Sumitomo. Historically they have accounted for nearly half of Japan's imports and more than three-fifths of its exports. In recent years though, as many Japanese industrial companies (e.g., Sony and Toyota) have expanded their international operations and have gained expertise in overseas marketing and production, the reliance on the traditional sogoshosha has diminished.

What do the sogoshosha do? They are involved both in domestic distribution of goods and services and in export and import transactions on behalf of diverse Japanese firms. By engaging in business on a worldwide basis, they reap economies of scales, are able to link buyers and sellers of widely disparate products anywhere in the world, and provide a variety of supporting services such as financing, insurance, transportation, warehousing, and market intelligence.

The ability to function effectively is helped by the creation of a sophisticated and state-of-the-art communication network among the firm's far-flung offices, customers, and affiliates. For instance, Mitsui & Company uses four computerized centers: Tokyo, covering all Asia; New York, spanning North and Latin America; London, encompassing Europe and Africa; and Sydney, covering Oceania. Satellites connect these centers and phone, computers, and mail also link local offices in more than 80 countries. These systems operate day and night because somewhere in the world, at any given time, deals are being made and customers need to be serviced. Because of the diversity of their business, their clientele, and geographic theater of their operations, sogoshosha emphasize both long-term relationships while being flexible in their approach and arrangements. Profit margins are slim, but on huge turnovers, even small percentages translate into billions of dollars.

What can a client expect from using a Japanese sogoshosha? Sogoshosha provide the client with expert knowledge about a particular market. Smaller firms, as discussed earlier, are often unable to gather relevant data about foreign markets. Sogoshosha, through years of extensive business dealings in numerous markets, have built up an enormous database about individual countries and companies. The client can rely on a sogoshosha's ability to deliver up-to-date and reliable information about particular and potential markets.

Second, sogoshosha, given their huge economies of scale, are able to provide their services to small firms and firms that are financially and managerially weak, at an attractive price. The marginal cost of servicing another customer for a sogoshosha, especially with regard to tapping into its huge information network, is minimal. Sometimes, large firms use sogoshosha's informational and distribution networks for the purpose of developing new markets and to service markets not equipped with their own distributors.

Third, sogoshosha provide exporters access to markets that would be otherwise impossible or too costly to identify. Because sogoshosha deal in a large variety of goods and services for clients all over the world, they can effectively barter goods and services among themselves. Thus, a Costa Rican firm that wants to sell bananas and buy fertilizers can use the sogoshosha, which has clients who need bananas and sell fertilizers. For the sogoshosha, these transactions bring out their ability to serve as effective intermediaries, linking together numerous buyers and sellers who would not be able to do business on a bilateral basis with the same ease and inexpense.

A final service that the sogoshosha provides is in financing business transactions. The sogoshosha, again because of its global scope of activities, can access financial markets, and obtain the most economical terms for loans, which it, in turn, advances to both exporters and importers. The clients are spared the financial risk, including currency risks (discussed later) of international trading, and provided the necessary export financing. By dealing with numerous currencies, sogoshosha have both the experience and the ability to minimize the risks that come with fluctuations in foreign exchange rates.

PRICING STRATEGIES

Broadly speaking, a firm can choose between three alternative policies with regard to pricing.

1. A standard worldwide base price
2. A domestic price and a standard export price
3. A market differentiated price

The standard worldwide pricing (followed by the Swiss maker of Swatch watches) allows the firm to present a global product and include all manufacturing, distribution, and overhead costs. Because cost structures vary from country to country as does economic conditions, the standard worldwide pricing may not allow the firm to be successful in all markets. Such a pricing strategy does not distinguish between the domestic and foreign markets, but considers both the same.

An export price separate from the domestic price can be justified on the grounds that the product is being sold to two different markets. The export price can be lower or higher than the domestic price. A lower price may occur if the exported good is of lower quality or where the research and development costs as well as most other overhead have been recouped from domestic sales. Another reason is to engage in the practice of **dumping,** which is defined as the sale of a product in an export market at a price lower than that normally charged in the domestic market. Dumping is a contentious issue in international trade, and many countries have laws and policies that bar dumping. In the United States, dumping is determined to have occurred when imports sold in the U.S. market are priced either at levels that represent less than the cost of production plus an 8 percent profit margin or at levels below those prevailing in the producing country and, in addition, results in injury, destruction, or prevention of the establishment of a U.S. industry. The International Trade Commission in the U.S. Department of Commerce handles complaints from U.S. firms about dumping in the U.S. market by foreign exporters. Fines and damages can be imposed on exporters found to be dumping in the United States. Management Focus 5-4 discusses the case of Chilean salmon being dumped in the United States.

MANAGEMENT FOCUS 5-4

SMELLY FISH?

In July 1997, the International Trade Commission (ITC) accepted a case filed by eight U.S. salmon farmers in Maine, which claimed that they were being unfairly priced out of business by inexpensive imports from Chile. The lawyer for the group that employed about 440 workers argued that a rapid, uncontrolled expansion of the farmed salmon industry around the world had resulted in an over-capacity. To stay in business, Chilean producers were willing to just cover cash costs to keep growing. He charged that action in turn translated into prices at 40 percent below full production costs. "In 18 months and with prices the way they are, we are goners," he said.

The Chileans had an explanation: they have better weather and sea conditions than U.S. farmers, cheap and plentiful feed from the country's big fishmeal industry, and relatively moderate labor costs. Furthermore, the industry had invested heavily in such new technologies as computerized feeding systems and lights that even out maturity rates. With regard to marketing, they had spent a fortune creating the ready-to-eat filets, shorn with scissors of pin bones, which U.S. home cooks preferred. Said Francisco Ruiz, chairman of the Association of Chilean Salmon and Trout Farmers, whose members accounted for 40 percent of all salmon sales in the United States, "We've made the product user-friendly and available at a consistent quality year round." The head of Darden Restaurants, which owned 656 Red Lobster restaurants, Roger Chapin,

agreed with this assessment noting that fresh salmon steaks were a best-selling item in his chain. "We buy 1.7 million pounds of salmon annually, 70 percent of it from Chile." Supporting the Chileans in the dispute, he continued by saying, "U.S. producers can't manage the volume and with their labor costs, they can't manage the pin bones."

An adverse decision from the ITC would hurt a company like Eicosal SA, a fish farming company based in Puerto Montt, Chile, which had annual sales of $22 million. In 1990, Eicosal produced 600 tons of fish from its pens in the fjords of southern Chile. With investments from its Chilean, Norwegian, and Dutch owners, Eicosal's 650 workers now sold 8,000 tons of salmon and sea trout annually, 30 percent of it to the United States. The general manager of the company rejected the charge of dumping. He said that for the last five years, "We have been making money. That includes cost of sales, depreciation, everything." Another loser would be U.S. consumers including patrons at Red Lobster restaurants because their baked salmon entrée would cost more.

The ITC in its ruling sided with the complaint and imposed duties on Chilean salmon. Fortunately for the Chileans, relatively modest tariffs, ranging from 0.16 percent to 10.69 percent, were imposed. Ironically, Chilean salmon, which had 40 percent of the U.S. salmon market, reached that position after Norwegian salmon were slapped with countervailaing taxes in 1990 for dumping in the U.S. market.

Source: Friedland, Jonathan. 1997, October 13. Chilean salmon farmers test free trade. *The Wall Street Journal,* p. A18; Mulligan, Mark. 1999, October 27. Chilean fish farmers fend off poachers, predators, and lawyers. *Financial Times,* p. 26.

A higher export price reflects the fact that export operations are more risky, expensive, and time consuming than domestic sales. Often transportation, packaging, insurance, customs duties, and distribution costs add up to a substantial sum, which pushes up the final cost to the foreign distributor or final consumer. Table 5-6 illustrates how the price escalates when sending a product overseas. In many cases, the price that the final consumer is faced with is several times the price quoted by the exporter. Where such prices are substantially higher than those of domestically produced goods, the imported product is obviously at a disadvantage. Sometimes the product may have to

Table 5-6	Price Escalation in Exporting		
		Domestic Market	*Export Market*
Factory price		$10.00	$10.00
Domestic freight		1.00	1.00
		$11.00	$11.00
Export documentation			0.75
Ocean freight and insurance			2.25
			$14.00
Import duty (10 percent of landed cost)			1.40
			$15.40
Wholesaler markup (15 percent on cost)		1.65	
		$12.65	
Importer markup (25 percent on cost)			3.85
			$19.25
Retail markup (50 percent on cost)		6.33	9.63
Final consumer price		$18.98	$28.88

Source: Albaum, Gerald, Strandskov, Jesper and Duerr, Edwin, *International Marketing and Export Management, 3/E.* © Addison Wesley Longman Ltd. 1998.

be positioned as a high-end product and targeted toward a consumer group different from its home country target market. The opening vignette discussed how the Chilean fertilizer company priced its product. Thus, a product may be priced differently in different markets. For instance, Sara Lee of the United States withdrew its Wonderbra women's underwear from the Chinese market after disappointing sales because the product was priced beyond the reach of most Chinese consumers. The company had overestimated the purchasing power of the Chinese consumer and had entered the Chinese market aiming at wealthy consumers who could afford the $36 to $72 for the product. The cost of a standard bra made by a local company sold for a tenth that of Wonderbra.[24] In India, in contrast, Reebok, the sports footwear company, initially found that the prices of its shoes approximated that of a junior bureaucrat's monthly salary. The company felt that to protect its brand quality, it had to resort to premium pricing. Thus, by pricing shoes at $50 to $75, Reebok was able to present itself as a prestige brand and in 1997, sold 300,000 pairs in the country.

In setting the base price for goods and services to be exported, the key variables are obviously production costs including overhead and out of pocket expenses, the elasticity of demand, the nature and extent of competition, the prestige value of the brand name and product, and the desired profit margin. The final cost will be determined by the costs of transportation, packaging, customs duties, exchange rate fluctuations, profit margins of intermediaries, government price control regimens, government subsidies, behavior of competitors, inflationary pressures in the export market, and market conditions. These factors, in turn, are influenced by the purpose of the exporter's pricing

---

[24]Harding, James. 1999, June 16. Wonderbra fails to lift off in cost-conscious Shanghai. *Financial Times,* p. 12; Nicholson, Mark. 1998, August 18. Where a pair of trainers costs as much as a cow. *Financial Times,* p. 10.

strategy, which might include penetration of a new market, obtaining a satisfactory or maximum return on investment, maintaining market share, meeting a specified profit goal, securing the largest possible market share, meeting a specific sales goal, profit maximization, meeting competition, presenting a high-end exclusive image, or charging whatever the market will bear.

Managers need to be familiar with the relationship between the volume of goods exported and the cost of the goods. Usually, unit costs decline as the size of output increases because of efficiencies that accrue through scale economies. Thus, while a firm may initially price a product low to enter a foreign market, increasing sales volume in turn reduces its costs and may indeed allow it to retain its low price advantage. In an innovative pricing technique, Chrysler, a U.S. automobile company, anxious to increase sales in Japan, offered its Neon cars to Japanese consumers for use for one year at the nominal price of 14,200 yen ($117) a month. Users who were not satisfied could return the car after a year at no additional cost.[25]

In 1997, General Motors' Saturn division began a concerted effort to sell its cars in the Japanese market. It priced its cars at about $14,000—competitive with Japanese models and below what most foreign imports cost. Saturn's strategy was to compete with Japanese rivals in their home market as an everyday car—unlike the upscale positioning other foreign car producers opted for. However, sales had been small, about 1,400 vehicles in 16 months. Analysts argued that Japanese consumers wanted something different from a foreign car, something that stood out. Distinctive European models accounted for about two-thirds of the imported cars sold in Japan. Successful imports from the United States included such quintessentially American cars as GM's Cadillac Seville and Chrysler's Jeep Cherokee. By trying to be an everyday car, Saturn found itself competing with dozens of different models from Japanese car companies.[26] These examples suggest that pricing is just one of several dimensions that exporters have to consider.

Figure 5-2 illustrates how prices are set in the United States and Japan. In Japan, the emphasis is on target cost which is determined by planned selling price minus the desired profit. For instance, if the planned selling price is 100 yen per unit and the desired profit is 10 yen per unit, design, engineering, and supplier prices have to fit within this target. In the United States though, cost is determined after design, engineering, and supplier considerations have been made; if the cost is too high, the process cycles back to the design stage.

Transfer Pricing   An important concept in international business is **transfer pricing,** which was discussed in Chapter 3. In setting transfer prices, the firm must consider the income tax rates, export or import tariff rates, and rules on repatriating profits in the countries the firm does business in. Among the approaches to transfer pricing are (1) transfer at direct cost, (2) transfer at direct cost plus a markup for profit and overhead, (3) transfer at market based price, and (4) transfer at "arms-length" price. No one method is perfect for all situations. Transfer prices are set at headquarters where managers have the entire picture of the firm's operations in their perspective. However transfer prices are set, they affect the prices of products and profitability margins.

---

[25]Nakamoto, Michiyo, and Jonathan Annells. 1997, March 6. Neon offer highlights U.S. troubles. *Financial Times,* p. 4.

[26]Shuchman, Lisa. 1998, August 25. How does GM's Saturn sell cars in Japan? Very slowly. *The Wall Street Journal,* pp. B1, B4.

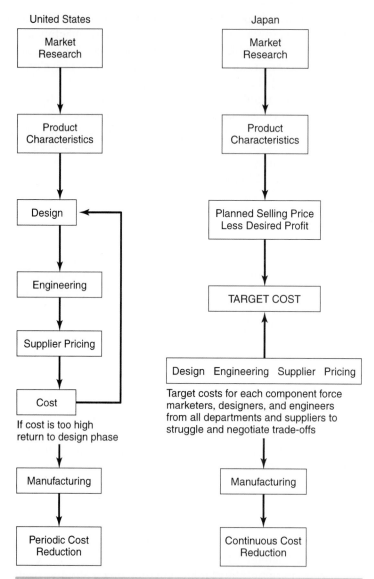

FIGURE 5-2 Setting Prices in the United States and Japan

Source: Strategy Pure and Simple: How Winning CEOs Outthink Their Competition, by Michel Robert © 1993. McGraw-Hill. Reprinted with permission of The McGraw-Hill Companies.

Trade Terms   Exporters and importers should be familiar with terminology used to quote the prices of their products. Two systems of **trade terms** are used: INCOTERMS (developed by the International Chamber of Commerce) and the Revised American Foreign Trade Definitions. Trade terms such as FOB (free on board) and CIF (cost, insurance, and freight) indicate what is included in the quoted price and whose responsibility it is. A price for a product quoted as, say $100,000 CIF, would mean that it includes, in addition to the price of the product, the cost of the insurance to the destination as well the freight or shipping charges. The most commonly used quotation in international trade is the CIF.

The price quoted would differ depending on what the exporter includes or leaves to the importer to pay. The quoted price is part of the marketing strategy and has to be carefully considered. Among the issues are the exporter's need for cash, in which case quote ex factory; the normal practice in the business, which is important to facilitate comparison if other bidders are quoting with a particular trade term; rules of the importing government; and the request of the importer. From the importer's point of view, a CIF quotation means it does not have to pay any charges until the goods arrive at the port of destination. Other factors to consider are the exporter's willingness or ability to handle the variety of tasks that shipping, packaging, and insuring entail.

FINANCIAL ISSUES IN EXPORTING AND IMPORTING

FOREIGN EXCHANGE RATES

As indicated earlier, exports and imports are vulnerable to fluctuations in foreign exchange rates. A decline in the value of the home currency would normally make a firm's products or services cheaper to customers overseas, which tends to increase sales. Conversely, an appreciation in the value of the home currency would make the products more expensive, which in turn would mean reduced demand. Both the exporter and their importer may see their sales and profits affected by the direction of the change in the currencies. Prices of imported inputs may go up and finished products, now more expensive, may have to be positioned differently in the home market. Managers may also have to reduce their profit margins to hold prices down, or withdraw totally from a market, or have to cut costs to keep their products competitive. In 1998, Minnesota Mining & Manufacturing Co., popularly known as 3M, reported poorer results because of the appreciation of the U.S. dollar.[27] It took more profit overseas to earn a dollar in the United States. Currency translations led to lower earnings and profits and sent the company's share prices tumbling. The high dollar also made the company's products more expensive, which leads to falling sales. As the dollar gained strength against East Asian currencies, customers there had to pay more for the same imported products they bought just weeks earlier. The company had major exposure in Asia—about 17 percent of its revenue and 23 percent of its earnings came from that region in 1997. And its profit margins were also disproportionately higher in Asia because of the high-tech, high margin products it sold there. Compounding the problems was stiff competition in 3M's domestic market in the United States, primarily from importers, whose depreciated currencies allowed them to sell in the United States at a discount.

Because all international business activities are affected by exchange rates, managers usually seek the help of specialists to manage this form of financial risk. Larger firms have in-house personnel while smaller firms may rely on advice from their banks or leave the exports to intermediaries (e.g., export houses) who are much more familiar with foreign exchange markets.

---

[27]Quintanilla, Carl. 1998, June 16. 3M expects earnings to decline due to Asia's turmoil. *The Wall Street Journal*, p. B4.

Various techniques exist to protect the firm against adverse exchange rates. This issue was discussed in Appendix 1-1. Of course, a firm may avoid foreign exchange risk by signing contracts that require payments in the home currency. This method, however, shifts the risk to the buyer. Firms may also negotiate a clause in the contract that allows for price adjustments should exchange rates change. Ipeco, a U.K. company that sells pilot seats to airlines and earns 60 percent of its revenues from Boeing of the United States, protected itself from a rising pound sterling by expanding its currency hedging activities and through gaining greater economies of scale by raising output to match Boeing's expansion.[28]

REAL EXCHANGE RATES

Our discussion has focused on nominal exchange rates, or the prevailing exchange rate, as reported in newspapers and quoted by banks. It is useful, however, to understand the notion of **real exchange rate** because they affect the competitiveness of firms. Real exchange rates take into consideration the inflation rates in the exporting and importing countries. A simple example will illustrate this point.

Assume that a Mexican firm is selling bicycles to Japan and the nominal exchange rate is 1 peso = 15 yen. Bicycles valued at 1,000 pesos are sold which translates in Japan into 15,000 yen. Let us also assume that a Japanese firm in Japan offers bicycles which are sold for 15,000 yen. Over the time period, say the prices have risen in Mexico by 10 percent because of inflation while in Japan, prices have risen by only 1 percent. The bicycles made in Mexico now cost 10 percent more or 1,100 pesos and are sold in Japan for 16,500 yen (@15 yen to the peso). On the other hand, the bicycles made in Japan are now selling for 15,150 yen. Because of the higher inflation rate in Mexico, the Mexican-made bicycles are now more expensive, even though the exchange rate has not changed. To remain competitive, the Mexican exporter will have to cut costs or reduce its profit margins.

What is the real exchange rate? We can calculate it as follows: (Inflation rate in Mexico/Inflation rate in Japan) × 100 or (1.1/1.01) × 100 = 1.089. This calculation states that the real exchange rate has risen by almost 9 percent (8.9). In order for the Mexican firm to remain competitive, nominal exchange rate would have to change to 1 peso = 13.77 yen (obtained by dividing 15,150 yen by 1,100 pesos), although it is currently at 1 peso = 15 yen. The manager of the Mexican firm should realize that the rise in real exchange rates adversely affects exports and conversely, a fall in real exchange rates is helpful. Another way to say it is that the Mexican peso is overvalued and thus, Mexican exports are hurt. For this reason, exporters need to keep a close watch on the movement of exchange rates.

TRADE FINANCING

International trade usually has major implications on the firm's working capital needs. Before payment is finally received from the importer, exporters need funds to produce and ship the goods overseas and importers need funds to store the goods before they are sold to the final customers. Because the time gap between the time a good is pro-

---

[28]Marsh, Peter. 1998, December 2. Exporter takes seat at Boeing's top table. *Financial Times*, p. 13.

duced and shipped and payment is received is usually longer in international transactions, managers need to have access to ample funds to meet their working capital needs.

Many financing methods are available. One such method is **factoring** in which the exporter sells its accounts receivable to the factor (a specialized financial institution or bank). Normally, the exporter would go to the factor before any contract is signed and shipment made and secure its willingness to buy the receivable. The factor will check out the credit rating of the prospective buyer before it agrees to buy the accounts receivable. Once the shipment is made, the exporter takes the necessary shipping documents to the factor for payment. The factor, in turn, collects the money through its representative (usually a correspondent bank) from the buyer.

Another well-established method is the use of a **letter of credit.** The importer establishes a commercial credit through its bank and specifies the condition under which payment would be made to the exporter. This letter of credit is sent to the exporter (or its bank) and acts as assurance to the exporter that it will receive payment for the goods shipped. To receive payment, the exporter presents to its bank (who is now in the role of a correspondent bank for the importer's bank), the necessary documents and invoice stating that the goods have been shipped. If the documents are in order and they are presented before the expiration date of the letter of credit, the exporter is paid in full.

Under both these methods, the exporter is assured of payment for goods shipped to importers. Payments are also received once the goods have been shipped and before they are actually in the hands of the customer, which may be several weeks later depending on travel times, customs clearances, and inland transportation. Of course, cash in advance is the surest way of receiving payment as well as to finance the costs of the goods and the transactions. This method is used in the case of uncertainty about receiving payment from the importer. For large transactions, partial payment in advance could be required.

Government organizations are available to help exporters financially. For example, the state of New Jersey's Economic Development Authority provides short-term working capital loans to help finance export activities of New Jersey's small businesses. The U.S. Small Business Administration, through its Export Revolving Line of Credit (ERLC) program provides guarantees of short-term financing for exporting firms. Under another program, the agency guarantees up to $1,000,000 of a loan to be used for the acquisition, construction, modernization, or expansion of facilities engaged in the production of goods and services involved in international trade. The Export-Import Bank of the U.S. (Eximbank) and Overseas Private Investment Corporation are two other U.S. government agencies that assist with export financing by guaranteeing short- and medium-term loans and by providing political risk insurance.

In some cases, importers themselves may need financial help to purchase the goods. Financing for importers is available from commercial banks. In addition, in many developing countries, funds for importing may be provided by international aid agencies and foreign governments. Most U.S. foreign economic assistance programs are administered by the Agency for International Development. This agency offers U.S. exporters opportunities to compete in the sales of goods or services to countries who will be using the aid provided by the United States to finance these imports.

Not all banks have the expertise to provide trade financing, and smaller firms may have a harder time obtaining assistance on affordable terms. For instance, in the United States, it is estimated that while small firms make up about 30 percent of U.S. exports, only about 150 to 200 of the country's 9,000 banks do a significant amount of trade financing for them.[29] Small firms, more often than their larger counterparts, need financial assistance to both export or import products. One of America's largest banks, NationsBank, offers an electronic trading system, known as TradeCard, for small and medium-sized companies. Under the system, the bank issues credit lines to importers based on a credit rating method similar to that used to issue corporate credit cards.

BARTER AND COUNTERTRADE ARRANGEMENTS

International trade, where purchases are paid for in kind (either goods or services) instead of cash, has been quite widespread and was common in the 1970s and 1980s. Today, many of these barter arrangements, referred to as **countertrade,** take highly sophisticated forms and are designed to achieve multiple goals on the part of both the exporter and the importer.

The primary pressure for countertrade arose because communist countries and many underdeveloped nations did not have the necessary freely convertible currency to pay for imported goods. Exporters who saw opportunities for sales in these countries agreed to novel "payment" arrangements for the goods they supplied. However, other reasons also explain why two parties may enter into a countertrade agreement, some of which are presented in Table 5-7. Countertrade arrangements are often entered into by governments (as opposed to individual firms) or required by a government.

The following is a brief description of the various forms of countertrade arrangements:

- *Pure barter.* Here the exporter agrees to accept products from the importer as payment. PepsiCo arranged with the then Soviet Union to supply Pepsi-Cola syrup and in exchange agreed to take Stolichnaya vodka as payment. PepsiCo sold the vodka and kept the receipts.
- *Clearing arrangements.* Two countries agree to exchange a number of products during a specified time period. The parties agree on the quantity and values to be exchanged and by the final settlement date any surpluses must be cleared up, usually by accepting more goods. The then Soviet Union entered into such arrangements with many developing countries such as India and Morocco.
- *Counterpurchase.* This approach uses two separate but linked contracts where (1) the exporter sells its products to an importer, and (2) the exporter agrees to purchase and market products from the importer (or other firms in the importer's country). The exporter keeps the receipts from selling the products.
- *Switch trading.* When one party has a good that the other party does not want, switch trading may be used. For example, a Danish firm agrees to sell dairy equipment worth 1 million krone to a Colombian firm in exchange for coffee of equivalent market value. The products are exchanged but the Danish firm does not really want the coffee. Using a switch specialist, the coffee is sold to a Japanese firm for 950,000 krone. The Danish firm gets the

---

[29]Fairclough, Gordon, and Matt Murray. 1998, February 24. Small banks expand their trade financing for exports. *The Wall Street Journal,* p. B2.

Table 5-7   Purposes for Countertrade

Exporter's Objectives	*Importer's Objectives*
Increased profits	Access necessary products
Enter a formerly inaccessible market	Conserve foreign currency reserves
Dispose of surplus production	Reduce debt burdens
Establish long-term relationships	Develop local industries
Make full use of production capacity	Establish long-term relationships

Source: Adapted from Albaum, Gerald, Jesper Strandskov, and Edwin Duerr. 1998. *International marketing and export management.* 3rd edition. Harlow, England: Addison Wesley Longman Publishing Company.

currency it wants less a small commission for the switch specialist. Because the Danish firm had planned all along to divest itself of the coffee, it would have incorporated the discount and the commission in the price for the dairy equipment.

- *Buyback.* In a buyback arrangement, the exporter supplies plant and equipment to the importer and agrees to buy a portion or the entirety of the production from the importer. Levi Strauss sold equipment and technology to a Hungarian firm to make jeans. Levi, in turn, received as payment jeans made at the plant, which it sold in Western Europe and retained the proceeds.
- *Offsets.* Under this arrangement the exporter agrees to buy or arrange to sell products made by the importer. This format is often used in transactions involving large government purchases as when the Japanese government required the U.S. exporter of fighter aircraft, McDonnell-Douglas, to buy some of the components of the airplanes from Japanese companies in exchange for receiving an order.
- *Debt-equity swaps.* In lieu of receiving payment for exports, the exporter is allowed to convert the debt into equity in the business of the importer or other businesses in the importing country. In effect, the exporter ends up becoming a foreign direct investor.

As this brief discussion would suggest, countertrade arrangements can easily become complicated to negotiate and administer. Specialists are available to counsel those new to countertrading. Large trading firms such as the sogososha play a mediating role in the consummation of many of these contracts. Some of the issues that come up in countertrading negotiations include determining the value of the transaction, transferability of obligations, choice of goods to be accepted as payment, length of time for completing the transaction, and method of settling disputes. Smaller firms and firms new to international business should be wary of such transactions. It is the larger and internationally astute firms that have the resources and the skills to successfully negotiate and implement countertrading arrangements. These arrangements require substantial managerial time and capability and often force the firm into types of business that it is not prepared for or capable of running.

A study of 211 countertrade arrangements undertaken by 152 firms in Canada, the United States, and Japan found that significant barriers to entry into countertrade operations existed for small firms, firms selling relatively low-value products, firms that were not heavily engaged in exporting, and firms that were inexperienced in countertrade. Countertrade was found to be beneficial to large firms with extensive trade operations for large, complex products, firms that were vertically integrated or could accommodate countertrade takebacks, and for firms that traded with countries with import restrictions and foreign exchange problems.[30]

CONCLUSIONS

Even though exporting and importing are the easiest and most common of international business activities on the part of a firm, they nevertheless introduce significant new challenges in how the firm conducts business. For firms new to international business it takes time to master these challenges before the benefits of international trade become fully realized. A wide variety of intermediaries and government agencies exist to provide a full gamut of services to the international firm and to help managers take the initial leap. Public policy has been supportive of exporting, because it creates domestic employment, earns valuable foreign exchange revenues, and improves the range and quality of products offered in the domestic market. As managers gain experience exporting (or importing) and the firm earns more of its revenues and profits abroad, the need to be closer to overseas customers assumes importance. It may take the form of licensing or joint ventures or even the establishment of wholly owned ventures abroad. Thus, exporting (or importing) is only an initial step in the path toward a more complete internationalization of the firm.

> ### OPENING VIGNETTE EPILOGUE
>
> Mr. Contesse pursued a creative strategy. SQM's agronomists worked with university researchers around the world, persuading them to experiment with the company's fertilizers on small plots of land owned by local farmers willing to be guinea pigs. Converts to the fertilizer were not hard to find. "They could probably sell every bit they bring up here," said an agriculture professor at the University of Kentucky. In 1997, the company's exports were more than $380 million, or 75 percent of total revenues.[31]
>
> ---
> [31]Dolan, Kerry A. 1998, March 23. Patricio Contesse's white gold. *Forbes*, pp. 100–101.

Key Terms

- management contract
- turnkey
- build-operate-transfer (BOT)
- build-operate-own (BOO)
- demand pattern analysis
- income elasticity measurements
- estimation by analogy
- lead-lag analysis
- cluster analysis
- multiple factor index
- regression analysis
- primary sources
- secondary sources
- channel
- agent
- distributor
- foreign sales corporation
- sogoshosha
- dumping
- transfer pricing
- trade terms
- real exchange rate
- factoring
- letter of credit
- countertrade

---
[30]Lecraw, Donald J. 1989. The management of countertrade: Factors influencing success. *Journal of International Business Studies* 20(1), pp. 41–60.

Discussion Questions

1. How does the creation of a free trade zone affect firms within the zone? How should firms from countries that are not members of a free trade zone react to the creation of such blocs?

2. How do changes in exchange rates affect the export and import operations of firms? What can firms do to reduce their exposure to exchange rate changes?

3. How should a firm go about selecting a potential foreign market to export its products? Why should it choose one country over another?

4. Under what conditions should a firm engage in countertrade arrangements? Identify some of the management issues that would arise under countertrade.

5. What are the various distribution channels an exporter can choose from? Why would a firm choose one type of channel over another?

6. The British pound appreciated 20 percent over the past year, which adversely affected the export of Scotch whiskey. Suggest a set of steps that the Scotch distillers in the United Kingdom can take to ensure that their product remains competitive in foreign markets.

Writing Assignment

You and your manager are flying to Hong Kong to complete the negotiations for a contract to buy 50,000 pieces of men's trousers from a garment company there for distribution through your retail stores in the United States. Your manager has asked you to prepare a two-page memorandum outlining the various clauses that should be included in the final contract. She would like to have it in time for tomorrow's meeting with the executives of the garment company.

Internet Exercise

Use the Internet to access Web sites of the U.S. Department of Commerce and identify a list of countries and a list of products that are prohibited from being exported out of or imported into the United States. Determine the penalties for violating such restrictions.

Internet Resources

Vast and varied information on exporting and importing is now available through the Internet. The Bureau of Export Administration of the U.S. Department of Commerce has a Web site at *www.bxa.doc.gov* with linkages to many other sites. The U.S. Small Business Administration's site at *www.sba.gov* provides information and advice for small businesses. The New Jersey Small Business Development Center has a site at *www.nj.com/njsbdc/*. To obtain current and past foreign exchange rates for the world's currencies, check out *www.x-rates.com*. A list of Incoterms and other helpful information on trade intermediaries can be found at *http://logisticszone.com*. To find out about the various types of services offered by freight forwarders, F.P. Freight Forwarders site at *www.fpexpress.com* is quite informative.

✍

Case 5–1   MORRISON LAMOTHE, INC.

John Pigott, president and CEO of Morrison Lamothe, Inc., a Canadian manufacturer of frozen prepared foods, was worried and disappointed. The lobbying efforts and public relations campaign the company had mounted in concert with a large group of small and medium-sized Canadian firms to forestall the passage of the Canada-U.S. Free Trade Agreement (FTA) had failed. The Canadian government had approved the treaty. Mr. Pigott pondered the consequences of the law that would open the Canadian market to duty-free entry by U.S. companies, who were larger and more resourceful than their Canadian counterparts. His challenge was to devise a strategy that would enable Morrison Lamothe to survive and grow despite what he saw was an adverse turn in the business environment in Canada.

THE COMPANY

Morrison Lamothe was Canada's leading producer of frozen meat pies and a major supplier of frozen dinners, entrees, and desserts. As an independent processor, the company produced for its own labels and as a copacker for others. The company had a combined staff of 179 people with annual sales of approximately $40 million.

The company has been in the food industry since 1933 when a bakery was founded by Cecil Morrison and Richard Lamothe. They were brothers-in-law who took over a small insolvent bakery in Ottawa, Canada's capital. By the 1960s, the bakery had grown to be the city's largest. During that period it had diversified first into the catering business in the late 1940s and later, in the 1960s, into frozen food manufacturing.

In the late 1970s, the company decided to focus its investment in the frozen food industry because it showed strong growth potential. Given the changes in the retail markets for bread, the company sold its bakery in 1980. A specialty bakery operation was closed down in 1987 at the conclusion of a copacking relationship. In 1995, the company shut its restaurant operations because they were no longer part of the focus on frozen food processing.

"Our investments in the Prepared Meals Division was designed to position it as an efficient, low-cost producer specializing in frozen meat pies and dinners.

Expansion and modernization of the plant located in suburban Toronto allowed us to acquire the Holiday Farms brand in 1984 and move into the frozen entrée category. As a result, we have become a market leader in the Canadian frozen food industry," explained Mr. Pigott. As part of a broader corporate strategy to serve the growing copack and private label segments of the frozen food market, the company acquired Northern Fine Foods. Now operating as the Fine Food Division of Morrison Lamothe, it produced under the company's own labels as well as for a growing number of customers who call on its capacity to handle specialized short and medium-sized production runs.

Since its early days, the company had remained in the family. Cecil Morrison's daughter, Jean Pigott, succeeded him as president in 1967. Marguerite Hale, another of Cecil's daughters, took on the position in 1978. Morrison's grandson, John Pigott, became president in 1989.

THE CORPORATE STRUCTURE

The company was organized into two divisions. The Prepared Meals Division focused on the retail grocery market. Its products included Savarin and Holiday Farms brand frozen dinners, meat pies, and entrees. The division also produced private label products for the Canadian market. The division's plant was located in Etobicoke, Ontario.

The Fine Food Division specialized in the preparation of meat pies, fruit pies, appetizers, and entrees for private label and copack customers. The division also marketed hors d'oeuvres and fully baked meat pies under the Morrison Lamothe brand and other names to the retail grocery trade. Its modern facility was in Scarborough, Ontario, and it had the flexibility to make a wide variety of pies and entrees. With that flexibility, the Fine Food Division could prepare custom products with production runs, small or large as required.

PRODUCT LINES AND DISTRIBUTION

The company produced pies, frozen entrees, hors d'oeuvres, and frozen vegetables in different sizes for both the retail and food service markets. For both market segments, the company produced under its own brands as well as under private labels. Some of the private labels for which Morrison Lamothe produced were President's Choice, No Name, Elegant, Western Classics, Coming Home, Our Best, Our Complements, Mrs. Paterson's, M & M International, McDonald's, McCain, Master Choice, and Shurfine. These private labels were owned by different food companies (such as Hormel Foods), supermarket chains (such as A&P), and restaurants (McDonald's). Private labels now constituted 36 percent of the dollar sales of the company. In addition, it sold products under its own brand names of Morrison Lamothe, Savarin, Authentic Pub Pie, and Holiday Farms, among others. The Savarin brand had the largest market share nationally in the frozen meat pie category and was the second largest seller among frozen dinners. Savarin's Chicken Pot Pie and its Fried Chicken Dinner were the top-selling products in their respective categories. The fact that other companies contracted with Morrison Lamothe reflected the industry's acknowledgment of the company's modern production processes, quality of the products, and managerial capability.

The company distributed its products through multiple channels, although traditional supermarkets were the most common. Other channels included club stores and specialty retailers.

THE FROZEN FOOD INDUSTRY

The size of the frozen food industry in Canada was estimated at about $2 billion and growing at about 7 percent annually. With a share of 23 percent, frozen dinners and entrees, the segment in which Morrison Lamothe competed, was the single largest segment in the industry. This segment was growing faster than the rest of the industry, which also consisted of ice cream, frozen fruit beverages including iced tea, frozen seafood, frozen confections, and frozen regular vegetables.

In terms of both overall volume and dollar sales, the company had been growing. However, because of competitive pressure, prices in some segments such as single entrees and dinners had declined. Frozen dinners and entrees constituted the bulk of the company's products. Certain segments such as the meat pie market had matured and the company experienced modest declines in the past few years. It remained though the dominant player in that segment and was the only company who could supply products in all segments.

FREE TRADE AGREEMENT

In 1988, the Free Trade Agreement came into effect. It brought together the two largest economies of North America—the United States and Canada—into one large common market. Duties on the movement of goods between the two countries would be removed permitting unhindered trade. The United States dominated the economy of North America. It was 10 times larger than the Canadian economy. With its population of 270 million, the United States dwarfed Canada (28 million). However, Canada and the United States were each other's largest trading partners.

The opposition to the FTA in Canada came from various groups including small and medium-sized businesses, labor unions, and Canadian nationalists. Small and medium-sized manufacturing firms particularly were worried that the removal of trade barriers including tariffs would expose Canadian firms to a high level of competition from U.S. firms who had the advantages of economies of scale, experience in catering to a diversified market, strong advertising power and savvy, and deep pockets to sustain a strategy of increasing and retaining market share. Canadian firms, many of whom had come into being, grown, and prospered, because of the tariff walls created by the Canadian government now saw their dismantling as the death knell for their business. Most Canadian firms did not have the resources or size to match most U.S. companies in most industries including frozen food. Labor unions were worried that Canadian firms would move production facilities to larger plants in the United States. They were also concerned that U.S. subsidiaries that had come into Canada to avoid the tariff wall would now be closed down because the cost differential created by the wall that led to the setting up of the subsidiary was no longer in effect. Canadian nationalists were concerned that left to the forces of free competition, Canadian companies would fare poorly against larger and richer U.S. companies, which would, in turn, destroy homegrown Canadian industry and enable U.S. firms to dominate the Canadian business landscape. Despite vigorous opposition, the Canadian government approved Canada's accession to the treaty.

THE U.S. THREAT

Morrison Lamothe genuinely feared the implications of FTA. Mr. Pigott observed, "We did not know what awaited us. We thought we would rapidly lose market share as American products rushed in and probably with lower prices. With our sales weakening and profit margins falling, we would be ripe for a takeover." However, a silver lining hovered around the cloudy horizon. First, the U.S. frozen food market was somewhat different from that of Canada. Frozen dinners and entrees had not grown at the same rate in the United States as they had in Canada; private label share in the United States was a tiny fraction but was growing fast; the family segment was underdeveloped in the United States where the emphasis was on individual size; the premium quality segment was also much smaller in the United States and the appetizer market there was underdeveloped. However, the average retail price of frozen food products in the United States was cheaper than in Canada. Second, Lamothe Morrison had built up a reputation for its brand names, and the private labels it produced for were also highly regarded. The company had modern plants and, although the workforce was unionized, labor-management relations were excellent. The company produced a comprehensive range of frozen foods and catered to a wide range of niche markets including salsa hors d'oeuvres, steak and kidney pies, and mini Jamaican jerk patties. Third, the company was looking into joining as a partner the Frozen Newtork, Inc., a joint venture of five independent family owned frozen food processors. Smaller firms had realized that consolidation may occur in the industry once the trade treaty came into being. Mr. Pigott said, "We have a 20 percent share in the joint venture. The joint venture has set up a subsidiary in Chicago, the Coming Home Foods Company, to market a range of premium frozen prepared food products to retail grocers in the United States. This is very new to us, selling to the Americans." Although exchange rates were favorable for Canadian exports, Morrison Lamothe imported quite a bit of the raw materials that were now more expensive from the United States.

Fourth, strength of the U.S. firms lay in producing in large quantities, which reduced unit costs. Given the huge size of the U.S. market, this strategy made sense. However, these companies lacked the flexibility to change product lines on short notice or produce smaller batches.

STRATEGIC CHOICES

Morrison Lamothe was at a crossroads. The business environment was now particularly challenging. The company had several strengths and some new opportunities. The task for Mr. Pigott as he put it, "Was to fashion a strategy that would let us survive and succeed. We could not hope to take the Americans head-on but then we have some advantages, given our size and experience, that American firms do not have. I have to be optimistic." He continued, "With the removal of tariffs, we woke up. The difference between us and those who failed was attitude. We realized we could compete." Mr. Pigott was determined not to let the company go under or be sold off. In the conference room of the company's offices in downtown Ottawa, hung two large portraits of Morrison and Lamothe gazing down benignly. He said, "I could not come to work, look at their eyes, and let this company fail. It has survived three generations and has grown, and adapted to opportunities and circumstances. We will meet this challenge."

The prospect of the elimination of Canadian tariffs was eagerly awaited by U.S. companies. The president and chief executive officer of Campbell Soup Co., one of the largest food companies itself, David Clark, observed, "It doesn't matter what you do at Morrison Lamothe. You'll be dead in two years."

QUESTIONS

1. What strategic options are available to Mr. Pigott? Discuss them.
2. Evaluate the strategy of exporting to the United States. What may make this strategy succeed? Why might it fail?
3. Evaluate the strengths of Morrison Lamothe. What are its weaknesses?
4. Are small firms doomed to fail when trade barriers fall? Discuss.

References

Fraedrich, John P., and Connie Rae Bateman. 1996. Transfer pricing by multinational marketers: Risky business. *Business Horizons* 39(1), pp. 17–23.

International Chamber of Commerce. 1990. *INCOTERMS 1990.* Paris: ICC.

Keegan, Warren J. 1995. *Global marketing management.* Upper Saddle River, NJ: Prentice-Hall.

Leonidou, Leonidas. 1997. Stimuli and barriers to global business: Exporters versus importers. *Journal of Global Business.* Fall, pp. 15–32.

Liberalizing international transactions in services—A handbook. 1994. New York: United Nations.

Moini, A. H. 1997. Barriers inhibiting export performance of small and medium-sized manufacturing firms. *Journal of Global Marketing* 10(4), pp. 66–93.

Root, F. R. 1994. *Entry strategies for international markets.* Lexington, MA: Lexington Books.

The tradability of banking services—Impact and implications. 1994. Geneva: UNCTAD. United Nations.

U.S. global trade outlook 1995–2000. March 1995. Washington, DC: U.S. Department of Commerce.

Verzariu, P., and P. Mitchell. 1992. *International countertrade: Individual country practices.* Washington, DC: U.S. Department of Commerce, International Trade Administration.

Walters, Peter G. P. 1997. Global market segmentation: Methodologies and challenges. *Journal of Marketing Management* 13(1–3), pp. 165–177.

The World Bank. 1995. *World Development Report 1995—Workers in an integrating world.* Washington, DC: Oxford University Press.

6
LICENSING AND FRANCHISING

OPENING VIGNETTE

Infogrames S.A. of France makes video games and is the only European company to rank among the top 10 global games producers by sales. "We feel we've made our name in Europe," said Bruno Bonnell, Infogrames' chief executive officer. "Now the hard part . . . the rest of the world."

Years of hit titles, careful acquisitions, and smart licensing agreements helped Infogrames, based in Lyons, grow. With sales of $230 million in 1998 (up from only $16 million five years earlier), the company planned to raise it fourfold within the next three years so that it could compete with the Japanese titans, Electronic Arts, Sony, and Nintendo. To be able to do that required not only staying abreast of new technology, but also entering the highly competitive U.S. market. Infogrames carved out a European niche with titles created around popular cartoon characters such as Asterix, Smurfs, and Tin Tin. The company understood European culture and had a penchant for creating games that appealed to its main European customers.

Infogrames led in new technology. Less revenue came from sales of games for traditional console and PCs, and more from mobile-communication devices, as well as the Internet, cable, and satellite systems that were changing the way people saw entertainment. Mr. Bonnell approached the market by putting Infogrames products on every new platform. It provided cable operators and television channels with games to broadcast across Europe. It entered into inflight entertainment and was working with a group of technology companies to create a new way of putting games on mobile phones.

The biggest challenge was how to break into the U.S. market. Infogrames' share of the U.S. market remained in the single digits and over the years, the company had only one or two big hits there. The U.S. market was the world's largest at $6 billion in annual sales and was hotly contested. To succeed, one had to be big. As one analyst noted, "The requirement for success is getting steeper. Companies are going to need about $500 million in revenue, a global presence, recognizable brands, a passionate but disciplined management team and a solid business plan to succeed in the home-entertainment market."

Despite the immensity of the U.S. challenge, Mr. Bonnell was optimistic about his company's chance to be at the top of the global game chart. He said, "In the game world, you often feel like a general trying to command troops with an earthquake going on around you. But we're just marching on."

The involvement of a firm in international business deepens when it goes beyond exporting and importing to actually sharing proprietary knowledge or trademarks with other firms. It happens through the mechanisms of licensing and its variant, franchising, where firms use a proven technology, process, or brand name belonging to another firm, to internationalize and expand their operations. Highly popular methods of internationalizing operations, licensing and franchising are intermediate stages in the firm's move towards partial or full ownership and control of its foreign operations. As with all types of business arrangements, they have their advantages and disadvantages and managerial challenges that are unique to these types of arrangements. This chapter discusses the management issues surrounding licensing and franchising and also examines a particular form of licensing—trademark licensing. Because the essential basis of this form of international business is the sharing of proprietary information and attributes, the legal mechanism for ensuring their integrity and for compelling the parties to comply with agreements assumes considerable importance. Hence, this chapter also looks at the legal framework available to resolve disputes that arise in connection with these arrangements. Another section discusses the typical components of a licensing agreement.

LICENSING

International **licensing,** defined broadly, comprises a variety of contractual arrangements, whereby a domestic firm (a licensor) allows its intangible assets or property rights (such as patents, manufacturing techniques—also called know-how, technology, designs and prototypes, and trademarks) to be used by a foreign firm (the licensee) for a fee, usually referred to as a **royalty.** The licensee incorporates the technology, know-how, or trademark in its production processes and products. It is the licensee who invests in the production and distribution systems, thus sparing the licensor additional capital outlays.

Licensing occurs in a wide range of industries including pharmaceutical, publishing, fast food, apparel, toys, and machine tools. Licensing a patent to another firm, sometimes referred to as technology licensing, is slightly different from licensing a trademark, which is also somewhat different from franchising. The distinctions are explained as follows:

- **Patent:** A legal protection given to new and useful inventions, discoveries, and designs. To be entitled to a patent, a work must be completely new. A patent is granted to the first inventor who files for the patent and once it is patented, no one else can make use of it without permission until it expires, usually after 17 years. Patents cannot be renewed. Patents registered with the U.S. Patent and Trademark Office must clearly explain how to make the invention so that when the patent expires, others will be able to freely make the product or use the process to make it. Most medicines are patented by pharmaceutical firms.
- **Trademark:** A legal protection given to a name, picture, or symbol that is used to distinguish one firm's goods or services from those of another. Thus, a trademark can consist of letters, numerals, packaging, labeling, musical notes, colors, or a combination of these. A trademark, which is registered with the U.S. Patent and Trademark Office, lasts indefinitely if it is used continuously and renewed properly. The swoosh that accompanies products made by Nike, a sporting footwear firm, is an example of a trademark.

- **Copyright:** A legal protection given to "original works of authorship" such as books, films, music, and software. A copyright gives the author and the author's heirs exclusive right to the work for the life of the author plus 50 years. In the United States, copyrights are registered with the Register of Copyrights at the Library of Congress.
- **Trade secret:** Information or process that is kept secret by a firm because it provides a commercial advantage. An example of a trade secret is the secret herbs used to cook chicken the original way by KFC (formerly Kentucky Fried Chicken). Trade secrets are not registered; they are protected by the fact that they are not disclosed.

Certain variables appear to be associated with the extent of licensing a firm engages in, including the following:[1]

- Investment in research and development (R&D) as a percentage of sales (the higher the percentage, the greater the licensing propensity)
- Relative size of a firm in its industry (the smaller the firm, the greater is the likelihood of licensing)
- Level of diversification (the greater the degree of diversification, the greater the likelihood of licensing)
- Extent of international business experience as measured by the amount of total sales accounted for by production abroad (the less the experience, the more the licensing)
- Recognition and integrity of brand names in the industry (the more well known a brand name or trademark, the greater the likelihood of it being licensed or franchised)

IMPORTANCE OF ROYALTIES AND LICENSE FEES

Licensing to foreign firms has been a long-established business strategy among companies in developed countries. Between 1952 and 1980, U.S. firms signed approximately 32,000 licensing agreements. In the 1990s, the pace of licensing continued unabated because of growth in high-tech industries such as computers, biotechnology, and pharmaceuticals. Because technological innovations tend to occur in advanced industrial societies, the majority of the licensors are firms based in these countries. Licensees, however, can be found in both developed and developing countries.

Royalties and license fees have become a growing and profitable component of U.S. foreign trade. For instance, in 1999, the United States earned over $36 billion in royalties and fees while paying out a much smaller $13.3 billion to foreign countries. Table 6-1 shows the rising trend of this form of export and import of services for the U.S. economy. The United States has enjoyed a surplus in this category of international trade reflecting its technological lead and the use of franchising for international expansion.

Table 6-2 identifies the leading countries from which the United States receives its income of royalties and license fees and makes payments to. While most of the countries on the list are advanced industrial nations, newly industrializing countries as users and creators of technology or franchising opportunities have also begun to appear. Readers

---

[1]Contractor, Farokh J. 1985. *Licensing in international strategy.* Westport, CT: Quorum Books.

Table 6-1	U.S. Income and Payments of Royalties and License Fees (in $millions)				
Year	1980	1985	1990	1995	1999
Exports	7,085	6,678	16,634	30,289	36,467
Imports	724	1,170	3,135	6,919	13,275

Source: *Survey of Current Business.* July 2000. Table 1: U.S. International Transactions, pp. 88–89.

may note that the United States earns nearly two times from Japan as Japan earns from the United States on this account. Half of all royalties and license fee payments made by U.S. firms go to Japan, the United Kingdom, and Germany, while almost one-sixth of all United States earnings come from Japan alone. The latter reflects the extensive reliance of Japanese firms on U.S. technology and the success of franchising in the retail industry.

ROYALTY

As noted earlier, royalty is the payment made by the licensee to the licensor for using the patent or technology or trademark. It is generally calculated as a percentage of the sales value of those products that use the licensed technology, process, or trademark. It can also be a percentage of the physical quantity produced or sold or even of the profits of the licensee. Royalties can also be adjusted—up or down—depending on sales volumes and over the length of the contract. They can be paid in lump sums or in a continuous stream over time.

The amount of royalty is difficult to negotiate because the potential market size for the licensed product is often unknown or cannot be easily determined. The licensor wants a royalty rate that allows it to recover as much of the cost of developing the technology as it can and where possible, earn a share of the profit from exploiting the technology.

The royalty rate, rarely more than 5 percent of total sales, reflects the bargaining power of the two parties. The risk taken by the licensee in terms of capital investment

Table 6-2	Top U.S. Export Markets and Import Sources for Royalties and Fees, 1999 (in $millions)			
Export to	Amount	Rank	Import from	Amount
Japan	6,053	1	Japan	3,162
United Kingdom	3,518	2	United Kingdom	1,749
Germany	3,110	3	Germany	1,287
Netherlands	2,990	4	France	895
France	2,149	5	Netherlands	782
Canada	1,696	6	Canada	607
Italy	964	7	Belgium/Luxembourg	219
Mexico	798	8	Mexico	104
Australia	723	9	Italy	98
Belgium/Luxembourg	669	10	Australia	69
All countries	36,467		All countries	13,275

Source: *Survey of Current Business.* July 2000. Tables 10 and 10a: U.S. International Transactions by Selected Countries, pp. 116–123.

and managerial effort is balanced against the quality of the technology offered by the licensor. In addition, the existence of other potential licensees or licensors will tend to reduce the royalty rate.

LICENSING AND FIRM STRATEGY

In deciding whether to license, the licensor has to ask the question: Can this technology, production process, design, or trademark be successfully used by another firm in another country? The answer may be no. It may be that the success of a product owes much to the firm's production methods, experience, linkages with marketing and the research department, and to that unique combination of skills and resources that are peculiar to every firm and that cannot be replicated at another setting. Much also depends on the licensee's abilities and resources and the nature of the foreign market.

The licensee's question is similar. "Can we replicate at our facilities what the licensor is able to do in its country and will it succeed in this market?" Again, the answer may not be obvious. A production process or way of managing that is successful in the licensor's country may be difficult to mimic in the licensee's country because of lack of skilled employees or poor engineering capabilities. Infrastructure may be insufficient, or difficulties may arise with input availability and product quality. And a licensee always runs the risk of misreading the market potential.

Licensing is embraced by a firm in all stages of a product's life cycle. In the introduction stage, licensing allows quick and easy penetration into key markets and to recover R&D costs. In the growth stage, the success in the home market may attract potential licensees, and by embracing them, the licensor can expand its market. In the mature and declining stages, licensing offers a way to prolong the life of the product by generating royalty income and to serve markets where the product is still younger. Indeed, royalty revenues from technology that is mature and facing competition at home are like windfall profits and could be substantial to finance other R&D projects.

As a global strategy, licensing imposes a constraint on both the licensor and the licensee. The licensor gives up much control over the production and sale of the goods by the licensee. Income is limited by royalty rates and the performance of the licensee. In the case of franchising, the franchiser does have much closer control over how the franchisee conducts its business and over minimum levels of performance. However, it is quite possible to have franchisees who fail to perform at the expected level. There may not be enough potential franchisees available in a particular market for the franchiser to expand. Because of this inability to exercise complete control over the licensees/franchisees, a global strategy becomes harder to pursue. It becomes apparent when the firm is unable to compete in a wide range of markets simultaneously and unable to move resources from one competitive environment to another. Thus, licensing is more likely to fit in with the multidomestic approach, where each country market stands alone and is treated as such or it is used to fill gaps in a company's presence in certain markets.

REASONS FOR LICENSING

The licensor may see licensing as a quick way to recover high R&D expenses; to expand overseas quickly without any significant financial outlay; to squeeze more life (and revenues) out of an asset that has matured or declined in the home country or other primary markets; and to test the potential of a foreign market before deciding on a more substantive investment there. Licensing may also be chosen because of the inability to enter a foreign market through exporting or direct investment because of government restrictions. A high level of political risk to direct investment in the foreign country or the small size of the foreign market that does not justify larger investments or scale economies may make licensing a good option. The possibility of obtaining useful feedback about the technology from the licensee and a chance to create a market for accessories, raw materials, and supporting inputs benefit the licensor. If the licensor is confident that its technological lead is so large that the licensee will be unlikely to emerge as a competitor then it is more likely to choose licensing. Due to the rise of counterfeiting in recent years firms are forced to license overseas as soon as products with a new technology are introduced in the home market. Reverse engineering allows copycats to imitate the product and offer it in foreign markets at lower prices. Early licensing can thwart this behavior of pirates by making the product available in the foreign market soon after its introduction.

In the 1970s and 1980s, when direct investment in East European countries was difficult, or even impossible, many western firms viewed licensing as a way to enter those markets and to set up a channel for future business.[2] The economic uncertainty following the collapse of communism meant that licensing remained a practical vehicle to build familiarity with those emerging markets and create a local partner for potential long-term and more involved relationships. At the same time it ensured an immediate flow of revenues through royalties and advances with a minimum of capital investment.

Licensing is also relatively risk free in political terms. Many host governments prefer licensing over foreign investment as the way to obtain technology. In addition, licensing is not subject to expropriation, because the licensor does not own physical assets in the host country. In a worst case scenario, the most that the licensor will lose is the licensing income. Although it could be substantial, it is much less than if a wholly owned subsidiary is expropriated or heavily regulated. All these reasons for licensing are summarized in Table 6-3.

From the licensee's perspective, the license allows the firm to acquire new and usually proven technology relatively quickly without incurring any substantial and uncertain R&D expenses. It also permits the firm to diversify into other lines of business and fill gaps in its product line, and to gain access to advanced know-how and well-established brand names to increase sales, productivity, and profitability. An examination of the intentions of Australian technology firms to become licensees showed that the determining factors were previous experience with licensing, perceived relative costs and benefits of licensing, awareness of opportunities afforded by the license, and the firm's own internal new production development and research capabilities.[3] Table 6-4 lists these reasons.

DISADVANTAGES OF LICENSING

Both from the licensor's and the licensee's perspectives, licensing poses some risks that managers need to be aware of. Some of the more important ones are discussed here.

Risks for the Licensor By licensing its technology, the licensor may unwittingly create a potential competitor in the future. The licensee gains access to proprietary technology and know-how and may be able to improve and adapt them to such an extent

[2]Langenecker, Juliane. 1993, September 27. Licensing lives on. *Business Eastern Europe* 22(39), pp. 1–2.
[3]Atuahene-Gima, Kwaku. 1993. Determinants of inward technology licensing intentions—An empirical analyses of Australian engineering firms. *Journal of Production Innovation Management* 10(3), pp. 230–240.

Table 6-3   Licensor's Reasons for Licensing

Firm-Specific Reasons:
- Shortage of funds for investment
- Absence of in-house managerial skills to exploit a technology
- Lack of knowledge of overseas markets
- Mature technology in the home market with revenue stream stagnant or dwindling
- Create a market of accessories, raw materials, and supporting inputs
- Obtaining useful feedback on the use of particular technologies and processes

External Reasons:
- Barriers to accessing foreign markets through other entry methods
- Host government pressures to license
- Small size of foreign market
- Discourage counterfeiting and piracy

that when the license expires, it can produce the good and compete against its erstwhile licensor. Sharing proprietary information should be considered carefully for it could mean loss of control over those elements of a company's assets that create its competitive advantage. Some technologies probably should not be licensed at all. Indeed, many firms license either older or peripheral, not core, technology they have fully exploited and are not concerned about losing control over or are confident of maintaining a sizable technological lead over their licensee through their own R&D innovations.

Because the licensor is dependent on the licensee in the particular foreign market, a second risk for the licensor is the possibility of the licensee failing to live up to the contract. Such failure can occur in many forms.

- Poor product quality or service, which would also reflect adversely on the reputation of the licensor and its products
- Inability to produce and distribute the product for reasons such as failure to absorb the technology or poor customer acceptance
- Outright violation of the agreement, such as not paying royalties or fees, not sharing any product or process improvement or information, or selling in markets that it is not permitted to do so

In many cases, the problems become known only after they have occurred (such as poor product quality); consequently it becomes harder to address them. Although the agreement must have specific clauses to prevent such developments and initial investigation may have screened the capabilities and history of the licensee, in reality, enforcement

Table 6-4   Licensee's Reasons for Licensing

- Absence of in-house R&D capabilities
- Opportunity to improve efficiency in production and introduce new products
- Profit from an established product, process, or brand name
- Opportunity to build up competency in a particular industry or product line in the future
- Inability to access technology because of government restrictions on imports or inward foreign investment

of the agreement may be expensive, time consuming, and difficult. The licensor may find that little can be done to compel the licensee to perform other than terminating the contract. Monitoring the performance of the licensee is not always easy and laws in different countries may favor the interests of the licensee.

A third consideration for the licensor is the revenue flows from the licensing arrangement. Licensing generally provides for lower revenues than if the firm manufactured the product itself in the foreign country, because the licensor has only an indirect involvement with the market. It is also limited in how much royalties and other fees it can realistically charge based on host government regulations and by changes in exchange rates. Moreover, unlike export or investment revenues, licensing arrangements are usually limited to a few years—generally five to 10—and this time frame may not generate as much profit as other entry options may and worse, as stated earlier, may create a potential competitor in the process. All combined, licensing may fail to provide even the minimum level of expected benefits to the licensor.

Risks for the Licensee Licensing arrangements also pose problems for the licensee. These problems include lengthy negotiating prior to the agreement and demanding reporting requirements once the agreement is in place. The likelihood is high that the licensor will be interested in audits and meddlesome inquiries into the firm's activities. The failure of the licensor to provide continuing technical, personnel, and knowledge support to successfully exploit the licensed technology, and the possibility that the adaptation costs to utilize the license is much higher than initially expected are real risks for the licensee. It also faces the possible negative effect on the firm's own in-house R&D activities, in terms of cutbacks, lower morale, or stunted growth prospects. Two other risks that need to be guarded against are the possibility of being technically dependent on the licensor, in a secondary role, because the licensor is less likely to provide its state-of-the-art or most advanced know-how to the licensee, and the possibility of the licensor violating the contract by licensing other firms in the market allocated to the licensee or by licensing a slightly different technology to other firms.

TECHNOLOGY LICENSING

Under **technology licensing,** the licensor lets the licensee use its patent, technical know-how, and production processes for a fee and royalty. Technology licensing can occur in several ways.

1. *Inventor-to-firm licensing.* This form of licensing occurs when an individual inventor, entrepreneur, or small firm secures a patent for a new invention. Lacking financial and organizational resources, they are unable to exploit the technology for commercial gain. Consequently, they seek licensees who are able to use the technology to manufacture and market the product. The Power Beat International Limited case at the end of this chapter describes the effort of a small firm in New Zealand to license a patent it obtained for developing a revolutionary automobile battery. Given the imbalance in the power relationship in such arrangements, the much weaker licensor essentially cedes all control over manufacturing and marketing to the more resourceful licensee in exchange for upfront fees and a stream of royalty payments.

2. *Firm-to-firm licensing.* This more common form of licensing occurs when one firm licenses its technology to another firm. The licensor has a choice of various foreign market entry methods and for many reasons already discussed chooses licensing over others. Similarly, the licensee chooses licensing as a way to internationalize its operations instead of importing or becoming a joint venture partner or being acquired by a foreign firm.

3. *Cross-licensing.* **Cross-licensing** usually takes place between firms of similar technological abilities in the same industry. They want to share the technical developments undertaken by the other firm or to share R&D costs. Not infrequently, the domestic and foreign firms enter a cross-licensing deal, which in effect gives the right of first refusal of any valuable patent or invention developed by one firm to the other. Cross-licensing agreements, more so than other licensing agreements, are difficult to write, and hence to protect the interests of both sides, expert legal counsel is retained. An example of a form of cross-licensing is presented in Management Focus 6-1.

4. *Intrafirm licensing.* It occurs inside a firm between the parent and overseas subsidiaries or among the subsidiaries of a multinational firm. For example, Nestle's R&D center in Switzerland, having developed new processes for manufacturing cereal, may license that technology to the company's subsidiary in Australia. Thus, both the licensor and the licensee are the same firm, though different divisions. Depending on the organizational structure, a division of the firm may not have a choice of declining the offer of a license from the parent or even another division.

Why would a firm license its own technology to other parts of its own organization? Headquarters managers may believe that it is a way to reduce political risk in the host countries where the subsidiaries are located. A nationalistic host government may impose control over transfers of profits and dividends to the parent firm and it may be easier for the firm to take out money in the form of royalties and technical fees. Also, headquarters may find that licensing is an effective means for transfer pricing and moving profits away from high-tax locations to low-tax locations. By allowing the firm's R&D centers to charge royalties for their inventions, it encourages research creativity, brings in revenues, allows them to function as profit centers, and enables the rest of the organization to benefit from the R&D activities in its subsidiaries.

TRADEMARK LICENSING

Ever since the French tennis player and champion, Rene Lacoste, nicknamed "Le Crocodile" because of his exceptionally long nose and speed on the court, put the alligator emblem on a white short-sleeved tennis shirt in 1926, thus creating the notion of designer labels, trademark licensing has become a popular method of market penetration and profit making.[4] U.S. licensors make billions of dollars in sales of licensed merchandise, of which more than a third is from overseas. The main markets are in Canada, Western

[4]Gallagher, Leigh. 1999, May 31. Endangered species. *Forbes,* p. 105.

MANAGEMENT FOCUS 6-1

FRENCH DRUG FIRM PROFITS
WITH OFFBEAT STRATEGY

Spend millions of dollars over many years developing a new product and then let others rake in profits by selling it? That may go against conventional wisdom, but it was a strategy that paid off handsomely for French pharmaceutical company, Sanofi SA. Tapping its erstwhile rivals for research funds in exchange for selling some of its most promising drugs—thus sharing both the risks and the rewards—helped Sanofi become a major player after entering the drug business in 1973. In addition to pharmaceutical products, Sanofi also had a perfumes and beauty products division (with brands such as Yves Saint Laurent, Oscar de la Renta, and Nina Ricci), and a bioactivities division.

Sanofi had come a long way from its origin as a diversification by the French oil company, Elf Acquitaine SA, which owned 52.3 percent of Sanofi. But the strategy followed by Sanofi chairman, Jean-Francois Dehecq, had much in common with trends in the petroleum business, in which he had worked for a decade.

Oil companies, he noted, once hoarded drilling rights. But these days they often shared the costs and risk of exploring new fields. "The pharmaceutical industry is heading in the same direction," Mr. Dehecq said, stressing that escalating financial risks had changed the old go-for-broke mentality in both industries. "We all have the same problem: the pharmaceutical business will never be what it was in the past." Efforts by governments to control runaway health care costs had slowed the sale of prescription drugs and squeezed profits. The only real cure, many pharmaceutical executives believed, was better drug research. But drug research was expensive. Sanofi, in 1996, had nearly 30 potential drugs under development. "Each project can cost up to $400 million," Mr. Dehecq said. "We obviously can't afford to spend that much on all the compounds we have in development—even if only half proceed to the final, most expensive phase of clinical tests."

The clinical trial for Plavix, the brand name of a drug called clopidogrel developed to prevent heart attacks, lasted three years, involved 19,185 patients, and cost more than $100 million. The solution for these high costs? Licensing. Sanofi shared the cost of developing clopidogrel with Bristol-Myers-Squibb Co., a U.S. firm. Plavix would be sold, when approved by regulatory authorities, in the United States by Bristol-Myers-Squibb. It was expected that the drug could become a blockbuster, with annual sales topping $1 billion within five years. But if it failed, the cost to Sanofi was much less than it would have been if it had not arranged this licensing agreement.

Such arrangements meant sharing potential profits as well as risks, of course. In 1995, licensees' sales of drugs discovered by Sanofi reached 10.4 billion francs ($2.05 billion) compared with revenue of 16.9 billion francs by Sanofi's pharmaceutical division. But over the years, such licensing arrangements helped underwrite Sanofi, allowing it to make dozens of acquisitions and pour 20 billion francs into research. The result? Sanofi had advanced to 25th place in global pharmaceutical company rankings.

Licensing arrangements were getting more and more lucrative. With truly innovative drugs in short supply, companies that discovered them could now wrest better terms than under old-fashioned licensing deals. Under the agreement with Bristol-Myers-Squibb, for instance, Sanofi would pocket an estimated 15 percent royalty on the drugs' total sales, plus a slice of profit proportional to its share of marketing overhead. Analysts believed Sanofi's share of sales of Plavix and two other promising drugs in its pipeline could boost the drug division's annual sales nearly 50 percent by the end of the decade, and fuel annual earnings growth of 20 percent or more during the same period, making Sanofi one of Europe's fastest growing drug makers.

Source: Moore, Stephen, D. 1996, November 14. French drug maker reaps profits with offbeat strategy. *The Wall Street Journal,* p. B4.

Europe, Japan, Australia, and New Zealand. U.S. firms dominate the world market for trademark licensing. It is estimated that 85 percent of total sales of licensed merchandise worldwide is attributable to properties originating in the United States. The Star Wars trilogy movies (*Star Wars, The Empire Strikes Back,* and *Return of the Jedi*) earned $2.7 billion from the box office and video sales. In contrast, trademark merchandising about the films' characters, clothes, and equipment topped $4.5 billion by 1999.[5]

Trademarks that have come to be associated with a particular product, image, lifestyle, or value are now frequently licensed by their original owners. Trademarks complement and reinforce the line of product offerings that a firm sells and generate recognition for the firm and its products. Disney characters such as Mickey Mouse are now found on virtually every type of product (clothes, notebooks, pencils) and as many product forms imaginable (the Mickey Mouse key chain, the Mickey Mouse coffee cup, and so on). The extensive licensing of Disney characters also ensures that the Disney name remains prominent in the marketplace and reminds the public about Disney's other products such as theme parks and movies. As with technology licensing, the licensees pay royalties and fees to obtain the right to use the trademark.

Trademark licensing's popularity can be partly attributed to the growth of international television broadcasting, media coverage, and travel. U.S. television shows and films have a worldwide presence and dominance. Television and film producers have recognized the synergy created by spinning off products based on shows and their characters. With satellite transmissions making television shows viewable around the world, viewers can recognize the products and feel an affinity for them. Licensing a variety of merchandise allows the firm to amplify and support other marketing efforts surrounding the show, bring the brand and its message into the retail setting, and expand the total number of people who hear about or are reminded of the show through various advertising and promotional vehicles. The ability to parlay a trademark into successful licensed products is illustrated in Management Focus 6-2. A British children's television program about a railway engine led to the licensing of a whole range of products carrying the name or logo of Thomas the Tank Engine and other characters from the show. The success of Thomas reflects how climbing the learning curve helps in adjusting the strategy and selecting the appropriate distribution system.

In a highly competitive environment, trademark licensing is one way to make one's presence noticed and felt in the marketplace. It also allows the licensor to gain access to funds (through initial licensing fees and advance payments of royalties) to finance production and development costs. It is particularly relevant in film and television production where funding is necessary to finance the production of a series of episodes for any title. From the licensee's point of view, associating its product line with a well-known trademark is an effective marketing tool to expand its sales. The products gain instant market recognition without the licensee having to invest in building up its own brand.

For many products, especially consumer products, brand names have become synonymous with quality, lifestyle, value, or prestige. They also distinguish one product from another. Licensing of foods and beverages, for instance, has made their markets expand internationally. Table 6-5 presents some of the brand names that have been licensed by firms to foreign companies.

---

[5]Pappas, Ben. 1999, May 17. Star bucks. *Forbes,* p. 53.

MANAGEMENT FOCUS 6-2

THOMAS THE TANK ENGINE

"Thomas the Tank Engine & Friends" was created as a television show in the United Kingdom in 1984 by producer Britt Allcroft. Based on a series of stories by the Reverend Wilbert Awdry written between 1948 and 1972, the television version in the United Kingdom ran as an 11-minute segment comprising two Thomas episodes. The show generated a great deal of licensing activity not only in the United Kingdom, but also in Australia and New Zealand. It started with puzzles and quickly expanded to include many children's toys, videotapes, books, and clothes. In the first year of licensing alone, 10 million Thomas books were sold in the United Kingdom.

The show caught the notice of WNET, the public television station in New York, which was at the time looking for new programs to strengthen its children's programming lineup. As a result, Britt Allcroft and her new production partner Rick Siggelkow, developed a half-hour program for American children called "Shining Time Station." Each show included five-and-a-half-minute episodes of the British films starring Thomas, a steam railway engine, and his friends. Public Broadcasting System (PBS) in the United States began distributing the series to public television stations in January 1989. At the same time, a licensing program was launched in the United States. The merchandise focused exclusively on the Thomas stories, rather than on the other "Shining Time Station" characters.

Attracting the interest of licensees to the Thomas stories and characters proved to be a challenge for several reasons. First, because the program was distributed through PBS, its audience was much smaller than network and syndicated shows aired by the commercial television stations. Second, aside from "Sesame Street," PBS was an unproven distribution channel for broad-based licensing programs. Third, Thomas was designed for the preschool audience, while the major buyers of licensed merchandise were older children aged 5–11. Finally, licensees thought that children in the United States would not be interested in steam trains.

The licensees that were signed on in the United States concentrated on the mass market, and the merchandise became widely available. However, despite good reviews, favorable press coverage, and a good sized audience (by PBS standards), the products did not sell well. In 1989, sales were less than $2 million. Consequently, Britt Allcroft Inc. changed its strategy. The company was receiving letters from viewers saying that they were looking for Thomas products at their local toy stores but could not find any. Because mass market licensees tended to underserve the low-volume specialty market, as well as the fact that the PBS audience was generally a more upscale demographic group, the company decided to refocus its efforts on the specialty market. In 1990, it began selling Thomas merchandise through specialty toy stores.

Licensees were still somewhat reluctant to sign on, based on the property's early track record. Britt Allcroft thought that the products may have been introduced too early in the market (before the show had become sufficiently well known) in addition to being in the wrong distribution channel. By the end of 1991, however, demand for Thomas products by parents of preschoolers boomed. Product shortages occurred, which piqued the interests of licensees. Even after Thomas became successful enough to attract the attention of mass market licensees, the company decided to stay with manufacturers who specialized in the upper end of the market (selling through specialty and department stores). It was estimated that by the end of 1993, the cumulative retail sales of Thomas licensed merchandise in the United States had reached $750 million. (The privately held Britt Allcroft Inc. does not release sales figures.)

Britt Allcroft Inc. planned its licensing efforts on a three-year cycle (paralleling the typical length of merchandise licensing contracts), and tried to maintain that schedule in terms of when promotions and expansion to new categories should occur. The company's goal was to manage Thomas as a long-term property, which meant carefully choosing markets and licensees.

The various products that were being licensed were designed to build up on the relationship between the child and steam engine. For example, home videos and books were important because

(continued)

Management Focus 6-2 (*continued*)

they advanced the television story lines and allowed children to interact with characters when they were not watching the television program. Toy trains allowed children to include the Thomas product into their play.

The decision to license new product categories depended to a large extent on requests from consumers who wrote to the company inquiring whether certain products were available and where they could be bought. As a result, the firm had licensed merchandise such as apparel, pajamas, flashlights, greeting cards, party goods, and more—about 2,000 products—all manufactured by about 75 licensees.

Promotions had also been an important part of the Thomas licensing strategy. In 1991, an appearance at Bloomingdales, an upscale department store, in New York City drew 14,000 people. The next year, a similar event attracted 25,000 people.

A traveling mall show called "Shining Time Station—Live!" featured music, dance, storytelling, and audience participation. Individual retailers also promoted Thomas with concept shops, contests, giveaways, and special displays. Licensed products based on the show are not advertised on television.

Britt Allcroft Inc. looked at itself as a producer, rather than a licensor, preferring to call the creation of products "off-screen production" rather than licensing. The income generated from merchandising was important, said the company, in that it provided the ability for it to remain independent and preserve its creative freedom: "We make money because we make magic, but we can only go on making magic if we make money." In terms of awareness, licensing created a link between the consumer and the property, spreading the word about the show and strengthening its viewership.

Source: Raugust, Karen. 1996. *Merchandise licensing in the television industry.* Boston, MA: Focal Press; Gates, Anita. 1997, March 23. W. Awdry, 85, children's book author, dies. *The New York Times*, p. 4D.

KEY STRATEGIC DECISIONS

Several key strategic issues need to be addressed when deciding on trademark licensing. They include timing issues, product categories, number of licensees, distribution channels, payment structures, and methods of keeping the trademark exciting over time. These issues are important to both the licensor and the licensee.

Table 6-5   Brand Name Licenses

Licensor	*Brand Name*	*Licensee*
Anheuser-Busch (U.S.)	Budweiser	Suntory (Japan)
Geo. A. Hormel (U.S.)	Spam	NewforgeFoods (U.K.)
Haute Brasserie (France)	Killian's Red	Adolph Coors (U.S.)
Jacob Suchard (Switzerland)	Toblerone	Sanborn Hermanos (Mexico)
Kirin (Japan)	Kirin	Molson (Canada)
Lowenbrau (Germany)	Lowenbrau Pils	Miller Brewing (U.S.)
RJR Nabisco (U.S.)	Planters	Britannia Brands (Singapore)
Rowntree Mackintosh (U.K.)	Kit Kat	Hershey Foods (U.S.)
Sunkist Growers (U.S.)	Sunkist	Rickertson (Germany)
Unilever (Netherlands)	Lipton	Morinaga (Japan)

Source: Henderson, Dennis R., Sheldon, Ian M. and Thomas, Kathleen N. "International licensing of foods and beverages makes markets truly global." *Food Review.* September-December, 1994, pp. 7–12.

1. *Timing.* The licensor has to decide the best time to launch products with its trademark. As the Thomas example in Management Focus 6-2 noted, initial sales of the trademark licensed products were low because the television show was not yet popular enough to have a large enough clientele base who would buy the show-related merchandise. Usually, a few products are licensed initially with expansion occurring over time, especially if the goal is to create a long-term awareness of the trademark. If, instead, the goal is to capitalize on a prevailing popularity of a product, it would make sense to launch a large number of different products in a variety of markets.

Managers should note that a lead time is involved between selecting licensees and the product becoming available on retail shelves. Product approval, development, manufacturing, and distribution take time. Some products such as video games and toys take longer time than others (such as apparel). Thus, for some products contracts need to be signed early to ensure timely arrival of the licensed merchandise in the shops. The total time from signing a contract to bringing a product on the market can take as long as 18 months. Sometimes a delay comes between a domestic launch and an overseas launch. The delay allows the firm to determine the success of the licensing and make changes if necessary. However, in more and more cases, U.S. firms are launching licensed products at home and abroad simultaneously. One reason is to prevent the emergence of counterfeiters. It is also a recognition that the property is available in many countries or customers in many countries have knowledge about it, usually through television programs.

2. *Product categories.* Today, virtually any type of product can be licensed to carry a particular trademark. A visit to any gift shop in a mall will introduce the reader to the wide range of products from apparel to videotapes that are now trademark licensed. For example, the products that were licensed with the Thomas the Tank Engine & Friends logo and features included story books, videotapes, and toy trains—an appropriate fit. It should also fit with the goals of both the licensor and the licensee. Not to be overlooked, the products must appeal to the customers.

3. *Number of licensees.* Some companies use numerous licensees in a single market while others use as few as one. The number of licensees is not related to the total amount of sales or to the number of products. Instead, it reflects careful managerial calculations. A single licensee may be signed on to produce a complete range of products for the entire market if it has the capability to design, produce, and market them. Where such abilities are absent, several licensees may be needed. The purpose of licensing also plays a part. If a goal is to obtain substantial advances (say, to finance the production of an episode of a television series), authorizing several licensees may allow that to happen. If the goal is to create a long-term licensing program, signing up few licensees with the aim of building up a trusting relationship may be the way to go, especially if licensing is a big part of their business.

4. *Distribution.* Although the licensee will distribute the product, the licensor has an interest in ensuring that the appropriate channel is used. Where the product is considered prestigious, expensive, and image sensitive, the best outlets may be high-class specialty or department stores as opposed to mass merchants. An upscale brand may suffer if it is sold through discount stores. In this context, the shopping behavior of the target customers needs to be carefully followed and new forms of distribution channels (such as the Internet, mail catalog, or company-owned shops) may have to be developed. The

Lacoste crocodile logo lost its cachet in the 1980s when it began to appear on cheap polyster shirts sold at discount stores. Devenlay, part of a French apparel maker controlled by the Lacoste family, spent $32 million to reclaim the U.S. rights to the Lacoste name and the crocodile logo in 1993. Lacoste knit shirts with the crocodile logo are now made in France from Swiss yarn and mother-of-pearl buttons and sold in upscale stores, alongside other designer clothes.[6]

5. *Terms of payment.* The royalty—usually between 5 percent and 12 percent—is typically paid on the net sales, or wholesale price of the product in the currency of the licensor. A minimum amount of royalty, or a "guarantee," is usually required. The guarantee protects the licensor from licensees who tie up a category but then do not adequately market the licensed merchandise. Of course, a guarantee adds risk to the licensee who is responsible for the payment even if the license as a whole fails.

The amount of royalties and guarantees depends on the goals and resources of both parties. Where the licensor is looking for funds to pay for its own business, it may ask for high advances. If the trademark is relatively unknown, a smaller guarantee and royalty rate may be negotiated—partly to attract the licensee to sign on. Successful brand names can command high royalty rates and advance monies. Market factors in the industry also play a role. Where many licensors are seeking licensees, the rates tend to drop. Licensees of low-priced novelties pay lower rates than licensees of luxury items. Finally, a licensee who has high product development costs or requires substantial retooling of facilities will try to negotiate a lower advance to compensate for these investments.

6. *Promotional support.* While the licensee usually works with retailers to push the licensed product, the licensor often is involved through advertising and promotion of various kinds. The licensor's goal is to keep the brand name in the public's eye, and present it appropriately. Sometimes the costs are shared between the licensor and the licensee. To prevent a trademark from becoming stale, the licensor often resorts to massive advertising.

IMPLEMENTING A TRADEMARK LICENSING PROGRAM

Similar to the issues of technology licensing, firms that wish to license their trademarks have to convince potential licensees about the value of the trademarks. That is, why is it important to make coffee mugs in the shape of a Disney cartoon character? Licensees would require detailed information about the market in which the product will be sold. A style book is an important sales tool for licensors and licensees alike. Such a book illustrates the various trademarks and other property depictions available for use on products. It includes detailed specifications, including colors and dimensions, tips on how to draw logos and characters, and visuals of photographs and art works available. It also has mockups or sketches of how the property can be incorporated into various products such as notebooks, party goods, footwear, scarves, action figures, or plush animals.

In selecting the licensee, the licensor should examine the quality of the licensee's products based on sample merchandise, price range, production capabilities, financial resources, and ability to innovate by bringing out new products. Another key issue is the ability of the licensee to translate ideas about a product into a creative, marketable product line.

---

[6]Gallagher, Leigh. 1999, May 31. Endangered species. *Forbes*, p. 105.

POTENTIAL PROBLEMS

The two main issues that trademark licensors have to be concerned about are counter-feiting and debasement of the trademark. Popular trademarks, especially those with a premium cachet (priced high and associated with images of prestige and success such as Gucci handbags) are prone to be copied illegally. Often the copies are so good that they cannot be distinguished from the genuine ones. Licensees are hurt when the market is flooded with counterfeit products. Because they are sold at a cheaper price, inferior copies adversely affect the value of the genuine article and reduce the size of the latter's market. The issue of counterfeiting is discussed in greater detail in Chapter 12.

The second concern for the licensor is the ability of the licensee to maintain the agreed-upon quality of the licensed products. Because trademarks give products their distinctive, and often distinguished image, shoddy quality naturally reflects poorly on the product's reputation. The issue of quality assumes even more importance in the case of toys where safety is a key factor, ensured through proper product design. A related concern is the "overlicensing" of the trademark. By failing to limit the type and variety of products licensed and the outlets where they are sold, the licensor runs the danger of creating an image that is no longer unique or exclusive.

LICENSING AGENTS

Many firms, especially those new to licensing or small in size, use licensing agents to help them set up the merchandise licensing arrangements. Such agents have expertise, contacts throughout the industry, and experience. They help with negotiating a contract, assist with administering it, collect royalties, and maintain ties with the licensees. The agents are generally paid a commission on all licensing receipts.

The characteristics to look for in an agent are the extent and nature of its experience, the number of companies it represents, compatibility with the firm's own objectives, and the size of its operations. Licensing agents range from individuals representing one or a few properties to fairly large organizations handling a number of properties.

FRANCHISING

Franchising is a variation of licensing. In franchising, a firm (the franchiser) licenses an entire business system as well as other property rights to an independent company or person (the franchisee). The franchisee organizes its business under the franchiser's trade name and runs it as per the rules and procedures laid down by the franchiser. In return for letting the franchisee use its trade name and way of doing business, the franchiser receives fees, royalties, and other payments.

Despite similarities, franchising and licensing differ. Franchising contracts are much longer in duration. While licensing is typically used by manufacturing firms, franchising is employed by service organizations. 7-Eleven convenience stores, Hilton hotels, McDonald's hamburger restaurants, and Avis car rental agencies usually expand through franchising. Unlike licensing, the franchisee is bound to operate its business as per the guidelines set by the franchiser, which is one reason why McDonald's restaurants appear similar the world over. As with licensing, franchising agreements usually require payment of a fee upfront and then a percentage of revenues. In addition, the franchisee may have to buy supplies and other materials from the franchiser. The franchiser's aim is to ensure quality goals are maintained as well as a standardization in the materials used.

International franchising is particularly attractive to a company when its product cannot be exported to a foreign country; when it is not interested in investing in that country as a producer; and when its production process (or business system) can be transferred to an independent company in the foreign country without much difficulty. Therefore, physical products whose manufacture entails significant capital investment and/or high levels of managerial or technical skills are usually not favorable candidates for franchising. Consequently, international franchising is most popular in consumer service products that can be produced with relatively low levels of capital and skills.

The growth of franchising as an international entry method has been phenomenal. It has been a successful method of doing business in the United States. As domestic markets have matured, overseas markets have opened up, and awareness of franchising as a concept has grown in countries where it was virtually unknown a few years ago, U.S. companies have been expanding abroad at a rapid clip. In 1971, about 156 franchising companies were operating 3,565 outlets abroad. Twenty-five years later, more than 400 U.S. firms had more than 40,000 franchisees abroad.[7] According to the International Franchise Association, more than four-fifths of foreign outlets of U.S. franchisers were located in Canada, Japan, Western Europe, Australia, and the United Kingdom. Also international franchising by non-U.S. companies has increased. For example, Benneton, an Italian clothing company, has more than 4,000 franchised outlets worldwide.[8] Table 6-6 lists the top ten franchisers in the world, all of which have their origins in the United States. As with trademark licensing, the success of many franchising businesses reflects the worldwide attraction of a lifestyle associated with the United States. Although large companies have traditionally entered franchising, in recent years smaller and newer companies have also expanded overseas.

Table 6-6	The Largest Franchise Chains	
Rank	*Chain*	*Number of Outlets*
1	McDonald's Corporation	16,796
2	The Southland Corporation	15,520
3	Subway Sandwiches and Salads	11,500
4	KFC	8,187
5	Burger King	7,506
6	Tandy Corporation	6,600
7	Century 21 Real Estate	6,000
8	Taco Bell	5,644
9	International Dairy Queen	5,347
10	Domino's Pizza	5,300

Source: International Franchise Association, 1996.

---

[7]Jha, Alok K. 1997, August 7. Consolidating at home, setting sights abroad. *The Wall Street Journal,* p. B11.
[8]Walker, B. J. 1989. *A comparison of international vs. domestic expansion by U.S. franchise systems.* Washington, DC: International Franchise Association, pp. 1–24.

Here are some examples of the use of franchising as a method of overseas expansion.[9]

- The Southland Corporation, based in Dallas, Texas, owns the 7-Eleven name, which is the leading convenience store in the world. It owns fewer than half of the 5,360 stores in the United States—the rest are franchised. The Southland Corporation, which has been majority-owned by a Japanese retail firm, Ito-Yokado, since 1991, runs more than 5,800 stores worldwide through franchising. This chain of convenience stores in Japan is the biggest in the country with a 15-percent share of the annual market of $104 billion. It sets the standards for the rest of the industry. 7-Eleven has been able to keep ahead of its rivals with state-of-the-art point-of-sale information systems and a well-trained crew of travelling instructors to tutor franchisee store-owners. In addition, being an early entrant into the business, 7-Eleven had the pick of sites and shrewdly handed out franchises to lots of former liquor stores. Having a liquor license adds 100,000 yen to the daily sales of an average convenience store.
- Gymboree, a Burlingame, California, firm that offers the world's largest child development play program through weekly classes and custom-designed equipment, has 468 units, of which only five are company owned. The rest are franchised, with 65 units outside the United States.
- The Body Shop International, based in Littlehampton, United Kingdom, specializing in "natural" cosmetics, has more than 1,000 stores in 45 countries, most of them franchised. Founded in 1976, the first franchise was awarded in 1978.
- McDonald's Corporation, the largest global food service retailer, has more than 15,000 restaurants in 80 countries. Only 30 percent are owned by the company and its affiliates; the rest are operated by franchisees. Fees from franchised restaurants contributed 30 percent of the total sales. McDonald's has been financially stronger primarily because it has been able to use other people's money (the franchisees') to expand and increase its cash flow.
- Hilton Hotels franchises 160 hotels, owns 23 hotels, and manages 40 of them.

In the fast food industry, U.S. franchising companies dominate worldwide. In Belgium, for instance, U.S. firms' share of all franchises is 64 percent, while in Germany it is a whopping 93 percent. McDonald's is the market leader in most European countries. In addition to their highly regarded brands, U.S. companies are technologically advanced with regard to operations management and possess strong marketing and advertising know-how as well as extensive experience.

TYPES OF FRANCHISING

One approach, called direct franchising, seeks out individuals or firms abroad who are interested in operating franchised businesses in their own countries. Direct franchising requires more franchiser involvement but gives the franchiser much greater control

---

[9]Japanese retailing—A matter of convenience. *The Economist.* January 25, 1997, pp. 60, 62.

over the foreign operations. Another method is to form a partnership with another company, resulting in the formation of a third company, which then develops franchises in other countries. For example, Coca-Cola owns or controls bottling companies, which in turn franchise other bottlers. A problem with having such joint ventures is that control is somewhat restricted and the financial issues tend to get complicated. A third and more typical approach involves the establishment of a **master franchisee** who is then given the rights to develop units within a particular country or area. Master franchisees are selected because of their resources, experience, and knowledge of the local laws and marketplace. Master franchisees provide local expertise and oversight of the subfranchisees thus reducing franchiser's cost, oversight, and control requirements. American FastSigns, a Texas-based chain of custom sign and lettering stores, expanded overseas through master franchisees, although it awarded direct franchises in Canada and Mexico. In Brazil, it gave its franchise to a local company, which in turn opened 11 stores.[10]

REASONS FOR THE POPULARITY OF FRANCHISING

The popularity of franchising is easy to understand. The reasons are akin to why licensing occurs. Franchising affords the franchiser an efficient and standard way to rapidly enter a market without the need for large capital outlays. Usually, the franchisee will raise the resources to establish the business itself though often, the franchiser will provide a variety of assistance including market research data, advice on site selection, lease negotiations, arranging of loans, advertising, training, and technical consulting. For example, Gymboree's franchising contracts provide for a royalty of 6 percent and advertising contribution of 1.8 percent; the contract period is for 10 years, renewable for 10 years. Subfranchising agreements and opportunities to expand are offered in the allocated territory. By requiring the franchisee to purchase its supplies from it, the franchiser creates another source of revenue, is able to exercise control over many quality issues, secures scale benefits, and is able to transfer out revenues from the host country should restrictions on payments of royalties be imposed.

Franchising enables a company to expand without using its own resources. For instance, PepsiCo owned and operated 60 percent of its restaurants whereas McDonald's franchised all but 30 percent of its restaurants. Thus, PepsiCo had tied up a lot of its capital in the costly equipment and decor of the stores while McDonald's had been able to tap into the resources of its franchisees. It was estimated that PepsiCo spent $1 billion in capital expenditures for building and acquiring restaurants, an amount greater than its operating profits. To be competitive with McDonald's, PepsiCo changed strategy and decided to reduce its ownership of restaurants worldwide to about 40 percent.[11]

From an inward perspective, an advantage is that the franchisee does not have to be a large organization. Indeed, sole proprietors or small firms are usually interested in and are able to secure a franchise. A franchise allows a formerly unknown business with limited prospects to hitch itself with an internationally recognized brand name or product. The franchisee's business prospects look up and it is able to draw upon the resources of a successful foreign organization to expand and improve its potential in ways it may not have been able to do otherwise. Of course, the franchisee has to be careful as to

[10]*Franchising World.* 1996.
[11]Rudnitsky, Howard. 1995, March 27. Leaner cuisine. *Forbes,* pp. 43–44.

which franchiser it enters into business with. A product or a way of doing business that is successful in one country does not always translate as well in another country, especially if it is economically and culturally different. In such a case, both the franchiser and the franchisee take a risk, which market research should obviate. The franchiser runs the risk of franchising a business in a country not ready for this product or type of business; the franchisee risks paying for a franchise that does not succeed.

SELECTING MARKETS

To be successful in international franchising, franchisers must do a geat deal of homework before venturing abroad. Some franchisers expand abroad by "rolling out" the standardized package that had worked successfully in the home market. Such format franchisers, therefore, select foreign markets because they are proximate and similar to the home market. While in some cases the home format has been transferred abroad intact successfully, in others minor adjustments are made.

Franchisers new to a country sometimes use pilot projects. These franchiser-financed market-testing ventures introduce new concepts, ideas, services, and products to the foreign consumer and help acquaint the franchiser to a market that has considerably different consumer habits. Pilot projects have been successfully used by firms such as Domino's Pizza and KFC to overcome unfamiliar market conditions, high start-up costs, weak brand recognition, and new or unusual training requirements in foreign countries.

Japan is a popular destination for many franchisers.[12] Two of the best examples are convenience stores and fast food operations. Both these retail concepts were brought into the country from the United States. Small Japanese companies like franchising as a way to import the latest ideas and goods in a quick, effective, and comprehensive manner. Larger Japanese firms like franchising because they can leverage their personnel and other operations to expand their business in a predictable and low-risk manner.

OTHER KEY ISSUES IN FRANCHISING

Issues of Quality and Brand Image   Because franchising is commonly used by service firms, the issues connected with manufacturing—building or adapting a facility, integrating technology, moving up the learning curve—are not as strong. However, quality issue is a top priority. The appeal of a Holiday Inn hotel in Bangkok to American tourists is that they are familiar with the name and expect a certain level of facilities and service when they check into the property. Should this expectation not be met, the image of Holiday Inn hotels, not just the one in Bangkok but also those elsewhere, in the mind of the traveler, is tarnished. Thus, the franchiser has to be concerned with the ability of the franchisee to maintain the quality and image of the products, the service, and the facilities, so that the international image of the organization is not sullied. To ensure that, franchisees have to be selected carefully, trained properly, and provided with a full range of support services. Companies like McDonald's maintain schools for training the managers of their food restaurants. The training programs also enable the company to foster the corporate culture across a widely disparate group of franchisees

---

[12]Japan—Retail Entry Strategies, National Trade Data Bank. 1996, June 11. Item ID IT Market IM 960611.019.

and their managers. Sheer numbers of franchisees and their distance from the parent country contribute to laxity in quality control. With more and more franchisees, difficulties tend to arise over maintaining oversight on quality and training, and may strain headquarters resources with regard to providing assistance, advice, necessary equipment, and supplies. One way firms handle this potential problem is by being close to the franchisees through offices in various locations. By placing headquarters personnel at these regional offices, the franchiser has in effect a local presence, and can liaison on a continuous basis with the franchisees in that region. This practice enables closer oversight over quality, brand integrity, and market performance. For instance, McDonald's manages its Belgian franchises through its own local subsidiary in that country.

Franchiser Support   Franchisees are dependent on the franchiser not only for the brand name and image but also the formula for doing the business. Thus, sales and profits are contingent on how well established and well known the franchiser's product and business are and how that image is protected and enhanced. Failure of the product or the business at headquarters or even at an unrelated franchisee will adversely affect other franchisees. Yet another concern is the extent of support they actually receive. In some cases, the complaint of the franchisee is the marked lack of autonomy available to it as to how to organize its business and take advantage of local opportunities. Given the franchiser's desire to maintain a high level of standardization, the opportunity for autonomous decisions on the part of the franchisee is usually constrained. In recent years, franchisees have begun to band themselves into associations to protect their rights and advance their interests with respect to franchisers. Thus, maintaining the proper relationship between the two parties is a necessary and vital task for managers.

Selecting the Partner   Choosing the right partner is just as important as choosing the right market. Each concept and country must be considered separately in relation to a multitude of issues about the market, potential franchisees, legal matters (e.g., rights of the franchiser, protection of trademarks and trade secrets, and termination of contracts), receptivity to franchising, and feasibility of the particular concept.

A key to success in franchising is a sound relationship between the parent firm and the franchisee. As operations become more complex in terms of capital, technology, and market knowledge required, maintaining good relations is often easier said than done. Management Focus 6-3 discusses the experience of a franchising relationship between a U.S. fast food company and its South Korean franchisee.

MANAGERIAL ISSUES IN LICENSING/FRANCHISING

A licensing arrangement has four sequential components: (1) selecting the licensee (or licensor), (2) negotiating the licensing agreement, (3) administering the agreement, and (4) terminating the contract.

SELECTING THE LICENSOR (OR LICENSEE)

A firm with an outward perspective would evaluate firms with the potential to use its technology to manufacture and sell the product in specific markets. The inward-looking firm would be scouting firms with the technology it needs to build up its product line, bolster the quality of its products, or introduce a new and advanced product in the markets

MANAGEMENT FOCUS 6-3

A ROCKY RELATIONSHIP

In 1998, after 14 years, Wendy's International Inc., a U.S. hamburger restaurant company, ended its relationship with its franchisee, Kim Young Il, and withdrew from South Korea. Wendy's experience illustrates the difficulties that exist in operating international franchises.

Mr. Kim, a former oil company executive, got the idea of opening a franchise while studying and teaching in the United States in the 1960s. His children loved hamburgers, but in South Korea, the dish could only be found at expensive restaurant hotels. So when he returned to South Korea in 1974, he used his retirement funds and some inherited money to win an exclusive right to open Wendy's restaurants in that country.

In 1993, Wendy's became concerned that Mr. Kim did not have the resources to compete with rivals such as McDonald's and Burger King. "He was undercapitalized and needed financial assistance," said Denny Lynch, a Wendy's spokesperson. Mr. Kim's preference was that Wendy's invest more of its money in his operations or allow him to expand through subfranchising. But Wendy's wanted Mr. Kim to team up with a partner from one of Korea's large industrial conglomerates, the *chaebol.* In 1994, Mr. Kim and Wendy's began to search for a new partner. But efforts to find a new partner with deep pockets failed and Wendy's finally told Mr. Kim that the franchising contract would be terminated if a new partner was not found by the end of 1997.

During the same period, other problems marred the relationship between Wendy's and Mr. Kim. Wendy's tried to force Mr. Kim to buy supplies of food from more than one vendor with the goal of reducing food prices at the restaurants. Mr. Kim, however, bought some of the key ingredients, such as beef patties, from a distributor that he controlled. Shifting to other suppliers would obviously cut into Mr. Kim's

profits from his distributorship. The two sides also disagreed over whether the franchising agreement permitted Mr. Kim to subfranchise in South Korea and over the amount of royalty paid by Mr. Kim and what Wendy's was obligated to provide in return.

Then, in 1997, a financial crisis hit South Korea and most companies there stopped entering into new ventures. It ended Mr. Kim's and Wendy's efforts to find a partner for the franchising operations in South Korea. Furthermore, banks stopped providing Mr. Kim and many other businesses with credit to import food. Mr. Kim imported much of his food from U.S. suppliers in order to meet quality standards as laid out in his contract with Wendy's.

With access to trade finance cut off, Mr. Kim had to use his own money to buy the food. As the value of the Korean won plummeted, the cost of imports skyrocketed. Mr. Kim tried to get Wendy's to accept locally produced food to replace imports but this proposition was rejected by Wendy's whose main concern was that the food served met prescribed specifications.

As the economic crisis snowballed, foreign firms became a target for Korean xenophobia. Foreign restaurants came under attack as symbols of excess and of money leaving the country. Mr. Kim stopped paying royalties to Wendy's but later he paid back all that was owed after Wendy's extended the deadline to end the franchising agreement to June of 1998. But by then, the relationship had reached a breaking point. Saying that he "had to be independent," Mr. Kim bought a local fast-food chain called Winner's and gave its name to each of the 15 Wendy's outlets he owned. Wendy's withdrew entirely from South Korea. But Mr. Kim did not harbor any grudges. "I really liked Wendy's," he said. "If they decide to come back to Korea, we can join."

Source: Schuman, Michael, and Richard Gibson. 1998, November 27. Following Wendy's exit, Koreans munch on Winner's. *The Wall Street Journal,* pp. B1, B6.

it serves. How do these two firms end up being licensor and licensee to each other? In many instances, a prior relationship may exist between the two parties as exporters and importers. Positive past relationship means the parties are familiar with each other, have been able to successfully work out their differences, and are aware of each others strengths and capabilities. Thus, they are able to proceed to the new level of relationship embodied in a licensing arrangement.

The licensor is interested in the following aspects of the licensee: manufacturing facilities, the size of operations, financial position, compatibility with the licensor, and the motivation for wanting the license. The licensor also evaluates the potential size of the market to be served, often difficult to accurately estimate, which is dependent on the licensee who, being in the market, has a better grasp of its size and trend. The legal framework in terms of enforcement of the agreement and the availability of dispute settlement procedures is another issue for the licensor to consider. In expanding overseas, the licensor is in effect marketing to two constituencies: the prospective licensee and the prospective consumers.

What is the licensee looking for in a licensor? The major attraction of course is the technology or trademark in terms of its proven efficacy, name recognition, and complete access to all the necessary details. The licensee would check to see whether the licensor has other licensing agreements elsewhere with other firms with other products and determine how those arrangements have performed. The reputation of the firm, the performance and consumer acceptance of the product in the home country, and its own ability to absorb the new technology are other factors for the company seeking a license to consider.

When choosing a potential partner, it pays to be selective. Firms need to be assured that the potential partner in the foreign country has sound business experience, a reputation for ethical practices, and has had no involvement in criminal activities or serious litigation. It is important to know the partner's reputation in business dealings and its banking and credit history. In addition, firms may also want to know how well placed a foreign firm or individual is in the country's political and business community.

Although the characteristics of the licensor and the licensee are important, managers need to be cognizant of factors in the overall licensing environment that may favor some relationships and not others. One such factor is the regulatory framework governing licensing in individual countries. In some countries, a licensing agreement is not valid until approved by the respective governments or has been appropriately registered. In others, antitrust laws prohibit giving exclusive rights to certain products or markets. The length of the agreement may also be limited by government policy. Governments in many less-developed countries place restrictions on the amount of innovations that the licensee can be required to transfer back to the licensor on the grounds that any such grantback clause violates the local firm's rights of ownership in new technology. Certain countries, such as the United States, prohibit the overseas licensing of strategic technologies—technologies that can be used for military purposes. Other restrictive factors to be aware of are controls on foreign exchange that may make the payment of fees and royalties in the desired currency difficult, the level and nature of withholding taxes, and caps on royalty rates and other fees.

Numerous resources are available to introduce a licensor to a "real" company who is capable of entering a licensing agreement. Sources of such introductions are government privatization ministries, trade associations, consultants, chambers of commerce, accounting firms, lending institutions, and business newsletters. The best approach is to use lawyers and consultants as introducers, because they are familiar with the laws and restrictions of the local government. It is wise to send a company representative who knows the language and the customs of the country of interest, along with the lawyer.

NEGOTIATING THE LICENSE AGREEMENT

Negotiations over a licensing agreement can be a long, drawn-out affair. The next section on components of a licensing agreement points to the issues over which the parties must negotiate intensely. In many cases, experienced licensors create a standard form for these contracts that outline the key provisions. The agreement is a legal document and is the essential commercial contract that governs the relationship between the licensor and the licensee.

As with any negotiations, much bargaining takes place over issues such as royalty rates and other fees, technology grantback, performance requirements, sublicensing rights, and protection of trade secrets. Each side uses its relative bargaining power to win concessions on some issues while yielding ground on others. For instance, when agreeing to provide exclusive selling rights in a given area, the licensor is often able to demand and obtain a sizable down payment or a minimum annual royalty payment.

International technology licensing agreements, in a few cases, can restrain trade in violation of U.S. or foreign antitrust laws. U.S. antitrust law, as a general rule, bars international technology licensing agreements that unreasonably restrict imports of competing goods or technology into the United States or unreasonably restrains U.S. domestic competition or exports by U.S. persons/firms. The U.S. Department of Justice's Antitrust Enforcement Guidelines for International Operations contains useful advice regarding the legality of various types of international transactions, including licensing.

Foreign countries, including the European Union, also have strict antitrust laws that affect technology licensing. Because of the potential complexity of international technical licensing agreements, firms seek legal advice before entering into such agreements. In many instances, U.S. licensors retain qualified legal counsel in the host country in order to obtain advice on applicable local laws and to receive assistance in securing the foreign governments' approval of the agreement. Sound legal advice and thorough investigation of the prospective licensee and the host country increase the likelihood that the licensing agreement will be a profitable transaction and help reduce or avoid potential problems.

ADMINISTERING THE AGREEMENT

The licensor has to ensure that the licensee is keeping its end of the bargain. This requires the licensee to keep full and accurate records of all licensed products manufactured and sold. Independent auditors are used to confirm the credibility of these accounts. Setting up a mechanism to monitor the performance and gain access to accurate records can be both difficult and costly. A key element of the administrative support provided by the licensor lies in the creation of a good database containing all licensing and relevant agreements, with a focus on contractual deadlines and commitments.

Major concerns for the licensor are the protection of its technology or trademark from piracy, sublicensing by the licensee (if prohibited by the agreement), timely receipt

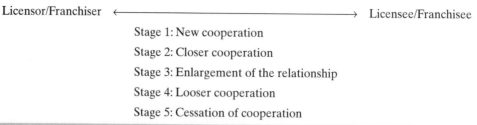

FIGURE 6-1 Life Cycle of a Licensing/Franchising Relationship

of properly calculated royalty payments, illegal use of the technology, retention by the licensee of any innovations it makes or finds, and possible quality deterioration in the products made by the licensee. All these require continuous monitoring, use of inspectors, frequent visits to the licensee's country of operations, and expensive legal help.

For the licensee, the concern is whether the licensor is indeed providing the technology and the support services it agreed to. Should difficulties arise in fully grasping the transferred technology or if the technology fails to perform as expected, the licensee would expect the licensor to provide a full package of services such as training of personnel, testing of equipment, and prompt and frank sharing of information.

TERMINATING THE AGREEMENT

Licensing agreements are for a certain number of years and can be renewed. However, contracts may have to be terminated, and sometimes before their normal life. With the end of the contract, the licensor is free to sign up with another licensee (assuming an exclusive contract had existed until then) or it may enter the market itself through exports or on-site manufacturing or direct ownership of facilities. Sudden cancellation of an agreement may end up shutting out the licensor from the entire market. In 1996, the Venezuelan licensee for Pepsi Cola, claiming inadequate support from the U.S. food and beverage company, switched its business to Coca-Cola. By this decision, Pepsi Cola lost its entire production and distribution system in Venezuela.[13] This example suggests the need for a close relationship between the two parties and provisions in the agreement for a satisfactory settlement of disputes.

Figure 6-1 depicts how the relationship between the licensor/franchiser and the licensee/franchisee evolve over time from being relative strangers through increasingly close cooperation to ultimately, a parting of ways. Managerial attention is necessary to prolong the relationship and make it profitable to both sides.

COMPONENTS OF A LICENSING AGREEMENT

A licensing agreement is a written contract between the licensor and licensee that sets out the rights and obligations of the two parties. The precise contents of an agreement depend on the objectives of the two parties and their respective bargaining power, the

---

[13]Deogun, Nikhil. 1997, February 21. Pepsi's domestic bottlers may expand to run overseas franchise territories. *The Wall Street Journal*, p. A3.

nature of the intellectual property that is being licensed, and the application of the national laws relevant to the contract. While the clauses of such a contract will thus vary from one agreement to another, certain key provisions must be included in an agreement.

1. *Scope of the license.* This clause identifies the precise nature of what exactly is being provided by the licensor to the licensee in exchange for royalty and fees. The clause should clearly state whether the license is exclusive (where the licensor gives up the right to issue licenses to others in the licensee's territory), or nonexclusive, and whether the licensee can grant sublicenses. Another issue that should be clarified is whether the licensee should be required to transfer back to the licensor any, some, or all of the inventions or improvements it may have made to the licensed technology.

2. *Restrictions on use.* Several types of restrictions are usually imposed on the use of the license by the licensee. Usually, a licensee will be limited to producing and selling in specific geographical markets. The licensor reserves for itself or other licensees other markets. Sometimes the licensor may prohibit the licensee from purchasing goods, services, or technology from competing sources. The licensee's R&D activities may be curbed or it may be asked to use technical experts from the licensor. Yet another restriction may be on the use of the technology after the agreement expires.

3. *Performance requirements.* As indicated earlier, the success of the licensing venture is contingent on the licensee's ability and commitment to produce the licensed product as per agreed-upon standards of quality and to fully exploit its sales potential in the licensed market. Therefore, the licensor seeks performance provisions regarding production, quality, and sales. Quality is often ensured by giving the licensor the right to monitor the licensee's operations or to place experts from the licensor inside the licensee's facilities. When Heineken, a Dutch brewery company, was expanding in Europe in the 1980s, it posted brewmeisters in its licensed operations to ensure the quality was synonymous with a premium brand such as Heineken.

4. *Compensation.* The licensee's payments of royalties and fees can be structured in various ways. As discussed earlier, the licensee may agree to pay a single lump sum in advance of the transfer of the technology. At other times, installment payments may be negotiated. The basis of payment of royalties—total production, total value of sales, a minimum amount, before or after taxes—must be clearly stated as well as the dates and the currency of payments.

5. *Intellectual property protection.* The agreement would clearly specify the rights and privileges of the licensee with respect to the licensed technology. What constitutes misuse of the patent may be suggested. When the license is about a trade secret, the agreement would contain a confidentiality clause that restricts the licensee's right to disclose the information.

6. *Dispute settlement.* Provisions for settling disputes that could arise during the life of the agreement must be outlined. Although the agreement should provide mechanisms to clarify any differences of interpretation or resolve conflicts, often references have to be made to external dispute settlement procedures. Thus, the agreement would cover issues such as the legal jurisdiction in which the disputes should be settled (under home, host, or third country laws and at what location) or the use of arbitration including the source and selection of arbitrators and the binding nature of their decisions.

7. *Duration.* The length of the licensing agreement should be specified. The agreement should also state how the relationship may be terminated. Common reasons for termination would be bankruptcy of either party, the failure on the part of the licensee to perform as per the agreement, nonpayment of fees and royalties, or failure to protect trade secrets. The licensee may terminate the contract if the licensor fails to provide the promised technology or supporting services or if the licensor issues a license to another firm to serve the same exclusive territory as the licensee. Alternately, the two parties may decide on a different type of relationship, say, a joint venture, and hence end the licensing relationship.

COMPARING LICENSING, TRADEMARK LICENSING, AND FRANCHISING

As this discussion has indicated, the managerial issues connected with licensing technology and trademark and franchising are similar in many respects. However, each one of these methods of international business affects a firm in different ways and has important implications for the success of the venture, human resource management, and organizational design. For instance, the risk to technology licensing is the possibility of creating new rivals; for trademark licensing the issue is ensuring the integrity of the trademark; for franchising the focus is on quality control. Table 6-7 summarizes these issues.

INTERNATIONAL LITIGATION

Even though under most circumstances managers from both sides can reach a mutually acceptable settlement to their disputes, in some cases, litigation may be the only way out. However, litigation is not the favorite choice of the parties because it is complicated, expensive, and time consuming, especially because no international court system exists in which to settle commercial disputes between private parties. Lawsuits also lead to unwanted publicity and may wreak long-term damage on a relationship, foreclosing future cooperation. When litigation is pursued, the determining issues are which country's laws have jurisdiction over the dispute, whether the decision of one nation's court can be enforced in another, and what does the licensing agreement say about dispute resolution.

Jurisdiction refers to whether a court has power over the firms involved in the dispute. If one country has jurisdiction, the managers from the other country should be aware that they can be sued in a foreign country. In determining whether it has jurisdiction, courts look at where the most important contacts of the relationship occurred—the place where the contract was negotiated and signed, the place of performance, the place of the business, the home of the parties, and the place of incorporation.

Each party prefers to opt for the court most advantageous to it. Therefore, they challenge the suitability of a particular forum. Enforcing a court's decision in another country is not easy, because the losing party may simply ignore it. The help of the foreign court would have to be sought and cooperation cannot be assumed. No international institution enforces judgments of the courts of sovereign nations. In such cases, the winning party may have to seek the help of its home government to intercede with the government in which the other party is based.

Table 6-7   Comparing Technology Licensing, Trademark Licensing, and Franchising

Strategy	Organizational Design	Advantages	Disadvantages	Critical Success Factors	Human Resource Issues
Technology licensing	Technologies	Early standardization of design; ability to capitalize on innovations; access to new ideas	New rivals created; possible dependence on licensee; possible eventual exit from industry	Choose licensees carefully to avoid future competitors; enforce patents and licensing agreements	Technical knowledge; training local managers
Trademark licensing	Product and geography	Fast market entry; low capital cost; no manufacturing concerns	Protecting the integrity of the trademark; monitoring the licensee	Specified use of the trademarks; partners share same values and objectives	Integrate licensees into the business
Franchising	Geography	Quick and easy entry into new markets; low capital cost	Exercising quality control	Partners share same values and objectives; maintain performance standards	Integrate franchisees into the business; training services

Source: Adapted from Levi, David and Slocum, John Jr. "Global strategic alliances: Payoffs and pitfalls." *Organizational Dynamics.* Winter, 1991, p. 48.

ALTERNATIVE DISPUTE RESOLUTION TECHNIQUES

In addition to litigation, the parties have the choice of using **mediation** or **arbitration** to settle disputes. The principal difference between the two is that arbitration decisions are binding on the parties. In mediation, the mediators provide an ongoing link between the disputants and provide suggestions to break deadlocks. Arbitration as a dispute resolution technique received a big fillip when the World Bank created the International Center for the Settlement of Investment Disputes to promote mutual trust between private foreign investors and host governments. Arbitration has many advantages: it is faster, cheaper, conducted privately, can be conducted without lawyers, and has a better chance of being enforced. Consequently, international contracts often designate arbitration as the exclusive form of dispute resolution. Table 6-8 provides a brief listing and description of well-known institutions that offer international arbitration.

The legal issues that arise in international licensing and how they are settled was aptly illuminated when Pepsi Cola's franchisee in Venezuela abruptly cancelled its contract and switched to archrival Coca-Cola. This incident is described in Management Focus 6-4.

PROTECTING PATENTS AND TRADEMARKS

International agreements specify how firms should apply for patent protection. U.S. patents give rights only within the United States. In order to protect a patent in foreign countries, a firm must obtain a patent in the foreign country. An understanding of the laws surrounding patent registration and patent protection is important if a firm is not to lose out in international markets. Under the Patent Protection Treaty, a single international

Table 6-8   Institutions that Provide Arbitration Services

- International Chamber of Commerce, Paris, France

The ICC has regional offices in various parts of world. It hears disputes in any of these locations under whatever law the parties concerned choose. It is the best known and probably the most frequently used of the arbitral institutions.

- The World Intellectual Property Organization Arbitration Center

This new agency was established under the aegis of the United Nations to provide administrative and organizational support to arbitrators deciding on international intellectual property disputes.

- American Arbitration Association

Based in New York City, the AAA handles both domestic and international disputes. The AAA provides arbitrators, and the rules follow closely the American judicial system.

- London Court of International Arbitration

The English courts support the LCIA by readily supporting the latter's decision. The LCIA provides detailed procedural rules for arbitration.

- Other institutions

Other organizations that provide arbitration include the Zurich Chamber of Commerce, the Canadian-American Commercial Arbitration Commission, the Japan Commercial Arbitration Association, and the Stockholm Chamber of Commerce. In addition, the disputants can themselves work out arbitration procedures and select their own arbitrators without having to rely on any of these established formal organizations.

THE PEPSI-COCA SWITCH

In August 1996, without warning, the Cisneros Group of Venezuela informed PepsiCo, the world's second largest maker of soft drinks, that it was ending its five-decade-old relationship as the franchisee of the U.S. company. Simultaneously, the Cisneros Group announced that it was forming a joint venture with Coca-Cola Company, PepsiCo's archrival, and would now produce Coca-Cola drinks for the Venezuelan market. With that decision, PepsiCo's market share of the $400 million Venezuelan market plummeted overnight to zero from about 45 percent, while Coca-Cola's shot up from 10 percent to more than 55 percent.

Venezuela was one of the few countries where Pepsi Cola had successfully held out against Coca-Cola's world market domination. Now, the company had to buy bottling assets or find another route to market its products in that country, where Pepsi's volume was 225 million unit cases annually, the fourth largest in Latin America. The loss of the franchise came at a time when PepsiCo was struggling to revamp its international operations.

PepsiCo reacted furiously to the news that its Venezuelan franchisee had defected to Coca-Cola, leaving it with no presence in a market it had a dominant and profitable position. It contended that it had a contractual agreement with the Cisneros Group until the year 2003. A spokesperson for PepsiCo said, "We believe this sale is illegal on several counts, and Pepsi will exhaust all legal measures both in Venezuela and the United States to insure that our rights and those of our consumers are protected." Indeed, the affront was so great that the spokesperson described Cisneros's action as "an outright betrayal of the Venezuelan people, and—as an attempt to deny the Venezuelans their freedom of choice in soft drinks—it should be opposed by everyone." In response, Coca-Cola replied, "We believe there is no basis for any legal action. The agreement that exists between the Cisneros Group and Pepsi recognizes the possibility of a change." The chief executive officer of Coca-Cola, Douglas Ivester, crowed that "for decades, Venezuela had been the only dark spot on the global Coca-Cola map. Today, it has become one of the brightest." The Cisneros Group said it had aligned itself with Coca-Cola to ensure future expansion. In a statement, Oswaldo Cisneros, chief executive of the Embotelladoras

Coca-Cola y Hit de Venezuela, the new name of the group of 18 bottling plants, said that the company would "undoubtedly become a participant in major expansion in the north of Latin America." The expectation was that the Group would be an anchor bottler for that region for Coca-Cola in due course.

PepsiCo claimed compensation of $118 million for damages. The amount covered sales of soft-drink concentrate that Pepsi would have sold the Group through the 18 months notice period the Cisneros Group should have given, according to the franchising contract. It also included PepsiCo's marketing spending on the bottling operations for the 18 months before the breaking of the contract. The Cisneros Group contested this claim in the Caracas Civil and Commercial Court, saying that Pepsi's figures were exaggerated. Pepsi also moved the Venezuelan Anti-Monopoly Commission to block the proposed venture between its former franchisee and Coca-Cola arguing that it violated Venezuela's antitrust laws.

In December 1996, the venture between Coca-Cola and the Cisneros Group received the green light to proceed from the Anti-Monopoly Commission. While rejecting Pepsi's challenge, the Commission did place some restrictions on a few regional soft drinks that Coca-Cola had bought from Cisneros in August. It also ordered Coca-Cola and Cisneros Group to pay a fine of $1.9 million. PepsiCo said that the decisions confirmed that "Coke and Cisneros broke the law. We're glad they clearly moved to deem this illegal. The situation in Venezuela has been a matter of principle and not of money." However, PepsiCo had asked that the joint venture be dissolved, and that did not occur. Coca-Cola, however, began negotiating with PepsiCo about its $118 million claim of damages.

In September 1997, the International Court of Arbitration in Paris awarded PepsiCo $94 million to be paid by the Cisneros Group. The amount was comprised of $87 million for breaking its Pepsi contract and $7 million in cost and fees. PepsiCo commented, "We are pleased with the award. We think that the court simply recognized that this action in Venezuela was an attempt to destroy our business. The award amounts to many years of profits for us." It was believed that PepsiCo's profits in Venezuela were between $5 and $8 million annually.

Source: Sellers, Patricia. 1996, October 28. How Coke is kicking Pepsi's can. *Fortune,* http://www.fortune.com/ *fortune/1996/961028/cvp.html*; press release September 5, 1997, Pepsi wins $94 m award from Coke bottler, *www.pepsico.com*; Leon, Roger. Pepsi Cola vs. Coca Cola. *The Monthly Report.* Accessed through google.com (*www.cyberven.com/spontaneous/colasing.html*), March 31, 2000.

patent application can be filed, which is then reviewed by the patent offices of individual member countries. Firms wishing to register their patents in other countries merely check off those countries on a form. Most developed countries are signatories to this treaty. Other international agreements govern trademarks and copyrights.

Problems arise for licensors in those countries that are not signatories to such international agreements. Although pursuing the matter through the host country's judicial system is one alternative, another option is to sue in the home country. Sometimes, the assets of the licensee in overseas locations may be seized to enforce court decisions. U.S. courts, although not bound to abide by and enforce the decisions of foreign courts, historically have recognized foreign judgments.

The European Union has a directive that provides a legal framework for the franchising business. The directive outlines a series of provisions of fair behavior and includes provisions for arbitration in case of disputes. The directive is summarized in Table 6-9.

CONCLUSIONS

Licensing and franchising are used successfully by many firms to increase their profitability and to tap into the opportunities provided by a global market. Technical superiority has allowed many firms to profitably exploit their patents and unique production methods without being directly involved in overseas manufacturing and operations. Integration of country markets and the creation of successful brand names have helped many service industries to grow enormously through franchising. Before selecting this option, however, managers should consider other alternatives that are available, which might conceivably earn higher incomes and provide greater growth opportunities. Negotiating a licensing/franchising agreement requires forecasting future market potential and mutual trust that both sides will deliver what they promise. These forecasts are often difficult to make, and expectations may have to be lowered. The danger of losing control over one's core competencies or proprietary knowledge together with the possibility of creating potential rivals strongly suggests carefully negotiating licensing

---

Table 6-9 Summary of the European Union Directive on Franchising

The directive aims to protect the identity and reputation of the franchise network by placing certain obligations on the parties involved:

- The franchisee is required to sell products manufactured by the franchiser or parties designated by it
- The franchisee is prohibited from engaging, directly or indirectly, in a similar business in a territory where it would compete with a member of the same franchise network
- The franchisee is required to sell, or use exclusively, goods matching minimum objective quality specifications defined by the franchiser
- The franchisee is prohibited from assigning the rights and obligations under the agreement without the consent of the franchiser
- The franchiser is prohibited from exploiting the franchise in the franchisee's territory
- The franchisee is required to comply with the franchiser's standards for maintenance of the operation and allow the franchiser to carry out checks on the inventory

Source: Belgium—Fast food franchising. 1995, May 17. *National Trade Data Bank.* Item ID IT Market IS9412.073.

agreements and being highly cautious in ceding of knowledge and technology. Even though individual firm circumstances often determine the adoption of market entry strategies, managers need to remember that in most cases, licensing is an intermediate stage in the move toward becoming a multinational firm. Consequently, in entering into licensing arrangements, the future possibilities and implications should be kept in mind.

OPENING VIGNETTE EPILOGUE

The company's strategy of entering the U.S. market reflected Mr. Bonnell's desire to "grow from the inside out." Wanting to avoid what he called an American tendency to simply export popular local games to foreign countries, Mr. Bonnell entered into licensing arrangements based around characters Americans already knew well. One of these, the rights to create a game around the hit movie "Mission Impossible," was already successful. The game jumped to the top three on U.S. game charts and sold more than 800,000 copies worldwide in 1998, nearly hitting the prestigious one million mark. Infogrames also entered into a licensing arrangement with Warner Brothers Interactive Entertainment and secured the rights for the entire Looney Tunes crowd, including Bugs Bunny, Daffy Duck, Elmer Fudd, and 250 other characters. The company expected these games to give it its first major foothold in the U.S. market.[14]

[14]Strassel, Kimberley A. 1999, March 19–20. Infogrames seeks big scores on global market. *The Wall Street Journal Europe*, p. 15.

Key Terms

- licensing
- royalty
- patent
- trademark
- copyright
- trade secret
- technology licensing
- cross licensing
- franchising
- master franchisee
- mediation
- arbitration

Discussion Questions

1. Under what circumstances would a firm choose to become a licensee instead of being an importer?

2. What are the major concerns of a firm when it licenses its technology or know-how to a foreign organization? What proactive steps can the licensor take to address such concerns?

3. Companies such as the McDonald's Corporation have thousands of franchisees and the number continues to grow. Does such expansion impose constraints on the company's management to effectively supervise the individual franchising relationship? Explain.

4. A U.S. company is negotiating agreements to provide a license to a firm in an advanced industrial country, say Sweden, and also to a firm in a developing country, say Egypt. Would you expect these two agreements to differ in substance? Why or why not?

5. Explain the managerial concerns of the licensee with regard to the use of the license. How can the licensee effectively address these concerns?

6. How should a firm go about identifiying potential franchisees? Identify a list of important criteria that the franchiser should use to select franchisees.

Writing Assignment

Your firm is negotiating a licensing agreement with a Chilean firm that will include sharing your patented information and technology with the Chileans. You have been asked by your superior to research and prepare a report on patent protection laws in Chile and the extent to which the laws are enforced. Prepare a three-page memo that includes the requested information and list of the sources of the information.

Internet Exercise

Use the Internet to identify at least three international franchising events—the dates, location, and organizers—in the coming year where franchisers and franchisees would meet to consummate business deals.

Internet Resources

A variety of sites offer information about franchising and licensing. The U.S. Small Business Administration offers valuable advice at its website, *www.ussba.gov*. For information on franchising, the International Franchise Association can be accessed at *www.entremkt.com/ifa/*. Many specialist legal firms provide advice on licensing and franchising agreements, patent protection, and trademark rights. The law firm of Sim, Hughes, Ashton & McKay has a site at *www.sim_mcburney*. Individual companies provide information on franchising as McDonald's does at its website *www.mcdonalds.com*. For information on franchising and intellectual property, the American Bar Association's site at *www.abanet.org* provides a wealth of information.

Case 6–1   POWER BEAT INTERNATIONAL LIMITED
(prepared with Verl Anderson)

In June 1994, following the failure to consummate a successful licensing agreement for the manufacture and sale of its new invention—an innovative automobile battery—Peter Witehira, the chief executive officer of the New Zealand-based Power Beat International Limited, was faced with deciding on a way to commercialize the new technology. Apart from finding a new licensee or even building a factory to manufacture the battery on his own, he wondered what other options he could pursue. He was also concerned that the company would be a target for a hostile takeover. The company's total revenue in 1993 was less than NZ$1.2 million and retained earnings was about NZ$400,000. (Financial statements are included in Exhibits 1 and 2; exchange rate was approximately US$1 = NZ$1.6).

PETER WITEHIRA, THE ENTREPRENEUR

Given its remote geographical location and the pioneering spirit of its original settlers, New Zealanders developed a reputation as a great nation of fixers,

Exhibit 1	Balance Sheet, 1990–1993: Power Beat International Ltd. (in NZ$)			
	1993	*1992*	*1991*	*1990*
SHAREHOLDERS' FUNDS				
Share Capital	2,520,000	2,520,000	12,600	11,338
Share Premium Account	92,620	92,620	2,600,020	1,336,662
Foreign Currency Translation Reserve	—	101,096	92,259	—
Retained Earnings	409,521	70,633	(165,925)	(233,364)
Total Shareholders' Funds	$3,022,141	$2,784,349	$2,538,954	$1,114,636
CURRENT ASSETS				
Cash	623,034	161,314	756,877	619,812
Receivables	149,070	42,032	281,384	25,926
Stock of Finished Goods	17,624	30,600	—	—
Amount Due by Witehira	—	322,500	—	—
Deposits & Prepayments	81,430	—	—	102,867
	871,158	556,446	1,038,261	748,605
CURRENT LIABILITIES				
Payables	(135,063)	(102,788)	(101,484)	(113,328)
Provisions for Deferred Taxation	(205,219)	(48,280)	—	—
WORKING CAPITAL	530,876	405,378	936,777	861,933
INVESTMENTS	1,863,413	2,003,042	1,361,222	—
FIXED ASSETS	274,483	108,670	90,092	432,145
INTANGIBLE ASSETS				
Patents	353,369	267,259	150,863	47,214
NET ASSETS	$3,022,141	$2,784,349	$2,538,954	$1,114,636

adapters, and tinkerers. Peter Witehira (pronounced weetee-heera) belonged to that tradition and drew on a family heritage that was part Maori and part Scottish.

In school he was an average student. In 1966, at age 15, he left school and became an apprentice in the aluminum joinery industry. There he met Harry Dean, a tradesman who became not only his work mate but also his "buddy and mentor." Harry taught the young Witehira the principles of pride in the job and of doing things properly.

Like most kids growing up in New Zealand in the 1960s, motor cars had a huge influence on him. As he said, "I loved cars. My first car was a one owner, Ford Popular. I was just 15 and found it wasn't fast enough." The Popular was followed by a Humber 80 and then a Wolseley 6/90. "Cars really were a major factor in my life. I helped build hot rods. I got to know the local racing drivers and would traipse off to Pukekohe for all of the major race meetings."

In 1974, Peter became a police officer. Ten years later he quit at a time when the most radical economic and social changes in New Zealand were being ushered in. After years of protectionism, the government opened up the economy. The country embarked on a roller coaster ride that saw fortunes made. Peter went into construction. "I was not only building houses but also designing them and about as busy as I could be. But there wasn't a lot of money in it. Because of the extreme competition, you had to keep profit levels low to get the work." In 1987, the stock market crashed. "The building boom was over. I wanted something new to do and decided to invent something. I didn't really know what it was that I wanted to invent, but I knew I had some potential in that area. I had earlier invented a scrambling device to stop people stealing videos."

The disciplines instilled in him by Mr. Dean played a strong part in developing his work ethic and now it really came to the fore. Always a keen reader, he started reading anything and everything. "One

Exhibit 2	Income Statement, 1990–1993: Power Beat International Ltd. (in NZ$)			
	1993	*1992*	*1991*	*1990*
INCOME				
Sale of Licenses	1,100,000	1,527,093	751,221	—
Interest Received	7,751	36,971	31,237	39,373
Sale of Prototype Samples	5,628	47,211	—	—
Consultancy & Engineering	74,520	—	—	—
TOTAL INCOME	1,187,899	1,611,275	782,458	39,373
EXPENSES				
Administration	195,426	254,416	252,741	123,625
Audit Fees	8,000	15,000	6,000	6,000
Depreciation	37,658	17,990	18,186	3,426
Foreign Exchange (Gain)/Loss	(35,712)	2,676	—	—
Operating Expenses	185,121	136,304	270,347	67,904
Rental & Lease Costs	18,827	7,703	—	—
Research & Development	105,432	99,194	154,331	—
Promotion & Marketing	166,554	182,051	—	—
Purchase of NZ License	—	645,070	—	—
Interest	667	7,647	13,129	928
Loss on Sale of Fixed Assets	10,099	936	285	916
Other	—	7,798	—	69,938
TOTAL EXPENSES	692,072	1,376,785	715,019	272,737
NET OPERATING PROFIT/(LOSS)	495,827	234,490	67,439	(233,364)
TAXATION	(156,939)	(48,280)	—	—
NET PROFIT AFTER TAXATION	338,888	186,210	67,439	(233,364)
EXTRAORDINARY ITEM				
Gain on Sale of Subsidiary	—	50,348	—	—
NET PROFIT ATTRIBUTABLE TO SHAREHOLDERS	338,888	236,558	67,439	(233,364)
RETAINED EARNINGS BROUGHT FORWARD	70,633	(165,925)	(233,364)	—
RETAINED EARNINGS CARRIED FORWARD	$ 409,521	$ 70,633	$(165,925)	$(233,364)

Source: Company annual reports.

book changed everything for me. It was called *Inventions that Changed the World*. There was a section that listed the ten inventions that the world still needed the most. The first four were medical inventions—cure for arthritis, for cancer, and so on. It was number five that interested me—the world needed a better battery. I thought that was something I could handle."

Mr. Witehira found few books about the principles of a battery. After reading all that he could, he decided to go about learning in the most direct way. He bought a brand new battery, took his hacksaw and cut the top off it and started prodding and poking and learning. "The principles were reasonably complex but I bought more batteries and cut them up and gradually got to the stage where I began to understand how they were constructed."

In his mind he had visualized the car battery as a "refrigerator—instead of storing food and milk, the battery was storing electric power. But to me it seemed car batteries were a refrigerator without a deep freeze unit. I began to think of ways to include the battery equivalent of a deep freeze unit, and that's where the concept of the Power Beat battery came from."

THE POWER BEAT BATTERY

The Power Beat battery was an alternative to the existing automotive batteries. As late as 1987, the technology incorporated in the standard car battery had been virtually unchanged for 70 years. The standard automobile battery could well be the only item that could be taken out of a 60-year-old car and be placed into a new vehicle (though voltages have changed). By contrast, automobiles in the 1990s bore little resemblance to vehicles manufactured in those early years. No one had thought of producing a standard car battery that didn't go dead if the electrical components were left on for an extended period of time. Meanwhile, sophisticated automobile design and the demand for more accessories (such as radio, compact disk player, cell phones, electric windows) were multiplying the electric load placed on batteries.

A lead acid starter battery, referred to as starting, lighting, and ignition, or SLI, battery, must provide electric power for starting in all conditions. Once the engine starts, the vehicle's alternator recharges the battery thus replacing the power used to start the engine. Two to three years was the average life for conventional SLI batteries—less if the unit was subjected to overcharging and/or repeated deep discharges because auxiliaries (such as the headlights) had been left on.

All vehicles require at least two levels of power. High current is needed, temporarily, for starting a vehicle. Lower current is required for auxiliaries such as lights and radios, for extended periods of time. Recognizing this distinction, the Power Beat battery used advanced lead acid battery cells in an ingenious configuration. This battery supplied different current to match a vehicle's two different power needs. Thus, if lights, radio, ignition, or accessories were left on, only separate, heavy duty, rechargeable auxiliary cells were discharged, which did not affect the starter portion of the battery. Therefore, the likelihood of the battery dying due to the lights or other accessories being on was greatly reduced, if not eliminated.

Instead of the conventional six-cell design, this 12-volt battery used a 12-cell configuration split into two groups. One six-cell group, constructed from low density, thin electrode plates, produced the fast, high discharge current needed for engine cranking. The other six cells contained specially designed, double grid, high-density plates capable of withstanding repeated slow, deep discharge cycling and thus provided needed power to the vehicle's accessories and electrical auxiliaries for much longer.

Controlling the operation of these two different six cell groups was an integrated electronic control unit called the discharge management system (DMS). Through an electronic sensor, the DMS unit determined whether the vehicle was in use. If the vehicle was not in use, the sensor isolated the starting plates so they could not be discharged. The sensor reconnected the starting and auxiliary plates when the driver started the vehicle.

The lead acid battery was a standardized, mass produced, commodity-like product for the automobile industry. It was cheap to produce relative to its output of energy. The Power Beat battery, on the other hand, was a premium quality battery that cost more to produce and more to install than standard batteries. The new battery was assumed to last between seven and 10 years longer than the common lead acid battery.

POWER BEAT INTERNATIONAL LIMITED

Mr. Witehira obtained a patent for his invention in the United States in 1987. With that initial patent, he developed a crude prototype battery and had it approved by a government scientist in Auckland who gave a written letter confirming the system would work. Armed with that confirmation, and little else, Witehira approached friends and relatives who put up NZ$40,000 toward development costs. He now needed the support of a scientific body to test his prototypes. The positive attitude of the Hamilton-based University of Waikato's physics department so impressed him he moved his family—a wife and their six children—to Hamilton.

Mr. Witehira formed a company to exploit the binary battery technology. He named his new company Power Beat International Limited (PBIL). Beat was an acronym for binary electric automotive technology, which was the technical description of the electric system. But the word needed some marketing clout and Mr. Witehira added "Power" to the name so it could be used in future publicity. It was registered as a New Zealand company in September 1989 with a paid-up capital of NZ$10,000 and with Witehira as the majority shareholder.

With no source of venture capital for budding entrepreneurs in New Zealand, PBIL was launched as a nonlisted public company. A float was made of 2,600,000 new shares at a price of NZ$1 each. Nearly NZ$1.4 million was immediately raised. To obtain extra funds, shares worth NZ$180,000 were sold to the Maori Development Corporation—a majority-owned New Zealand government agency for promoting economic activity among the country's leading ethnic minority—and to Australian and Canadian interests.

In October 1993, PBIL was listed as a public company on the New Zealand Stock Exchange. On the first day of trading, the shares were sold for NZ$18. The company now had more than 900 shareholders who had invested NZ$4.8 million. Among the shareholders was Mr. Witehira's local paperboy. Brendan Mitchell, aged 10 at the time, heard about the company. He told his sister, Desiree, aged 16. Together they bought NZ$1,000 of shares—he with savings from his paper route, she from baby-sitting money.

The firm was now focusing on commercializing its battery, convinced that the technology had been demonstrated to be practically feasible. Technical praise for the battery had come from many sources. In 1994, it won the prestigious RD100 Award—the so-called Nobel Prize for technology innovation—which in the past had been given to the development of products such as desktop computers and photocopying machines.

The company's approach was to take an idea from invention through the prototype and the evaluation stage to establish a proven, test-manufactured product. When a satisfactory consumer market had been demonstrated, the resultant business opportunity would be ready for transfer to outside interests for mass-manufacture and marketing.

PRODUCT DEVELOPMENT

PBIL did not have the financial resources, technical ability, or managerial skills to mass-produce its battery. To determine the reliability and functional characteristics of the battery, it was necessary to carry out a limited volume test production run. This test would give the company valuable technical information about the product and the manufacturing process.

A family-owned independent battery company, Amplex Consolidated Private Limited, in Sydney, Australia, agreed to make Power Beat batteries under contract. Amplex was one of only three automotive SLI battery manufacturers operating in Australia and New Zealand. The first batteries were produced in February 1990. It was not an ideal situation though because PBIL needed to exercise control over the product quality and manufacturing procedures, deeming them critical for any new product. So, PBIL purchased a majority shareholding in Amplex, changed the name to Power Beat Australasia Limited, and for a short period operated the business. Capital had to be injected and production facilities improved. Once safe and reliable production was underway, PBIL sold the company back to the previous owners in 1993 retaining only a 19 percent shareholding to protect its interests. Nearly two years were spent fine-tuning the battery, developing various versions for specific applications, and establishing marketing contacts for the company. The company had deliberately avoided the giants of the worldwide battery manufacturing industry in the belief that they would have quietly killed the design because of the threat it presented to their own technology. Witehira felt his new battery would not be attractive to any of the established producers.

MARKETING

The battery was configured and designed as an after-market, drop-in replacement for (but not limited to) most modern cars made after 1976. A heavier version was planned for trucks and a different dimensioned battery for European cars. Installation was straightforward on many modern vehicles that divided the starter motor cable from the auxiliary power harness at the battery's terminals. Where they were not divided, auxiliary and alternator wires had to be separated from the starter motor cable for connection to the smaller positive terminal. The battery was therefore being promoted to automobile dealers, not manufacturers. To be sold as original equipment by car manufacturers, the battery required certain modifications. Although priced higher than the conventional battery—the recommended retail price was NZ$146 compared with between NZ$80–$110 for a conventional battery—PBIL touted the advantages of the product in terms of security, convenience, safety, and longer life. However, because of the product's youth, it was not yet known for certain how long the average Power Beat battery would last. Some had been in use since 1988. The company claimed that the binary battery's life expectancy would be more than double that of conventional batteries.

Power Beat Australasia sold batteries under the Power Beat name in Australia, and since the middle of 1993 had been shipping fewer than 1,000 units a week to New Zealand. Production costs in Australia were high and the small size of the output militated against scale economies.

Few retail outlets in New Zealand carried the Power Beat battery. Some new car dealerships acted as marketing agents for the product. Among them were Jaguar and Nissan dealerships. When the first batteries were produced in Sydney, Witehira went to Nissan

New Zealand with some samples in the hope that they would appreciate the new product. This tactic was successful and Nissan New Zealand now offered the battery as an optional equipment to new car buyers. It also offered the Power Beat battery as a replacement for all vehicles checked for battery replacement at Nissan service centers in the country. In Australia, Power Beat batteries began to be fitted to all Toyota Previa ambulances manufactured in Australia and in some four-wheel-drive vehicles used by the Australian government, in particular the defense department.

Various efforts had been made to enter into arrangements with overseas firms to produce, market, or license Power Beat batteries. Mitsubishi, a giant Japanese conglomerate, signed a cooperative marketing agreement in 1990 that covered Japan, Europe, and the United States. Mitsubishi acquired a 6 percent shareholding in PBIL. After three years, the agreement was ended with no sales developing. Mitsubishi sold its stake. According to PBIL, Mitsubishi wanted to cash in a lot quicker than was appropriate for this sort of project. With the termination of the Mitsubishi connection, PBIL turned to U.S.-based Standard Communications, a subsidiary of electronics giant Philips, and signed a licensing deal in late 1993. It was envisaged that Standard Communications would introduce a special version of the power distribution system developed by PBIL together with the binary batteries for use in boats in the U.S. marine market. That agreement had been put on hold, however, following a row over a technology transfer agreement with a Canadian firm, Trend Vision Technologies, because Standard Communications wanted to see the outcome of the dispute before proceeding. In early 1994, Hyundai, the Korean automaker, signed an agreement to test Power Beat batteries in its cars. In the United States, a New Zealand racing driver, Steve Millen, was test marketing the Power Beat battery on a selection of Nissan luxury and high-performance vehicles.

By the time PBIL went public with its share offering, the already-tested manufactured versions of its battery were available on the market. The yearly advertising budget had been less than NZ$50,000 per year, with some television and newspaper and magazine print advertisements. Brochures and other printed material had also been produced. PBIL planned a major advertising launch during 1994 with a budget of NZ$150,000.

PBIL was competing against conventional battery manufacturers. As yet, though, these competitors had not reacted to PBIL's efforts to produce and sell its bi-nary batteries. However, no real incentives motivated the battery industry, because the expected extended life of the Power Beat battery could reduce industry volume.

OTHER PRODUCT LINES

PBIL's expertise lay in the design of energy management systems. The company's main income was drawn from the sale of licenses, technology transfer fees, and royalties. Apart from the binary battery, the company also held patents for advanced electrode plates for use in various battery applications; a new low-cost technology for power distribution and multiplexing; a load leveling system that could allow homes to be powered from a trickle-fed storage battery system; and a variable stroke internal combustion engine.

Although the firm was developing new technologies, much of Mr. Witehira's energy and efforts were directed toward obtaining a partner who would take the Power Beat battery technology and use it to mass-produce the product for the world market. Nearly all of the company's revenues derived from royalties and technical fees related to the battery.

FACILITIES AND ADMINISTRATION

The company's modern offices and research center were located just south of Hamilton in North Island of New Zealand. Within easy reach of Auckland, 75 miles away, Hamilton was itself the country's fourth largest city. The firm employed a total of 14 workers. A team of three scientists worked on developing and improving the various technologies. With Mr. Witehira as the managing director, the members of the board of directors included a prominent Maori businessperson as chair, a University of Waikato electronics' professor, an owner of a plastics company, and a representative of minority shareholders. Mr. Witehira and his wife held 51 percent controlling interest in the company.

Mr. Witehira was the brain and driving force behind the company. He was the inventor of the Power Beat battery and other technologies. He served as the firm's spokesperson, gave press interviews, and explained the technology to curious audiences at home and abroad. He negotiated with potential partners and clients and supervised the research and development work. The workload, by any measure, was heavy and his daily schedule, hectic.

LICENSING ARRANGEMENT WITH TREND VISION TECHNOLOGIES

As part of its efforts to commercialize the battery technology, PBIL was always on the lookout for overseas partners. In March 1993, Trend Vision Technologies Inc. (TVT), a public company registered in Vancouver, Canada, but operating from offices in Arizona, approached PBIL to obtain manufacturing and marketing rights for the Power Beat battery in North America, Europe, and Asia. TVT was listed on two stock exchanges—the Vancouver stock exchange in Canada and NASDAQ in the United States. PBIL understood these listings to mean that TVT had financial credibility and the ability to raise funds. In May 1993, an agreement was signed between TVT and PBIL by which TVT would pay a minimum license fee of US$9 million over three years for the rights to Power Beat's technology. In addition, royalties of 4 percent on sales of batteries and power management technology would be payable as well as a separate royalty payment of US 1 cent per plate (an average automobile battery requires between 50 and 84 plates) to cover the new electrode plate technology designed by the company. The agreement also required TVT to have manufacturing facilities in place within three years capable of producing a minimum of 3 million Power Beat batteries annually. An escape clause in the agreement said that should any problem arise with the payment of the license fee, TVT would forfeit all monies paid and would have no further rights on Power Beat's battery.

Initially, no cash payment was exchanged. Instead, based on business trust between Peter Witehira and Massimo Fuchs, chairperson and CEO of TVT, PBIL agreed to a series of payments for the first US$750,000 deposit. TVT advised PBIL that raising cash for future payments would present no problem. TVT even provided a letter stating their shareholders included a number of Swiss, Canadian, and U.S. banks. Soon after the agreement was signed, Fuchs issued a statement saying that TVT's capital structure would be increased to allow them to fund commercial manufacture of Power Beat batteries.

Under the schedule of installments included in the agreement, TVT was to make the first payment of US$100,000 to PBIL on the 12th of May 1993. That payment was late in arriving. The second payment of US$150,000 was also late. In mid-June, Fuchs tried to persuade PBIL to take US$150,000 worth of shares in TVT in lieu of the cash. "At first, we said no thank you," says Mr. Witehira. "But, finally, we agreed on a specific one of departure to facilitate the completion of the already overdue second payment, and accepted US$100,000 cash and US$50,000 in TVT shares." Mr. Fuchs insisted that it was simply taking longer than TVT had anticipated to raise the cash to complete the purchase of the battery technology. "The next payment was

for half a million dollars (US) due on the 15th of July 1993," recalled Mr. Witehira. "We had some thoughts that were beginning to nag a little." The payment of US$500,000 was to signal the point at which PBIL would officially hand over the technology in the form of technical specifications and a Nissan Infiniti Q45 sedan that was fitted with a Power Beat battery.

The payment was late again. However, Mr. Fuchs made a dramatic appearance at the annual general meeting of PBIL shareholders in New Zealand in July. He gave a rousing speech at the meeting outlining TVT's payment commitments to PBIL. After the meeting, Mr. Fuchs handed a check for US$500,000 to Mr. Witehira. The check, though, was post dated to September 29, 1993. PBIL declined to accept it and was already thinking of terminating the agreement with TVT. When PBIL threatened to do so, Mr. Fuchs offered to immediately arrange for a bank check to be sent via overnight mail from the United States. A check drawn on an Arizona bank did come, and was deposited by PBIL. It finally appeared that the contract was on track. The information on the battery technology was transferred to TVT and so was the Nissan demonstration car.

On receipt of the technology and the car, Mr. Fuchs issued media releases stating that TVT had now made all required payments to PBIL and that a technology license for North America and Asia would be issued in addition to forming an Asian joint venture. In October, PBIL's bank informed it of problems in clearing the bank check issued on behalf of TVT—in fact, the check had effectively been dishonored. While TVT continued the appearance of business as usual, maintaining consistently that all they needed was more time and issuing media statements about the technology, PBIL was both frustrated and concerned as it had listed itself on October 12, 1993, on the New Zealand stock exchange. It was now becoming clear to PBIL that TVT was using the agreement to promote their own stock. After deciding on legal advice, the relationship with TVT was formally terminated in mid-December.

Because PBIL was a minority shareholder in TVT and in view of the misleading statements and claims Fuchs was making to the U.S. media, PBIL informed the U.S. Securities and Exchange Commission about TVT's failure to meet its contractual obligations. TVT shares were suspended from trading for a few days in mid-January 1994. It was forced to make announcements to NASDAQ and the Vancouver stock exchange where TVT finally admitted that they had failed to make all payments, and as a direct result had been denied the licensing rights for the Power Beat technology. However, no mention was made of the fact that TVT had issued a bounced check for half a million dollars. Instead, it stated its intention to initiate legal action against PBIL for withholding its technology from them. Although trading in TVT shares recommenced following the issue of this statement, it was suspended again when the company failed to file its annual financial statement or annual return, a requirement for all publicly listed companies. In early January 1994, PBIL issued a press release announcing the termination of the agreement with TVT. TVT's threat of a lawsuit against PBIL did not materialize. Subsequently, TVT was delisted from NASDAQ.

The continuing controversy was reported in the New Zealand media, but in a one-sided way, according to Mr. Witehira. Newspapers presented TVT's press releases without referring to PBIL for comment. PBIL's share prices dropped and were trading for NZ$6.

The failure of the TVT licensing agreement was most disappointing for PBIL because until now, it had appeared to be the most lucrative and successful effort to commercialize the Power Beat battery technology. The media publicity, though, brought renewed attention and interest in the company, both domestically and overseas. It forced Mr. Witehira and his senior managers to consider other options, such as domestic manufacturing. He was, however, reluctant to sell outright the technology to another firm.

FUTURE DEVELOPMENTS

While Mr. Witehira traveled around the world presenting details of his inventions to highly appreciative technical audiences, the head office in Hamilton continued to receive eager inquiries from firms seeking licensing or production rights. One of the proposals being considered was to build a plant to produce its batteries at Huntly, an industrial town near Hamilton. The factory would cost NZ$15 million and would require joint venture partners. According to Mr. Witehira, potential partner companies, several of them foreign, had already expressed interest, although he refused to divulge their identities. Cautious after the TVT setback, Mr. Witehira said, "We need to pick the right partner, somebody who can do it right. It'll crack the battery industry worldwide because we will be able to produce a very high-quality battery at a relatively low price." Given the small size of the domestic market, the plant would certainly have to export the bulk of its output, most likely to New Zealand's major and growing trading partners—Australia, Southeast Asia, and Southern California. Producing batteries would also mean a major departure for the company, which had seen itself only as a technology development outfit. Also, it was not apparent that the firm had the resources and competency to engage in manufacturing and sales.

Saddled with a proven technology that he was finding difficult to commercialize, Mr. Witehira was also forced to consider selling the technology of the Power Beat battery. This sale might mean the end of all prospects of the battery being available on the market. On the other hand, it would provide funds to PBIL to continue its research and development on new technologies.

With all the difficulties that PBIL had encountered and the various options he had, Mr. Witehira may have felt disappointed. He however needed only to look out of his office to see an example of Kiwi ingenuity that succeeded. PBIL's office complex was directly opposite Hamilton airport, where a New Zealand-built Fletcher crop-dusting aircraft was mounted on a podium.

INDUSTRY NOTE: THE WORLD AUTO BATTERY INDUSTRY

The total market for automobile batteries was about 240 million units annually. The market size was determined by the number of motor vehicles produced; the total car population as it influenced replacement sales; and the average battery life measured from the date of installation in the vehicle. Worldwide demand for car batteries was expected to grow at an annual rate of about 2.5 percent until the year 2000 but the growth was expected to be lower in Japan, the United States, and Europe. The car battery industry in Europe and the United States already had excess production capacity and Japanese battery makers had diversified to cater to the country's electronics industry.

ORIGINAL EQUIPMENT AND REPLACEMENT MARKETS

Out of the 240 million automotive batteries shipped in 1991, 24 percent or almost 57 million units were to meet original equipment manufacturer (OEM) needs. The demand for OEM batteries was the highest in those countries that were major automobile producers—the United States, Japan, and Western Europe. Demand for replacement batteries was particularly high in Latin America, Africa, and the Middle East as these regions had little motor vehicle production. However, because of stagnating car production and sales in the developed world, the sale of OEM batteries had correspondingly slowed. Demand for batteries for replacement was estimated at about 20 percent of the registered vehicles in a country.

Table 1	1991 Automotive Battery Shipments (millions of units)	
Region	*Units*	*Percent*
United States	76.8	32.2
Canada	4.6	2.0
Asia/Pacific	58.8	24.6
Western Europe	47.9	20.1
Eastern Europe	21.7	9.1
Latin America	18.9	7.9
Africa/Middle East	9.6	4.0
Total Volume	238.2	100.0

Source: George Kellinghusen. 1992. Five year forecast report. Proceedings of the 104th convention of Battery Council International. May 17–20. Monte Carlo, Monaco. pp. 44–47.

The regions of North America, Western Europe, and Asia/Pacific made up almost 80 percent of the market for automotive batteries (see Table 1). North America (United States and Canada) was the largest market, almost one-third of the world.

An advanced industrial economy, New Zealand had a population of 3.5 million with a gross domestic product of about NZ$75 billion. The total stock of all motor vehicles in 1992 was 2,352,000, of which two-thirds were cars. The relatively small size of the domestic market was indicated by the number of cars sold annually. In 1993, fewer than 53,000 cars were sold, equal to a single day's sales in Japan and half a day's sale in the United States. About 600,000 batter-

ies were being made in New Zealand annually at two relatively old plants. As a consequence, automotive battery sales in New Zealand were quite small and any plans to either manufacture the product or license it necessarily involved international markets.

The worldwide auto battery market (except China and the former communist countries) was about US$12 billion in 1992. The 10 largest car battery companies (see Table 2) accounted for 68 percent of the market.

The elimination of trade barriers among the European Union (EU) members had created fierce competition among the various battery manufacturers. Currently, about 35 percent of the batteries of various types sold in one country were manufactured in an-

Table 2	Major Car Battery Producers in the World, 1992 (in sales)

1. CEAC (Italy-France)
2. Varta Batterie (Germany)
3. Pacific Dunlop (U.S.-Australia)
4. Yuasa (Japan)
5. Johnson Controls (U.S.)
6. Tudor Spain (Spain)
7. Delco Remy (U.S.)
8. Japan Storage Battery (Japan)
9. Exide (U.S.)
10. Matsushita (Japan)

Source: George Kellinghusen. 1992. Five year forecast report. Proceedings of the 104th convention of Battery Council International. May 17–20. Monte Carlo, Monaco. pp. 44–47.

other EU country, compared with a figure of about just 10 percent in 1980. Following the internationalization of the automobile market, the battery industry too was undergoing restructuring.

In 1990, out of some 40 battery manufacturers in the European market, 18 accounted for 92 percent of the total. The four leaders—Varta, CEAC, Chloride, and Tudor Spain—alone controlled 41 percent of the market. In two years, these 18 manufacturers had been reduced to only ten and accounted for almost 95 percent of the market. Among them, the four leaders—CEAC, Varta, Tudor Spain, and Hawker-Siddeley—controlled 75 percent of the total. A number of firms were acquired by others.

TECHNICAL DEVELOPMENTS

Intensive competition among battery makers had made the products more reliable. Historically, technical changes in batteries had taken place under the influence of the car manufacturers. With changes in the design of the vehicles themselves, the batteries too were changing. For instance, the reduction in space under the streamlined hoods, the increase in temperatures around the engine, and the increase in electricity consumption due to the greater number of accessories all placed additional demands on the battery's design and power. Continued movement had been away from the traditional battery and toward reduced maintenance units (topping up of water levels once every six months or once a year) or sealed units (maintenance free).

Among the electrochemical cells, lead held the strongest position by far both in terms of its price/performance ratio and recycling potential when compared with the other cells currently available. The superior physical characteristics of other cells such as, for example, nickel-cadmium or nickel-hydride, sodium sulfur, and the different lithium based systems suggested opportunities for additional research by battery manufacturers.

ENVIRONMENTAL ISSUES

Scrapped automotive batteries constituted one of the more visible sources of lead contamination. Although battery recycling was close to 97 percent, concern over environmental pollution remained high. For example, in the United States, as of 1992, more than 35 states had laws banning the disposal of wet cell lead acid car batteries; 15 of these states had mandatory takeback laws. Congress was formulating a plan to tax all lead at the smelter, with a view to discouraging lead usage. The tax on both new and reclaimed lead would increase the price of lead by 200 percent, and add to the cost of batteries. Imported batteries would be taxed on their lead content.

Severe air pollution in many urban areas had forced public opinion and regulatory authorities to mandate strict emission rules. The electric vehicle concept was being advanced as a potential solution. Two main factors restricted the use of the electric vehicle—the recharging ability of batteries and the purchase price of such vehicles. However, from 1996, 10 percent of U.S. cars would be required by law to run on alternative power. Thus, a demand was created by U.S. car and component manufacturers for a battery to meet alternative power requirements.

Source: Battery Council International. 1992. Proceedings of the 104th Convention. Monte Carlo, Monaco.

QUESTIONS

1. What are the options available to Power Beat International? Which option should be selected? Why?
2. Why has Power Beat found it difficult to find a licensee for its invention?
3. Evaluate the role and importance of Peter Witehira in the company.
4. If you were a potential licensee, what would your evaluation be of Power Beat International Limited and its battery?

References

Bond, Robert E., and Jeffrey M. Bond. 1994. _The source book of franchise opportunities._ Burr Ridge, IL: Irwin.

Chen, Min. 1996. _Managing international technology transfer._ London, UK: International Thomson Business Press.

Contractor, Farokh J. 1985. _Licensing in international strategy._ Westport, CT: Quorum Books.

Fladmoelindquist, K. 1996. International franchising—Capabilities and development. _Journal of Business Venturing_ 11(5), pp. 419–438.

Fladmoelindquist, K., and L. L. Jacque. 1995. Control modes in international service operations—The propensity to franchise. *Management Science* 41(7), pp. 1238–1249.

Gutterman, Alan S. 1995. *The law of domestic and international strategic alliances.* Westport, CT: Quorum Books.

Hadjimarcou, John, and John W. Barnes. 1998. Case study: Strategic alliances in international franchising—The entry of Silver Streak Restaurant Corporation into Mexico. *Journal of Consumer Marketing* 15(6), pp. 598–607.

Hill, Charles. 1992. Strategies for exploiting technological innovations: When and when not to license. *Organization Science* 3(3), pp. 428–441.

Hoffman, Richard C., and John F. Preble. 1993. Franchising into the twenty-first century. *Business Horizons.* November–December, pp. 35–43.

Kogut, Bruce, and U. Zander. 1993. The knowledge of the firm and the evolutionary theory of the multinational corporation. *Journal of Internatonal Business Studies* 24(4), pp. 625–645.

Londa, Bruce S. 1994. An agreement to arbitrate disputes isn't the same in every language. *Brandweek* 35(37), p. 18.

Raugust, Karen. 1996. *Merchandise licensing in the television industry.* Boston: Focal Press.

Shahrokhi, Manuchehr. 1987. *Reverse licensing—International technology transfer to the United States.* New York: Praeger.

Sherman, A. 1991. *Licensing and franchising.* New York: Amacom.

Shivell, Kirk, and Kent Banning. 1993. *Running a successful franchise.* New York: McGraw-Hill.

Telesio, Piero. 1979. *Technology licensing and multinational enterprises.* New York: Praeger.

Thunman, Carl G. 1987. *Technology licensing to distant markets—Interaction between Swedish and Indian firms.* Uppsala, Sweden: Acta University.

7
STRATEGIC ALLIANCES
AND EQUITY INVESTMENTS
❧

OPENING VIGNETTE

In 1998, when Travelers, part of Citigroup, acquired an equity stake in Nikko Securities of Japan, the concern was whether the corporate and national cultures of the two financial companies were compatible. This concern was highlighted by the disagreements that arose during negotiations to create a joint venture in wholesale banking.

The goal of the joint venture was to unite the Tokyo operations of Citibank's Salomon Smith Barney unit and Nikko's wholesale and investment banking business. One of the first issues that arose was who would control it. Nikko executive Junichi Arimura said he felt a wave of relief when he heard Sanford Weill, cochair of Citigroup, offer a 51 percent to 49 percent ownership shares. Then he realized that Mr. Weill meant 51 percent Travelers. Nikko, despite its weak position as a smaller company with serious problems, was determined to own a majority stake. Citigroup offered an even 50:50 split. Nikko refused. "It must be a Japanese company," Mr. Arimura told the Americans. "There is no compromise."

Another issue was management. Nikko wanted "co-heads of everything," as a Travelers official complained. Salomon officials were pushing to have their Tokyo branch head, Toshiharu Kojima, a Japanese who had risen through the ranks of Wall Street financial firms, designated the venture's leader. The discussions had all been in English, but then Mr. Kojima and the Nikko officials burst into a flurry of Japanese. Suddenly, all the Japanese stood, bowed, and walked out of the room. Mr. Weill looked at his team who had worked with Mr. Kojima. They shrugged and suggested that they sit tight.

For more than an hour, the Japanese on both sides of the deal talked in an adjacent office. Nikko officials worked hard to convince Mr. Kojima that they were interested in working with him—even having him run the business—if he was sensitive to their need for a strong voice in the venture.

A third issue was what to do with Nikko's so called "relationship managers." In addition to the 400 pure traders, salespeople, and investment bankers Nikko would send to the joint venture, the Japanese company fielded an army of 600 workers whose job was to wine and dine, flatter, chat up, and keep open ties with thousands of client companies. To Nikko, the relationship managers nurtured corporate ties that were crucial, even if many of the relationships weren't immediately profitable. For many Salomon officials, however, they simply spent too much time chasing too few profits. Nikko argued to retain these employees. It feared that many of its long-time clients would not work with the joint venture, which was viewed as a foreign company.

A look at the business section of any daily newspaper will inform the reader of how common joint ventures, outright purchase of foreign firms, and the formation of strategic alliances have become as methods of business expansion abroad. These forms of international business are evidence of a deeper involvement in international operations on the part of the firm. They provide the investor with increasing control of the foreign operations and affect in important ways how the firm is managed and organized. In recent times, the marked trend has been toward the creation of intercorporate linkages between otherwise competing firms. These strategic alliances enable firms to pursue the same goals as equity investments allow, but without the complexities and direct financial commitment that come with ownership. This chapter first discusses strategic alliances, then joint ventures, and finally wholly owned subsidiaries. The discussion examines the reasons for creating these forms of businesses, distinguishes their particular relevance, discusses the management issues encountered in operating and establishing such ventures, and identifies the factors that contribute to the success and failure of alliances. A section also discusses the qualities that managers need to successfully manage alliances.

DEFINITIONS

We start by briefly defining three related forms of international business: strategic alliance, joint venture, and wholly owned subsidiary. A **strategic alliance** is an interfirm collaboration over a given space and time for the attainment of mutually defined goals. Thus, the term covers agreements between two or more firms in which all parties must contribute some input. It may operate locally, regionally, or globally and has specified goals. The word *strategic* is included to suggest that the alliance has long-term goals and is consistent with a firm's overall strategy. In 1997, six airlines—Air Canada, Lufthansa, SAS, THAI, United, and Varig—formed the "Star Alliance," a strategic alliance with the goal of providing integrated worldwide travel service to travelers. Even though the six companies retained their individual corporate identities, they cooperated and coordinated their operations in areas of flight schedules and ticket issuance, pooled frequent flier programs, and arranged for seamless baggage and cargo handling, information sharing, and even purchase and stockpiling of supplies and materials from aircraft to toilet paper.[1] The alliance enabled each member airline to access cities not on its route by enabling each to sell tickets to passengers traveling to any city served by any of the members.

A form of strategic alliance is a **joint venture.** It has two distinctive features: (1) an equity investment is usually involved; and (2) a separate organization is often formed. Thus, a strategic alliance can be referred to as a nonequity joint venture, where firms collaborate but do not create a new organization. It may be viewed as an interim step toward the creation of an equity joint venture. Equity participation by a partner in joint ventures may be less than 50 percent (thus holding minority ownership), 50 percent itself, or more than 50 percent (majority ownership)—the balance in all cases being held by one or more partners. Where ownership in the foreign venture is entirely held (i.e., 100 percent of the equity) by one firm, the venture is referred to as a **wholly owned subsidiary.** The opening vignette is an example of an equity joint venture.

---

[1]Tagliabue, John. 1997. May 15. Five airlines extend limits of alliances. *New York Times,* p. D4.

Strategic alliances, joint ventures, and wholly owned subsidiaries can be considered as three forms of progressively more internationally involved activities of a firm. Each one requires more resources of various sorts for its execution than the previous mode of international business. Similarly, each new mode allows the firm to exercise even greater control over its overseas operations. This relationship is illustrated in Figure 7-1.

Because many of the issues regarding strategic alliances and equity joint ventures are similar, much of the discussion for one applies to the other. Sometimes these two terms—strategic alliance and joint venture—are used interchangeably. However, where their differences impact international management, those distinctions are noted.

THE MOVE TO ALLIANCES AND FOREIGN INVESTMENT

When and how does a firm make this move to enter into strategic alliances, joint ventures, and wholly owned subsidiaries? That point is determined by the intersection of various forces—both internal and external to the firm—that impel firms to expand operations through closer ties with other firms and through investments of capital and other resources. The stages theory suggests that strategic alliance is the logical next step in the international evolution process after trading and licensing. Overseas markets, sales volumes, profit margins, and profit potential may reach such a size that exports and licensing become suboptimal methods of international operations. Overseas distributors may not be able to handle additional sales or may not give the necessary attention to a particular line, especially if it is distributing multiple products. Foreign governmental restrictions of all sorts directed against imports make exporting less attractive. Licensees may not have the capacity to produce in quantities needed or be able to absorb higher levels of technological sophistication in the product. As a next step, the firm forms a strategic alliance where it teams up with another firm to enter a foreign market, obtain capital and raw materials, and increase its potential and reach. Over time, the firm decides that it needs to become more actively involved in the foreign market,

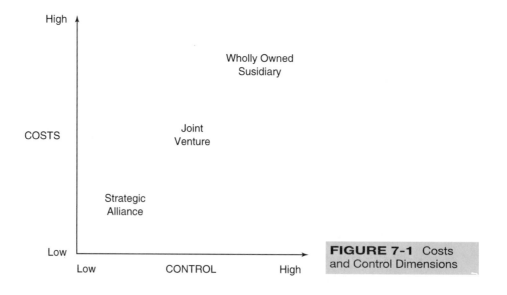

FIGURE 7-1 Costs and Control Dimensions

to fully leverage its home country strengths in the foreign market and to use its economic and technical resources to make the foreign operations more successful. The involvement takes the form of investing in existing or new ventures, first in the form of joint ventures and finally as wholly owned subsidiaries. Accumulated experience from exporting and licensing also gives the firm the confidence to engage in foreign direct investment. Investing abroad constitutes a major incremental change in the international aspirations and activities of a firm.

Taking the inward perspective, a domestic firm moves beyond importing and being a licensee to the stage where it enters into closer, contractual relationships with its business partners abroad, such as suppliers, bankers, designers, or information technology providers, or even competitors. In the joint venture stage, a part of the domestic firm is bought by one or more foreign investors. The transition to becoming a wholly owned subsidiary occurs when the foreign firm acquires all the shares of the domestic firm.

An example of inward perspective is the experience of Empresas ICA, Mexico's largest construction company, which had traditionally depended on Mexican government contracts for its revenues. Since 1947, the company had served almost as an appendage to Mexico's government building dams, bridges, and roads. However, declining oil prices in the 1990s, a major source of tax revenues for the Mexican government, had reduced public works expenditures. Government policies on obtaining bids on construction projects had also changed, as a result of which Empresas had to compete with other private sector and foreign firms for projects it normally got as a matter of routine.

To compete in this changed environment, the company formed a joint venture with a U.S. engineering company, Fluor Corporation, in 1993. The venture bid jointly on all Mexican projects. For Empresas it meant eliminating a potential rival and enjoying access to Fluor's extensive U.S. customer base and U.S. banking relationships. For Fluor, it meant locking up Mexico's largest and most respected civil-engineering firm. While the partnership gave the Mexican company a new roster of clients, those of Fluor's, it also had to share 50 percent of the profits with its joint venture partner.[2]

CHOICE OF COUNTRIES

In selecting countries to invest in, just as with countries to trade with, the distance theory suggests that a firm, in its first overseas venture—strategic alliance or wholly owned subsidiary—go to a "near" country in terms of culture, economic development, and geographical distance. For this reason, Canadian and British firms are among the leading investors in the United States. Similarly, Greek firms have invested in businesses in its geographical vicinity—Bulgaria, Macedonia, and Romania. A study showed that companies are 2.4 times more likely to acquire firms in neighboring countries than elsewhere.[3] At the same time though, European firms saw their neighboring countries as presenting the most difficulties in buying operations (e.g., Germany for Eastern Europe, France for Germany, Switzerland for Italy). This viewpoint suggests that managers tend to be more aware of difficulties in their neighboring countries, perhaps from their greater experience of trying to acquire there.[4]

[2]Millman, Joel. 1998, July 10. Mexico's Empresas ICA copes with new times. *The Wall Street Journal,* p. A12.
[3]Hope, Kerin. 1998, December 8. A big market close to home. *Financial Times Survey,* p. II.
[4]Angwin, Duncan, and Brett Savill. 1997. Strategic perspectives on European cross-border acquisitions: A view from top European executives. *European Management Journal* 15(4), pp. 423–434.

Many Canadian firms first go to the United States when they expand internationally for the same reasons U.S. firms go to Canada. The assumption that the U.S. market and ways of doing business are similar to those in Canada may blind the firm when evaluating the U.S. market. Evidence from 32 Canadian retail companies showed that only 7 (22 percent) were functioning successfully in the United States.[5] This result was because assumptions of similarity prevented the Canadian executives from learning about critical differences. It is quite possible that an asymmetry in the distance may make Canada closer to the United States, but it does not then follow that the United States is closer to Canada. The apparent cultural similarity between countries may not always be a relevant factor for firm performance, a point that was further supported by a large study of internationally active firms. After controlling for a variety of organizational and industry characteristics, researchers found that the direction of a firm's international expansion in terms of cultural relatedness had no effect on subsequent accounting and market measures of performance.[6]

The conclusions one can draw about selecting close countries for foreign direct investment are (1) treat even psychically close markets as foreign markets; (2) test assumptions and perceptions prior to entry; (3) interpret information correctly (usually through direct experience); and (4) develop the ability to learn about other countries.

REASONS FOR FORMING STRATEGIC ALLIANCES AND JOINT VENTURES

Alliances can be found in all types of industries and between large and small firms. Firms seek alliances for various reasons. They enter into them to obtain advantages, which on their own, they cannot get. Some of these objectives are presented in the following discussion and also apply to why firms enter into joint ventures.

1. *Foreign market entry.* Strategic alliances enable a firm to enter into foreign markets by relying on the partner's distribution network and established market presence. This established presence saves the firm from building its own distribution network, especially in a new, difficult, small, or uncertain market, or to invest in an expensive publicity campaign to build up awareness in the foreign country about its own products and services, and to avoid legal and trade barriers. The rise in alliances between airlines is primarily attributed to the existence of national government laws that restrict foreign investment in the commercial aviation industry.

2. *Increased market share.* Strategic alliances allow firms to secure a larger share of the market by offering customers a comprehensive range of services obtained by bundling the product lines, servicing centers, support services, and other complementarities.

3. *Reducing risk.* By forming strategic alliances, firms can spread the risks inherent in large projects among the member firms. Alliance also enables a firm to complement and diversify its own product and service offerings. In addition, it enables the firm to

[5]O'Grady, Shawna, and Henry W. Lane. 1996. The psychic distance paradox. *Journal of International Business Studies* 27(2), pp. 309–332.
[6]Gomez-Mejia, Luis R., and Leslie E. Palich. 1997. Cultural diversity and the performance of multinational firms. *Journal of International Business Studies* 28(2), pp. 309–335.

move faster—get products to a market, acquire market intelligence, transfer new ideas from the laboratory to the production floor—and thus obtain a quicker payback on investment. Partnering with a local firm, especially in less-developed countries about which a foreign firm may be less familiar or comfortable with, may limit the latter's exposure to risk.

4. *Economies of scale and synergy.* By combining specific functions (say manufacturing, information systems, marketing, or research and development), members of the alliance are able to lower the costs through economies of scale. Waste and duplication are reduced or eliminated and the overall effect is lower costs and more efficiency. Excess capacity can be utilized. In 1997, United Grain Growers (UGG) of Winnipeg, Canada, sold a 45 percent stake to Archer-Daniels-Midland Company (ADM), the largest food processor in the world, based in the United States. The sale created a vertically integrated unit: UGG supplied the grain; ADM turned it into finished products such as flour and bread.[7]

5. *Access to technology, patents, and trademarks.* Strategic alliances enable a technologically challenged firm to access the more advanced research, engineering, and production methods of another firm so that it can upgrade its own products lines, production processes, and seek new business as a subcontractor. Sometimes, one of the partners may have the facilities the other needs, such as production plants, because its own plant's capacity may be be limited. Hilton Hotels (U.S.) and Ladbrook Group (U.K.), two hotel and gambling companies, formed an alliance to expand international growth by leveraging the powerful Hilton brand name.[8]

6. *Acquisition of information.* Alliances can plug the member firms into a much wider web of information than they might otherwise be able to access. Such information may be about business opportunities, new products, sources of cheaper inputs, or new research and development.

7. *Coopting or eliminating competitors.* "If you can't beat them, join them" is a well-known proverb. By allying with current or potential competitors, a firm may be able to reduce the competitive threat to itself and thus be able to spare resources to build up its strengths. Such alliances also strengthen smaller individual firms especially where they have to contend with large, resourceful, or well-established firms. Alternatively, larger firms may ally to eliminate the competition and try to secure the bulk of the market for themselves. Alliances, thus, can alter the competitive environment of a firm by coopting current or future rivals by creating allies out of competitors. Thus, they can be seen as a defensive ploy to eliminate destructive competition; alternately, it could be an offensive strategy to isolate and put pressure on a common competitor. Because of their

[7]Greenwood, John. 1997, December 27. UGG's new alliance increases odds for survival. *The Financial Post,* p. 34.
[8]McDowell, Edwin. 1996, August 30. Hilton-Ladbroke agreement is broader than expected. *New York Times,* p. D2.

effect on competition, in many countries large ventures and alliances require government approval and antitrust immunities. In 1999, the French government disallowed Coca-Cola's purchase of Orangina, a carbonated orange drink from a French company, because of its concern that it would give Coca-Cola an unfair advantage over its competitors in France.[9]

8. *Trends in the industry.* If forming alliances is a trend in the industry, all the firms believe they have to be involved and cannot be left out. Delaying participation may also leave a firm with fewer choices should it later decide that entering an alliance is desirable. In the 1990s, many firms, responding to changes in the industry, the regulatory framework, market conditions, and technology formed new alliances. The goal was to take advantage of global business opportunities and to survive in an increasingly competitive environment. The automobile industry saw a spate of takeovers, mergers, and equity ownership as firms consolidated to gain scale efficiencies and market access.

9. *Government influence.* Both host and home country governments may encourage firms to form alliances. National governments may believe such alliances are in the interests of their domestic businesses. In some cases, government permission is needed to form an alliance; as noted earlier, the government's role often is to ensure that the alliance does not violate antitrust laws and do not eliminate competition. An example of a strategic alliance backed by national governments is the Airbus Industrie, which was founded in 1969.[10] It was backed by the governments of the United Kingdom, France, Germany, and Spain. Airbus was essentially a marketing company that sold the planes its four partners jointly manufactured. Typically, British Aerospace (BAe) made the wings, Germany's Daimler-Chrysler Aerospace S.A. (Dasa) the fuselage, Spain's Construcciones Aeronauticas S.A. (CASA) parts of the tail, while France's Aerospatiale Matra produced the cockpits and assembled the aircraft. Even though Airbus had all the trappings of a company—including a modern headquarters complex in Toulouse in southern France, a logo, a managing director, and a board of directors—it was not one. It was a *Groupement d'Interet Economique,* a French legal construct that published no detailed accounts and made no profits or losses in its own right. All profits and losses went directly to the four partners.

A study of the motives behind alliance formation by 94 U.K. firms with partners from Western Europe, the United States, and Japan suggests that market access and geographical expansion are the leading reasons. A rank order listing of the reasons for forming joint ventures and strategic alliances are summarized in Table 7-1. Management Focus 7-1 discusses the reasons why Japanese aerospace companies sought strategic alliances.

REQUIREMENTS FOR FORMING STRATEGIC ALLIANCES

Firms that seek to benefit from strategic alliances and joint ventures need to be cognizant of a set of simple but powerful principles.

---

[9]*http://augustachronicle.com/stories/091898/bus_124-2798.shtml*
[10]Tagliabue, John. 1996, May 2. Airbus tries to fly in a new formation. *New York Times,* pp. D1, D9.

Table 7-1	Motivation for Entering into Joint Ventures and Strategic Alliances		
Motivation	*Rank**	*Mean*	*Standard Deviation*
To gain presence in new markets	1	2.46	0.73
To enable faster entry into the market	2	2.39	0.78
To facilitate international expansion	3	2.35	0.84
To effectively compete against a common competitor	4	1.80	0.77
To maintain position in existing markets	5	1.69	0.76
To exchange complementary technology	6	1.60	0.69
To lower joint operations costs; economies of scale	7	1.59	0.71
To enable product diversification	8	1.53	0.71
To enable faster payback on the investment	9	1.50	0.68
To concentrate on higher-margin business	9	1.50	0.69
To share research and development costs	11	1.46	0.67
To spread risk of a large project over more than one firm	11	1.46	0.68
To reduce existing or potential competition	13	1.34	0.60
To shift production to lowest-cost location	14	1.28	0.56
To exchange patents or territories	15	1.25	0.48
To conform to foreign government policy	16	1.13	0.42

*Rankings are based on a mean measure of importance, and the mean is the average on a scale of 1 (of no importance) to 3 (of major importance).

Source: Glaister, Keith, and Buckley, Peter. "Strategic motives for international alliance formation." *Journal of Management Studies.* 1996, 33(3), pp. 301–332.

- *Collaborating is competition in another form.* Firms must remember that their alliance partners could be out to get hold of their trade secrets and strategic plans. Such managers enter alliances with clear objectives and they also understand how their partners' objectives will affect their own success.
- *Harmonious relationship between partners is only one measure of success.* Alliances rarely remain a winning proposition over the long term. Occasional conflicts may indeed signify an active interest in the relationship and a determination to protect each party's core skills.
- *Cooperation has definite limits.* Top managers need to instruct lower level people of what to share and what not to share with their strategic partners. Strict gatekeeping of information and skill sharing is necessary to avoid wholesale loss of proprietary capabilities to the partner.
- *The goal is to learn from the partners.* The alliance is a means to understand and use the partner's capabilities and learn and incorporate them in one's own firm.
- *Strategic alliances have important implications for the firm's overall strategy and goals.* An alliance allows the firm to concentrate its attention on those activities that it has kept for itself while sharing or obtaining other activities from the alliance. Therefore, it is essential that senior managers be involved in managing the strategic alliance.

Although strategic alliances remain highly attractive, firms should resist the temptation to rely on their partners for services and skills they should develop themselves for

MANAGEMENT FOCUS 7-1

JAPAN ABANDONS HOPES OF FLYING SOLO

The decision of Kawasaki Heavy Industries, one of Japan's leading aerospace manufacturers, to take a 6-percent stake in Rolls-Royce's Trent 900 program, represented an important element of its strategy to remain a player in the global aerospace market. "It is impossible for Japanese companies to do it on their own. This is the best way, in terms of technology and costs, to participate in global engine projects," said one Kawasaki official.

In recent years, Japan's aerospace industry had been one long crusade to develop a home-grown aircraft, including engines, that could compete in the fierce world aircraft market. Collaboration with foreign aerospace makers was initially intended as a means toward that goal. By taking a stake in foreign projects, Japan's fledgling aerospace manufacturers hoped to acquire technological expertise and marketing know-how in order to one day go their own way.

From the late 1950s to the early 1970s, the 60-seat YS-11, a part-state, part-private venture, was to be Japan's first postwar indigenous civil aircraft. But just as the propeller-driven YS-11 came to market, the world had moved on to jet engines. The industry and government recognized that the YS-11 was not commercially feasible and terminated the project in 1973. Hopes of developing a jet aircraft were abandoned when it became apparent the project had to be large scale to be commercially successful. Japanese manufacturers chose to take part in developing Boeing's 767 instead. They took a 15-percent stake in the 767, and the success of the project led to a 21-percent stake in the creation of the Boeing 777.

The Japanese joined in engine projects as well. Kawasaki alone was involved in engine projects earlier with Rolls-Royce, the British airplane engine maker and later with Pratt and Whitney, a U.S. firm. In addition, Japanese manufacturers had taken a 23-percent stake in the V2500 project to build a turbo fan engine for mid-sized commercial aircraft and were to share in GE's CF34-8C engine. Such projects provided Japanese aerospace companies with lucrative subcontracting work in which they had developed expertise. Kawasaki, for example, had strength in turbines and was responsible for the turbine nozzle and case, among others, of the V2500. By taking a stake in these projects and becoming risk-sharing partners, Japanese companies also participated in the profits that the engines and aircraft eventually made. But most important perhaps, "Japanese companies want to continue participating in global projects as a means to maintain work," pointed out Miki Sugiura, vice president of the Society of Japanese Aerospace Companies.

As aerospace development had become increasingly costly and dominated by the big players, the chances of Japanese companies making a commercial aircraft or engine on their own had receded. For one thing, it was difficult to develop something new or different that might help it compete with the offerings of established players. While Japanese companies probably did have the technology to make a civil aircraft on their own, without the proven reliability of companies such as Boeing or Airbus Industrie, and with no marketing expertise, it was unlikely that such an aircraft would be commercially viable.

Furthermore, in an industry where being big counted, the scale of Japanese aerospace operations was far too small for companies to compete globally. The industry was less than half the size of the U.K. or French aerospace industries and only one-seventh that of the United States. As Mr. Sugiura noted, "The development of Japan's aerospace industry will depend on participation in international alliances."

Source: Nakamoto, Michiyo. 1997, January 10. Japan abandons hopes of flying solo. *Financial Times,* p. 6.

their own future growth and success. Otherwise, the danger lies in becoming dependent on the partner and the potential decay in the firm's competitive ability. As the firm is able to offer less and less to the partner, it exposes itself even more to the partner with the likelihood that it may either lose the partner or be taken over by the partner.

CREATING A STRATEGIC ALLIANCE

One of the major challenges of building a strategic alliance is choosing the right partners. The key criterion is whether the potential partner (or partners) provides a strategic fit to each others' needs and goals. It means the potential partners must have the necessary capabilities and resources that would be valuable and available to the other parties. A related issue is the number of partners that should comprise the alliance. Once the alliance partners have been chosen, attention has to be directed to identifying the roles and responsibilities of each partner. The relationship becomes complex when the number of partners increases and when the alliance has multiple goals. Two other issues that are important are the possibility of a clash between corporate and national cultures as the different firms try to collaborate and succeed and the need to create a sense of trust between the parties. This point was illustrated in the opening vignette. Firms from different countries have to cope with cultural differences as well as differences in operating systems, decision-making structures, and corporate practices. Because the alliance members are still competitors and retain their own legal identities, the ever-present fear is that one or more of them might act opportunistically at the expense or the interests of the others. Management Focus 7-2 discusses how the Star Alliance has coped with these challenges.

EQUITY JOINT VENTURES

An equity joint venture, as defined earlier, is a company that is owned by two or more firms. It can be a totally new company or it can be formed by one or more companies acquiring portions of another company. Firms form equity joint ventures for several reasons. One, the other entry methods—exporting/importing, licensing/ franchising, and strategic alliances—may no longer provide the desired benefits or provide only suboptimal returns. Two, the political and regulatory environment that formerly prevented foreign direct investment may have changed, permitting such investment now. Three, the ability to exercise greater control over the foreign operations and integrate worldwide activities is enhanced by foreign direct investment. Four, the firm may have reached that level of experience, growth, maturity, and size where equity ownership in foreign operations is seen as a worthwhile venture.

For many firms, the joint venture may serve as an intermediate step on the way to wholly owning the overseas subsidiary. The period of the joint venture is treated as a learning opportunity—acquiring new skills, becoming familiar with local customers and market peculiarities, and operating in a foreign environment—until the firm feels it is confident and experienced enough to sally forth on its own. Ralston-Purina, a U.S. firm, ended a 20-year joint venture with Taiyo Fishery Company and established a wholly owned subsidiary in Japan, after learning enough of the Japanese market and business environment that it no longer needed a local partner.[11]

---

[11]Reuer, Jeffrey. 1998. The dynamics and effectiveness of international joint ventures. *European Management Journal* 16(2), pp. 160–168.

MAKING ALLIANCES WORK

Lufthansa's CEO, Jurgen Weber, the force behind the Star Alliance, asked about its permanence, replied, "We will cooperate as long as we like it. But we can stop if it's not win-win. At most we are engaged"—but not married. "Anyway, that's usually more fun." He believed that Lufthansa needed alliances because, "We can explore the global market, which we couldn't on our own, with more powerful distribution than before. We have the tickets to prove positive results from alliances."

Once allied, the key issue to Mr. Weber was "increasing trust in one another. We must sell the others' seats with the same intensity as our own. In some cases, where dukes like to keep their kingdoms, the working level must be reminded, and we have done so." Paul Paflik, head of airline cooperations for Austrian Airlines, a member of another alliance that included Swissair and Delta AirLines, shared that sentiment. "It was most difficult at the beginning. Each airline had a different philosophy and not everyone agreed the alliance was of absolute benefit, so we had problems. Strong personalities on both sides had determined why the others worked as they did. Plus Delta was so much bigger than the rest. It had different problems."

Even though the members of Star Alliance claimed no major problems had arisen in the first year, it didn't mean that coordination had been easy. A spokesperson said, "Trying to coordinate six different airlines is a logistical nightmare." But Star learned from others and reorganized the coordination structure after the official launch. "We couldn't continue as we were." Star reduced its alliance committees from 25 to 15, keeping those key to customer benefits. A business policy group oversaw the committees. That group reported to a board composed of the members' chairpersons. In addition, working groups that wrestled with specific problems reported to an alliance development committee. Working group leaders were sent to group dynamics training.

However, these committees did not work as smoothly as desired. Nobody was authorized to make a decision for the alliance. Individual airlines

had officers or representatives on an executive committee, steering committees, and working groups to do so. Star executives emphasized to managers the role alliances play in their carriers. As a manager of United Airlines in London admitted, "I know it's not acceptable to turn a blind eye to Star. It's in my 1998 business objectives, as it was in 1997. Star is always in my mind." His sales staff considered first if something should be sold as Star. If not, it pushed United. The United States was different. "They aren't exposed. So, the goal this year is to win the hearts and minds of everyone, showing that their pay depends on Star and the effect of that extra passenger in Des Moines."

Gradually, Star-based systems and procedures were introduced, giving employees something to work with: A common baggage tracking system and a plan to assign responsibility for it; common airport lounge access, though each airline kept its own name and displayed a Star nameplate; a linked, not merged frequent-flier program, especially for elite travelers; joint ticket offices and joint Star terminal space, first at home hubs such as Frankfurt, then the top 35 stations where members meet, such as Hong Kong, Tokyo, and London Heathrow. But common check-in, a much touted customer benefit, would cost $100 million and take two to three years to deliver. Joint facilities, Star's "landlord" concept, were not easy to set up. The pertinent committee had to wrestle with merging sites that partners spent months and years choosing and decades using. Local peculiarities interfered too; for example, where long-term leases precluded sharing of facilities or where immigration and customs procedures differed. Star also was in a quandary over how to assign costs with decisions being made bilaterally.

The biggest problem though had been to integrate the computer systems of the six airlines as they related to reservations, frequent fliers, baggage tracking, and check-in. Mr. Paflik admitted, "We way underestimated the IT-revenue accounting link. But as soon as you start revenue sharing, everyone calculates prorates differently." Merging technical systems proved to be difficult not only

(continued)

Management Focus 7-2 (*continued*)

because of the reluctance on the part of the information technology staff but also because many airlines regarded certain IT tasks such as yield management as proprietary. Developing a common technical system was expensive and as a yield management expert for United noted, "We are not convinced that we could handle one that size. It's a huge project and we all have big investments in our own, customized systems. The international benefits are not worth all the money and effort. One hundred million dollars in added revenue from Lufthansa is a relatively small number in a $16 billion company." The emphasis was now on making sure the various company's systems could communicate with each other.

Another issue that the Star Alliance faced was obtaining landing slots at airports. For instance,

Lufthansa's request for slots at Chicago was received unenthusiastically by alliance ally United, which wanted to hold on to all its slots because of its important domestic competition with American Airlines. American opposed the slots being given to Lufthansa for antitrust reasons, though the Department of Transportation ruled against it.

The Star alliance was dominated by two airlines—United and Lufthansa. The smaller airlines, Air Canada, SAS, Thai, and Varig, found the relationship challenging, but also immensely rewarding. One United manager commented, "This is like a free consulting service." Mr. Paflik observed that "for a smaller carrier, it really involved a lot of effort because we don't have the resources. For a big carrier, it just means devoting more people to it [the alliance]."

Source: Feldman, Joan M. 1998. Making alliances work. *Air Transport World.* June, pp. 29–35.

EXTENT OF EQUITY OWNERSHIP

The extent of ownership levels is linked to how much control the parent firm wishes to exercise over its foreign operations. As greater control is desired, larger degrees of ownership in the subsidiary are required. Studies indicate that the nationality of the firm affects ownership policies among multinational firms. U.S. firms appear to have a strong preference for majority or full-ownership in foreign subsidiaries. European companies, although preferring majority ownership, were more flexible with regard to joint ventures; and Japanese multinational firms often preferred joint ventures to 100 percent ownership. A study of the subsidiaries of the world's major advertising agencies showed that firms headquartered in countries that have high power distance and uncertainty avoidance and whose home market was large were more likely to establish majority-owned subsidiaries.[12]

The higher the percentage of ownership, the more capital is required. The partner who puts in more of the money takes more of the risk should the venture fail, while being in a position to reap most of the profits should it succeed. Hence majority ownership is preferred if the partner wants the venture to be operated in the way it would like.

How important is it to own 51 percent or 49 percent of a joint venture? Not very. Control can be exercised by an even smaller holding, particularly if the other owners are numerous or wish to be passive participants. Ford Motor Company, for instance, has effective control over the Japanese automobile firm, Mazda, even though it holds only

---

[12]Erramilli, M. Krishna. 1996. Nationality and subsidiary ownership patterns in multinational corporations. *Journal of International Business Studies* 27(2), pp. 225–248.

about a third of its shares.[13] What the partners bring to the venture probably determines the extent of control. Injection of capital at a key time or highly specialized (or hard to duplicate) skills would give a partner considerably more clout.

The partner that provides technology (interpreted broadly to include brand names and processing of commodities) is more likely to have majority ownership. In contrast, local knowledge is the contribution most consistently associated with a minority share of equity (and over time, the tendency is for this share to go down). However, government restrictions on the extent of foreign ownership in a venture give the local partner greater clout and majority ownership. Successful companies tend to focus on what they will learn from the venture and at what speed, rather than on being fixated on a certain percentage. Of course, at times of conflict, the partner with the majority ownership may forcefully assert control, which is usually reflected in its naming its own personnel to key posts in the venture.

NEGOTIATING THE JOINT VENTURE

As with strategic alliances, with joint ventures too, it is necessary to pay great attention to selecting the right partner(s). Joint ventures should be formed when complementary skills are offered by the partners, cooperative cultures exist between the firms, the firms have compatible goals, and commensurate levels of risks are involved.

Complementary Skills   The first step in finding a partner with complementary skills is to conduct a comprehensive search that focuses on skills, technologies, and markets. Such a search can be broad, encompassing all major players in a particular market, or keyed initially toward a targeted partner. Firms with partners already in place (in strategic alliances) may seek to upgrade their level of involvement (into joint ventures) without scanning a full range of potential partners. Firms should form alliances only with firms that fulfil a specific need. Ideally, all partners should learn from the venture; otherwise, it becomes a one-sided affair where one partner acquires new knowledge, insights, and experiences, and over time, emerges as a strong competitor of the other partner.

Initially, such ventures should take up projects that are clearly within the capability of both firms. This factor is especially important when one of the firms is much smaller and could easily be overwhelmed by its larger collaborator. A firm may possess technology and knowledge skills but lack the managerial and marketing expertise necessary to take products to market. Thus, this firm will seek large established firms with resources in management and marketing but who lack new product lines or technological ability. In such cases, the needs and capabilities of both partners complement each other well.

Cooperative Culture   Although the need for each other's assets and capabilities may bring firms together, to be able to work in unison, the partners need to be compatible. Joint ventures and strategic alliances work well when managers show a sensitivity and understanding of the corporate and national cultures of the respective parties. Internationally experienced firms build up cadres of managers who are well experienced in working with people from different geographical regions of the world. While

---

[13]Pollack, Andrew. 1996, April 13. Ford, in Mazda investment, is revered as well as feared. *New York Times,* p. 35.

good relationships between the senior managers are obviously essential to set the tone and the atmosphere for the venture, opportunities to develop trust through regular meetings, constant exchange of information, rotation of personnel, and frequent visits to each other's facilities are key ways to develop personal bonds that not only forge a human commitment to the venture but also allow for the effective handling of problems that invariably arise.

Of course, cultural differences are not always based on nationality. Corporate cultures vary too in terms of a firm's history, its size, risk-taking propensity, human resource policies, reward systems, and organizational structure. In addition, firms from less-developed countries or from smallish places have characteristics different from firms from advanced nations or those based in larger cities. Finally, differences based on the functional specialization of workers may be an issue. Engineers in two different firms are likely to find that they share many common interests and concerns whereas they may find the finance managers in their own companies to be an alien group of colleagues.

Compatible Goals   Joint ventures fail when they do not further the goals of all the partners. Thus, the goals have to be clearly defined from the outset. However, they do change over time as the goals are achieved or the place of the venture in the parents' overall scheme of activities becomes enhanced or reduced. The rationale for the venture no longer exists. A good example of compatible goals is the Airbus Industrie. Each of the four partners, on its own, did not have the ability to compete with the industry leader, Boeing. However, by focusing on designing and building advanced planes they have become an alternative source of aircraft to the world's airlines.

Clear goals focus the attention of the partners on what the venture should strive for. When goals vary, conflicts are inevitable. Differing goals influence the types of managers that are assigned to the venture, the amounts of capital and other resources allocated, and the way the venture is run. The climate of the venture is also affected. Where the partners have competing goals, the relationship is more likely to fail. A careful examination of partners' goals helps to see whether they are commensurate with one's own goals. Managers evaluate the past actions of potential partners as a way to glean actual motives or by hiring former employees of theirs or by contacting their customers and previous partners. Table 7-2 lists the criteria used by Korean and American executives to choose joint venture partners. Note that only one factor—ability to provide quality products—was on the list of both groups.

Table 7-2	Partner Selection Criteria (in order of importance)
Korean Executives	*American Executives*
1. Technical capabilities	1. Financial assets
2. Industry attractiveness	2. Managerial capabilities
3. Special skills we can learn from partner	3. Capability to provide quality products/services
4. Willingness to share expertise	4. Complementarity of capabilities
5. Capability to provide quality products	5. Unique competencies

Source: Reprinted from *Journal of World Business,* Vol. 32, No. 1, Dacin et al, "Selecting partners for successful international alliances: Examination of U.S. and Korean firms," pp. 3–16, © 1997, with permission from Elsevier Science.

Commensurate Levels of Risk   Because entering into joint ventures is one way to reduce the risk that would exist if the firm should venture forth solo, it means that all the partners in the venture must benefit from risk reduction. If nothing is at stake for one of the partners, then this firm has little reason to stay on in the venture. Given the exceedingly high cost and uncertainty of successfully developing new ethical drugs, pharmaceutical companies try to protect themselves from major failures by forming into consortiums or conducting joint research. Thus, managers must be hesitant about entering into ventures in which they are required to contribute more resources than they can afford.

Among the issues that have to be negotiated are the inputs that each partner will bring to the venture and how the venture will be supported during the initial phase. Another issue is the extent of autonomy that the parents will give the venture with regard to purchasing, marketing, product development, and product lines. No less important is the manner in which profits will be allocated to the parents and who will contribute what in terms of key managers. Shared management is often a cause for conflict and it may make good sense to let one partner dominate the relationship. The difficulty of creating a joint venture is illustrated in Management Focus 7-3.

MANAGING THE JOINT VENTURE

Because the long-term intentions and behavior of the partner cannot be predicted, it makes sense to start with a small-scale relationship. With positive experience on the part of both sides, the relationship can be expanded into more complex arrangements. Thus, it is not uncommon for ventures to be formed with one's foreign distributor; both firms have presumably worked with each other and know what their respective capabilities and strengths are. Successful ventures depend greatly on trust and mutual respect on the part of the partners.

Whereas contracts are drawn up and signed and have legal bearing, it appears that successful ventures rely less on the legal obligation of the parties and more on the human relationship built up between the parties. Although this aspect is not always addressed, the contract should spell out the procedures to be followed in case the arrangement has to be unwound or changed.

Safeguarding Core Competencies   While one of the goals is for the partners to learn from each other, the partners need to remember that they do not share all their knowledge, experience, and technology. The firms have to carefully identify what skills and technologies they pass on to their partners and develop safeguards against unintended, informal transfers of information. The aim is to limit the transparency of their operations and protect the core competencies of the firm from being eroded. Thus the firm has to devise appropriate organizational safeguards to prevent leakage of its proprietary knowledge and core competencies. This can be accomplished through several ways including curtailing the scope of the formal agreement, which might cover a single technology rather than an entire range of technologies or part of a product line rather than the entire line, or limiting distribution to a specific number of markets or for a specific period of time. The objective is to circumscribe a partner's opportunities to learn. Another approach is to establish specific performance requirements. Additional information is provided only after the other party delivers on its promise to do its part.

THE VENTURE THAT DID NOT TAKE PLACE

In 1990, Volvo of Sweden and Renault of France established a strategic alliance through a complicated scheme of cross-share holdings, joint production and R&D agreements, and supervisory boards. Since 1971, the two automotive firms had cooperated on a cross-supply agreement that involved the swapping of gasoline engines for gear boxes.

The 1990 alliance was motivated first by the desire to exploit potential synergies in joint product development, purchasing, quality, and manufacturing, and second to create a firm of sufficient size, breadth, and depth to compete effectively on a global basis. The Volvo-Renault alliance was part of a trend in the automotive industry to consolidate through alliances, joint ventures, acquisitions, and mergers. As shown in Table 7-3, the two firms complemented each other in several areas though important differences were evident too.

The key features of the alliance were as follows:

- Substantial cross-holdings by each firm, and a poison pill to discourage any attempt to end the relationship
- Equality of the partners as reflected in the equal divisions of management appointments to the joint operating committees, the creation of two alliance headquarters in Gothenburg and Paris, and the use of English as the official language
- Comprehensive structure of 21 committees to engage both the firms at various levels in the hierarchy

- Integration of the operational side of the two firms, while retaining each firm's downstream activities of marketing, brand names, and dealer networks

Three years later, senior executives of both firms indicated that the alliance was healthy and successful. Joint purchasing and exchange of components had worked well. Progress had been made on quality issues as well as on developing a new family of rear-axle drives and the setting up of a joint venture to make buses in France. Language differences were still a problem, though the French were making strides in mastering English. By 1993, the alliance had exploited the easy gains.

Problems arose over two projects. Between 200 and 300 engineers from both firms were engaged in developing a new common platform for a high-end executive car. The French were proud of their styling and cost containment skills. The Swedes were equally proud of their safety and engineering skills. The French thought the engineering gains of Volvo came at a high price in terms of money and delays. The French proposed that the new platform be a front-wheel drive car; the Swedish engineers wanted it to be a rear-wheel drive. A front-wheel drive design would require the engine to be transverse mounted; Volvo's modern engine that met European and U.S. emission standards were too long to be mounted transversely. Renault could supply its own V-6 engine, which was shorter, but it did not meet U.S. emission standards,

Table 7-3	Differences and Complementarity Between Volvo and Renault	
Characteristics	*Volvo*	*Renault*
Home country	Sweden	France
Culture/Language	Anglo-Saxon; Swedish; Use of English common	Latin; French
Ownership	Publicly owned	Government owned
Size	Small niche player in cars; dominant in heavy trucks	Large and broad product lines; weak in heavy trucks
Core competencies	Safety	Styling
Management structure	Decentralized; informal flow of information	Centralized; formal flow of information
Market orientation	Scandinavia, U.S., Asia	Continental Europe

(*continued*)

where Volvo had a major presence. Subsequent tests showed the platform needed to be strengthened to survive crashes which further raised the weight, cost, and development time.

The second problem was over truck production. Truck buyers perceived Volvo engines to be superior to Renault's. Because Volvo trucks were priced higher than Renault trucks, it was conceivable that Volvo engines could be installed in Renault trucks and sold for less. Volvo suggested that it concentrate on the production of all heavy trucks (it ranked second in the world in that category) and that Renault focus on the production of medium and light trucks. Renault resisted noting that it had a strong heavy truck position in France.

With a 50:50 control arrangement, both sides had the power to veto decisions. Many decisions were highly sensitive such as where to locate production and thus jobs. Renault, as a state-owned enterprise, was particularly sensitive to protecting jobs. Although both firms also wanted to protect their respective brands, to obtain real cost savings, duplication had to be eliminated. Decisions by committees were slow and expensive.

Pehr Gyllenhammer, Volvo's executive chair and Louis Schweitzer, Renault's chief executive officer, impatient with the slow progress towards integration, proposed a merger of the two firms. In 1993, a conservative party gained power in France and announced its intention to privatize Renault in late 1994. Mr. Gyllenhammer believed that the merger had to take place soon, before privatization occurred, which would put a market value on the company. In September 1993, Volvo and Renault announced the terms under which the two companies would merge their car and truck manufacturing businesses.

The proposed merger would create Renault-Volvo RVA to be owned 65 percent by the French government and 35 percent by AB Volvo. The firm would be headquartered near Paris where Renault's head office was situated. The new company would be directed by a management board under the supervision of a supervisory board. The supervisory board would be headed by Mr. Gyllenhammer, and the management board, which would be responsible for the running of the firm, would be headed by Mr. Schweitzer.

The merger was justified by the two managers on three grounds: (1) it would create the second largest truck producer and the sixth largest car producer in the world; (2) substantial sums would be saved in purchasing, research and development, and production; and (3) it would make for a financially strong company, which was necessary to meet the capital requirements of both firms.

Support for the merger could not be found in Sweden. The proposal touched on a nationalistic nerve among the Swedes who felt that Volvo was a national symbol. Volvo's stock prices fell. At the stockholders' meeting, representative of the company's white collar workers announced their opposition to the merger. Nine hundred engineers in the company called for the merger to be postponed. Reports began circulating that strategic alliance projects had not gone smoothly between Swedish and French workers. The media presented Mr. Gyllenhammer as an ambitious man who ignored economic realities in favor of personal advantage. Volvo dealers in the United States and Canada expressed strong concern that the merger would dilute Volvo's favorable brand image. Managers feared that with a 65:35 ownership ratio in favor of Renault, control of Volvo would be lost. Finally, with the latest financial results showing a dramatic increase in profits, it was argued by some executives that the company did not need to merge to survive.

On December 2, 1993, the directors of Volvo withdrew their recommendation of a merger with Renault. Mr. Gyllenhammer and four other directors resigned immediately. The next day, he sold his family's shareholdings in the firm. In January 1994, a new board of directors was elected. It was announced that Volvo would focus on its core automotive businesses; all noncore assets would be sold by 1996 with the proceeds used to retire the firm's outstanding debt. On February 17, 1994, Renault and Volvo announced the dissolution of the strategic alliance. This ending was expensive for Volvo because it had to pay Renault under the poison pill provision, repurchase Renault's shares in Volvo, and write-off goodwill. All joint projects were terminated except for the 1971 arrangement to swap engines for gearboxes.

Source: Bruner, Robert, and Robert Spekman. 1998. The dark side of alliances: Lessons from Volvo-Renault. *European Management Journal* 16(2), pp. 136–150.

Many of the skills that get transferred from one partner to another are not covered in the formal agreements that govern a collaborative relationship. Although top managers put together the agreements and set the legal parameters of the relationship, it is the day-to-day interactions of engineers, marketers, and product developers from the two firms far down in the hierarchy that determine what gets discussed, shared, and transferred. To limit unintended sharing of information at this level means appointing and monitoring gatekeepers. For instance, the other partner may be required to go through a particular office (and nowhere else) to access people and information. Certain facilities and factories may need to be out of bounds for employees of the partner. While collegiality is an essential ingredient for success in collaborative ventures, too much of it can hurt the company. Senior managers should regularly meet with their staff assigned to the venture to ascertain what information the partner is requesting and what information is being provided.

SUCCESSFUL JOINT VENTURES

A much studied joint venture was Toppan Moore, formed in 1965 by the Canadian office forms company, Moore Corporation, and Toppan Printing, a major Japanese printing company.[14] Toppan Moore, based in Japan, was initially owned 55 percent by Toppan Printing, the rest being owned by Moore Corporation. Moore supplied the venture with its advanced technology for making business forms. In return, it relied on Toppan's salesforce to access the Japanese market. Toppan obtained the technology it needed for making forms. Over the next 30 years, the joint venture flourished—sales rose, new products were introduced, subsidiaries in other Asian countries were formed.

Several explanations can be advanced for this success. First, the joint venture was allowed to function as an independent company with little interference from either of the parents. Moore let the company be organized and managed as a Japanese, rather than Canadian company, with the initial management team being drawn almost entirely from the Japanese parent. The reason for this decision was that Moore had no knowledge about the Japanese market while Toppan Printing had the marketing expertise and clients. Second, a close relationship between the managers of the venture and Moore was developed. Once a year, managers from Toppan Moore and Moore met to share technical information. Visits to each others' plants were common. Moore initially shared its most advanced machines with the venture, which created the basis for a trusting and open relationship. Third, by leaving the management of the joint venture to Japanese hands and giving it autonomy, Moore was unable to acquire for itself the local knowledge about the Japanese market. Thus, Moore was not in a position to buy out its Japanese partner. Fourth, the venture being successful, provided Moore with a steady stream of royalties and profits and later on, new products and technologies. Moore itself was learning and benefiting from its joint venture. However, given Moore's strong R&D activities, the joint venture continued to gain from its access to new technological developments. (In the mid-1990s, following top management changes at Moore in Canada, the company reduced its share in the joint venture to 10 percent and in 1996, sold off that remaining stake too. This move allowed Moore to form relation-

[14] Toppan Moore (case study). In *International management—Text and cases* by Paul Beamish, Allen Morrison, Philip Rosenzweig, and Andrew Inkpen. New York: Irwin McGraw-Hill, 2000.

ships with other Japanese firms while exposing itself to competition from its former joint venture in many markets.)

General Electric, the U.S. conglomerate, had 14 joint ventures in Japan.[15] A study of the most successful of these ventures identified three key success factors:

1. *Careful planning and execution.* Both partners carefully evaluated their partners. From the start of the joint venture, both sides contributed some of their best managers to staff the new company. They clearly identified their respective strategic needs and objectives. The top management of both partners was committed to the success of the ventures and developed a common vision. In the implementation phase, the partners developed a work plan and established a decision-making process. From this first step, management commitment was probably the key priority. As a top Japanese executive suggested, "If the top man in the company believes in the joint venture, it is hard to go back to him with excuses on why it is difficult to make the joint venture work."

2. *Assignment of key personnel.* Because it was often difficult for foreign firms to hire both junior employees and first-class experienced managers, the Japanese partner was often the source of key personnel for the joint venture. Expatriates, small in number, comprised a permanent staff whose members served five years on assignment and a temporary staff whose members served three years. The purpose was to prevent corporate amnesia and to maximize organizational learning. Recruiting people from outside the partners also helped in building employee loyalty toward the new company and not have dual loyalties to the joint venture and the partner firm.

3. *Adopting an evolutionary approach.* Most of the joint ventures started on a small scale (e.g., with a distribution agreement) and progressively grew to include other activities such as manufacturing. Both partners treated the ventures as truly independent companies and did not interfere in their day-to-day management. Each new step in the joint venture had been planned and negotiated separately. Another success factor was the ability to transfer knowledge. With top management support, GE learned from its Japanese partners lean production technology, continuous improvement, and managing innovation while the Japanese partners learned marketing skills, a strategic approach, creative management, and access to new technologies.

In a study of Sino-U.S. joint ventures, it was found that their performance was better when control was divided along functional lines.[16] This result was attributed to the fact that Chinese culture, economy, and politics were so far removed from the experience of most Westerners that dominant control was risky. However, the lack of managerial skills on the part of the Chinese made dominant control by them similarly risky. For U.S. managers, having dominant control was important for psychological and economic reasons. From the perspective of efficiency, dominant control can be perceived as more efficient than split control. Less interpartner conflict arises where one partner makes the business decisions.

A survey of managers and government officials representing eight Sino-American joint ventures identified four strategic tasks as particularly critical for effective performance

[15]Turpin, Dominique. 1993. Strategic alliances with Japanese firms: Myths and realities. *Long-Range Planning* 26(8), pp. 11–15.
[16]Child, John, and Yanni Yan. 1999. Investment and control in international joint ventures: The case of China. *Journal of World Business* 34(1), pp. 3–14.

in the Chinese environment.[17] These tasks were gaining decision-making control of critical business functions, developing an effective salesforce, retaining trained joint venture managers, and influencing government officials. Gaining decision-making control of critical business functions enabled one side of the joint venture to be able to coordinate and implement its strategies. Although these findings were specific to joint ventures with Chinese organizations, the general conclusions can be applied in other geographical settings too.

FAILURE OF JOINT VENTURES

Because a joint venture is dependent on the goals and needs of the partner firms, its continued existence may often have little to do with its own performance. Alliances end in several ways, and it is fair to say that that they are inherently unstable. They need to be seen, not in isolation, but as part of the broader activities of the partner firm. Where a firm has multiple alliances, performance and experience in one can affect the partner's perspective on the others. Similarly, the partner's interests, which coincided when the venture was formed, can easily diverge over time making the venture no longer necessary. Table 7-4 reports on a study of how 272 international joint ventures were terminated during the period 1985 to 1995. The most common way a joint venture ceases to exist is when one of the partners buys out the other partner.

The major difficulty in managing alliances arises because they have more than one partner; disagreements among them are quite natural. Over time, a joint venture may develop its own identity and cultural traits and thus pose even more difficult problems of coordination and integration for the partners. Where the partners are from different political, economic, and cultural settings, the potential for conflict is greater. Paradoxically, it is the existence of these differences in the marketplace that in the first instance led to the creation of the joint venture.

Joint ventures go under for other reasons as well. One common cause is lack of clarity regarding the sharing of responsibilities between the partners. Other reasons include corporate amnesia caused by the turnover of expatriates and managers in the partner company (which makes people forget the original motivations and the past lessons of the relationship), lack of continuity in the personal relationships between the

Table 7-4	How Joint Ventures End	
	Status of the Joint Venture	*Percentage of Firms*
1.	Foreign partner acquires the share of the other partner	34.2
2.	Foreign partner sells out its share to the other partner	49.6
3.	Foreign firm sells out its share to a third party	4.0
4.	Foreign firm and partner sell the joint venture to a third party	2.9
5.	Foreign firm and partner liquidate the assets of the joint venture	9.2

Source: Reuer, Jeffrey. "The dynamics and effectiveness of international joint ventures." *European Management Journal.* 1998, 16(2), pp. 160–168.

---

[17]Luo, Yadong. 1995. Business strategy, market share, and performance of international joint ventures: The case of joint ventures in China. *Management International Review* 35(3), pp. 241–264.

top management of the partners, and no preparation to end the venture should the relationship go awry.

Ideally, managers of the partners of the joint venture should have a mechanism or process to terminate the relationship. Because the parties enter into a joint venture to pursue temporary goals, they should have little expectation that the venture will last indefinitely. Even in short-lived ventures, it is possible for the partners to have learned valuable lessons from each other. That many joint ventures are short-lived can be explained by their nature and by the strategic intentions of the partners.

Some of the issues managers should consider regarding the end of a joint venture include the following:

- *Importance of the joint venture.* The ending of the joint venture is likely to be contentious and harmful when the venture plays an important role in one of the partner firm's corporate portfolio. Failure to recognize this point early on in the relationship would result in one party unwittingly losing control over key assets and loss of bargaining power.
- *Pricing the venture.* The issue here is how to determine the value of the venture and how to reallocate it among the partners. If one partner wants to buy out the other, how much should it pay? If the venture has been successful and is particularly attractive to one of the partners, the price will be high and it will also be affected by the bargaining power of the parties. Sometimes the purchase price may be set at the outset of the venture with each party retaining the right to call the option. Another option is to have a **shotgun clause** in the contract, where a partner firm is allowed to name a price and the partner elects to acquire the venture or sell out at this price. Other pricing options can be negotiated by the parties
- *Transferring resources.* The partners should have in place arrangements that deal with the transfer of funds, physical assets, personnel, and information systems, and how to handle organizational cultures and administrative systems should one of them end up owning the joint venture. The joint venture would have to be effectively integrated into the firm's overall activities and some adaptation would be required to ensure integration.
- *Creating and sharing value.* The partner firms can focus on the joint venture to either create value (increasing the size of the pie) or distribute the value (sharing the pie). Both these goals are sources of tension between the partners. While ideally the focus should be on increasing the size of the pie, in reality the partners emphasize their share of the pie through various control mechanisms (such as majority ownership) rather than focusing on issues such as trust or developing synergy. The gains or losses the partners make from the venture are ultimately dependent on both value creating and value appropriating.

Management Focus 7-4 discusses the negative consequences for one of the joint venture partners after the alliance broke up. It points to the loss of key competitive attributes because the joint venture allowed the firm to become dependent on the other partner.

MANAGEMENT FOCUS 7-4

ONE GAINS, THE OTHER LOSES

In 1987, Ford and Volkswagen (VW) combined their subsidiaries in Brazil and Argentina when hyperinflation, weak growth, and a ban on car imports had badly hurt sales in both countries. Their joint venture, known as Autolatina, became highly profitable even in this hostile environment by closing surplus Ford and VW assembly plants and offering aging models that were cheap to build. The plant in Pacheco, on the northern outskirts of Buenos Aires, Argentina, was originally a Ford factory, with Volkswagen moving in. Ten years later, a six-foot high chain link fence divided the plant roughly in half, on one side the operations of Ford, on the other side those of VW—a symbol of a joint venture that had broken up.

The basic mistake of Ford, its officials acknowledged, lay in assuming that a marriage made in the late 1980s would last indefinitely. The union looked good on paper: the companies would make cars together for Brazil and Argentina, sharing all the profits and producing no competing models. The trouble was that Ford let VW make the subcompacts, a segment that had since come to account for half the region's auto sales, with Ford still struggling to catch up. Ford was also caught off guard by rapid economic changes that turned the once stagnant countries into attractive markets. As a result, Ford endured heavy losses in a region that has become the most profitable in the world for rivals such as General Motors and Fiat. "We've essentially started over; we're building a new company from the ground up in Argentina and Brazil," said Alex Trotman, Ford's chair and chief executive. In 1996, Ford's South American division lost $645 million.

In the 1990s, the Brazilian and Argentine economies staged a complete turnaround, and Autolatina was caught unprepared. The import ban on cars was replaced with steep tariffs, prompting nearly a dozen automakers to start exporting their latest models to those countries and begin planning new factories. Suddenly faced with true competition—and reluctant to share the technology needed to build their own latest models—Ford and VW decided in early 1995 to break Autolatina apart.

The break up helped VW and hurt Ford. VW held onto a third of the regional auto market and produced steady earnings. But Ford's operations emerged from the venture in disarray, with much lower market shares, mainly because of its lack of small cars. The moral, as Ford officials saw it, was that companies combining operations should look hard at what might happen if the venture later comes undone. "Emotionally, you know, the last thing you want to do is contemplate coming apart," said Jacques Nasser, president of Ford's worldwide automotive operations. "At some stage up front, you kind of need to brainstorm the conditions under which the partnership stops providing the added values and synergies."

The biggest problem for Ford had been that almost all growth in both auto markets had come in subcompacts, particularly the smallest subcompacts, called "popular cars." But Ford specialized in midsize cars before Autolatina, while VW built mainly smaller cars. During the joint venture, the two companies made all Autolatina's cars together and shared all the profits. The larger cars mostly bore Ford nameplates and went to family-owned Ford dealers, though, while the smaller cars tended to have VW nameplates and went to VW dealers.

Ford dealers begged for a small car as the Brazilian market in particular shifted in the early 1990s. But Ford executives were reluctant to erode Autolatina's profits by developing a subcompact from scratch and then placing it in competition with VW's Golf, from which Ford was already taking half the profits. At the same time, VW officials were reluctant to share their subcompact designs with Ford for fear that Ford would use them in other world markets.

Yet the result of Ford's decision to focus on Autolatina's profits rather than on Ford brand cars was that Ford emerged from the alliance with a reputation for making cars bigger than most consumers wanted. "Obviously, we should have nurtured our brand better in those years," said Ivan Silva, the new president of Ford of Brazil. "It would be much less painful now."

(continued)

(continued)

VW officials were pleased with the breakup of the joint venture, having retained their dominant market position in Brazil and gained a larger share in Argentina from just 10 percent in 1987 to being the market leader with 18.6 percent in 1996. In addition, they claimed that they learned a lot from working with Ford in Autolatina, improving their abilities to track costs more closely and cut the number of management meetings. As an auto analyst put it on the break up of Autolatina, "Be careful who you marry, and have a good prenuptial agreement."

Source: Bradsher, Keith. 1997, May 16. One thrives, the other doesn't. *The New York Times*, p. D1, 3.

LIFE CYCLE OF ALLIANCES

The preceding discussion suggests that strategic alliances and joint ventures are dynamic entities that rarely stay the same over time. Ventures successful at one time later falter and dissolve. For instance, Volkswagen (VW) of Germany created a highly profitable joint venture in China with the Shanghai Automotive Industry Corporation to manufacture cars. Believing it could replicate this success, VW formed another joint venture with First Auto Works in another Chinese city. But this venture failed largely because of a weak distribution network of First Auto Works. A growing overcapacity in car production in China forced a big cut in prices. On top of the price cuts, the Shanghai company began putting more resources into a new venture with VW's rival, General Motors, to build sedans.

In the mid-1980s when China opened up its economy to foreign investment, it demanded that foreign firms set up joint ventures with Chinese firms and transfer modern production technology to the ventures. VW accepted this situation and although initial investment was modest, it spent heavily to build components and engines locally as the venture grew. Over time, 95 percent of the components of the cars made by the joint venture were produced in China. As the first joint venture to offer a fully localized product, the company earned sizable profits while competitors had a hard time selling cars assembled from imported kits, which because of high tariffs were priced high. In 1996, the venture produced 200,000 cars.

In later years though, the venture was no longer as profitable. China now had about 100 automobile producers, many of them certainly small. Because of competition for market share, prices of cars had fallen. Also, VW had only a share in the manufacturing side of the joint venture and not in distribution. As the car from the venture became a local product and Chinese engineers acquired the skill to make it, distribution and sales grew in relative importance. The Chinese joint venture partner was able to use its control over distribution to squeeze VW's profit share.[18]

This case illustrates how a joint venture changes over time. Activities in one stage affect activities in the following stage. Three broad stages can be identified.

---

[18]Kahn, Joseph. 1997, April 18. Departure of VW's China unit head reveals flaws in a rare success story. *The Wall Street Journal*, p. A15.

1. *The Formative Stage.* At this stage, usually in the initial years, different firms come together because they have a shared vision about the industry and a need for complementary resources. In the early stage, the parties show a lot of enthusiasm for the venture, founded on high expectations and hope. Unfortunately, a heightened expectation and positive early results often set the stage for quick disenchantment as realities of marketplace competition and doubts of the partners' complete commitment to the enterprise arises.

2. *The Metamorphosis Stage.* As the joint venture gets ready to "take off," the partners begin grappling with the depth and breadth of their relationship. In fact, the relationship sort of evolves where the partners make adjustments, yielding or asserting control where necessary, and coordinating each other's structures, processes, and activities for the good of the venture. The parameters of partner behaviors are established. Committees are set up. A dense web of interpersonal relationships between the various partners are built up. The focus is on operationalizing the venture.

At a subsequent point in the metamorphosis phase, the parties discuss and determine additional commitment in terms of funds, technology, human resources, knowledge, and personal ties to the enterprise. Tensions in the relationship arise when the venture performs less than optimally for one or more of the partners, thus prompting reluctance to maintain the same level of commitment.

3. *Stabilization/Deterioration Phase.* A few years into the relationship, the issues are whether to maintain the alliance (usually because it has performed to expectations) or to manage the decline and dissolution of the venture (because of its suboptimal performance or due to a change in the priorities of the partners). If the business is doing well, the partners may be reluctant to confront each other with underlying problems that over time may hurt the relationship. Alliances that have lasted have arrangements where both sides regularly review the relationship in meetings between key managers, where a trust has been built up through constant exchange of communication, personnel, and key resources, and where the goals of all parties continue to be met. However, the parties may decide, jointly or individually, to terminate the venture. In many cases, instead of outright termination, the parties may redefine their relationship by narrowing or limiting it, often by one or more of the parties reducing their respective stakes in the alliance.

THE ALLIANCE MANAGER: WHAT DOES IT TAKE?

The central role and importance of the manager in the success of a strategic alliance or joint venture cannot be overemphasized. Such a person is usually selected by one of the partners. Depending on specific cases, the chief executive officer may be appointed by the majority partner. Often times, depending on the specific skills that a partner brings in (such as say, sales and distribution capabilities), the main position in that function (in this case, the marketing position) would be held by a manager sent from this particular partner.

The role and responsibilities of the head of the alliance change with every stage of the relationship. Understandably, the person wears several hats in order to play various roles, often mediating between the demands and expectations of the various owners. In the early stages, the **alliance manager** is a *strategic sponsor*—a combination of a visionary and an emissary. Such a manager is able to translate and communicate for all employees in the venture, the visions and goals of the partners. The manager is also an *advocate* for the interests of the venture. As the alliance grows and flourishes, coordinating various activities become important. Here the role is that of a *networker* and *facilitator,* linking functions, people, partners, and resources. Because disagreements are bound to occur, another role served by the alliance manager is that of a *mediator*—an honest broker who resolves conflicts for the good of the venture. If the manager is an expatriate, then that person also plays the role of an *ambassador* to the business and government community. In addition to all these roles, the person is also a *manager* with the task of running the venture and achieving its goals. In mergers especially, combining two different corporate cultures and assuring employees of continued opportunities require strong and imaginative leadership skills. The alliance manager most often finds an exodus of capable and experienced managers when mergers occur because they may fear limited career opportunities and corporate cutbacks to eliminate duplication.

Given the high likelihood that managing the joint ventures will be difficult, the selection of the right managers is clearly important. Table 7-5 presents a set of teachable and unteachable competencies alliance managers should possess. Effective managers are born with certain traits; they are also trained in various other dimensions, including the ability to gain the confidence and admiration of peers and subordinates; and they also learn from experience.

Given the important role of the alliance manager, such a person should hold the position for a period much longer than the two or three years that usually characterize such assignments. Building trust, credibility, rapport, and a personal relationship are time-intensive activities whose pace should not be forced. Frequent changing of such managers disrupts the stability of the relationships and creates conditions for the breakdown in communication between the partners. As the examples reported in the previous section suggests, building up institutional memory through longer-term appointments of key personnel contributes to the success of the venture.

Table 7-5	Alliance Manager Characteristics	

Unteachable Competencies:
- Willing to change self to accommodate others
- Willing to consider other person's point of view
- Able to simultaneously consider multiple points of view
- Can learn from past but not be constrained by it
- Willing to take losses in return for future gains

Teachable Competencies:

Functional	*Earned*	*Interpersonal*
Line skills	Credibility and respect	Social skills
Staff skills	Extensive networks:	Process skills
Educational background	-organizational	Tact/sensitivity
General business knowledge	-alliance	Cross-cultural awareness
	-industry	

Source: Adapted from Spekman, Robert E., et al. 1996. "Creating strategic alliances which endure." *Long Range Planning.* 29(3), p. 353.

WHOLLY OWNED SUBSIDIARIES

The next and even deeper involvement of a firm in its international operations occurs through the creation of wholly owned subsidiaries. Wholly owned subsidiaries imply that the parent firm is the sole owner of its overseas operations.

One hundred percent ownership occurs through acquisitions, greenfield investments, and mergers. A foreign firm may purchase an existing firm outright. Following the economic crisis in East Asia in the late 1990s, many local firms, weakened by debts and losses, were put on the market by their owners. For instance, Korean chaebol such as Hyundai, Samsung, LG, and Daewoo sold off several of their noncore businesses, which were purchased by U.S. and European firms.[19] Privatization of state-owned enterprises in many countries afforded foreign firms the opportunity to fully acquire firms in industries and countries that formerly had been closed to them. In other cases, a firm buys off its partners in a joint venture relationship and acquires complete ownership. For instance, Whirlpool first acquired a majority ownership in a home appliance operations owned by Philips and within three years, the U.S. company acquired the rest of the Dutch firm. When two or more separate and independent international firms join into a new entity, a merger occurs. In 1998, Daimler-Benz AG of Germany and Chrysler Corp. of the United States merged to create a single united company called DaimlerChrysler.[20]

The full ownership entry strategy is pursued where the firm clearly does not believe that it needs the resources and expertise of another partner or other partners. Obviously, such a firm would be quite resourceful, with ample funds to build a subsidiary from scratch or purchase existing operations outright. It would also require deep knowledge about the foreign market and considerable positive experience in overseas operations. A superior line of product/service is also a must. Success would mean retaining all profits (just as losses mean that all of them must be absorbed by the parent).

REASONS FOR 100 PERCENT OWNERSHIP

A firm may have any one of many reasons for wanting to own 100 percent of its overseas subsidiary. One set of reasons can be found in the parent's experience with strategic alliances and equity joint ventures. If past experience has been negative, the firm may understandably want to avoid those forms of relationships again. In addition, the firm may be hesitant about joint ventures and strategic alliances based on the following factors:

- Uncertainty about the capabilities and integrity of the partners
- Concern about the possible pressure in the future to share more and more decisions, authority, and resources with their partner(s)
- Concern about to whom the current joint venture partner may sell its shares or ally with in the future
- Worry about a conflict of interest between it and the foreign partners (over say, pricing, product development, quality control, or personnel matters)
- Conviction that 100 percent ownership is necessary to effectively integrate the subsidiary with the rest of the firm's activities and operations and exercise control

---

[19]Psst! Want a nice piece of chaebol? *Business Week.* 1998, May 18, pp. 50–51.
[20]Lipin, Steven. 1998, May 7. Chrysler approves deal with Daimler-Benz: Big questions remain. *The Wall Street Journal,* pp. A1, A11.

The last point is probably the principal reason why a firm seeks to own fully its over-seas operations. It eliminates the need to seek the permission of partners or to exhaust precious time and resources in negotiating and accommodating the interests of the other parties. It allows the firm to pursue its strategic goals unequivocally. As noted ear-lier, a firm may initially enter as a joint venture partner but over time as it acquires ex-pertise and confidence in operating in the host country, it may buy out its other partners and become the sole owner. The reasons for having a joint venture partner may have been accomplished and thus the partner is no longer required. A firm may also find that the joint venture partner is unable to deliver what it had promised at the outset and thus its presence in the venture is no longer necessary. Alternatively, a local partner may de-cide to sell out its share to the foreign firm because of various reasons such as a change in the business focus of the local partner, an inability to meet its commitments to the joint venture, or difficulties with the foreign partner.

Other related issues merit consideration by a firm. The firm may have a compelling desire to shield technical know-how and marketing plans from outsiders and especially competitors, both current and future. Quality control issues may be so paramount that full control is necessary to ensure the necessary level of quality. The firm may believe that its foreign image may be tarnished if it is associated with either host country part-ners or any other partner for that matter. A firm pursuing a global strategy would, by definition, need to exercise centralized control over its global operations and such con-trol may be thought by managers to be more effectively exercised if the parent had full control over its subsidiaries. One hundred percent ownership bestows total control and is necessary to accomplish corporate objectives whether they are maximizing profits, re-turn on investment, sales growth, market share, and the like. In 1998, Johnson Controls, Inc., a U.S. manufacturer of automobile components and controls for buildings, pur-chased the Becker Group of Germany, a manufacturer of door systems and instrument panels and other automobile components. The acquisition by Johnson Controls re-flected the firm's strategy to become the global leader in automotive interior systems by having the capability to produce, design, and engineer the products in Europe, one of the company's largest markets.[21]

Absence of host government restrictions on total ownership, opportunity to counter protectionist tendencies in the foreign country, and a weak currency may make complete ownership of foreign operations easy, desirable, and affordable. Following the decline of the Canadian dollar against the U.S. dollar to its lowest levels ever in 1998, U.S. companies such as Pope & Talbot Inc., a forest products firm, found Canadian firms to be a bargain. Cross-border takeovers increased significantly as the strong U.S. dollar made Canadian firms less expensive to acquire.[22] The creation of a single market in Eu-rope opened up opportunities for cross-border acquisitions as firms sought to expand their scale of operations to match the competition from U.S. and Japanese firms.

Purchasing a foreign firm gives ready access to a foreign market as well as to valu-able assets such as a distribution network. Sometimes, the stock prices may be lower, and a company flush with large retained earnings may spot a bargain. When General

---

[21]Rose, Robert L. 1998, April 28. Johnson Controls agrees to purchase of Becker Group. *The Wall Street Journal*, p. B19.
[22]De Santis, Solange. 1998, February 7. Canada's weak currency turns its companies into U.S. targets. *The Wall Street Journal*, p. A18.

Motors Corp. invested money and technology in ailing Ssangyong Motor Co., a Korean company, it did so to gain access to Ssangyong's vehicle distribution system in that country. This move was important because South Korea represents a rapidly expanding automobile market and to be able to fully participate in the market, a local presence is necessary in the face of tariffs and quotas that limit the potential of exports.[23]

When acquiring another firm, the managers of the acquiring firm hire professional experts such as international accounting firms, strategic business consultants, merchant banks, local accounting firms, and lawyers to perform **due diligence.** The main purpose of due diligence is to obtain independent input on the condition of the firm that will be acquired, confirm the wisdom of the proposed transaction, obtain insights into the management and commercial practices of the firm, set the price of the acquisition, and determine cultural and corporate fit.

DRAWBACKS TO 100 PERCENT OWNERSHIP

Several impediments block the path of a firm's ability to expand through creating wholly owned subsidiaries. For one, it is simply much more expensive. Buying 100 percent of the shares of a firm costs the buyer much more than say, buying 60 percent of the shares. Similarly, building a new subsidiary from scratch on one's own is also an expensive proposition. The firm may not be able to sustain a 100 percent ownership strategy over the long haul.

Secondly, host governments are more likely to impose restrictions of various sorts on 100 percent foreign ownership. In certain industries, outright purchase by a foreign firm may not be approved. Some industries may be barred from majority ownership by foreign firms (such as the airlines industry in the United States). Sometimes, the host government, citing concerns that a monopoly is being created, may refuse the acquisition of an existing firm that would eliminate a competitor as the earlier example of Orangina noted.

As discussed in Chapter 3, host country nationalists are more likely to target wholly owned foreign subsidiaries and make them an object of any popular or demagogic protests. The political risk may be perceived to be higher. Should the business climate turn negative, the foreign subsidiary may find itself unable to repatriate to the parent capital, dividends, and profits. Regulations of various kinds including restrictions on converting local money into foreign currency, especially hard currency, may prevent the firm from liquidating its assets and transferring the proceeds to home. In effect, by investing money the firm signals an irrevocable, at least in the short run, commitment to the foreign country—a commitment from which the foreign firm may be unable to extricate itself.

A third issue is the need to establish the organizational linkages between the parent and the subsidiary. Apart from reporting and control mechanisms (discussed in Chapter 9), the parent may wish to appoint home country managers in its foreign operations, especially in key positions. Quite possibly, the parent firm may not have the requisite numbers of qualified home country managers who could be posted overseas. As a consequence, it may be forced to rely on host country managers or even managers from third countries resulting in managers at headquarters believing that their ability

---

[23]GM seen investing in South Korea firm. *The Wall Street Journal.* 1997, March 24, p. A14.

to effectively integrate the overseas operations into the firm's overall activities is substantially reduced. Alternatively, the firm may have to change its culture as well as its policy toward training, promotion, and integration of foreign managers into the company's executive ranks. Several Japanese firms with wholly owned operations in the United States in their early years would create a twin-track management system—one staffed by U.S. managers, the other by Japanese managers sent by headquarters. In many cases, this system created suspicion and resentment among the U.S. managers, inefficiency in overall operations, and conflict between the two groups.

As South Korea's giant chaebol expanded overseas, they needed hundreds of world class managers and there were not enough capable Korean managers. To compete with multinational firms from other countries, especially Japan, South Korean firms had to give their foreign managers a significant level of responsibility and authority as well as higher pay than what Korean managers received.[24]

Fourth, when a wholly owned subsidiary is created by acquisition or merger, it presents the challenge of meshing different corporate and national cultures and practices. As discussed in Chapter 2, culture is deeply embedded in the human psyche, and it is reflected in corporate culture. Changes are often not easy to introduce because of well-established practices in the acquired firm, resistance from employees, and a desire sometimes to maintain a local face even while trying to exercise control. Usually cultural adjustments have to be made and certain practices in the subsidiary retained. Inability to handle the cultural differences make the acquisition difficult to operate with attendant implications for profits, sales, and integration with the rest of the firm. Following the merger of Daimler-Benz and Chrysler car companies, the company appointed Andreas Renschler as head of global executive development to smooth the differences and to oversee and prepare appropriate career paths for the top 3,000 executives from the two companies. To establish credibility, he said he would feature Chrysler's U.S. managers as prominently as Daimler-Benz's German managers. *"I have to get to a point where people can trust us."* The new company created more than 100 integration teams following the merger to bring the two companies together, eliminate duplication, and reduce costs.[25]

Depending on the extent of autonomy given to the management of the subsidiary, disagreements may arise with the parent over a variety of issues:

- Distribution of profits versus reinvestment
- Borrowing versus equity to fund projects
- When, where, and by how much the capacity would be expanded
- The level, purpose, and location of R&D activities
- Degree of capital intensiveness in the production process and its integration with the rest of the firm
- Transfer prices for raw materials and finished products
- The variety of products produced and product mix
- Access to distribution channels
- The geographical markets serviced by the subsidiary

---

[24]Foreign bodies in South Korea. *The Economist.* 1996. December 14, p. 66.
[25]Simonian, Haig. 1999, February 3. All eyes on the mega-merger integrator. *Financial Times,* p. 12.

- Pricing, extension of credit, and post-sales servicing
- Human resource issues such as selection and source of managers, compensation levels, decision-making styles, and relationship with unions
- The need to project a certain image

Given the preceding list of potential sources of conflict with headquarters, firms must focus on the cost and benefit of 100 percent ownership. The parent may seek to exercise control through the following avenues:

- Ownership (controlling the majority of the governing board)
- Market access (control over trademarks, brand names, or distribution channels)
- Technology (control over patents and sharing of R&D)
- Finance (by providing low-cost or ample capital on its own or by arrangements through financial institutions)
- Personnel (by providing qualified technical and managerial personnel)
- Political assistance (by effectively dealing with the government to temper any restrictive practices)
- Supply (limiting the availability of raw materials to the subsidiary)
- Physical assets (control over sites, capacity size, and specialized equipment)

It would certainly appear that a firm may be able to achieve most, if not all of its goals, through a strategy of less than 100 percent ownership.

CONCLUSIONS

Strategic alliances and equity joint ventures, increasingly common and eagerly entered into, are generally short-term arrangements in a firm's evolution toward becoming a multinational firm. Recognizing that, managers need to devise steps so that the collaboration yields as much benefit as possible to the partners, and at the same time ensuring that their core competencies are not lost and potential rivals are not created. Great care has to be taken in defining the purpose of the collaboration, in selecting the partner(s), in negotiating the alliance, in making the relationship work to mutual benefit, and to terminate it when appropriate. Strategic alliances and joint ventures will not disappear from the portfolio of business arrangements for the international firm. They will exist, being constantly created, altered, and terminated. Wholly owned foreign subsidiaries represent the final extension of a domestic firm. Even though they afford the parent control over its overseas activities and effective integration into its overall strategy, they are often expensive and could be difficult to divest should the need arise. Shortages of capable managers and other resources as well as host government reservations may constrain a firm's ability to wholly own its foreign operations or fully exploit the purported advantages of 100 percent ownership. Equity joint ventures and wholly owned subsidiaries also impact in crucial ways how the firm is organized and operated. The three forms of doing business internationally discussed in this chapter are appropriate under certain circumstances and all require specific managerial attention. The challenge in every case is to ensure that the choice of international business arrangement is consistent with the strategic goals of the organization.

OPENING VIGNETTE EPILOGUE

After more discussions, Mr. Weill huddled with his team and decided that it was not worth breaking the joint venture by insisting on majority ownership. Nikko was given a 51 percent share. When the Japanese returned to the room where Mr. Weill and his team of Americans were waiting, Mr. Arimura joked, "We have all decided to go to work for Kojima securities." Nikko officials proposed that Mr. Kojima run the business with a "joint" CEO from Nikko, a solution modeled on phrasing from bond-underwriting advertisements that describe a "lead" and subordinate "joint lead" underwriter.

With respect to the "relationship managers," the gap between the two sides proved too large to bridge. A compromise was reached. The managers would continue to report to Nikko, but the joint venture would pay most of their salaries. This solution was thought to be the best to ensure that Japanese clients did not desert the proposed joint venture. Within days of reaching these agreements, the joint venture was approved and began operations in March 1999.[26]

[26]Spindle, Bill. 1999, May 19. Travelers, Nikko union is many things: Easy is not one of them. *The Wall Street Journal*, pp. 1, A10.

Key Terms

- strategic alliance
- joint venture

- wholly owned subsidiary
- shotgun clause

- alliance manager
- due diligence

Discussion Questions

1. The joint venture method of international operations has several disadvantages. Discuss them and suggest specific ways by which managers can overcome them.
2. In forming a strategic alliance or joint venture, should a company seek a partner similar in size, organizational culture, and resources, or should it seek a firm that is dissimilar? Explain.
3. Identify a set of circumstances under which a firm might form a strategic alliance, an equity joint venture, and a wholly owned subsidiary in a foreign country.
4. A joint venture is often described as a dynamic relationship that requires constant attention of the owners. What makes a joint venture dynamic, and why do the owners have a difficult time managing change in joint ventures?
5. Joint ventures have high mortality rates, yet they are popular. Explain this seeming contradiction.
6. Identify the elements that are necessary for strategic alliances and joint ventures to succeed. Why are they difficult to replicate in most settings?

Writing Assignment

Renault, a French automobile company, acquired a 38-percent stake in Nissan, a Japanese car manufacturer. Prepare a two-page report discussing how Renault may exercise effective control holding only a minority ownership in Nissan.

Internet Exercise

Select any industry and select a particular foreign country. Use the Internet to access sites that will identify or provide leads on potential strategic alliance or joint venture partners in the foreign country for that industry. Some useful sites may include the chambers of commerce, trade associations, host and home government offices and agencies, and consulting firms.

Internet Resources

Many organizations specialize in bringing firms together to form alliances. One such firm is Global Opportunities, Inc., which has a Web site at *www.global-opportunities.com/joint-ventures.cfm*. A newsletter called "CIO Magazine" also provides useful information through *www.cio.com*. Consulting firm Booz, Allen & Hamilton can be accessed at *www.bah.com*. A list of companies seeking joint venture and strategic alliance opportunities can be found at *www.tradenet.ca/common/jnt_ventures.html*. The International Finance Corporation, a member of the World Bank Group, publishes scholarly reports on foreign investments in developing countries. Their Web site is *www.ifc.org/DEPTS/OPS/ECON/*.

Experiential Exercise

It's a Deal! Negotiating a Strategic Alliance

(This experiential exercise illustrates the reasons why firms seek strategic alliances and focuses on the nature and dynamics of the negotiations that have to be conducted by the parties to reach a mutually acceptable arrangement. The exercise also emphasizes the role of firm power in alliance building and how to effectively use scarce resources. The instructor will provide additional information.)

The direct air route between the countries of Amberland and Roseland lies over the kingdom of Jade. Until recently, foreign air transport companies were not allowed to overfly Jade, necessitating the taking of a circuitous route that bypassed the entire kingdom. However, in a recent relaxation of its stringent overflying policies, the kingdom of Jade has agreed to allow one round-trip flight over it every day.

Two airfreight companies are in the business of shipping goods between Amberland and Roseland and welcome the new decision of the government of Jade because it would cut costs and increase profits. However, only one round-trip flight could be operated over Jade every day, making the two companies eager to reach an agreement on how to use this route so that both of them benefit. Inability to reach an agreement means both firms will have to use the long, circuitous route. Each company can load and fly one plane per day (round-trip) from Amberland to Roseland, and vice versa. The two companies are not direct competitors, and they are different with regard to their size and profitability.

The following information is available about the two companies:

	Company A	Company B
1. Air freight capacity of plane (in tons)	150	100
2. Profit from transporting over kingdom of Jade (the direct route)	$120/ton	$60/ton
3. Profit from transporting by the circuitous (or long) route	$ 20/ton	$20/ton

Goal: The goal of this exercise is to reach an agreement on the use of the direct route that will allow each company to achieve the largest possible profit.

Rules:

1. Participants are formed into two equal groups, one representing Company A, the other Company B, and separated.
2. Each group plans its negotiating strategy. Allow 10 minutes.
3. Each group selects its sequence of negotiators. Negotiations will be on an one-to-one basis in front of both groups.
4. Each negotiation round lasts 3 minutes.
5. At the conclusion of the round and if no agreement is reached, the negotiators return to their respective groups. Allow 5 minutes for the groups to consult before the next round of negotiations are held.
6. The sequence of negotiations continues until a deal (or agreement) is reached. Every round of negotiation is conducted by a different player.
7. While the negotiations are underway, the rest of the two teams remain quiet and observe the process. They cannot provide any advice or help to their negotiator.
8. Negotiators in subsequent rounds are not bound by commitments made by negotiators in previous rounds.
9. The number of negotiating rounds is limited by the number of players in each team.

A game played with 20 players, divided into two equal teams of 10 each, would have a maximum number of 10 negotiating rounds in which to reach an agreement.

Case 7–1   THE DATING GAME

It had been more than a year since John Hutchinson, chief executive officer of Noctel, a small telecommunications company in Bankaland, had read in *The Wall Street Journal* that the government of Urugustan was planning to privatize its state-owned telephone company. Soon thereafter, Mr. Hutchinson, had initiated efforts to become a player in Urugustan's telephone industry. Fourteen months later, Noctel found itself without a local partner, a Urugustan government requirement for entering a bid to own the would-be privatized company. The deadline for submitting bids was less than two months away, and Mr. Hutchinson was worried.

NOCTEL INC.

Noctel Inc. was a small telephone company that operated both mobile and fixed line systems in Bankaland, a highly advanced industrial society. Noctel's strength lay in its technological innovation and high level of customer service. The company had flourished following the deregulation of the telecommunications industry in Bankaland where all restrictions on the entry into the industry had been removed.

The company had been started in 1995 by a group of communication engineers who had been laid off from AT&T, a giant U.S. phone company. Using state-of-the-art technology, which could yield high returns even with relatively small-scale operations, and benefiting from a flat hierarchical structure with a small bureaucracy and relatively negligible overheads, the company had successfully used venture capital to grow rapidly. It offered local and long-distance phone services, Internet connections, and a high-speed data and video transmission network. Connectivity was rated by industry groups as among the highest and Noctel had gained a reputation for excellent customer service. The company had been posting profits every year and was now looking to expand, preferably abroad, as the domestic market remained highly competitive and growth rates were slowing.

PRIVATIZATION IN URUGUSTAN

As with many other countries in the 1990s, Urugustan decided to privatize its antiquated phone system. The government did not have the resources to modernize the system, though it recognized that a modern telecommunications network was essential for rapid economic development. Urugustan was a developing country with a population of 15 million and per capita income of $6,250.

Under the government's privatization plans, it planned to invite tenders from foreign telecommunications companies. The government wanted foreign firms to bid in alliance with a local partner so that home country firms and nationals would have a stake and a say in the telecommunications industry. The government had announced its plans in an official notification and had set March 1, 2000, as the deadline to receive bids. The winner would be announced on June 1, 2000. A license to provide monopoly telecommunication services in the country would be issued for 10 years.

NOCTEL'S PLANS

Noctel felt that Urugustan offered a good opportunity for the company to expand. It had the financial, human, and technical resources to operate the system and based on data available, the venture would be successful. The Urugustan economy was expanding rapidly and with rising per capita income, Noctel would be able to offer various value-added services whose margins were much higher.

Noctel, however, had one problem. It did not have any presence or connections in Urugustan and its international experience was extremely limited, although this issue did not daunt Mr. Hutchinson. He had about 15 months to lay the groundwork, find a local partner, work together on preparing a winning bid, and submit it by the March 1 deadline. In addition to the challenge of finding a suitable local partner, Noctel had to be concerned with Nokia, a large Finnish telecommunications company, which had an office in the Urugustan capital and operated a small local franchise for providing limited mobile phone service.

Soon after reading *The Wall Street Journal* news item about the privatization plans, Mr. Hutchinson had called a meeting of his senior managers, who generally agreed that Urugustan offered a new opportunity for Noctel. Success in Urugustan would allow Noctel to seek other foreign markets, especially when many other countries in that region were also planning to modernize and privatize their telecommunication services. The challenge was to identify a local partner in Urugustan, determine whether Noctel and the local partner were a good fit, assess the ability of the local partner, and finally negotiate a detailed agreement with the local partner. This agreement would form the basis for preparing the formal bid to the Urugustan government for buying the country's telecommunications system.

LOCATING A LOCAL PARTNER

Noctel had obtained from the Urugustan's embassy in Bankaland a directory of major businesses in Urugustan. It had also contacted its own country's embassy in Urugustan and found the commercial attaché there extremely helpful. Based on information obtained and a background study of the culture, politics, and economics of Urugustan, Noctel sent a senior marketing manager and a technical services manager to Urugustan to talk with local managers there. As Mr. Hutchinson noted at a meeting with his managers, "The only way to find a partner is by being there. That is how we can establish connections."

Urugustan's private sector economy was dominated by both local businesses and multinational firms. Most of the locally owned businesses were controlled by leading families, united by blood, marriage, and ethnicity. Some of these businesses had entered into joint ventures with foreign firms or were licensees and importers of foreign products. A few of these family-owned business houses had a well-deserved reputation for quality of products and services, reliability and integrity, and deep pockets.

IN URUGUSTAN

Peter Reid and Jonathan Duncan, the two Noctel managers, leased two suites long term at the Hilton hotel in the capital. Many foreign companies were located in the hotel, which served as an excellent site both for staying long term and to meet local people. The hotel was equipped with a full-scale business center and had excellent telecommunication links with foreign countries.

Soon after arriving, the two managers received a call from a person who identified himself as a "matchmaker"—someone who brought local businesses and foreign firms together. He wanted an appointment and faxed over a long list of successful deals he had clinched, a sort of resumé. Mr. Reid and Mr. Duncan were excited at the prospect. "We may not need the long-term lease at the hotel. This guy seems to know everyone in this city and has dealt with some big international names. He will be our ticket," said Mr. Reid.

When Mr. Reid and Mr. Duncan met the matchmaker, they were surprised to find that he wanted a fee up front for providing information. The Noctel managers were hesitant because they were not sure what sort of information they would get. They took the chance, paid him his fees, and received a talk about the major business families in Urugustan, their business specializations, and how he could introduce them to the two Noctel managers. The matchmaker said that each introduction would cost additional sums.

One evening, Mr. Reid and Mr. Duncan attended a party at the residence of the commercial attaché. At the party were quite a few prominent Urugustanis and members of the expatriate Bankaland community. The party enabled the Noctel managers to establish contact, share business cards, and get invited to local clubs, golf games, and a tour of business facilities. They told the attaché about the matchmaker who cautioned them to be careful about self-styled matchmakers. While some were genuine, others were not.

WHICH LOCAL FIRM?

Within days, Mr. Reid and Mr. Duncan had a stack of business cards. They identified a list of firms and began calling to set up meetings. The matchmaker called offering his services to introduce them to the patriarch of this family, the scion of that family. Mr. Duncan was undecided what to do. "Can he really deliver or can we get the meetings with these folks by ourselves. At $20,000 a meeting, it is expensive, and we are not sure of the outcome. But what if he can deliver something useful?" They decided against taking up the matchmaker's offer.

In choosing which local firm to contact, Noctel's managers were less concerned about their telecommunications expertise, but more about their knowledge of the local economy, connections with the government, and ability to obtain qualified people. Because most of the larger local firms were family-owned businesses, obtaining hard, reliable financial and performance data was difficult or not available at all. "We really did not know how strong these firms were. We were merely forming impressions. It certainly helped that we talked with our embassy friend and a couple of Bankaland guys who had been living in this country for a long time," recalled Mr. Reid.

In talking with the managers of the local company, Mr. Reid and Mr. Duncan found that they were not the only foreigners looking for local telecommunication partners. Some of the local firms had already committed to partner with other international firms. "We knew the Finns were here. But it was surprising that so were the Swedes, the Canadians, the Japanese, the Americans, even the Spaniards," said Mr. Duncan. "We thought we had moved pretty fast having flown out here only two weeks after reading the privatization news in *The Wall Street Journal*. But the others clearly had a head start on us."

Another surprise was that Mr. Reid and Mr. Duncan soon realized that the local firms were checking them and Noctel out too. Some of the local firms wanted to learn more about Noctel, its history, its owners, its products, and its overseas experience. The two Noctel managers provided as much information as needed; they handed out brochures about the company and its capabilities, financial reports, and favorable Bankaland media reports. Some local firms declined to pursue any further conversations on the subject of forming an alliance. However, after nearly three months, the two managers had established an ongoing relationship with three local companies.

ASSESSING COMPATIBILITY

"Well, we have been talking with these three groups for three months now, we probably should decide on who to pursue," said Mr. Reid. Mr. Duncan agreed, saying, "We need a partner who will fit well with our Noctel culture and way of doing business. We have to have the right chemistry between us. After all we cannot run a phone company quarreling with each other. But how do we determine who is compatible and who is not?"

In communication with managers at headquarters and during visits home, Mr. Reid and Mr. Duncan drew up a checklist of characteristics to look for in the potential partner. These included core values as evidenced by how they treat visitors and women, how are phone calls handled, the ease of interacting between managers and subordinates, formality or informality of communication, feeling comfortable with Noctel people and vice versa, and of course, acceptance to the board and top management of Noctel. Most of these core values could only be discerned through extended interactions with the local managers. Based on these criteria, Mr. Reid and Mr. Duncan continued their conversations with higher-level managers of the three business houses they had identified. At the end of three more months, they settled on Pratchat Industries Ltd., a diversified conglomerate, as the potential local partner.

NEGOTIATING THE ALLIANCE

Pratchat Industries Ltd. had no experience in telecommunications. However, they had a track record of entering into new businesses with considerable success. For instance, they were the biggest producer of frogs, which were exported almost entirely to France. They also produced, on contract, for U.S. pharmaceutical companies, generic drugs for a wide range of ailments. Within the country itself, they owned a radio station and an English language newspaper, among other businesses. Ben Abdul, a member of the family that owned Pratchat Industries Ltd., had been negotiating with the Noctel managers for the past three months. He had become familiar with Noctel and was interested in exploring an alliance with them. Telecommunications was a new business with tremendous growth potential and Pratchat wanted to be part of it.

It was now eight months since Mr. Reid and Mr. Duncan first came to Urugustan. They flew back to Bankaland with a profile of Pratchat Industries. After discussion with Mr. Hutchinson and other top managers, they drew up a 40-page draft agreement to present to Mr. Abdul. The agreement was a business plan as well as a joint venture arrangement in which Noctel would hold a 60 percent interest. The joint venture would submit a bid to the Urugustan government for purchase of the local telephone firm. Mr. Hutchinson flew with Mr. Reid and Mr. Duncan when they returned to Urugustan. Mr. Hutchinson met Mr. Abdul, members of the Pratchat family, and senior civil servants in the telecommunications department of the ministry before returning to Bankaland. He gave Mr. Reid and Mr. Duncan the green light to have the agreement approved with Mr. Abdul.

The agreement was quite detailed. It included technical specifications about operating and modernizing the telephone system; about the financial contributions of each party; basis for evaluating performance of the venture; basis for distributing dividends; the staffing of senior level positions; and the role of Pratchat Industries. Mr. Reid said, "We had the agreement looked over with a fine tooth comb by a legal consulting firm at home before presenting it to Pratchat. We wanted to know what we were getting into and we wanted Ben to know what he was getting Pratchat into. We did not want misunderstandings later on."

Mr. Abdul took a copy of the agreement back to his office. It was two weeks later that he returned with a team of Pratchat family members and top managers. They went over each point in the agreement with Mr. Reid and Mr. Duncan. The Noctel managers realized that they had to explain many aspects of the draft agreement to the other side. The negotiations dragged on. One evening, as they sat at the Hilton bar drinking local beer, Mr. Duncan commented, "Pete, do you get the feeling that they are getting cold feet over the deal? I think they want to get the technology from us and reduce their share of the equity. I can understand the reduced equity contribution, but I don't see the technology angle. With the changes in the technology, they need us to keep up-to-date. They don't have the engineers or the technical ability to upgrade. Our bid will succeed because of our advanced technology and low cost and superior service. So why are they not moving faster?" Mr. Reid replied, "Jon, I have a gut feeling that this is not going anywhere. We have had discussions over which side will exercise control, who will staff what positions, and what each side will bring to the table. The frustrating thing is that they are unwilling to agree on the procedures for ending the relationship. It is almost as if they expect us to sign the deal and walk away from it. But we need to have the dispute resolution clauses clear and agreed upon. Otherwise we will be in big trouble should we fall out." "Let's not get discouraged, Peter. We may have to be a little more flexible on some of the issues. After all, we need them for this bid and they certainly have good contacts, know the set up, and a good track record."

After a few more rounds of negotiations, the two sides were deadlocked. Pratchat wanted the following: to retain control even with a minority equity stake; it wanted as much of the components and parts to be bought in Urugustan from Pratchat Industries family of firms; it wanted the right to buy out Noctel's share of the venture after five years; it wanted several key positions filled by members of the Pratchat family; it wanted dividends to be declared on the basis of annual revenues, not profits; and it wanted disputes to be resolved in Urugustan courts under Urugustan law. Reid and Duncan flew back to Bankaland for further instructions from headquarters.

Noctel adjusted its position on several of these issues and met Pratchat's demands fully on purchasing and dispute resolution. It was willing to share control and allocate several executive positions to the Pratchat family; and it was willing to sell the venture back after a longer time frame. It however would not compromise on the basis of dividend distribution.

Mr. Reid and Mr. Duncan returned with their new negotiating briefs. A meeting with Mr. Abdul was arranged. Over cocktails, the three men met. Mr. Reid started by saying, "We are willing to go the extra yard and be flexible on some of the positions we have held." Mr. Abdul was quiet. After he heard out Mr. Reid's new offer, he said. "Look, Pete. This is going to be hard on you. But last week, we signed an agreement to ally our-selves with Nokia to bid for the privatization deal. They gave us a deal we are happy with. I am sorry."

Mr. Reid and Mr. Duncan were shocked. One year in Urugustan had come to naught. The cost (nearly $500,000), the time, the energy, all seem to have been wasted. Gathering his wits around him, Mr. Reid told Mr. Duncan, "I guess we better call Hutchinson and give him the bad news."

QUESTIONS

1. What options does Noctel have in Urugustan?
2. How can Noctel find another local partner in the short period remaining before the bid deadline arrives?
3. If Mr. Reid and Mr. Duncan had to do it again, how should they have approached the opportunity in Urugustan?
4. How should Noctel have approached its negotiations with Pratchat Industries Ltd?
5. Evaluate Noctel's choice of entering Urugustan as the first place for its international expansion.

References

Au, Alan Kai Ming, and Peter Enderwick. 1994. Small firms in international joint ventures in China: The New Zealand experience. *Journal of Small Business Management.* April, pp. 89–94.

Beamish, Paul W., and Andrew C. Inkpen. 1995. Keeping international joint ventures stable and profitable. *Long-Range Planning* 28(3), pp. 26–36.

Blodgett, Linda Longfellow. 1991. Partner contributions as prediction of equity share in international joint ventures. *Journal of International Business Studies.* First Quarter, pp. 63–78.

Blodgett, Linda Longfellow. 1992. Factors in the instability of international joint ventures: An event history analysis. *Strategic Management Journal* 13, pp. 475–481.

Brouthers, Keith D., Lance Eliot Bouthers, and Timothy J. Wilkinson. 1995. Strategic alliances: Choose your partners. *Long-Range Planning* 28(2), pp. 18–25.

Dussauge, Pierre. 1995. Determinants of success in international strategic alliances: Evidence from the global aerospace industry. *Journal of International Business Studies.* Third Quarter, pp. 505–530.

Glaister, Keith W., and Peter J. Buckley. 1996. Strategic motives for international alliance formation. *Journal of Management Studies* 33(2), pp. 301–332.

Hamel, Gary, Yves L. Doz, and C. K. Prahalad. 1989. Collaborate with your competitors—and win. *Harvard Business Review.* January–February, pp. 133–139.

Hinterhuber, Hans H., and Andreas Hirsch. 1998. Commentary: Starting up a strategic network. *Thunderbird International Business Review* 40(3), pp. 185–208.

International joint ventures in developing countries: Happy marriage? Statistics for 1970–1995. IFC Discussion Paper Number 29. Washington, DC.: International Finance Corporation.

Meschi, Pierre-Xavier, and Alain Roger. 1994. Cultural context and social effectiveness in international joint ventures. *Management International Review* 34(3), pp. 197–215.

Mills, Roger W., and Gordon Chen. 1996. Evaluating international joint ventures using strategic value analysis. *Long-Range Planning* 29(4), pp. 552–561.

Pearson, M. 1991. *Joint ventures in the People's Republic of China: The control of foreign investment under socialism.* Princeton, NJ: Princeton University Press.

Reuer, Jeffrey. 1998. The dynamics and effectiveness of international joint ventures. *European Management Journal* 16(2), pp. 160–168.

Sasaki, Toru. 1993. What the Japanese have learned from strategic alliances. *Long-Range Planning,* 26(12), pp. 41–53.

Shaughnessy, Hadyn. 1995. International joint ventures: Managing successful collaborations. *Long-Range Planning* 28(3), pp. 10–17.

Shenkar, Oded, and Yoram Zeira. 1992. Role conflict and role ambiguity of chief executive officers in international joint ventures. *Journal of International Business Studies.* First Quarter, pp. 55–75.

Smith, Anne, and Marie-Claude Reney. 1997. The mating dance: A case study of local partnering processes in developing countries. *European Management Journal* 15(2), pp. 174–181.

Spekman, Robert E., Lynn A. Isabella, Thomas C. MacAvoy, and Theodore Forbes, III. 1996. Creating strategic alliances which endure. *Long-Range Planning* 29(3), pp. 346–357.

Turpin, Dominque. 1993. Strategic alliances with Japanese firms: Myths and realities. *Long-Range Planning* 26(8), pp. 11–15.

Walter, Bruce A., Steve Peters, and Gregory G. Dess. 1994. Strategic alliances and joint ventures: Making them work. *Business Horizons.* July–August, pp. 5–10.

8

OPERATIONS MANAGEMENT AND LOGISTICS

OPENING VIGNETTE

The holiday season was only a few weeks away. Greg Zitzer was frantically searching for a ship to carry loads of carved figurines from Hong Kong to the United States. His company, Willitts Designs International Inc., had been deluged with holiday orders but stranded overseas were shipments of his most popular items: 1,000 statuettes of Jesus and angels, and 38,000 collectible models of historic footwear. Even though his shipping agent had started seeking space for the delivery in the beginning of August, calling 15 different shipping companies every day, Mr. Zitzer was without a boat. "I'm desperate," he said, as he prepared to fly to Asia to negotiate with suppliers and shipping lines.

For U.S. companies in the fall of 1998, the boats from China and other parts of Asia were slow to arrive. U.S. importers saw record numbers of delays and foul-ups on shipments of everything from teddy bears to furniture, all stranded by a shipping jam between Asia and the United States. The pre-holiday shipping season had turned into a logistical headache with some consignments lost for days in overloaded ports and others getting loaded onto ships after long delays, only to be bumped off for another cargo. Companies were "begging and groveling and paying anything the shipping lines want," said Tom Craig, general manager of LTD Shippers Association, which represented U.S. importers. "It's on the brink of chaos."

Some frustrated importers accused shipping lines of breaking contract agreements to illegally charge higher rates. Importers had planned to have all the merchandise in place before the Christmas shopping season began in earnest. Because transportation costs accounted for 5 to 10 percent of the price of goods, higher shipping services would show up on retail price tags.

The cause of the shipping problems was the enormous increase in the demand for products from Asia that year. Because the financial crisis in that region had devalued local currencies, Asian goods were particularly cheap for U.S. buyers. At the same time, U.S. products were now much more expensive for Asian buyers, which led to a fall in demand. As a result, nearly empty ships were sailing to Asia and packed ships were returning to North America. Shipping companies claimed that they were losing money on their Pacific runs. Consequently, they had withdrawn shipping capacity from the Asian trade creating the space crunch. Denying that they were breaking contracts, they explained that spot prices had risen along with demand for space. "It's the basic free market supply and demand structure," said Tom Cowan, senior vice president at SeaLand Service Inc., the biggest U.S. shipping line.

B oth international manufacturing and service firms can organize the various elements of the operations process in a way that enhances their competitive advantage.
Organizing the operations starts from deciding where to locate facilities, determining
their size, and assigning appropriate roles to such facilities. An analysis of what a firm
does enables managers to decide which activities can be contracted out and which can
be retained in-house; however, new managerial challenges emerge in coordinating the
various operational activities to ensure smooth and efficient functioning. Changes in information technology and new management ideas such as just-in-time (JIT) and total
quality management (TQM) have opened up new strategic opportunities. The competitiveness of many firms now arises in large part from improvement in processes, new
product introductions, and product quality, in addition to reducing input costs. This
chapter looks at the location and purpose of overseas facilities, the importance of appropriate plant capacity, the concept of the value chain, the various issues surrounding
the decision to subcontract elements of the firm's activities to outside entities, and the
relevance of effective distribution, inventory management, and quality control in international business.

LOCATION OF FACILITIES

Where should a firm locate its overseas office, warehouse, distribution center, or manufacturing facility? Location decisions are important for at least two reasons. One, this
decision usually involves committing substantial sums of money. Facilities, once established, cannot be easily moved. Therefore, great care needs to be taken in selecting the
site in the first place. A mistake may be harder to rectify. Second, location affects production costs and access to customers. A bad location may lead to interruptions in supplies or poor quality of workforce. Thus, site selection is a long-term, strategic decision
that has a major impact on the firm's ability to compete, on how the various worldwide
operations of the firm are integrated, and on its image in the host country.

Managers have several options in location planning. They can expand an existing
facility, which is generally less expensive if physical space is available. Another option
is to establish new facilities, either by acquiring existing operations or building a totally
new setup, which is often necessary to enter new markets, to be near customers, or because existing facilities can no longer be expanded or modernized. A third option is to
close down operations at one place and build (or acquire) one elsewhere usually because of rising costs, lack of physical space, or erosion of the customer base at the present location. A final choice is simply to do nothing. The firm may find the other options
unattractive and could cater to customers by contracting out production to other firms.

The decision as to which country to enter to set up operations is clearly a top management decision and is guided by more general factors such as size of the market, stability of politics, transparency of rules, predictability in exchange rates, and availability
of the necessary infrastructure. These issues were discussed in Chapter 5 with regard to
selecting an overseas export market. The actual site to locate the facility in the foreign
country is selected much more carefully and often after following a structured list of
necessary attributes. Headquarters not only selects the country in which investment will
occur but also is involved in selecting the type of specific facility at a specific location
in that country.

Prior to the formation of the European Union, foreign firms were likely to establish multiple plants, many of them small in size, to cater to the individual country markets of Europe. With the integration of the member countries and the consequent elimination of tariffs, quotas, and differential standards, firms began setting up fewer but larger plants to serve the entire market created by the Union. Firms also establish facilities to cater to a regional market and not just a specific country market. The product is specifically designed for the regional market, transportation costs are reduced, and the need for being near to customers is desirable and even encouraged by the host government. For instance, General Motors decided to build a plant in Thailand to make cars for the Southeast Asian market.[1] Under a global strategy, a few or even a single large plant may be used to supply the entire world market. Large facilities provide economies of scale, eliminate duplication, and enhance coordination of activities by concentrating all activities at a particular place, especially where the production process is complex and hard to control, such as with computer chips. Companies do not have to duplicate expensive equipment, facilities, and highly trained personnel. For this approach to succeed, transportation costs cannot be high.

Companies sometimes exert a great deal more effort in selecting a site within a country than in selecting the country itself. As Management Focus 8-1 illustrates, Daimler-Benz, a German automaker, had already decided on building a plant in the United States to produce utility vehicles. It finally chose to build it at a new or **greenfield site** in Alabama, due largely to the financial incentives and tax breaks that the state government provided.

As should be evident, many factors determine location decisions. Usually firms try to narrow the search for an acceptable site to one geographic region. Thus, for instance, German automobile firms decide on the United States for locating their new factories because the United States is their largest overseas market. With that decision behind them, the focus is on finding a site in the United States, which would be optimal in terms of building and operating costs. A list of the more common factors that determine plant location is presented in Table 8-1. Of the many reasons to build a plant overseas, some advantages are more tangible than others. Benefits such as reduction in labor, capital, and transportation costs are tangible and easy to measure. Others such as learning from suppliers, customers, and foreign research centers are intangible and difficult to determine. When a firm pays more attention to the intangible benefits, it places itself in a stronger position to gain a competitive advantage from its foreign operations.

LABOR FACTORS

The availability of the right type of labor, its cost in terms of wages and benefits, labor productivity, attitudes towards work, and existence, role, and militancy of labor unions are key locational determinants. Because restrictions (in the form of immigration laws, work permits, or nonacceptance of foreign credentials) on the free movement of workers exist among most countries, labor markets are segregated on a country-by-country basis. These restrictions allow differential wages, labor conditions, and labor policies to exist among nations. For labor intensive industries, such as garments and electronic

---

[1]GM chooses Thailand over Philippines for its big plant. *The New York Times.* 1996, May 31, p. D4.

BUILDING MERCEDES IN ALABAMA

When Daimler-Benz, the German maker of luxury cars, announced its intention to establish a plant in the United States, it set off a bidding war among American states, each of whom wanted the prestige project. Alabama got the plant but not before extensive courting of the company by everyone from the governor down to county officials and by offering extensive tax breaks. The company was expected to create 1,500 new jobs at the plant and 15,000 to 17,000 other related jobs around the state. The tax breaks and subsidies promised by the state amounted to nearly $300 million (equal to about $200,000 for each job). This amount was eighteen times what Tennessee paid for a Nissan plant in 1980, four times what Kentucky paid for a Toyota plant in 1985, and three times what South Carolina paid for a BMW plant in 1992.

The deal to produce Mercedes vehicles in their home state illustrated the extent to which politicians go to create jobs in the private sector, especially at a time when firms are downsizing. Companies, no longer loyal to a city or a state or even country, found that their most valuable asset was the leverage they held in choosing a site.

Regardless of how many jobs Mercedes ultimately created in Alabama, the state's concessions had brought the United States only what would have gone there anyway. To avoid high German labor costs and to penetrate a booming U.S. market for family trucks, known as sport utility vehicles, Daimler-Benz had decided by early 1993 to build a plant in the United States.

Andreas Renschler, who managed the site selection for Mercedes and then ran the plant, said his aides had initially suggested 62 sites. None were in Alabama. The Germans knew all about Tennessee, as well as the Carolinas and other coastal states. However, "Alabama," Mr. Renschler said, "was totally unknown."

But Alabama's businesspeople and politicians recognized the many advantages of having Daimler-Benz locate in their state. Not only would it bring jobs, many of them at wages twice the state's prevailing rates, but it would also propel the state, with this prestige investment, into the economic ranks of the other fast-growing southern states.

The state governor flew three times to Stuttgart, the company's headquarters in Germany, and steered an incentive package through the state legislature. The state bought the land for the factory in the town of Vance, about a half-hour drive northeast of Tuscaloosa, and used the National Guard to clear and level the land on a "training mission." The state offered $77.5 million in sewer, water, and other utility improvement, $92.2 million to buy and develop the site and about $5 million annually for employee training and other programs. The company was allowed to keep its corporate income taxes and keep most of its employees' personal state income taxes as long as the company had debt payments on plant construction. The state also agreed to buy 2,500 Mercedes utility vehicles, for use by everyone from highway construction supervisors to agricultural agents. The expense: about $75 million.

Simple economics argued for the Carolinas to be the site of the new plant. Daimler-Benz already had two truck plants there and those states had easy access to Atlantic ports. The company planned to import parts from Germany and to export about half of the finished vehicles.

But North and South Carolina, the other finalists, found that the tax breaks or payments they extended were matched or bettered by Alabama. Although Mr. Renschler said that the company did not play one state against another, officials from all three finalists disputed that claim.

The generous subsidies and tax breaks however proved too much for the state to bear and the governor who brought Daimler-Benz to Alabama was defeated in a reelection bid. The new governor negotiated limits on some state commitments to the company. He made sure that the company agreed to eventually buy back a visitors' and training center, paid for by the state, at market value, not just a nominal price. The plan for a Mercedes fleet was cancelled. Daimler-Benz executives said they were satisfied with the revised incentive package. "We are not coming into Alabama because there is a nice governor." Mr. Renschler said. "We still feel at home here."

Source: Myerson, Allen R. 1996, September 1. O Governor, won't you buy me a Mercedes plant? *New York Times*, pp. 1, 10.

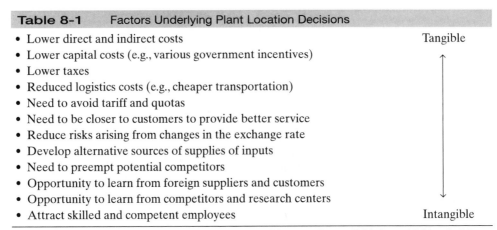

Table 8-1   Factors Underlying Plant Location Decisions

- Lower direct and indirect costs   Tangible
- Lower capital costs (e.g., various government incentives)
- Lower taxes
- Reduced logistics costs (e.g., cheaper transportation)
- Need to avoid tariff and quotas
- Need to be closer to customers to provide better service
- Reduce risks arising from changes in the exchange rate
- Develop alternative sources of supplies of inputs
- Need to preempt potential competitors
- Opportunity to learn from foreign suppliers and customers
- Opportunity to learn from competitors and research centers
- Attract skilled and competent employees   Intangible

Source: Adapted and reprinted by permission of *Harvard Business Review.* Table from "Making the Most of Foreign Factories" by Kasra Ferdows, March-April, 1997. Copyright © 1997 by the President and Fellows of Harvard College; all rights reserved.

components assembly, labor costs are a big chunk of total costs. Semiskilled workers can perform many production processes, and technological innovations have made it possible to easily train workers in the operations of sophisticated tools. This evolution has led firms to relocate facilities in countries with lower labor costs. However, labor costs change over time. Many one-time low-wage countries attracted huge amounts of investments, which pushed up the demand for labor and thus wages. Firms moved away from these locations to other now comparatively cheaper places. As wages rose in South Korea, South Korean firms relocated to Taiwan, and as Taiwan prospered and labor costs there rose, the firms moved to Indonesia where the costs were still lower. This pattern is exemplified by the migration of the plants in which Nike's shoes were made. Initially made in South Korea, over time, in search of lower labor costs, the production of the shoes was shifted to Taiwan, then Indonesia, and subsequently, Vietnam.

Lower wages usually reflect lower productivity. The main lead recipients of manufacturing investments in the world are the 10 leading industrialized countries where labor, materials, and capital costs are certainly not the cheapest. Table 8-2 shows the relative labor productivity per worker in selected countries. For instance, labor productivity in Mexico has been only a third of that of the United States. In Germany, while productivity is lower than that of the United States, wage rates are much higher, leading to overall high labor costs.

ACCESS TO MARKETS

Because products have to be sold, easy access to the market is another key factor. Most service firms tend to situate their offices in major cities of the world (e.g., London, Tokyo, New York) where potential clients as well as support businesses have their offices. Improvements in transportation and telecommunications, and declining real costs have made it possible to cater to customers from far-off distances. For instance, refrigeration and long-haul aircraft (capable of flying vast distances without stopping to refuel) now

Table 8-2	Relative Labor Productivity per Person Employed (U.S. = 100)	
Country	*1973*	*1996*
United States	100	100
Canada	81	67
Mexico	34	33
Japan	55	76
Australia	50	50
France	66	69
Germany	73	63
Sweden	66	74
United Kingdom	52	58

Source: Statistical Abstract of the United States: 1998, 118th ed. Washington, DC: U.S. Bureau of the Census, 1998.

make it possible for cod fish caught off the coast of Iceland to be shipped the same day from Reykjavik to be served in restaurants in Tokyo that same evening. As Management Focus 8-1 showed, foreign firms have established facilities in the United States primarily to be close to their customers because the United States is often the single largest market for them. Proximity is particularly relevant when close interactions with customers are needed for designing products, to provide after-sales services, and to solve glitches. Having a facility in the country where the customers are is a good way to deflect any hostile attitude that may develop among the population toward the foreign firm; now the firm can present itself as one with strong commitments to the local community. For example, Softek, a Mexican software company, established its facilities in Monterrey in northern Mexico to take advantage of its lower labor costs and close geographic proximity to the U.S. market. The company provided a wide range of software programming services to U.S. companies, in direct competition with companies in India. Softek's engineers earned about $12,000 annually, less than a third of the pay typical in the U.S. software industry, but more than double that received by their Indian rivals. However, the Mexican workers were often more culturally attuned to the rhythms and demands of U.S. businesses and more importantly, Monterrey was in the same time zone as most of Softek's customers and only four hours from major U.S. cities.[2]

COMMUNICATIONS INFRASTRUCTURE

A reliable and modern telecommunications system has become a prerequisite for conducting business efficiently. Locations with good phone systems that can carry voice, data, and video transmissions are able to attract new businesses. The Internet, which has opened up opportunities for direct marketing as well as transferring information quickly, efficiently, and inexpensively, relies exclusively on telecommunications. This

---

[2]Lapper, Richard, and Henry Tricks. 1999, May 17. Nearshore contracts flow Mexico's way. *Financial Times,* p. 10.

new medium of communication has enabled remote places to overcome their locational disadvantage. For example, Douglas Locke runs 800 Hampers, an Internet-based Scottish specialty food service. He supplies Scotch whiskey, marmalade, smoked salmon, oatflakes, haggis, and shortbread around the world from a remote village in the Scottish Highlands. His Web site receives half a million hits a month.[3] Similarly, Ireland has emerged as the choice location for telemarketing call centers in Europe primarily because of its heavy investment in a telecommunications infrastructure.[4]

TAXES AND INCENTIVE PROGRAMS

Income/corporate taxes, property taxes, sales taxes, customs duties, and many other forms of government-imposed levies constitute a cost of doing business. High-tax locations tend to discourage potential investors. Many governmental authorities encourage investors to come in and create jobs, advance employee skills, and develop the area by giving tax breaks or even tax holidays as illustrated in Management Focus 8-1. Tariffs and quotas, when they exist, raise the price of imported/exported products and consequently affect total sales and revenues. The world trade in garments is governed by the Multi-Fiber Agreement (MFA), which places quotas on how many of individual product items (such as blouses or shirts) each country can export to the developed countries. As countries such as Hong Kong exhaust their quotas, manufacturers there open new operations in countries whose quotas are as yet unfilled. For this reason, garments in the U.S. market, which once came from Hong Kong, Taiwan, or South Korea, are now being made in Bangladesh, Sri Lanka, and Honduras. The developed countries have committed themselves to phasing out the MFA.

Many countries, to encourage inward foreign direct investment, create industrial areas equipped with the necessary infrastructure—developed sites, water, sewage, and electricity lines, telecommunication services, roads, housing, and community services. Some of these areas are **free trade zones** where the host government waives all import and export duties on raw material and finished goods brought in or taken out of the zone. A firm can import raw materials and use local labor and local inputs and reexport the product out of the zone either to the host country or other countries. These zones tend, understandably, to be located near airports and seaports.

A special type of free trade zone exists on the Mexican side of the U.S-Mexican border. Known as the **maquiladora,** raw materials and semifinished goods are sent to these special zones in Mexico where additional work is completed on the goods. They are then shipped back to the United States. All duties are waived by both the governments, except on the value added by the additional manufacturing processes taking place in Mexico. Maquiladoras were created to provide jobs to Mexican workers and dissuade them from migrating, illegally, to the United States. Under NAFTA, the maquiladoras will lose their tariff-free advantage, and thus technically no longer exist.

Like many countries, the government of Ireland used a combination of low corporate taxes, a large supply of skilled workers, and low inflation to successfully attract foreign investment. By the late 1990s, the country had emerged as the world's second

---

[3]Nicholson, Mark. 1999, November 30. Internet can overcome geographic drawback. *Financial Times Survey,* p. II.
[4]Nuala, Moran. 1999, November 4. Finding a place at the cutting edge. *Financial Times Survey,* p. III.

largest exporter of software. Foreign companies generated three-quarters of Ireland's manufacturing exports, over half of its manufacturing output, and more than two-thirds of manufacturing employment. U.S. electronic companies chose to locate in Ireland over any other EU country to establish their European operations.[5]

FOREIGN EXCHANGE RATES

Fluctuations in exchange rates may make a location desirable or unattractive. When a currency appreciates, a firm's products cost more in the foreign market typically resulting in declining sales. A simple example will explain this tendency. Assume that one U.S. dollar equals 125 yen. A camera costing 12,500 yen will be sold in the United States for $100. However, if the yen appreciates and the new exchange rate is 100 yen to the dollar, the same camera will now cost $125 in the United States. Much of the Japanese foreign direct investment in the United States can be partly attributed to the rising value of the yen in relation to the dollar. By both producing and selling in dollars in the United States, Japanese firms insulated themselves from fluctuations in the exchange rates. However, exchange rates change both ways over time and investment decisions rarely are solely based on them.

REGULATORY REGIME AND POLITICAL STABILITY

Although governments generally have liberalized their rules to encourage inward investment, as discussed in Chapter 3, many forms of regulations and rules can be considered by prospective investors to be onerous. Sometimes, investors may see advocacy groups as overly prying. In other cases, the selection and acquisition of a site can be time consuming as well as bureaucratic. Large sites for, say, chemical factories often require extensive documentation to prove to local authorities that the operations will not have an adverse impact on the environment. Elsewhere, protests from indigenous groups may delay land acquisitions.

"Green harassment" by environmental groups has forced United States forest products companies to look overseas for timber supplies. In the United States, extensive regulations on harvesting forests have limited growth opportunities. Given the long-term nature of investments in this industry (trees usually require at least 15 years to reach harvesting stage), political stability in the foreign country is an important concern for timber companies. For example, Russia, which has more timber than any other single country in the world, is perceived as politically unstable, where private ownership rules are not clearly defined and protected, and transportation infrastructure is poor and inadequate. For these reasons, timber companies have kept away—but not from long-stable New Zealand. Rayonier, a company based in Stamford, Connecticut, purchased cutting rights to over a quarter million acres of New Zealand cultivated forests in a 1992 privatization program. One reason for the New Zealand investment was that it was close to Asia where the company had many customers. The company, however, did not want to be overly dependent on one region and was considering investing in Chile.[6]

[5]Brown, John. 1998, November 2. Ireland—Advantages come under fresh attack. *Financial Times Survey*, p. III.
[6]Bulman, Robin. 1996, October 24. "Green harassment" spurs overseas quest. *Journal of Commerce*, p. 3C.

QUALITY OF LIFE

Availability of facilities such as educational and cultural institutions, quality housing, medical services, and easy access to the modern conveniences of life are also key factors in determining where to locate a plant or an office. Many countries and cities lack these facilities, and this scenario may discourage a firm from being able to send managers there. Family members may be reluctant to move to such places. The firm has to offer additional bonuses and benefits to encourage people to accept a transfer to such places. In other cases, the cost of living may be quite high. Language and cultural differences, or an unwelcoming attitude toward foreigners and foreign firms in the host country may also dissuade the firm from setting up a facility there.

TRANSPORTATION

Transportation systems provided by roads, railways, ships, pipelines, and airplanes are necessary to bring in raw materials or semiprocessed products from suppliers and send out finished or semifinished goods to customers or other processing centers. Reliability, frequency of service, and costs are important variables. The opening vignette illustrates the importance of a reliable transportation system for successful business operations. Thus, the existence of the necessary infrastructure in the form of adequate roads, railway lines, seaports, and airports with supporting services (such as equipment to load and unload goods, storage areas, and trained and qualified workers) assume key importance. Good transportation influences the amount of inventory that needs to be maintained, the continuity of operations without interruptions of supplies and deliveries, and enables emergency requests of customers to be met.

Thus, a variety of factors are considered in deciding on the location of facilities. For example, many western computer companies have subcontracted parts of their needs to software firms in India and have even established research centers in that country. The attraction of India stemmed not only from the low labor costs but also the high educational standards of Indian programmers and their command over the English language. Timing also played a part. The Year 2000 (Y2K) computer date problem and the Euro currency conversion triggered a huge demand for services that could not be met by the available number of programmers in the United States and Europe, and so western companies looked to India to get some of the technical work done. With the growing competence of Indian engineers, foreign firms set up sophisticated operations in India.[7]

A study comparing the location patterns in the United States of foreign-owned and U.S.-owned manufacturing facilities found that foreign firms preferred to establish plants in the coastal states, and those with low unionization rates and lower wages. The differences can be attributed to the fact that foreign firms and U.S. firms are dissimilar. Foreign firms in the United States are more dependent on imports than their U.S. counterparts and hence they prefer to locate near seaports. They choose no-union, low-wage locations to neutralize the cost disadvantage vis-à-vis domestic U.S. firms. Also, because they may be investing in firm-specific training for their workforce, they perceive

---

[7]Guha, Krishna, and Paul Taylor. 1999, March 15. Silicon subcontinent. *Financial Times,* p. 14.

employee skills across the country to be uniform, thus choosing to locate where wages are the lowest.[8]

SITE SPECIFIC FACTORS

The particular site that is finally chosen needs to have certain attributes. Usually engineers and architects will be involved in evaluating the piece of property. Issues that arise are the size of the property with scope for future expansion and its cost. The speed with which the facilities can be constructed and whether building materials and expertise are locally available must also be considered. Easy accessibility to transportation networks, customers, and suppliers, as well as the availability and price of utilities such as water, power, and sewage lines are major factors in any evaluation. For some firms, the requirements of environmental standards and the disposal of wastes are critical factors.

EVALUATING LOCATION ALTERNATIVES

Often firms select a site not because it promises the highest return on investment but because it is likely to cause the fewest problems. The actual evaluation of competing sites is somewhat subjective. However, several evaluation techniques are available.

Factor Rating Sometimes, companies use a checklist to compare selected sites. Once the requirements of a new facility are decided, the firm compares the merits of various locations against a set of factors. Depending on the importance of each location factor, weights are assigned.

Assume that the following criteria are important in a site to manufacture scooters: labor costs, access to raw materials, transportation services, living conditions and community services, and building costs. For each of these five criteria, different weights are assigned depending on the relative importance of each. Each factor is usually given a score on a common scale (say, 0 to 100). Thus, for instance, if labor costs are attractive in one place, a higher score is assigned. If living conditions and community services are less attractive, a lower score is assigned. The scores are multiplied by the weights for each factor. All the weighted scores for a particular location are then added to obtain the composite score. Thus, as Table 8-3 shows, two (or if necessary more) competing sites

Table 8-3	Using Weighted Criteria Method to Compare Sites					
			Scores (out of 100)		*Weighted Scores*	
Factor		*Weight*	*Penang*	*Bangkok*	*Penang*	*Bangkok*
Labor Costs		.50	80	70	40	35
Access to Raw Materials		.20	60	70	12	14
Transportation Services		.10	80	50	8	5
Living Conditions/Community Services		.15	40	60	6	9
Construction Costs		.05	80	60	4	3
Total		1.00	340	310	70	66

[8]Shaver, J. Myles. 1998. Do foreign-owned and U.S.-owned establishments exhibit the same location pattern in U.S. manufacturing industries? *Journal of International Business Studies* 29(3), pp. 469–492.

can be easily compared. This scenario would suggest that Penang, Malaysia, should be selected. Keep in mind that criteria change over time and criteria relevant in one country may be less crucial in another. In many cases, managers establish minimum scores in each factor, which every site must meet or a minimum overall composite score for a location to be accepted.

Of course, one set of factors that may be important for a steel plant would not be equally relevant to a bank location. For the latter, usually downtown urban locations and good telecommunication facilities are key determinants. In cases of mining, drilling, or hydroelectricity companies, the location is determined solely by where the deposits of minerals lie or where a river flows.

Locational Cost-Volume Analysis   Under this technique fixed and variable costs of operations are compared for each of the locations under consideration. The location that has the lowest total cost will be preferred. This technique assumes that fixed costs are constant for a given output, the level of output is predetermined, and only one product will be produced. This technique is illustrated here as fixed and variable costs for four potential sites. Assume that the total output is 10,000 units annually.

Location	Annual Fixed Cost	Variable Cost per Unit
Dubai	$100,000	$10
Kuwait	$150,000	$15
Doha	$200,000	$15
Manama	$125,000	$5

Using this information, we can calculate the total cost for each location as follows:

Location	Fixed Cost + Variable Cost	= Total Cost
Dubai	$100,000 + $100,000	= $200,000
Kuwait	$150,000 + $150,000	= $300,000
Doha	$200,000 + $150,000	= $350,000
Manama	$125,000 + $50,000	= $175,000

From these results, at 10,000 units, Manama provides the cheapest location. But at 5,000 units, the cost is the same between Manama and Dubai and thus at that level, managers are indifferent in their selection of the location. However, because other costs, most notably, transportation, also play a role, they should be included too. Keep in mind that changes in currency rates may distort these cost figures.

Transportation Model   If the proposed facility will be the sole source or destination of products, the transportation costs per unit can be added to the variable cost in the preceding model. Where multiple facilities receive and send shipments and a new location is being considered, a transportation model of linear programming is used. Here, a special purpose algorithm determines the minimum transportation costs that would result if a new facility were to be added. In the following simple example, a company will set up a new parts distribution warehouse for 800 units every week. It is considering three new locations: Bangkok, Singapore, and Jakarta. The costs are as follows:

Location	Fixed Cost	Variable Cost	Transportation Cost
Bangkok	$4,000	$4	$19,000
Singapore	$5,000	$6	$18,000
Jakarta	$3,500	$5	$22,000

Annual total cost for these three cities are:

Location	Fixed Cost	+ Variable Costs	+ Transportation Costs	= Total Cost
Bangkok	4,000	+ $3,200	+ $19,000	= $26,200
Singapore	5,000	+ $4,800	+ $18,000	= $27,800
Jakarta	3,500	+ $4,000	+ $22,000	= $29,500

Hence, Bangkok has the lowest total cost for this weekly volume.

Center of Gravity Method   This method is used to determine the location of a facility that will minimize distribution costs. The quantity to be shipped to each destination is assumed to be fixed over time. It is possible for the amounts to change as long as the relative amounts stay constant. To determine a location, a map, drawn to scale, showing the possible destinations is required. A coordinate system is used to determine the relative distance of each location.

To determine the coordinates of the center of gravity (which is the location of the proposed facility), one needs the average of the x coordinates and the average of the y coordinates. These averages are determined by adding and averaging all the x coordinates and adding and averaging all the y coordinates. When the amounts to be shipped are not the same for all markets, then a weighted average is used to determine the center of gravity. The weights are the quantities shipped. A simple example is used to show how this method works.

A U.S. company is planning to build a plant in Western Europe to supply several cities. The destinations and coordinates of these cities are:

	Dublin	London	Frankfurt	Brussels	Average
x	1	2	4	3	2.5
y	4	3	2	2	2.75

The center of gravity is $2.5x, 2.75y$, which places it between Brussels and London, and just below London. However, let us assume the monthly shipments to these destinations are different, say Dublin 100 units, London 400 units, Frankfurt 400 units, and Brussels 200 units. The weighted average is calculated as follows:

$$x = 1(100) + 2(400) + 4(400) + 3(200) = 3100/1100 = 2.8$$
$$y = 4(100) + 3(400) + 2(400) + 2(200) = 2800/1100 = 2.5$$

The coordinates of the center of gravity are approximately $2.8x$, $2.5y$, which would be just west of Brussels.

STRATEGIC ROLE OF OVERSEAS FACILITIES

Successful firms use their foreign operations to learn more about their customers and suppliers, to attract skilled and capable employees to work for them, and to create centers of expertise to benefit the entire firm. Companywide success is achieved by assigning specific roles to individual foreign operations. This approach reflects an understanding of the strategic importance of foreign operations as a competitive weapon.

The opportunity for a firm to learn from its foreign operations stems from three developments. First, the reduction in trade barriers reduces the need to establish facilities to skirt tariff walls and quota restrictions. Second, for many industries, low-cost locations have become less important; the need to introduce new products, and the availability of sophisticated production methods, often relying on highly competent suppliers of components, are now more relevant. Third, managers are under enormous competitive pressure to introduce new products into the marketplace quickly and efficiently, which requires combining research and production in the same location. Firms that recognize these developments are more likely to locate their operations at places where learning is maximized and to assign increasingly complex and important roles to them.

DIFFERENT TYPES OF FACILITIES

Overseas production facilities can be categorized into one of six types depending on the strategic role assigned to them by the firm's headquarters.[9] These are:

1. *Offshore factory.* The purpose of the **offshore factory** is to take advantage of low wages or other input costs that are essential for low-cost production. The products are either exported for additional work or for final sale. Investments in technical and managerial resources are minimal with all decisions made at headquarters.

2. *Source factory.* The **source factory** is also set up to take advantage of low costs of production but its strategic role is broader than that of the offshore factory. Source factory managers have greater authority over purchasing, production planning, customization, and production processes. The factory produces a part or a product for the firm's worldwide markets.

3. *Server factory.* The **server factory** is set up to meet the needs of a specific national or regional market. This factory has the autonomy to make changes in products and production methods to meet the requirements of the market it serves.

4. *Contributor factory.* Unlike the server factory, the **contributor factory** has additional responsibilities that include product and process engineering and selecting and developing suppliers. A contributor factory competes with a firm's home-based factories as a testing ground for new products and processes.

---

[9]Ferdows, Kasra. 1997. Making the most of foreign factories. *Harvard Business Review.* March–April, pp. 73–88.

5. *Outpost factory.* The **outpost factory** is an intelligence-gathering facility located near suppliers, competitors, customers, and research centers. Because they also make products, they tend to have a secondary role too, say as a server or source.

6. Lead factory. The **lead factory** creates new products and processes for the entire firm. The lead factory managers have the authority and the capability to choose their own suppliers, carry out their own research, and maintain close links with customers and other research organizations.

The strategic roles of foreign factories are illustrated in Figure 8-1. The vertical axis measures the competence of the factory while the horizontal axis identifies the reasons for its overseas location. Thus, for instance, the outpost factory has very low competence in what it can do or what it does as opposed to the lead factory, which has more authority and bigger responsibilities. Both factories, however, are located to take advantage of technical skills and knowledge.

Usually, a foreign factory serves two or more strategic roles. For example, in 1998, Häagen-Dazs, a U.S. ice cream company, introduced successfully a new flavor, *dulce de leche,* in supermarkets and its own 700 retail stores across the world.[10] Named after the carmelized milk that was one of the most popular flavors in Argentina, Häagen-Dazs first recognized its success at its stores in that country. The company's U.S. managers learned of the dulce de leche at one of its brand conferences and decided to target it to the United States' growing Latin population. The Argentine stores functioned both as an outpost factory and a server factory. Similarly, many foreign firms have set up plants in China not only to take advantage of low labor costs (offshore factory) but also to serve the huge and rapidly prospering Chinese population (server factory).

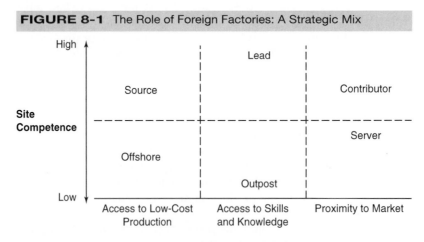

FIGURE 8-1 The Role of Foreign Factories: A Strategic Mix

Source: Adapted and reprinted by permission of *Harvard Business Review.* Figure from "Making the Most of Foreign Factories" by Kasra Ferdows, March-April, 1997. Copyright © 1997 by the President and Fellows of Harvard College; all rights reserved.

[10]Leonhardt, David. 1998, September 7. It was a hit in Buenos Aires—so why not Boise? *Business Week,* pp. 56, 58.

The roles of the factories change over time as their managerial and employee capabilities are enhanced and proven. Changes in the firm's own mission (brought on by reorganization, mergers or divestments) and external developments in the form of rising wage rates, increasing productivity, government incentives, and expanding foreign markets also lead to reevaluation of the strategic role of the foreign facility. For example, Hewlett-Packard first built a factory in Singapore in 1970 to produce simple, labor-intensive components at a low cost. Over time, its responsibilities and capabilities increased so that by the mid-1990s, it had grown into one of the company's global centers for the design, development, and manufacture of portable printers for markets worldwide.[11]

To be able to make this transition and learn from the overseas facilities, managers have to:

1. Periodically review the strategic role of a facility in the firm's global network. As part of this assessment, the current roles of each facility should be compared with the desired roles, based on the firm's overall strategy.
2. Increase the competencies of the foreign facilities by investing in equipment and technical training, emphasizing quality, and helping with purchasing and transportation.
3. Allocate an appropriate combination of technical, financial, and human resources to a site with the ultimate goal of creating a factory that should be able to acquire a world class specialty.
4. Staff each facility with appropriately skilled managers. The qualifications, capabilities, and responsibilities of the manager differ depending on the role of the factory. A manager of a server factory needs to be highly knowledgeable about local market conditions whereas the lead factory manager would be one who is not only highly technically proficient and familiar with local conditions but also knows the company well.
5. Make a sustained commitment over many years to get the most out of the foreign operations. Such commitment is not always easy to come by however, because of both external and internal changes.

RESEARCH AND DEVELOPMENT ACTIVITIES

There are two types of international R&D centers: (1) the corporate laboratory, which concentrates on research and is closely connected to an international research program directed by corporate headquarters (such a facility may or may not interact with overseas manufacturing facilities), and (2) the support laboratory, the main activities of which are to act as a technical service center (e.g., adapt products for a specific market) and to adapt home country technology to local conditions, or vice versa.

Traditionally, innovation in multinational firms has taken place in the home country of the firm. The focus of the firm in the early stages is essentially on the domestic market, and thus R&D is typically organized to meet the needs of that market. Given the need to coordinate the various research projects and to share results with the relevant functional managers, locating R&D in the home country appears to be the right way to

---

[11] Ferdows, Kasra. 1997. Making the most of foreign factories. *Harvard Business Review.* March–April, pp. 73–88.

organize this activity. A centralized R&D center that serves the entire firm is also less expensive than maintaining several facilities and hiring researchers and is less difficult than the task of overseeing and coordinating several research projects around the world. Of course, the important dimension of R&D is not cost control but how effective the research is. When R&D is done overseas, it usually takes the form of product modification or adaptation to meet the particular needs of foreign markets.

An increasing number of companies, particularly in technologically intensive industries such a electronics and pharmaceuticals, are moving away from centralizing R&D toward creating a globally dispersed network of research centers. For example, Canon, a Japanese optical imaging company, has eight dedicated research facilities in five countries. Nestle maintains a large number of research centers whose activities are coordinated through a central office at headquarters in Switzerland. This coordination of research also allows research results to be shared among the various centers. Other companies rely on technical experts to serve as a link between the foreign market and domestically based R&D activities. The experts provide researchers information on needs, problems, competitors, and products in the foreign market. At the same time, the experts function as a conduit for new products, processes, and solutions to the managers in the host country.

The internationalization of R&D follows, with a lag, the internationalization of production. Siting R&D facilities in different locations is now seen as a normal part of a strategy to broaden the technology base and expand abroad. Firms benefit, at relatively little transaction cost, from the results of foreign technological and scientific systems and from the exchange of know-how and services, which can take place with the various overseas operations of the firm. If R&D can be done or used more efficiently abroad, it reinforces the development of competing concentrations of high-tech activities. A frequent criticism of decentralized research is the likelihood of duplicate activities occurring in various laboratories. Researchers naturally wish to become involved in the most promising projects. This tendency can lead to the deliberate disguising of projects in order to counter charges of duplication.

The activities of Texas Instruments Inc., a U.S. computer company, in India provide a good example of intrafirm dispersion of R&D activities. In 1986, the company established Texas Instruments (India), a wholly owned affiliate, to perform R&D in Bangalore. The affiliate represented an investment of about $15 million and employed about 300 Indian engineers. The primary driving force behind the location of this facility was access to R&D personnel of required ability to cater to the needs of the parent firm's manufacturing affiliates worldwide. The Bangalore facility was one of the company's four, with others situated in Dallas, Tokyo, and Bedford, United Kingdom.

Texas Instruments had been able to perform geographically dispersed, but globally integrated, R&D activities because of information and communication technologies that allowed the exchange of detailed integrated chip designs and scientific simulations across the world without a time delay. The Indian center had the latest work stations and a variety of computers that were interconnected by a local area network, which in turn was connected to Texas Instruments' worldwide data communications network. All the software, databases, and designs developed by Texas Instruments (India) were exported to the parent firm in the United States via satellite link for distribution and use by the entire firm and its customers.[12]

---

[12]Kuemmerle, Walter. 1997. Building effective R&D capabilities abroad. *Harvard Business Review.* March–April, pp. 61–70.

Management Focus 8-2 discusses the development of a new car in Europe by a U.S. firm. It illustrates how firms draw on experiences worldwide to bring together the right mix of talent and technology to develop a new product.

The main driving forces for the dispersion of R&D activities include the following:

- Competitive pressures increase the need to tap knowledge, expertise, and skills wherever they are located in the world and before rivals appropriate these assets. The dispersion has also been aided by the availability of a large pool of scientifically and technically trained personnel throughout the world. In less-developed countries and those in transition (e.g., Eastern European countries), labor and research costs are lower. At the same time, a growing scarcity of R&D personnel hampers many developed countries.
- Advances in communication and information technologies allow the division of R&D into multiple projects that could take place in geographically separate locations, to be subsequently integrated. They also allow, where needed, R&D activities that are conducted in an integrated, on-line manner across borders.
- Liberalization, particularly with regard to foreign participation; ownership and access to local universities and science and technology centers; and the strengthening of intellectual property rights encourages the dispersion of R&D by international firms. In addition, the proactive policies adopted by some countries (in the form of providing tax breaks for research and creating science parks) positively influence the decision of international firms to locate R&D abroad.
- The increasing level of manufacturing and sales of a firm occurring abroad also hastens dispersion. As a consequence, firms are forced to address the product and process needs of the foreign market and thus some R&D activities are now conducted close to the host market. For instance, when Mazda introduced a sports car, Miata, for the U.S. market, it had the vehicle designed in Southern California, by mostly U.S. engineers.
- As more and more sources of potentially relevant knowledge emerge across the world, firms must establish a presence at an increasing number of locations to access new knowledge and to absorb new research results into their own organizations.
- A final argument for maintaining a research facility in the host country concerns corporate social responsibility. Such a facility is evidence of the company's commitment to the country and a recognition that local resources, scientists, and market peculiarities demand research in the host country. Employing host country scientists, using host country resources to develop new products, transforming home country processes and products to the needs of the host country, and building up the technological base of the country, all contribute to muting undue criticism the foreign firm may attract in the host country.

Despite this changing trend, the reasons for locating R&D facilities in the home country still remain strong. Facilities already exist and are generally easier to expand rather than creating new facilities elsewhere. In addition, numerous costs are involved in organizing and coordinating geographically dispersed R&D activities. Firms also

BUILDING A NEW GLOBAL BESTSELLER

Not since the astounding success of the Model T between 1908 and 1927, which sold about 880,000 units annually, had the Ford Motor Company put so much hope on a new car, the Focus. The company was gearing the car to sell at the rate of one million vehicles every year across the United States, Europe, and South America. Of course, building cars in the competitive 1990s was different from the early stages of the automobile industry. The cost of developing the Focus would be more than $2 billion and in a global market, no car could expect to remain competitive for more than four years.

The Focus was designed to replace Ford's long-established small car, the Escort. The Focus would offer substantial improvements in interior room, ride and handling, crash protection, occupant comfort, and attention to detail, and yet be priced about the same as the Escort. More importantly, the Focus was expected to be profitable, something that could not be said for the Escort. How would all these be possible?

With capacity in the automobile industry far outstripping demand, automakers that could offer the best set of features for the lowest prices and still make profits were the most likely to survive and have the capital to cash in on long-term growth in developing markets. Ford managers said the company's leaner, more-disciplined development process under its "Ford 2000" reorganization had cut development costs by 25 percent. The cost of building each car was lopped off 10 percent or $1,000.

Ford had long tried to build a car that it could sell in both Europe and the United States, with a minimum of changes. It had failed in its attempts in the early 1980s with the Escort and again in the 1990s with its Mondeo-Contour-Mystique family of mid-sized cars. With the Focus, though, the company was more hopeful. "I think we've finally got it," said Jacques Nasser, the president of Ford's global auto operations.

In developing the Focus, Ford was determined to cut waste and duplication. In 1994, the Focus began to take shape in Dunton, United Kingdom, and in Merkenich, Germany, where Ford of Europe had its design studios. Earlier that year, the company had combined its North American and European operations. "I smashed the two programs together and tried to draw the best elements of both," recalled Al Kammerer, the manager who was then in charge of global small-car development. He started with a team of 100 to 150, which later grew to 600. He avoided regional jealousies and factionalism—a problem in previous global-car attempts—by assembling an international team: a Briton as chief program engineer, a German as chief technical officer, an Irishwoman as chief technical officer, and an Anglo-Australian as chief designer.

By September 1994, on a display board in the design center in Germany, Ford workers using different-colored tapes had outlined the shape of every car competing with the Escort. The full size outlines were nearly on top of each other. On the same display, Ford designers also had outlined the proposed shape of what became the Focus. It had a roof line about 3 inches higher than the others, which altered nearly all the rest of the car's dimensions. Because the length of the Focus was set by the designated size for that class of vehicles, the only way to create more cabin space was to raise the roof. It allowed occupants to sit up straighter and higher, gave them more legroom, and made the car easier to get into and out of. To make the car more competitive with the European and Japanese offerings, Ford put extra effort into giving the car a tight, responsive steering. To make it more appealing to consumers, the car was designed to be less expensive to repair. The time taken to remove the engine was cut by one and a half-hours; more of the body was bolted together rather than welded; and rear lights were mounted near the roof to keep them from being damaged in parking lots. To cut manufacturing costs, Ford built an automatic transmission in the United States, rather than importing it from Japan, as it did for the Escort. "That type of efficiency is a little hidden, but it's real," said Mr. Nasser. Fifteen major subassemblies, including instrument panels, seats, and suspensions, were outsourced rather than made inside the company, as before, further reducing costs.

Source: Simison, Robert. 1998, October 8. Ford hopes its new Focus will be a global bestseller. *The Wall Street Journal*, p. B10.

benefit from the presence of supporting industries and there are potential advantages of being near to downstream operations to test and use new inventions and processes.

CAPACITY AND PLANT SIZE

Capacity refers to the upper limit of the goods that can be produced or the work that can be done at a given time in a plant or building. Selecting the capacity of the plant, warehouse, or office is determined by a number of factors, including the following:

- The availability of capital to invest
- The costs of the facilities
- The pace of technological innovation
- The possibility of expansion in the future
- The likelihood of losing potential customers if the capacity is too small to meet growing needs
- Access to the necessary inputs including workers
- The availability of suitable sites
- The approval of the host government
- The size of the market
- The advantages that accrue from economies of scale

Companies that use their capacity to the fullest often tend to subcontract orders to other producers, especially if the demand for the product is high and it is for a short term. Expansion of capacity usually takes time and the company many not wish to turn away customers if it is already operating at full capacity. It turns to companies operating at lower capacities and places orders.

The automobile industry reflects how individual firms approach the issue of size. Although worldwide the industry had excess capacity and sales growth was flat, most automobile firms were busy building new plants in North America. Manufacturing capacity in North America was expected to rise by 11 percent between 1999 and 2005. Toyota and Honda, both Japanese companies, were pursuing a long-established strategy of building most of their cars and light trucks in the markets they sold. As they moved away from exporting, Japanese companies now faced idle capacity at home. General Motors, the world's largest automotive firm, was setting up new factories to build cars in radically different ways, options not easily available in existing plant facilities and where union work practices were entrenched. Another reason for new plants in North America was demographic. Compared to Europe and Japan, the market in Canada, Mexico, and the United States continues to grow. Japan, on the other hand, faces a rapidly aging population. In North America, plants worked at 90 percent capacity in the 1990s—almost full capacity. In fact, the industry experienced a shortage of capacity for making pickups and sports utility vehicles, the segment for which most of the new factories would produce vehicles.[13]

Given the high cost of developing a new car, a company had to be confident of sales large enough to recover these R&D costs. In the late 1990s, a flurry of mergers and

---

[13]Simison, Robert L. 1999, May 6. Automakers plan factories in North America. *The Wall Street Journal,* p. B12.

acquisitions took place in the industry. However, it is worth noting that the share of the three largest companies in 1969 was 51 percent; in 1996, the share of the three largest companies was only 36 percent. The number of companies that produced more than 1 million vehicles was nine in 1969; in 1996, the number was 14. Thus, mergers and alliances have not been enough to offset the trend for the industry to become less concentrated.[14]

The role of size is also noticeable in the service industry where the trend has been toward "big." Royal Ahold, the Dutch food retailer, is one of the largest in the world. It is the biggest supermarket chain in the Netherlands and fourth in the United States. It operates in six countries in Latin America, five in Europe, and five in Southeast Asia. The company's determination to become big stemmed from the small size and maturity of its home market. The retail industry has also benefited from technological advances, and being big allowed Ahold to spread the high expenses of technology across its global sales. A smaller sales base would effectively prohibit large spending on technology. Also, large size enabled the firm to exercise buying and distribution power.[15]

A firm pursuing a global strategy could conceivably operate a few large-scale facilities to cater to its worldwide markets. A multidomestic strategy requires many more facilities of varying sizes located in individual countries where the firm is competing. Many countries have policies that require purchases by government agencies be made from either domestic firms or firms with facilities in the home country. This sort of policy effectively bars nonlocal producers from bidding on lucrative contracts.

The creation of free trade areas such as NAFTA and the EU has led firms to consolidate smaller plants into a few larger plants after barriers to trade within the area were removed, making the market bigger. Mergers and acquisitions were common in the late 1990s. However, closing down an office or plant is not always easy. Opposition from the workers who may lose their jobs and from host country labor unions and politicians often become an issue. Government regulations may require the payment of substantial severance amounts to workers losing their jobs or long, drawn-out procedures to justify the closure.

A firm may also establish plants of differing technological sophistication in different countries. At the mature stage of the life cycle of the product, the firm may shift the entire plant or build a similar one in a less-developed country and thus prolong the life of the product by selling it in the host country. The need to be innovative and a first mover, however, may force the firm to commit to building a state-of-the-art facility and new product lines in its home country or in another developed country. The facilities in less-developed countries tend to be smaller, using older technology that is being phased out in the advanced home country, requiring less maintenance or skilled technicians, and the products meet lower quality specifications. The smaller market and the absence of local producers with the capability to produce high-quality components or parts affect facilities size, as does the presence of large number of workers, lack of technical sophistication, lower wages, lower economic development, and poor infrastructure.

With multiple plants around the world, and sometimes each plant making a different component, integrating operations becomes a major managerial challenge. Transportation and production schedules have to be coordinated. Tariff and nontariff restrictions have to be taken into account. In addition, many of the processes at the vari-

---

[14]Kay, John. 1999, March 3. Where size is not everything. *Financial Times,* p. 10.
[15]Hollinger, Peggy. 1998, November 20. When size matters. *Financial Times,* p. 25.

ous facilities have to be standardized. Standardization allows costs to be reduced and makes it easier to compare costs and data across various locations. Central purchasing and distribution can lead to enforcement of quality standards, appropriate pricing, reduced inventories, and uninterrupted production and deliveries.

Flexible production systems, use of robots, Internet communication, and computer-aided designing and manufacturing have allowed facilities to produce multiple models, customize products for different markets and buyers, introduce new products at a faster pace, and be profitable with comparatively smaller production runs. To remain competitive in the marketplace, managers have drastically cut down the product life cycle and hurry the product from the R&D center to the factory floor and on to the customers.

Leading firms in countries that have industrialized in the latter quarter of the twentieth century have grown by borrowing and learning from their more advanced rivals. This approach to growth is in sharp contrast to the behavior in the past when inventions and innovations were the main impetus. The case study of Hyundai Heavy Industries (HHI), presented in Management Focus 8-3, illustrates how the company became the world's largest shipbuilder by learning from firms in other countries.

VALUE CHAIN ANALYSIS

Every business is a collection of interrelated activities that design, produce, market, deliver, and support its products. This set of business activities is referred to as the **value chain.** Managers evaluate every component of the value chain and determine how to reduce its costs and/or how to do it differently. To the extent the manager is able to do so, the firm gains a competitive advantage by either producing at a price lower than its competitors or offering new types of products relative to its competitors.

The components of the value chain can be categorized as primary activities and support activities. Primary activities include inbound logistics (such as receiving and storing raw materials), actual operations (transforming raw materials into finished products), outbound logistics (storing and distributing the finished products), marketing and sales (advertising and promotion), and customer service (after-sales service, training users, and repairing). All these primary activities are concerned with the creation and sale of the product or service for which the firm exists. Support activities are needed for the primary activities to be carried out without interruptions and problems. Support activities include procurement (purchase of raw materials, spare parts, computers, and buildings), technology (information systems and R&D), human resource management (recruiting, selecting, training, compensating, and retaining employees), and the firm's infrastructure (consisting of staff functions such as planning, finance, accounting, law, and public affairs). Each component of the value chain—both primary and support—contributes to the final value of the product that the firm produces. These activities translate into sales of the product.

By analyzing the value chain, managers are able to identify areas that need improvement (such as customer service), strengthen linkages between the components (as between R&D and manufacturing), determine the contribution of every activity to the overall value of the final product, and recognize the nature and size of the impact of the various activities on each other. Such analysis indicates which activities contribute the most (and also the least) to the product's value. To maintain a competitive advantage,

HOW HYUNDAI BECAME THE BIGGEST BUILDER OF SHIPS

Hyundai is one of South Korea's diversified business groups known as *chaebol*. A chaebol is typically owned by a single family and has subsidiaries in a wide variety of unrelated industries. Hyundai Heavy Industries (HHI) began building its first ship, a large crude oil tanker, in March 1973. Ten years later, the company was the world's largest shipbuilder. How did it accomplish this meteoric rise especially when it had no prior experience in shipbuilding and in a business environment marked by excess production capacity and cutthroat price competition?

The initial encouragement came from the South Korean government, which secured financing for HHI's shipyard and underwrote the massive infrastructure construction that was required. The government also helped HHI win its first order and when HHI could not sell its ships, the government insisted that crude oil to Korea be delivered in HHI-made tankers.

HHI's main competitors were Japanese shipbuilders; the productivity rates of the Japanese were higher, which compensated for their higher labor cost. Labor productivity in shipbuilding was largely a function of the degree of equipment automation, the skill level of the workers, the quality of ship designs, and the length of time it took to complete building a ship. From the outset, HHI's goal was to raise productivity and to reduce building time in order to meet delivery deadlines. To gain firmer control over the construction process, to ensure timely delivery of both inputs and outputs, to reduce costs, and to achieve parity with the Japanese shipyards on all fronts, HHI decided to develop basic design capability in-house and to produce its own engines and core electrical equipment. The guiding slogan became: "Our own ships, our own engines, our own designs." The strength of HHI came to rest on its total capabilities.

In the absence of a capability to create new technology, learning can take place through imitation and reverse engineering or by buying technical licenses and other forms of assistance from foreign firms. HHI followed the latter route. It bought dockyard designs from a Scottish naval architecture firm; ship designs and operating instructions from a Scottish shipbuilding firm; production know-how from the Kawasaki Shipbuilding Co. of Japan; and benefited from the experience of European shipyard workers it employed.

Faced with large orders in 1974, Kawasaki subcontracted HHI to build two tankers and provided them with the ships' proven designs. The Japanese trained HHI engineers and technicians both on-site and in Japan, and Japanese foremen were stationed at HHI to help. As a consequence, HHI learned how to read blueprints, coordinate drawings to the job, and install machinery.

HHI won its first order for two 260,000 DWT large crude carriers from a Greek shipowner on the condition that it build an exact replica of a ship that had been built in a Scottish shipyard. HHI obtained the detailed drawings from the Scottish yard, procured identical equipment, and mimicked every design detail. Nevertheless, replication was not 100 percent successful, which led to the establishment of a design office employing 300 people. Problems in hull construction delayed the launching of the first ship by several months; the second ship too was delayed. When the deadlines expired, the buyer refused to accept delivery. Deliveries of other ships to buyers in Japan and Hong Kong were also stalled.

At this time, the Hyundai group established the Hyundai Merchant Marine Co. (HHMC) to provide shipping services to Hyundai's newly founded general trading company and to absorb HHI's undelivered ships. The Korean government favored HHI's strategy of forward integration. As owner of Korea's oil refinery, the government dictated that all crude oil deliveries to Korea be carried in Korean-owned vessels, namely those of HMMC.

Little by little, HHI acquired capability in design modification which was necessary for cost control. The company still lacked capability in basic design of ships. To solve this problem, it began buying basic designs from European consulting firms. However, HHI discovered that consulting firms took no responsibility for reaching rated capacity and failure to do so delayed deliveries and earned HHI stiff penalties. To avoid such delays, HHI in-

(continued)

(continued)

vested in a basic design capability, even though most shipyards do not possess such a set of skills. In 1978, the design department expanded to include 500 people and by 1983, it included 900 designers, eliminating the need to buy designs from outside, except for special purpose vessels.

HHI decided to invest in a marine engine shop. Until then, it bought the engines from Japan. Japanese engine manufacturers charged foreign buyers higher prices than what they charged Japanese buyers. To secure an alternative source to the high-priced Japanese engines, the Hyundai Engine and Heavy Machinery Manufacturing Co. (HEMCO) was established. To improve quality standards and bring it up to the levels of Japanese and European shipbuilders, HHI opened a small training center where foremen were sent for periods up to three months. Workmanship standards were set for welders, pipers,

fitters, and painters. The training center received feedback from inspection stations, and inspection stations fed information to the line. The department of quality control focused on meeting the schedule to build ships and later on establishing standards of statistical quality control.

With control over all aspects of shipbuilding, HHI was able to monitor costs, introduce savings and reduce overheads, and focus on enhancing workforce capabilities. By being part of a chaebol and because of critical support from the Korean government, HHI was able to obtain the necessary resources, hire competent people, assume risks, and adopt a long-run approach to maximization. However, two elements of this success stood out: (1) HHI moved closer and closer to the innovative mode through heavy investments in R&D; and (2) it diligently scanned the world technology frontier for new know-how and ideas.

Source: Adapted from Amsden, Alice H. 1989. Learners as producers: Hyundai Heavy Industries, the world's largest shipbuilder. *Journal of Manufacturing and Operations Management* 2, pp. 124–144.

the firm should strengthen and hold on to those activities it is good at, in comparison to other companies, and that contribute distinctive value to its product. These key activities are the ones a firm should not consider outsourcing.

GLOBAL SOURCING

A firm has a choice to do in-house all that is necessary to make and sell its products. At the other extreme, it can contract out to external suppliers to provide all or most of the components and services needed to make and sell the products. Thus, firms fall on a continuum between 100 percent manufacture and 100 percent purchase and operate at some combination of the two. How much of the work of producing and selling should be done in-house and how much should be purchased from outside vendors is referred to as the **make-or-buy decision.** Ford Motor Company buys from other companies, both in the United States and abroad, about half the components it needs to manufacture cars.

TYPOLOGY OF OUTSOURCING

Sourcing involves both contractual as well as locational decisions. A firm may outsource to other plants or subsidiaries, branches, or even firms in the same organization or industrial group. Such intrafirm sourcing allows multinational firms to obtain supplies in-house from within their own extensive corporate network. As a result, much of international trade today is between subsidiaries of the same firm located in various countries. Alternatively, the firm may contract with a vendor that is entirely independent of the firm. This latter version is what is referred to as **outsourcing.** Outsourcing is not limited to goods only; even services are outsourced. Most international firms outsource several dimensions of their human resource functions such as cross-cultural training for managers, tax preparation, and employee relocation. International consulting firms such as KPMG Peat Marwick and Price Waterhouse Coopers often provide such services.

DETERMINANTS OF SOURCING

When a firm decides to purchase rather than do it itself in-house, one key question that arises is where should it look for suppliers—within or outside the country? Whether it sources offshore (outside the home country) or onshore (inside the home country) is dependent on a number of factors, including the following:

- Better quality
- Lower prices
- Lack of spare capacity at the firm's factories
- Absence of domestic suppliers
- Lack of in-house capability
- Need to meet a sudden or short-term increase in demand, which the home country facilities cannot meet
- Technologically advanced nature of products
- Unavailability of item locally
- Ability to deliver on schedule
- Readiness on the part of the foreign supplier to work with the firm to re-design products and troubleshoot
- Willingness to negotiate deals over size, value, delivery, and length of contracts
- Organizational links with the supplier (either as an associate firm of the same industrial grouping or a subsidiary of the same organization)

Exchange rate differences make offshore outsourcing attractive if the home currency appreciates heavily. Indeed, by having multiple offshore suppliers, the firm would be able to neutralize the impact of foreign currency fluctuations on the cost of its inputs.

POPULARITY OF OFFSHORE SOURCING

Many factors contribute to the growing trend and willingness of firms to outsource offshore either components or even entire products.

- Improvements in transportation, infrastructure, and communication
- Lowering of tariffs
- Greater sophistication on the part of purchasing managers
- Growing technical competency among firms in many parts of the world
- Availability of production capacity, often excess, in many foreign countries
- The need to cut costs and downsize in an increasingly competitive environment
- A desire to focus on the core competencies of a firm and thus divest nonessential activities

- The trend toward establishing a network of manufacturing facilities around the world to take advantage of special breaks
- The ability to offer a full line of products without having to invest in and manage production facilities.

Table 8-4 lists the determinants of a good source.

CAUTION ABOUT OFFSHORE OUTSOURCING

Offshore outsourcing requires the firm to closely and effectively coordinate production, supplies, and deliveries between different locations and different entities. However, the tendency to rely on outside firms may leave the buying firm vulnerable to disruptions in supply and to a loss of bargaining power over time. As suppliers become proficient, the buying firm is tempted to outsource even more aspects of the company's activities so that in time, the company may well end up being a sort of "empty" or "hollow" corporation relying entirely on contractors to provide its product or service. Such firms are often able to parlay their well-known brand names on outsourced products and thus maintain a strong position in the marketplace. More likely, the firm may lose its technological and managerial ability to make the product on its own, so much so that should a need arise to make the product internally in the future, the firm may simply be unable to do so. Thus, certain capabilities, advisedly should not be surrendered, especially if they involve the primary competency of the firm. The reliance on outsourcing particularly hurts the firm's manufacturing or operations abilities, and over time intraorganizational power shifts away from engineers and operations managers toward, usually, finance and marketing groups. The weakening role of the production/operations people in the firm further exacerbates the decline of the firm's in-house production capabilities and further increases the amount that is outsourced. Such a weakened in-house production team is less likely to be able to take advantage of emerging technologies or innovations and incorporate them in its own design and production regimen. It is not unusual for contractors to gain the capability over time to fully manufacture a quality product at a low price and emerge as competitors to the firm that outsourced in the first place.

Other operational difficulties may arise with outsourcing. The lines of transportation are usually much longer (compared to domestic sourcing), and they are prone to disruptions whose effects could be quite harmful. Transportation systems may break down or supplies be interrupted because of a myriad of reasons including labor strikes, maritime or air accidents, political events such as wars, embargoes, or congestion at ports,

---

Table 8-4   Determinants of a Good Source

1. Price
2. Quality and capabilities
3. Support services, which include replacement of defective items, instruction in the use of equipment, and repair of equipment
4. Location in relation to shipping time, transportation costs, and response time for rush orders or emergency service
5. Inventory policy
6. Flexibility of the supplier

or bureaucratic snafus. The opening vignette illustrates these problems. The implication of this aspect is quite severe in those cases where firms rely on keeping a low inventory. Delays or disruptions in supplies effectively shut down production or distribution where stockpiled inventory would likely be minimal.

Another problem sometimes arises over quality. It is often harder to monitor the quality of goods produced, and defects are not detected until they have been received. Replacement consignments require time, and the firm is often locked into long-term contracts necessitating painstaking and time-consuming work between the firm and its suppliers to work out the quality glitches.

Finally, the firm needs to be aware of the environmental and human rights situation in the countries where it outsources. In the home country, negative press accounts or determined action by advocacy groups protesting violations of human rights or wanton degradation of the physical environment in a foreign country may vitiate the trading ties between the two nations. This situation forces the firm to explain its conduct and in some cases, to cancel orders with suppliers and move them to other countries. For example, to Nike, Inc., China was an important production base; in 1995, the company sourced 32 percent of its shoes—mostly low- to medium-value products—there. Nike liked the cheap labor and China's excellent infrastructure for getting finished goods from factories to ports. Nike, however, was cautious about overexposing itself to China because of political pressures in the United States to revoke that country's most favored nation trading clause because of human rights violations. If most favored nation status was removed, tariffs on shoes imported into the United States would rise from 6 percent to 60 percent in some categories. If that happened, Nike would be forced to export shoes made in China to Europe and Asia.[16]

Other issues that may cause problems include inadequate knowledge about business practices in the foreign country, adverse changes in the currency rates between the buying and selling countries, and possible resurgence of nationalistic sentiments in both countries.

ROLE OF SUPPLIERS

Japanese firms have demonstrated the importance of forging close relationship between the firm and its suppliers. Historically, suppliers delivered the goods contracted for at the given schedule and at the agreed-upon price. Different suppliers competed among themselves to win contracts. Poor performance by a supplier would generally mean that its contract would not be renewed. Japanese firms, however, work with a few suppliers on a wide range of issues: design of the products, defect rates, delivery schedule, quality component, and feedback to and from suppliers. Such an extensive relationship builds up trust and a mutual reliance on each other. Suppliers would often identify problems and suggest solutions and would work more as a partner of the buyer rather than an arm's length contractor. One consequence of this practice is that as Japanese manufacturing firms have established facilities abroad, they have been followed by the firms that provide components, parts, and other business services at home. In imitation of the Japanese model, firms in other countries including the United States, have striven to develop

---

[16]Studwell, Joe. 1996, October 24. Prime target Nike runs own course through maze of labor practices. *Journal of Commerce*, p. A5.

Table 8-5   The Supplier as a Partner, Not Adversary

Characteristic	Contemporary Approach	Traditional Approach
Number of suppliers	Few	Many
Length of relationship	Long	Short
Low price	Less important	Very important
Reliability of deliveries	Very high	May not be high
Sharing with supplier	High	Low
Quality of products	Supplier certifies	Buyer verifies
Volume of business	High	Low per supplier
Location of suppliers	Close to buyer	Scattered
Flexibility of suppliers	High	Low

long-term relationships with their vendors. Table 8-5 compares the modern and traditional views of the buyer-supplier relationship.

LOGISTICS AND SUPPLY CHAIN MANAGEMENT

Logistics refers to the movement of materials within a production facility and to incoming and outgoing shipments of goods. On a broader level, it involves the procurement, distribution, transportation, maintenance, and replacement of material and personnel. Logistics require managers to adopt an extremely practical approach to the realities and opportunities that exist in this field. A related but broader concept that has gained currency in recent years is **supply chain management.** It usually refers to the manufacturer receiving information from the retailer on daily sales of particular products and using that information to decide on issues of designing, sourcing, and production volumes. Managing that supply chain requires that parts of the supply process that were previously considered as separate be brought together. Many large firms are employing logistics specialists who work not only to reduce costs but also boost revenues for the firm.[17]

As discussed earlier, one of the determinants of location is transportation facilities and costs. In most cases, firms use or need to use a combination of transportation facilities to move cargo between different destinations. The use of two or more modes to handle a shipment is referred to as **intermodal.** The choice of transport systems and the route taken is determined by the freight charges including insurance, nature of the product, the time taken to reach the destination, the availability of the service (e.g., scheduled sailings), type of equipment used (e.g., refrigerated carriers), reliability of the service, governmental regulations, likelihood of interruptions because of civil disturbances, worker militancy, congestion at ports, and the experience and reputation of the firm.

International logistics is more difficult than domestic distribution. Firms experience problems with export documentation, transportation costs, tariffs, finding foreign representatives with appropriate know-how to market products, delay in transfer of funds, currency fluctuations, language barriers, and post-sales servicing. In addition, international logistics is also costly. It is estimated that international logistics costs range

---

[17]Batchelor, Charles. 1999, June 17. Logistics aspires to worldly wisdom. *Financial Times,* p. 13; Batchelor, Charles. 1998, December 1. Moving up the corporate agenda. *Financial Times Survey,* p. I.

from 25 to 35 percent of a product's sales value, as opposed to 8 to 10 percent for domestic shipment.

The complex nature of international logistics and why an understanding of it is necessary for efficient management is illustrated by the following example.[18] Japan's port services are the world's most expensive. Carriers estimate that the cost of waterfront services averages 25 to 100 percent more in Japan than in other countries. Furthermore, Japan is the only major port nation in the world that has no-Sunday work rules and lacks 24-hour operations. These practices force carriers to adjust their entire Asian schedules at great cost and inconvenience.

The Japan Harbor Transportation Association (JHTA), which runs Japan's waterfront services, exercises unilateral control over the availability of maritime labor to serve ocean carriers. Both labor and management are represented by the association that controls which stevedores and longshoremen work at which berths, so as to eliminate competition for services.

The process by which the association controls Japan's ports is known as "prior consultation." It requires that all carriers receive approval from the association for virtually any operational change involving port-related services, no matter how minor and meaningless.

The JHTA, therefore, wields an enormous amount of leverage over carriers, shippers, and intermediaries involved in port terminal operations. Such control also can lead to discrimination against foreign carriers in Japan. It costs a foreign shipping company approximately $100 more, compared with other countries, to unload or discharge a 20-foot container in Japanese ports.

Japanese carriers, however, have their own terminals and stevedoring operations, which levy lighter charges on their own ships. This difference is substantial, because most container ships entering Japanese ports carry about 2,000 to 4,000 20-foot containers.

When a ship enters a port, it usually is required to take a local pilot to navigate through local waters. In Japan, however, while all foreign cargo ships are required to use a pilot, Japanese ships with experienced Japanese captains on board are allowed to navigate on their own. Further, pilotage fees in Japan are the highest in the world, averaging 50 to 100 percent higher than in most other countries.

ROLE OF GOVERNMENT

Both home and host governments play a determining role in international logistics. Their involvement has special relevance for those firms that make up the logistics industry as well as all those who use their services. Nearly all governments support ocean and air carriers owned by their nationals or based in their countries. One form of support is subsidies for the manufacture and operating of ships as was illustrated in Management Focus 8-3.

Because transportation systems are also essential during times of national emergencies (such as wars or natural disasters), nearly all governments support the maintenance of a certain level of domestic-based logistics companies. Governments also encourage companies, especially in airline and shipping, to project a national image abroad for prestige purposes and to ensure that part of the foreign trade is transported

---
[18]Budwick, Phillip. 1996, October 30. A tilted port policy. *Journal of Commerce*, p. 6A.

by carriers of the home country. In addition, governments may also own transportation companies. One reason is to earn foreign currency. In recent years, many governments have privatized their transportation companies and encouraged private enterprise to enter formerly government-reserved businesses.

Many countries have cargo preference rules that require certain types of merchandise or certain proportion of merchandise to be used by home country-based transportation firms. For instance, three-fourths of the food shipped overseas as aid or as export promotion by the U.S. Department of Agriculture is required to be shipped on U.S.-flag vessels. This practice is opposed by U.S. grain farmers and companies because U.S. carriers charge higher rates, which effectively reduces the amount of money that foreign buyers have to buy grain.

Countries enter into bilateral agreements that demarcate the percentage (in weight) of cargo that should be handled by carriers belonging to different countries. In many such agreements, the 40:40:20 formula is used. Here, cargo traffic between nations Y and Z is reserved in the following manner: 40 percent moves on vessels of nation Y; 40 percent moves on vessels of nation Z; and 20 percent moves on vessels from any other nation.

Considerable regulation exists with regard to international aviation, both for passenger and cargo traffic. The number of airplane flights and their capacities are usually established through bilateral air agreements reached between national governments. The U.S. Department of Transportation negotiates with foreign governments in granting access to foreign air transport companies to U.S. airports and obtaining agreements for U.S. air transport companies to gain access to foreign cities. Over the years, air traffic agreements have tended to become liberalized as international business has grown.

NEED FOR INTERMEDIARIES

Because of the large number of transportation options available, their constantly changing prices, and the many different types of documents that are needed to accompany goods crossing national boundaries, a firm's international logistics department is usually responsible for the management, communication, control, and planning of the logistics activities. These activities include the following:

- Order processing
- Packaging
- Labeling
- Documentation preparation
- Answering customer queries
- Handling deliveries and returns
- Warehousing
- Material handling
- Providing parts and servicing
- Planning, arranging, and purchasing international transportation services

Many firms, however, are unable to provide the complete range of services. Instead, they outsource all or portions of this function to specialist logistics providers such as freight forwarders, export management companies, export packers, customhouse brokers, container leasing companies, banks, and goods surveyors, among others. For firms new to international business, the use of an intermediary is recommended. Thus, when Boots, a U.K.-based pharmacy chain, decided to expand into Thailand, it went to MSAS Global Logistics to ensure that supplies would reach its newly opening stores in a timely manner. MSAS Global Logistics, a London-based firm, first sourced and designed a suitable warehouse and installed appropriate air-conditioning, insulation, lighting, racking, and communication systems in Thailand. A skilled warehousing manager joined the operation to set up and manage the facility. MSAS Global Logistics was also responsible for the management of store fittings for the new stores, supplying inventory to the stores, transporting the products by sea and air from abroad, and handling Thai customs and licensing requirements. The logistics provider employed about 85 people to support the Boots work—mainly Thai nationals, although three senior managers were from the United Kingdom.[19]

The most common logistics provider is the **freight forwarder** who can handle nearly all the logistical aspects of a transaction. Large forwarders can assume responsibility for managing the firm's international supply and distribution activities. They work with various transportation companies and are able to secure the best prices as well as create the necessary documentation that would need to accompany the goods being shipped. For example, UPS Worldwide Logistics, a subsidiary of the U.S.-based United Parcel Service, a delivery company, had a contract from guitar manufacturer Fender International of the Netherlands, to manage shipments coming into Europe by sea and land from manufacturing sites around the world, inspect the products for quality, oversee inventory, fulfill distributor and dealer orders, and manage multicarrier deliveries to 22 countries in Europe and 10 countries in the Middle East and Asia. UPS Worldwide Logistics also handled the return of damaged guitars for repairs. According to Fender's managers, one of the key benefits of using UPS Worldwide Logistics was that it centralized distribution, which reduced delivery times, cut back on inventories held by dealers, and enabled the company to come closer to the final consumer by getting to know their tastes and preferences.[20]

Although price is important, timely and efficient service from customs brokers and forwarders is crucial when exporting and importing merchandise. Timely transmittal of documentation and real-time information on shipments is important when exporting food products overseas. Because the operations of many firms are global in scope, these firms work with both exporters and importers. Firms need one-stop shopping from their brokers and forwarders—it may have to be the same office. The work of logistics providers has been helped by advancements in **telematics,** an omnibus term that includes technologies such as in-cab devices to track a vehicle's progress, automatic toll collection devices, "smart" roadside signs linked to sensors monitoring traffic volumes, automatic vehicle control systems, and package-in-transit tracking systems. Telematics brings together advances in satellite navigation, digital mapping, and telecommunications to allow a more intelligent use of transport networks.

The most sophisticated distribution management systems and the most extensive geographical networks have traditionally been operated by courier companies such as UPS, FedEx, DHL, and TNT. Many of these companies have been developing logistics operations as the example of UPS and Fender indicated. Retailers such as Wal-Mart in the United States have a reputation for supply chain expertise. Close ties with suppliers,

---

[19]Chemists take scientific approach to expansion. *Financial Times.* 1999, June 17, p. 16.
[20]Another string to its bow. *Financial Times.* 1999, June 17, p. 15.

manufacturers, and customers are being forged through the use of computer software systems such as **enterprise resource planning.** These systems provide the information backbone to cope with the complexities of modern businesses. They bring together information that was previously dispersed throughout the organization and turn it into a tool that managers can use. The major providers of enterprise resource planning systems are SAP, Oracle, PeopleSoft, J. D. Edwards, and Baan.

JUST-IN-TIME PRODUCTION

The time required to create a good or service for the customer is known as the cycle time. In the competitive environment, reducing the cycle time assumes critical importance, because customers prefer suppliers who can deliver faster than others. The effort to reduce cycle time is best represented by the advent of **just-in-time** concepts. At one extreme it means that an organization has absolutely no inventories of raw materials, semi-, or even finished goods and yet can respond immediately to changing market conditions. Technological innovations have contributed to the widespread application of just-in-time concepts as Management Focus 8-4 shows.

The concept of just-in-time inventory first originated at Toyota, the largest Japanese automobile firm. For it to succeed, Toyota needed the cooperation of its suppliers and distributors. All three entities had to make adjustments and changes in their operations and coordinate their schedules to ensure that cycle times were reduced. To reduce cycle time, the number of defects had to be brought down substantially especially because few spare parts were being stocked. Limited space and expensive land in Japan discouraged construction of large storage yards. The ideas behind just-in-time are not limited to the production dimension only; it has been extended to other business areas such as distribution, procurement, after-sales customer service, and accounts receivable.

The success of just-in-time ideas has prompted companies around the world to adopt it. As discussed in the section on sourcing, firms have changed their relationship with their suppliers from an adversarial one to being a partner requiring sharing, trust, and confidence. The concept also needs highly reliable transportation systems so that raw material can be delivered quickly and finished products distributed efficiently.

QUALITY

A quality revolution has been occurring around the world. It began in Japan in the early 1950s and has since spread to North America to Europe. The importance of quality in managerial processes and outcomes is now widely recognized as a key determinant of increasing a firm's effectiveness and efficiency. The success of Japanese products in the U.S. market in the 1970s and 1980s dramatized the effect of high quality. Customers had the opportunity to compare products and in many cases they preferred the imported one. As Japanese firms gained market share, U.S. firms understood the key role of quality in business success.

What is quality? Broadly speaking, **quality** refers to the ability of a product or service to consistently meet or exceed customer expectations. In recent years, the notion of quality has been extended to include organization-wide efforts to integrate all dimensions of managerial activities. This approach, commonly known as **total quality management (TQM),** is characterized by continuous improvement of processes and

MANAGEMENT FOCUS 8-4

SPARE PARTS ON THE INTERNET

Boeing Co., the world's largest manufacturer of airplanes, based in Seattle, Washington, designed a new Internet site to give airlines fast access to the 410,000 different types of spare parts the company keeps in stock for maintenance and repair of commercial aircraft.

Boeing Commercial Airplane Group's worldwide Web site, called the Boeing PART page, was demonstrated in October 1996 at a company-sponsored spares symposium. "There was widespread interest in it," said Dick Schleh, a company spokesperson. "It's just now getting going, but we anticipate it will be the preferred way of ordering spare parts."

The site simplified the ordering process, reduced paperwork and errors, and instantly gave order and shipping status as well as information on price, inventory, and part interchangeability. The PART page was available to airlines and repair services that used standard computer workstations with Internet access. Customers would access the Boeing parts database, which listed the entire parts inventory at spares facilities in the United States and around the world, including London, Brussels,

Singapore, and Beijing. Built-in safeguards limited usage to registered individuals only, and workstations had to have a Web browser able to handle a security protocol.

The PART page "provides an easy, economical way for spares customers to access our mainframe database," said Darce Lamb, vice president of Boeing Spares. "It's a fully interactive on-line service that extends the advantage of electronic commerce to every customer regardless of size," he added.

Until the PART site, only larger Boeing customers had the resources to link into the Boeing mainframe, using private-line services. More than half of Boeing's customers, including small carriers and repair stations, used phone, fax, or telex to place orders or request prices. Boeing then had to relay the messages for processing, creating the chance for an error. "With PART, the process is point-and-click and fill-in-the-blanks," Mr. Lamb said. "Plus the cost for local Internet access is cheaper than private line costs." Mr. Schleh said Boeing tested a pilot site with three companies—Alaska Airlines, Canadian Airlines International, and Tramco—a repair and modification outfit in Everett, Washington.

Source: DiBenedetto, William. 1996, October 31. Boeing's PART of Web a site for spare wares. *Journal of Commerce*, p. 3B.

products, competitive benchmarking of performance standards with those of other firms, empowerment of employees, the use of teams for problem solving and decision making, and a knowledge of quality control and improvement tools among the workforce. A comparison of organizational cultures of a traditional firm and a TQM firm is presented in Table 8-6.

INTERNATIONAL QUALITY AWARDS

The recognition that improvements in quality translate into a competitive advantage has encouraged governments to institute awards to honor firms that demonstrate excellence in quality. In Japan, the Deming Prizes, named in honor of W. Edwards Deming, an American statistician and proponent of quality control techniques, have achieved great prestige, and winners are organizations against which competitors benchmark themselves. In the United States, the Baldrige Award was created in 1987 by the U.S. Department of Commerce to promote quality awareness, understand the requirements for quality excellence, and share information about successful quality strategies and the

Table 8-6	Features of a Traditional Firm and a TQM Firm	
Variable	*Traditional Firm*	*TQM Firm*
Overall mission	Maximize return on investment	Meet/exceed customer satisfaction
Objectives	Short term	Both short and long term
Management	Often closed; sometimes inconsistent	Open; employee input welcomed
Manager's role	Issue and implement orders	Coach subordinates
Customer needs	One of many priorities	Key priority; need to understand
Problems	Assign blame and punish	Identify causes and resolve
Problem solving	Not systematic	Systematic; use of teams
Improvement	Discontinuous	Continuous
Supplier relationship	Adversarial	Partnership
Job design	Narrow and specialized	Broad and general
Focus	Product oriented	Process oriented

Source: Nakhal, Behnam and Neves, Joao S. "The Deming, Baldrige and European Quality Awards." *Quality Progress,* 1994, April, pp. 33–37.

benefits. In 1988, 14 large European multinational firms formed the European Foundation for Quality Management to promote total quality management principles in West European countries. With support from the European Organization for Quality and the European Union, the Foundation established the European Quality Award, the first of which was given out in 1992.

Although the overall approach of the Deming Prizes is the control of processes that ensure the quality of goods and services, the Baldrige Award places the highest emphasis on customer satisfaction to achieve competitiveness. The European Quality Award extends the notion of quality even further to include corporate social responsibility and overall firm performance. These awards emphasize the importance of quality dimensions in a firm's competitive ability, and winning an award lends valuable prestige and recognition.

INTERNATIONAL STANDARDS ORGANIZATION

The **International Standards Organization (ISO)** is an international body composed of national standards organizations of more than 90 countries. Based in Switzerland, its purpose is to promote worldwide standards that contribute to improvements in efficiency, productivity, and cost reduction. The work of the ISO is carried out by various technical committees. The Quality Management and Quality Assurance Committee created a set of standards on quality issues. Known as **ISO 9000 Series,** these standards have assumed importance for doing business internationally. Companies that have been certified as having met ISO standards are often given priority in the award of contracts over noncertified firms, especially in European countries. To obtain ISO certification, a firm must engage in a rigorous self-review of its managerial and production processes. The process takes 12 to 18 months, and on certification, the firm is registered in an ISO directory that companies seeking suppliers refer to for a list of certified companies. The popularity of the ISO in Europe means that obtaining ISO 9000 certification is an essential requirement for doing business in the European Union.

In the United States, the ISO 9000 Series has been issued as the American National Standards Institute (ANSI)/American Society for Quality Control (ASQC) Q90 Series. The ISO 9000 and the Q90 are technically equivalent except that the latter uses terminology customary in the United States, which makes it easier for U.S. firms to use the ISO 9000 Series. These international standards also help companies with guidelines on how to set up a quality management system if they do not have one presently.

CONCLUSIONS

This chapter has highlighted several of the key operational issues that face managers as their firms expand internationally. With the entire world to choose from, location of facilities requires careful analysis and consideration of several competing factors. Where to site R&D centers and how to integrate them with the production facilities and customer needs require a thorough understanding of these interlocking relationships. With operations on an international scale, the scope for outsourcing has increased. However, such decisions have to be evaluated in terms of long-term implications. Integrating widely scattered operations requires managers to analyze the value chain, realize the role of efficient logistics, and choose appropriate plant or office capacities. Global operations enable firms to learn new managerial techniques and adapt them to their own business. Among the operations innovations gaining favor are quality and just-in-time systems. The international business manager has to be able to organize the firm's production or service operations in such a way that it can cross-transfer effective practices in one part of the world to the entire firm, increase the value of its primary and secondary activities, and use logistics management to bind together its scattered facilities with both suppliers and customers. Advances in technology have focused attention on increasing efficiency in purchasing and distributing goods and services and have led to the emergence of specialist firms to help companies earn a competitive edge.

OPENING VIGNETTE EPILOGUE

Mr. Zitzer would end up paying 50 percent more than usual to squeeze the shipment onto a vessel. Other companies had to resort to drastic measures. Samsonite Corp., a Denver, Colorado-based luggage maker, split its business among several ship lines to guarantee space. Hartz Mountain Corp., a New Jersey pet products company, obtained its supplies on an alternative shipping route through the Suez Canal. Hoping to guarantee deliveries, big retailers like Dayton Hudson Corp. warned suppliers to book overseas transportation at least two weeks in advance.[21]

[21]Mathews, Anna Wilde. 1998, September 22. Holiday imports from Asia jam shipping lanes. *The Wall Street Journal*, pp. B1, B4.

Key Terms

- greenfield site
- free trade zone
- maquiladora
- offshore factory
- source factory
- server factory
- contributor factory
- outpost factory
- lead factory

- value chain
- make-or-buy decision
- outsourcing
- logistics
- supply chain management
- intermodal
- freight forwarder
- telematics
- enterprise resource planning

- just-in-time
- quality
- total quality management (TQM)
- International Standards Organization (ISO)
- ISO 9000 Series

Discussion Questions

1. For each of the following four types of businesses, rate the importance of each factor in terms of making international location decisions. Use L for low importance, M for moderate importance, and H for high importance:

Factor	Airline Hub	Auto Plant	Accounting Firm	Copper Smelter
Labor costs	_____	_____	_____	_____
Availability of skilled labor	_____	_____	_____	_____
Transportation costs	_____	_____	_____	_____
Nearness to customers	_____	_____	_____	_____
Cost of living	_____	_____	_____	_____
Pollution control regulation	_____	_____	_____	_____
Nearness to raw materials	_____	_____	_____	_____
Construction costs	_____	_____	_____	_____
Presence of similar firms	_____	_____	_____	_____
Exchange rate stability	_____	_____	_____	_____

2. Explain how superior value chain management can increase a firm's competitive advantage. How is telematics impacting the internationalization of service industries?

3. Most international pharmaceutical companies have their plants in advanced industrial countries of North America, Europe, and Japan. In contrast, most sports footwear companies source their products from developing countries such as China and Indonesia. Explain this seeming inconsistency.

4. How important is it for a firm to win one of the major quality awards? What competitive benefits can be gained by a firm that obtains ISO 9000 certification? Explain.

5. Identify a list of criteria that a firm should use to decide which aspects of its value chain it should outsource. What aspects should not be outsourced? Why or why not?

6. How should a firm determine the strategic role of its foreign factories? Are some roles preferable to others?

Writing Assignment

Following poor performance, a U.S. apparel firm has decided to close down its two factories located at different sites within the member nations of the European Union. As an assistant in the office of the chief executive in New York City, you have been asked to investigate and prepare a report outlining the steps that need to be followed as per the rules of the EU and the host countries to close down operations. The company is anxious to comply with all procedures in place.

Internet Exercise

Use the Internet to identify a list of products, firms, and industries that are using cyberspace for conducting international business transactions such as exports and imports of goods and services. Describe the nature and quality of the technical/computer facilities needed to consummate such transactions.

Internet Resources

Many government agencies around the world have Web pages that provide information on incentives offered to foreign firms for investing in that country. The Industrial Development Agency of Ireland's home page is *www.idaireland.com*. For information on locating in Chile, one source is *www.finanzas.cl/deloitte*. Leading logistics companies such as Exel Logistics, Royal Nedlloyd, Tibbet & Britten Group, Sea-Land, C.H. Robinson, Air Express International, Fritz Companies, and Ryder Integrated Logistics provide information about the extensive range of services they offer. *www.ups.com* is a good source of information about UPS's package delivery and other services. SAP's Web site is at *www.sap.com*.

Case 8–1 SIEMENS AUTOMOTIVE SYSTEMS

In early 1995, Stephen Drake, product marketing manager at Siemens' electrical motors division in London, Canada, under heavy pressure from customers to reduce prices, was evaluating various cost-cutting options. With materials accounting for 60 percent of total cost, Stephen knew sourcing components offshore and moving assembly operations to low-cost, soft-currency locations were two alternatives. He wondered what additional information he might require and what options he should recommend.

GENERAL COMPANY BACKGROUND

The Electric Motor/Electrical Motor Systems division (henceforth referred to as EM division) was part of the Automotive Systems group of Siemens, a German multinational firm, the sixth largest electronics and electrical engineering company in the world. The world headquarters of the Automotive Systems group was located in Regensburg, Germany, with research and development, testing, production, assembling, and sales and service facilities situated worldwide. The group was one of the leading suppliers of automotive electrical and electronic components and systems to the automobile industry.

The EM division's facilities in London, Canada, produced heating, ventilation, air conditioning (HVAC) fan motors, engine cooling motors, and antilock braking system (ABS) pump motors. London had the mandate to supply engine cooling motors worldwide and HVAC fan motors to North America. Because headquarters assigned mandate responsibilities, competition among EM's many plants were kept to a minimum. Having a mandate meant London could devote talent and resources exclusively to certain products and assigned geographical markets.

Just as Regensburg assigned mandates, so could it reallocate them—often for political, not just economic reasons. In 1994, London lost its North American mandate to produce ABS pump motors to a new plant established for the purpose in Georgia in the United States. The loss of the ABS pump motors mandate meant that London no longer accepted new orders for that product and all production would cease in two years when current orders were filled. Because resource availability, growth opportunities, sales, and profits were closely tied with the mandate a plant had, London's managers had to lobby headquarters constantly to ensure that mandates were not lost or eroded, or alternatively, to retain or expand them.

PRODUCTION

Employing nearly 1,300 workers, the London facilities had a capacity to produce approximately 30,000 motors per day. These motors were assembled entirely from components made and supplied by outside vendors from across Canada and the United States. In 1994, when automobile sales were at record high levels, the EM division was hard-pressed to obtain adequate and continuous supplies. When some vendors were unable to provide certain components in ample quantities, the division was forced to look outside North America and placed orders with off-shore manufacturers in Brazil and South Korea.

Siemens' engineers complied with stringent quality standards and worked with the vendors to ensure that components met acceptable norms. While the products made by London were standardized across all manufacturers and no components were produced in-house, the competitive advantage of the firm lay in its ability to work closely as a team with customers to supply technically advanced, cost-competitive products on time, precisely as specified. A flexible approach to engineering design allowed customization of the motors for a wide range of applications and performance requirements. At the same time, advanced manufacturing processes and techniques and close proximity to customers allowed for high quality standards, fast execution of orders, compliance with tight scheduling requirements, and swift troubleshooting.

MARKETING

The products of the EM division were sold as original equipment (OE) to automobile manufacturers. With its North American mandate for HVAC fan motors, the division's customers were the three U.S. auto companies: General Motors, Ford, and Chrysler. Japanese manufacturers in North America relied on Japanese suppliers and until now, the EM division had been unable to break that close relationship.

The mandate for cooling motors being worldwide, the division sold to European automakers such as BMW, in addition to the three U.S. firms. Because products made by the division were sold as OE in automobiles, the total number of potential customers were the 28 companies worldwide that made motor vehicles.

The division's main competitor in both North America and Europe was another German firm, Bosch. Other suppliers were smaller firms from the United States, France, Italy, and Japan. All these firms, including Siemens, typically signed multiyear contracts to provide specific numbers of different types of motors at agreed prices. Negotiations over such contracts were intense as various suppliers tried to undercut each other over price, delivery schedules, and specifications. Because the products were generally standardized and delivery schedules were set by the buyers, the competition was usually over pricing. In 1994, the EM group lost the entire contract to sell to Volvo, a Swedish automaker, by a small margin. Volvo opted for a less sophisticated, though cheaper product, over that offered by the EM group.

The EM group at London, when selling to automakers in Europe, had to cope with higher transportation costs and longer delivery times when compared to European-based suppliers. Also, the crucial need to be close to the customer was not met. Stephen, a Canadian, was concerned about remaining competitive in the European market.

Marketing of the various motors required working closely with the automobile companies. Engineers from both buying and selling firms were aware of technical needs and developments, product modifications and innovation, as well as prices and costs. Given the relatively small number of buyers and sellers in the industry, the competition to win contracts was intense, and all parties were familiar with each other's strengths and capabilities.

CUSTOMER RESISTANCE

Throughout the 1990s, the automobile companies, mostly because of Japanese competition, had been on a relentless cost-cutting spree. This objective was reflected in the demands from purchasing managers at the automobile firms that suppliers like Siemens hold, or even reduce, the price on their motors.

As Stephens said of his recent negotiations with Ford, "We are being pushed to the wall. The auto companies, far from allowing us increases to compensate for rising costs, now demand that we give discounts for large volume orders and that we absorb all labor and overhead costs, and even a part of the materials cost increase. Our profit margins are being squeezed and I don't know how long this can continue. But so long as our competitors are willing to bid lower, we have to keep up with them."

This determination by automobile purchasing managers to hold prices down compelled Stephen to seek efficiencies and cost control in his assembly operations in London. It meant working with plant engineers to redesign products, produce in modular forms, improve assembly operations, and reduce the markup, sometimes to less than three percent.

COST STRUCTURE

A breakdown of the costs indicated that the cost of components and materials accounted for 60 percent of the final price of the product, with 25 percent for overhead, 10 percent for labor, and the rest, profit. The relatively small proportion of the labor costs was partly due to the extensive use of robots and automation in the assembling process. Labor costs offered virtually no scope for any significant reduction. While costs of overheads such as utilities rose, new sales contracts barred these costs from being passed on to the automobile companies.

Recognizing the high proportion of material costs, EM London took a leaf out of the negotiating book of its customers and was now demanding cost containment, even price reductions from its vendors.

Long-term multimillion-dollar contracts were being offered to suppliers who kept price increases to a minimum and gave discounts on large volume purchases.

In recent months, Stephen's efforts to control costs had been helped by the relative decline of the Canadian dollar against the U.S. dollar. Because 80 percent of the sales were to the United States, the decline in the Canadian dollar's value had provided a cushion to absorb some of the costs. It was neutralized though, to some extent, because many of the components suppliers were based in the United States and had to be paid in U.S. dollars.

Despite this respite, cost-cutting and cost-holding options were running out at London. Attention had to be focused elsewhere and Stephen, who had been with the company for six years, prepared a report on alternative courses of action for George Granieri, the director of the Aftermarket Business Unit.

FOREIGN EXCHANGE RATES

Stephen had closely followed the fluctuations in the world's foreign exchange rates. The London factory, as with many other multinational firms, dealt with a large number of currencies and consequently was affected by exchange rate changes. Since the early 1990s, the changes that had occurred included the rise of the Japanese yen and German mark, the fall in the Canadian dollar, and the softness of currencies such as the Spanish peseta and the Italian lira. See Exhibit 1 for foreign exchange rates for selected currencies.

For cooling motors, London competed with other manufacturers for the business of European automakers. Exchange rate differentials impacted on profit margins, especially because they were already narrow. Similarly, for HVAC motors, EM's units in soft currency countries were gaining a cost advantage and were a competitive threat. Spanish and Italian companies were able to produce even cheaper than Canada and had begun to undercut the London operations when bidding for contracts, especially in Europe.

The rise of the Japanese yen and the German mark affected the EM division in different ways. With C$1 trading for less than 65 Japanese yen, manufacturers in Japan were finding production costs increasingly unbearable. Stephen believed that Japanese auto companies in both North America and Japan might soon buy motors from Siemens. Unlike in the past, Stephens was now receiving inquiries about prices and product performance from the Japanese auto firms. On the other hand, the rise of the German mark reduced the value of sales and profits denominated in Canadian dollars.

As in most multinational firms, the finance function, including the management of foreign exchange risk, was centralized at headquarters in Germany. There, specialists used hedging strategies to reduce losses arising from exchange rate changes and provided guidelines on future rates for up to four years to aid in planning and sales negotiations. For Stephen, exchange rate differentials suggested an attractive way to reduce component and assembling costs.

OFFSHORE OUTSOURCING

The EM division was now looking to outsource offshore many of the components that it usually bought from the United States and Canada. Offshore manufacturers in Mexico, Brazil, and emerging market economies of Asia, such as Korea and China, and in soft-currency, developed countries such as Spain and Italy, were able to provide components at lower prices than their U.S. and Canadian counterparts.

Sourcing offshore posed some difficulties. Experience with the Brazilian supplier in 1994 pointed to unreliability over delivery. The EM division had to work with its major customer, Ford, to pressure the Brazilian firm to expedite production and delivery. Expensive air freight had to be used instead of the traditional, yet cheap, though time-consuming, ocean transport. While deliveries to European customers were not interrupted, thanks to enough supplies in transit, the danger was there.

The EM division at London maintained inventories of five days and hence it had to be able to rely on foreign suppliers and transportation firms to deliver components in a timely fashion. As suppliers became more far-flung, the possibility of schedule slippages and transportation hitches arose.

Yet another problem arose over the quality of magnets supplied by a Korean firm. Entire consignments had to be returned and since then, London had instituted an elaborate system of controls and checks to ensure that quality expectations were met. There was always the danger that lower prices of offshore components might come at the expense of the high quality that Siemens strove for in its finished products.

The automobile companies preferred to have their motor suppliers in close geographical proximity. For EM London, the European market was much farther than the U.S. one. Automakers in Europe had turned in some cases to European suppliers who benefited not only from being closest to the automakers, but also had shorter shipping times, cheaper transportation, and in some cases, gained from a weakening currency. The loss of the ABS motor mandate was due to the willingness of the Automotive Systems group to set up a plant in the United States near the facilities of the main buyer of the motors who insisted on that as the price for continued patronage.

Stephen foresaw the possibility of the EM division establishing facilities to make cooling motors and HVAC motors in southern Europe, East Asia, and Mexico. Relocation would reduce assembling costs and ensure availability of cheap components. Spreading out facilities would also even out the effects of exchange rate fluctuations. Stephen also noted the phenomenal growth—actual and forecasted—of the automobile industry in countries of South America and China. He would like his division to be positioned to take advantage of these opportunities as he struggled to protect his shrinking profit margins from the tough purchasing managers at the world's automobile firms.

Stephen knew a meeting would be called soon by George Granieri to discuss the best strategies for dealing with the cost-price squeeze. He wondered whether he needed additional information and what the total range of options might be.

Exhibit 1	Foreign Exchange Rates (US$1 = Foreign Currency)				
Country/Currency	*1991*	*1992*	*1993*	*1994*	*1995*
Canada (dollar)	1.1556	1.2711	1.324	1.4028	1.3633
Germany (mark)	1.5610	1.6140	1.7263	1.5488	1.3763
Japan (yen)	125.20	124.75	111.85	99.74	83.575
Spain (peseta)	96.69	114.62	142.21	131.74	122.94
Italy (lira)	1151.1	1470.9	1704.0	1629.7	1698.5
Korea (won)	760.8	788.4	808.1	788.7	758.0
Brazil (real)*	.19	2.20	.05	.85	1.0905

*per thousand

QUESTIONS

1. What, if any, additional information would help Stephen Drake decide on what recommendations to make to his superior?
2. How can a multinational company such as Siemens address the issues caused by changes in exchange rates?
3. What will be the role of the London facilities if more and more work is outsourced?
4. Given the drawbacks to outsourcing that Siemens Automotive has experienced, why should the company persist with this option?
5. Siemens Automotive is competing with other divisions in the same company and with other companies in the industry. What is the basis of this competition? How can Siemens retain its mandate and competitive edge?

References

Coughlin, Cletus C., Joseph V. Terza, and Vachira Arromdee. 1991. State characteristics and the location of foreign direct investment within the United States. *Review of Economics and Statistics* 73(4), pp. 675–683.

Ferdows, Kasra. 1997. Making the most of foreign factories. *Harvard Business Review.* March–April, pp. 73–88.

Gidwitz, Betsy. 1980. *The politics of international air transport.* Lexington, MA: Heath Books.

Jungnickel, Rolf. 1996. Globalization: Exodus of Germany industry? *Intereconomics* 31(4), pp. 181–188.

Kuemmerle, Walter. 1997. Building effective R&D capabilities abroad. *Harvard Business Review.* March–April, pp. 61–70.

MacCormack, Alan David, Lawrence James Newman III, and Donald B. Rosenfield. 1994. The new dynamics of global manufacturing site location. *Sloan Management Review.* Summer, pp. 69–79.

Nakhal, Behnam, and Joao S. Neves. 1994. The Deming, Baldrige, and European Quality Awards. *Quality Progress.* April, pp. 33–37.

Schmenner, R. W. 1979. Look beyond the obvious in plant location. *Harvard Business Review.* January–February, pp. 126–132.

Stalk Jr., George. 1988. Time: The next source of competitive advantage. *Harvard Business Review.* July–August, pp. 41–51.

Sullivan, Daniel C. 1996. General considerations involving logistics management companies. *Journal of Transportation Law, Logistics and Policy* 63(4), pp. 443–468.

Ulgado, Francis M. 1996. Location characteristics of manufacturing investments in the U.S.: A comparison of American and foreign-based firms. *Management International Review* 36(1), pp. 7–26.

Weimershirch, Arnold, and Stephen George. 1994. *Total quality management: Strategies and techniques proven at today's most successful companies.* New York: John Wiley & Sons.

World Investment Report 1995. *Transnational Corporations and Competitiveness.* United Nations. New York.

9

ORGANIZATIONAL DESIGN AND CONTROL

❧

OPENING VIGNETTE

In 1996, executives at Procter & Gamble (P&G) boldy declared that the U.S. consumer products company would double its net sales by the year 2006, to $70 billion. Since then, the company had consistently missed its growth targets. Its fat substitute product, Olestra, had shown poor sales; global economic turmoil hurt its foreign operations; and its share price had dropped considerably.

In response, the company began to reorganize itself. The chief executive officer, John E. Pepper, planned to step down earlier and the focus shifted away from the traditional approach of cutting costs and dropping under-performing tasks. Goaded by big supermarket chains such as Carrefour and Wal-Mart Stores who wanted global products at a global price and noting organizational changes at companies such as Kellogg, 3M, and General Electric, the message to Mr. Pepper was clear: "What thousands of people have been telling us is that we need to be simpler and move faster."

The result was the project called Organization 2005. It called for restructuring the company's hierarchy and a new product development process designed to speed innovative offerings to the global market. The old structure, based on geography, was being reshaped into seven global buisness units organized by category, such as baby care, beauty care, and fabric-and-home care. The global business units would develop and sell products on a worldwide basis, ending the previous system that gave P&G's country managers full autonomy over product pricing and what products to make and sell. In addition to marketing and pricing, global business units would supervise new product development. P&G would move away from its traditional method of first testing products in mid-sized U.S. cities before introducing them on a global basis.

Making the transformation was not expected to be easy or quick. The restructuring would mean that many country managers would be replaced or downsized. Most of the extra revenue the company was counting on would come from emerging markets such as Russia and from Asia—areas suffering through a harsh economic slowdown. P&G's top managers however believed that they could make all the structural changes and achieve the sales goals by the year 2005.

Organizing a firm that can successfully compete in the global business environment is a challenging task for business managers, and it is a task that is never complete. Even though top managers recognize that a proper fit between how a firm is organized, its goals, and the operating environment is essential for competitive success, no magic formula determines for them which type of organizational structure is appropriate. Indeed, no single best structure fits all firms. A structure that works well in one setting does not in another. Furthermore, because the goals of the firm and the environment in which it operates change, organizational structures have to be regularly altered. This chapter identifies key determinants of organizational structures, examines some of the more commonly used structures with illustrations of how firms use them, analyzes the competing forces that determine centralization and decentralization of decision making, and discusses the control mechanisms used by managers to ensure that the firm is functioning along the desired lines. Although the tendency may be to design an elegant architecture, the key underlying goal is to coordinate a firm's various value-added activities into an integrated whole that can function effectively to achieve organizational goals.

DEFINING ORGANIZATIONAL STRUCTURE

Organizational structure refers to the architecture of the firm in terms of how it is set up and how it answers the following questions:

- Who is in charge of what activities?
- Who reports to whom?
- What activities are grouped together?
- How are the different activities of the firm coordinated?
- Where are key decisions made?
- What are the rules and procedures to ensure that all parts of the firm are tied together and function as a coherent whole?

Usually, an organization's structure is presented in the form of a diagram or picture, the **organization chart,** which outlines departments, job titles, lines of authority and communication, staff functions, how the departments relate to each other, and how they are coordinated. In actuality, these impersonal diagrams are infused with life by managers and employees who have tasks and responsibilities that are carried out on a continuous interactive basis to achieve organizational goals. Designing an organizational structure is usually not easy, except maybe for the smallest of firms. As goals, performance, and operating environment changes, and managers gain experience, the firm is likely to be restructured. Thus, organizational structures are ever changing and managers are forever engaged in creating new and improved versions.

EVOLUTION OF AN ORGANIZATION'S STRUCTURE

The stages theory of internationalization of a firm posited that in the initial phase, the firm's structure is necessarily simple because its activities are on a small scale and domestically focused. As overseas sales increases, the firm hires specialized personnel and even creates an export unit in its marketing department to cater to foreign inquiries and to handle the tasks that international exports require, such as customs declarations, payments in foreign currencies, and shipping requirements. For example, U.S. airlines set up separate phone lines (and sometimes staff them with operators with foreign language competency) to handle reservations and inquiries for overseas travel when they started flying to foreign destinations. With increasing overseas sales, the firm may set up an office abroad. As opportunities for licensing and joint ventures become available, the firm creates a separate international department to handle all its international activities and invest it with all necessary authority and resources. In effect, the foreign operations of the firm are now clearly delineated from its domestic activities. As more and more revenues start coming from overseas and foreign subsidiaries are established, the firm restructures its organization on a geographic basis in which the domestic market is just one of several areas. Where the firm has multiple product lines, it organizes on a product basis. The international department, in essence, disappears. Finally, as the operations of the firm become more diverse and worldwide with key activities scattered around the globe and the home country relegated to being one more market or another location for a value-added activity, coordination becomes difficult. The firm looks to designing unique and complex structures to remain competitive. Figure 9-1 shows how a firm's organizational structure evolves over time, as overseas sales or purchases grow, and as the complexity of business activities (e.g., number and type of products, markets, suppliers, and facilities) increases.

Of course, not all firms expand in this step-by-step, methodical fashion but this simple model does illustrate how as a firm evolves from a small domestic-focused organization to doing business on a global scale, the organization's structure has to contemporaneously change to accommodate the new tasks, the new goals, and new challenges. Coordination and control become more complex. The old structure becomes ineffective over time as the firm outgrows the systems and procedures designed to meet earlier market conditions, organizational goals, technology, and firm capabilities. Hence, firms experience a constant pressure and need to restructure.

DETERMINANTS OF STRUCTURE

How should a firm be designed? Several factors influence that decision.

1. *The firm's long-term goals or strategy.* Since Alfred Chandler advocated the linkage between strategy and structure, it has been widely accepted that for a firm to be able to

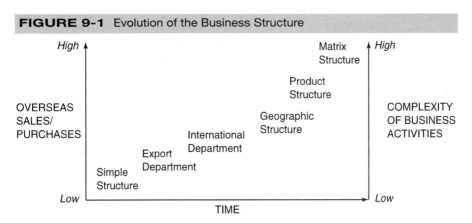

FIGURE 9-1 Evolution of the Business Structure

Source: Adapted from *Organizing for Global Competitiveness.* 1995. The Conference Board, New York.

effectively implement its strategy, it needs to create an appropriate organizational structure.[1] Hence, once the organization's mission has been set and the long- and short-term goals identified, the next task is to organize the firm in such a way that employees, managers, and departments can work and be coordinated to achieve those goals. The structure needed to pursue a global strategy is quite different from that needed for a multidomestic strategy. This distinction, in effect, implies that organizational structures are indeed unique and vary from firm to firm. As an example, a firm such as Nestle whose goal is to compete in every major market in the world in the food industry, has a geography-oriented structure with widely dispersed research facilities and considerable authority to individual country managers. In contrast, the Finnish company Ahlstrom, which specializes in paper manufacturing, paper-making machinery, glass making, and electricity generators, has a structure organized by product lines.[2]

2. *The operating environment of the firm.* The operating environment for a firm can range from stability to volatility. Firms operating in a rapidly changing environment need to have organizational structures that are easily adaptable. As discussed in Chapter 4, changes in the environment take place in the economic, political, social, and technological realm. Since the creation of the European Union and its integrated market, many firms operating there have restructured to prepare for the increased competition and to cater to the pan-European consumer. For instance, firms such as Unilever, Marks & Spencer, and IBM have centralized their manufacturing, information technology, and other infrastructural activities to improve efficiencies and cut costs. In 1995, Alcatel Alsthom, a French telecommunications equipment manufacturer, reorganized itself around product lines, rather than around countries, which had been its traditional structure. The old system made sense in an era when Alcatel got the bulk of its business from European state-owned telephone companies such as France Telecom. But as the European phone monopolies were being privatized and challenged by new competitors, these companies were demanding lower prices for equipment and instituting competitive bidding for contracts. Alcatel hoped that the new structure would enable it to compete more effectively with other equipment makers.[3] The opening vignette illustrates how firm performance forces managers to redesign structure in order to remain competitive.

3. *The nature of technology that undergirds the firm's operations.* Technology refers to the process that transforms information and raw materials into finished goods and services. It not only means machines, information processing capabilities, and plant layout, it also includes employee knowledge base, skills, and experience. The technologies used by firms impact how an organization is designed. For example, Deutsche Bank, the largest bank in Germany, expanded in the 1990s to more than 2,400 offices at home and abroad. A fundamental driving force behind its expansion was technology. In the banking industry both new "hard" and "soft" technologies had become available. Hard technologies included telecommunications, computers, ERP software, and video communication, which enabled managers and customers to have better information at lower costs and to distribute services to clients efficiently and effectively. Soft technologies, or financial inno-

---

[1]Chandler, Jr., Alfred D. 1962. *Strategy and structure.* Cambridge, MA: MIT Press.
[2]Kosonen, Paavo. 1994. *Corporate transformation and management.* Helsinki School of Economics and Business Administration, Acta Universitatis Oeconomicae Helsingiensis.
[3]Landler, Mark. 1995, October 6. Alcatel to be reorganized along product lines. *The New York Times,* p. D6.

vation (such as the use of derivative instruments of interest rate and currency swaps) used these hard technologies for delivering the services. Out of these hard and soft technologies came the opportunity to expand overseas and redesign its structure.[4]

Revolutionary advancements in **information technology**—the computerized hardware and software that is used to process information—has profoundly impacted organizational design and management control. Information technology has given rise to flatter organizations in place of centralized, hierarchical bureaucracies because of the easy access to and dissemination of information throughout the organization. Because information can be shared instantly and inexpensively among many people in many locations, the value of centralized decision making and bureaucracy decreases. It has also enabled firms to outsource certain functions and departments. For instance, soon after British Petroleum acquired Amoco in 1999, as part of the restructuring, the entire human resource department of the merged company was outsourced. Only those aspects that required judgment and policy were retained in-house.[5]

4. *The organizational age, experience, and managerial capabilities of the firm.* Business success is also linked to factors such as the vision and dynamism of the firm's leadership and workforce, the quality of its products, the historical experience of the firm with various structural designs, and the "fit" or alignment among important variables such as staffing, rewards, and tasks. As the stages model suggested, a firm's structure changes as it expands into new businesses and new markets. Usually, this expansion occurs over time; with accumulation of experience, the firm is likely to diversify into new product lines, new ways of doing business, and new markets. In addition, managers learn what works and what does not. They become aware of their own and their firm's capabilities and limitations, and thus are able to organize the firm's structure accordingly. For instance, large companies, such as IBM, Royal Dutch/Shell, and Caterpillar, have substantial amounts of international business experience with many of their executives having served in foreign locations. Older firms, as in the steel and textiles industries, in contrast, have faced technological and competitive challenges that have forced them to adopt new technologies, introduce new product lines, or simply go out of business. Sometimes, the structure grows in a way that it becomes dysfunctional. For example, Gambro, a Swedish medical technology company, saying that its complex structure was the main barrier to cutting costs and improving profit margins, moved toward creating a simpler structure.[6] The firm sold off its various noncore businesses leaving it only with three distinct businesses—renal care, medical equipment, and dialysis equipment. These three businesses were run almost as separate companies with distinct manufacturing, logistics, and R&D divisions. The restructuring was done to integrate the three and eliminate duplication in management, purchasing, and production.

5. *The behavior of competitors.* Changes in organizational design in one company in an industry sometimes trigger similar changes in the other firms as they attempt to retain their competitive position in a rapidly transforming industry. Thus a design that might

---

[4]Bryan, Lowell L. 1993. The forces shaping global banking. *The McKinsey Quarterly* 2, p. 60.
[5]Lester, Tom. 2000, January 4. An alternative strategy. *Financial Times,* p. 8.
[6]Burt, Tim. 1998, September 3. Gambro hopes to straighten its tangled medical lines. *Financial Times,* p. 17.

have been appropriate in an industry characterized by a large number of similar-sized firms may not be suitable when mergers and acquisitons create a few dominant firms. Novo Nordisk, a Danish producer of pharmaceuticals and industrial enzymes, restructured, splitting the two product divisions into separate legal entities. Until now, the two product divisions were combined because of manufacturing synergies. Products ranging from genetically engineered insulin to brighteners used in laundry detergents were brewed in huge fermentation vats, and economies of scale enabled the company to compete effectively in both businesses. The company was forced to restructure because of the large number of mergers that occurred in the pharmaceutical industry since 1993. Falling behind bigger rivals, the company focused on conserving scarce funds for its main product line—diabetes treatment.[7]

TYPES OF ORGANIZATIONAL STRUCTURES

Organizational structures come in all sorts and sizes. Each structure is appropriate under particular circumstances and has its own strengths and weaknesses. Several structures together with examples are discussed in this section. It should be recognized that in reality, individual firms have structures that may differ in substantial ways from the "models" discussed here. Only the top positions are shown here; space does not permit showing the organizational layout of an entire firm.

BUSINESS UNITS

Most organizational structures apply to the entire firm; however, large and diversified firms usually have separate organizational entities that provide one or more products or services to a particular market. These individual entities are referred to as **business units** and usually operate as **profit centers.** A profit center is accountable for both the revenues generated by its activities and the costs of those activities. As an example, United Technologies Corporation (UTC) was a U.S.-based conglomerate whose business units included Pratt & Whitney (jet engines), Sikorsky (commercial and military helicopters), Carrier (heating, ventilating, and air conditioning systems), USBI (solid rocket boosters), Hamilton Standard (flight systems), and Otis Elevator Company (elevators and escalators). Business units are the basic building blocks of a large firm's organization.

SIMPLE STRUCTURE

In the infancy stage of an organization's life cycle, the firm is created and run by a single individual or a small group of individuals. Such an organization may have what is referred to as a "simple structure" characterized by a small number of employees and few coordination and control mechanisms. The owner (or owners) have full knowledge of the activities of the firm and the employees, and they supervise the entire workforce.

FUNCTIONAL STRUCTURE

The **functional structure** is the most logical and unsophisticated form of organizational structure. In this structure, employees and their tasks are grouped by functionally special-

---

[7]Moore, Stephen D. 1999. Novo Nordisk opts for new prescription. *The Wall Street Journal,* p. B5B.

ized areas such as operations, marketing, finance, human resources, R&D, and accounting. This structure is often used by firms in the early stage of their internationalization. An office within the marketing function may have the task of handling all export issues or alternately, an office within the purchasing department may handle all imports. Another form may occur when the individual functional areas are expanded to the global level. Thus, senior executives have worldwide responsibility for the various functions such as production, marketing, R&D, and human resources management. In the case of production, global responsibility would mean direct control over domestic and foreign manufacturing units. These senior managers report to the president who is responsible for coordinating all these functions. The president is responsible for the business's profit and loss; the functional heads run cost centers and are evaluated on performance measures like productivity, volume, quality, cost control, market share, and response time. When functionalism occurs on a global level, the marketing department handles all marketing activities, which may mean the end of any separate export unit.

The functional structure works well when the business emphasizes efficient use of specialized resources, economies of scale, and cost controls. By organizing on the basis of function, it puts people of similar skills, interests, and capabilities together. It makes supervision easier when the manager needs to be an expert in only a narrow area. This structure is suitable for firms that make only one or two product lines, when the technology is relatively routine, the environment is stable, and the need is low for interdependence across functional units.

The principal weakness is its unwieldiness should the firm have several product lines. Decision making becomes difficult because the president is the only person in a position to make the interfunctional decisions. Decisions can also be slow under this structure if communication between departments is minimal. It also becomes difficult to determine responsibility and evaluate performance. If a new product fails, who is responsible—manufacturing? marketing? R&D? By being organized by function, employees tend to be loyal to their area, which makes coordination among the functions harder. In times of environmental volatility, this structure is slow to respond.

Illustration of the Functional Structure   At Bechtel Corporation, a leading U.S. engineering and construction firm, one of its business units, Bechtel Civil Company (BCIV), provides technical, management, and related services to develop, build, and operate infrastructure projects and facilities for its customers worldwide in five areas: aviation services, highways, transit and rail, buildings and urban development, and water resources. The structure of BCIV is presented in Figure 9-2.

The functional departments are Infrastructure Resources, Business and Planning Services, Regional Planning and Strategic Project Development, and Regional Offices. The purpose of the infrastructure resources department is to provide the regional offices with specialized technical and managerial capabilities including cutting-edge technologies and work methods. The business and planning services department helps the regional offices to define and understand BCIV's markets and to manage the assets and financial activities of the company. The unit also houses the company's human resources, legal, and public and community relations functions. The regional planning and strategic project development department develops long-term, complex, and multibusiness line engineering and construction opportunities for the firm. The regional offices, located in San Francisco, London, and Hong Kong, develop and implement a regional business

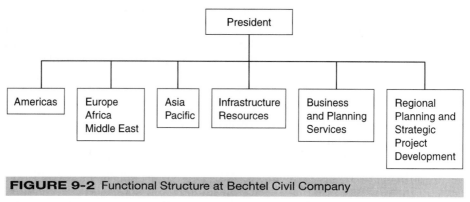

FIGURE 9-2 Functional Structure at Bechtel Civil Company

Source: Adapted from *Organizing for Global Competitiveness.* 1995. The Conference Board, New York.

strategy to win projects in its five market sectors, manage project operations and performance, and establish and maintain relationship with clients, much like the marketing function. The office of the president provides business leadership, establishes company goals and profitability targets, and leads the implementation of these goals and other business initiatives.

INTERNATIONAL DIVISION STRUCTURE

Through the **international division structure,** the firm gives exclusive authority and responsibility for overseas operations to a separate department. This international department usually handles all exports or imports. However, it could also be responsible for manufacturing and sales, licensing, planning, policy, and administration connected with the overseas markets or sources. International divisions are common in many firms and have the advantage of putting in one place all the international needs and capabilities of the firm. The structure is preferred by firms with a large domestic-oriented business but which is seeking to develop its international business. Gerber Products, a leading U.S. producer of infant food and infant products, uses the international division structure to provide a clear focus to the company's international operations and uses a cadre of experienced international managers to achieve its objectives. Figure 9-3 describes Gerber's organizational structure. A potential negative of this structure is that by concentrating all foreign activities in a separate department, a disconnect is created with the rest of the organization, which is primarily domestic-oriented.

PRODUCT STRUCTURE

The **product structure** is adopted by firms with multiple product lines. Every product (or a family of products) comprises a department that is responsible for its worldwide design, production, and marketing. Consequently, all of the required functional resources necessary to carry out these tasks are placed within the particular department. This format is widely used.

The strength of this structure lies in its ability to direct all resources for the successful production and marketing of a particular product on a worldwide basis. Man-

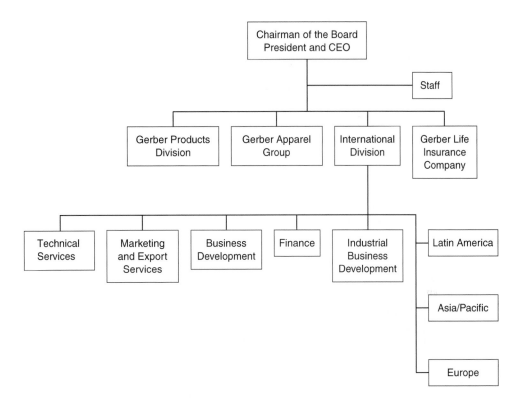

FIGURE 9-3 International Division Structure at Gerber Products Company

Source: Adapted from *Organizing for Global Competitiveness.* 1995. The Conference Board, New York.

agerial performance (linked to the product) is easily measured. The main weakness is duplication of overheads, difficulty in coordinating different product lines in different markets, and the possible loss of economies of scale. Another danger is that the product departments may not be able to recognize differences in markets and change the product accordingly.

Illustration of the Product Structure   Corange Limited is a British-based diversified health care company. Its core areas of expertise are in diabetes, cardiovascular care, cancer therapy, bone disorders, and infectious diseases. Its largest business unit, the Diagnostics Division, offers a wide range of products that aim at temporary treatment of various human diseases through rapid, accurate diagnosis and monitoring. It is a leading supplier of biochemicals to research institutions and clinical laboratories, as well as raw materials to other diagnostic and pharmaceutical manufacturers. The division consists of five businesses (biochemicals, diabetes care, laboratory diagnostics, molecular diagnostics, and point of care diagnostics) and several support activities. Each business has its own R&D, business development, finance, and strategy functions. Figure 9-4 presents the organizational structure of Corange's Diagnostics Division.

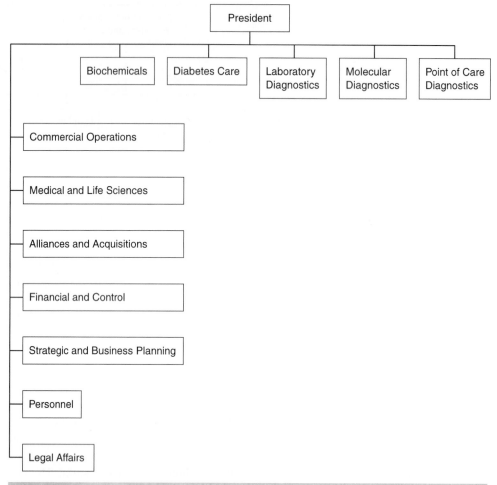

FIGURE 9-4 The Product Structure at Corange Ltd.

Source: Adapted from *Organizing for Global Competitiveness.* 1995. The Conference Board, New York.

GEOGRAPHICAL STRUCTURE

The **geographical structure** organizes the firm on the basis of the geographical areas it does business in. Traditionally, it was adopted by firms that sold goods in a diverse set of countries when the firms needed to adapt both the products and the management styles to the peculiarities of each geographical area. In recent years, several environmental and company specific factors have combined to make this structure attractive.

The emergence of integrated regional markets makes it plausible for a firm to establish a regional office to handle all of its activities (e.g., R&D, manufacturing, purchasing, distribution, and marketing) in those countries. Secondly, in many countries, laws or regulations may constrain ownership, local product content, employment, natural resource exploitation, or marketing, which forces a firm to set up an autonomous local unit to cater to that particular country. Thirdly, in the service sector, because of the necessity of being close to customers, firms (such as in banking, accounting, insurance, advertising, and law) organize their worldwide activities on a geographical format. Finally, because of competitive reasons, firms compete at several levels, including local, regional, and global; they need to be closer to their customers to, say, provide after sales service; and they often have to customize their product to meet local needs. All these factors suggest a geography-based approach to organizing.

In addition to these external environmental factors, company-specific forces recommend such a structure. For instance, in the initial stages when firms establish subsidiaries and branches abroad, they often give their overseas operations considerable autonomy. Secondly, small and medium-sized firms do not have the resources and skills that larger organizations have and therefore, they settle for less complex structures such as the geographical format. Thirdly, when firms expand overseas through acquisitions of foreign firms, it may not be always possible to integrate these acquired businesses, because they are different from the rest of the firm's business or because it makes sense to leave them alone to cater to their markets. Finally, firms with the geographical structure may find that any reorganization is expensive, or is likely to trigger resistance from country managers, or because the historical experience and organizational culture requires its continuance.

Firms that use the geographical structure are likely to have a big slice of their sales coming from overseas; have mature, homogeneous, and stable product lines; and are in the food, automotive, pharmaceuticals, cosmetics, and farm equipment industries. Examples of firms that use this structure or versions of it include Nestle, Sony, Ogilvy and Mather advertising agency, and Unilever.

Among the obvious disadvantages of this structure are the duplication of staff, business systems, infrastructure, and capital resources in multiple markets—a high organizational cost. The structure also insulates one geographic unit from another, which may make it difficult to share technologies, lessons, and products across markets. Thus, mistakes made in one market may well be repeated in others because open communication is likely to be thwarted under such a structure.

Illustration of the Geographical Structure   Otis Elevator Company is the world's largest manufacturer of elevators and escalators. It was the market leader and had a double-digit market share in every market. Based in Farmington, Connecticut, more than four-fifths of the company's sales came from outside the United States.

Otis's business was organized by geography. Four regional heads (Europe/Africa/Middle East, Latin America, North America, and Pacific Asia Area) reported to the president. Each region contained a mix of subregions and countries at the next level of management. For example, reporting to the head of the Pacific Asia Area were executives responsible for operations in North Asia and Southeast Asia, as well as individual country managers of Australia, India, and Japan. The subregional executives had responsibility for countries in their area. As an example, country managers for China, Korea, Taiwan, and Hong Kong were accountable to the head of North Asia, who was based in Hong Kong. The structure is shown in Figure 9-5.

The heart of the company was the local branch manager who was located in a major city. The manager had a salesforce and crews for maintenance, modernization, and installation. Each branch manager was responsible for developing and achieving a business plan and for the financial outcomes of the profit center. In a small or medium-sized

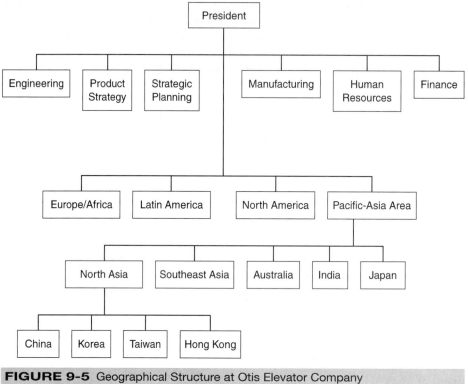

FIGURE 9-5 Geographical Structure at Otis Elevator Company

Source: Adapted from *Organizing for Global Competitiveness.* 1995. The Conference Board, New York.

country, branch managers reported directly to their country manager. A larger country with many branches was generally divided into zones to which branch managers were accountable, and which reported to the country manager. Each level of Otis operated within the boundaries of an approved business plan and was accountable for its performance. Joint venture relationships were managed by the country manager.

Staff personnel, though varying in size, in finance, human resources, marketing, installation, and maintenance were found both at the country manager's level as well as the branch manager's level. Regional managers also had support staff in these areas as well as manufacturing, purchasing, law, and other. Thus, the firm had considerable redundancy of staff personnel. Otis, however, believed that it was important to have the necessary support staff as close to the local market as possible. The local operations were run by a host country national who functioned within the ambit of the laws and cultural practices of the country. By allowing local managers to have their own team, they could function successfully in the foreign country.

MIXED OR HYBRID STRUCTURE

In most firms, the organizational structure is a mix of two or more structures and hence are referred to as **mixed** or **hybrid structures.** The main reason a firm may combine elements from several structures is because it has a highly diversified product line whose strategies, technologies, markets, and competitors vary greatly. It is quite possible that the mixed structure is a result of a historical event, such as an acquisition. Such structures are found in all sorts of businesses—those just beginning to internationalize and those that have long been internationalized, as well as small and large firms.

The advantage of the mixed structure is that it permits managers to emphasize what is important for each of its subunits. Product, geographic, or functional needs can receive the requisite amount of attention depending on the situation. For instance, a mix of function and geography allows for specialization within each regional market, while a mix of product and geography can encourage easier transfer pricing. As can be anticipated, the principal weakness of such a structure is the duplication of various activities, which can prove to be expensive. Of course coordination and control become more complicated and difficult for managers to handle.

Illustration of a Mixed Structure   Alcan Aluminum Ltd. (Alcan), a Canadian company, is among the largest producer of aluminum in the world. Nearly 90 percent of its sales come from outside Canada. Driven by the need to make and implement decisions quickly and at lower cost, Alcan created a mixed structure. The staff functions (research and technology, corporate affairs, finance, personnel, occupational health and safety, legal and corporate secretary, and environment) report to the chairman and CEO. The mixed nature of Alcan's organization is presented in Figure 9-6 where the line operations report to the COO. The mix includes four geographical regions (Brazil, Germany, Pacific, and United Kingdom), along with three North American businesses of primary smelting, rolled products, and downstream fabricating (Alcan Enterprises). In addition, Alcan Raw Materials and Metal Management handles purchasing, logistics,

FIGURE 9-6 Mixed Structure at Alcan Aluminum Ltd.

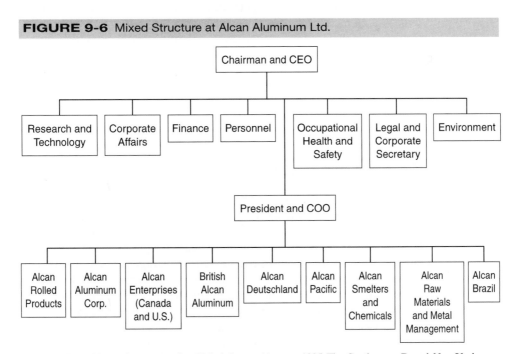

Source: Adapted from *Organizing for Global Competitiveness.* 1995. The Conference Board, New York.

and sales of aluminum and its associated raw materials on a worldwide basis. Reporting to these senior line executives are national companies, together with some businesses that operate on a regional basis and a few that operate worldwide in a niche market. Meanwhile Alcan Aluminum Corporation handles government compliance and regulatory matters (such as taxes) in the United States for Alcan Rolled Products and Alcan Enterprises. These three entities operate in a matrix format in the United States.

Alcan's mixed structure means that corporate management does not try to force widely differing parts of the company into a uniform and rigid organization mold. It allows each of the firm's operations to adapt to meet its unique business circumstances.

MATRIX STRUCTURE

The **matrix organization** is a gridlike structure that employs multiple chains of command. Some employees report to two or more managers and often deal with multiple systems of decision making, career planning, and budgeting. The matrix structure draws its historical roots from the project manager concept in the aerospace industry and the product manager approach in the consumer goods industry. Only in recent years have firms engaged in international business adopted this structure.

No single global matrix model provides a standard. Combinations of product and geography models are the most common; but other dimensions such as function are also added to the design. Firms use this structure to balance their product, geographic, and functional elements. For example, the product division is responsible for global product policy, manufacturing, and product profitability. Country divisions are responsible for marketing and overall country profitability, whereas functional departments deal with R&D, corporate policies, budgets, and the like. Examples of companies that use two-dimensional matrix formats are Asea Brown Boveri (ABB), Caterpillar, and Deutsche Bank (all of which combine geography with product). Companies that use three or more dimensions in the matrix format include Dow Chemical Company and International Business Machines, both of which combine geography, product, and function.

In the two-dimensional format, the managers responsible for the various product lines throughout the world and the country managers each report to the business general manager. These executives jointly supervise the head of the relevant product business in each country. Thus, the manager of the Product X business in Brazil reports to the country manager of Brazil and to the regional product executive for Product X. Both of these managers are required to cooperate in overseeing the creation and execution of the business plan and to use jointly the resources at their disposal. Thus, matrix structure requires collaboration and participation. Figure 9-7 describes this structure.

An advantage of the matrix design is that it forces the firm to consider all the important business factors, which can help it function better in a changing environment. With it, multiple expertise is brought to bear on a problem to resolve it in a manner that enhances the entire business. The structure leverages the company's core technologies and provides an opportunity for global economies of scale. It also gives more individuals the opportunity to develop into business generalists and thus increase the number of managers from which high level executives may be selected.

Although it seems to be an attractive design, in reality, it is a difficult structure to both create and live by. A great deal of time, effort, and energy is needed by managers to establish the process and understand it. The possibility of conflict among managers

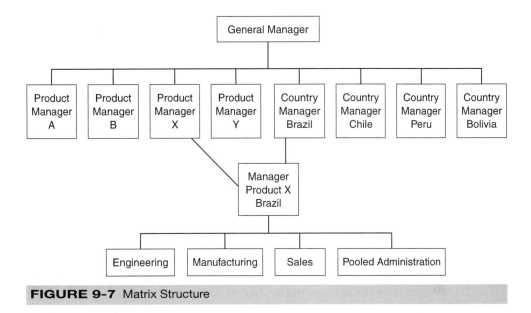

FIGURE 9-7 Matrix Structure

is high, which can be exacerbated because of cultural differences and physical distance between the managers. It is also an expensive system because of the need for frequent communication, which is usually achieved through face-to-face meetings, which in turn requires traveling and is thus costly. Decision making is also slow, and the ambiguity of the structure may make some managers incapable of functioning effectively and further is compounded by the fact that a manager has to report to two supervisors.

Attraction of the Matrix Design   The main goal of the matrix design is to enable managers to effectively cope with a highly complex and ever-changing operating environment by allowing them to draw upon the firm's resources in various ways. Matrix structures are suitable for managing several products or services, several markets, and a variety of skills and knowledge in a balanced way. Its attractiveness has been bolstered by changes in the business environment.

Trade blocs have forced firms to consider geographic factors in designing their structures. These blocs have created opportunities for consolidating R&D, purchasing, and production on a regionwide basis and thus pursue more of a global (albeit on a regional scale) rather than a multidomestic strategy. Second, the matrix structure allows a firm to deal with the demands of nationalism, which translates into local manufacturing and job creation, while retaining a global product focus. Third, with business drivers such as technology, specialized skills, customers, trend setters, and key competitors spread throughout the world, firms locate operations elsewhere to take advantage of the business drivers in order to remain competitive and to find new sources of revenue. And finally, deregulation and technological change have spurred competition to highly intense levels in most industries. Large international firms compete at various levels in various markets and must take into account both local and international factors. The matrix structure helps such firms to form a clear perspective of what its goals ought to be and in the appropriate allocation of resources.

In addition to these external factors, several company-specific factors also play a determining role. One of them is the availability of and ability to use information technology. Such technology encourages lateral communication patterns, decentralizes decision-making, enhances the role of the staff departments to become more active and supportive, and relocates value-added activities to various places that are optimal in terms of nearness to customers, raw materials, inputs, and competitors. With further improvements in information technology and its mastery by managers, the matrix structure is likely to become more viable than ever. Secondly, the matrix structure is suited for those firms that have business units specializing in related products, technology, and markets. These firms are able to utilize headquarters in an effective coordinating manner over key issues such as transfer pricing, dissemination of best practices, and executive development. A third determinant is the experience of the firm in international business. Extensive experience creates an institutional knowledge and learning that may embolden the firm to adopt such a structure. The firm is likely to have a team of highly capable and knowledgeable internationalized managers who are aware of the challenges of international business and thus are better able to create and manage the matrix structure. Finally, with increasing emphasis on meeting customer concerns, all the activities of the firm have to be geared toward that important goal. The matrix structure allows the firm to be organized in such a way that teams of managers can effectively addresss customer needs.

Illustration of a Matrix Structure National Westminster Bank PLC (NatWest) is one of the largest banks in the United Kingdom, with operations in more than 30 countries. The bank's Global Treasury division offers customers solutions to their currency and interest rate exposures using cash and derivative instruments. It is among the top 10 treasury operations worldwide and trades in 60 major currency/currency pairs globally, making it a market leader in foreign exchange, money markets, and their derivatives through 16 dealing rooms worldwide. Treasury's marketing and sales staff are located in 12 countries.

The senior managing director of Global Treasury supervises the three regional directors, four product heads, and the heads of the main support functions. These three regional directors work with the global product heads to develop regional business plans and strategy and are jointly responsible for profitability in their respective geographic regions. They are also accountable for managing risk, marketing, and for administrative matters. The four global product heads are responsible for currency options, money markets, foreign exchange, and proprietary trading on a worldwide basis. The heads of each of these units have staff located in various offices around the world, where they execute the local product strategy in conjunction with the local Treasury managers. Treasury has its own support staff in technology, finance, operations, and human resources and could draw on other centralized services such as audit and credit risk. The structure is shown in Figure 9-8.

NEW TYPES OF ORGANIZATIONAL STRUCTURES

Several new organizational designs have emerged in an attempt to address the need to leverage advanced technology, be near to customers, and coordinate widely dispersed activities. Four such structures are discussed here. In the **front-end/back-end structure** some activities (such as sales and sales service) are placed in the front of the organiza-

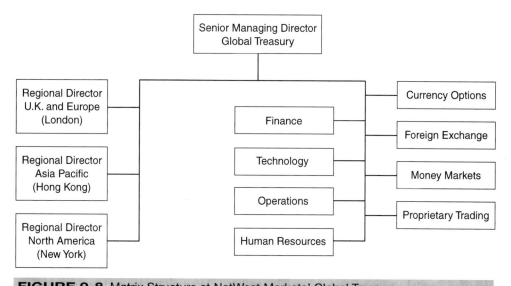

FIGURE 9-8 Matrix Structure at NatWest Markets' Global Treasury

Source: Adapted from *Organizing for Global Competitiveness.* 1995. The Conference Board, New York.

tion to serve customers, while other activities such as R&D, engineering, and manufacturing are put in the back end. The two ends are tied together through various mechanisms including information systems, joint teams of product managers and customer accounts managers, and business development activities. This structure is a modification of the traditional functional structure.[8]

The key strength of this structure is its response to customer needs by providing all the firm's products in an interrelated manner (and not stand-alone basis) with the full gamut of sales services. Also, both ends can be organized as profit centers and be assessed accordingly. The biggest challenge of this structure is to find ways to link the two ends to avoid disputes and interruptions. Compagnie des Machines Bull (Group Bull), a French manufacturer of automatic teller machines, smart cards, scientific minicomputers, and banking systems use a front-end/back-end organization format. Important back-end functions include R&D and manufacturing. The front-end comprises four geographical units that are responsible for applications, distribution, sales, and services. The front and back ends were integrated through several means. A line operating unit, Bull Systems Products, develops and manages the worldwide offering of several of the company's line of products. Various strategies, plans, policies, guidelines and teams are also used. This structure is provided in Figure 9-9.

The **process structure** symbolizes a new trend toward decentralized structures consisting of autonomous, cross-functional teams staffed by engineers and marketers. Managers look at firms as temporary entities and accordingly, design networks of autonomous companies coordinated through a central office and bound by a relationship of exchanging goods and services. For example, the production of apparel involves a

---

[8]Galbraith, Jay. 1992. *Organization design: The past, present and future.* Center for Effective Organizations, School of Business Administration, University of Southern California. Unpublished paper.

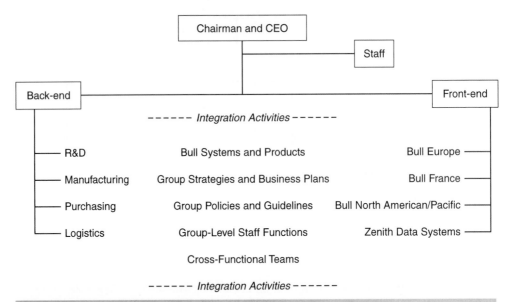

FIGURE 9-9 Front-End/Back-End Organization at Group Bull

Source: Adapted from *Organizing for Global Competitiveness.* 1995. The Conference Board, New York.

loose coordination among specialized textile, coat, dress, shirt, button, trim, and accessories manufacturers, designers, and retailers. Its strength lies in the flexibility of the network and its ability to quickly innovate and easily adapt to changing fashions that make some types of fabric trim popular one season, and another the next. Because each unit in the process structure is specialized, they are highly efficient. Should the unit prove to be inefficient, managers can easily lop it off without extensive damage to the overall company. Under this process structure, operational decision making is decentralized—member units strive for continuous improvements—which allows them to be responsive to market changes.

Tasks are handled by polyfunctional teams. The work of the teams is structured around carefully designed and integrated processes. Each of the business's major processes comprises several teams that are accountable to a process owner who, in turn, reports directly to the general manager. Individuals who work in the teams are usually not specialists; they have several skills. Rewards are based on both team and individual performances. Obviously, to succeed, employees must be capable of working in a group setting.

What is a process? It is a set of linked activities that takes an input and transforms it to create an output. A bank's processes include obtaining deposits, evaluating and approving credit, providing loans, processing payments, and customer service. In order to create a process organization, management must first identify the key processes of the business—usually about five—and then determine their areas of performance emphasis, such as quality, cost, and cycle time. Figure 9-10 illustrates the process structure. Process organizations are found at the business unit level, rather than at the corporate level, where their usage would be impractical and unwieldy. They are effective where product life cycles are short and the external environment is highly competitive.

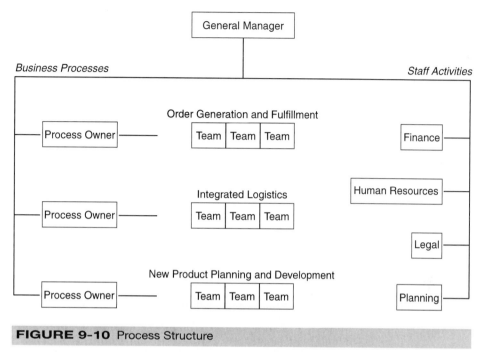

FIGURE 9-10 Process Structure

Source: Adapted from *Organizing for Global Competitiveness.* 1995. The Conference Board, New York.

The strength of this structure is that it relates firm activities to customer needs. Nonvalue-added work can be identified and eliminated to reduce the cost of doing business. Because self-management is emphasized, layers of supervisors are not needed. The elements associated with the hierarchical structure (authority, power, protection of privilege) are not present. The disadvantage lies in identifying the firm's main activities and in creating the right type of workforce who can work in this egalitarian setting.

Fuelled largely by information technology, another way of organizing businesses—called **temporary networks**—is emerging.[9] Powerful personal computers enable both large and tiny businesses and even individuals to reach into global reservoirs of information, expertise, and financing, and conduct transactions throughout the world. Often, these businesses join together electronically into fluid, temporary networks to produce and sell goods and services. Tasks are not assigned and controlled through a stable or fixed chain of management but are carried out autonomously by these independent businesses. When the job is done, the network dissolves and its members go off to seek new tasks. The work of the temporary network is coordinated by the individuals who compose it, with little or no centralized direction, control, or supervision. Instead, the results emerge from the individual actions and interactions of the different players in the system.

A consequence of temporary networks is the break-up of large firms into smaller units. For example, General Motors has split into several divisions, which are now small

---

[9]Malone, Thomas W., and Robert J. Laubacher. 1998. The dawn of the e-lance economy. *Harvard Business Review* 76(5). September–October, pp. 144–152.

companies, each concerned with managing their brands and funding new car development. Many tasks have been outsourced. Cars are developed by independent engineers and designers, who join together in autonomous and self-organizing coalitions. The entire job depends on a high-speed computer network—the Internet—for communication.

The notion of a **transnational-network structure** is relatively new.[10] It is a structure that has three essential elements: (1) providing managers with multiple perspectives about environmental opportunities and demands; (2) internationally dispersed yet interdependent physical assets and management capabilities; and (3) a set of flexible internal mechanisms to integrate the various activities of the firm.

The complex and volatile environment in which the firm operates means that managers must have the ability to sense and analyze the numerous and conflicting opportunities and demands that arise. An inability to do so may lead to lost opportunities or potential problems. Consequently, managers in the subsidiaries should be able to recognize the changing needs of local consumers and host governments, keep track of the strategy of competitiors and respond appropriately, and transfer corporate knowledge, information, and expertise among the various units of the firm.

After identifying opportunities and demands, managers must be able to make choices and respond in an effective manner. Under this structure, the goal is to ensure that viable national subsidiaries or facilities achieve global scale by giving them the responsibility of becoming the company's main source for a given product or expertise. The firm accesses important technological advances and market developments worldwide by securing the cooperation of the relevant subsidiaries in upgrading the company's technology, developing new products, and shaping marketing strategies, thereby increasing the interdependence of the the firm's various units.

The third element is the need for a management decision-making process that can resolve the variety of interests and perspectives in the firm and effectively integrate the dispersed responsibilities. Such a process is necessarily quite sophisticated and subtle and functions on three levels. First, it allows top management to intervene directly in the content of certain decisions—a form of centralization. Second, it creates formalized roles and administrative systems in a way that lets key managers influence important decisions. Third, top management creates an organizational culture through socialization, which provides the appropriate context in which decisions are delegated.

As is evident, this approach to designing an organizational structure is different from the ones discussed earlier. The transnational-network structure links the different worldwide parts of a firm. Each part evolves to take advantage of resources, knowledge, and markets wherever they exist in the firm and in the world. While such a structure is suggested for firms operating in highly complex environments, creating and managing such a firm is inordinately complicated.

ORGANIZATIONAL RESTRUCTURING

The designs already discussed are what may be called standard models. Throughout the business world, numerous variations of these standard models evolve as firms constantly grapple to find the "right" design. The new designs have certain common features. Firms

---

[10]Bartlett, Christopher A., and Sumantra Ghoshal. 1995. *Transnational management,* 2d ed. Chicago, IL: Irwin.

are looking more and more at their value chains and designing their activities around them through a greater use of teams, self-contained units, and information technology. Flexibility of the structure remains a key requirement, guided to a large extent by the need to understand and respond to customer preferences quickly. Management Focus 9-1 discusses the change toward customer responsiveness in the organization structure at Ericsson.

RECASTING BUSINESS STRUCTURES

Because of the short time between product development and marketing and the business strategies of product differentiation and customer satisfaction, firms are caught between different pressures to organize their structures accordingly. These issues are presented in Table 9-1. Similarly, environmental pressures impact on the structure. Economic downturns reduce the demand for a firm's products and thus revenues. Managers look to cut costs and stress efficiency. For example, Reuters Holdings, a news and information company based in London, in a bid to become more efficient, changed its long-standing geographic structure and reorganized along global product lines. Before the restructuring, the company's various divisions were organized by three geographic areas: the Americas, Asia, and the Middle East and Africa. The company was responding to changes in global financial markets, the need to remove barriers to intracorporate communication between divisions, and stiff competition from rivals such as Bloomberg and other Internet-based information service providers.[11] Table 9-2 summarizes how different environmental triggers impact an organization and how structures are adapted accordingly.

Historically, firms have reacted to the need for change by altering their organizational structures. Senior managers believed that changes in formal roles and reporting relationships would alter the linkages between the different parts of the firm and create new decision-making paradigms. These changes would in turn reshape the way individual managers think and behave. This model of change is presented in Table 9-3.

However, merely redrawing an organizational chart rarely brings about meaningful change. Moving boxes and changing reporting lines ignore interpersonal relationships, individual stakes, and informal ties. Thus it is no surprise that structural changes do not always yield desired results or that strong opposition precedes any plans to reorganize. Where changes have been instituted, it takes months or years to bring about a reorientation in individual (and group) attitudes, behaviors, and beliefs. As stated in Management Focus 9-1, the chief executive officer of Ericsson had to resign because he could not execute his restructuring plans swiftly. The executive, Sven Nilsson, found Ericsson's slow, consensus-based management style a big hindrance that failed to centralize decision making or decentralize production and research and development quickly. In the nine-month period following the initiation of restructuring the company, Ericsson saw its archrival Nokia become the leader in global mobile phone sales, its profits and share prices fell steeply, the launching of new products were delayed, and several models were recalled for technical problems.[12]

As a result, a different approach to instituting organizational change has emerged. Within this approach, change is initiated at the level of the individual, and through

---

[11]Reuters plans to change its geographic structure. *The Wall Street Journal.* July 20, 1998, p. B10.
[12]Latour, Alar. 1999, July 8. Ericsson chief ousted in dispute over reforms. *The Wall Street Journal,* pp. A10, A12.

REORGANIZATION AT ERICSSON

In October 1998, Ericsson, a large Swedish telecommunications firm, announced a major organizational restructuring designed to focus on customers and markets with decision making decentralized and profit centers located to smaller units. The impetus to restructure came because of a sudden slowdown in Ericsson's mobile phone sales and reports that at least a fifth of some models of its mobile phones were defective. Other factors included a decline in the prices of some of the company's products by as much as 23 to 25 percent, the fall by nearly half the price of its traded shares, and continuing losses in its Infocom segment. The general uncertainty affecting the global telecommunications industry, as well as the need for more research and development to keep up with competitors such as Nokia and the rapid convergence of telecoms and data in the form of stiff competition from U.S. data network companies such as Cisco Systems, also provided impetus to restructure.

The new organizational structure replaced the existing one based on three product divisions. Under the new structure, Ericsson's operations were divided into three business segments to serve different customer categories. Each business segment would be headed by an executive vice president, with consolidated profit and loss responsibility. The three segments were (1) network operators, which included operations for both wireless and fixed solutions for data and telecommunications, (2) consumer products, whose main core was mobile phone operations, and (3) enterprise solutions that focused on developing comprehensive solutions for business communication requirements.

These three customer-focused business segments consisted of 20 business units, which in turn comprised a number of product units. These units had global responsibility for developing and delivering products. The company's operations in the area of defense electronics, cables, and components remained unaffected by the restructuring.

In order to ensure a strong focus on customers and markets, customer responsibility was established at both the local and global levels. Four new corporate offices, besides the one in Stockholm,

Sweden, were established. These offices would also enable the company to recruit executives on a worldwide basis. The new offices covered the four geographical areas—Europe, Africa, and the Middle East; North America; Latin America; and Asia and Oceania—and were managed by an executive vice president. This geographical focus was to ensure that operations were conducted quickly, with optimal utilization of resources and focus on customers. This combination of customer units and geographic units was expected to bring the company closer to the customer and, in the simplest case, could be regarded as a product specialist and a customer representative working side by side. The geographical units would be locally responsible for customer relations, marketing, and sales. In most cases, they would be the same as Ericsson's local companies.

In additon to the three managers responsible for the business segments and the four managers in charge of the geographical markets, a separate manager would be responsible for each of the six corporate functions: finance, technology, supply, marketing and strategic business development, human resources, and information. The marketing function, which was new, would be responsible for global marketing, brand management, business development, and market coordination. These corporate functions then act in a coordinating role by utilizing resources more efficiently within Ericsson by adopting a common strategy. These 13 managers together with the president and chief executive officer comprise the corporate executive team.

The new structure, resembling a matrix, was meant to make the company more transparent and its decision-making process faster. "None of this is cast in iron," said Sven Nilsson, the company's president and chief executive officer. "But we expect this structure to be in effect for the next few years." He also indicated that he expected the company would benefit from "synergies" among the reshuffled business units and that the units were likely to experience some reduction of the workforce.

The restructuring did not elicit positive comments from observers. A telecommunications spe-

(continued)

(continued)

cialist noted that while the restructuring was a big step forward, "The reorganization does not change anything fundamental. Compared with the strategic imperatives they face, it is not that important." More fundamental changes were needed, such as investing heavily in research and development of data networking, Internet protocol, and other Internet-related technologies. These areas were considered more promising than mobile telecommunications and were areas that Ericsson had neglected because it was preoccupied with the booming mobile technology market. Other observers believed Ericsson should divest its underperforming products and exploit the datacom opportunities by making a big acquisition. Less than 10 months later, Mr. Nilsson was forced to resign. The company's chairman, Lars Ramqvist said, "We have certain problems. We have to come out with more new products and we need to do it faster. We need to step up the pace of restructuring."

Source: Latour, Almar. 1998, October 1. Ericsson unveils big overhaul of its structure. *The Wall Street Journal,* p. B9; McIvor, Greg, and Tim Burt. 1998, October 9. Ericsson's behavior wins it no friends in the markets. *Financial Times,* p. 20; Latour, Almar. 1999, July 8. Ericsson chief ousted in dispute over reforms. *The Wall Street Journal,* pp. A10, A12.

personnel assignments and socialization, the firm reshapes individual attitudes and expectations. These events are followed by altering the communication flows and decision-making processes among the departments and individuals. Once these goals are achieved, the changes are consolidated by restructuring the firm. The new change process is shown in Table 9-4. When ABB Asea Brown Boveri redesigned its structure, the chief executive officer carried out extensive discussions beforehand with the firm's top 70 managers. Then, to ensure he had the necessary support, he conducted a 40-question survey of those managers and obtained 90 percent support of the decision to do away with regional reporting lines and replace them by product divisions.[13]

Structural reorganization introduces changes in order to make a new strategy work. Often they are aimed at cost cutting but usually the goal is to increase the firm's responsiveness to customers and other stakeholders as was illustrated in the opening

Table 9-1	Strategy and Organizational Structure
Business Strategy	***Corresponding Organizational Structure***
Innovate	Decentralize Decisions
	Encourage Networks
Differentiate	Centralize Decisions
	Develop Specialists
Customize	Make Team Decisions
	Remove Management Layers

Source: From *Turning Points: Creating Strategic Change in Corporations* by Charles Fombrun, © 1992. McGraw-Hill. Reprinted with permission of The McGraw-Hill Companies.

---

[13]Taylor, William. 1991. The logic of global business: An interview with ABB's Percy Barnevik. *Harvard Business Review.* March–April.

Table 9-2	Environmental Change and Structure		
Environmental Trigger	*Improvement Issues*	*Capabilities*	*Controls*
Efficiency	Timing and productivity	Automate, just-in-time	Centralize, specialize
Customer Responsiveness	Quality and service	Customize, differentiate	Networking, delayering
Technological change	Innovation and speed	Build skills, invest in R&D	Flatten pyramid, decentralize

Source: From *Turning Points: Creating Strategic Change in Corporations* by Charles Fombrun, © 1992. McGraw-Hill. Reprinted with permission of The McGraw-Hill Companies.

Table 9-3	Traditional Model of Change
Step 1: Change in formal structure and responsibilities	
Step 2: Change in interpersonal relationships and processes	
Step 3: Change in individual attitudes and mentalities	

Source: From *Turning Points: Creating Strategic Change in Corporations* by Charles Fombrun, © 1992. McGraw-Hill. Reprinted with permission of The McGraw-Hill Companies.

vignette. The goal is to create cross-functional teams and task forces as well as provide more autonomy and leeway to managers down the hierarchy. By sharing successful strategies and practices throughout the firm, layers of management positions can be eliminated and outsourcing becomes a possibility for much of the work done in-house. Successful restructuring cuts costs, reduces the bureaucracy, and instills an entrepreneurial attitude among employees. Management Focus 9-2 discusses the creation of a new structure following the merger of Exxon and Mobil, two U.S. oil companies.

CENTRALIZED VERSUS DECENTRALIZED DECISION MAKING

In designing its organizational structure, a traditional question is whether decision making should be centralized or decentralized. **Centralization** and **decentralization** of decision making refers to where in the organizational hierarchy key decisions are made.

Table 9-4	Emerging Model of Change
Step 1: Change in individual attitudes and mentalities	
Step 2: Change in interpersonal relationships and processes	
Step 3: Change in formal structure and responsibilities	

Source: From *Turning Points: Creating Strategic Change in Corporations* by Charles Fombrun, © 1992. McGraw-Hill. Reprinted with permission of The McGraw-Hill Companies.

MANAGEMENT FOCUS 9-2

A NEW STRUCTURE AT EXXONMOBIL

In 1999, Exxon and Mobil merged to become the world's largest oil company with operations in nearly 200 countries. As the leaders of the two companies considered the organizational structure of ExxonMobil, they did not simply ask themselves which of the two companies' structures was the better choice. They started with a clean slate, asking: How can we best organize to strengthen the synergies created by the merger? What kind of structure can help give us the competitive edge to pull away from the pack?

ExxonMobil went global. Under the new structure, 11 business line companies oversee individual businesses worldwide. In addition, a twelfth company provides key centralized services for the other 11. Discarded were entities that managed multiple business lines such as oil production, refining, and marketing within one company. Thus, under the new corporate structure, for example, ExxonMobil Production Company produces oil and natural gas in the United States and oversees the production business in affiliates around the world. In a separate business, ExxonMobil Refining & Supply Company runs the firm's U.S. refineries and guides refinery operations in the affiliates. In short, ExxonMobil has entrusted its vast and diverse operations to a slate of business units with global responsibilities. Each company has responsibility for a focused portfolio of operations around the world, with a president at the helm and significant authority to run itself.

Each of the 11 companies receives key support from ExxonMobil Global Services Company.

Embracing a concept formerly employed by Mobil, this company centralizes certain staff activities in ExxonMobil. Global Services comprises three functions—Procurement, Information Systems, and Facilities—that can reap big advantages from worldwide centralization. Those advantages include, among others, global consistency in standards and practices, large-scale purchasing power, and the application of common platforms for electronic communications and data flow. Other staff functions, such as human resources, law, controller's, and public affairs, are structured to ensure that services are supplied globally.

Why change and not use Exxon or Mobil's proven model instead? Exxon and Mobil determined that neither company's structure was sufficiently "leading edge" to justify keeping it. And, in any case, differences between the two corporate structures made change inevitable. In addition, reorganizing at its inception would enable the merged company to realize its goal of saving $2.8 billion in annual synergies by year three of the merger.

Rene Dahan, a senior vice president of ExxonMobil, while praising the new structure noted that no structure was perfect. "We must anticipate any shortcomings and deal with them effectively when they arise. We also have to bear in mind that an organizational model, no matter how good, is never an end in itself. It's a tool—an important tool—that will help us achieve the goals of the business."

Source: Moore, Shelly. 1999. What's new and better about ExxonMobil? *The Lamp.* Fall, pp. 7–9.

Centralization suggests concentration of authority at the top of the organization, at headquarters, and in the parent firm. Decentralization distributes decision making throughout the organization, among the subsidiaries, and to managers further down in the hierarchy. Throughout corporate history, a natural tension characterizes the question as to whether to centralize and to decentralize. One set of forces calls for greater strategic direction from the top of the organization while the other set talks of the need to be close to the customer. In reality, the locus of decision making is scattered throughout the organization where some are reserved for top management, others left to managers in the

Table 9-5	General Levels of Centralization-Decentralization

COMPLETE DECENTRALIZATION

- *National Autonomy:* Each national unit functions on its own and no coordination exists with other national units.
- *Informal Cooperation:* Each subsidiary operates almost independently but they all share informally best practices, lessons learned, new ideas, and other information.
- *Coordinating Mechanisms:* Formal systems and committees bring subsidiary managers together to share key decisions and resolve regional issues.
- *Central Coordination:* Headquarters staff play active coordinating and supporting roles, framing the agenda for key decisions, consolidating and distributing information, and pushing forward integrated plans.
- *Central Direction:* Headquarters managers exercise clear line authority in directing subsidiary executives in specific functions or product areas.
- *Central Control:* All decision-making is centralized at headquarters.

CENTRALIZATION

Source: Blackwell, Norman, Jean-Pierre Bizet, Peter Child, and David Hensley. 1991. Shaping a pan-European organization. *The McKinsey Quarterly* 2, pp. 94–111.

field and low in the hierarchy, and yet others reserved for somewhere in between the two ends. Table 9-5 illustrates the six general levels of the centralization-decentralization continuum.

The sheer size of many modern firms make it virtually impossible to concentrate decision making at the top. Most experience a pressure to delegate decision making further down. Decentralization also allows decisons to be made by managers who are closest to customers, vendors, operations, and the rank-and-file workers. By empowering managers at the lower end of the hierarchy or in far-flung operations, decentralization makes the organization more flexible and nimble and increases the commitment of employees throughout the firm.

CHANGING ROLE OF HEADQUARTERS

Largely because of the emergence of information technology, the number of functions that can be handled further down the hierarchy has increased sharply. It has raised questions about the purpose and effectiveness of a head office. Indeed, a study reported that not a single company claimed to be able to systematically measure the value and effectiveness of what a head office did.[14] However, of the 89 large companies in the United States, Europe, and Asia that were studied, in those that were well managed, the head office was small: 2 percent or less of the total headcount. Financial service companies were more likely to have more than 2 percent of personnel at head office. Royal Bank of Canada had a corporate staff of 5,000 while the much larger Shell had a corporate staff numbering about 150.

During the 1990s, most companies reorganized their headquarters significantly. Certain functions such as business development, procurement, and the exchange of knowledge and best practice were strengthened. The use of information technology

[14]*Organizing for global competitiveness: The corporate headquarters design.* 1999. New York: The Conference Board.

pointed to a more lateral, team-based organization, with decision making being pushed downwards. This dilution of central authority is hard for many managers at headquarters to accept.

FACTORS DETERMINING CENTRALIZATION AND DECENTRALIZATION

Whether decision making is centralized or decentralized depends on several factors. Centralizaton occurs when a global strategy is pursued and in family owned or controlled firms. In contrast, a multidomestic strategy requires the firm to decentralize decision making to the subsidiaries.

Companies in certain industries tend toward centralized control (e.g., drug manufacturers because they require product consistency and high R&D outlays). In contrast, international accounting and law firms tend to be decentralized because of government regulations about qualifications and licenses of accountants and lawyers and because of the differences in accounting and auditing rules and legal practices across countries.

As discussed earlier, the various organizational structures enable more or less centralization depending on a specific design. The functional structure allows centralization by concentrating all aspects of a function in a single department. The geographical structure shifts decision making and responsibility to country and regional managers. The product structure centralizes decision making in the office of the product manager who is responsible for the worldwide production and marketing of a product line. In this case, knowledge of the product is more important than familiarity with the nuances of different markets. Subsidiaries with a wide range of products sold in a variety of markets tend to be more autonomous than affiliates with uniform products and markets. The transnational-network structure diffuses decision making throughout the organization.

The nature of a function also affects whether it would be centralized or decentralized. Manufacturing is generally more tightly controlled than marketing units. Finance tends to be centrally controlled in virtually all cases and so are accounting procedures, sales reporting, executive personnel policy, sources of supply, quality control, trademark and brand name, and advertising. Although R&D have usually been centralized at headquarters or at few locations with research results shared with the rest of the organization, as discussed in Chapter 8, many firms now also conduct R&D operations closer to the customers, at different locations, and in conjunction with subsidiary goals and needs. A high degree of interdependence among the units favors centralization (for example, an integrated petroleum company with its low level of product diversification).

Human resources functions including labor relations tend to be decentralized because of variations in working conditions, labor markets, and employment laws across countries. However, human resource departments exist at the headquarters not only to handle personnel issues there but also to address executive development for the entire organization, implement best practices across the firm, and foster uniform human resource policies and practices. Staff functions such as taxation, strategic planning, public relations, and legal services are found at headquarters, and yet some of these functions (public relations and legal services for instance) are also found at the subsidiary level to respond to local operating needs.

Companies with a few large subsidiaries in a region tend to be more decentralized than those with many small units. Distant subsidiaries tend to have greater autonomy, particularly if located in countries with unstable political conditions and stringent legal requirements. Joint ventures tend to have considerable local autonomy, which is not surprising because of the need to work with one or more partners. Newly acquired subsidiaries that continue to manufacture their old product lines under their former management tend to have greater autonomy. Over time though, as the new owners become familiar with the working of their new acquisition, it becomes more closely wedded to the rest of the firm.

In addition, several managerial dimensions impact on the decision to centralize or decentralize.

- The costliness of decisions
- The need for consistency throughout the organization
- The corporate culture and historical experience
- The availability of competent managers
- The size of the firm and the scale of its operations
- The multinationality of ownership
- The experience and confidence of managers with overseas operations
- The quality of the intrafirm communications systems
- The nature of the in-house planning process
- The stage the firm is in its life cycle

Absence of sufficient numbers of competent and experienced managers, especially with regard to overseas operations, and unfamiliarity with foreign operating environments, particularly those culturally and economically distant from the home country, tend to encourage firms to decentralize. Similarly, the lack of a cohesive and strong organizational culture coupled with inadequate communication systems, both technical and human, may compel the parent firm to appropriate to itself as many decisions as are necessary for the firm to succeed.

In this context, the experience of BMW, the German automaker's purchase of the ailing British company, Rover, is instructive. After acquiring Rover, the German parent treated it at arm's length, keeping it as a separate company. BMW was concerned that a heavy-handed overhaul of one of the world's oldest and proudest carmakers might arouse anti-German feelings within Rover's workforce and alienate the British public. Rover's managers had almost complete autonomy because it was thought important that Rover retained its distinct British identity as a unique selling point. However, since the acquisition in 1994, Rover reported mounting losses every year. Sales stagnated or declined. Although BMW had invested over $3.3 billion in Rover, productivity continued to lag behind BMW's German factories by as much as 30 percent. In late 1998, BMW realized that its decentralized approach was not working. To turn around Rover required more involvement of headquarters at all levels of management at Rover. As Bernd Pischetsrieder, chairman of BMW noted, *"We were too careful in trying to protect the company culture.... But we will now take our Rover colleagues more closely in hand."* Since then links between the two companies have been strengthened and BMW has adopted a much more interventionist approach with job cuts, flexible scheduling, and more German managers at Rover.[15] These efforts were, however, unsuc-

---

[15]Bowley, Graham. 1998, December 29. A hard-driving pilot for Rover. *Financial Times,* p. 9; Simonian, Haig. 1998, December 3. BMW reins in unruly charge. *Financial Times,* p. 20.

cessful and Rover was sold off. In contrast, when Deutsche Bank of Germany acquired Bankers Trust of the United States, it was made clear that the former would closely supervise the latter. Deutsche Bank folded the U.S. bank's management into its own centralized structure based on global product lines. Deutsche Bank's chairman pointed out, *"We don't believe in autonomy. We will continue with our centralized management, so there will be no autonomy."*[16]

Many Japanese firms centralize their decisions at headquarters, which means that the foreign subsidiary is less of a partner with the home office and is instead an implementor of headquarters plans, technologies, and ways of operating. As overseas operations grow in number and as business conditions become more competitive, a centralized organization and management style may overload the capability of the home office to run the foreign operations in an effective manner.

The extensive use of Japanese managers rather than host country nationals in key positions in the foreign subsidiary of Japanese firms has been criticized by host country residents. But the issue is complex. The Japanese managerial style is predicated on good communication and most non-Japanese do not speak or read the Japanese language, which hinders effective communication. Even host country nationals who are fairly proficient may still not really and fully understand Japanese culture. Conversely, Japanese managers do not fully understand local foreign cultures.

As has been noted, information technology has impacted the issue of centralization and decentralization. Using the Internet to sell products and services has changed some aspects of the organizational structure. For instance, the giant German media company, Bertelsmann, expected that in the year 2000, half of its revenues would come from electronic businesses ranging from book retailing to multimedia products. The firm expected some parts of its print-based activities—books, magazines, and journals—to shift to the Internet. The impact of the Internet on Bertelsmann's organizational structure as seen by Thomas Middlehoff, its chairman, is discussed in Management Focus 9-3. This case illustrates the centralization dimensions of information technology.

As should be apparent, the preceding issues represent only broad considerations for managers. The extent of centralization and decentralization varies vastly across firms, and even then the locus of decision making is not firmly set. As firms restructure, this locus shifts. The challenge, as always, is to make decisions that allow the firm to secure the benefits of globalization while addressing the disparate needs that diversity of customers engender.

CONTROL AND CONTROL MECHANISMS

Control refers to the devices created to ensure that managers are making decisions that conform to the firm's strategic goals. Control mechanisms enable all parts of the organization to be coordinated and to function in harmony. They keep upper-level managers informed on the direction and level of the firm's activities and alert them to deviations and shortfalls. Consequently, as appropriate, corrective actions can be taken.

The issue of control is complicated in an international firm. Because the geographic location of facilities and activities are worldwide, the firm may be organized differently

---

[16]Rhoads, Christopher. 1998, December 1. Deutsche Bank to give BT no autonomy. *The Wall Street Journal,* pp. A3, A4.

<MANAGEMENT FOCUS 9-3>

THE IMPACT OF THE INTERNET

Thomas Middlehoff thought that no part of his company would be untouched by the Internet. "The Internet will grow across our entire value chain," he said. As such, the development of a companywide approach to the Internet, and in particular, electronic commerce was now "strategically important." But implementing this strategy was difficult. Bertelsmann prided itself on a decentralized management culture arranged around 300 profit centers. Communication between these centers was sometimes close but also often nonexistent.

The effects of decentralization—which the company considered a cornerstone of its success by encouraging managers to act as entreprenuers—could easily be seen in information technology. Eighty different electronic data programs and 12 different e-mail systems operated across the company. Bertelsmann's various subscription busi-

nesses, with about 40 million members, still lacked links between the various units.

Mr. Middlehoff believed that one of the reasons Bertelsmann found it difficult at times to respond quickly to technology was its inability to fully exploit its resources. He conceded that "Amazon [Amazon.com, an Internet book distributor] has one great advantage over us—they have one database." However, he wanted to be careful not to promote more decentralization when developing a uniform strategy for the Internet. "Every part of the value chain will at some point follow its own Internet strategy—but at the moment we need coordination," he said.

One big obstacle to the creation of a common Internet strategy was the company's bureaucracy. Mr. Middlehoff lamented that "we discuss who is responsible, while other start-ups just get out and do it." He hopes these obstacles would soon lie in the past.

Source: Studemann, Frederick. 1999, January 13. Responding to the call of the Internet. *Financial Times Survey,* p. VII.

in different markets (e.g., licensing operations in one country, a joint venture in another, and a wholly owned operation in a third country), and performance standards do vary across the world. Also, currency differences require careful interpretation of foreign financial statements. Product pricing, working capital management, and sources of funds are all affected by currency fluctuations. In addition, managers in the foreign operations may have little control over many important decisions made by the parent firm, which in turn, affect how managerial performance is evaluated.

The organizational structure of the firm itself is a control mechanism. It is designed to ensure that organizational goals are effectively realized. Even heavily decentralized firms are held together by efficient control systems, an international executive committee, and by the energy and vision of presidents and chief executive officers. As the discussion on centralized versus decentralized decision making indicated, control is exercised by stipulating where key decisions in the organization are made. By establishing the locus of decision making, individual managers are held accountable for their performance. Profit centers are the typical means of assigning responsibilities and assessing performance.

CREATING EFFECTIVE CONTROL SYSTEMS

Creating effective control systems is a complex task because many variables have to be accounted for. For starters, the costs of controls should be measured against the benefits. Control systems should also be linked to the organizational goals, such as market share and return on investments, and be as objective as possible, which is measured by number of units produced or sold. To be complete in the sense that all key performance variables are evaluated, control systems need to provide timely information to managers. For instance, in 1995, Barings Bank of the United Kingdom learned—too late—that it had in effect gone bankrupt following losses suffered in illegal trading by its representative in Singapore. Control systems are only effective if they are accepted by the managers who must comply with them. Management Focus 9-4 discusses the unhappiness of some European managers with the control mechanisms introduced by the new U.S. owners of their firm.

TYPES OF CONTROLS

Two broad types of control tools available to managers are **direct control** and **indirect control.** In direct control, senior managers rely on face-to-face communication, frequent inspection tours, and carefully chosen personnel in key positions to monitor the firm's operations. Club Med, the French hospitality firm that operates paid-in-advance resorts, has a policy of regularly transferring most of its employees and managers among its resorts as a way of keeping its managers and products fresh. In indirect control, managers rely on frequent and detailed reports, including financial results and budgets, from subordinates to gauge how the firm is doing. Management Focus 9-4 discussed how Upjohn extended its reliance on regular reports to its new acquisitions. Indirect control is usually less expensive than direct control. In practice, managers use a combination of direct and indirect control mechanisms.

Control systems are also characterized as bureaucratic or cultural. **Bureaucratic controls** refer to rules and procedures, standard operating manuals, and top management-mandated requirements that outline individual responsibilities, reporting requirements, and explicit performance standards. These controls suggest a rather rigid dimension to management, which could become a hindrance in periods of fast change. However, they provide a systematic and standardized measure of performance and easy determination of deviations. Management Focus 9-5 discusses the control techniques at a large multinational company.

Cultural controls, often seen as the opposite of bureaucratic controls, rely more on corporate culture to induce conformity with the firm's goals and performance standards. The firm uses selection and training techniques to acculturate individuals into the firm's philosophies and values. A corporatewide ethos is fostered and managers are imbued with it to such an extent that they implicitly understand what is expected of them and they work accordingly in the pursuit of the organization's goals. Unilever, an Anglo-Dutch consumer goods company, fosters a common corporate culture among its many scattered and decentralized units by sending every year 300 to 400 managers from all over the world to its international management training college near London. The company also recruits the best college graduates—people who can work in teams and understand the value of cooperation and consensus—in the markets it operates, assigns managers on short- and long-term projects at head office or another subsidiary, and hosts annually two major conferences in Rotterdam and London, which are attended by 350 to 500 senior managers from all over the world.[17]

---

[17]Maljers, Floris A. 1992. Inside Unilever: The evolving transnational company. *Harvard Business Review.* September–October, pp. 46–51.

EUROPEANS CHAFE UNDER U.S. RULES

When Upjohn Company, a drug company based in Kalamazoo, Michigan, merged with Pharmacia AB of Sweden and introduced new control and reporting measures, it sparked resentment and resignations. International mergers require the meshing of two different organizational systems, which, as Upjohn's experience suggested, is not an easy task.

The first problem was where to locate the firm's headquarters. Pharmacia had previously acquired an Italian concern, Farmitalia, giving it centers in Stockholm and Milan. Most of Upjohn's operations were in Michigan. Under merger accounting rules, the newly formed company had to be registered in the United States, but the Swedes and Italians feared that a U.S.-headquartered company would wrest control from Europe. Jan Ekberg, who led Pharmacia at the time of the merger, proposed a compromise site. The company would maintain the Milan, Stockholm, and Kalamazoo centers but create a new headquarters in London. The structure, however, proved unwieldy. Executives in Italy and Sweden, accustomed to reporting to the local chiefs, now had to report to officials in London, who often had little knowledge of their daily operations. The extra layer of management slowed approvals, product launches, and staffing decisions. "London calling" became a joke phrase among executives, a reference to pestering by distant higher-ups. "Suddenly I had two bosses, and I had to explain everything twice," said Karl Olof Borg, who ran the research division in Milan. "London was like an artificial limb.'"

The biggest irritants were created by the new control systems. The Swedes were used to an open system, in which small teams were largely left on their own. Executives preferred getting the whole group's approval before making a big decision, not handing down orders: *Alla aer i baten,* "Getting everyone in the boat," as the Swedes called it. Upjohn, however, was used to commanding captains. After the merger, John Zabriskie, Upjohn's CEO, quickly divided the combined company into departments, all reporting to London. He put managers on a tight leash, requiring frequent reports, budgets, and staffing updates. The Swedes bristled at having to write detailed monthly reports as demanded by the Americans.

Dr. Borg in Milan was used to describing his research through brief presentations a couple of times a year; now he had to file detailed monthly reports. "I was spending hours and hours on these reports, which no one could possibly read," Dr. Borg says. "Eventually I just stopped writing them in such a detailed way. It was all just extra process." He left the company.

The head of the Stockholm office had to tell London executives where he was each week. At Pharmacia, his reports had been monthly, if that. One manager was surprised to find Dr. Zabriskie appearing at a meeting to discuss ads that were running in small markets in Europe. During one tense meeting, Dr. Zabriskie overruled a top development executive on the pricing of a generic drug.

Italy posed another problem. In Kalamazoo, the Italian business center came to be referred to as "Fortress Milan" because of its impenetrable fiscal controls and management defense mechanisms. Before the merger, Pharmacia itself had been having a hard time integrating its Italian acquisition. Dr. Borg said he often had to leave meetings "just so the Italians would speak out honestly." To make them feel more comfortable, he went out of his way to have lunch with lower-level employees or even play tennis with them, an unheard-of move at most Italian businesses. The Italians also placed a higher value on their families—leaving work for sick relatives or to care for children—which the Swedes mistook for lack of company loyalty, Dr. Borg said.

Compounding the problems were difficulties in uniting the separate computer technologies of the two firms. Shortcomings in the computer systems made it harder to track product developments and financial performance of its units. The company was late to realize that a year-earlier gain from currency hedging wasn't going to be repeated again.

As a consequence of all these, the costs of merger rose to $600 million, $200 million more than originally estimated. Several top R&D people, at odds with senior executives, departed. With stock prices declining, the chief executive, Dr. Zabriskie resigned citing "personal reasons."

Source: Frank, Robert, and Thomas Burton. 1997, February 4. Cross-border merger results in headaches for a drug company. *The Wall Street Journal,* pp. A1, 13.

In a traditional society, such as China, kinship serves as a control mechanism, especially for family-owned firms, where assets are subdivided and reallocated to family members through guanxi ownership. Guanxi networks and guanxi building lead to access to capital, markets, information, and other inputs, and the creation of business organizations. Although these organizations sometimes employ workers and managers who are not part of the guanxi, key decision making, responsibility, and autonomy are primarily reserved for those who are part of the "relationship" based on the existing trust within the guanxi. Thus, shared values provide one means of exercising control.

The nature of control mechanisms differs across firms, industries, and countries. As would be expected, in integrated firms and those with highly interdependent components, strict controls are usually in effect. Financial institutions, often because of regulatory requirements, have detailed bureaucratic controls and stringent record-keeping requirements. Firms new to internationalization are more likely to institute demanding controls whereas more experienced international firms may rely more on marketing and financial controls. Manufacturing firms invariably resort to machine controls to keep track of production goals, defect rates, quality control, and raw material usage.

Studies show that U.S. multinational firms are more likely to rely on bureaucratic controls and performance data than European firms who tend often to use cultural controls and direct controls to manage their overseas subsidiaries.[18] Headquarters at U.S. firms are heavily staffed with people assigned to information collecting, processing, comparing, and generating and preparing reports and budgets. European firms, in turn, need a large pool of capable managers who can accept overseas assignments. A study of manufacturing firms in Japan and the United States found that U.S. managers, compared to their Japanese counterparts, tended to use communication and coordination more extensively, build in greater slack in the budget, use budgets as a control tool, and evaluate performance over the short run.[19] These differences are attributable partly to the strong sense of individualism in the United States and the pronounced group orientation in Japan. Other studies showed that U.S. companies report to headquarters more frequently than do their Japanese and European counterparts, who seem to prefer "management by exception." They are also more likely to hold regular management meetings on a regional or worldwide basis and to rely much more on personal visits between the head of the subsidiary and a superior at headquarters.

COMMUNICATION SYSTEMS

To implement the control mechanisms, communication systems need to be in place. More and more international firms are using English as the their lingua franca. Even where firms use teams with members from diverse linguistic backgrounds such as ABB, English is usually the preferred language. For example, the language used at Alstom, the Anglo-French electrical engineering company, was English.[20] Six months after the company was formed by GEC of the United Kingdom and Alcatel of France, it ended its

---

[18]Egelhoff, William G. 1984. Patterns of control in U.S., U.K., and European multinational corporations. *Journal of International Business Studies.* Fall, pp. 76–90.

[19]Ueno, Susumo, and Uma Sekaran. 1992. The influence of culture on budget control practices in the U.S.A. and Japan: An empirical study. *Journal of International Business Studies* 23(Winter), pp. 659–674.

[20]Marsh, Peter. 1998, November 30. Language poser resolved. *Financial Times Survey*, p. III.

CONTROL TECHNIQUES
AT ASEA BROWN BOVERI (ABB)

ABB's organization is flat, with responsibility delegated to as low a level as possible. The group comprises 1,300 companies, each having an average of 200 employees, and 4,500 profit centers with some 50 individuals each. As Percy Barnevik, the president and CEO of the company said, "The only way to structure a complex, global organization is to make it as simple and local as possible . . . all of our operations must function as closely as possible to stand-alone operations. Our managers need well-defined sets of responsibilities, clear accountability, and maximum degrees of freedom to execute."

But despite extensive decentralization, a sense of general direction and leadership emanates from the center, especially from Mr. Barnevik himself. He said, "Decentralization does not mean abdication . . . you still have to know what is going on." Besides corporate strategy, the review and approval of unit plans and operations, and the president and CEO's forceful leadership style, some of the more centralized aspects include the following:

- A common reporting system for every business area and geographic region. A management information system collects performance data on all profit centers and compares it with budget and forecast information.

- A constant effort to communicate the group's central values. Mr. Barnevik and his colleagues at headquarters travel frequently and meet thousands of employees every year. Corporate values are also communicated through various documentation including a booklet, Selected ABB Policies, which describes key aspects of the corporate culture such as openness to foreign cultures, ethics, and individual responsibility and initiative.

- An annual three-day seminar for the top 400 line and staff executives in the group, which provides both information and an opportunity for personal networking.

- Groupwide use of the name ABB. Thus, new acquisitions, such as that of Combustion Engineering, are renamed ABB Combustion Engineering.

- The use of English as the official company language. The heads of major countries and regions, business areas, and corporate headquarters functions must be able to communicate in English.

The company relies heavily on budgets and plans to execute its strategy. Mr. Barnevik noted, "We have the glue of transparent, centralized reporting through a management information system called ABACUS. Every month, ABACUS collects performance data on our 4,500 profit centers and compares performance with budgets and forecasts. The data are collected in local currencies but translated into U.S. dollars to allow for analysis across borders. The system also allows you to work the data. You can aggregate and disaggregate results by business segments, countries, and companies within countries.

"We look for early signs that businesses are becoming more or less healthy. On the tenth of every month, for example, I get a binder with information on about 500 different operations—the 50 business areas, all the major countries, and the key companies in key countries. I look at several parameters—new orders, invoicing, margins, cash flows—around the world and in various business segments. Then I stop to study trends that catch my eye."

Source: Taylor, William. 1991. The logic of global business: An interview with ABB's Percy Barnevik. *Harvard Business Review.* March–April.

experiment in "language sharing"—maintaining both French and English as its official languages. It quickly became evident that the complexities of putting all company literature in both languages easily outweighed any benefits. The company switched to English even though the headquarters were in Paris and 38 percent of its 110,000 employees were in France as opposed to just 17 percent in the United Kingdom. Of its top 300 managers, 130 were French, 80 British, and 40 German while the remaining 50 came from 10 other countries. At the level of the executive board, 7 of the 11 members were French, the rest British.

Technological advancements in communication (e.g., telephone, facsimile, e-mail, Internet, Intranet, and teleconferencing) and transportation (e.g., faster air travel, overnight courier services, lower costs) have undoubtedly made it easier for head office and subsidiary managers to exchange more information and meet more frequently. Centralized firms, however, complain about the time it takes to get information from the subsidiaries and the tendency of managers in the subsidiary to make decisions on their own. An additional complication is that managers sent from headquarters end up adopting the local point of view.

Indeed, communication between the parent and the subsidiaries is typically better in quality (clarity, accuracy, and timeliness) where less control is exercised by headquarters personnel over subsidiary operations and where top management is more likely to stand by decisions made by the subsidiary that deviates from established norms. Also, greater teamwork between headquarters and subsidiary managers contributes to the quality of communications. In addition, where firms have greater experience in international markets or where managers have experience in working overseas, communication tends to be better. Because effective communication is the key to control, it is important to have good quality communication flows in the firm. Schlumberger, a U.S. company specializing in providing oil field services and high-tech measurement devices, has more than 2,000 offices in 100 countries. It maintains communication links with all its offices through the Internet and creates teams of workers located at various sites to address operational problems. Consequently, it can tap into the experience and insights of its employees anywhere while reducing the need for time-consuming and expensive business travel.

How do firms enforce control? Usually, the headquarters can enforce its control mechanisms through legal pressure, business pressure, persuasion, and appealing to mutual benefit. Legal pressure operates when the parent firm has a legal claim through guarantee, contract, financial obligation, or ownership. Even then, the pressure may not be effective if important political considerations are involved or the subsidiary is nominally dependent on the parent for human, financial, technological, and managerial resources. Control is also exercised by placing home country nationals in key positions in the subsidiary. Business pressure can be generated when the affiliate is dependent on the parent for sales, supply, management, or finance. Where the subsidiary is totally autonomous, the parent may appeal to the local management by emphasizing group loyalty. Persuasion is effective only if the subsidiary feels it is in its interest to be persuaded. The control structure is defective and likely to collapse if the parent is unable to emphasize the mutual benefit to both parties that comes from adhering to the company's strategy. Thus, in reality, considerable flexibility and mutually acceptable policies are needed for the control procedures to succeed.

REINTRODUCING CONTROL

Too much decentralization and autonomy can lead to substantially weakening the influence of headquarters on the functioning of the firm's subsidiaries. A set of administrative mechanisms can be used by headquarters to reassert its control over the subsidiaries, including the following:

- Information management systems that provide data relevant to the overall performance of the firm and its constituent parts
- Human resource management programs that appoint and reward managers who have an organization-wide, rather than a narrower subsidiary perspective
- Conflict resolution tools to resolve disputes inherent in the process of reestablishing headquarters control

Information management mechanisms, for instance, allow headquarters to collect and present data in numerous ways and to compare one subsidiary with another. Through appropriate packaging, the data can be used to show a subsidiary in a poor or good light. Because access to information and its selective use provides power within the organization, the manner in which the information management mechanisms are used enables headquarters to justify the exercise of control over the subsidiary.

Similarly, managers appointed to lead the subsidiaries could be individuals with pronounced administrative rather than entrepreneurial skills. Human resource programs would socialize managers in the ways of the headquarters and career rewards would go to those who advance the agenda of the headquarters and not just that of the subsidiary.

Finally, various committees, preferably headed by skillful and senior executives, provide a forum to introduce new proposals, a method to implement them, and a way to settle differences. Who is selected to staff the committee sends a more powerful signal to the subsidiary about the importance and role of the committee than the establishment of the committee as such.

In deciding which mix of mechanisms to use and when, managers at headquarters must consider the characteristics of these mechanisms. Some mechanisms can be easily established and discarded while others have a much longer time frame. Task forces, by definition, have a specific purpose and are temporary. In contrast, career paths of managers take years to develop and the results are available only at an indeterminate future date. Similarly, some mechanisms are more effective than others. The budgeting process has both a strong and symbolic effect, but not so coordination committees. In addition, the timing of the use of the mechanisms is important. Sudden changes in resource allocation procedures may hurt the subsidiary and thus the firm. It should also be recognized that all mechanisms may not be available to managers in all firms or in all settings. The history of the firm and the current organizational culture are crucial determinants.

In companies where these control systems are instituted, the first step is usually the appointment of a key executive—a capable and respected individual—to a new position with a broad mandate to improve performance through the coordination of subsidiary activities. The driving logic behind such coordination is usually cost reduction through eliminating duplication of activities and securing scale economies. This stage is followed by the creation of teams and other coordinating councils to enable the consideration of strategic issues from a global rather than a regional perspective. Only late in the transition process, which might take several years, would changes in the authority of managers and allocation of resources occur.

CONCLUSIONS

This chapter discussed a wide variety of organizational structures and explored the various control mechanisms used by managers to successfully run far-flung operations. New forms of structures have been developed to enable firms to compete in a more dynamic, deregulated, and turbulent global environment. These structures have changed the centralization-decentralization decision-making locus, and they increasingly rely on information technology for control purposes.

Given the wide variety of organizational designs and the many variables determining them, certain conclusions can be reached. For one, organizing is an important management task that is linked closely to strategy. Secondly, successful firms set challenging goals for their managers—goals that the structure should be able to deliver. Thirdly, the need for a strong organizational culture gains prominence as the firm extends itself and becomes differentiated because of the need to respond to regional requirements. Corporate culture serves as the tool for control especially when bureaucratic controls are not effective. And finally, successful operations require that firms have competent and globally experienced managers—individuals who are not only technically proficient but can function in complex environments that are culturally different. The managerial challenge is to create structures that are flexible and speedy, to encourage motivation and creativity, and at the same time ensure efficiency and control.

OPENING VIGNETTE EPILOGUE

The new global structure had already yielded some positive gains. In 1997, the company introduced an extension of its Pantene shampoo line. The advertising campaign for the product was almost entirely visual, with images of beautiful women and their lustrous hair, and had a limited script. The visual emphasis meant the campaign was easily translated and shipped to P&G's overseas markets without the usual months of testing and adapting. The result: P&G was able to introduce the brand extension into 14 countries in six months, versus the two years it took to get the original shampoo into stores abroad. The company hoped to reproduce the Pantene success with its other products under its new structure.[21]

[21]P&G's hottest new product: P&G. *Business Week.* October 5, 1998, pp. 92, 96.

Key Terms

- organizational structure
- organization chart
- information technology
- business unit
- profit center
- functional structure
- international division structure
- product structure
- geographical structure
- mixed or hybrid structure
- matrix organization
- front-end/back-end structure
- process structure
- temporary network
- transnational networked structure
- centralization
- decentralization
- control
- direct control
- indirect control
- bureaucratic control
- cultural control

Discussion Questions

1. Select any multinational firm and obtain a copy of its current organizational chart and one that is at least 10 years old. Identify any differences between the two. Explain the reasons for any changes or lack of changes.

2. A U.S. bank opened a branch in London to provide credit card services to residents in that country. Identify and explain a set of control mechanisms that the head office in the United States should institute to ensure that the London branch performs in accordance with the bank's objectives of being the number one credit card issuer in the United Kingdom in three years. Also explain how the control mechanisms will be enforced.

3. Explain the conditions under which the matrix structure works best. Why is it generally difficult for companies to work with this structure?

4. Compare and contrast the geographic, product, and functional structures. Why would managers prefer one structure over another?

5. Explain how information technology is impacting organizational structure, locus of decision making, and control in international firms.

6. As foreign sales grow, the export department in a firm tends to disappear. Explain.

Writing Assignment

A small firm that manufactures running hats has been experiencing a steady increase in overseas orders necessitating extra work and specialized attention on the part of the marketing department. Recently, inquiries had been fielded from foreign firms who were interested in licensing agreements to make and sell the hats abroad. Write a two-page memorandum justifying the creation of an international department in the organization to handle all these foreign inquiries and opportunities. Explain how such a department will fit in with the rest of the organization.

Internet Exercise

Identify a set of companies in a particular industry (e.g., Ericsson, Nokia, and Motorola in the mobile telephony industry). Use the Internet to obtain information about the organizational structure of each of these companies. Compare and critically evaluate the information provided by the companies on their Web sites.

Internet Resources

Most firms that have a Web site post press releases there, which include information about organizational changes that the firm may have announced. Reading the business papers or magazines informs the reader about organizational changes in a firm. To learn more about these changes directly from the firm, access the firm's Web page. For instance, websites such as *www.ericsson.com, www.abb.com, www.PG.com,* and *www.nokia.com* give the reader access to corporate information about the organizational structures of Ericsson, Asea Brown Boveri, Procter & Gamble, and Nokia, respectively. Where the Web site of the company is unknown, find it by using a search engine such as Yahoo! at *www.yahoo.com/Business_and_Economy/Companies/.*

Case 9–1 THE ROYAL DUTCH/SHELL GROUP OF COMPANIES

Since taking over as chairman of the Royal Dutch/Shell Group in July 1998, Mark Moody-Stuart, a geologist by training and a lifelong Shell employee, had literally shaken up the giant Anglo-Dutch oil company by introducing radical changes in how the firm was organized and decisions made. The challenge for Mr. Moody-Stuart was to institutionalize the changes in a 92-year-old company where autonomy among the various divisions was highly treasured, by making tough and tradition-breaking decisions, at a time when, despite disappointing financial results, the company was not in a financial crisis.

BRIEF HISTORY

The Royal Dutch/Shell Group of Companies (or Group) grew out of an alliance made in 1907 between Royal Dutch Petroleum Company of the Netherlands and The Shell Transport and Trading Company Limited of the United Kingdom, by which the two companies agreed to merge their interests while maintaining their separate identities. This arrangement had continued till today with Royal Dutch Petroleum owning 60 percent of the Group and Shell Transport and Trading holding the rest. As parent companies, Royal Dutch Petroleum and Shell Transport and Trading did not engage in operational activities. They were public companies, one headquartered in the Netherlands, the other in the United Kingdom, whose shares were traded internationally. Each had its own board of directors and Mr. Moody-Stuart, before becoming chairman of the Group, was chairman of Shell Transport and Trading.

The two parent companies directly or indirectly owned the shares in the Group. The Group's several hundred operating companies—all separate legal entities—were engaged in various aspects of oil and natural gas, coal, chemicals, metals, and other businesses. However, oil and gas accounted for nearly 90 percent of the Group's sales. It was among the world's largest oil company with operations in more than 100 countries.

As with other leading international integrated oil companies, the operations of the Group had been always on a large scale. On average, annual capital investment topped $11 billion in recent years. The Group did not hesitate to invest in huge projects throughout the world and when any project faced difficulties, the attitude was "to throw money at a problem until it was fixed."

BUSINESS ENVIRONMENT

The petroleum industry was going through a period of great change in the 1990s. Crude oil prices had fallen steeply and so had oil company earnings in all three major businesses in the industry—exploration and production, refining and marketing, and petrochemicals. Supply of oil and petroleum products exceeded demand.

The regulatory environment was also changing. European governments started privatizing oil companies, with British Petroleum as the first. New and nimble competitors were emerging. Consolidation in the industry was accelerating. Exxon and Mobil were engaged in merger discussions, which had been preceded by the takeover of Amoco by British Petroleum. Total Fina was poised to take over its French rival Elf Aquitaine. The danger was that the Group would no longer be number one in the industry. Other oil companies around the world were seeking alliances and acquisitions.

The Group was slow to react to the changes in the business environment and make the appropriate changes. It continued to increase capital spending and refused to shut down poorly performing operating companies. Managers failed to meet production goals and return on capital targets. Profits fell and shareholders started unloading their holdings. The Group's shares plunged 30 percent in 1998, wiping $43 billion off the company's market capitalization.

ORGANIZATIONAL STRUCTURE

The basic business unit of the Group was the local operating company for which the local management team assumed full accountability. A company general manager headed the management committee of the local company, which might include managers of supply, distribution, production, marketing, chemicals, finance, legal, and personnel. These individuals were frequently a mix of local nationals and Shell's international cadre.

The Group was managed by a committee of managing directors. In 1999, this committee comprised three British members and two Dutch members. The committee considered, developed, and decided upon overall objectives and long-term plans to be recommended to operating companies. Decisions were made on a consensus basis. The chair of the Group lacked decisive executive authority.

The Group did not exist as a legal entity and had never had a headquarters or board of management. Headquarters alternated between The Hague and London depending on where the chairperson of the Group came from—Royal Dutch Petroleum or Shell Transport and Trading. Attempts over the years to create a strong chief executive had failed. The boards of the two parent companies met in "conference" to decide on the future of the Group. On retirement, the executive chairs of the two companies assumed nonexecutive directorships on their respective boards ensuring continuity of views, policies, and practices. The operating companies enjoyed almost complete autonomy. Country managers possessed considerable clout. Most operating decisions were decentralized to the level of the operating companies. One executive described the relationship between the Group and its operating companies as follows: "It's like a federal system, so at times for an operating company, it's like Texas against Washington [D.C.]." The central coordination and integration of the Group's activities were ensured through a complex matrix of geographic regions, business sectors, and functions.

The matrix structure lengthened and complicated the Group's decision-making processes. An executive noted, "We are sensitive to everything and this generally results in our moving too slowly." In 1995, Mr. Moody-Stuart's predecessor scrapped the matrix structure and replaced it with a product structure. The operating companies were organized into five divisions—exploration and production, oil products, gas, coal, chemicals and renewables—that reported to one of the five managing directors of the Group.

The previous organizational structure worked until the mid-1990s. With U.S. companies dominating the giant oil fields of West Asia, the Group went elsewhere to find oil, developed a vast and efficient distribution organization, and acquired a pioneering stake in the fast-growing natural gas business. When nationalistic governments in West Asia expropriated foreign oil companies in the 1970s, the Group escaped unscathed even as many of its competitors were rudely jolted. Furthermore, in an age when communications were poor, the Group's system of decentralization and giving autonomy to country managers worked smoothly. The strong national operating companies that identified closely with the countries in which they did business was viewed as one of the Group's main attributes.

WEAKNESSES OF THE STRUCTURE

By the time Mr. Moody-Stuart took over, the problems with the Group were plainly visible. Over the years, country managers and operating companies had established fiefdoms and resisted directives from the top. The national orientation of the operating companies also made it more difficult for the Group to compete as markets became more regional and global in character, especially in refined oil products and chemicals.

The strong national companies also contributed to a chronic misallocation of capital within the Group. National "barons" had always demanded their share of the capital budget but until recently, the collegial committee of managing directors had been unable to resist their demands. The committee also dithered over difficult decisions on whether to sell or close losing operations. Mr. Moody-Stuart admitted that, "Too often in the past we've said let's spend a bit more time and a bit more capital to fix this business." But in too many cases that fix never occurred.

Two events in recent years drew negative attention to the Group and highlighted the problems of giving unfettered freedom to the various operational units. One was the furor over the proposed destruction by one of its British operating companies of an outdated offshore oil rig, the *Brent Spar,* by sinking it in the North Sea. The proposal was abandoned following protests throughout the United Kingdom and other countries in Western Europe. The second was a reported collusion between an operating company and a Nigerian military dictatorship to extract oil without concern for environmental degradation and the quality of life for the people in the drilling area.

With the Group's performance trailing those of archrivals Exxon and British Petroleum, pressure mounted to streamline the executive structure. One outside observer argued that the collegiate management system had "served Shell (the Group) well in the past, but today had become part of the problem—reducing accountability, blurring responsibility, and increasing costs."

RESTRUCTURING

Although Mr. Moody-Stuart recognized the problems faced by the Group and plunged into a program of restructuring, few would have thought that a Shell insider would now be a reformer. He had a doctorate in geology from Cambridge University. The birthplaces of his children—Netherlands, Brunei, Australia—charted the postings of an oil man. A strong religious ethic pervaded his entire family. One brother ran Transparency International, an anticorruption advocacy group. He admitted that the Group had not been as clear as he would have liked on human rights.

Confounding expectations that he would be "Mr. Continuity," Mr. Moody-Stuart announced a set of steps in December 1998, which would drastically restructure the organization. Acknowledging concern over the Group's laborious process of decision making by consensus and committee and the absence of one powerful chief executive, he said, "We have entered a new period where executive decisions have to be made rapidly and business accountability must be absolutely clear." The main elements of his plan included the following:

- End decades of consistently ill-disciplined capital allocation
- Improve the Group's performance by focusing more on short-term improvement in return on average capital employed
- Sell poorly performing assets in the chemicals division
- Reduce budget allocations for new exploration and production
- Exercise greater control over operating companies
- Appoint chief executives for each of the Group's five major divisions
- Maintain the existing dividend policy

Mr. Moody-Stuart's plans and accompanying actions drew approval from external analysts. He began to demand accountability from his managers. Future ˌupstream projects would have to be fully profitable with average oil prices of $14 a barrel and must be able to cover their costs at $10 a barrel or less. He shut down some head offices in Europe, began hiring outside managers, and appointed chief executives to head the five major divisions. He sold off 40 percent of the Group's chemical business and cut back capital spending by a third. He stripped Shell Oil of the United States (one of the largest operating companies) of its

freedom over investment decisions. He also confirmed that "there will be no sacred cows" as the Group restructured. "If we see things that get in the way, whether they are individuals or fundamental structures, we'll change it." The initial results seemed positive: profits were looking up and so was the stock price.

The idea of creating a U.S.-style chief executive officer with decisive powers was yet to gain ground. One concern was that doing so would upset the delicate balance between the British and Dutch arms of the firm. However, the dilution of consensual decision making would increase the power of the chair of the five-person committee of managing directors.

THE FUTURE

While the restructuring plans were welcomed by analysts and investors, doubts remained as to whether the cooperative nature of the Group's management, which was so embedded in the organization's culture, could altogether disappear. A radical change in the autonomy of the operating companies might trigger opposition within the organization. For instance, in 1985, Shell Oil of the United States had to give up its separate listing on the New York Stock Exchange. That move triggered widespread resentment among many Shell Oil employees, some of whom filed a class action suit to try to stop the parent company from making the U.S. operation a wholly owned subsidiary. The resentment still lingered, and it was not uncommon to hear employees openly criticize the rest of the Group.

Mr. Moody-Stuart's desire to take the best of the Group's old structure and culture (he had called the independent national character of the operating companies "a pearl beyond price") and blend it with a new, more commercially savvy and accountable core will require making tough decisions. "There is an obsession [among outsiders] about our structure," he said. "But the important issues are behavior and action." That may be so but the Group now had to prove that the structure was not too limiting.

QUESTIONS

1. Will Mr. Moody-Stuart's restructuring plan succeed? Why or why not?
2. What are the difficulties that may arise in fully implementing the plan? How should they be anticipated, prepared for, and overcome?
3. Describe the changing business environment in which the Royal Dutch/Shell Group of Companies currently operate.

4. If the ownership structure of the Group was changed, would it improve the firm's performance? Why or why not?
5. The Group is enormously successful—it is the largest oil company in the world, it is profitable, it has cash reserves exceeding $11 billion. Why, therefore, does it need restructuring?

References

Ackenhusen, Mary, Daniel Muzyka, and Neil Churchill. 1996. Restructuring 3M for an integrated Europe: Part one—Initiating the change. *European Management Journal* 14(2), pp. 21–35.

Ackenhusen, Mary, Daniel Muzyka, and Neil Churchill. 1996. Restructuring 3M for an integrated Europe: Part two—Implementing the change. *European Management Journal* 14(3), pp. 151–158.

Aharoni, Yair. 1996. The organization of global service MNEs. *International Studies of Management & Organization* 26(2), pp. 6–23.

Bowman, Edward, and Bruce Kogut. 1995. *Redesigning the firm.* New York: Oxford University Press.

Carroll, Glenn, and Michael Hannan, eds. 1995. *Organizations in industry—Strategy, structure, and selection.* New York: Oxford University Press.

Doz, Yves L., and C. K. Prahalad. 1991. Headquarters influence and strategic control in MNCs. *Sloan Management Review.*

Fombrun, Charles. 1992. *Turning points: Creating strategic change in corporations.* New York: McGraw Hill.

Hirschhorn, Larry, and Thomas Gilmore. 1992. The new boundaries of the "boundaryless" company. *Harvard Business Review.* May–June, pp. 104–115.

Kramer, Robert J. 1996. *Organizing for global competitiveness: The European regional design.* New York: The Conference Board.

10
HUMAN RESOURCE MANAGEMENT

❧

OPENING VIGNETTE

In the fall of 1996, Bandag, America's leading maker of retread tires for trucks and buses, tapped Gerald Borenstein to join its Hong Kong office. For Mr. Borenstein, transferring to Hong Kong meant giving up living in a small town in Iowa for the excitement of Asia and exchanging a mid-level finance job for a high-visibility post in a fast-growing market. "The company was saying, 'We are going to go global,' and I said, 'I want to play,' " said Mr. Borenstein.

Mr. Borenstein had joined Bandag in 1989 as an accountant and had advanced to the rank of a plant comptroller. With the company projecting that overseas sales would one day contribute 60 percent of total revenues from the current 35 percent, he decided to position himself for an overseas management job by enrolling in 1993 in a company-paid executive MBA program.

As part of his MBA program, Mr. Borenstein traveled to Hong Kong and Shanghai, where he visited a rubber plant. He wrote a three-page paper suggesting ways in which U.S. retread tire companies could expand into China. Impressed, his boss sent it to corporate headquarters. There, his ideas fitted with other efforts under way to enter the China market. In 1996, Mr. Borenstein was called to headquarters to explore business opportunities in China. After a year of commuting to China, he produced a 100-page report outlining a five-year plan under which Bandag could become the dominant player there. He lobbied for an Asian posting and when Bandag decided to expand into China, he was sent in as the deputy to the company's director in Hong Kong. Don Chester, then international vice president, offered Mr. Borenstein no guarantees as to what his next assignment would be. However, the company's expectation was that if he did well, he might get another overseas posting.

Although Mr. Borenstein's salary did not increase, the Hong Kong appointment offered him a higher profile. "I was going to do finance, strategic thinking. It was a career move, a chance to be at front lines, to create something new and exciting in virgin territory," he said. The job also came with perquisites typical for expatriate executives: a large apartment on a hill overlooking Hong Kong, a full-time housekeeper, and private school for his two children, aged three and six.

Mr. Borenstein moved to Hong Kong in January 1997. He traveled across Asia, hired new employees, and prepared for expansion in Southeast Asia.

(continued)

Opening Vignette (*continued*)

Sales for the first half of 1997 exceeded expectations in China, Indonesia, and South Korea. Mr. Borenstein met regularly and exchanged electronic mail with top corporate officers; the company's CEO visited Hong Kong and attended his briefings back at headquarters. As Mr. Borenstein said, "Things were booming in Asia."

Things changed suddenly. In the summer of 1997, the currency in Thailand and Indonesia collapsed. Soon, throughout the region, economic growth and sales prospects stalled. Profits vanished. At home, Bandag faced increased competition from other tire companies. Its stock price fell to $28 from $54. About the same time, Mr. Chester, the man who had sent Mr. Borenstein to China, retired, and several other executives that he knew were reassigned.

As the Asian crisis spread, so did the pressure to cut costs. Mr. Borenstein, however, believed that the company needed to be fully prepared for the time when the Chinese economy was ready to take off, and kept on spending on new hires and offices.

The successful operation of a business enterprise depends to a great extent on the quality of its managers. Hiring, developing, and placing qualified and competent executives in key positions throughout the organization are important tasks for the human resource department as well as top management. The caliber of the managers to fashion and implement the firm's strategy is a vital source of sustainable competitive advantage because other factors of production such as capital and machinery can be more easily duplicated around the world. As the international scope of business grows, firms recognize the need to employ globally savvy managers. In response, firms develop new policies and standards on recruitment, training, performance evaluation, and compensation so that the right managers are available at the right place at the right time. At the same time, firms need to recognize the restraints imposed by national laws, exchange rates, cultural differences, economic reality, and social changes. This chapter discusses the human resource issues connected with the employment of managers and executives and how international firms deal with the challenge of preparing managers for overseas assignments.

ROLE OF THE HUMAN RESOURCE DEPARTMENT

Broadly defined, **international human resource management** is the process of procuring, allocating, and effectively utilizing human resources in an international firm. Unlike human resource management in the domestic setting, international human resource management requires a much broader perspective, such as determining salary levels and income tax rates in a variety of countries. It also encompasses a wider range of activities, such as organizing training programs to increase cultural adaptation or helping spouses find jobs in a foreign location, and a higher degree of uncertainty, such as a manager's inability to perform effectively overseas or change in government rules regarding work permits for foreigners. Table 10-1 identifies some of the major issues in international human resource management.

The nature and type of the human resource function is dependent on the internationalization stage of the firm and whether it has adopted a multidomestic or a global strategy. For instance, a firm that exports to a foreign distributor may need little, if any, change to its human resource activities. Increasing exports may require sending sales, service, or maintenance people to the foreign markets either on short-term or long-term assignments. Should the firm enter into a joint venture arrangement with a company in a foreign country, it may require assigning managers at various levels to work in the joint venture's operations. If the firm has a multidomestic strategy, the parent or headquarters would leave much of the human resource function to be determined and implemented at the level of the subsidiary. A global strategy would require a considerable alteration in the role of the human resource department at headquarters where a large number of human resource issues (recruitment and assignment of managers, compensation, performance appraisal, employment law, among others) would assume critical importance.

Given the strategic continuum between multidomesticity and globalization, firms are moving to a two-tier structure of the human resource function. The decentralized multidomestic dimension acknowledges the need for human resource functions to accommodate and adapt to practices in the host country environment. The centralized global strategy, in contrast, seeks to integrate human resource management with overall corporate strategy and to ensure a consistent and economically viable approach across national borders. Where foreign operations are closely controlled by the parent, the influence of head office personnel practices would be markedly felt in the subsidiary.

Coca-Cola Company, a U.S.-based producer, packager, and distributor of juices and soft drinks, illustrates the role of human resources in an international firm.[1] The company is managed through 25 operating divisions making up six regional groups. Even though the company sells the same products in most countries, they are distributed in different ways depending on how business is done in individual countries. Because of this diversity, the role of the global human resource managers is to maintain a link between the divisions and the corporation. The human resource department supports this role and enables businesses to act locally while thinking globally. Each of the operating divisions has a director of human resources, as does each of the six groups. They are

Table 10-1	Key International Human Resource Management Issues (in descending order of importance)

- Finding candidates for international assignments
- Coordination of a manager's assignments between line managers and human resources
- Manager's adjustment to working in different cultures
- Spouse's career
- Expatriate participation in training
- Decentralized human resource programs
- Resistance to relocation

Source: Global Relocation Trends 1996 Survey Report. Windham International, New York City.

---

[1]Anfuso, Dawn. 1994. HR unites the world of Coca-Cola. *Personnel Journal.* November, pp. 112–121.

supported by human resources in Atlanta, but work fairly autonomously. The Atlanta office functions as custodian for international equity, by making decisons for such issues as benefits, compensation, and training, and infusing the corporate philosophies in human resource functions throughout the organization. This philosophy dissemination is done through a human resource orientation, held twice a year in Atlanta for international staffers and once for those working at headquarters. The two-week orientation is for people who have recently joined Coca-Cola as human resource representatives or for longer-term employees who can benefit from fresh exposures. The company has designed a performance development system, an industrial relations negotiation model, and regional expatriate programs that its human resource managers around the world can adapt.

EMPLOYMENT LAWS

International human resource management is affected by employment laws in both the host and home countries. Such laws cover many issues including discrimination, immigration and work permits, salaries and benefits, and taxation. Foreign firms and their employees are bound by the laws of the country in which they operate. They have to develop rules and train managers in such a way that the laws are understood and followed.

U.S. employment laws apply to foreign wholly owned subsidiary firms incorporated in the United States.[2] This precedence was established by the Supreme Court in a 1982 case, *Sumitomo Shoji America, Inc. v. Avagliano*. The court also held that the Friendship, Commerce, and Navigation Treaty between the United States and Japan (and thus similar treaties with many other nations), which excluded certain executive personnel decisions from the application of antidiscrimination laws, was void because by locally incorporating in the United States, the firm was no longer a "foreign" corporation. This decision left open the question about the applicability of U.S. laws to foreign firms in the United States that function not through legally incorporated subsidiaries but as branches, representative offices, or other unincorporated entities.

U.S. citizens employed abroad in U.S.-owned or controlled firms are covered by certain federal employment laws. Thus, these employees can seek redress should their rights under these laws be violated. Among the most important employment laws that have extraterritorial application are Title VII of the Civil Rights Act (1964), Age Discrimination in Employment Act (ADEA), and Americans with Disabilities Act (ADA). The Civil Rights Act bars discrimination on the basis of race, religion, national origin, gender, and color. The ADEA protects employees who are aged 40 and above from discrimination, while the ADA enjoins employers from discriminating against individuals who are disabled. The extraterritorial application of these laws is limited to U.S. citizens and only if these laws do not violate the laws of the country in which the workplace is situated. As an example of the application of these legal provisions, it would be unlawful for an employer in the United States to refuse to send a female manager overseas because of the belief that foreign customers would feel uncomfortable dealing with a woman.

---

[2]Brown, Ronald. 1995. Employment and labor law considerations in international human resource management. In Oded Shenkar, ed. *Global perspectives in human resource management* (pp. 37–59). Upper Saddle River, NJ: Prentice Hall.

The Civil Rights Act also bars sexual harassment. In response, some firms have developed policies on the topic that apply to their foreign operations. For example, Colgate-Palmolive, a U.S. toiletry products company, has a strict worldwide policy that opposes sexual harassment in the workplace regardless of the cultural mores of the country in which it is operating.[3] Charges are investigated by the in-country human resources department. Findings are communicated to the senior person at the location and appropriate action is taken, which could range from reprimand to termination.

IMMIGRATION

Another piece of legislation that affects international human resource management has to do with immigration and work permits. Every country has rules that regulate the number and qualifications of foreigners who will be admitted and the duration of their stay. Procedures for obtaining work permits or visas for foreigners in most countries are cumbersome and time-consuming. In many cases, while a manager may be granted entry to work, the manager's spouse is usually not given a work visa. The human resource department has the task of applying for and obtaining relevant work papers for its managers going abroad or for foreign managers coming to headquarters.

RECRUITMENT AND SELECTION FOR OVERSEAS POSITIONS

Firms send managers to their overseas operations to serve in the following roles:

1. As the chief executive officer of the foreign branch or subsidiary. An example would be Renault sending a manager to Japan to head Nissan, the auto firm in which Renault has 50 percent ownership.
2. As a functional manager in the foreign branch or subsidiary. For instance, Fuji Film of Japan sends a manager to be in charge of production at one of its factories in the United States.
3. As a technical expert sent abroad to either train host country and/or third country nationals, or to install, repair, or maintain technical facilities. For instance, Exxon, an oil company, sends engineers to repair oil installations in Venezuela.

An employee sent abroad is referred to as an **expatriate.** Traditionally, in the United States at least, a foreign assignment was viewed with apprehension. The worry was that the overseas posting was not a promotion but more an exile away from headquarters. Leaving home would mean abandoning the best opportunities to those who stayed behind. The role of foreign posting in the entire career development pattern of executives was often not clear. However, as revenues from overseas operations have grown, many firms have moved to encourage a stint abroad as helpful to build up a globally conscious and trained managerial team.

Who are the expatriates? Table 10-2 provides a profile of the expatriate population based on a 1999 survey of 264 companies employing more than 74,709 expatriates worldwide.

---

[3]Anfuso, Dawn. 1995. Colgate's global HR unites under one strategy. *Personnel Journal.* October, pp. 44–54.

Table 10-2	Profile of the Expatriate Population
Gender	
Male	87%
Female	13%
Marital Status	
Married	69%
Accompanied by a spouse	77%
Not accompanied by a spouse	23%
Single	28%
Single males	75%
Single females	25%
Other Relationship	
Male with significant other	2%
Female with significant other	1%
Employment Status of Spouse	
Spouse employed before assignment	49%
Spouse employed during assignment	11%
Accompanying Children	
Children accompanying on assignment	61%
No children	39%
Length of expatriate assignments	
Less than 1 year	8%
1–2 years	30%
2–3 years	39%
3 or more years	23%
Current employees	78%
New hires	22%

Source: Global Relocation Trends 1999 Survey Report. Windham International, New York City.

The need to send employees abroad is dictated by many factors such as the firm's human resource strategy, stage of internationalization, and the labor market for different types of skills. Such employees may be available in the firm itself or may have to be recruited from other firms, either within or outside the country where they are needed. In some cases, firms tap into their pool of retired employees for short-term assignments overseas.[4] The overall number of people sent abroad has increased; however, within a particular firm the numbers, time frame of the assignment, and the nature of the assignment may have changed significantly.

In general, assignments are getting shorter. Business trips are being made more frequently and longer as a substitute for long-term postings. Aided by advances in communication technologies in the form of electronic mail, Web sites, teleconferencing, facsimile, and telephones, managers are able to function across the globe—as a virtual

---

[4]Lublin, Joann. 1998, March 2. Companies send intrepid retirees to work abroad. *The Wall Street Journal,* p. B1.

expatriate—without being permanently posted abroad.[5] A survey by The Conference Board indicated that the average period of expatriation was three years or less. Practices vary concerning the appropriate duration of an international assignment: U.S. and U.K. companies tended to send out expatriates for two to three years while Continental European companies sent them for four to six years. This difference did not appear to follow a strict logic, but rather a different national appreciation of the benefits and costs of short versus long expatriate assignments.[6]

AT&T, a U.S. telecommunications firm, has three diffferent type of assignments.[7] Long-term placement occurs when the company enters a new market. Expatriates start the business, establish an infrastructure that can manage the business, hire and train people to work in the organization, and localize the project so that host country nationals can handle it. Mid-range assignments can last as long as 24 months. The tasks may include overseeing the building of a plant or handling an installation in the country. Short-term assignments can last up to 11 months and are for supplemental assistance to build up staff in a country or for specific training programs.

Regardless of whether it uses short- or long-term overseas assignments, an international firm can use such assignments to attain three strategic goals:

1. *Management development.* In many companies, a foreign assignment is the way to develop among future top managers the capability to formulate global strategy. Middle managers get to learn about suppliers, customers, and competitors, acquire specific expertise, and learn how the company works.
2. *Coordination and control.* Because the trend for international firms is to build widely dispersed production and marketing organizations and then integrate them tightly through better communication and transportation, foreign assignments serve as effective means to reassert headquarters control over subsidiaries.
3. *Information sharing and exchange.* The third strategic role of overseas assignments is particularly relevant for technology-driven firms. Expatriates provide the means to transfer complex new ideas, processes, and technology to the subsidiary employees and also bring back to the parent the knowledge and skills present in the subsidiary. It also gives the managers time to develop a rapport and trust at the host location to facilitate future information exchanges across geographical and organizational boundaries.

INPATRIATE MANAGERS

An **inpatriate** refers to host or other foreign country nationals who are transferred to headquarters or to the parent's facilities. As international activities have expanded, employing foreigners as managers at the parent has become more and more common. Nearly a quarter of all cross-border managerial postings are made to the firm's headquarters country.[8]

[5]Solomon, Charlene. 1998. Today's global mobility. *Global Workforce.* July, pp. 12–17.
[6]*Managing expatriates' return.* Report Number 1148-96-RR. The Conference Board. New York. 1996.
[7]Solomon, Charlene. 1994. Staff selection impacts global success. *Personnel Journal.* January, pp. 88–101.
[8]*Global relocation trends 1997 survey report.* 1997. New York: Windham International.

Foreign managers are brought to the parent for several reasons:

- For training and development
- For assignment to technical projects
- To absorb the corporate culture and understand the firm from the parent viewpoint
- To participate in project teams
- To reduce the need for sending out expensive home country managers to the foreign location
- To tap qualified and capable individuals for organizational growth

Inpatriates face the same issues that expatriates face when they go abroad, including immigration and legal issues, compensation and benefits questions, family concerns, and cultural adjustment. Once a foreign individual is selected for an assignment to the United States, the topmost priority of the human resource department at headquarters is to arrange for a visa, which involves working with the Department of Labor and the Immigration and Naturalization Service (INS). Employers can avail of two types of work visas in the United States. One is the H-1, commonly used when recruiting foreign students from U.S. college campuses and to hire highly skilled foreigners. The other is the L-1 intracompany visa that allows managers and executives to enter the United States for up to seven years if they meet specific requirements. Although many inpatriates come on a two- or three-year assignment, most make an effort to obtain permanent residency often because of the accompanying spouse's need to secure employment, for which resident status is required. The alternative is for the spouse to independently qualify for a work visa.

As with going abroad, for a foreigner coming to the United States, especially on assignment for the first time, anxiety and uncertainty are understandable. The head office can take various steps to smooth the transition to life in the new location. Table 10-3 identifies a list of stategies that the human resource department at headquarters can consider to assist the inpatriate adjust to the United States.

WOMEN MANAGERS

The increasing number of women in managerial ranks in the United States and Canada and to a lesser extent in Western Europe has invariably led to an examination of the status of women in international management. The number of women expatriates, though small compared to the number of men, continues to increase. The small number of women (13 percent of all expatriates) may reflect the fact that expatriates are usually selected from upper-middle to senior corporate ranks, where women are still a minority. As more women rise up in the corporate hierarchy, it is likely that women will be considered for overseas appointment in the same manner as men. A study of North American female managers in Asia found that larger companies sent more women overseas than smaller firms, with financial institutions more likely than other industries to do so.[9]

---

[9]Adler, Nancy J. 1993. Women managers in a global economy. *HR Magazine.* September, pp. 52–55.

Table 10-3	Tips to Help Inpatriates Adjust to the United States

1. Insure that the paperwork is initiated as early as possible for the inpatriate and family members to get social security numbers, which they will need for a driver's license, bank account, and credit card.
2. Give managers who will have responsibility for inpatriates training in cross-cultural awareness, especially in ways that the United States may differ from the rest of the world.
3. Use the firm's diversity programs to instruct the inpatriate about recognizing and handling diversity in the U.S. workplace.
4. Train managers to become sensitive to different communication styles.
5. Link the inpatriate to community resources.
6. Choose a relocation company that can provide an array of services for the inpatriate, including help with real estate, schools for the children, as well as visits to the local supermarkets, and generally getting them settled.
7. Remind managers not to assume the international corporate culture is the same as the one at headquarters.
8. Help the manager realize that the inpatriate, if coming from a subsidiary, may not be used to the scrutiny of working at headquarters. The same holds true for the bureaucracy at headquarters.
9. Try to help the inpatriate establish credit.
10. Provide assistance to the accompanying spouse who may have given up an income. A spouse can be offered educational reimbursement, career guidance, and assistance with volunteer activities.

Source: Solomon, Charlene M. "HR's helping hand pulls global inpatriates onboard." *Personnel Journal.* 1995, November, pp. 40–49. Used with permission, Workforce, www.workforce.com.

Given that the status and role of women vary across countries, a recurring question is whether women expatriate managers would be successful in countries where women hold low-level jobs or where they are expected to be primarily homemakers and child rearers. Firms may refrain from sending women abroad on the presumption of foreign prejudice against female managers or that a foreign assignment would cause problems for dual-career marriages. However, studies have found that women managers were willing to go on overseas assignments and were successful abroad.[10] In Japan and Korea, where few women managers are to be found in the higher echelons of firms, foreigners, including foreign women, are treated as foreigners, and not locals. Therefore, the rules governing the behavior of local women, which limits their access to managerial ranks, do not apply to foreign women. With regard to dual career couples, the concern over accepting a transfer overseas applies equally to men whose wives are more and more likely to have their own careers.

CHOICE OF SOURCES OF MANAGERS

Firms look to the home country, host country, and third countries to find managers to staff positions overseas.

---

[10]Adler, Nancy J. 1987. Pacific basin managers: A gaijin, not a woman. *Human Resource Management* 26(2). pp. 169–191.

HOME COUNTRY NATIONALS

In many situations, firms use home country nationals in managerial positions abroad. In addition to the strategic reasons outlined earlier, some of these situations include the following:

- During startup or initial period of the foreign operations
- To fill a special managerial skill that is lacking or is expensive at the overseas office (more likely in poor countries or in highly sophisticated industries)
- Headquarters' need to exercise a high degree of control over its foreign operations (because of the highly integrated nature of the firm's operations; desire to protect proprietary knowledge or activities from falling into the wrong hands; to maintain certain unique features of a product or service, which cannot be assured if the managers are not from the parent). In addition to control, home country managers may be preferred simply because they are familiar with parent firm procedures on various matters such as financial reporting or research and development routines.
- The short-term nature of the foreign operation, which eliminates the reason to hire and train local or third country nationals
- The need to maintain a foreign image in the foreign country
- To apply greater clout with the local government in negotiations than a host country national could, because of a susceptibility to pressures from the local government, colleagues, and media
- To ensure greater acceptability to all groups in a multicultural society, especially where conflict and tension infuse inter-communal relationships (a host country person may not have the support of one or the other groups)

HOST COUNTRY NATIONALS

In recent years, international firms have come to rely more and more on host country nationals at all levels of operation at the foreign location. The main reasons for this trend, called **management localization,** are lower costs and familiarity with the working environment. The average one-time cost of relocating an expatriate family is $49,000—not including domestic U.S. home sale costs.[11] This figure includes the cost of moving household goods, home finding and settling-in assistance, home property management, travel, interim living expenses, and cross-cultural preparation. In addition, salaries and allowance often triple the total compensation cost. Other reasons include nonavailability of home country nationals, difficulty in adapting to the cultural environment of the host country, especially if it is significantly different from the home country, and reluctance of the host government to issue work visas to expatriates. Economic difficulties abroad and consequent diminution of business opportunities also force foreign firms to cut down on the number of expatriates abroad as a way of reducing costs.

The practice of Japanese firms to use expatriates from home in senior positions in their U.S. operations had negative consequences in many Japanese subsidiaries, which

---

[11]*Global relocation trends 1998 survey report. 1998.* New York: Windham International.

compelled them to promote or appoint U.S. nationals to key managerial ranks and decision-making roles.[12] The problems experienced that led to the localization of management included the following:

- The perception by U.S. managers that upper-level positions were out of bounds for them, in effect limiting career progression. This led to a high turnover among U.S. executives.
- Several cases of employment discrimination suits brought by U.S. managers denied promotion were settled at high financial costs and also created negative publicity for the company.
- Japanese firms were seen as unattractive places to work, making it harder to recruit competent and ambitious U.S. managers.
- To do business with U.S. firms and to be seen as a business that was committed to the U.S. market, it was essential to have U.S. managers in the upper echelons.

THIRD COUNTRY NATIONALS

A third option is the use of third country nationals for foreign assignments. Third country nationals are neither from the home or host country. Third country nationals provide a potentially large and talented pool from which to draw managers. Less-developed countries such as India and Egypt have seen a huge increase in the education of managerial personnel. However, lower wages and their relatively small economies compared to population size and growth, induce many managers to seek positions abroad. In countries with a paucity of indigeneous managerial talent and where home country expatriates may be too expensive or even unavailable, third country nationals offer a viable choice. As international operations expand, a firm is more likely to send third country nationals to its various overseas postings.

CHANGING PATTERNS OF STAFFING

The longer a firm operates in a foreign country, the more likely it is to use fewer home country nationals and more and more host country nationals. As the firm's overall international activities grow, the number of third country nationals as well as host country nationals being sent to the parent country (inpatriates) tend to increase.

Staffing positions overseas is also linked to a firm's management philosophy. For instance, an ethnocentric orientation is reflected in greater reliance on home country nationals; polycentric orientation leads to the use of host country nationals; and the geocentric orientation is consistent with the inclusion of third country nationals at home and abroad.

The oil company Chevron starts with as few U.S. expatriates as possible when it expands abroad and quickly turns the operation over to host country employees.[13]

---

[12]Serapio, Manuel. 1995. Management localization in Japanese subsidiaries in the United States. In Oded Shenkar, ed. *Global perspectives of human resource management* (pp. 211–225). Upper Saddle River, NJ: Prentice Hall.
[13]Solomon, Charlene. 1994. Staff selection impacts global success. *Personnel Journal.* January, pp. 88–101.

Typically, the company sends a management team to review the skills of local employees. Firms in a developing country typically have a higher proportion of expatriates to local national employees. As the operation matures, and as local national employees are trained, the proportion changes. For example, in the United Kingdom where the operations are fairly mature, oil exploration having started in the late 1960s, the ratio of Britons to Americans is 10 to one. In contrast, when Chevron does frontier exploration in less-developed countries, the geologists, engineers, and earth scientists tip the ratio the other way. Management Focus 10-1 discusses the staffing philosophy of Coca-Cola.

MANAGEMENT FOCUS 10-1

COCA-COLA'S STAFFING PHILOSOPHY

The Coca-Cola Company sees itself not as a global organization, but as a multilocal enterprise. Its global strategy is to allow its buinesses in more than 200 countries to act according to local needs, local laws, and local cultures. For this reason, the company's philosophy is to employ as many host country nationals in its businesses as possible.

However, the system still needs expatriates for two reasons. One is to fill a need for a specific set of skills that may not exist at a particular location. When it started operations in Poland it brought in an expatriate from Chicago, an American of Polish descent, to fill the position of finance manager. The second reason is for the employee's own executive development. At Coca-Cola, before managers are promoted to senior executive level, they are expected to have international exposure.

The company has an international service program that focuses on the development of a core group of workers for international mobility. About 500 high-level managers and professionals are part of the program. Said Michael Semrau, assistant vice president and director of international human resources, "The cost of the program is significant, so we tend to focus on people who have knowledge of their particular field plus knowledge of the company, and who can do two things in an international location. One is add value by the expertise that they bring to each assignment, and two is enhance their

contribution to the company by having that international experience."

Of the 500 people in the program, approximately 200 move each year. The typical duration of an international assignment is three to five years, although that can vary based on need. The international service program group supports the expatriates. The specialists in this group work with local division or regional human resources people to coordinate the transfer of the international service people and to ensure that the appropriate compensation elements are in place and provided on a timely basis. The company's goal is to have a compensation program that will enable employees to move around the world without hesitation. It has been done by setting up a U.S.-based compensation package, where expatriates are paid according to U.S. benchmarks rather than changing salaries for each move they make.

To ensure equity within the international ranks, the company has a worldwide job evaluation system. The program evaluates the same positions in different parts of the world on a single standard. A human resource development committee in every functional area of the company is generally set up to identify talent within their particular functions and then take the steps necessary to make sure those workers achieve their potential.

Source: Anfuso, Dawn. 1994. HR unites the world of Coca-Cola. *Personnel Journal.* November, pp. 112–121.

METHOD OF SELECTING MANAGERS
FOR OVERSEAS ASSIGNMENTS

Firms identify employees for international assignments in various ways. The most common method is the recommendation of a manager, followed by previous overseas assignment, self-nomination, job postings, and recommendations from the firm's human resource information system. As the opening vignette indicated, Mr. Borenstein's posting to Hong Kong was largely the result of his own initiative.

Interviews by managers are the most frequently used method for selecting candidates for international assignments. Interviews by human resources departments occur only half as frequently and only a small minority of firms utilize assessment programs. The infrequent use of assessment tools is probably the result of a shortage of qualified candidates, particularly within the firm.

Given the importance of family, especially spousal support, both employees and their spouses should be involved in the decision to be posted abroad and be briefed on the full implications of the financial, career, and cultural aspects of the assignment.

CHARACTERISTICS OF THE SUCCESSFUL EXPATRIATE

It is not easy to identify the individual who will succeed in an overseas location. It cannot be assumed that someone who has performed well in the domestic arena will necessarily succeed abroad. The foreign environmental context may be so different that the manager's experience and skills may not transfer.

Studies show that the qualities deemed most important for overseas success include independence and ability to achieve results with limited resources, sincerity and integrity, technical knowledge, and a positive attitude towards overseas work. In addition, a positive attitude on the part of the spouse and family are also desirable qualities.[14]

Individuals being sent abroad must be well versed in the company's mission, goals, products, and strategies. Because expatriates will function often at a considerable distance from home, they will have to be relied upon to make decisions that do not have to be second-guessed by headquarters.

Expatriates should be competent to do the job they are being sent to do. Technically and managerially competent individuals are likely to be self-confident and able to recognize the problems and identify the issues. They are also going to be more easily acceptable by the rank and file as well as colleagues in the host country.

As noted in Chapter 2, while foreign language skills are useful, they are not an essential requirement. Interpreters and translation services are widely available and used. Knowledge of the host country language (or languages) leads to a better understanding of the country's culture and a greater appreciation of nonverbal cues and nuances. Language allows the expatriate to associate socially and outside the workplace with a cross-section of society instead of being drawn only to other fellow expatriates. The important point is that a good manager must have the capability to communicate effectively. How it is done is less important.

---

[14]Solomon, Charlene. 1994. Success abroad depends on more than job skills. *Personnel Journal.* April, pp. 51–60.

Sensitivity to the foreign culture is another important and related attribute especially if the job involves active interaction with host country employees and citizens. As Kenneth Davis has suggested (adapting a concept from Stephen Covey's *Seven Habits of Highly Effective People*), the effective expatriate is one who is high on two dimensions: courage and consideration. Courage refers to the extent individuals display their feelings and convictions while consideration refers to the amount of respect and understanding one has for the feelings and convictions of others. A high-courage/high-consideration communication style creates a win-win situation; any other combination offers suboptimal results. Figure 10-1 presents a communication matrix with four main types of expatriate communication style: isolationists, ugly tourists, gone natives, and global communicators.

- *Isolationists* are low-courage, low-consideration communicators who bring a low embodiment of their own cultural identity and convictions and also have a low regard for the cultural identity of the host population. Real communication is difficult with such persons, and the result is a lose-lose situation.
- *Ugly tourists* are high-courage, low-consideration communicators who have a high regard for their own culture but are disdainful of the host culture. These individuals see the world through their own cultural filters, and the result is a win-lose approach.
- *Gone natives* are low-courage, high-consideration communicators who are highly appreciative and understanding of the host country culture while deprecating their own. Such individuals fail to advance the headquarters' goals, and the result is a lose-win situation.
- *Global communicators* are high-courage, high-consideration communicators who have a strong sense of their own cultural identities and a high level of consideration for the cultural values of the host society. Such individuals contribute to a win-win situation by drawing out the positives from both the home and host country cultures.

Another criteria is the extent to which the manager is familiar with the foreign country. Personal experience in terms of having lived or visited or even worked abroad

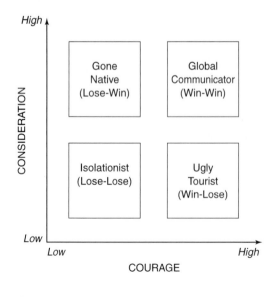

FIGURE 10-1
Matrix of International Communicators

Source: Davis, Kenneth, DeRycker, Teun and Verckens, J. Piet. "Become a global communicator." *Global Workforce,* October, pp. 10–11. Copyright © 1997 Kenneth W. Davis, Indiana University-Purdue University Indianapolis.

is important because such a person has a perspective different from those who have not. This person is more likely to recognize similarities rather than differences among societies and may be better able to adjust in a foreign country. However, previous experience abroad may not necessarily translate into success in a second overseas assignment especially if the country or the nature of the task is different.

The state of a person's health is important for at least two reasons. One, the overseas assignment could be physically and mentally taxing, especially if adequate support staff is not available and a large cultural adjustment has to be made. Two, especially in poor countries or in hard-to-access locations (such as a copper/gold mine in Irian Jaya in Indonesia), medical care may not be adequate.

Overseas assignments are often stressful because the family has to cope without the familiar social network of friends and families. The support of the spouse and children are essential for the manager to be able to work effectively. A prior and accurate knowledge of the working and living conditions in the country destination assist in their proper preparation.

The manager's career plans should be considered when evaluating the person for overseas posting. At Caterpillar, a heavy equipment company, which receives more than two-thirds of its revenues from abroad, to be able to rise to the senior ranks, managers with overseas experience have an edge.[15] When managers understand this requirement, they are likely to prepare themselves accordingly.

FAILURE IN OVERSEAS ASSIGNMENTS

Most expatriate assignments are successful, and both the individual and the organization benefit. However, in some situations, the expatriate fails overseas and either returns home prematurely or stays on but functions at a suboptimal level. Assignment failure is hard to define and thus hard to measure. Data on assignment failure are extremely difficult to obtain. A study of 1,824 British expatriates over a three-year period found early return to be only 8 percent, suggesting that most expatriate postings are successful.[16] Other studies have suggested a higher rate of failure.[17] The costs of a failure is quite high in money terms given the large salaries of the expatriate and the expenses incurred in sending the expatriate abroad, foregone business opportunities, and the career setback experienced by the failed expatriate. Some of the most common reasons managers fail in their foreign assignment are provided in Table 10-4.

Managerial failure has less to do with competence, since capability and experience are often the reasons for selecting the manager. Instead, failure stems primarily from an inability of the expatriate and spouse to adjust to a different physical or cultural environment and other family-related issues such as children's education and aging and ill parents. It was reported that Henry Wallace, the first foreigner to head a Japanese automobile company, Mazda Motors, returned to the United States because his wife was unhappy living in Hiroshima, where Mazda was based.[18]

---

[15]Briscoe, Dennis. 1995. *International human resource management.* Upper Saddle River, NJ: Prentice Hall.
[16]Forster, Nick. 1997. The persistent myth of high expatriate failure rates: A reappraisal. *International Journal of Human Resource Management* 8(4), pp. 415–433.
[17]Solomon, Charlene. 1996. Danger below! Spot failing global assignments. *Personnel Journal.* November, pp. 78–85.
[18]Strom, Stephanie. 1997, November 14. First foreigner to lead Japanese company retires. *New York Times,* p. D6.

Table 10-4	Commonly Cited Reasons for Assignment Failure

- Spousal or partner dissatisfaction
- Family concerns
- Inability to adapt
- Job fails to meet expectations
- Wrong candidate
- Unsatisfactory job performance
- Unsatisfactory quality of life
- Dissatisfaction with compensation

Source: Global Relocation Trends 1999 Survey Report. Windham International, New York City.

DUAL CAREER COUPLES

With increasing numbers of **dual career couples,** where both husband and wife work, the employment of the spouse overseas is the single most important hurdle in getting first-choice candidates to accept assignments. Potential candidates decline the offer of an overseas assignment because they cannot afford to lose the income or they worry it may derail the spouse's career entirely to be out of the workforce for a few years. Only 11 percent of the spouses who were employed before the assignment were employed during the assignment. This problem has no easy solution. Some companies, in response, have shortened the length of assignments, hoping that this alternative would be less disruptive to a spouse's career. Some examples of innovative programs that firms have created to support spouses include:

- Helping the spouse overcome cultural and emotional hurdles at a new location by offering cross-cultural counseling and connecting them with a network of spouses in the host community
- Arrranging work permits and offering career counseling
- Creating a consortium of companies and pooling resources in a specific location or within an industry and creating a job bank to find a job for the trailing spouse
- Providing a prelocation tour of the country to see what opportunities may exist
- Retaining professional international placement service
- Providing for and encouraging higher education

Spousal assistance programs vary from firm to firm. For example, Shell International, the Anglo-Dutch oil company with more than 5,500 expatriates from 70 different countries, has a Spouse Employment Centre which focuses on partner education and employment issues.[19] A companywide survey had indicated that employees were unhappy with the inadequacy of predeparture information about the destination and a failure to listen to spouses who had been abroad and were willing to share their experiences. Out of the idea to have spouses share information, The Outpost was born. Spon-

---

[19]Frazee, Valerie. 1998. Tearing down roadblocks. *Workforce.* February, pp. 50–54; Harvey, Michael. 1998. Dual career couples during international relocation: The trailing spouse. *Human Resource Management* 9(2), pp. 309–331.

sored by the company and staffed by expatriate partners, The Outpost headquarters office opened in The Hague in November 1995. Two years later, 40 local hubs known as information network centers had been established worldwide. The Outpost maintained a database of 11,000 volunteer briefers, or families who had agreed to discuss informally their experiences with another family about to relocate to any area they had lived. Other programs included assistance with job search fees, professional skills maintenance, course fees, and career counseling. Shell reimbursed 80 percent of agreed costs up to $4,000 per assignment on expatriation and $2,500 on repatriation.

CULTURE SHOCK

As discussed in Chapter 2, people experience culture shock when they find that familiar cues are missing.[20] Their absence causes stress and affects the manager's ability to function in the desired manner, leading to tension, frustration, a feeling of alienation, and often depression.

The expatriate typically goes through a cycle as shown in Figure 10-2. The first stage in the cycle is the honeymoon period where the expatriate is new to the foreign country and excited about it. In second stage the initial enthusiasm is replaced by irritability and hostility as the expatriate encounters difficulties and notices enormous differences in the culture. In the third stage, the expatriate begins the process of coming to terms with the differences and figures out how to function in the foreign country. In the final stage, the expatriate adapts to the host country culture and is able to function successfully. Studies show that the entire cycle could last up to 50 months.[21] Because most expatriate assignments for U.S. managers are on the average less than three years, it is quite likely that many do not get over culture shock.

How can managers cope with culture shock? Proper predeparture cross-cultural training would prepare managers to expect and steel themselves against the possibility that they will experience culture shock. The more the person knows about the foreign country before arriving in the country, the better that person is able to recognize the symptoms of culture shock. Many expatriates seek relief in clubs or associations that exist in the foreign city and cater to expatriates. Although such kinship may be reassuring

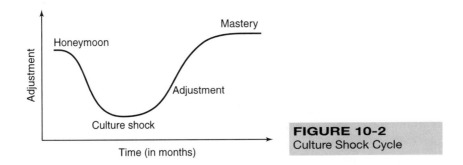

FIGURE 10-2
Culture Shock Cycle

[20]Harris, Philip R., and Robert T. Moran. 1996. *Managing cultural differences.* Houston: Gulf Publishing.
[21]Black, J. Stewart, and Mark Mendenhall. 1991. The U-curve adjustment hypothesis revisited: A review and theoretical framework. *Journal of International Business Studies* 22(2), pp. 225–247; *Global relocation trends 1998 survey report.* 1998. New York: Windham International.

initially, it may also serve to isolate the expatriate from the host community and strengthen the negative feelings associated with the second stage of the culture shock cycle. Keeping an open mind and seeking rational explanations for apparently irrational behaviors of the host population helps in understanding the local culture.

CROSS-CULTURAL TRAINING

As discussed in Chapter 2, the purposes of cross-cultural training are developing cross-cultural skills, assisting with cross-cultural adjustment, and with improved job performance among managers.[22] Many firms, having recognized these needs, have established cross-cultural training programs for their managers. However, most cross-cultural training programs are not comprehensive in nature. They are limited to environmental briefing, basic culture orientation, and some language training. The most common reason for not offering comprehensive training is that it is considered unnecessary or ineffective by top management.

Many different types of training methods are available. Landis and Brislin (1993) proposed a typology that differentiates between alternative training methods.[23] A graphical representation of this typology can be found in Figure 10-3.

1. *Information or fact-oriented training.* Trainees are presented with various facts about the country in which they are about to live via lectures, videotapes, and readings.
2. *Attribution training.* This approach focuses on explanations of behavior from the point of the host culture. The goal is to learn how host country nationals process information on how to behave so that the trainee can understand why people in the host nation behave the way they do. This information would enable the trainee to adapt personal behavior to approximate that of the host country nationals.
3. *Cultural awareness training.* Here the focus is on teaching trainees about their own culture and its many attributes and how culture impacts behavior. The theory is that once their awareness is raised, trainees are better able to appreciate the role of culture in human behavior in other countries.
4. *Cognitive-behavior modification.* Trainees identify what they find to be rewarding and punishing in their own subcultures (e.g., religion, work, and family) and then examine the reward and punishment structure in the host country. Evaluating similarities and differences lets the trainees develop strategies that will enhance rewarding behavior and avoid punishment in the foreign country.
5. *Experiential learning.* Trainees are actively introduced to the foreign society and learn first-hand through role-playing exercises, visiting the foreign country, and cultural simulations.
6. *Interaction training.* Trainees interact with host country nationals or returned expatriates and thus learn first-hand about life and culture in the foreign country.

---

[22]Harrison, J. Kline. 1994. Developing successful expatriate managers: A framework for the structural design and strategic alignment of cross-cultural training programs. *Human Resource Planning* 17(3), pp. 17–35.
[23]Landis, D., and R. Brislin. 1983. *Handbook on intercultural training,* vol. 1. New York. Pergamon Press..

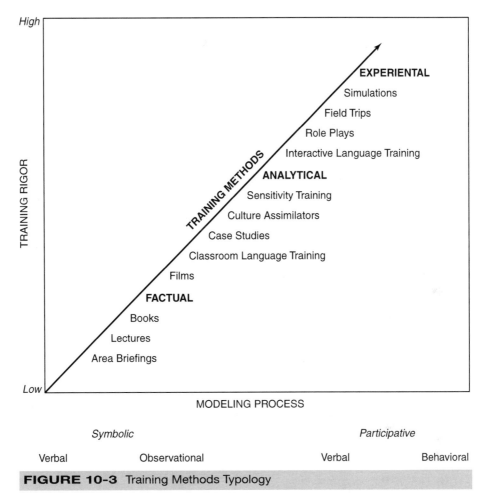

FIGURE 10-3 Training Methods Typology

Source: Black, J. Stewart, and Mark Mendenhall. 1989. A practical but theory-based framework for selecting cross-cultural training programs. *Human Resource Management* 28(4), pp. 511–539.

While valuable in identifying the many different types of training methods, this typology does not suggest which method may be appropriate in one case and not another or how effective they are. Several frameworks exist to help in this matter.

TUNG'S FRAMEWORK

Rosalie Tung (1982) suggested that the choice of training method to be used depends on the degree of interaction required of the expatriate in the foreign country and the extent of similarity between the expatriate's own culture and that of the assigned posting.[24] Thus, if the degree of interaction is low and the similarity of the cultures is high, less emphasis on cross-cultural training is needed. In contrast, if the degree of interaction is

---

[24]Tung, Rosalie. 1981. Selection and training of personnel for overseas assignments. *Columbia Journal of World Business* 16(1), pp. 68–78.

going to be high and the similarity of the cultures is low, then cross-cultural training would assume great importance.

MENDENHALL AND ODDOU FRAMEWORK

A more advanced training framework presented by Mark Mendenhall and Gary Oddou (1986) builds on Tung's work by specifying appropriate training methods and categorizing them as low, medium, and high in rigor.[25] The more rigorous the training, the more likely it is to make a lasting impression on the trainee. This framework is shown in Figure 10-4.

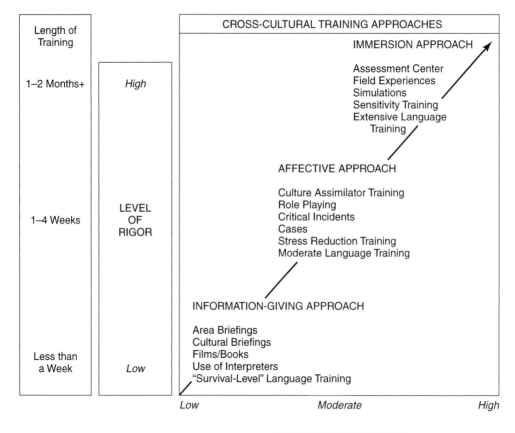

FIGURE 10-4 Mendenhall and Oddou's Model of Cross-Cultural Training

Source: Mendenhall, M., and G. Oddou. 1986. Acculturation profiles of expatriate managers: Implications for cross-cultural training programs. *Columbia Journal of World Business.* Winter, pp. 73–79.

---

[25]Mendenhall, Mark, and Gary Oddou. 1986. Acculturation profiles of expatriate managers: Implications for cross-cultural training programs. *Columbia Journal of World Business* 21(4), pp. 73–79.

BLACK AND MENDENHALL'S COMPREHENSIVE MODEL

Building on the foundations of the social learning theory, which explains the learning process as getting the trainee's attention, ensuring that the trainee retains what is learned, and confirming the trainee's ability to translate the learning into actual behavior, Stewart Black and Mendenhall (1989) offer a comprehensive model of how an expatriate training regime should be organized.[26]

The various training methods are treated in a continuum based on two dimensions. The first is the extent to which the methods involve actual participation by the trainees (e.g., lectures on culture has minimal or no participation on the part of the trainee to field trips where the involvement is deep). And second is how rigorous they are (e.g., lectures are low in rigor compared to a field trip). Which of these methods would be appropriate for a particular expatriate is dependent on three factors: (1) the extent to which the foreign country is culturally similar or dissimilar to that of the expatriate's own; (2) the expected degree of interaction with the nationals of the host country; and (3) the extent to which the assigned job is similar or dissimilar to the work the expatriate is currently doing or has done previously. Figure 10-5 presents a decision tree framework to apply this model.

Thus, for example, where the culture of the foreign location is highly different, the level of interaction with host nationals high, and the nature of the job is going to be significantly different, the training program designed for the would-be expatriate would have a high level of rigor, requiring longer time, using a wide range of methods from lectures to role playing and field experiences, and consisting of topics such as the culture and history of the foreign country, interpersonal skills, language skills, and how to handle job-related stress. Conversely, in an overseas appointment to a country similar to that of the expatriate, where little interaction with local people is required, and the job is similar to the one at home, the expatriate has to make the minimum of adjustment. Consequently, a training regime would be low in rigor, lasting only a few hours at best, and presented through a lecture, a film, or other readings.

A typical cross-cultural training program is structured in the following sequence: (1) self-assessment, (2) cultural awareness, (3) knowledge acquisition, and (4) skills training. The training methods could include area briefings, lectures, readings, films/videos, classroom language training, case studies, culture assimilators, sensitivity training, interactive language training, role-playing, field trips, and simulations. Table 10-5 provides an overview of the costs and the range of services for language training that are available from specialized vendors.

PERFORMANCE EVALUATION

Performance evaluation is a process that enables an international firm to evaluate and continuously improve the individual, subsidiary, and corporate performance against clearly defined goals and targets. Evaluating an expatriate manager's performance overseas is complicated for a variety of reasons. Performance is affected by changes in exchange rates, the pace of inflation in the host economy, the local cost of various inputs, local tax rates, time delays in reporting, and the constraints imposed by the policies of

---

[26]Black, J. Stewart, and Mark Mendenhall. 1989. A practical but theory-based framework for selecting cross-cultural training programs. *Human Resource Management* 28(4), pp. 511–539.

FIGURE 10-5 Black and Mendenhall's Decision Tree Model

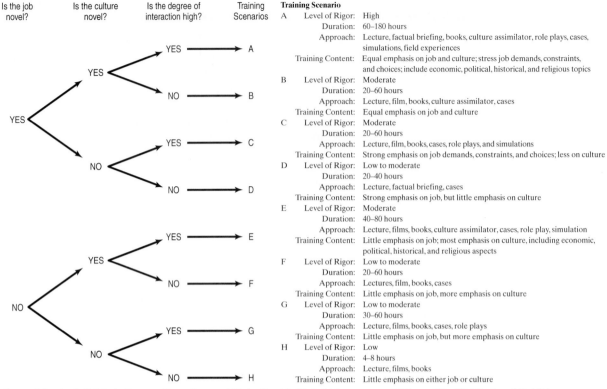

Source: Mendenhall, Mark, Punnett, Betty Jane and Ricks, David. *Global Management.* 1995, pp. 452–453. Blackwell Publishers, Oxford, UK.

Table 10-5 Cost of Training Programs

$50	A language training CD-ROM and a microphone for speech recognition
$275	One person participating in a group language training course
$475	A language training CD-ROM, 12 interactive lessons with a teacher over the Internet, and homework incorporating Web sites in foreign languages
$1,050–$3,000	One day of post-arrival on-site culture training for the family
$3,000–$5,000	Cost per family member for one post-arrival on-site culture training session per week for the first six months of the assignment
$3,500–$5,000	A two-day predeparture culture program for the employee and partner (another $1,375–$2,500 for the children)
$4,000	A one-time fee to set up videoconferencing equipment ($1,500) and 50 hours of instruction from a language training teacher ($50/hour)
$5,500	A five-day predeparture culture and language program for the employee and partner
$10,000	A two-day cross-cultural program and eight days in a language immersion program for the employee and partner

Source: Frazee, Valerie. "Send your expats prepared for success." *Global Workforce.* 1998, May, pp. 15–22. Used with permission, Workforce, *www.workforce.com.*

the parent firm or headquarters with regard to transfer pricing, product line, plant capacity, and financial support. The expatriate manager usually has little, if any control, over these factors and they vary from country to country. Should performance be poor, the head office may find that the expatriates cannot be easily replaced because of the high cost and the likely unavailability of suitable managers in the firm who can take up an assignment on short notice. Furthermore, because most expatriates serve an average of three years or less abroad, this period is often not long enough for the person to adjust to the new post and perform at full potential. By the time the expatriate has figured out the job and the foreign culture, it is time to go home or to another posting.

For evaluation to be valid, a match between the strategic business purpose of the position and the person doing the job is needed. Such a match is often not easy because the human resource department is not involved in the company's strategic planning process and is not involved early enough in a manager's overseas assignment. Evaluating the expatriate from headquarters or another foreign location (e.g., regional head office) requires that the supervisors be thoroughly knowledgeable about the foreign work environment. One option is to use two supervisors—one local, one at headquarters—to increase agreement on performance goals and performance measurement. This focus on the contextual factors in determining performance would tend to be country-specific, which in turn would make it difficult for both cross-country comparisons of expatriate performance as well as comparison with the performance of managers at headquarters. Another issue relates to the performance evaluation instruments that have to be used. If evaluation is in the context of a country or geographical area, then evaluation instruments could not be standardized across the firm although they would have the desirable feature of including items relevant to the particular job.

How do international firms carry out performance evaluation of their expatriates? Structured expatriate evaluations have become more frequent in recent years. Host country performance reviews are the most widely used method for evaluating expatriates followed by performance review in the home country, regular expatriate visits to the home office, regular manager visits to the host country, and annual surveys of expatriates. Management Focus 10-2 discusses examples from two multinational firms.

A study of performance evaluation in 58 U.S. multinational firms found that their human resource managers were in favor of using standardized instruments that were customized for local contexts and using multiple evaluators from home and host countries. They also preferred evaluations be conducted annually or semiannually.[27] The study also reported that many firms do not actually follow these practices, which require greater effort, time, and resources. Such corporate indifference may lead to problems for the firm and the expatriate. By not accounting for local contextual variables in evaluating managers, the firm relies more and more on headquarters' notion of appropriate performance, which might reflect poorly on the expatriate even to the point of hurting career advancement. In assessing the performance of the expatriate, it is important to consider the impact of the following variables and their interrelationship:

- The compensation package
- The level of the position (e.g., chief executive officer) and dimensions of the job

---

[27]Gregersen, Hal, Julie Hite, and J. Stewart Black. 1996. Expatriate performance appraisal in U.S. multinational firms. *Journal of International Business Studies* 27(4), pp. 711–738.

MANAGEMENT FOCUS 10-2

EXAMPLES OF PERFORMANCE EVALUATION IN INTERNATIONAL FIRMS

Monsanto Company, an agricultural products firm, based in St. Louis, Missouri, makes sure that employees sent overseas speak with their sending and receiving managers to produce an action plan for development. This plan includes not only the business goals, but also the cross-cultural competency they need to achieve on site.

Before employees attend cross-cultural training sessions, they take time to think about the overseas position and write a job description listing expected accomplishments. Cross-cultural trainers help in preparing these documents. When the employees are abroad, they meet with receiving managers to garner support for their action plan and its accomplishment. The sending and the host managers are jointly accountable for the development and progress of the action plan. On returning from their stint abroad, employees go through a formal repatriation process where they showcase their knowledge to superiors, peers, and subordinates through formal presentations and informal get togethers.

In Asea Brown Boveri (ABB), the Swedish-Swiss electrical engineering firm, when expatriates join another division of the company, the local practices relative to performance prevail. These expatriates are considered to be full-fledged employees of the foreign division and with the exception of how their taxes, benefits, and housing are handled, everything else—performance evaluation and bonuses—are treated like other employees in that country. Because half of the company's expatriates work on large projects, their performance is evaluated on the project through site visits by managers from the division offices or through managers working on the project. Employees sent abroad for advanced training are evaluated on their learning by managers in the sending organization but based upon the feedback of the assigned host manager.

At ABB, the organizational culture requires that employees have an international perspective and thus they are evaluated on their cultural sensitivity and their relationship with the host community. This aspect of the evaluation is done by the host unit's local manager. Appraisals are done annually.

Source: Solomon, Charlene Marmer. 1995. Repatriation: Up, down, or out. *Personnel Journal.* January, pp. 28–37.

- Support provided by headquarters to the expatriate and family
- The working environment in the host country
- The extent to which the expatriate and family adjust to the host culture

REPATRIATION ISSUES

Repatriation refers to the return of the expatriate to the home country after completing a tour of duty in a foreign location. Successful reentry is reflected in employees advancing in their careers and securing personal fulfillment from the foreign experience at the same time the firm benefits from the development of an internationally competent manager.

Returning expatriates bring back the following benefits:

- A global perspective on the firm's business
- Stronger intercultural communication skills

- An ability to conceptualize and comprehend business trends and events better because of their exposure to contrasting cultural, political, and economic work systems
- Improved planning skills
- The ability to be better motivators of subordinates as a result of working with culturally diverse personnel abroad

Despite these positive attributes, most firms fail to fully utilize and integrate their returned expatriates in the company's operation. Within two years of repatriation, 25 percent of employees leave their company.[28] This number is higher than typical employee turnover rates at similar employee levels. When they leave, repatriates take with them valuable knowledge, usually to a competitor.

The primary cause of this turnover is a combination of greater opportunity elsewhere and an apparent lack of appreciation for the global experience gained by these employees. The vast majority of returning expatriates do not have the benefit of comprehensive human resource programs to help them. Instead of looking at repatriation as the final link in an integrated, circular process that connects good selection, cross-cultural training, relocation assistance, global career management, and successful work performance, it is often overlooked or neglected. Ideally, repatriation planning should begin at the time of expatriation.

Repatriation is often a painful experience for the returning executives and families for a number of reasons, including the following:

- The firm does not know what they have been doing these past several years, does not know how to use their new knowledge, and appears not to care.
- The job provided by the firm on their return does not use their experience, skills, and capabilities, or sometimes the job is temporary.
- Salaries and benefits are reduced as many of the overseas allowances are no longer provided.
- They feel a sense of loss of influence, autonomy, and prestige that came with the overseas posting but does not exist at the home country.
- They may experience a sense of alienation especially if social, technological, and organizational changes have been rapid during their years abroad.
- They encounter difficulties in obtaining appropriate housing and other social services.
- The firm offers insufficient assistance with relocation problems.
- Friends, colleagues, and neighbors show little interest in their experience.

Why do many firms not have comprehensive repatriation programs? The main reasons are lack of in-house expertise in repatriation training, high cost of repatriation programs, and no perceived need for training by top management.[29] Firms can improve the repatriation process through a variety of methods.

- Communicate realistic expectations about reentry to employees at the time the overseas position is offered

---

[28]Storti, Craig. 1997. *The art of coming home.* Yarmouth, ME. Intercultural Press.
[29]Harvey, Michael. 1989. Repatriation of corporate executives: An empirical study. *Journal of International Business Studies* 20(1), pp. 131–144.

- Send job postings to the expatriate while abroad and circulate resume to all potential hiring units
- Prior to return (one year to six months), arrange a networking visit to home office to establish visibility with line and human resource managers
- Establish fallback position if no job is available in the event that, largely because of reengineering and downsizing, companies have difficulty guaranteeing a specific position to the returning expatriate
- Arrange for expatriates to maintain visibility through regular business trips home and through contact with visiting home country personnel, as well as encourage expatriates and families to visit home during home leave
- Create communication links to the expatriate via e-mail, newsletters, copies of important memos and relevant publications, and enable family members to stay in touch with changes at home through news publications
- Set up mentoring programs that match expatriates with company executives to give them a touch point high up in the company (Before sending their managers abroad, 3M pairs them with mentors who hold at least the rank of vice president. These "reentry sponsors" stay in regular contact with their expatriates and provide news about goings-on at the home office and serve as an early warning system about potential job or family problems that the expatriate may experience.[30])
- Sponsor gatherings of former expatriates, which give them a chance to share experiences and frustration with others who have lived through the shock of coming home
- Create a housing program that provides company-sponsored house-hunting trips or home financing

Policies and procedures vary from company to company.[31] Volvo, the Sweden-based automobile company, sent every year 15 fast-track managers from at least six countries on five-months assignments to other centers, meeting regularly to pool their experiences. At the end of their training, they made a presentation to top management. Monsanto Corporation, which has approximately 50 expatriates and 35 inpatriates in the United States, operated a repatriation training program in which expatriates learned what they should expect upon reentry. They are warned about the culture shock of returning home, about how colleagues and friends might be different, about how the office environment might have changed, about how much the expatriate experience had changed them and their children. Monsanto's program is a model of human resource planning with the human resource department involved in predeparture assessement, cross-cultural counseling, performance management, and other aspects of the international assignment.

Because repatriation has as much to do with personal adjusment as with work-related matters, the company offers repatriated employees the chance to meet three months after their return, for about three hours at work with several colleagues of their choice. The debriefing segment is a conversation aided by a facilitator who has an outline to help the expatriate cover all the important aspects of the repatriation. This de-

---

[30]Solomon, Charlene. 1995. Repatriation: Up, down or out? *Personnel Journal.* January, pp. 28–37.
[31]Maitland, Alison. 1998, December 3. New paths to global thinking. *Financial Times,* p. 23.

briefing serves several goals: it allows the employee to share important experiences; it educates managers, colleagues, and friends about the expatriate's expertise; and it functions as a resource in the organization regarding overseas work.

Novo Nordisk, a Danish pharmaceutical company, offers a good example of how a reentry session might proceed. Eight months prior to return the human resource manager meets with returning expatriates to focus on career objectives and to develop a list of key potential contact people including a designated person responsible for carrying out the reentry action plan.[32]

The increasing use of third country nationals results in more diverse and complicated workforces. Repatriation frequently is impossible for such managers when they are promoted beyond the opportunities that their original foreign operation could offer. Even though third country nationals offer the prospect of lowering the cost and increasing the diversity of the entire expatriate workforce, they also pose major challenges for managing global teams equitably.

COMPENSATION

The strategic purpose of any compensation system is to attract, motivate, reward, and retain capable employees. An appropriately designed compensation system is necessary to enable the firm to employ people who will work toward the organization's goals. Although expatriates usually comprise a small percentage of a firm's total employees, they are an important and expensive group.

Establishing a compensation package is complicated by issues such as foreign exchange rates, currency controls, currency of payment, national pension and social security contribution rules, cost of living, home leave and attendant transportation costs, and differences in tax rates. In addition, a firm must address the issues of maintaining pay equity and control over compensation costs.

Several approaches are used by international firms in compensation planning. No single approach is ideal. Factors such as the number of expatriates, the firm's experience in international management, length of assignments, size of the firm, the geographical destination, and the firm's product lines are all relevant factors. Some of the more common approaches that firms have adopted are presented in the following discussion. These approaches are not mutually exclusive, and a firm may use a combination of these approaches.

NEGOTIATION

Firms new to international business tend to negotiate mutually acceptable compensation packages with each prospective expatriate. This approach is appealing when the firm has only a few expatriates. It requires a minimum of information, keeps the system simple and less burdensome to administer, and keeps everyone's options open. The actual compensation package depends on the negotiating skills of both sides and the desire of each to have the foreign assignment take place.

When compensation packages are set by negotiations, inequities are likely to occur. Expatriate managers are likely to find out, given their small number in the firm, the

---

[32]*Managing expatriates' return.* Report number 1148-96-RR. 1996. The Conference Board. New York.

differences in their individual compensation packages, which may lead to unhappiness on the part of the lower-compensated employee. Payment of host country taxes is the responsibility of the expatriate under this approach but the host government is likely to hold the firm responsible if tax payments are not on time or not correct.

LOCALIZATION

Localization is the practice of paying expatriates the same compensation as host country nationals. This approach makes sense when a manager is posted to another country permanently. It is also used when a manager from a country with lower salaries and lower standards of living is transferred to a more advanced country, as when a manager from Mexico, for example, is posted in the United States. Inpatriates to the United States and Canada are compensated on the basis of the localization approach. The reverse is harder to implement though. Americans sent to Mexico are unlikely to accept the compensation levels paid to Mexican managers in Mexico. In such a case, various types of allowances—housing, automobile, English-language schools for children, health insurance—are paid to supplement the compensation package. The nature and size of supplements provided can easily take on the features of a negotiated package and would tend to vary from individual to individual and from country to country. The use of local market compensation packages declined in the 1990s.[33]

BALANCE SHEET

Under the **balance sheet approach,** the goal is to ensure that expatriates are able to maintain abroad a standard of living that closely approximates the one they lived in their home country. The expatriate is expected neither to lose or gain financially compared to peers in the home country.

The balance sheet approach is most frequently used by North American, European, and increasingly, Japanese firms to compensate their expatriate staff. Under this approach, salaries are evaluated and determined the same way as they are for domestic employees. In creating the compensation package, the expenses of an individual or family in the home country are divided into four categories—housing, goods and services, income taxes, and a discretionary or reserve amount (e.g., savings, alimony payments, university education for children). Each category varies with the income level of the expatriate and the size of the expatriate's family. Costs of comparable housing, goods and services, and income taxes in the host country are compared to those in the home country for the expatriate and appropriate adjustments made to ensure that the expatriate's living standard is "equalized." However, the reserve component is not protected or equalized because it represents expenses that the manager would have in the home country and not in the host country. The balance sheet approach is illustrated in Table 10-6. It assumes an American expatriate with an income of $100,000 is sent to Finland. The expenses in Finland (in markka) have been converted into U.S. dollars at the prevailing exchange rate. The last column shows the extra sums, in addition to the salary of $100,000, that the company will have to pay the expatriate to enable a replication of the standard of living in Finland.

---

[33]Gould, Carolyn. 1997. What's the latest in global compensation? *Global Workforce.* July, pp. 17–21.

Table 10-6	Illustration of the Balance Sheet Approach for a U.S. Expatriate in Finland			
Expense Category	*U.S. Expenses (in US$)*	*Costs in Finland (in Finnish markka)*	*Conversion to U.S. Dollars (1US$ = 5M)*	*Additional Payments in US$*
Income Taxes	$ 20,000	M110,000	$ 22,000	$ 2,000
Housing	$ 15,000	M120,000	$ 24,000	$ 9,000
Goods and Services	$ 40,000	M240,000	$ 48,000	$ 8,000
Reserve/Discretionary	$ 25,000	—	$ 25,000	—
TOTAL	$100,000	M470,000	$119,000	$19,000

In using this approach, the compensation analysts will have to determine and monitor costs of living in foreign locations on a continuous basis. In addition, exchange rate fluctuations will have to be taken into account. Also, the issue of whether to pay the additional sums in host country or home country currency must be addressed. All these issues tend to make the balance sheet approach quite complicated to devise and administer. It also overlooks the role of compensation as an incentive and reward tool.

LUMP SUM

Under the **lump sum approach,** a firm provides the expatriates with a sum of money, in addition to the salary and other normal incentives, to be spent by the recipients as they deem appropriate. If an expatriate wants to live in a small apartment and shop where the locals shop, it would not affect compensation. Similarly, living in style would be the prerogative of the expatriate independent of the compensation package. The most difficult part of this approach is to determine the size of the lump sum, the currency in which it will be paid, the exchange rate, and tax implications, problems similar to the ones encountered in the balance sheet approach.

The lump sum approach is used by companies in high-tech firms that exercise tight control over the length and timing of the overseas assignments of their managers. Expatriates in these firms generally go abroad for two to three years followed by repatriation to the home country.

CAFETERIA

Unlike the lump sum approach, in the **cafeteria approach,** the expatriate is provided with options from which to choose, subject to an overall limit. This option is designed to allow expatriates to seek compensation package elements that are more important and pass over those that the individual expatriate may not need. Thus, while an expatriate with school-going children would want company-paid tuition, a single person may opt for membership in a country club. The cafeteria approach is more common in the investment banking and legal professions, where salaries tend to be a small percentage of high overall incomes. In many countries, tax liabilities on benefits are lower than on cash payments.

ADDITIONAL COMPONENTS OF A COMPENSATION PACKAGE

The different approaches just discussed are presented in Table 10-7. In most cases, firms pay additional amounts of money or benefits to induce employees to take an overseas assignment, especially those that are in undesirable locations. This foreign service premium has become less common in the 1990s as firms have become more international in their activities. The additional premium paid also tends to discourage expatriates from returning or alternately, as seen earlier, create financial problems when the expatriate returns home and loses the perquisite.

Firms typically reimburse employees for educational expenses for children in elementary and secondary schools; provide some type of transportation allowance in the form of a company car and annual trips home; and pay for relocation expenses including a familiarization trip before the assignment.

In recent years, European firms, in particular, have adopted a regional approach to compensation. This approach eliminates discrepancies between employee compensation packages by paying one rate expressed in a common currency (the Euro in the EU, or the currency of the headquarters country) for a job across the whole region. Complications arise when adjustments have to be made for social security, pensions, and taxes. British Petroleum, because of its need to attract and retain a professional, mobile staff while reducing costs and ensuring equality of treatment has adopted this approach and offers its employees a "Eurocontract."[34]

Table 10-7	Executive Compensation Systems		
	Circumstances	*Advantages*	*Disadvantages*
Negotiation	-Special situations -Firms with few expatriates	-Conceptually simple	-Difficult to apply when number of expatriates increase
Localization	-Long-term assignments -Entry-level expatriates	-Simple to administer -Equity with host country nationals	-Expatriates come from economic conditions different from host country nationals -System usually requires supplemental pay
Balance Sheet	-Experienced senior and mid-level expatriates	-Keeps expatriates whole compared to home country peers -Facilitates mobility	-Complicated -Can lead to entitlements -Intrudes into expatriate finances
Lump Sum	-Relatively short (less than 3 years) assignments	-Closely replicates home country compensation	-Exchange rate variation makes this system hard to use except for short assignments
Cafeteria	-Senior expatriates -Expatriates with high overall incomes	-Can be more cost effective than other approaches	-Difficult to apply to traditional expatriates with varying needs

Source: Compensation basics for North American expatriates. 1995. Scottsdale, AZ: American Compensation Association.

---

[34]Mazur, Laura. 1995. Europay. *Across the Board.* January, pp. 40–43.

Another policy followed by some international firms is that of paying an international base salary without regard to nationality or place of hiring, plus expenses for relocating and cost of living with the firm's headquarters' country as the base for calculations. In this way, an international cadre of executives is created. This **international approach** is particularly useful for senior-level executives who move from one foreign post to another.

INCOME TAXES

Calculating and paying income taxes to different government agencies is a complex matter. The United States taxes all its citizens and resident aliens, whether they make the money in or live in the United States or abroad. This practice leads to **double taxation**— by the host government in addition to the home government.

International firms address taxation in two ways—through **tax protection** or **tax equalization.** Under tax protection, the expatriates pay no more tax than they would if they lived in the United States. The company reimburses employees for any taxes paid in excess but would allow them to keep the difference if the taxes were lower. This situation would actually create a windfall for the employee. Under tax equalization, the actual tax payments are not important to the expatriate because they are paid by the company. The company withholds the hypothetical home country tax liability from the expatriate's salary. Ninety-two percent of all U.S. firms use tax equalization and in the vast majority of cases, the firm administers their employees' tax responsibilities.[35]

PROBLEMS WITH DIFFERENTIAL COMPENSATION SYSTEMS

Compensation packages for expatriates can easily become expensive and complicated to administer. Where differential compensation systems are used, the following problems may occur:

1. Differences, sometimes quite large, between the total compensation of home country nationals and that paid to host or third country nationals, often for the same job, can create tensions between the locals and the expatriates.
2. A uniform companywide pension plan is difficult to establish.
3. Transfering managers overseas becomes expensive.
4. Expatriates resent repatriation back to home or a transfer to another foreign location if it means lower salaries and perquisites.

In developing a sound international compensation policy, the firm should address several issues, such as:

- Should the expatriate come home or stay abroad indefinitely?
- Are the assignments short or long term?
- What is the purpose of sending someone abroad?
- Is the cost worth it in terms of increased sales/profits or acquisition of knowledge/technology?
- Why does the individual want to go abroad?

---

[35]*Global relocation trends 1996 survey report.* 1997. New York: Windham International.

Developing and administering the compensation policy for expatriates is done at the firm's headquarters. Compensation managers must be familiar with the various issues at home and abroad and be able to justify decisions. For instance, when FedEx, a U.S. courier service, expanded to Germany, in accordance with German practices, the company provided its managers there with cars, Mercedes-Benz at that. When this information became known to managers at headquarters in Memphis, they reacted harshly because it was not the custom in the United States for a firm to provide its managers with vehicles, let alone Mercedes cars.[36] Management Focus 10-3 discusses how high salaries are needed to bring managers to Australia.

MANAGEMENT FOCUS 10-3

BIG COMPENSATION PACKAGES NEEDED TO LURE CHIEF EXECUTIVES

As Australia opens its economy to international competition, firms there are forced to seek out first-rate top-level managers to make sure their businesses are up to speed. The country's relatively small population means the domestic pool has to be supplemented by recruits from overseas. And to attract and retain top managers from abroad, Australian firms pay generously.

"There's been a fundamental recalibration of the expectations of a chief executive in Australia," said Ashley Stephenson, a recruiter at executive search firm, Egon Zehnder International, in Sydney. Headhunters, searching for the world's best, often end up recruiting in the United States. One of the first executives to be hired was Frank Blount, an American and former executive with AT&T who was hired to run the government-controlled telecommunications firm, Telstra. Another hire from the United States was Dennis Eck, a former retailing executive, to run Coles Myer Ltd., Australia's biggest retailer. Several executives in the financial industry in Australia have been lured down under with compensation packages that are generous by that country's historical standards.

George Trumbull who was recruited from Cigna Corporation in the United States to head

AMP, Ltd., Australia's biggest fund manager, was reported to have received annual cash salary of A$1.33 million (about US$813,700), plus annual performance bonuses. In addition, provided that he met specified performance objectives, he could receive "at no monetary cost" to him as many as 1 million AMP shares over the next two years. At current market prices, the shares were valued at A$20 million.

"Rightly or wrongly," said Brett Hoffman, a principal at Towers Perrin Forster & Crosby Inc., a compensation consulting firm, when international recruiters create a competitive compensation arrangement, "they tend to use an American package as a model," which means generous sums.

The compensation packages of chief executive officers in Australia are comprised of approximately 50 percent base pay, 25 percent to 30 percent short-term incentives (e.g., annual cash bonuses), and the balance in the form of long-term incentives such as stock options. Mr. Hoffman thought that such performance-linked compensation packages were likely to grow. Such packages tended to widen the gulf between top management and those below them, riling some shareholders.

Source: Witcher, S. Karene. 1998, July 31. Big pay packages needed to lure CEOs from abroad rile some Australians. *The Wall Street Journal*, p. B5D.

---

[36]Real, Les. 1997, June 3. Personal conversation with the author. Denver, CO.

MANAGEMENT DEVELOPMENT

For truly global companies, the whole issue of expatriates—selection, training, and repatriation—should simply be an extension of the company's management development program. It should be built into it, integrated, and not be a separate issue. Many firms, though, do not have comprehensive management development programs that focus on early identification of talent, appropriate training, systematic postings abroad in increasingly responsible positions, repatriation arrangements, and integration of overseas experience into the individual's long-term career goals. A little more than half the companies formally addressed long-term planning with their expatriates. When they did, it was most often at the preassignment stage, and less frequently during the assignment or on return at the end of the posting.

Firms adopt different approaches toward management development. Archer Daniels Midland, a U.S. agricultural products firm, sends employees abroad only to fill specific technical needs, not for career development.[37] The company has no formal preparation for employees sent overseas or returning, largely because it lacks the personnel staff to do it and because future assignments are not a certainty. In contrast, GE Medical Systems has a comprehensive career development and career management program that helps employees throughout the organization. The company uses predeparture and cross-cultural workshops, ongoing roundtables for expatriate support, and an expatriate peer mentor program. The company stays in touch with workers coming and going. Honda of America Manufacturing, Inc., the U.S. subsidiary of Honda, the Japanese automobile firm, sends U.S. managers to the parent company in Tokyo for up to three years, after preparing them with six months of Japanese language lessons, cultural training, and life style orientation during work hours. Standard Chartered, a British bank that employs 90 percent of its workers outside the United Kingdom, instills global thinking in its managers by recruiting college graduates from up to 21 nationalities every year. Trainees recruited in Singapore are sent to London and vice versa for a couple of months to learn the business and to hone their interpersonal skills. Managers recruited into cross-border roles at a more senior level learn about global thinking and corporate culture as part of their induction. Selected groups attend the international management program at a university.[38]

Formal management development programs are also provided by universities and businesses where curriculums are geared toward creating an international cadre of managers. Examples are the American Graduate School of International Management in Glendale, Arizona, corporate-sponsored business schools such as Theseus (set up by France Telecom), and private consulting firms. In-house corporate schools such as McDonald's Hamburger University provides training in 22 different languages, simultaneous translation, and even teach in two languages at the same time.[39] It also has training centers in Munich, Tokyo, Sydney, and London. A training department in China prepares managers on how to give performance reviews and feedback, how to listen, and what to do if a person becomes defensive. In addition, all the training centers train managers in every facet of operations.

---

[37]Engen, John. 1995. Coming home. *Training.* March, pp. 37–40.
[38]Maitland, Alison. 1998, December 3. New paths to global thinking. *Financial Times,* p. 23.
[39]Solomon, Charlene. 1996. Big Mac's mcglobal HR secrets. *Personnel Journal.* April, pp. 46–54.

TEAMWORK

Inevitably, international companies organize employees to work in teams. As Management Focus 10-4 highlights, the opportunities offered by cross-cultural teams are plentiful, and they require support to be functional. For Texas Instruments, with 62,000 employees in more than 30 countries, technology affords operating units a great deal of autonomy and limits the use of expatriates.[40] Employees worked in teams but they did not relocate. Communication occurred through phone, fax, teleconferencing, and computers. It was much more cost effective and less disruptive.

CULTURAL TRANSFORMATION

A major goal of management development is the creation of host and third country managers who can think, work, and behave in ways that are compatible with the corporate culture, which is, in many cases, greatly influenced by the home country culture. Inpatriation is one way of developing compatible managerial talent. Management Focus 10-5 describes the efforts of an Italian truck manufacturer to introduce European practices in China.

OUTSOURCING HUMAN RESOURCE FUNCTIONS

Many of the human resource functions discussed in this chapter are quite complicated. Small firms and those new to international business do not have the in-house capability to provide many services that internationalization requires and are compelled to contract them out to specialized outside vendors. To cut costs, increase efficiency, and focus on core competencies, many firms outsource nonstrategic human resource functions. Some functions, such as tax planning and preparation, have long been provided by outside vendors, but increasingly more tasks are being outsourced. The leading functions that are outsourced are shown in Table 10-8.

Accounting and consulting firms such as PWC (Price Waterhouse Coopers) and KPMG Peat Marwick have traditionally provided services in taxation and compensation planning. Firms such as Berlitz and Windham International specialize in providing cross-cultural training, relocation assistance, and stress counseling. Executive search companies such as Korn/Ferry, Heidrick & Struggles, and Spencer Stuart have seen their revenues grow as they have expanded to serve clients on a worldwide basis.[41] Organization Resources Counsellors collect and provide data on housing and living costs in cities around the world.

CONCLUSIONS

The growth of international business has created new and complex tasks for the human resource department and has transformed its role in numerous ways. International firms employ managers from home, host, and third countries in their operations. In turn, human resource issues of selecting, evaluating performance, and compensation have become

---

[40]Solomon, Charlene. 1995. Global teams: The ultimate collaboration. *Personnel Journal.* September, pp. 49–58.
[41]Donkin, Richard. 1997, November 14. The expatriate experience. *Financial Times,* p. 1.

GLOBAL TEAMS: THE ULTIMATE COLLABORATION

As firms form strategic alliances and joint ventures and utilize a globally diverse group of employees, the use of teams is becoming more and more common. Teams maximize expertise from a variety of people, provide companies a more accurate picture of international customers' needs, and profit by the synergy necessary to unify the varying perspectives of different cultures and different business functions. It all adds up. Global teams are one way of cross-pollinating—they move people who are successful in one branch of the firm to work with people in another country and another branch.

The fundamentals of global team success are not all that different from the practices that work for domestic teams. But they entail more variables, such as culture, language and communication, and group dynamics. In addition the issue of logistics must be overcome: challenges inherent in working in different time zones, travelling vast distances, and conflicting schedules.

To become productive units, global teams must evolve, usually through four phases. In Phase One, each team member comes with personal expectations, culture, and values. The first step involves team members recognizing that values are merely a set of norms particular to their society; they are not universals. In Phase Two individuals begin to respect the cultures of other team members even as they acknowledge problems and differences. During Phase Three, team members begin to trust each other. They start to share knowledge. At this time, they begin to focus on achieving team goals. And then, in Phase Four, the team begins to work in a collaborative way.

The Dallas-based Maxus Energy, a wholly owned subsidiary of YPF, a large Argentine energy company, successfully uses cross-functional teams of Americans, Dutch, British, and Indonesians to maximize oil and gas production. The self-directed teams receive clear guidance from the company:

- Limit team size to 10
- Create representation on each team of varied functions and cultures
- Clearly define the role of the teams
- Understand the function of the team leaders and team facilitators
- Allow experimentation with rules and structures
- Establish clear operational guidelines
- Include specific times for meetings and finished reports
- Thoroughly monitor the team's progress through updates and reports

Equally important, Maxus provides its teams with technical, verbal, monetary, and decision-making support that helps them to meet their objectives.

Intel Corporation, the California-based computer chip maker, has used global teams for more than a decade for a medley of projects from formulating and delivering sales strategies for specific products to developing and manufacturing new products. Whatever their purpose, Intel's teams are frequently composed of a combination of employees from many of the company's locations in Ireland, Israel, France, Taiwan, and the United Kingdom. Many of the teams come together quickly, do their work, then disband and regroup with other team members. The main reason for the success of the teams is their simple, basic processes and procedures. Setting clear expectations and having clearly defined goals, roles, and responsibilities make teams work.

Source: Solomon, Charlene M. 1995. Global teams: The ultimate collaboration. *Personnel Journal.* September, pp. 49–58.

MANAGEMENT FOCUS 10-5

LITTLE ITALY IN CHINATOWN

Camillo Donati is the chief representative in China of Iveco, the truck-making subsidiary of Fiat and the largest Italian investor in that country. Since 1988, he had lived in the Jinling Hotel in Nanjing and was the author of the most ambitious training and cultural exchange program ever undertaken by a European company in China.

"We have given the Chinese the possibility to understand our industrial culture and the opportunity to live our social life," said Mr. Donati. Iveco selected nearly 400 Chinese-trained engineers and workers, trained them in Italian language, and transferred them to Italian factories in the late 1980s. "We tried to eliminate the differences in style—how we live and how we speak," he continued.

In 1986, Mr. Donati arranged for 32 Italians to come to Nanjing to teach 370 local mechanics and other staff basic Italian. Then the Chinese employees were all transferred to Iveco's factories in Italy to gain on-site technical expertise in how the trucks

and vans were assembled, as well as a sense of the corporate and national culture. For Iveco, more than most international automobile firms, such a substantial language program was a necessity, "At that time we had a problem in how to communicate," Mr. Donati explained. "The Chinese didn't speak English and, in fact, the Italians too didn't speak such good English either."

Iveco's extensive training program had yielded results. Iveco was the best-known name in light commercial vehicles in China. It had invested $200 million in a 50:50 joint venture to produce 60,000 light commercial vehicles annually. Because of its training programs, the number of Italians employed in Nanjing had shrunk. The main plant had 3,000 workers, only eight of which were Italian expatriates. Even that number was expected to decrease. Mr. Donati acknowledged, "We are developing the local managers."

Source: Harding, James. 1999, February 2. Little Italy comes to China town. *Financial Times,* p. 11.

important. To be successful, the right manager has to be selected and provided with appropriate cross-cultural training. Many firms fail to make good use of repatriated executives thus squandering valuable talent. The complexity of international human resource management has meant that many functions are outsourced to specialist service providers. New competencies and knowledge are being demanded of human resource managers as they create and assist the international manager to function effectively in the global environment.

Table 10-8	Most Frequently Outsourced International Human Resource Activities

- Tax preparation
- Cross-cultural training
- Work permits/visas
- Household goods move coordination
- Settling-in services
- Expense reimbursement
- Review of pay
- Compensation development

Source: Global Relocation Trends 1996 Survey Report. Windham International, New York City.

OPENING VIGNETTE EPILOGUE

Three years after sending Mr. Borenstein to Hong Kong, Bandag closed its office there and laid him off. A search for another job with a U.S. company in Asia proved fruitless. In mid-January 1999, he returned with his wife and two small children to Newport Beach, California, uncertain when and where he would work next.

Reflecting on his plight, Mr. Borenstein blamed it on the economic turmoil that had started in East Asia in 1997. He also acknowledged that he did not keep close enough touch with headquarters and failed to cultivate allies back home. He did not cut costs quickly enough in response to falling sales. Even his pride in his expensive company-paid apartment worked against him. "When executives came out from Iowa to visit Hong Kong, I brought a lot of people home," Mr. Borenstein said. "That was not wise. They said we lived in a palace. I got a lot of flak over that. That's the kind of thing they remembered."

When he first arrived in Hong Kong, "I felt we had control of our destiny," he said. "But you're not in control of your career anymore. With globalization, the winds change dramatically. You're a hero one day; the next you're a goat."[42]

[42]Kaufman, Jonathan. 1999, January 21. An American expatriate finds Hong Kong post a fast boat to nowhere. *The Wall Street Journal*, pp. A1, A8.

Key Terms

- international human resource management
- expatriate
- inpatriate
- management localization

- dual career couples
- repatriation
- balance sheet approach
- lump sum approach
- cafeteria approach

- international approach
- double taxation
- tax protection
- tax equalization

Discussion Questions

1. What are the advantages and disadvantages of using host country and third country nationals? Under what circumstances may a firm use third country nationals?

2. Given that finding expatriate candidates is the largest single challenge faced by international human resource managers, suggest a plan of action as to how a firm can deal with this problem.

3. You have been hired by a Japanese firm to design a cross-cultural training program for a group of Japanese functional managers who will be transferred from Tokyo to their zipper manufacturing plant in Georgia in the southern United States. What will be the components of this program, and what will the program serve to achieve?

4. Evaluate the alternative approaches to determining compensation for expatriate managers. Why would a firm select one approach over another?

5. A U.S.-based firm has operations and offices in many foreign countries. It has a strict corporate policy on sexual harassment based on U.S. laws and court decisions.

Should the company extend the policy to its overseas locations or should it develop singular policies for every country in which it operates? Discuss.

6. Explain the role of the human resource department in a large multinational firm. How has its role been changing and why?

Writing Assignment

Your company plans to transfer to its headquarters a manager from one of its foreign locations. The transferee is a citizen of the foreign country and will require a work permit. You have been asked by the human resource department to investigate with the immigration authorities and prepare a short manual outlining the specific steps that have to be followed to obtain the necessary legal papers so that the foreign manager can be transferred to the country where the headquarters is located.

Internet Exercise

Use the Internet to find out the personal income tax rates and the corresponding income amounts for 10 different countries. Prepare a report comparing the results with the tax rates in your home country. Web sites of the U.S. Bureau of Labor Statistics, U.S. Department of Commerce, Arthur Andersen, Price Waterhouse Coopers, Towers Perrin, and Eurostat (Statistical Office of the European Communities) are some initial places to explore.

Internet Resources

An excellent source of information on international human resource management is *www.workforceonline.com*, the online version of Workforce magazine. Windham International, a global relocation firm, can be accessed at *www.windhamworld.com*. Berlitz, a language and cross-cultural training firm has a site at *www.berlitz.com*. The Society for Human Resource Management's site is at *www.shrm.org*. Examples of recruitment Web sites are Monster Board (*www.monsterboard.com*), Career Mosaic (*www.careermosaic.com*), *The Wall Street Journal* (*www.@careers.wsj.com*), *International Herald Tribune* (*www.iht.com*), Career Path (*www.careerpath.com*), and Recruiting Consultants (*www.iirc.com*).

Case 10–1   THE AMERICAN VIRUS

On Monday morning in Tokyo, Noburu Sato, director of international operations for Kinoman Specialty Foods (KSF), arrived at his office to find a fax from Tadashi Kijimura, the company's technical advisor in Atlanta in the United States. Mr. Kijimura had resigned from his position. Mr. Sato swore under his breath and muttered, "Tadashi has also succumbed to the American virus." With Tadashi's resignation, the company had lost in four years, three of its executives it had sent to its U.S. subsidiary. While the immediate issue was to arrange for Mr. Kijimura's responsibilities to be handled by someone else, the bigger question that Mr. Sato worried about was how to stop the loss of its internationally experienced managers when posted in the United States.

KSF AND ITS OPERATIONS IN THE UNITED STATES

KSF was a well-established Japanese company that manufactured a wide range of food products including sauces, condiments, and bottled beverages. In the late 1980s, the company established a plant in the United States to manufacture products for the U.S. market in response to the growing popularity of Asian foods there. The plant employed about 100 American workers. Although most of the senior managerial staff at the U.S. subsidiary were Americans, several positions were held by Japanese managers sent from headquarters, including the president of the subsidiary, the manager for technical maintenance, the chief financial officer, and the director of food chemicals and preservatives. Sensing a need to develop products specifically for the U.S. market and to adapt a wider range of Japanese products to suit the American palate, the company established a research and development laboratory alongside its factory in 1992. The lab employed two Japanese technical advisors who worked with a small team of U.S. food products researchers.

The U.S. subsidiary was not the company's only overseas venture. Earlier, it had established plants in Malaysia and Thailand and sourced raw materials from many other countries. Several Japanese expatriates served at its production plants in Asia, and over the years many managers from headquarters had served a stint in Kuala Lumpur and Bangkok, respectively. Sales from overseas operations had risen steadily and by 1999 accounted for more than a quarter of the company's total revenues.

MANAGEMENT DEVELOPMENT AT KSF

The descendants of the founders of the company owned a controlling share of the parent company and were involved in the day-to-day operations. However, the company was run by professional managers. An ethnocentric philosophy characterized the company's operations. The formula that had served the company well and contributed to its success was unquestioned— no one knew of another way to run the business.

To run the overseas operations, managers from headquarters would be sent out on a three-year assignment. The managers were selected on the basis of their technical capabilities and proven record of performance in Japan. All managers sent abroad were men in their mid-forties, with substantial experience. A tour of duty overseas was considered just another appointment in the manager's career with the company. With lifetime employment and job rotation considered the norm in the company, managers were expected to accept the foreign posting. Until the resignations from expatriates in the United States, the company had not experienced any problems with its expatriate policy. Certainly, no expatriate had ever resigned while in Bangkok or Kuala Lumpur.

CONCERN OVER FOREIGN POSTING

Most Japanese managers did not look forward to the overseas posting. It did not count specifically towards career advancement, and many feared that being abroad would mean that they would be "out of the loop." Although financially the overseas appointments were attractive, with company-paid bonuses, opposition to accepting the overseas posting also came from the potential expatriate's wife. Although she did not have a career on her own, she was unwilling to give up her social circles in which she was active and comfortable. She feared that abroad she would be isolated and be totally dependent on her husband. Believing that hours of work overseas for her husband would just be as long as they tended to be in Japan, she foresaw a lonely, boring time, her only company her children.

Many also were greatly concerned about the educational opportunities abroad for the children. Especially for those with teenagers, families were reluctant to take the children out of Japan. The high school exit exam required extensive preparations, and success determined admission to the more prestigious universities. Parents felt that foreign educational systems would leave their children unprepared for Japanese higher education. The lack of foreign language skills was another factor that discouraged the wives, and although the company provided tutoring for the husband in the language of the host country, no such provision existed for the wife or children. Finally, both the employee and his family tended to harbor a sense of insecurity about living outside Japan. They were concerned over issues such as crime, health, availability of food they were accustomed to, and ability to get along with non-Japanese.

The company provided minimal predeparture training to its expatriate managers. Information was provided about the living conditions, Japanese communities, other Japanese companies, and official contacts. Efforts were sometimes made to enable returned expatriates to share their views and experiences with those tapped to be sent abroad. However, such networking was informal at best and depended on the initiative and interests of the individuals concerned.

THE KIJIMURAS IN THE UNITED STATES

On June 23, 1996, Tadashi with his wife Michiko and their two children, aged 10 and 12, flew into Atlanta from

Tokyo. It was Tadashi's first posting overseas. They were both excited and apprehensive. Thanks to television and the printed media, they had a general idea about life and culture in the United States, which seemed very different and overwhelming to the Kijimuras. All the Japanese employees at KSF's operations in Atlanta were at the airport to welcome them. Arrangements had been made for their housing in a Japanese hotel for the time being.

Within a week, Mr. Kijimura began working at the company in the R&D department. A Japanese colleague picked him up for work and dropped him off at the hotel at the end of the day. In the welcome packet provided to him was a manual for obtaining a Georgia driver's license; it came in a Japanese translation and he was told that he could take the exam in Japanese. Michiko was visited by the wives of the other Japanese managers and they took her and the children to the Georgia-Japan Friendship Club where Michiko was surprised to find that more than a thousand Japanese nationals lived in the area. A Japanese language school that went up to grade eight offered an opportunity for the children.

Soon Michiko with the help of a Japanese-speaking real estate agent was looking at houses to buy. Every time Michiko would meet her new Japanese friends, she would say, "The houses, they are so big and they are so cheap!" Soon, they bought their new house and moved in. Tadashi now had his driver's license and his own car. Michiko, who had never driven a car before, decided to learn to drive too. She thought it would help her buy the groceries, visit the club on her own, and pick up and drop off the children. Apprehensive about learning how to drive, she signed up with a driving school and was astonished at the ease with which cars with automatic transmission could be driven. In a few weeks, she had her license and a new car with automatic transmission.

The children adjusted well. Although their friends were Japanese, they became friendly with the children of their U.S. neighbors. On Labor Day, one of the neighbors invited them over for Southern-style barbecue. They had a pool and the children took their bathing suits for a pool party. Mr. Kijimura was so impressed by the huge gas grill of his neighbor that he bought one the next day, amazed at the low "end-of-summer sale" price he paid. He invited both his neighbors with their families, and served food with a full selection of products from his own company.

On weekends, Tadashi played golf. It was easy to reserve the links and the costs appeared to him to be minimal at numerous courses from which he could choose. He encouraged his wife to take up golfing too

and Michiko was surprised to see many American women playing golf; until now, she thought only men, and businessmen at that, played golf.

Whenever they could, the Kijimuras did some traveling. They found it easy to drive around. Everything was cheap and everything worked. Their fears about crime and safety appeared to be unfounded. Despite their weak English, though it was improving rapidly, they had no difficulty in obtaining services at hotels, restaurants, shops, and banks. They found the Americans always smiling, greeting them, making them feel at home.

Michiko got involved with a local university that had a Japanese language program. The program wanted to develop links with the local Japanese community to provide a full range of learning experience to the students. The children were now avid followers of baseball and football and were in the neighborhood's Little League. They were also doing well in school. Tadashi's work was going well too. He found his American research colleagues to be remarkably open to new ideas with an easy-going approach to their job.

In their letters and phone calls to family and friends at home, the Kijimuras were enthusiastic. Michiko would include in every letter some aspect of American life and compare it with that in Japan. She would also occasionally write, "You may not believe it, but here in America, you can get whatever you want, even shitake mushrooms and plum wine." On their annual three weeks vacation to Japan, they would take gifts for their families and friends. Their language now included many English words when they spoke Japanese; Tadashi dressed more casually; Michicko had bobbed, permed, and streaked her hair; and the children, to the shock of uncles and grandparents, wore baseball caps backwards.

END OF ASSIGNMENT

In April 1999, Tadashi was informed by Mr. Sato at headquarters that his new posting to the research lab in Tokyo would start in July. He had known that the appointment to Atlanta was for three years and his term was almost over. Yet, he received the transfer order with a sense of sadness; he was not excited at the thought of returning to Japan. That night, over dinner with his family, he announced that they would soon have to begin planning and packing their return. Michiko was quiet and then asked slowly, "Can you get an extension?"

Tadashi responded, "For how long can I ask? Three months? Six months? That will be the most they will give. And what excuse can I give? To ask for some additional time to complete the two research projects we are working on?"

The children weighed in, "Do we really have to go back to Tokyo, Dad?"

Over the next two months, Mr. Kijimura, even as he raced to complete his projects at work, wondered what he should do. His mind was made up when he received a call from a U.S. executive search company, based in New York. He was told about a job with a large U.S. multinational food company that could use his technical skills as well as knowledge about Japanese foods and the Japanese market. Although the job required frequent travel to Japan, it was based in the United States. The job was available immediately.

When he told this to his wife, she exclaimed, "I can't believe it. We are meant to stay here. Accept it right away!" But Tadashi now worried about how he would tell his boss, the president of U.S. operations. In the past few years, two Japanese managers in the U.S. operations had quit soon after their transfer orders had come. The president had always spoken of them as traitors, a disgrace to the company, men with "back-bones of eels." So, on Friday, when he met his boss and told him that he wanted to resign, the president replied, "Tadashi, I don't want to hear this. If you want to leave the company, let headquarters know and tell them why you want to leave."

QUESTIONS

1. Should the company make changes on how it prepares its managers for cross-cultural experiences abroad?
2. What can the company do to stop the defection of highly qualified managers?
3. Why did the U.S. culture appeal so greatly to the Kijimuras?
4. What does the transformation of the Kijimuras say about the corporate culture of KFP, Japanese culture, and U.S. culture?
5. Should Mr. Sato try to dissuade Mr. Kijimura from resigning? Why? What would it take for Mr. Kijimura to reconsider his decision?

References

Black, J. Stewart, and Mark Mendenhall. 1992. Evaluating the performance of global managers. *Journal of International Compensation and Benefits* 1, pp. 35–40.

Compensation basics for North American expatriates. 1995. Scottsdale, AZ: American Compensation Asociation.

Global relocation trends 1999 survey report. 1999. New York: Windham International.

Hanami, Tadashi. 1992. Employment discrimination in U.S.-based Japanese companies. *Economic Eye* 13(4), pp. 28–32.

Hugenberg, Lawrence, Renee LaCivita, and Andra Lubanovic. 1996. International business and training: Preparing for the global economy. *The Journal of Business Communication* 33(2), pp. 205–222.

International sources of salary data. 1998. *Compensation & Benefits Review.* May–June, pp. 22–27.

Kobrin, Stephen. 1988. Expatriate reduction and strategic control in American multinational corporations. *Human Resource Management* 27(1), pp. 63–75.

Mendenhall, Mark, and Gary Oddou. 1991. Expatriate performance appraisal: Problems and solutions. In Mark Mendenhall and Gary Oddou, eds. *Readings and cases in international human resource management.* Boston: PWS-Kent.

Pucik, Vladimir. 1985. Strategic human resource management in a multinational firm. In H. V. Wortzel and L. H. Wortzel, eds. *Strategic management of multinational corporations: The essentials.* New York: John Wiley and Sons.

Rogovsky, Nikolai. 1998. What type of knowledge is needed in the foreign branches: Staffing practices in large U.S. law firms. *The International Journal of Human Resource Management* 9(2), pp. 296–308.

Spreitzer, Gretchen, Morgan McCall, Jr., and Joan Mahoney. 1997. Early identification of international executive potential. *Journal of Applied Psychology* 82(1), pp. 6–29.

Swaak, Reyer. 1995. Expatriate management: The search for best practices. *Compensation & Benefits Review.* March–April, pp. 21–29.

Tung, Rosalie. 1988. Career issues in international assignments. *Academy of Management Executive* 2(3), pp. 241–244.

11
MANAGEMENT OF
EMPLOYEE RELATIONS

✍

OPENING VIGNETTE

At the end of 1987, Ford Motor Company tried to introduce major innovations in its labor relations practices at its plants in the United Kingdom. Management wanted to introduce new production methods using teams, remove the hierarchical set up that existed on the shop floor, harmonize pay structures, and have supervisors focus on making production more efficient, rather than enforcing work rules. The company's goal was to emulate Nissan U.K., the British subsidiary of the Japanese automobile company. Nissan had achieved flexibility in its greenfield operation by hiring temporary workers during peak production periods and using terms and conditions common to the entire workforce. It had only two categories of shop floor employees—technicians and assembly line workers. Status differentiation among all employees was neutralized by requiring them to wear overalls and eliminating preferential parking spaces and separate cafeterias.

Ford's proposals were greeted by wildcat (illegal, unauthorized) strikes. Workers, by an overwhelming majority, voted to strike. Ford's offer of higher salaries was rejected by the workers. With production disrupted in the United Kingdom (and workers idled at dependent plants in Europe) and mounting losses, Ford gave up its efforts to reorganize the workplace.

Why did Ford fail? Nissan had succeeded because it had a new plant while Ford with its greyfield facilities had an already established labor relations culture and practice where change was harder to introduce. At that time, unemployment in the United Kingdom was declining and the increasing shortage of skilled labor strengthened the ability of the union to oppose the company. Ford U.K. was also vulnerable due to management practices such as just-in-time inventory (which meant it had no stockpiles of either raw materials or finished goods) and single sourcing of parts and components (to reduce costs and ensure standardization). It was also possible that the workers and their leaders were not consulted nor provided with relevant information in a timely manner.

In March 1988, Ford abandoned plans to build a new electronic components plant in the United Kingdom after an interunion squabble over representing the 450 workers that would have been hired. Trouble had erupted after the firm's managers at its parent headquarters in Detroit, Michigan, had agreed with the Amalgamated Engineering Union (AEU) to be the sole representa-

(continued)

Opening Vignette (*continued*)

tive of the workers at the proposed plant. Other unions protested this exclusive arrangement and accused the AEW of breaking with the procedures of the British Trade Union Congress, the apex body of labor unions in the country.

In late 1989, Ford negotiated a new collective bargaining agreement with its U.K. workers, which called for increased wages and cost of living allowances. Threatened with a strike, Ford offered even more money. Skilled workers were still unhappy and went on strike. They objected to Ford training unskilled people to do the work previously done by skilled workers, which was seen as a threat to their jobs. Because of their strike, thousands of workers were laid off in the United Kingdom and in other European plants—reflecting the interdependence of Ford's European facilities. On March 2, the strike ended and work resumed. On April 10, 1990, workers at one of the plants accepted wide-ranging reforms in working practices to allow greater flexibility and integrated manufacturing teams. The use of group leaders replaced foremen, and it increased employee responsibility on the assembly line with fewer job categories.

The overwhelming majority of the workers employed by international firms in their overseas facilities are not expatriate managers or even managers at all. Instead they are the rank and file workers and shop floor employees who perform the countless duties connected with the production and distribution of goods and services for the firm as well as the attendant office functions. The management of these workers including their wages and working conditions is determined by factors such as labor market conditions, host government laws and policies, presence of labor unions, and the firm's own human resource policies. As business has become internationalized, so have labor markets. New pressures are being felt on wages and working conditions in every country. This chapter examines the managerial issues connected with the employment of the rank and file workers, who are mostly citizens of the host country. Particular attention is given to how international managers handle the workplace relationship when labor unions are present and on understanding the role and attitudes of unions toward multinational firms.

THE LABOR MARKET

For most positions, the international firm recruits from the labor market in the host country. Depending on the job, the labor market may be local, regional, or national. When Deutsche Bank of Germany needs secretarial staff for its New York City office it hires them from the New York area labor market. If the bank was seeking experienced accountants, the search may encompass the entire country, the national labor market. The predominant use of host country nationals to staff positions is understandable. The number of such positions is relatively large. Workers can be paid host country wages without expensive premiums for crossing borders. The host country government and society expects an investor—domestic or foreign—to employ local nationals. For non-managerial jobs, it is difficult to secure government work permits to bring in home or third country nationals unless a compelling need can be demonstrated.

In certain situations, the international firm may have to expand its search for skilled and even low-skilled workers to include the entire world or a region of the world. In the late 1990s, shortage of computer software engineers and other highly skilled technology workers in the United States led technology firms to seek greater numbers of H-1b work visas issued by the U.S. government for foreign workers. Many U.S. companies recruited in Canada, advertising in Canadian newspapers and on Canadian university campuses. Canadian high-tech workers were attractive because they spoke English and had few problems adjusting to the American workplace. In addition, under the North American Free Trade Agreement (NAFTA), Canadians (and Mexicans) could readily obtain permits to work in the United States.[1]

Customer preferences encourage firms to widen the labor markets from which to draw potential employees. Swissair, an airline based in Zurich, Switzerland, which operates flights throughout the world, had since the mid-1970s, employed Japanese flight attendants on its services to Japan. In 1996, it began employing Indian and Thai flight attendants on its Asian routes. The majority of Swissair's passengers were non-Swiss, and the company felt that employing non-Swiss cabin staff acknowledged the realities of its client base without diminishing the company's Swiss standards.[2]

When employers find wage costs, especially for low-skilled jobs, high they are more likely to look to other countries to base operations. To take advantage of Mexico's abundant supply of cheaper low-skilled workers, many firms have invested in garment manufacturing plants there. Jeans labeled "Assembled in Mexico" start with cotton, usually grown in the United States, which is woven into denim at a U.S. mill, and then sliced by cutters into about 17 pieces. These pieces are then shipped by truck to garment factories in Mexico where they are stitched together by workers laboring 48 hours or more a week for about $1.25 an hour. The finished jeans are transported back to the United States for distribution and sale.[3]

In countries with small populations or workforces such as Kuwait and United Arab Emirates, international construction firms like Bechtel of the United States and Hyundai of South Korea hire workers from the Indian subcontinent (India, Pakistan, Bangladesh, Nepal, and Sri Lanka) to work on projects for a specific number of years. Specialized labor companies provide the requisite number of workers with different skill levels and arrange for work documentation, travel, housing, and medical care. In the 1950s and 1960s, West Germany arranged with Turkey for Turkish workers to come and work in Germany's postwar reconstruction. Some of these "guest workers" stayed on and formed a minority population in Germany. These examples show how labor markets have expanded and changed.

---

[1]Tamburri, Rosanna. 1998, May 12. Canada frets high tech "brain drain." *The Wall Street Journal*, p. A16.
[2]Swissair to recruit 80 flight attendants in India and Thailand. 1996, October 15. *www. swissair . . . _ media_release.html*.
[3]Lounsberry, Emilie. 1998, February 22. In Mexico, jeans and empty pockets. *The Philadelphia Inquirer*, pp. A1, A16.

LABOR FORCE CHARACTERISTICS

The characteristics of the labor force in a country affect how employee relations are organized and managed. In this section, the issues of immigrants, women, children, and prison labor for international firms are discussed.

IMMIGRANTS

The labor force in many countries has been affected by the influx of legal immigrants from culturally diverse countries. The international movement of people has been taking place since the beginning of civilization. However, national governments try to regulate the influx of immigrants by limiting residency and work permits. A recent exception is the decision of the European Union to allow citizens of its member countries to freely move about the EU in search of employment. The presence of immigrants, especially from ethnically and culturally different countries, has led to issues related to managing a diverse workforce and fair employment practices.

Immigrants, particularly those less-educated and from less-developed countries, are often willing to work long hours at low wages. Firms prefer to hire such workers especially for menial, unskilled, or semiskilled jobs, the so-called 3-D jobs—dirty, dangerous, and difficult—which local nationals in developed countries are averse to accepting.

Given the wide disparity in economic conditions across nations, people cross borders illegally in search of employment. In the United States, employing illegal immigrants is a violation of the law. Employers are required, under the **Immigration Reform and Control Act** of 1986, to verify a job applicant's documents to determine whether the individual is eligible for employment. Given their status, illegal immigrants avoid the primary labor market, and instead, throng to the secondary labor market. Many employers find it tempting to hire them because of the low wages that can be paid with little attention to working conditions, knowing that workers are unlikely to complain to the authorities. Given the potential risks of government investigations and negative publicity, the firm's recruitment policy should be to avoid the employment of illegal immigrants.

WOMEN

The proportion of women in the workforce varies from country to country, which in turn affects the size of the total labor force. In many countries because of lower education levels, their subservient societal role, or social restrictions on workplace participation, the percentage of women in the labor force is smaller. Table 11-1 presents data on the labor force participation rate for women in selected countries. Over time, the number of women in the labor market has increased. The growth in assembly operations, especially of electronic products and garments in less-developed countries, has impacted the labor market by enticing more and more women to seek employment. Female workers are valued for their patience, diligence, and compliant attitude. In some electronics plants in Mexico, women comprise more than 95 percent of the workers.

In most countries, the number of upper-level positions held by women is proportionately fewer than those held by men. This discrepancy has given rise to the notion of a **glass ceiling,** where although formal restrictions on women's participation in the workplace may not exist, social, educational, and organizational factors may limit the employment of women in the higher echelons of a firm. In Japan, for instance, many

Table 11-1	Labor Force Participation Rate for Women (aged 15–64) for Selected Countries	
Country	*1980*	*1997*
Australia	52.1	64.7
Canada	59.1	67.8
France	54.4	59.8
Germany	52.8*	61.8
Japan	54.8	63.7
Mexico	33.7	42.8
South Korea	51.3**	54.8
Sweden	74.1	74.5
United Kingdom	58.3	67.5
United States	59.7	71.3

*West Germany

**1990

Source: Statistical abstract of the United States 1999. 119th ed. Washington, DC: U.S. Census Bureau, 1999.

women are employed as secretaries and office assistants. Often referred to as *shokuba no hana* or office flowers, they are hired for their appearance, their manners, and their obedience—in a sense, decorations for the office. They are expected to resign when they marry or have children. This practice creates opportunities for western firms operating in Japan to recruit qualified female workers ignored by their Japanese competitors.[4] Table 11-2 presents data on women's share of administrative/managerial and professional/technical jobs in selected countries.

CHILD AND PRISON LABOR

Two labor market issues that have come to the fore in recent years are the use of child labor and prisoners. Children in the labor market are common in poverty-ridden nations such as Bangladesh, and the use of prison labor to manufacture products for export takes place in many countries. Both these groups receive close scrutiny from social advocacy groups, labor unions, home country governments, and investigative media. The reactions are usually negative and managers need to be careful that they are not employing child or prison labor or importing products from suppliers abroad who directly or through subcontracting use such workers. In 1998, Adidas-Salomon, a Franco-German sporting goods company, admitted that some of its licensees and subcontractors in China used Chinese prisoners to produce thousands of soccer balls branded with Adidas and official World Cup logos. In reaction, the company cancelled all soccer ball orders coming out of China, decided to create a full-time human rights department within the company, and centralized all Chinese production in one location to avoid any possible diversion of production to prison labor camps.[5] Various welfare organizations are working with

---

[4]Whitehall, Arthur. 1991. *Japanese management: Tradition and transition.* New York: Routledge.
[5]Copetas, Craig, and Craig Smith. 1998, July 1. Adidas concedes that some soccer balls likely were made by Chinese prisoners. *The Wall Street Journal,* p. A14.

Table 11-2	Women in Administrative/Managerial and Professional/Technical Jobs	
Country	*Administrative/Managerial Jobs* (% of total)	*Professional/Technical Jobs* (% of total)
Canada	42.2	51.1
China	11.6	45.1
France	9.4	41.4
Germany	26.6	49.0
Greece	12.1	44.2
India	2.3	20.5
Japan	9.3	44.1
Mexico	19.8	45.2
Singapore	34.3	16.1
Sweden	27.9	63.7
United Kingdom	33.0	43.7
United States	44.3	53.1

Source: Human development report. 1999. *United Nations Development Program.* New York: Oxford University Press.

international firms to create programs to reduce the employment of children and to provide a humane, meaningful work environment to these young workers, and to ban the import of goods made by prison labor. Management Focus 11-1 looks at the response of Nike, Inc., to criticism of its labor policies at the plants of its overseas contractors.

HUMAN RESOURCE ISSUES

RECRUITMENT

Workers are generally recruited in developed countries on the basis of competence and qualifications. However, it is not uncommon, especially in traditional societies, to rely on social status for hiring. Social status may include family background and ties, wealth, education, race, religion, or connections to the military or the ruling elite, among other factors. Foreign firms need to understand the interrelationship between various ethnic, racial, religious, and linguistic groups in diverse and contentious societies. In the United States, civil rights laws not only bar discrimination in employment on the basis of a wide range of personal attributes (such as race, religion, national origin, color, age, and handicap status) but also requires employers to engage in affirmative action to actively recruit from certain groups who may be underrepresented in the firm. In Malaysia, government policy favors the recruitment of Malays over the Chinese and Indian populations, in a policy known as *bumiputra* (sons of the soil) and employers—foreign and domestic—are required to abide by it.

In many countries, foreign firms are seen as the employers of choice. More prestige is attached to such employers, and applicants often believe that working conditions there are better and career advancement opportunities more generous. These perceptions make recruiting capable employees easier. McDonald's, the U.S. fast food chain, finds recruiting employees for its stores quite easy because its name, logo, and brands

MANAGEMENT FOCUS 11-1

NIKE LISTENS TO ITS CRITICS

In an effort to defuse criticism of the labor practices in the plants of its overseas suppliers, Nike Inc., an athletic gear manufacturer based in Beaverton, Oregon, named Maria Eitel, a former Microsoft Corporation public relations executive, to the newly created position of vice president of corporate and social responsibility. She was responsible for Nike's labor practices, environmental affairs, and "global community involvement."

Unions, church groups, social activists, college students, and politicians had criticized Nike for allowing underage and inadequately paid workers to make its products in underdeveloped countries. The appointment of Ms. Eitel, the company said, "signals Nike's commitment from the top to be a leader not only in developing innovative footwear, apparel and equipment, but in global corporate citizenship."

The company's chairman and chief executive, Philip Knight, also agreed to a demand that the company had long resisted—pledging to allow outsiders from labor and human rights groups to join its independent auditor, PWC, to inspect the factories in Asia, interview workers, and assess working conditions. "We believe that these are practices, which the conscientious, good companies will follow, in the twenty-first century," he said. "These moves do more than just set industry standards. They reflect who we are as a company."

Following protests by college students who accused Nike of manufacturing its products in foreign sweatshops using underpaid, poorly treated workers, the company agreed to let 10 students accompany teams from PWC on their audit tours of the 41 foreign factories it uses to make athletic gear for U.S. universities. Nike also said it would raise the minimum age for hiring new workers at shoe factories to 18 and the minimum for new workers at other plants to 16 in countries where it was common for 14-year-olds to hold such jobs. It would not require the dismissal of underage workers already in employment. Footwear factories have heavier machinery and use more dangerous raw materials, including solvents that cause toxic air pollution. At overseas factories that produced Nike shoes, the company planned to tighten air quality controls to ensure that the air breathed by workers met the same standards enforced by the U.S. Occupational Safety and Health Administration (OSHA) at home in the United States. The company, however, did not mention raising wages, which were less than $2 a day in China and Vietnam, and less than $1 a day in Indonesia. These wages were claimed to equal or exceed the minimum wage laws in those countries. All of Nike's clothing, shoes, and sports gear were made in plants owned by third-party manufacturers.

Source: Griffith, Victoria. 1999, November 12. Nike agrees to show students its factories. *Financial Times,* p. 6; Cushman, John. 1998, May 13. Nike pledges to end child labor and apply U.S. rules abroad. *The New York Times,* pp. D1, D5; Richards, Bill. 1998, January 15. Nike hires an executive from Microsoft for new post focusing on labor policies. *The Wall Street Journal,* p. B14.

are widely known and easily recognized. When it began hiring for its first restaurant in Moscow, Russia, 27,000 people applied.[6]

A trend in North America that has spread to Western Europe is the increasing use of temporary workers. Instead of hiring workers on a permanent basis, firms rely on vendors to provide them with employees with specialized and specific skills for a fee for indefinite periods of time. This contractual relationship enables the firm to adjust its number of workers to the demand for work. Long-term costs such as training, pensions, and health care are avoided, and the employer is better able to control labor costs while

---

[6]Solomon, Charlene M. 1996. Big Mac's mcglobal HR secrets. *Personnel Journal.* April, pp. 46–54.

retaining workforce flexibility. Temporary workers are used for virtually all types of jobs—skilled and unskilled, high-paid and low-paid.[7] Even multinational firms have emerged to provide temporary help in various parts of the world.

COMPENSATION

Wages are determined by the supply of and demand for particular skills in the labor market as well as government regulations (such as minimum wages) and prevalent practices in the industry or area. Table 11-3 compares compensation costs for production workers in manufacturing in several countries using U.S. compensation as a base. Note that between 1980 and 1996, the compensation costs in most countries grew fast, reducing the gap with the United States, and in several cases, even exceeding the United States. Compensation costs include all pay made directly to the worker and legally required employer expenses for insurance and benefits.

The total wage bill is often inflated because government requirements regarding benefits leave little flexibility on the part of the employer. The level of benefits vary widely across countries. In the United States, employers match contributions of employees to a national pension system—social security. In Germany, seven weeks of paid

Table 11-3	Indexes of Hourly Compensation Costs in Selected Countries for Production Workers in Manufacturing	
Country	*1980*	*1997*
United States	100	100
Canada	88	91
France	91	99
Germany	124*	155
Israel	38	66
Japan	56	106
Mexico	22	10
Singapore	15	45
South Korea	10	40
Sri Lanka	2	3**
Switzerland	112	160
Taiwan	10	32
United Kingdom	77	85

Note: Data adjusted for exchange rates.

*West Germany

**1996

Source: Statistical abstract of the U.S. 1999, 119th edition. Washington, DC: U.S. Census Bureau. 1999.

---

[7]French-Swiss deal to create no. 1 temporary agency. *The New York Times.* May 9, 1996, p. D6.

vacation for all employees is mandated by law. In Mexico, all employees are entitled to an additional month's wage every year.[8]

Nonmandatory benefits also vary from country to country. In the United States, where medical care is not provided by the state, health insurance is a treasured employee benefit. This benefit is not an issue in countries where the government provides health benefits to all citizens. In China, where housing shortages in urban areas are acute, provision of housing is a much sought after benefit and one way to keep employee turnover low.[9] The European Union has been working toward a convergence of employee benefits among member nations. However, given the wide range of economies that make up the Union, major disparities will probably persist for some time.

In many countries, employers share profits with the workers. The employers may do so on their own, through union-negotiated arrangements, or as required by the law of the country. Variable pay—bonus, profit sharing, and stock options, common in the United States—has become more acceptable in Europe.[10] By shifting a larger percentage of their total employee compensation bill to variable pay, employers protect themselves in the event of a business downturn and reward employees when the business is doing well. In less-developed countries, the employer-employee relationship is sometimes paternalistic where the firm is expected to provide an extensive range of services to the employees. Foreign firms in the extractive industries (e.g., petroleum and mining) and commercial agriculture (e.g., tea and banana plantations) have provided housing, transportation, roads, utilities, medical care, and other attributes of urban living for their employees. In many cases, these facilities have to be provided to enable the effective exploitation of the natural resources at hand. In other cases, the government is simply unable, because of limited funds, to provide such facilities and may require the foreign firm to provide them as a condition for the issuance of the necessary authorization to mine the gold or grow bananas. When difficulties arise in the townships, the company may get blamed. If possible, the firm should try to hand over the operations of as many of these civic services to either the local government or other private organizations as early as it can so as to not create a potential grievance or hostility against the firm or private investment in the future.

Rules regarding layoff and termination of workers also vary. Justification, advance notices, and severance payments are often required. They all have the effect of turning labor costs into fixed costs. Consequently, hiring has to be done carefully. In contrast, the **employment-at-will** doctrine is prevalent in the United States. This practice gives employers the freedom to terminate employees with or without cause, and severance payments are not required by law. In contrast, in Mexico, workers can be terminated only for just cause. In India, the government's permission is needed before an employer can terminate workers. However, as Management Focus 11-2 illustrates, the laws can be and often are skirted.

High labor costs at home have forced many companies to build facilities at low-cost locations abroad. The Taiwanese computer manufacturer, Acer, has experienced difficulty in finding both production line and R&D workers in Taiwan. Wages for produc-

[8]Reynolds, Calvin. 2000. *Guide to global compensation and benefits.* San Diego, CA: Harcourt Professional Publishing.

[9]Swaak, Reyer. 1995. The role of human resources in China. *Compensation & Benefits Review* 27 (September–October), pp. 39–46

[10]Flynn, Julia. 1999, November 17. Performance-based pay spreads across Europe. *The Wall Street Journal,* p. B9D.

MANAGEMENT FOCUS 11-2

LAYOFF RULES IN INDIA

India's laws make it virtually impossible to sack workers, and the country's weak government does not dare rile unions by tackling labor reform. In this country of 960 million and widespread poverty, labor is so sensitive an issue that government officials speak only of protecting and creating jobs. Yet big changes are under way in India's labor market as foreign and local companies find it relatively easy to lay off excess workers by buying them out.

The Indian subsidiaries of appliance maker Whirlpool and electronics giants, Siemens and Philips, extended golden handshakes to thousands of Indian workers, with the blessings of the government and the cooperation of unions. "The perception of India is that there are a lot of labor problems and the strictest laws, but the reality is that the market is so flexible," says Sudhir Jalan, chairman of Bells Controls Ltd., a Calcutta firm that makes process-control systems. The lack of formal labor reform does not matter, he adds, because the "revolution is quietly under way."

Quietly is right. With little fanfare, nearly 1,300 of Siemens' 7,500 employees in India opted in September 1997 for early retirement, after the company embarked on restructuring following poor financial results. The maximum payout to any employee was the equivalent of $16,160, which though low by Western standards, was a large one in India. Anil Nadkarni, Siemens' personnel director in Bombay, said that because the program was voluntary, union leaders did not resist, and Siemens "helped the employees in identifying investment options for the (retirement) cash received."

Under Indian labor law, an employer with more than 10 workers cannot fire anyone without permission of a government labor commissioner, which is usually impossible to get. Industrialists like Mr. Jalan sidestep the law by contracting or subcontracting. Foreign investors, by establishing new ventures, can set their staff levels and hire nonunion workers, especially in the fast-growing high-tech field.

Problems for foreign investors can arise in joint ventures with weak Indian partners or ventures whose union labor is highly politicized, as in the automobile, food processing, and consumer-durable sectors. Takeovers, a growing focus of foreign investment, can also prove troublesome, as Whirlpool found when it acquired two Indian appliance makers. Whirlpool had to shed 1,350 workers through voluntary retirement in the past two years.

Source: Karp, Jonathan, and Michael Williams. 1997, October 13. Firms in India use buyouts to skirt layoff rules. *The Wall Street Journal,* pp. A16, A18.

---

tion line workers in Taiwan were five times higher than in the Philippines and at least 15 times more than in China. Consequently, the company has shifted production to plants in the Philippines and China.[11]

EMPLOYMENT LAWS

Human resource management has become increasingly legalistic. Every country has laws and regulations governing a whole host of employment issues. However, the application and effectiveness of these laws vary greatly from country to country. In the United States, the violation of antidiscrimination laws leads to stiff penalties on erring firms. In New Zealand, a person's sexual orientation, marital status, or political beliefs

---

[11]Taylor, Paul. 1999, November 24. Only people pose problems. *Financial Times,* p. IV; Banks, Howard. 1997, May 5. Deutsch hegira. *Fortune,* pp. 130–133.

cannot be a consideration in employment decisions. In Japan, in contrast, employers routinely ask such information of applicants and make decisions on them. One of Japan's few antidiscrimination laws is the Equal Employment Opportunity Law, which is aimed at promoting equality of the sexes in the workplace. The law has no criminal penalty for violators; it only requires employers to do their best to abide by the law. Thus, no effective legal remedy is available in Japan for discriminatory practices.[12]

The issue of sex discrimination has rapidly become a managerial problem as the number of women employed has increased. In 1991 and 1992, the U.S. House of Representatives held a series of public hearings on alleged employment discrimination by Japanese firms in the United States. The president of Astra U.S.A., Inc., the U.S. subsidiary of a Swedish pharmaceuticals company, was dismissed in mid-1996 for sexual harassment of its saleswomen. The company settled with the Equal Employment Opportunity Commission (EEOC) and apologized for what happened.[13] U.S. firms, faced with expensive lawsuits and negative publicity, have introduced policies to combat sexual harassment at their foreign subsidiaries because U.S. civil rights laws apply to U.S. citizens working in U.S. firms abroad. Complaints of sex discrimination have risen in other countries too, and many governments have enacted laws making it unlawful to discriminate on the basis of a person's gender.

EMPLOYEE PARTICIPATION IN DECISION MAKING

The view of the human relations school of management, which has gained ascendancy since the Hawthorne studies of the 1920s, suggests that employees are satisfied and motivated if they are included in the firm's decision-making process. Today, firms use a variety of techniques to engage the rank and file workers in the running of the business.

Participation of employees in the decision-making process is governed by several variables.

- The philosophy of the firm as expressed by top-level management
- The nature of the industry and work processes
- The educational level, motivation, and capabilities of the employees
- The firm's historical experience
- The patterns of consultation in the industry and country
- Legal mandates from the government
- Labor market conditions

Codetermination   Employee participation in decision making takes place in many forms. One such method is known an **codetermination** in which managers share decision making and information with workers. The system is legally mandated in Germany and other Northern European countries such as Sweden and Norway. At lower levels in the firm's hierarchy, works councils function as information sharing forums in most West European countries. Employees and their managers meet regularly to share information that is of interest to both parties. The issue of codetermination arose when

---

[12]Hanami, Tadashi. 1992. Employment discrimination in U.S.-based Japanese companies. *Economic Review* 13(10), pp. 28–32.
[13]Maremont, Mark. 1998, January 27. Astra U.S.A.'s former president Bildman admits tax charges, gets prison term. *The Wall Street Journal,* p. B5.

Daimler-Benz of Germany merged with Chrysler of the United States in 1998.[14] Under German law, union officials and representatives of a company's workforce get half of the seats on a company's supervisory board, which oversees management and ratifies all major strategic decisions, akin to a board of directors. But the supervisory boards only represent employees based in Germany. However, the German union that sits on Daimler-Benz's supervisory board agreed to give one seat to a representative of the United Auto Workers (UAW) union, which represents Chrysler's workers. This arrangement gave a UAW official familiar with Chrysler, a boardroom say in matters involving not just Chrysler operations in the United States, but also Daimler and Chrysler operations worldwide. This level of responsibility is unprecedented in U.S. companies, where unions seldom share responsibility for a company's management.

European Works Councils   In 1994, the European Union issued a directive requiring the establishment of **European Works Councils** (EWCs) in multinational firms operating in the member countries of the European Economic Area. Multinational firms that employ 1,000 or more workers in the member countries and have a subsidiary employing at least 150 workers in at least two of these countries are required to set up an EWC. An estimated 617 companies, including 76 non-European firms, fall under this definition.[15] Companies that already had such arrangements were not affected by this directive. The EWC is a forum for the employees and their representatives to receive information from the firm's headquarters about crucial transnational issues that bear on the well-being of the employees. An example of the issues dealt with by EWCs in a particular firm—the Finnish telecommunications company, Nokia—is provided in Table 11-4.

The EWC Directive was issued over strong opposition from international companies. Employers argued that a single method of informing and consulting employees was inconsistent with the complex and dynamic organizational structures of firms. They felt that employee involvement was best done as close to the shop-floor level as possible rather than at headquarters level. The costs of EWCs would be substantial because the directive required that costs be borne by the employer. Another issue was that the EWCs would delay key business decisions and ultimately lead to collective bargaining at a pan-European level.

Based on the functioning of EWCs thus far, it appears that at best they exercise a low level of influence over decision-making processes. Sometimes, they are not consulted on strategic issues and the annual meeting, which is the norm, does not respond to the needs of prompt information and discussion. The enforcement of the directive is left to individual nations, and the mechanism in place to punish employers who fail to inform and consult are weak or nonexistent.

Job Enrichment   A **job enrichment** model advanced by Hackman and Oldham (1980) suggests that workers be given autonomy on the job, feedback on their performance, a sense of identification with the task they do, variation in their tasks, and greater use of their skills. Implementing the job diagnostic model may require redesigning the

---

[14]Mitchener, Brandon. 1998, May 18. German union to cede a board seat at Daimler to UAW in Chrysler merger. *The Wall Street Journal,* p. A4.
[15]Hall, Mark, et al. 1995. *European Works Councils: Planning for the Directive.* Coventry, UK: Industrial Relations Research Institute, University of Warwick.

Table 11-4	Information and Consultation With the EWC at Nokia

- Market situation/competition
- Financial situation (budget/profit, profitability and finance, long-term budget)
- Outline of investment plans
- Technological level and technological development
- Research and development activities
- Strategic changes (changes in the environment, changes/transfers in production)
- Outlines of personnel policy
- Qualifications of employees and development of skills/training
- Employment situation and outlook
- Crises
- Topical issues
- National issues

Source: *European Works Councils: Planning for the Directive.* 1997. Coventry, UK: Industrial Relations Research Institute, University of Warwick.

social and technical dimensions of a job. The most celebrated example of empowering workers was the experiment by the Swedish automaker, Volvo, at its plants in Kalmar, Sweden. Instead of building cars in the traditional format of assembly line operation, the workers were divided into autonomous groups who could use their skills as they saw fit, on schedules that suited them, at the pace of their liking, and with interpersonal relationships that were comfortable to them. As a result, the quality of the cars produced increased as did employee morale, while absenteeism and tardiness fell. However, fewer cars were produced and the costs were higher. In 1995, the Kalmar plant was shut down as Volvo, suffering heavy losses due to stagnant sales in its largest single market, the United States, looked for ways to cut costs.[16]

LABOR-MANAGEMENT RELATIONS

This section examines various management issues that arise as a result of the interaction between international firms and labor unions. The nature and role of unions and how they function in three major economies are discussed.

LABOR UNIONS

Labor (or **trade**) **unions** are associations of workers whose goals are to improve wages, benefits, and working conditions for their members. By banding into a group and dealing with management accordingly, the union expects to realize its goals more often and more completely than could an individual employee. The relationship between the union (representing the workers) and employers is referred to as labor-management relations, which is a component of a broader concept called **industrial relations.** The industrial relations system, first conceptualized by Dunlop (1957), consists of three main actors—the employer, the union, and the government. These three interact with each other to create the rules and standards of the workplace. Even though the union and the employer,

---

[16]Gordon, Judith. 1996. *Organizational behavior.* Upper Saddle River, NJ: Prentice Hall.

through the exercise of their respective strengths, set the rules at the workplace, these rules are influenced and guided by the broader policies established by the government.

Membership in labor unions varies from country to country and industry to industry. Membership depends on various factors including the following:

- Government policies and their enforcement that encourage or discourage membership
- The rights and capabilities of the union
- The level of industrial development in a society (Unions are more likely to be found in manufacturing firms.)
- The human resource practices of firms
- The educational level and psychological outlook of the workforce
- The nature of the firm and industry

Although many countries are signatories to international conventions that give workers the right to form unions, in reality, the exercise of this right is constrained in many less-developed countries.

Union membership has declined in many industrialized countries as shown in Table 11-5. The decline can be attributed to several factors: reduction in manufacturing activity where unions have been historically strong; growth in the service sector where unions have less experience; legislation that has improved working conditions and guaranteed rights; globalization of the economy forcing firms to become competitive; deregulation and privatization of industries; shifts in public policy inimical to union interests, and changes in the work structures in the form of greater reliance on part-time work, telecommuting, contract labor, and temporary employment.

FUNCTIONS OF THE UNION

The most common way by which unions advance the interests of the workers is by engaging in **collective bargaining** with employers. Collective bargaining results in an

Table 11-5	Unionization of Labor Force in Selected Countries, 1995	
Country	*Labor Force Unionized (%)*	*Percentage Change 1985–1995*
Australia	35.2	−29.6
Canada	37.4	1.8
France	9.1	−37.2
Germany	28.9	−17.8
Israel	23.0	−77.0
Italy	44.1	−7.4
Japan	24.0	−16.7
New Zealand	24.3	−55.1
Poland	33.8	−42.5
Sweden	91.1	8.7
United Kingdom	32.9	−27.7
United States	14.2	−22.1

Source: Human Development Report 1998. United Nations Development Program.
www.undp.org/hdro/iwork.htm.

agreement that sets out the rules of the workplace. By bargaining with the employer on behalf of its members, the union replaces individual employment contracts with a collective contract. The topics covered in collective bargaining contracts vary from country to country depending usually on the extent to which employment issues are covered by the laws of the country. In the United States, health insurance has to be negotiated, whereas in Germany, state provided universal health coverage means it is not a topic of bargaining. Decentralized bargaining occurs between a single employer and its unions usually at the plant level. In centralized bargaining, all employers in an industry bargain with all unions in the industry with the resulting contract applicable to all employers and workers. Collective bargaining contracts normally apply to workers in unionized facilities. In many countries, however, employers or the government extend these agreements to cover workers in nonunionized firms. In recent years, centralized industrywide bargaining in many countries have given way to single-firm bargaining.

Unions are also political institutions and serve as a voice for workers' protests. In the early 1980s, union workers at the Gdansk shipyard in Poland formed the world's single largest union, Solidarity, under the leadership of Lech Walesa. Solidarity spearheaded the movement for societal reform and ultimately the collapse of communism in Poland. In the United States, where labor unions are independent of the government, they have historically focused on "bread and butter" or economic issues. In Mexico, in contrast, the *Confederacion de Trabajadores de Mexico* (Mexican Workers Confederation), the most influential of Mexico's labor federations, enjoyed a quasi-official relationship with the *Partido Revolucionairo Institucional* (Institutional Revolutionary Party), Mexico's long-time ruling party, and worked to further national political goals. In the United Kingdom, the national federation of labor unions, the Trades Union Conference, has historically been a partner of the Labour Party and has had a dominant say in the party's election manifesto and when it has been in power, in the formulation of public policy. In less-developed countries, where union income is low because of high labor mobility (difficulty in retaining members), small membership, low wages, and the lack of labor homogeneity, unions look elsewhere for support. Limited resources means unions are unable to provide a full range of services to its members. Hence, unions form alliances with political parties (usually left wing), religious organizations, or even the government. When governmental alliances are involved, political and ideological issues become important in labor-management relations.

INDUSTRIAL DISPUTES

A breakdown in relations between the employer and the union is typically manifested in the form of strikes and lockouts. A **strike** takes place when employees as a group refuse to work until changes are made in working conditions and wages. The strike and the threat of strike represent the principal means by which unions apply pressure on employers. In a **lockout,** the employer closes its facilities, denying employees work and wages, as a way to put pressure on the union to make concessions.

In all industrialized societies, labor unions have the right to strike. However, important restrictions in every country limit the unfettered exercise of this right. The incidence of industrial disputes varies from country to country, year to year, and industry to industry. The level of strikes is affected by many factors including the size and militancy of labor unions, the maturity of union-management relations, economic conditions, the structure of collective bargaining, and the general social and political state of the country. In 1960, two well-known economists, Arthur Ross and Paul Hartman, predicted the "withering away of the strike" in the world as countries develop and unions and managers learn about each others' concerns.[17] Although strikes have not withered away, they have been declining in many countries. This decline is attributed to several factors:

- Greater managerial sophistication in preparing for and handling strikes
- Availability of mediation and arbitration services to help parties resolve disputes amicably
- Greater maturity in labor-management relations
- The ability of international firms to move or at least to threaten to move operations to another location in a foreign country
- The greater use of automation in the production process
- The opportunity to outsource and subcontract work
- The decline in union membership itself
- The increased fear among workers, even skilled workers, that they can be easily replaced by other workers in the labor market

The integration of production activities across countries means the international firm is exposed to disruptions by industrial action. Strikes in one country can seriously interrupt work at a firm's plants in other countries as the opening vignette illustrated. In 1998, workers at General Motors' plants in Flint, Michigan, struck over the issue of outsourcing production.[18] With supply of parts from the striking plants stopped, GM's operations in the United States, Canada, and Mexico came to a halt.

The nature and consequence of strikes are complicated for the firm when these industrial actions are politically motivated. Strikes are expressions of protest and they are used to bring pressure on governments and employers to institute change. Following the advent of democracy and the lifting of restrictions on union activity in South Korea in 1987, the country experienced widespread industrial unrest as workers sought to test the limits of democratic freedom and articulate long-suppressed demands. In such situations, worker demands may appear extravagant and, with no established procedures to handle disputes, strikes last longer and settlements, when reached, may be so expensive to the firm as to drastically impair its competitiveness. Management Focus 11-3 describes how a labor dispute emerged and the response of the various actors of the industrial relations system.

UNION ATTITUDE TOWARD INTERNATIONAL BUSINESS

Labor unions are suspicious of multinational firms. Multinational firms are seen as "exporting" jobs when, instead of building a new facility or expanding existing facilities in the home country, they invest in facilities in a foreign location. Sometimes such overseas expansion is accompanied by closure of facilities in the home country. Furthermore, goods produced overseas are then exported back to the home country. The results are job insecurity and deteriorating working conditions. Unions also believe the ability

[17]Ross, Arthur, and Paul Hartman. 1960. Changing patterns of industrial conflict. New York: John Wiley & Sons.
[18]Greenhouse, Steven. 1998, July 30. For UAW, huge price and tiny victory at GM. *The New York Times,* p. D5.

MANAGEMENT FOCUS 11-3

A U.S. FIRM CHALLENGES A NEW ZEALAND UNION

New Zealand is composed of two main islands separated by the 90-mile wide Cook Strait. Ferries cross the strait in about three hours carrying passengers, cars, and cargo. Owned and operated by New Zealand Rail, the interisland ferry service was sold in 1994 to a U.S. firm, Wisconsin Central Transportation. The new owners announced that the number of employees on the ferries would be reduced because the ferries had about twice as many workers as needed, and working hours could be increased because ferry service would now be provided around the clock.

The Seafarers Union opposed these changes and the company threatened to lock the workers out. The union also argued that safety would be compromised if the number of workers were reduced. To put pressure on the union to negotiate, the company announced that the ferries would not accept reservations during May 1–3, soon after the current contract expired. May is the beginning of the winter holidays for schools and is a busy travel period. Under New Zealand labor law, neither the management nor the union could engage in a lockout or strike respectively until existing collective bargaining contracts expired.

The management of the ferry service announced that it was determined to get what it wanted and hired a former cabinet minister belonging to the Labour Party to lead negotiations with the maritime unions.

The company's managers visited Britain to study how four European firms had fired workers and offered to rehire them on less attractive terms. The company also acknowledged that its contingency plans included placing advertisements for strikebreakers using the fictitious "Alternative Ferry Service." Another union, the Merchant Service Guild, labeled these tactics "totally unacceptable," while the Seafarers Union said the company was adopting an "American-style union-bashing" approach.

The company argued that the changes it wanted would cut about NZ$12 million off the firm's wage bill and would help ward off potential competitors while meeting the needs of customers. While the wages of employees retained would remain the same, a "very generous" once-only payment would be made to those willing to work more days a year.

As negotiations dragged on, it was reported that replacement workers were being assembled at ferry terminals. These were workers who had flown in from Australia and several South Pacific countries. The government's Maritime Safety Authority cautioned that masters, deck officers, and engineers with foreign certificates needed to get sea-going licenses from the Authority but had not done so. The unions announced that other unions in the country were being advised of the situation and would be asked for help if the company locked them out.

Source: Various articles from *The New Zealand Herald* and *The Waikato Times.*

---

to go on strike to pressure management is sharply reduced because the multinational firm can continue to supply a market by merely switching production to plants elsewhere in the world. These issues were vividly illustrated when the German automobile firm, Volkswagen, closed its sole U.S. plant in western Pennsylvania with the loss of 2,500 jobs. The company continued to serve the U.S. market through imports from lower-cost facilities in Brazil and Mexico. The plant was closed because of slow sales caused by the high cost of producing its line of small cars. The competition sold cars cheaply because they were being built in low-wage countries.[19]

---

[19]Holusha, John. 1987, November 21. Volkswagen to shut U.S. plant. *The New York Times,* pp. 1, 37.

Unions also find multinational firms complicated organizations to deal with. For one, unions often cannot find the individual or the office where key decisions are made. They believe that actual decisions are not made at the plant level or even the host country but at the firm's headquarters abroad. Therefore, the interests of the local workforce are not heard and union leaders are unsure whether the managers they are dealing with have the authority to make commitments and make decisions. Workers in one location are played off against workers in other locations as firms seek concessions and flexibility in work rules. For another, multinational firms are an unequal partner to labor unions during collective bargaining negotiations. Firms typically have large resources and efficient communication systems allowing them to collect, analyze, compare, and share data among their world offices and headquarters. Thus, they come to the bargaining table better prepared. Also, information about the firm's financial position or its global goals is difficult to assess by the union and may not be accurately presented to it.

Unions oppose free trade, which they see as benefiting mostly multinational firms. Multinational firms are charged with taking advantage of low workplace standards and low wages in less-developed countries to produce goods and services, which are then marketed in the developed countries, jeopardizing jobs, careers, and living standards there.

Unions use a variety of measures in efforts to improve their influence and bargaining power when dealing with multinational firms.

- *Political activism.* Drawing on their strength in numbers and as voters, unions have lobbied for curbs on international trade. Allied with other advocacy groups, they successfully opposed the start of a new round of global trade liberalization talks in 1999. Although they failed to halt the creation of NAFTA, they were able to attach a side protocol, the North American Agreement on Labor Cooperation (NAALC), to the treaty. Under NAALC, the National Administrative Office (NAO) has responsibilities to review each country's employment laws and to consider labor rights issues and was established in each member country. The office reports its findings and makes recommendations about the extent to which disputed actions have been consistent with a member country's own labor laws. While the NAOs lack the power to enforce decisions, and in many cases do not have the authority to make decisions, they nevertheless draw attention to labor conditions and practices in member countries, and may embarrass employers into making necessary changes. Beyond the NAOs, additional methods of advancing the labor objectives agreed upon by the member countries are available. However, all these organizations and procedures are still in their infancy and their impact on improving employment conditions is as yet unknown.
- *International labor union cooperation.* Labor unions have tried to form global alliances with unions in other countries. National unions or apex federations have formed international groups that function as information clearing houses, issue joint declarations, and forge links with unions on a country-to-country basis. Individual workers are not members of these confederations. At least three such international confederations exist: (1) the Brussels-based International Confederation of Free Trade Unions (ICFTU), which has as its members unions from the western democratic countries and Japan; (2) the World Federation of Trade Unions (WFTU), representing

unions from the former communist countries of Eastern Europe and its allies; and (3) the World Confederation of Labor (WCL), a smaller gathering of Christian trade unions of Europe. In addition, the **International Trade Secretariats** are international federations of national labor unions operating in the same or related trades or industries. They cooperate with the ICFTU. Similarly, unions are affiliated with the WFTU, called Trade Union International, and the WCL, known as Trade Internationals. These secretariats study transnational labor issues and coordinate the responses of national unions to multinational firms. With the collapse of communism, the ICFTU is presently the leading world trade union center representing more than 125 million members in 136 countries.[20]

A major goal of interunion cooperation is to exchange information among workers and unions about international firms in a timely manner so they may prepare themselves better, and to reduce the firm's advantage of playing off workers in one country against those in another. Unions seek information on matters such as the following:

- Whether the managers with whom they bargain have the authority to make decisions
- The organizational structure of the firm in order to determine the locus of decision making on labor matters
- The firm's history of behavior in other countries
- Which plants are crucial, where expansion is planned, and where the links are weak.

Information is shared through reports, publications, and meetings. Speaking of assisting U.S. unions, Michael Boggs, the secretary of the International Chemical, Energy and General Workers Union (ICEF), said, *"Early warning is the key to preventing multinationals from union-busting. Since these companies are unionized in their home countries, pressure can often be exerted to dilute their union-busting abroad—but only if American unions give early notification to the ICEF, before positions harden."*[21] An example of successful international union cooperation is presented in Management Focus 11-4.

- *Coordinated industrial actions.* To ensure that strikes are effective, unions aim to organize strikes, slowdowns, sit-ins, boycotts, and cyberpicketing at a multinational firm's operations around the world. Such actions are not common given the obvious difficulties including the unwillingness of workers in one country to go on strike in support of workers in another country and the differences in laws with regard to the legality of such strikes. However, with the creation of the European Union, many national labor unions have created Europe-wide associations and have been able to organize coordinated industrial action.
- *Transnational collective bargaining.* One goal of unions is to conduct collective bargaining between an international firm and all its employees in various countries. Little evidence indicates that such bargaining takes place.

---

[20]*World Labour Report.* 1997–1998. (ICFTU).
[21]*IU Digest.* 1990, January. 12(1), p. 12.

THE CAMPAIGN AGAINST RAVENSWOOD ALUMINUM COOPERATION

From November 1990 to April 1992, the United Steelworkers of America (USWA), with the support of the AFL-CIO, conducted a comprehensive and successful campaign against the Ravenswood Aluminum Corporation (RAC) in Ravenswood, West Virginia. The events that led to the campaign began when Kaiser Aluminum sold RAC in December 1988. When negotiations for a new collective bargaining contract stalled in 1990, the union offered to continue working under the old contract. However, just before the contract expired, on the midnight of October 31, the company declared an impasse, and immediately replaced all the workers. The fact that replacement workers arrived immediately suggested a premeditated strategy on the part of the company. All bargaining ceased and it was announced that the replacement workers would become permanent.

The union local immediately started a campaign. It met with the staff from the American Federation of Labor-Congress of Industrial Organizations (AFL-CIO) and the head office of the USWA to develop a strategy to target RAC's international connections. Research into RAC's ownership led the union to Marc Rich and Company, the largest metal trader in the world and based in Zug, Switzerland. The company was run by its namesake Marc Rich, who had fled the United States in 1983 to avoid prosecution for fraud and tax evasion. Rich's right-hand man, Willy Strothotte, was the controlling owner of RAC, and had an office in the same building as Mr. Rich in Switzerland.

The international campaign by the union was one of three fronts opened by the union to get back the jobs of its members. The other fronts included an end-user campaign, which targeted RAC's major clientele (primarily beverage companies using aluminum cans) through a "don't buy" proposal, and Fort Unity—a union program designed to sustain membership during the campaign.

The international effort was assisted by the International Metalworkers Federation and the International Federation of Chemical, Energy and General Workers. Both these International Trade Secretariats provided information about Rich's extensive business operations. Together the investigative efforts of the USWA and the AFL-CIO unearthed information about Rich's operations around the world. Ten countries were identified where campaigns against RAC could be initiated.

The U.S. union met with officials of the Swiss trade union confederation, the Swiss metalworkers union, and the Dutch trade union federation. Letters signed by five members of the Swiss parliament were sent to Rich and a press conference was called in Switzerland. A meeting was arranged with the officials of RAC's banks. News coverage on television and in the print media followed.

Although Rich denied that he was connected to RAC, the efforts to publicly embarrass Rich and his business partners were maintained throughout 1991 and well into 1992. A "wanted" poster of Marc Rich was printed in seven languages and distributed worldwide. The union was able to halt a bid by Mr. Rich to acquire a state-owned Czech aluminum plant by appealing to President Vaclav Havel.

On April 15, 1992, the president of the USWA, George Becker announced that months of recent negotiations between himself, Mr. Strothotte, and Mr. Rich's attorney had resulted in the removal of the CEO of RAC. In addition, Mr. Strothotte hired a former NLRB general counsel with instructions to bargain in good faith with the USWA and reach an agreement. The union campaign was suspended.

A new collective bargaining agreement was reached which included the termination of replacement workers, back pay for each worker, and amnesty for all union workers charged with disciplinary violations. The contract was overwhelmingly supported and all 1,700 workers were fully reinstated.

Documents later revealed how effective the coordinated international campaign had been. RAC was defaulting on its loans to its Dutch bank and other creditors; its revenues had declined 30 percent; and it owed large sums to its suppliers.

Source: Multinational corporations: Expanding influence in the 1990s. 1995. Washington, DC: AFL-CIO.

Working conditions differ greatly from country to country, as does the level of economic development. Similarly, unions differ in their goals and political affiliations, which makes cooperation among them difficult. Government policies too differ over wages, multinational firms, and labor unions.

MANAGEMENT ATTITUDE TOWARD UNIONS

International managers prefer not to deal with unions at their facilities. The presence of unions imposes additional costs on the firm and reduces managerial freedom. These issues are illustrated in the opening vignette. In addition, union opposition to trade liberalization and their advocacy for workers' rights in less-developed countries run counter to corporate interests. Although international firms prefer to function without the intrusive presence of labor unions, in reality, largely because of legal requirements in the host country and the activism of advocacy groups, the presence of unions either at the workplace or in the larger economic environment cannot be avoided.

Differences in the industrial relations systems across countries force international firms to make adjustments in how they organize and manage their employee relations. In Sweden, where labor unions are strong, employers have to work closely with them. This interaction involves sharing information, obtaining union input into the firm's decision-making processes, and placing union representatives on decision-making boards. In the United States though, the laws permit employers to actively oppose labor unions. Thus, U.S. firms in Sweden adapt to the mores and practices of the Swedish labor system while maintaining a different system at home.

In a study of U.S. foreign direct investment abroad, Cooke (1997) found that U.S. firms were less likely to invest in countries where union membership was high, where collective bargaining occurred on a centralized basis (at the national or industry level), where governments restricted layoffs, and where policies bound employers to sectoral or regional bargaining agreements.[22]

In countries with a choice of unions, the firm would benefit from dealing with unions that are strong locally, essentially nonpolitical, genuine representatives of the workers, and responsive to their member's best interests. Foreign firms sometimes embrace unions that are closely linked with the government believing that such a strategy would ensure labor peace and a compliant workforce. Problems arise when governments change, when firm policies diverge from the expectations of the host government, and when employees try to form independent unions.

Managers access a variety of options to reduce or mitigate the influence of unions. One technique is to locate or expand facilities in countries or regions where unions are weak or where the industrial relations system is stable. The threat of closing operations or shifting production to a foreign location and the consequent loss of employment for many workers is a potent weapon increasingly used by employers to obtain work rule changes and cuts in wages and benefits from their unionized workers. Globalization, deregulation, privatization, overcapacity, and reduction in trade and investment barriers have put unions on the defensive. Workers are anxious to save their jobs and are willing to make the con-

---

[22]Cooke, William N. 1997. The influence of industrial relations factors on U.S. foreign direct investment abroad. *Industrial and Labor Relations Review* 51(1), pp. 3–17.

cessions demanded by employers.[23] For example, when workers at Ford Motor's factory in Sao Bernardo in Brazil went on strike in 1990, they smashed parked cars and vandalized the bosses' offices. In 1998, despite the company laying off 2,800 workers and reducing wages, the workers did not strike because of a growing fear of unemployment. As one laid-off worker noted, *"People used to be very aggressive towards the management. But today they are behaving like angels. Unemployment has scared them."* Instead, the union blamed the government for creating adverse economic conditions.[24]

However, industrial relations is a dynamic process and the nature and extent of union activism changes over time. What might have been a stable location at one time may in due course become a center of labor union militancy. South Korea is a good example of this process.

Sometimes, to induce inward investment, a government may change labor laws and practices. In 1988, Nissan, a Japanese company, offered to build an automobile plant in Britain if the British government would ensure that the employees at the proposed venture would agree to be represented by a single union. In the United Kingdom, multiple unions at a single workplace had been common, which presented the employer with competing demands. Nissan was able to wrest this concession when it signed a "one plant one union" agreement with the electricians union. (This action by the union triggered a conflict in the Trades Union Congress—the apex union body—and led to the expulsion of the electricians' union from its membership.) To the employer, a single union offers many advantages: dealing with one set of leaders, no rivalry among unions to increase membership and no showing off that one is more effective than another, not having to cope with competing demands, less conflict among the workers, and the opportunity to develop a long-term stable relationship with the union.

Other strategies used by employers include replacing workers with automated facilities, linking wages and bonuses to productivity (in effect reducing the fixed costs of labor), and working closely with unions in a win-win relationship. Mangers also institute practices such as teamwork, quality circles, and other consultative arrangements. Through lobbying efforts, coalition building with other businesses, and because of their role and resources in creating economic wealth and employment, international firms have been able to limit the exercise of union power.

INDUSTRIAL RELATIONS SYSTEMS: A PROFILE OF THREE COUNTRIES

Although it could be argued that national industrial relations systems should converge because urbanized societies face similar situations with respect to competition, technological changes, costs, and workers' needs, it appears that they remain divergent on many issues. It is beyond the scope of this chapter to study all the national industrial relations systems. However, those of the leading economic countries—United States, Japan, and Germany—are discussed here to illustrate their distinguishing characteristics and to identify the sorts of adjustments in employee relations that foreign firms going into these countries must make. A summary is presented in Table 11-6.

---

[23]Bernstein, Aaron. 1998, March 2. Why workers still hold a weak hand. *Business Week,* p. 98.
[24]Dyer, Geoff. 1999, January 10. Ford workers embark on game of patience. *Financial Times,* p. 1.

Table 11-6	Summary of Industrial Relations Systems of the United States, Germany, and Japan		
	United States	*Germany*	*Japan*
Unionization Rate and Trend	14.2 percent; declining	28.9 percent; declining	24.0 percent; declining
Union Organization	Craft, industry, both	Industrywide	Enterprisewide
Apex Union Body*	AFL-CIO	DGB	Rengo (dominant)
Political Affiliations	Weak	Strong	Very weak
Bargaining Structure	Largely decentralized	Centralized; industrywide	Decentralized
Bargaining Topic	Wages and benefits	Quality of worklife	Wages
Grievance Handling	Voluntary arbitration	Labor courts	Agreed-upon rules
Strike Occurrence and Frequency	At expiration of contract; few	At expiration of contract; few but large	During contract negotiations; frequent and short
Collective Bargaining Coverage	Limited to the parties to the contract	Extended to entire industry or region	Firm-specific
Employee Involvement in Management	None	Codetermination; works councils	Frequent consultation with employer
Union-Employer Relationship	Adversarial	Consultative	Highly cooperative

*AFL-CIO = American Federation of Labor-Congress of Industrial Organizations; DGB = Deuscher Gewerkschaftsbund (German Trade Union Federation); Rengo = Japanese Trade Union Confederation

UNITED STATES

The industrial relations system in the United States is a mix of legalism and volunteerism. A large number of laws and decisions of administrative agencies have established the parameters within which the system functions while at the same time given workers and employers considerable leeway to determine many of their own rules without governmental intervention. The principal federal law that governs labor relations in the private sector is the National Labor Relations Act of 1935, which is enforced by the National Labor Relations Board (NLRB). The law gives workers the right to form their own unions, bargain collectively, and engage in strikes. It also prohibits both employers and unions from engaging in behaviors—known as unfair labor practices—that would prevent the exercise of these rights. The NLRB has two main roles: (1) assist in the process of union creation at a workplace, and (2) investigate and prevent unfair labor practices.

The typical manner in which unions come into existence in a workplace is by winning a representation election where a majority of the workers seeking unionization votes for the union. The holding of the election is preceded by active campaigning by the employer to dissuade the workers from voting for the union. If the union wins, it is certified as the legal representative of the workers and the employer is bound to work with and through the union. Unions are organized by craft or industry, or a combination of both.

Collective bargaining between the union and the employer represents the principal forum in which wages and benefits, hours of work, and terms and conditions of employment are negotiated. Virtually any topic can be a subject of negotiation, and both parties are required to bargain in good faith although they are not required to reach an agreement. Collective bargaining contracts are legal documents and are enforceable in the courts of law.

Most collective bargaining contracts contain a grievance procedure to handle workplace complaints. The procedure lays out a series of steps the employer and union will go through to resolve disputes that arise during the life of a contract (which is determined by the parties themselves). Nearly all such procedures end in arbitration where an independent outside individual or panel of individuals determine the merits of the case and render a final decision binding on both parties. Arbitration represents a private and voluntary system of dispute resolution in the United States; its legitimacy has been recognized by the courts. Typically, a grievance process in a contract is accompanied by a "no-strike" clause. Thus, while workers are assured that any violation of the contract or complaints against the firm would receive a fair hearing ending with independent outside arbitration, the employer is assured of uninterrupted work by its employees during the period of the contract.

Labor unions are primarily organized for the economic welfare of their members and have not been closely involved with the government or political parties. Most of the unions are affiliated to a national confederation, the American Federation of Labor-Congress of Industrial Organization (AFL-CIO). National unions, by definition, have membership in many firms across the country. An example of a national union is the United Auto Workers Union (UAW), which is predominant in the automobile industry. The UAW has affiliated unions in many plants across the country, and these affiliate unions are known as local unions. Local unions actually represent workers at a particular workplace and work on a day-to-day basis with the firm's management.

Collective bargaining negotiations may take place in a variety of formats. A local union may directly negotiate with a single firm or a group of area firms. A national union representing many locals may negotiate with a single firm or with a group of firms. Similarly, a single firm may negotiate with a large number of unions. In general, negotiations are decentralized.

Membership in labor unions in the United States has been declining, and currently less than a tenth of all private sector nonfarm employees are represented by unions. Union membership is largely concentrated in the old manufacturing industries (e.g., steel, auto, and rubber), located in the industrial states of the Northeast, Great Lakes, and the West Coast, among middle-aged workers with high school education. Although the United States is the largest recipient of foreign direct investment, U.S. unions have not been particularly successful in organizing workers in foreign-owned firms. One reason is that they have not specifically targeted foreign-owned firms when it comes to mounting organizing campaigns. Unions are just as likely to lose representation elections in foreign-owned firms as they are in domestic firms. Because unions lose more than half the elections, the number of new union members has not risen appreciably. Even when the union wins and is able to represent the workers, it may be unable to secure a collective bargaining contract for its members. Unions have a harder time negotiating a successful contract with foreign-owned firms, especially those from Germany and Japan. All these factors suggest that foreign-owned firms, which may have close relations with unions at home, tend to work to operate a nonunion facility, just as the domestic U.S. firms do.[25] The American industrial relations system affords firms, domestic and foreign, the opportunity to function without unions and it appears that foreign firms do just that.

GERMANY

Germany is the world's third largest economy (after the United States and Japan) and the second largest international trader (after the United States). Compared to most major countries, the manufacturing sector employs a large proportion of the workforce. Union membership, about 29 percent of the employed workforce, has declined since the 1980s largely because of the continued shrinking of the country's manufacturing sector. German unions are well-staffed and well-financed through membership dues.

The industrial relations system, unlike that of the United States, is highly centralized. Most national unions are members of the *Deuscher Gewerkschaftsbund* (DGB, the German Trade Union Federation), which consists of 17 industrial unions. These unions organize both blue and white collar workers in the public and the private sectors in specific industries such as chemicals, metal working, and transportation. In effect, each industry (not firm) has a single union. The goal of the DGB is to safeguard and advance workers' rights not only at the workplace but also in the larger society.

Private sector employers too are organized at the national level through the *Bundesvereinigung der Deutschen Arbeitsgeberverbande* (BDA, the Federal Association of German Employers Organizations). The BDA, which represents 47 different industry groups, in turn accounts for between 80 and 90 percent of all private employers. Neither the DGB nor the BDA participate directly in collective bargaining, but they coordinate and provide information to their members.

The government plays a strong role in the German industrial relations system. All political parties have strong factions representing workers' interests; however, it is the Social Democratic Party that has the closest links with the unions. Extensive legislation covers labor standards, benefits, discrimination, plant closures, and employee rights. The country also has a comprehensive vocational training system, which is jointly managed by unions, employers, and the government.

Collective bargaining agreements are negotiated at the industry level, either nationwide or regionally. Thus, no direct bargaining takes place between unions and employers at the enterprise or plant level. A few industrial unions negotiate agreements with industry associations, which set the pattern for other unions and industry associations to agree upon. Consequently, interindustry wage differentials are not large. The topics in a collective bargaining contract cover wages, training, layoffs, union responsibilities, and management rights. In the 1980s and 1990s, industrial disputes were not over wages, but over the length of the work week and quality of work life issues. Contracts are legally enforceable and binding on the signatories and their members. In addition, such contracts can be declared by the government to be binding on all firms in an in-

---

[25]Sanyal, Rajib N. 1989. An empirical analysis of the unionization of foreign manufacturing firms in the U.S. *Journal of International Business Studies.* First Quarter, pp. 119–132; Sanyal, Rajib and Joao Neves. 1992. A study of union ability to secure the first contract in foreign-owned firms in the U.S.A. *Journal of International Business Studies.* Fourth Quarter, pp. 697–713.

dustry regardless of whether they are members of the particular industry association. As a result, collective bargaining contracts cover nearly all workers in an industry, even though all firms are not involved in the negotiations.

Given the centralized, industrywide collective bargaining, strikes, while rare, when they do occur are at a high level. Usually strikes are matched by lockouts by employers. Because the union pays members a generous stipend when they are on strike, the limitation of the size of the strike fund forces the union to select a group of firms in a particular geographical region to mount its industrial action.

Employment disputes and disputes over collective bargaining agreements are settled through labor courts, consisting of three persons—a professional judge who is a specialist in labor law, a union representative, and a representative of the employer's association. Labor courts have jurisdiction over individual employment contracts and collective contracts including industrial disputes.

Mitbestimmung or codetermination is a unique feature of the German system. Employees are represented through works councils, which are elected every three years. All workers in a firm are eligible to vote and stand for election regardless of union membership. In reality, though, most works councilors are union members. The works councils serve as a vehicle for consultation with the employer and joint decision making, including implementing collective bargaining agreements. They are, however, barred from negotiating over issues already settled in collective bargaining agreements such as wages, and they are not permitted to call strikes. The consent of the works councils is required for issues such as discipline, daily working hours and breaks, temporary overtime work, the fixing of job piece rates, suggestion plans, holiday schedules, evaluating employee performance, safety regulations, welfare services in the plant, and administration of employee housing, among others. In addition, the Codetermination Acts of 1951 and 1978 require that in large firms, representatives of workers and unions hold half the positions on the company's board of directors. One of the representatives of the workers has to come from the ranks of middle management. Although in the vast majority of cases, the board makes decisions unanimously, in cases of a tie, the chairperson, who always represents the shareholders, casts the deciding vote.

This extensive system of worker involvement in the running of the firm has created a highly stable system. Technological change has been easier to adopt with comparatively little opposition from unions and workers, largely because the codetermination system allows the expression and protection of employee interests. The need to consult workers has also compelled managers to adopt a comprehensive long-term perspective on the management of human resources.

Foreign firms operating in Germany are required to involve workers in the consultative process as already outlined. The system requires a greater degree of information sharing between employers and the union than is traditionally done in the United States. In recent years, businesses have complained about the rising cost of labor and the inflexibility of the labor market in Germany and are trying to change this environment. For instance, one plant of Opel, the German subsidiary of General Motors, which uses lean manufacturing techniques and teams to produce cars, is not a member of the employer's association and thus is able to negotiate contracts with workers separate from the rest of the automobile industry. The union's goal has been to bring the company into its fold. At BMW's plants, the standard eight-hour day, five-days-a-week shifts have been replaced by variable shift patterns, which means workers put in an average of nine hours each day four days a week, and are regularly required to work on Saturdays for no extra pay.[26]

JAPAN

Many elements of the Japanese industrial relations system were put in place by the United States during its occupation of Japan after the end of World War II. Drawing from the American National Labor Relations Act, the Labor Union Law was enacted in 1945, following which union membership rose greatly. The Japanese constitution permits workers to organize a union, to bargain collectively, and to engage in strikes. These rights have been defined and implemented through the Labor Union Law. As in the United States, supervisors and those high in the firm's organizational hierarchy are excluded from union membership under this law.

In the period after the war, unions mushroomed as workers joined them to protest unjust work conditions and the effects of runaway inflation. The spontaneity of workers' protests limited the size of a typical union to the workforce of a plant or enterprise. Plant unions of a multiplant firm later joined into an enterprise union to match the corporate structure of the firm. When the enterprise-wide federation of plant unions was formed, the plant unions often ceded large measures of organizational rights and powers to the federation and became its branches or locals. Thus arose Japanese style unionism—"enterprise unionism." The Labor Standards Law establishes minimum standards of working conditions and requires the employer to adopt written work rules.

Forming a union is fairly easy: any group of workers can claim to be a labor union as long as certain documentary requirements are met, organizational effectiveness is demonstrated, and the governance structures are democratic. Unions are protected from unfair labor practices on the part of the employer. Unlike in the United States though, there are no unfair labor practices on the part of the union. Charges for unfair labor practices are addressed by the National Labor Relations Commission, which consists of representatives of the unions, employers, and the public.

Within many nonunion firms are employee associations, which act like unions but are not considered unions because they are not registered with the government. These employee associations usually consult with the employer on a wide range of matters relating to the workplace.

The enterprise union usually enlists all employees in the firm, regardless of occupational classification, as members. Therefore, the union is familiar with, and its fortunes affected by, the performance of the firm. As a consequence, less mutual suspicion and greater cooperation characterize the relationship between the managers and the union.

To prevent the total loss of union identity in a firm, employees express their demands through joint labor-management consultative councils (which usually meet frequently) and collective bargaining, which takes place whenever the union demands. Refusal to bargain when the union demands it is an unfair labor practice.

The Labor Union Law outlines the process by which the union and the employer should negotiate, and because the topics of bargaining are not defined, in effect, any topic is fit for negotiations. In reality though, the consultative councils serve as a way to identify the issues that should be bargained over. Failure to reach an agreement in the

---

[26]Bowley, Graham. 1998, November 28–29. Flexibility cuts both ways. *Financial Times,* p. 7.

consultative councils implies a labor-management conflict, which is resolved through collective bargaining. Strikes and lockouts are used to force the other party to concede and allow the union to charge the employer with engaging in unfair labor practices. Grievances at the workplace are usually handled through the consultative councils.

The most common topic of bargaining and over which strikes take place is the size of the annual wage increases or the size of the semiannual bonuses. In what is known as *shunto* or the spring labor offensive, unions across the country launch demonstrations and work stoppages to force employers to grant wage raises. The unions are intimately familiar with the financial conditions of the firm, making collective bargaining negotiations over this issue essentially an effort to determine the best way to budget the firm's resources. Granting a larger wage increase may leave less for technological innovations and thus the employer may ask the union to accept a smaller pay hike this time for a larger one in the future.

Strikes occur early in the collective bargaining process. The margin of the workers' vote in favor of a strike sends a clear message to the employer about the extent of union solidarity behind its demands. Strikes can also occur intermittently even as negotiations continue. To the employer, the strike is not so much a financial setback but rather a loss of public prestige and image. Unlike in Germany and the United States, strikes are rarely long; most last from a few hours to a few days at a time. This lack of militancy today is attributed to the employee-oriented human resource management practices adopted by employers following the widespread labor unrest in the early 1950s. In general, the relationship between employers and workers is harmonious, and regular consultations allow the airing of concerns and their resolution without snowballing into major problems.

Individual enterprise unions form industrywide unions, which in turn are affiliated to national federations. Of the several federations the largest one is known as the *Rengo* (the Japanese Trade Union Confederation). Similarly, Japanese firms have formed national-level organizations such as the *Keidanren* (Japanese Federation of Economic Organizations), which exercises considerable influence over policy formulation at the government level through financial contributions to political parties, well-researched policy proposals, and extensive participation in the advisory and consultative forums of government. Another major employer organization is the *Nikkeiren* (Japanese Federation of Employers' Associations), which is the mirror rival of the labor union confederations. These national level organizations conduct research and report on the state and trends in the economy. They also cultivate relationships with all sections of the government to influence public policy and legislation.

In the 1990s, the Japanese economy stagnated. The result was enormous pressure on firms to regain profitability and growth. To cut costs, many firms abandoned one of the sacred cows of Japanese industrial relations—lifetime employment. Because of the *keiretsu* system, failing firms were often taken over by friendly affiliates rather than allowed to go under but that too is changing. Foreign firms, though, close plants and lay off workers. In 1991, when Procter & Gamble, the U.S. consumer products firm, shut down its medical and health care plant in Japan, workers and their union protested and led a legal challenge.[27] Japanese workers tend to take a tougher stance with foreign

---

[27]Ono, Yumiko. 1991, April 3. P&G's closure of plant causes protest in Japan. *The Wall Street Journal,* p. A16.

firms than with Japanese companies. As more foreign firms enter Japan, some concerns are being raised as to whether the traditional postwar system can survive. For instance, following Renault's effective takeover of Nissan in 1999, massive restructuring, plant closings, and job losses occurred.

ORGANIZING EMPLOYEE RELATIONS

The goal of a firm's headquarters is to organize human resources and labor relations practices in foreign operations in ways that reconcile conditions in the host countries with the goals of the parent firm. Because human resources and labor relations practices are, to a large extent, country-specific, most international firms tend to decentralize these functions to their overseas operations and adapt to local conditions. This strategy of decentralization is independent of the extent of foreign ownership—wholly, majority, or minority—in the subsidiary.

Decentralization does not mean that the parent firm has no interest in or influence on the organization and functioning of human resources and labor relations in its foreign affiliates. Kochan and Katz (1988) presented a three-level strategic decision matrix on labor relations, which is shown in Table 11-7. At decision level 1, as the firm decides where to locate its overseas facilities, human resources is one of the determining factors. Decision makers at this strategic level would be at headquarters considering wage rates and benefits, government regulations of employment contracts, union activism and influence, skill level and availability of workers, and productivity rates in the foreign location. The parent firm monitors human resource/labor relations developments in the subsidiary, and coordinates activities across the firm's many locations. For instance, headquarters can work to prevent industrial disputes in one location from spreading to another. Similarly, headquarters serves as a conduit for sharing best practices from one location to another. Headquarters intervention is more probable if the subsidiary is a key plant, such as a single source of supply within a production system, and where the investment in a given subsidiary is substantial.

At decision level 2, the managerial focus is on creating personnel policies and devising collective bargaining strategies at the level of the subsidiary. While to some extent headquarters philosophies and ideas have a play, usually they are crafted keeping in mind local practices. Management Focus 11-5 discusses the sort of changes in human resource practices that an international firm may introduce in its overseas operations.

Decisions at level 3 of Kochan and Katz's strategic decision matrix deal with individual workers or work groups and their relationship to the immediate work environment. The activities are at the shop floor level. Both levels 2 and 3 take place in individual geographical and political jurisdictions, and thus would be in the domain of human resource and labor relations managers at the subsidiary.[28]

Table 11-7	Levels of Human Resource/Labor Relations Decisions		
Level 1	Strategic	Headquarters	Evaluating various national practices
Level 2	Operational	Subsidiary	Adhering to national rules/practices
Level 3	Functional	Shop-floor	Employee-focused

---

[28]Kochan, Thomas, and Harry Katz. 1988. Collective bargaining and industrial relations. Homewood, IL: Irwin.

MCDONALD'S AS A CHANGE AGENT

McDonald's International, which operates in more than 90 countries through nearly 19,000 restaurants, reveres flexibility and sensitivity to local business practices. Rita Johnson, staff director in international human resources with responsibility for Central Europe, said, "One of our guiding principles is that our restaurants should always be a reflection of the communities they serve—not only the individuals we employ and the culture and ethnicity of those communities, but also the employment practices." That principle means taking the company's best practices from around the world and working with local staff to blend those into local practices. The result is the employment of the most positive people practices that exceed the expectations of their employees.

When the company evaluates a country prior to entering it, human resource managers prepare a list of employment-practice questions that must be answered as part of the fact-gathering process. Such questions include:

- What are the labor laws?
- Would the company be able to establish part-time and flexible work schedules?
- What specific number of hours would employees be allowed to work?
- Can the company employ youth under the age of 18?
- What other services must the company provide?

In many countries in central Europe, for example, employers must provide showers and lockers. In some locations, building a single restaurant means creating an entire network of support services such as engineers, construction workers, and agricultural experts.

In countries where the quick service restaurant industry is new or nonexistent, the culture, laws, and customs do not accommodate the many facilities needed to operate the business properly. It becomes an opportunity to bring some of these changes into a country, and to put some people into the workforce who would not normally be in the workforce, particularly homemakers and college students who are working for the first time.

The company often introduces the concept of flexible scheduling or part-time scheduling for the first time in a country. This practice is sometimes difficult to implement if the prevalent employment practice is to hire individuals full time. Companies must be in constant communication with labor ministry officials and local businesspersons to advise them of the advantages of having flexible or part-time scheduling as an employment practice. Given its worldwide reputation, McDonald's finds it easy to recruit capable workers. The company establishes itself as an employer of choice by paying top wages for high-quality employees and providing generous benefits packages.

Source: Solomon, Charlene M. 1996. Big Mac's McGlobal HR secrets. *Personnel Journal.* April, pp. 46–54.

One indication of the decentralized nature of the human resources/labor relations function is the use of host country nationals to head departments in subsidiaries. In nearly all foreign-owned firms in the United States, the officers in charge of this function at the U.S. headquarters and at the plant level are U.S. nationals. This reliance on employing host country nationals is not surprising. They are familiar with prevailing employment practices and the legal framework of the country. A home country or third country national would be unfamiliar (at least initially) with host country practices and the blanket imposition of alien work practices on host country rank and file workers by a foreigner could be resisted, resented, or be impractical. Host country nationals at the subsidiary present a local face to the workers, union leaders, and community groups, thus effectively masking the firm's foreign ownership, and consequently reducing some hostility.[29]

Reliance on host country nationals or adhering to host country practices are no guarantee that employee relations will be smooth. Nike's experience showed that despite having its contractors pay prevailing wage rates, it did not insulate the company from charges of exploiting workers in less-developed countries. Legal requirements regarding workers' participation in decision making as embodied in the European Works Councils are also forcing the headquarters of international firms to adopt a more proactive approach to the management of employee relations in their overseas facilities.

CONCLUSIONS

The international manager has to work with rank and file workers in countries with widely varying employment practices and legal systems. This chapter examined some of the key human resource issues faced by international firms. Given the differences across countries, a uniform worldwide policy towards employee relations cannot be pursued. The firm's headquarters typically provides considerable autonomy to the host country managers in overseas operations to devise and implement policies and programs regarding employment. At the same time, international managers need to recognize the unfavorable attitude of labor unions towards international business and prepare to counter worldwide the efforts of unions to impose costs and restrictions on the management of operations. The entire subject of managing employee relations is highly dynamic as well as legalistic. The international manager both at headquarters and at the overseas location needs to have a solid understanding of the changes and how to take advantage of them.

OPENING VIGNETTE EPILOGUE

On April 11, 1990, Ford announced the transfer of a $340 million planned investment in an engine manufacturing facility in the United Kingdom to Cologne in (then West) Germany. In speculating on the reasons for the transfer, *The Financial Times* of London wrote of the tense labor relations in Ford's British plants, a misjudgment of the industrial relations system in the United Kingdom, the strengthening of the European Union, the prospect of German reunification, and the pressure from unions in Germany and Spain complaining that Ford was biased towards Britain.[30]

[30]Blanpain, Roger. 1992. Labour relations in a changing environment: A general overview. In Alan Gladstone et al., eds. *Labor relations in a changing environment*. Berlin: Walter de Gruyter.

---

[29]Sanyal, Rajib. 1988. The labor relations function in foreign-owned firms. *Proceedings of the Eastern Academy of Management annual conference 1988*. Washington, DC: George Washington University.

Key Terms

- Immigration Reform and Control Act
- glass ceiling
- employment at will
- codetermination
- European Works Council
- job enrichment
- labor unions
- industrial relations
- collective bargaining
- strike
- lockout
- International Trade Secretariats

Discussion Questions

1. Explain the various ways in which workers participate in the decision-making process of a firm. Why would an employer welcome such input from workers?

2. How is the human resource/labor relations function in international firms organized? What is the relationship between headquarters and the subsidiary with regard to labor-management relations in the subsidiary?

3. Why would multinational firms prefer to operate without unionized workers? Explain some of the techniques used by firms to minimize union influence.

4. The general attitude of labor union leaders toward multinational firms is unfavorable. What rational basis could explain this attitude? As a manager of a multinational firm, how would you respond to the union's concerns?

5. Compare and contrast the industrial relations systems of the United States, Germany, and Japan. If the manager of a multinational firm based in a country other than these three could select one of these three systems as the most favorable to work in, which one would the manager choose? Why?

6. Andrew Grove, CEO of Intel, the world's leading manufacturer of computer chips, commented that the U.S. government should automatically grant residency (and work) permits to every foreign student it admits into the country. This measure, according to him, would take care of the labor market shortage of technical employees. Do you agree with his views? Explain the apparent dichotomy in the views of national governments and senior managers of multinational firms with regard to free movement of labor across countries.

Writing Assignment

Your company is considering investing in a manufacturing facility in the United Kingdom. One of the factors the company is concerned about is the level of union militancy in that country in the form of strikes. You have been asked to look at strike data in the United Kingdom for the past ten years, analyze the trend, and prepare a two-page report summarizing the nature and extent of strike activity in that country. (Note: The instructor may select other countries.)

Internet Exercise

Select any human resources or labor relations topic covered in this chapter. Access the Web site of labor union federations of two countries and ascertain their positions and views on the subject. Prepare a two-page report summarizing your findings. The Web site of the AFL-CIO (*www.afl-cio.org*) has a comprehensive list of Web sites for many foreign union federations.

Internet Resources

Many governmental, union, and employer Web sites provide information about employee and labor relations. The Web site of the European Union (*www.europa.eu.int*) gives access to all the EU's directives on social and labor policy and the actions of individual member governments. Labor-related statistics compiled by the U.S. Bureau of Labor Statistics is available at *www.stats.bls.gov*. The Canadian Labor Congress maintains a site at *www.clc-ctc.ca*. The Web site of the journal *Workforce* at *www.workforceonline.com* provides information on human resource practices. So does the Web site of the Society for Human Resource Management (*www.shrm.org*). The European Industrial Relations Observatory (*www.eurofound.ie*) collects information about labor relations developments in Europe. A site, *www.igc.apc.org/igc/labornet*, provides access to several other sites dealing with labor and employment issues. For a more academic approach, visit Cornell University's site at *www.ilr.cornell.edu*. The U.S. Census Bureau's Web address is *www.census.gov*. The United Nations Development Program's reports and statistics can be found at *www.undp.org/hdro/report.html*.

Case 11–1   THE CLOSURE OF RENAULT-VILVOORDE

It was early May in 1997, and Louis Schweitzer, chief executive of Renault, a French automobile company, was in his suburban Paris headquarters at Billancourt. He was pondering the extraordinary range of protests that his announcement on February 27 had unleashed. On that day, Renault announced that it would close its plant at Vilvoorde, north of Brussels, Belgium, by July with the loss of 4,600 jobs (3,100 in the factory itself and another 1,500 among component suppliers and subcontractors). Under strong pressure to rescind the closure decision, Mr. Schweitzer was also following the debate that had emerged about the effectiveness of European Works Councils (EWC) in preventing such plant closures.

THE AUTOMOBILE INDUSTRY

By the 1990s, the worldwide automobile industry was characterized by overcapacity and stagnating sales. As a consequence, the industry was consolidating through mergers and acquisitions. For instance, BMW (Germany) had purchased Rover (U.K.), Ford (U.S.) acquired Jaguar (U.K.) and obtained a controlling interest in Mazda (Japan), General Motors (U.S.) bought half of Saab (Sweden), and Volkswagen (Germany) bought a 70 percent stake in Skoda (Czech Republic). Despite overcapacity, automobile companies continued building new plants in East and Southeast Asia, South America,

and Eastern Europe to take advantage of lower input costs and to easily access those emerging markets.

The overcapacity problem in Europe was immense. Capacity exceeded demand by 2 million vehicles annually; only 80 percent of the productive capacity was currently being utilized. The European companies were facing ever-increasing competition from Japanese and Korean manufacturers who were building new plants in Europe, and from cars made at low-cost plants in Central and Eastern Europe. As a result, many jobs in existing plants were being lost. As the push for greater productivity grew, overcapacity increased, resulting in even more layoffs.

Because an automobile plant created high-paying jobs directly and indirectly (in component suppliers and distributors), governments, especially in countries or regions with high unemployment, were anxious to attract new investments. Various incentives were usually offered. The EU also provided subsidies, through its European Regional Development Fund, to firms locating facilities in the Union's impoverished areas.

Employers had long claimed that wages and indirect labor costs had an important impact on location decisions. Unions had rejected such claims arguing that other factors such as infrastructure, proximity to markets, level of workforce training, productivity, and quality were more important considerations.

Industrialists, both European and foreign, called upon the EU and the governments of its member countries to address the issues of high labor costs and a "suitable business environment to attract investment and boost job creation." Unions too had called for cuts in the indirect costs of employment, reduction in working times, and policies to encourage economic growth. At the same time, with the member countries preparing for admission to the European Monetary Union in 1998, the need to meet certain economic criteria in support of a single currency meant that generous aid to help laid-off workers or bail out financially strapped firms was not going to be forthcoming.

RENAULT

Renault was the largest automobile company in France. The French government had partially privatized the firm and in 1997, its share of the company's equity was less than half (46 percent). The company had set itself an ambitious target of doubling its global sales to 4 million by 2010. In 1997, sales were expected to slow in the French market after the removal of government-sponsored incentives, which had bolstered the market over the previous two years. Apart from Europe, the company also sold its cars and trucks in Southeast Asia, Russia, and North Africa.

Due to their small size, the two French carmakers, Renault and Peugeot-Citroen, were viewed as particularly threatened by the overcapacity in the industry. They were also more dependent on the European market than their other continental rivals such as FIAT and Volkswagen. It was generally acknowledged that they had too many plants. In 1997, Renault employed 140,000 workers throughout the world, with 75 percent of them in France alone, and most of the others in the rest of Europe. The company manufactured its vehicles in 29 plants in five European countries: France, Spain, Portugal, Belgium, and Slovenia.

In 1996, Renault suffered a loss of about $1 billion. This huge loss led Renault's chief executive, Louis Schweitzer, to announce that he had no other option but to close the Vilvoorde plant. He cited the 1,900 job losses at a Volkswagen plant near Vilvoorde in 1995 as symptomatic of the problems in the industry. In fact, Renault had been downsizing on a continuous basis for about 15 years and had already reduced its workforce by half. The company wanted to restructure production so that each factory would be the sole producer of a given model, except in the case of the Clio and the Megane. The restructuring plans also called for the closing of two Spanish assembly lines and the elimination of 2,800 jobs in France.

THE VILVOORDE PLANT

The plant in Vilvoorde was established in 1925 and had been modernized in the early 1990s. The plant produced the Clio and Megane models; both of which were also produced at other plants. The plant produced 820 cars a day. In 1992, the workers had negotiated a major work rules flexibility and investment package to keep the plant functioning. The plant was generally regarded as being highly productive and achieving high levels of quality.

Belgium had a long-standing expertise in car assembly. It assembled more cars per capita (500) than any other country. Besides Renault, other companies with important assembly lines in Belgium included Ford, Volvo, General Motors, Volkswagen, and in earlier years Citroen and British Leyland. These companies employed 33,000 workers in the country. The corporate headquarters and decision-making centers of these companies, however, were not located in Belgium. Indeed, although recent developments in the car assembly had promoted specialization and more decentralized decision making, key strategic decisions remained the prerogative of headquarters, and hence, foreign centers.

The decision to close the Belgian factory had been motivated by labor costs that were 30 percent higher than the French plants. The high costs had not been offset, despite modernization, by an increase in productivity. Renault noted that while average net pay in Belgium was similar to that in France, the high level of social security contributions meant that costs were in fact 30 percent higher in Belgium than in France, and 48 percent higher than in Spain. The company considered the closure of the factory in Slovenia, but rejected it on the grounds that it afforded access to the Italian and East European markets.

The decision to close was also justified by a continuing decline in the profitability of the company and by the need to redistribute production among the remaining plants, which would also lead to the cutting of jobs in France. The final straw was the refusal of the French government to grant early retirement at age 51 to 40,000 employees, a measure requested jointly by Renault and Peugeot-Citroen in exchange for hiring 15,000 "young" people.

The closure of the plant was thus part of a wider reorganization, which would save more than $150 million per year, consolidate production, and restore the company's profitability. The company noted that the action was necessary to streamline operations and would not be reversed.

With the closure of the Belgian plant, production of the Megane and Clio models would be moved to Valladolid in Spain. Renault was expanding its plant there (which was one of four plants the company had in that country). It had asked for a subsidy of $10 million from the EU and the Spanish government to support the expansion and create 500 new jobs. Valladolid was situated in the Castille-Leon province, one of EU's poorest regions. That meant subsidies could amount to as much as 40 percent of the total investment, which in the Renault case was valued at $69 million.

INFORMATION SHARING AT RENAULT

Following the EU directive to establish European Works Councils as a forum for informing and consulting with employees in the firm, Renault voluntarily created such a body called the European Group Committee (EGC). The role of the EGC at Renault was given more depth by the provision that documents were to be sent to committee members in sufficient time "to allow in-depth exchanges and the expression of remarks and propositions by the committee." The EGC at Renault dealt with the following issues:

- Major changes in the company's composition
- The company's economic, financial, and social situation
- The production and investment situation
- The commercial situation and the development of markets
- The development of work organization and of production technologies
- The general orientations of training

As required by the EU directive, the EGC had employee representatives from the EU countries in which Renault operated—Belgium, France, Spain, and Portugal. The EGC met headquarters management annually to be informed and consulted about the firm's progress and prospects. In "exceptional circumstances," particularly where corporate restructuring proposals had a significant effect on employee interests, the EGC could seek further information and consultation meetings with management. The operating expenses of the EGC were borne by the company.

In addition to the EWC, in several European countries national laws required the establishment of works councils as consultative and decision-making forums. In France, for instance, employee representatives were elected to works councils or union delegates appointed by unions to work with managers to address workplace issues. Similar arrangements existed in Belgium.

The EU directive did not provide specific penalties for infringement, but the European Court of Justice had ruled that member states of the EU were obliged to ensure that infringements incurred penalties. Individual states were required to establish measures and procedures to adopt should the parties fail to abide by the agreements reached under the directive.

THE CLOSURE ANNOUNCEMENT

Renault informed both the Belgian and French governments in advance of its plans to close the Vilvoorde plant. In fact, Renault had informed the Belgian prime minister, Jean-Luc Dehaene, on February 21 of the company's heavy losses and had hinted that the closure of the Vilvoorde was being considered as an option. Mr. Dehaene had told the company that its proposed action was "totally unacceptable." On February 26, the prime minister was told of the closure by the Flemish regional government. Meanwhile, the company set aside $436 million to meet the cost of closing the plant including paying workers severance wages.

The agreement with the EGC provided that the committee meet "at least once a year by order of the chair," who was also the chief executive of Renault. According to this agreement, Mr. Schweitzer was under no obligation to order an extraordinary meeting of the EGC to consult its members on the closure of Vilvoorde. Thus the EGC had not been informed or consulted. Although the scope of the agreement with the EGC would appear to cover the case of a mass layoff as announced at Vilvoorde, the agreement made no specific provision for an extraordinary meeting to be called in these circumstances.

A directive of the EC on mass layoffs specified that an employer should provide the relevant authority with written notification of any planned layoffs. It obliged the employer to forward a copy of this notification to employee representatives. In this case, the federal Belgian and the regional Flemish authorities were informed a few days prior to the official announcement of the closure. The worker representatives at the work council at Vilvoorde were informed just 10 minutes prior to the closure statement being made to the media. The company had decided to give as short a notice as possible to prevent efforts by various groups to delay or cancel the closure decision.

PROTESTS OF EMPLOYEES AND UNIONS

The company's unexpected announcement on February 27 to close the Vilvoorde plant led to widespread protests against the decision. It immediately triggered a strike by the plant's workers who occupied the plant and prevented the shipment of finished cars. Renault workers across Europe went on a sympathy strike for one hour. Automobile workers in Belgium, fearing a similar fate, as well as workers in other threatened industries, also went on strike. Workers at Volkswagen, Volvo, Opel, and Ford plants in Belgium staged sympathy strikes. The Spanish trade unions came out in support of their Belgian counterparts and criticized the Spanish government for its indiscriminate use of aid requests. More than 90 percent of the workers joined the one-hour strike. Much of this activity—including Europe-wide strikes in Renault and major demonstrations—was organized by Renault's EGC with the support of the European Metalworkers' Federation (EMF). Some commentators described the unprecedented protest as the first genuine "Eurostrike." This situation was a new development, because national interests had, in the past, tended to override European-level solidarity in the context of growing competition for jobs. Following the Eurostrike, more than 10,000 workers attended a demonstration outside Renault headquarters in Billancourt on March 11. Renault workers had come from Belgium, France, Spain, Portugal, and Slovenia. A mass demonstration was held in Brussels on March 16, at which 50,000 people from across Europe demanded action from the European Commission (EC) to protect jobs and blamed the Commission for the situation at Vilvoorde.

Mr. Schweitzer met union representatives "on neutral territory" in Beauvais in France on March 19 and reiterated that the company's decision to shut down the plant was irrevocable. Speaking after the meeting, one union official complained that Mr. Schweitzer had been "like a recording," repeating everything he had already said. Union leaders urged workers to keep up the pressure, arguing that the meeting had given some indication that the timetable of the closure of Vilvoorde could be flexible. They insisted that the factory stay open until a buyer was found. Unions argued that enough work could be created to keep Vilvoorde open if hours at Renault plants across Europe were reduced by 10 percent.

In a statement issued by Mr. Schweitzer after the meeting, he merely conceded that further talks would be held on internal transfers to ease the hardship caused by the closure. Then in early April came the news that the management at Renault's subsidiary in Spain expected to introduce a third shift, lengthen the working day, and introduce Saturday shifts to make up for the closure of Vilvoorde.

On April 10, by a two-thirds majority, Vilvoorde workers voted to end their strike of five weeks and returned to work. This move was seen as part of a strategy to begin lengthy negotiations on the terms and conditions of mass layoffs. It was also felt that staying out longer could have been held against the workers. The unions said they would sue Renault to force the company to pay wages to workers who had been on strike.

European and Belgian unions were unanimous in their condemnation of Renault's decision to close its Belgian plant without prior consultations. The European Trade Union Confederation (ETUC) condemned Renault's move as "brutal and unacceptable," and a "clear infringement of European legislation on collective layoffs." It had called for the massive demonstration in Brussels in support of employment solidarity and European social policy—"the corporate conflict at Renault once again highlights the gap between the Europe of profit and the social Europe." The ETUC also reiterated its demands for the inclusion of chapters on employment and social rights in the new EU Treaty, and called for the establishment of a European code of conduct in the event of large-scale layoffs. The World Labour Confederation said that Renault's unilateral measure demonstrated to what extent relocation played a part in Europe and "condemned the way a company can ridicule procedures adopted at the international level and the nonrespect of national laws on the matter."

Renault's EGC had immediately denounced the lack of consultation, which it saw as entirely against the spirit of the directive and the agreement with the company. It called for an immediate extraordinary meeting of the full committee. In the meantime, representatives from French and Belgian unions met on March 2, and were joined by their Spanish colleagues the next day. They agreed to seek to prevent a closure of the Vilvoorde plant and explore all possible legal avenues. A protest was also staged around the extraordinary meeting of the French works council on March 6 at which management refused to allow participation of the Belgian representatives. Management finally addressed the EGC at a meeting on March 11 where it reiterated the rationale behind the closure. The EMF attacked the symbolic nature of the consultation with the workers, without any intention to reassess the options, and asked management to suspend the decision pending further consultations. This option was rejected by the company.

REACTION IN FRANCE

The management of Renault was surprised by the hostile reaction of the French government, although the company had informed the government in advance of its plans to shut down the factory. Initially slow and embarrassed, the government refused to intervene in the dispute saying that the decision was the responsibility of the management and that the government's ownership in the firm was less than 50 percent. The French prime minister, Alain Juppe, observed, "It is an autonomous company decision and as the head of government I must also respect the company's autonomy." Subsequently, facing protests from the Belgian government and the EC, French president Jacques Chirac voiced his condemnation of the way the closure had been announced, but at the same time stated that he understood the rationale behind the closure. In his opinion "the closure of factories is, alas, part and parcel of life."

REACTION IN BELGIUM

Renault's announcement was fiercely condemned in Belgium. The closure of the plant, in the Belgian prime minister's own electoral district, was bound to further aggravate the high unemployment rate in the country. Initially, the Belgian government accused Renault of sacrificing Belgian jobs to protect jobs in France. However, Renault soon announced that nearly 2,800 jobs would be shed by the company in its French operations. In any case, the relationship between the two countries came under a lot of strain. The Belgian government accused Renault of violating the directives of the EC and Belgian rules on informing and consulting employees on strategic decisions. It was argued that Renault should have informed Vilvoorde workers about the planned closure ahead of time, and workers should have been asked advice on the plan.

The Belgian government and the regional Flemish government decided to sue Renault over the procedures followed when announcing the closure. They found support from the European commissioner responsible for competition, a former Belgian socialist politician, Karel Van Miert, who agreed that management had disregarded legislation on EWC and collective layoffs. He criticized Renault's decision to close a profitable plant and said that the EC was "scandalized by this kind of behavior."

The Belgian prime minister, Mr. Dehaene, even visited Paris to talk to the French government. The Belgian government filed a complaint with the Organization for Economic Cooperation and Development (OECD) for breach of the organization's code of conduct on multinational firms. However, during a visit to Brussels by the French president, Mr. Dehaene said "that Renault has perhaps been for too long a purely state company which did not react quickly enough to market problems."

Despite all public pronouncements, the Belgian government appeared only to have lodged a complaint with the OECD against the method adopted by Renault in the closure of the Vilvoorde plant. A government spokesperson noted that any ruling by the OECD would not be legally binding but would send a "strong signal" to Renault.

REACTIONS FROM EMPLOYERS

Belgian employers and their organizations (Federation of Belgian Enterprises and Flemish Federation of Enterprises) also reacted with dismay against the closure. Their reactions focused on the manner in which it was announced. According to them, it completely lacked social responsibility, infringed all codes of conduct, and constituted a decision made without any corporate ethic. At the same time, however, the employers said they understood the inevitability of economic logic in management decisions.

OTHER ACTS OF SOLIDARITY

Several government agencies and a number of cities and companies in Belgium canceled fleet orders for Renault cars. Some companies decided not to replace older vehicles with Renaults. Individual citizens put bumper stickers on their cars that said, "This is my last Renault." The Belgian and French Conference of Bishops officially stated that it was a sign of elementary respect for humans to inform and involve employees in decisions that have such an impact on their lives. Mr. Van Miert, the competition commissioner, said he would block Renault's application for subsidies for its operations in Spain. The Spanish government suspended EU aid payments for Renault's Spanish operations.

LAWSUITS

In a case brought by a Vilvoorde employee, with union support, a Brussels industrial tribunal ruled that Renault had failed to conform to the rules on information sharing and consultation under Belgian law. The labor tribunal concluded that Renault had ignored legal procedures concerning mass layoffs, the disclosure of information to the works councils at Vilvoorde, and its obligation to negotiate the plans with union representatives on the works council. The tribunal ordered the company to restart consultations with employee representatives, thus effectively postponing (though not canceling) the closure. Mr. Schweitzer replied that the tribunal's decision would not interfere with the plans to close the plant. Senior management at Renault reacted by announcing that it would reopen the procedures under the terms of collective agreements, which meant the closure will be postponed but not de facto annulled. "Procedural issues do not change economic realities," said Martin Baert, spokesperson for Renault. Renault also lodged an appeal against the tribunal decision. Indeed, labor law experts doubted that the tribunal's decision implied any obligation for Renault to renegotiate the closure.

In another legal case brought by the Renault EGC, a magistrate's court in Nanterre in France ruled that management at Renault had failed to observe its obligations to the EGW to inform and consult it on decisions "affecting its strategic orientations and the major development of a European subsidiary such as to have repercussions at the European level." The court fined Renault only about $2,750 and suspended the closure of Vilvoorde until management had fulfilled its obligation to inform and consult its EGW. The company appealed the decision and argued that it would make no difference to its plans—highlighting that the court's decisions did not make any judgment on the merits of the closure. Management stated that it believed that it had complied fully with Belgian laws but would now start the consultation procedure.

REACTION BY THE EUROPEAN COMMISSION

The ETUC called on the EC to introduce measures to strengthen and amplify existing legislation on EWCs and mass layoffs. Renault's application for EU funding to expand Spanish operations at the same time as closing Vilvoorde raised concerns about "subsidy shopping" by multinational firms. The EC promised to look into the issue of European funds being used to replace viable operations with production in cheaper locations.

The EC and the European Parliament called for tougher measures to protect the interests of workers in the event of large-scale layoffs, transfer of operations, and relocation. Padraig Flynn, the commissioner responsible for industrial relations, employment and social affairs, questioned the deterrent effect of existing legislation for ignoring EWC directive and promised to assess the legality of Renault's actions. The majority of the European parliamentarians condemned Renault's actions. EU's Council of Ministers met to discuss how to ensure that actions such as that of Renault could be avoided. At the same time, it was acknowledged that it was up to the Belgian authorities to take action if they felt that Renault was closing the Vilvoorde plant without due consultation. In fact, the EC noted that it had no further powers to bring infringement proceedings against a company. Once a directive had been properly implemented, which it determined Renault had, the enforcement was a matter for the national authorities. However, Jacques Santer, president of the EU, noted that Renault had handled the closure of the Belgian plant poorly: "Regardless of whether they did or did not follow the directives, the spirit of the law was not respected." He went on to describe Renault's action as a "serious blow to confidence in Europe."

Mr. Flynn said he believed it was necessary to complement the existing EU rules with more general rules to make information and consultation compulsory at the level of the member countries. "The Vilvoorde case shows that we still have some way to go in order to strike the right balance between corporate or economic needs and social requirements of workers and society as a whole." The Vilvoorde affair revealed the loopholes in European social regulations, which were in themselves insufficient to force reluctant management to negotiate economic and social options with worker representatives.

THROUGH THE STORM

Louis Schweitzer wondered how long the protests would continue. The decision to shut the plant had brought into the open a whole host of issues—the effectiveness of European Works Councils, trans-European labor union cooperation, adverse publicity, industrial disputes, relationship between governments, the role of the European Commission, the use of EU subsidies for business expansion, among others. It was possible that more European legislation on social issues may be forthcoming as a result of Vilvoorde. Mr. Schweitzer took comfort in the fact that Renault had not budged from its decision to close the Belgian plant as part of its strategy to survive and that the price of the company's shares had risen sharply. Business leaders like him were doing what the EU was supposed to do: treat Europe as one giant area and rationalize production across boundaries.

QUESTIONS

1. If you were Mr. Schweitzer, would you rescind the decision to close the Vilvoorde plant? Why or why not?
2. Looking back, should Renault have handled the announcement of the closure differently? Why or why not?
3. Evaluate the role of European Works Council in this case. Did it serve any purpose?
4. If Renault had consulted and informed its European Works Council, what would have been the outcome? Why?
5. Will the Renault case lead to more regulations on the part of national governments and the EU regarding plant closures and relocations? Why or why not?

References

Adams, Roy J. 1997. The impact of the movement toward hemispheric free trade on industrial relations. *Work and Occupations* 24(3), pp. 364–380.

Blanpain, Roger. 1991. *Labour law and industrial relations of the European Community.* Deventer, The Netherlands: Kluwer Law and Taxation.

Dunlop, John T. 1957. *Industrial relations systems.* New York: Holt.

Gladstone, Alan, et al., eds. 1992. *Labour relations in a changing environment: A general overview.* Berlin: Walter de Gruyter.

Greer, Charles R., and Gregory K. Stephens. 1996. Employee relations issues for U.S. companies in Mexico. *California Management Review* 38(3), pp. 121–145.

Hackman, J. R., and Greg Oldham. 1980. *Work redesign.* Reading, MA: Addison-Wesley.

Hall, Mark, et al. 1995. *European Works Councils: Planning for the Directive.* Coventry, UK: Industrial Relations Research Institute, University of Warwick.

Levine, Marvin. 1997. *Worker rights and labor standards in Asia's four new tigers.* New York: Plenum Press.

Morales, Gerard. 1998. A new era of international cooperation for trade unions. *Labor Law Journal* 49(3), pp. 920–924.

Parks, James B. 1997. Crossing borders: The rise of a global union movement. *America@Work* 2(4), pp. 16–17.

Sanyal, Rajib. 1989. Unionizing foreign-owned firms: Perceptions of American union officials. *Labor Studies Journal* 14(4), pp. 66–81.

Streeck, Wolfgang. 1993. The Federal Republic of Germany. In Miriam Rothman, et al., eds. *Industrial relations around the world.* Berlin: Walter de Gruyter.

Taira, Koji. 1993. Japan. In Miriam Rothman, et al., eds. *Industrial relations around the world.* Berlin: Walter de Gruyter.

12

MANAGING ETHICS AND
SOCIAL RESPONSIBILITY

OPENING VIGNETTE

The *Brent Spar* was a unique and massive installation in the North Sea. It had two functions: to store oil and to offload oil from its storage tanks into tankers offshore. It was constructed as a huge floating buoy, fabricated from steel, and moored to the seabed by six anchors. Its displacement was 66,500 tons, its floating draught 109 meters; its total height 137 meters and its dry weight 14,500 tons. The operation of the *Brent Spar* was the responsibility of Shell UK Exploration and Production (Shell Expro), an operating company of the Royal Dutch/Shell Group of companies.

Following the shutdown of the installation in 1991 after 15 years of operations, Shell Expro conducted some 30 studies to review various options to dismantle it. Initial studies looked at methods of bringing it offshore for scrapping, but this was determined to be technically difficult. The most viable and environmentally sound option that emerged was deep-sea disposal. This option was described as a practical balance of technical feasibility, environmental safety, and cost considerations. The company had the proposal evaluated by an independent team from Aberdeen University before submitting it to the British government for approval. With the permission of the British government, Shell Expro made plans to carry out deep-sea disposal of the structure in the summer of 1995. The British government informed 13 other parties (12 nations and the European Union), signatories to the Oslo Convention on protection of the marine environment, of its decision. The structure would be sunk in the North Atlantic, 150 miles from land at a depth of greater than 6,000 feet.

The announcement of this plan triggered a ferocious reaction from Greenpeace, an environmental advocacy group. On April 30, shortly before the *Brent Spar* was to be towed, a group of Greenpeace activists boarded and occupied the installation illegally. To extensive media coverage, the activists hung a banner reading "Save Our Seas." Greenpeace opposed the deep sea disposal of the installation arguing that the *Brent Spar* was a "toxic time bomb" containing nearly 20,000 tons of toxic rubbish, sludge, and oil. It also charged that the disposal would set a precedent for more than 400 North Sea platforms to be "dumped at sea." And lastly, Greenpeace claimed that the matter to dispose of the *Brent Spar* had been decided secretly and argued that it was wrong on principle to dispose of waste material of any kind in the ocean. The company

(continued)

447

Opening Vignette (*continued*)

denied all these charges. It noted that in some countries it was permissible to sink or topple offshore petroleum installations when they became redundant. In the United States, the government had, since the mid-1980s, encouraged oil companies to use structures as artificial reefs in the Gulf of Mexico, on which marine life had proliferated to the great benefit of fishermen.

Over the next two months, Greenpeace mounted a campaign in continental Northern Europe, particularly Germany, against Shell. The German government, facing elections and political challenges to its environmental credentials, changed its initial position and protested to the U.K. government. The activists who had boarded the *Brent Spar* were forcibly removed under the glare of media attention. At an international conference concerned with the broad issues of North Sea pollution, various European governments called for a ban on sea disposal of oil installations, isolating the United Kingdom and Norway, the only countries which faced the problem of eventual disposal of oil structures. As Shell Expro began towing the *Brent Spar* to the disposal site, Greenpeace called for a boycott of Shell products in Germany. Two hundred service stations were damaged, two fire-bombed, and one raked with bullets. On June 20, 1995, the British prime minister publicly defended the disposal plan in Parliament. Greenpeace effectively and speedily transmitted information through satellite links and the Internet about what it was engaged in. Their spokespersons appeared on live television programs all over Europe.

International firms experience situations in which practices and behavioral expectations vary from country to country. Competitive pressures abroad force managers to choose options that they would not consider at home. In many cases, no laws and regulations compel firms to adhere. The issues, instead, are of a moral and ethical nature in the sense of "what is right and proper." Different people in different parts of the world think and believe differently, as noted by the sixteenth-century French philosopher, Michel de Montaigne, *"There are truths on this side of the Pyrenees which are falsehoods on the other."* The firm often faces a difficult set of choices—trying to reconcile competing and conflicting demands. It has to decide on actions that fit with what the firm believes to be correct, with what the host society considers to be the norm, with what the home country of the firm believes is the proper standard, and with what various advocacy groups may demand. At the same time, international firms, because of their role as foreign change agents, are more vulnerable than domestic firms to criticisms from advocacy groups, governments, and the general public. Consequently, an important managerial task is the creation and maintenance of a favorable social and political climate in which to operate the business. This chapter discusses the ethical dilemmas that confront international managers, the increasing expectation that managers pay attention to social responsibility, and the strategic steps that the international firm can take to function successfully by combining ethical conduct with the bottom line.

ETHICAL DILEMMAS IN INTERNATIONAL BUSINESS

Consider the case of a clothing retailer in the United States, which buys its line of blue jeans from a garment firm in Bangladesh. In Bangladesh, children as young as 10 work long hours for meager wages in factories where jeans are stitched. In Bangladesh, a poor country with an annual per capita income of $300, it is "normal" for such young children to work while in an advanced country such as the United States, use of child labor is prohibited and, if done, arouses moral indignation. What should the clothing retailer in the United States do? Should it cancel the contract with the garment firm in Bangladesh or should it insist that the firm adhere to U.S. labor standards? Should it claim that it is not in the business of imposing U.S. values in a foreign society and thus continue to purchase products made by child labor? Or should it at the outset refuse to do business with firms that use child labor? Additionally, should the U.S. buyer be concerned about the nature of the Bangladesh government—whether it is democratically elected or is an authoritarian regime?

These difficult questions are further compounded by the different perception of ethics on the part of the various parties. In this example of the child workers, the ethical dimensions of the contract can be seen from the perspective of the various individuals/parties.

- *The buyer for the U.S. retailer.* A large contract at a good price could mean a bigger bonus, a promotion, and career advancement for the individual concerned. Conversely, failure to obtain the contract may lead to a lower income and a stunted career.
- *The U.S. retailer.* A lower purchase price would mean bigger sales, larger profits, opportunity to grow, higher dividends, and the ability to remain competitive. Conversely, a higher purchase price would squeeze profits, reduce dividends, and curtail expansion plans.
- *The American public.* While usually not directly involved in the transaction, and given the cultural values, this large group would likely adopt an attitude that would call for the retailer to cancel the contract. The public expects a firm's behavior abroad to mirror its conduct at home. The public, however, benefits from cheaper products.
- *The Bangladeshi garment manufacturer.* This business probably exists because of its access to low-cost labor, and its ability to secure the U.S. contract is dependent on its quoting a low price.
- *The U.S. government.* The U.S. government, for foreign policy reasons (such as advancing human rights around the world), may oppose trading with Bangladesh or alternately, turn a blind eye to human rights issues in that country because of national security reasons.
- *The Bangladeshi government.* The government of Bangladesh sees the exports of garments as one of the few options it has to earn foreign exchange, create jobs, and speed up economic development. Given the large labor supply, the poverty of the people, and the desire to develop by engaging in trade, the Bangladesh society in this stage of its development accepts the employment of child labor.
- *Labor, human rights, and other advocacy groups.* These organizations, concerned at harsh working conditions in Bangladesh and the employment of child labor, would strongly protest in the United States the action of the U.S. retailer of selling products made in "unacceptable" conditions.

The dilemma is palpable for American buyers and their U.S. firms. For the American public, the correct course of action is obvious. For the Bangladeshi firm and its government, the economic compulsions suggest a behavior diametrically opposed. The U.S. government has to balance national interests with corporate and individual interests. The advocacy groups seek to pressure U.S. retailers to introduce workplace changes in Bangladesh. The hapless child worker is usually given no choice.

This case is only one illustration of the numerous situations where practices and standards vary from society to society and where business imperatives place managers in ethical quandaries. Other common situations include the following:

- Employment practices that favor one ethnic, religious, racial, or gender group over another
- The giving and taking of bribes to secure contracts or sales
- The exploitation of natural resources at the expense of the natural and physical environment
- Cooperating with the government to silence protestors so as to be able to conduct business without interruptions
- Inaccurate bookkeeping to avoid paying taxes
- Misuse of proprietary and personal information
- Threatening to close and shift operations and facilities as a way to obtain concessions
- Industrial espionage
- Marketing banned chemicals in countries with lax or nonexistent regulations
- Disposing of toxic waste and garbage by ignoring rules or accepted practices
- Duplicating software, books, movies, videos, and music without respecting copyright and patent protections

The international firm and its managers are constantly faced with the need to make ethical choices, which are mostly ambiguous and rarely clearcut. Failure to make correct choices can cost the firm in many ways: expensive legal settlements or criminal penalties, damaging media publicity, loss of key executives or restrictions on business activities, and denial of access to markets and contracts.

WHAT IS ETHICS?

Ethics refers to what is good and bad in the context of what is moral duty and obligation. The ethical international firm or manager would be expected to make decisions that are good and moral for their own sake. They go beyond what the law may require. Ethical decisions are firmly anchored and steeped in a set of individual, corporate, and societal values, which derive from the cultural underpinnings of a society. Because every society has developed its own rules regarding business conduct, notions of permissible and impermissible actions abound.

The ethical principles that guide an individual's actions are influenced by several institutions: the nation's legal system, religious authorities and their pronouncements, professional associations, and the organization in which the person is employed. The importance of these institutions varies from situation to situation. In an orthodox Islamic country such as Iran, the role of religious leaders is prominent as compared to a secular nation such as India. In the United Kingdom, professional organizations, say of lawyers and accountants, have codes of conduct for their members to live by. Many organizations have created codes of conduct by which they expect their employees to work by. In the United States, an extensive system of laws and court decisions provide guidance to employers and individuals alike.

Even though it is not always recognized, most managerial decisions are suffused with ethical implications. Ethics is an integral part of decision making because:

- Managerial decisions affect people's lives and well-being, both inside and outside the organization.
- Managers must distribute organizational resources equitably.
- Managers establish and implement rules and policies in the organization.
- Managers, in making decisions, experience role conflict between personal values and organizational demands.
- Managers are accountable for their decisions to the organization's various stakeholders.

This intertwining of ethics with management places managers in the role of having to choose courses of action that ensure ethical integrity is preserved.

ALTERNATIVE PERSPECTIVES ON ETHICS

Managers tend to believe that their own ethical standards are superior to those of their peers. In the United States, considerable attention is given in the media, in educational institutions, and in public and commercial life to the topic of business ethics. The high visibility of this issue is in contrast with most other countries. However, in countries making a transition to democracy with independent opposition parties, press, and the judiciary, ethical questions are being raised more frequently and ethical lapses criticized.

In most societies, vast differences in ethical practices exist. In Japan, where occurrence of crime is low and acts of individual honesty high, governments are frequently wracked by financial scandals, and several government ministers have had to resign in recent years on charges of corruption. Thus, it becomes hard to predict national ethical standards, which is further complicated by real or perceived differences in ethics among subcultural groups and even by gender.

In looking at the garment example from Bangladesh, four dimensions about the issue can be identified.

1. **Individual relativism.** This concept is based on the premise that an individual person or organization would decide whether a certain course of action was acceptable or not. The controlling variable is the individual's notion of what is right or wrong based on the given context. Thus, a firm is free to do what it wants or what it does not want based on its own beliefs. With regard to placing the order with the Bangladeshi garment firm, the U.S. retailer evaluates its business options and determines that buying from Bangladesh is most profitable.
2. **Cultural relativism.** This concept is based on the premise that no culture is superior or inferior to another. Culture A considers its practices to be acceptable, but culture B may find them intolerable. Culture B must then adopt the

behavior embodied in the proverb "When in Rome, do as the Romans do." Because of unique economic circumstances, children in Bangladesh must work and Americans and other foreigners should accept this reality even though child labor is not permissible in their home countries.

3. **Ethical imperialism.** Under this concept, it is assumed that home country notions of ethical conduct are correct and that they should be practiced in the host countries. This notion is embodied in the saying, "What is good for the goose, is good for the gander." In the example discussed here, the American buyer would insist on U.S. levels of working conditions and labor standards in Bangladesh.

4. **Universalism.** In contrast to the individual and society-specific dimensions of ethics, the notion of universalism is based on the belief that fundamental values and principles guide human behavior worldwide, irrespective of practices in individual societies and countries. A belief in universalism leads to the acceptance of certain codes of conduct throughout the world. To the extent that universalism is widespread, the conditions for ethical dilemmas are consequently reduced. In the example, child labor would be universally considered as unacceptable.

Managers should be able to distinguish between practices that are merely different from those that are clearly wrong. For the relativists, nothing is sacred and nothing is wrong. For the imperialists, anything that is different is unacceptable. These extreme positions give credence to the need for identifying and supporting common universal standards of behavior. Thomas Donaldson, in an article in the *Harvard Business Review* (1996), suggested that companies be guided by three principles:[1]

1. *Respect for core human values, which would determine the absolute moral standard for all business activities.* Such values would include the right of every human being to good health and economic advancement, to recognize individuals not merely as workers and resources but also as human beings, and to support the communities through good corporate citizenship.

2. *Respect for local (home and host country) traditions.* As discussed in Chapter 2, culture is a defining element of the human condition. Different cultural traditions must be respected, especially because they determine business ethics for those societies. Thus, gift giving in Japan, lavish by Western standards, should not be seen as a form of bribery. Western companies, over time, have recognized this practice, and now engage in it themselves, by setting more generous limits there than in other countries.

3. *Place importance on context to determine what is right and what is wrong.* Managers should understand the context in which various behaviors work. The context explains particular ethical conduct and shows why an action unacceptable in one country is fully compatible with the conditions in another. In India, in many businesses, nepotism in recruitment is quite widespread. This practice has to be seen in the context of a country with a huge number of unemployed people. In the United States, nepotism is the exception, not the norm.

---

[1]Donaldson, Thomas. 1996. Values in tension: Ethics away from home. *Harvard Business Review.* September–October, pp. 48–62.

Ethical values change over time. Behaviors and actions condoned at one time may not be acceptable at another time. Internal forces in a society and external pressures both bring about a change in ethical values. For instance, public frustration with corruption and crime in Italy over a long period forced widespread changes in the nature and structure of government in 1995. Similarly, demand in the United States to spare dolphins and other mammals when fishing for tuna forced many fishing exporters to the United States to change the use of drift nets for deepsea fishing and to label packaged tuna accordingly. As consumption of tobacco products came to be viewed as a public health concern in the United States, U.S. diplomatic offices overseas, which in the past would help tobacco companies gain access to foreign markets, began to support host country laws and regulations against smoking.[2] In times of rapid political, economic, and social change, as was experienced by countries in Eastern Europe in the early 1990s following the collapse of communism, problems arose that led to new opportunities and behaviors for which the existing institutions for ethical guidance had no answers. The state of ethics in such cases were in flux and caused confusion for the international businessperson.

SOCIAL RESPONSIBILITY

The issue of **corporate social responsibility** has a special resonance in international business, because a profitable foreign firm may be perceived as exploiting the host country to benefit shareholders and owners in the home country. Hence, a compelling argument may be made that while the firm pursues profits, it simultaneously should engage in responsible social behavior.

Business ethics and corporate social responsibility are closely related notions. They reinforce each other. The ethical firm is typically also a socially responsible firm. While in the discussion on ethics the focus has been on choosing the right option where multiple choices are present, the concept of corporate social responsibility emphasizes management's obligations to its numerous stakeholders.

Corporate social responsibility takes form in many ways.

- Contributing to charitable organizations
- Sponsoring local sporting teams or museum events
- Establishing educational scholarships
- Assisting local governments with planning of events
- Donating items, knowledge, and expertise
- Providing free services to special needs groups
- Conserving the environment
- Manufacturing "ecologically friendly" products
- Investing in socially responsible firms
- Creating working conditions and work rules that adhere to the standards of developed countries
- Producing safe products
- Treating effluents and waste in an environmentally sound manner

---

[2]Robbins, Carla, and Tara Parker-Pope. 1998, May 14. U.S. embassies stop assisting tobacco firms. *The Wall Street Journal*, pp. B1, B18.

<table>
<tr><td>MANAGEMENT FOCUS 12-1</td></tr>
</table>

BODY SHOP

Anita Roddick, the founder of Body Shop PLC, Britain's most successful global retailer, was also a crusader for human rights, animal rights, environmental protection, and Third World development. Since 1976, when the first store was opened in Brighton, England, the company that pioneered the sale of natural or "green" cosmetics with a political message had expanded to more than 1,600 outlets in 47 countries. In 1998, the company's profits rose 20 percent to $63 million on sales of little over $1 billion. But recent sales had slowed, partly because of competition from imitators. Although it claimed to put principles before profits, the company had been buffeted by allegations, denied by Ms. Roddick, that it misled the public over animal testing of the ingredients of certain products. Its share prices had fallen from a high of $6.06 in 1993 to about $1.50 in early 1999.

Ms. Roddick cleverly linked her products to environmentalism. Her lotions and soaps, made primarily of wholesome, natural ingredients, attracted hordes of customers. However, as new competitors entered the market, she continued to devote more and more time on social activism. These activities included helping Greenpeace, an environmental group, launch a "save the whales" campaign in 1985; Amnesty International, a group that speaks out on behalf of prisoners of conscience; and the rainforest activists Survival International and Friends of the Earth. As Anita and her husband, Gordon,

the cofounder and chairperson of the firm, spent more and more time launching environmental projects, they were ignoring the need to revamp their aging product lines. For instance, the head of finance was sent to help set up a windmill that would produce electricity for the home office.

While sales in Europe grew, in the United States they fell. Critics argued that Body Shop failed to bring U.S-targeted products to its shops, which were regarded as cluttered. "It was a different culture which we didn't understand," acknowledged Ms. Roddick about the United States. Others said U.S. consumers no longer bought into the company's political message—still popular in Europe—though Ms. Roddick denied this premise. "It's not the message that affects sales, it's dull-looking shops," she said.

In 1998, Ms. Roddick stepped aside as chief executive to become cochairperson of the company with her husband, and was succeeded by a new executive brought in from outside the company. The company stressed that despite the changes Body Shop's "core values and value system" of social responsibility would not change. It was announced in early 1999 that the company's management structure and operations would be radically altered in a continued effort to enhance profitability. One analyst noted that "this reflects a coming of age for Body Shop. It is moving from being a radical retailer to an efficient corporate retailer."

Source: Body shop or shape up? *Fortune.* April 15, 1996, pp. 119–120; Beck, Ernest. 1998, May 13. Body Shop founder Roddick steps aside as CEO. *The Wall Street Journal,* p. B14; Beck, Ernest. 1999, January 27. Body Shop gets a makeover to cut costs. *The Wall Street Journal,* p. A18.

Management Focus 12-1 examines how a cosmetics company strove to be socially responsible and how it had to juggle social activism with bottom-line compulsions.

SELECTED ISSUES IN ETHICS

Any number of ethical issues create conflicts between international firms, advocacy groups, and governments. The following discussion addresses three of these issues—bribery, counterfeiting, and industrial espionage.

BRIBERY

A recurrent issue in international management is how managers should deal with the practice of **bribery,** prevalent to a greater or lesser extent in all countries. Bribery is defined as payment, in either cash or kind, with the intent to influence public officials to grant business favors. Some international business transactions depend on the payment of large sums of money to individuals—politicians, public officials, and people similarly placed—who exercise a decisive influence over the awarding of contracts.

Surveys regularly rank countries in terms of their level of corruption, often bribery. Transparency International, a Berlin, Germany-based organization devoted to stamping out corrupt business practices, gathers survey results from corporate management and risk analysis organizations as well as information volunteered by representatives of international companies, to create an annual ranking of countries by the amount of bribery, embezzlement, and trickery involved in doing business. Table 12-1 presents a listing of the ten least and the ten most corrupt countries based on perception of corruption as measured by an index. An index score of 10.0 signifies a totally corruption-free country whereas 0.0 means a country is perceived as highly corrupt. Ninety countries were studied in 2000.

The nature and extent of bribery varies not only across countries, but also by industry and specific firm. Business transactions involving large construction projects (such as an oil pipeline) or high-value products (such as the sale of a fleet of aircraft) or a turnkey project (such as the setting up of a cellular telephone network) are more susceptible to bribes than others, because the huge money value of the transaction makes it easy to disguise illicit payments. The size of the potential contract also fosters intense competition among rival firms to bid for the contracts. Because a few key officials may be in positions to award or reject the contract, the temptation and opportunity to bribe are great. A firm may be more willing to bribe because it does not have the product or the expertise to compete with other firms on an even basis, or it is in a financial bind and desperately needs a major contract to turn itself around. The lack of a code of ethics

Table 12-1   Transparency International Corruption Perceptions Index (CPI), 2000

Top Ten Least Corrupt Countries			*Bottom Ten Most Corrupt Countries*		
Rank	*Country*	*CPI Score*	*Rank*	*Country*	*CPI Score*
1	Finland	10.0	81	Mozambique	2.2
2	Denmark	9.8	82	Kenya	2.1
3	New Zealand	9.4	82	Russia	2.1
3	Sweden	9.4	84	Cameroon	2.0
5	Canada	9.2	85	Angola	1.7
6	Iceland	9.1	85	Indonesia	1.7
6	Norway	9.1	87	Azerbaijan	1.5
6	Singapore	9.1	87	Ukraine	1.5
9	Netherlands	8.9	89	Yugoslavia	1.3
10	United Kingdom	8.7	90	Nigeria	1.2

Note: The United States had a Corruption Perceptions Index of 7.8 and ranked 14th among the 90 countries.

Source: www.transparency.de/documents/cpi/2000/cpi2000.html

or the absence of ethics training for managers in such companies also contributes to their willingness to accede to demands for bribes.

Bribes not only add to the costs of doing business, but also pose difficult ethical dilemmas and in many situations, serious legal problems. Nearly all countries have a body of rules and practices designed to combat bribery and corruption. Yet domestic law, in general, only applies to acts committed in the country in question and to the bribing of national public officials. It does not expressly cover acts conducted abroad or the bribing of public officials in foreign countries. In the legislation of the United States, the Foreign Corrupt Practices Act (FCPA) has been an exception in this respect. In other cases, a company's public image can be severely affected by negative publicity and by Internet campaigns that highlight evidence of corruption. Such firms might also lose out on hiring and retaining quality staff.

Largely because of U.S. pressure and a growing realization that corruption, including bribery, tends to undermine good governance, especially in developing nations, 34 countries signed the first Convention on Combating Bribery of Foreign Public Officials in International Business Transactions in 1997. The signatories included the 29 member nations of the Organization for Economic Cooperation and Development (OECD)—a consultative group comprised of the world's major exporting nations, except China. The treaty made bribery of foreign officials by corporations of the member countries a crime and established procedures that the firms could follow to ensure compliance. In addition, firms in treaty countries could no longer deduct the bribes they paid to foreigners from their national tax returns, which was allowed in many countries including France and Germany. It is estimated that German companies alone spent as much as $5.6 billion a year on bribes to foreign officials, most of it added to the contract price and then written off on their taxes.[3]

In addition to national laws and international agreements, opposition to corrupt activities has emerged from various sources.[4] International development agencies such as the World Bank and the International Monetary Fund have linked aid disbursements to improvements in administrative practices to eliminate corruption. Monitoring groups such as Transparency International, through its annual rankings, draw negative media attention to corrupt nations. As democratic practices have spread, opposition political parties in many countries have demanded greater openness in the awarding of contracts. Overseas banks, which are often used by bribe recipients to keep such money, have been forced to disclose such accounts and freeze them on the order of courts. Public opinion too has turned against bribery as was evidenced by the uprisings against President Suharto and his regime in Indonesia in 1998 and defeat of corrupt politicians in elections in Italy and Japan in the early 1990s.

How changes in the political system of a country affect how companies traditionally do business is illustrated by the following example. In 1998, the Mexican subsidiary of International Business Machines agreed to pay $37.5 million in cash and computer products to Mexico City to resolve a dispute over a failed database system that it sold the city. IBM de Mexico admitted that its executives had acted inappropriately in the

---

[3]Yannaca-Small, Catherine. 1995. Battling international bribery. *The OECD Observer.* No. 192, February–March, pp. 16–17.
[4]Lewis, Paul. 1997, August 13. 2 global lenders use leverage to combat corruption. *The New York Times,* p. A14.

course of selling a computer system. It all began two years earlier when officials from Mexico's governing party bought the system from IBM without competitive bidding. But the district attorney for the city, who belonged to the opposition party that came to power the next year, questioned the deal and pressed criminal charges. He also found that the system was full of glitches and did not perform to specifications. This example shows how the rules of business change when opposition parties gain power in countries such as Mexico where one party rule has been the norm for years.[5]

Efforts to reduce bribery should be welcomed by international firms. With the act becoming illegal in many more countries, cooperation among national law enforcement agencies will make it more likely that violators will be detected and prosecuted. In addition to raising the cost of doing business, bribes induce increasingly unscrupulous behavior among firms eager to secure business opportunities. In turn, though, over time, such behavior undermines the economic and social structures of the country and hurts these business firms. U.S. firms can now expect a more even international playing field.

For more than two decades, U.S. firms have adjusted to the requirements of the FCPA. Firms in foreign countries, however, will now have to develop corporate compliance programs, educate and convince their managers and employees about top management sincerity and commitment to antibribery, train employees on what is permissible and what is not permissible conduct, and closely monitor the work of its managers, consultants, and subcontractors.

Foreign Corrupt Practices Act   The FCPA identifies certain permissible and impermissible behaviors with regard to bribery for managers of U.S. firms. The law was enacted in 1977 following disclosures of a number of questionable payments made by U.S. firms to foreign government officials to gain an advantage in bidding for contracts. In one instance, Lockheed Corporation, an aerospace firm in the United States, paid an estimated $25 million to Japanese officials to help in the sale of its aircraft to Japan. Investigations revealed that more than 100 of the Fortune 500 companies admitted making questionable foreign payments, totaling more than $300 million. The law, amended several times, has three important parts: antibribery, accounting and record keeping, and penalty.

The antibribery sections make it a crime for any U.S. firm and foreign firms that issue negotiable securities on American stock exchanges to offer, promise, or make payments or gifts of anything of value to foreign officials, politicians, and political parties with the intention of changing policies or to secure the suspension of a legal norm. The law however permits certain forms of bribery. For instance, payments made to "speed up" governmental actions by lower-level officials are legal. Such "grease" payments may be made to hasten the installation of telephones, improve mail pickup and delivery, or accelerate loading and unloading of cargo.

U.S. firms are liable if evidence indicates that the company had actual knowledge that an illegal payment was made to a foreign government official to obtain a contract. Oftentimes, a firm may appoint local agents to represent its interests in a foreign country and such an agent may pay a host country government official. The U.S. firm would be liable if it knew of such payments or should have known in the normal course of business.

---

[5]Dillon, Sam. 1998, July 24. IBM. to pay Mexico City millions for failed system. *The New York Times*, p. D24.

The law also requires firms to maintain detailed records and accounts. The intention of such control systems is to make it hard for firms to hide "slush funds," give bribes, or otherwise falsify transactions. Consequently, firms have created accounting systems that prevent unauthorized transactions and permit easy audit by outside regulatory agencies.

The law specifies stiff penalties for violations. Firms can be fined up to $1 million for each violation, and individuals are liable for fines up to $10,000 and up to five years in jail. The firm cannot pay fines on individuals. Further, the government can bar an erring company or individual involved from doing further business with the U.S. government. Export licenses can also be suspended.

The U.S. Supreme Court in its interpretation of the law has permitted firms to bring a civil suit against the accused firm. In the case *Kirkpatrick v. Environmental Tectonics Corp.,* Kirkpatrick obtained a construction contract from the Nigerian government by bribing Nigerian officials. Environmental Tectonics Corp., an unsuccessful bidder for the contract, sued Kirkpatrick for damages under the FCPA, and won.

U.S. firms claimed that this law would have a chilling effect on their ability to obtain overseas business because competitors from other nations were not subject to this law. This argument presumed that overseas contracts were awarded solely on the payment of bribes. The evidence is mixed. Studies show that the ability of U.S. firms to secure contracts overseas has not been stymied. Indeed, U.S. exports to so-called bribe-prone countries have increased faster than exports to countries that are not considered bribe-prone. While the payment of bribes to obtain business may often be exaggerated, over the years, several companies and their managers have been prosecuted for violating this law. Instead, U.S. firms have sought to create an edge over their rivals in the areas of customer service, quality of products, product features, a thorough study of the foreign market and its culture, and by competitive pricing.

To ensure that U.S. firms and their managers do not violate the FCPA, a firm's employees must be familiar with the law. Training courses should focus on the following aspects:

- The various types of permissible and nonpermissible payments
- Recognizing the rank, status, and position of the foreign person who is requesting payment or who is to be paid
- Selecting a reputable foreign agent
- Briefing foreign agents about the clauses of the act
- Payments for "miscellaneous" expenses
- Sources where legal counsel can be obtained, including the U.S. Department of Justice
- Familiarity with business customs, practices, and laws in the foreign country
- Reference to the company's own code of ethics
- Recognizing and resolving ethical dilemmas

Despite the law's strict provisions, a study revealed that more than 90 percent of the U.S. company directors believed their competitors occasionally or regularly used intermediaries to circumvent anticorruption legislation in competition for contracts. This claim would suggest that incidents of corruption appear to be widespread despite the FCPA. The study indicated that country managers and middle-ranking managers, as the persons under pressure to deliver results, were most likely to succumb to the temptation to pay bribes. Even though more education and support is needed for executives at this level, companies also need to pay attention to the conditions under which agents or intermediaries are employed. Of course, hiding behind agents does not exempt a U.S. company or its executives from prosecution under the FCPA.[6]

COUNTERFEITING

Losses from counterfeiting are difficult to measure. It is estimated, however, that it costs $200 billion every year to U.S. businesses alone. An estimated 5 percent of products sold worldwide are ersatz, and almost everything is copied, from Windows 98 software to Similac baby formula to Delco auto parts. According to one estimate, nearly 200 million illegal compact disks are stamped out each year, almost 60 percent of them from China. The International Anticounterfeiting Coalition, an industry-funded group in Washington, D.C., believes 70 percent of medicines sold in developing countries are knockoffs. An attorney for Microsoft, Anne Murphy said, *"We refer to some countries in Asia as one-disk markets. More than 99 percent of the software is illegal copies."* Multinational pharmaceutical firms estimate that they lose about $500 million in potential sales annually in India because the Indian government recognizes patents only on the process for making the drug and not on the product itself. Consequently, when Pfizer introduced its anti-impotence pill, Viagra, pharmaceutical companies in India were busy trying to duplicate the drug by changing the method of synthesizing its molecule.[7] Table 12-2 lists countries where the most piracy of computer software occurs. Piracy rate refers to the extent to which software is illegally copied. For instance, in China, only 4 percent of the software used has been legitimately acquired.

The issue of violating copyright and patent laws has assumed great importance in the United States, the world's largest exporter of films, videos, recorded music, books, and computer software. Although many countries are signatories to international copyright pacts that ban illegal duplication and sales, some countries have either failed or are unwilling to curb illegal duplication. In 1996, an estimated $414 million was lost to Mexican pirates of U.S. music, film, and software. U.S. industries complain that Mexico fails to enforce its own laws protecting intellectual property and violates the agreements on copyright included in the North American Free Trade Agreement. From the Mexican point of view, such illicit practice has to be tolerated because it sustains thousands of poor Mexicans, especially when the economy is in dire straits.[8]

Although these complaints are the basis of intergovernmental trade disputes, the firm whose products are being duplicated without receiving royalty or license payments is the loser. It is not just loss of sales and royalties that international firms have to be concerned about, but also the high possibility of purchasing and using defective components in their production process and in the final products. Fake parts are made of inferior material and have shorter life than the genuine article. In 1989, an airplane belonging to Norway's Partnair charter airline disintegrated 22,000 feet over the North

---

[6]Montagnon, Peter. 1998, October 14. Public turning against the use of bribery. *Financial Times,* p. 5.
[7]Karp, Jonathan. 1998, July 10. Awaiting knockoffs, Indians buy black-market Viagra. *The Wall Street Journal,* pp. B1, B5.
[8]Varelo, Rogelio. 1998, February 20. Mexican officials, companies working to fight piracy, heighten awareness. *The Wall Street Journal,* p. B9G; Greenberger, Robert, and Craig Smith. 1997, April 24. CD piracy flourishes in China, and West supplies equipment. *The Wall Street Journal,* pp. A1, 13.

Table 12-2	Illegal Copying of Software, Leading Countries, 1997	
Country	*Total Loss ($ billions)*	*Piracy Rate (%)*
United States	2.78	27
China	1.45	96
Japan	0.753	32
South Korea	0.582	67
Germany	0.509	33
France	0.408	44
Brazil	0.395	62
United Kingdom	0.335	31
Canada	0.295	39
Italy	0.272	43
WORLD	11.382	40

Source: 1997 global software privacy report. Business Software Alliance and Software Publishers Association.

Sea, killing all 55 people aboard. The cause? Counterfeit bolts and bushings in the plane's tail. A Boeing 747 has roughly 6 million parts. By the time it is 10 years old, many of these parts will be replaced five times or more. Airlines rely on a network of dealers to keep spare parts in stock for quick availability—they lose $20,000 to $100,000 in revenue each day their planes are grounded.[9]

What can a firm do when it finds that its products are being illegally duplicated, thus hurting its sales and revenues? Before answering that question, it would be helpful to understand why counterfeiting or copyright violations occur. Counterfeiting is highly profitable, easy to do, and low on the agenda of law enforcement agencies. The building of U.S. and European plants overseas has had the unintended effect of their designs, factory equipment, and expertise falling into the hands of shady entrepreneurs. The availability of well-known brands as inexpensive counterfeits enables consumers in less-developed and politically volatile countries to be kept happy. It tips the nation's trade balances, boosting exports, and damps down demand for imports of such products. The machinery to counterfeit perfect copies is easily available and affordable.

Anticounterfeiting Strategies   Businesses have responded to counterfeiting in numerous ways. A framework advanced by Harvey and Ronkaiken (1985) distinguishes between four sets of strategies that are presented in Figure 12-1.[10] In the *withdrawal* strategy, firms exercise greater control over or limit the distribution of their products in markets where counterfeiting is widespread. In the *warning* strategy, a firm alerts consumers about counterfeits of its products, such as taking out advertisements in the local newspapers. The ads attempt to educate the consumers on how to distinguish the fake from the genuine article and to list the legal consequences of buying counterfeit products (e.g., negation of manufacturer's warranty, component failures, safety risks). The

---

[9]Stern, Willy. 1996, June 10. Warning. *Business Week,* pp. 84–92.
[10]Chaudhry, Peggy, and Michael Walsh. 1996. The piracy paradox persists. *The Columbia Journal of World Business* 31(3), pp. 34–48.

FIGURE 12-1 A Framework for Opposing Counterfeiting

prosecution strategy focuses on firms pursuing criminal litigation against the counterfeiters. Under the *hands-off* strategy, the firm pursues a low-key campaign to curb counterfeiting, unwilling to let the consumers know that illegal facsimiles of its products are available on the market. The firm is concerned that such information would lead to customers switching to a competitor's merchandise whose authenticity may be less suspect. These strategies form a continuum between a passive and an aggressive stance.

Given the severity of the problem, firms have, either on their own or through industrywide associations, sought to limit or eliminate counterfeiting. The measures they have taken include the following:

- Financing law enforcement campaigns against the manufacture and sale of counterfeit goods
- Lobbying government officials and legislators to investigate and prosecute unscrupulous firms and dealers at home and abroad
- Buying parts and components from only approved dealers and manufacturers
- Making multiple checks during receiving, inspection, and installations
- Reducing the markup on the price of products (small markup reduces the attractiveness of counterfeiting)
- Working with the home government to put pressure on the host government to crack down on illegal production and distribution
- Working with host governments to enforce their own copyright laws and honor international treaty obligations by arguing that violation of such laws and obligations could undermine the confidence of foreign investors
- Licensing producers in the host countries to produce the product on the premise that it would create a class of legal entrepreneurs in the foreign country who would have an incentive and be able to pressure their own government to crack down on the bootleg producers
- Providing financial incentives to channel members to reject counterfeits
- Reducing the time gap between when the product is released in the home country and when it is available in the host country (the longer the time gap, the greater the chance of illegal duplication)

- Producing the product in the host country to take advantage of low production costs and thus allowing it to be sold at a price consistent with the economic earnings level in that country (the inducement to copy is partly because the price of the "legal" version is prohibitive for people in poor countries)
- Reducing licensing royalty rates (reducing per-unit revenues could be made up by large volume of sales)
- Using technology to make products that self-destruct if copied
- Using private investigators to investigate and uncover piracies and publicize such findings through the media (with the effect of shaming the governments where such violations are occurring, forcing them to crack down on bootleggers)
- Forming alliances with firms in the same industry or in other industries facing the same situation and lobbying both host and home governments to enforce existing laws and crack down on bootleggers

An innovative approach to address software piracy in developed countries has been adopted in New Zealand. Supported by Microsoft, the approach is designed to help New Zealanders understand the importance of protecting intellectual property by establishing a direct link between enforcement activities and resulting benefits to the New Zealand community. The support of the community for antipiracy enforcement activities is rewarded in the form of donations to organizations needing technological assistance, equipment, and training. Microsoft hoped that involving the general community would lead to tips on copyright violations that would in turn enable the company to mount criminal complaints against the offenders. Financial settlements, obtained through litigation, are donated back to the community.[11]

National laws regarding copyright, trademark, and patent protections vary with regard to their comprehensiveness and enforceability. Trade treaties such as NAFTA have provisions that require member countries to protect intellectual property rights. In 1997, under the auspices of the World Trade Organization, an international agreement to curb counterfeiting was signed. Known as the Agreement on Trade-Related Aspects of Intellectual Property Rights, Including Trade in Counterfeit Goods (TRIPS), it requires the signatory countries to imprison and fine individuals or organizations guilty of violating copyright, trademark, and patent rights. Illegally produced goods can be seized and destroyed. Firms believe that the agreement is a first step in cracking down on counterfeiting. Often times, the U.S. government, at the behest of individual firms or industry associations has taken up cases with foreign governments to curb violation of intellectual property rights. For example, in 1998, the United States signed a copyright agreement with Vietnam with the goal of reducing illegal duplication of books, magazines, movies, videos, software, and compact disks. Under the agreement, U.S. companies and individuals can take action in the Vietnamese courts against copyright abuse and are entitled to seek enforcement of their rights. However, enforcement of laws in

---

[11]Asia-Pacific: New Zealand gets proceeds from anti-piracy campaign. Microsoft anti-piracy report. (*http://microsoft.com/europe/antipiracy/english/spring98/asiasouthpacific.htm*), p. 2.

many developing countries is uneven, and the punishment meted out for violations is not seen to be sufficiently strong to act as a deterrent to other violators.[12]

The results of all these corporate and government efforts are mixed. It is clear that these efforts have to be multipronged, sustained over the long haul, and involve close work with host and home country governments. In Mexico, for example, the government established the Industrial Property Institute to address the problem of pirating intellectual property. It created an alliance of private businesses to work with the government to update copyright laws, step up enforcement of existing laws, create new laws that clearly define piracy and have harsher penalties, and mount advertisement campaigns to boost antipiracy awareness among the populace. One reason for this effort on the part of Mexico was the apprehension that the U.S. would impose sanctions on it for violating copyright laws under Section 301 of the United States trade law.

In recent years, multinational firms have been accused of "biopiracy" by governments of developing countries. Under biopiracy, international firms have taken nature-based products (plant or animal life) that have been in existence for and used in poor countries for thousands of years, and sought to obtain a patent protection for them. In effect, by obtaining patents, the firms would now be able to claim royalty payments on the indigenous production and use of the products. In 1997, the Indian government successfully challenged a patent awarded by the U.S. Patents and Trademarks Office to the Mississippi Medical Center for the use of turmeric as a medicinal product. Under the rules of the WTO, patents are provided for inventions that qualify for their novelty, nonobviousness, and utility. The turmeric patent failed to satisfy the criteria of novelty as turmeric paste has been used to treat wounds and stomach infections for centuries by Indians.[13]

ECONOMIC ESPIONAGE

Although obtaining trade secrets and strategic plans from a competitor have long been the practice among businesses, **economic espionage**—spying to obtain vital economic information—has been on the increase. The need to obtain an edge in an intensely competitive global business environment has contributed to a huge increase in the incidence of economic espionage. Corporate spying has also been aided by a more mobile workforce, technical gizmos that allow vast amounts of information to be compressed into small packages and smuggled out of offices and across borders, and the great value placed on a firm's intellectual property. With the end of the Cold War, rivalry among nations has shifted to the economic arena and in many countries, government intelligence and security agencies now direct their efforts to obtain economic information about other countries and firms on behalf of domestic firms and industries. In Russia, one of the KGB's spokespeople claimed that the secret service is *"gathering economic intelligence, which we can then sell to Soviet enterprises to help them from being hoodwinked by foreign trading partners."* And of course, today, many more secrets increase the opportunity to steal more than ever before.[14]

---

[12]Birchall, Jonathan. 1999, January 6. U.S. tries to close last Asian refuge of CD pirates. *Financial Times*, p. 7.
[13]India: Bio-piracy campaign victory against turmeric patent (*http://gen.free.de/gentech/1997/Sep-Oct/*), p. 3.
[14]Farnham, Alan. 1997, September 8. How safe are your secrets? *Fortune*, pp. 114–120.

It is estimated that in 1997 alone, intellectual property losses from foreign and domestic espionage in the United States may have exceeded $300 billion. The American Society for Industrial Security said that more than 1,100 documented incidents of economic espionage occurred and another 550 suspected incidents could not be fully documented. According to the Federal Bureau of Investigation (FBI), governments of at least 23 countries including France, Germany, Israel, China, Russia, and South Korea have targeted U.S. companies. The FBI's caseload of corporate spying doubled to 800 from 1994 to 1995.[15]

U.S. high-tech firms in California's Silicon Valley are the most frequent targets of foreign spies. The spies generally look for research and development strategies, new products and processes, manufacturing and marketing plans, and customer lists. Foreign companies use a variety of techniques to obtain the information they want. They might wire tap U.S. businesspersons flying on international flights or plant individuals as employees in a U.S. firm without revealing their true allegiance. Espionage might take the forms of outright theft or bribing employees. "Netspionage" or computer-based espionage has emerged as a new security risk for companies. About 80 percent of trade secrets are stored in digital form. Talented computer hackers can copy data without leaving any trace that they broke into a computer. In effect, a company could have all its documents stolen, and never know it. Following the dislocations in the aftermath of the collapse of the Soviet Union, thousands of Russian computer scientists have been recruited by organized criminal groups to penetrate the Internet's global web of computer networks.[16]

Because of widespread concern over the growing problem of corporate spying, particularly by foreign companies, the United States enacted the **Economic Espionage Act** in 1996. The law made the theft of trade secrets a federal felony. Armed with the law, firms have filed complaints with the authorities and brought criminal lawsuits. One such case is described in Management Focus 12-2. Although the fear of jail sentences may deter corporate spies, firms have to focus on their internal control mechanisms to prevent the loss of vital business secrets. To begin, firms must conduct thorough background checks of key employees and restrict access to important documents to a select group of individuals. They can also alert employees to the possibility of being approached for information and remove disgruntled employees from key positions. Installing appropriate surveillance and security systems is also critical.

It should be recognized that firms need information about their competitors, customers, suppliers, and the government to remain competitive. Obtaining timely and fact-based data on which managers can make decisions and formulate strategy is done through industry analysis. To give themselves an edge, companies resort to obtaining **competitive intelligence**—information about their customers, competitors, suppliers, and governments. Competitive intelligence is about mining public sources of information and then using appropriate analytical techniques to put the information together creatively. It becomes illegal and unethical when firms resort to industrial espionage to obtain competitive intelligence.

[15]Nelson, Jack. 1998, January 12. Spying against U.S. firms rising. *Richmond Times-Dispatch,* p. 2; McMorris, Frances. 1998, February 2. Corporate-spy case rebounds on Bristol. *The Wall Street Journal,* p. B5.
[16]Silverman, Rachel. 1999, January 11. Stop, thief! *The Wall Street Journal,* p. R50; Lloyd, John. 1998, December 19–20. Freedom to corrupt. *Financial Times Weekend,* p. 10.

MANAGEMENT FOCUS 12-2

THE CASE OF THE SPYING SCIENTIST

In January 1997, Victor Lee, age 47, a chemical engineer at label-maker Avery Dennison Corporation based in Pasadena, California, entered a colleague's office, turned off the lights and wearing winter gloves began rifling through confidential plans to expand the company's operations in East Asia. Soon thereafter, Dr. Lee passed on these plans to a Taiwanese competitor of Avery's in exchange for money. Avery discovered Dr. Lee's spying when a job candidate from Taiwan informed on him. The company called the FBI, which quickly caught Dr. Lee in the act. In June, Dr. Lee admitted his guilt, and as part of the agreement, became a temporary undercover agent for the FBI.

It all began in 1989, when Dr. Lee, a native of Taiwan and a U.S. citizen, spoke at an adhesives-industry conference in Taipei. There he met P. Y. Yang, chairman of Four Pillars Enterprise Co., a Taiwanese adhesive-tape maker. Mr. Yang was interested in Avery.

Dr. Lee began working for Avery in 1986 after obtaining advanced degrees from U.S. universities. He was described by his superiors as "hard working, bright and meticulous" and rose quickly to the rank of senior research engineer, which gave him access to computer passwords and many company secrets.

Despite his success, Lee worried about his finances. Soon after the speech in Taipei, Mr. Yang and Dr. Lee met for dinner at a restaurant. Mr. Yang offered Dr. Lee periodic payments of $10,000–$15,000 for Avery trade secrets. "Just teach or tell us something we don't know," Mr. Yang told Dr. Lee. Dr. Lee neither accepted nor refused the overture. He later admitted to the FBI that by Chinese tradition his silence meant he was accepting the offer.

Soon, Dr. Lee started mailing details of Avery's products to Four Pillars. Over seven years, he leaked highly confidential secrets such as the formula for Gillette's self-testing Duracell battery labels, reports on high-quality paper-coating methods, and details of a technology that allows for high-speed application of adhesives to paper. The thefts became so routine that Dr. Lee kept a sheet of labels preaddressed to Mr. Yang in Taiwan. It is calculated that he provided more than $50 million of secrets in return for a total of about $150,000 paid to a Taiwan account controlled by his mother-in-law.

His scheme started to unravel in August 1996 when Four Pillars objected to the hiring of one of its scientists by Avery. Four Pillars threatened to sue the scientist, prompting him to give up on Avery and seek work elsewhere. But in an act of revenge against Four Pillars, he revealed to Avery officials that Dr. Lee was a spy.

"We were all shocked," said Kim Caldwell, an Avery executive vice president. The FBI was called in. With help from company employees, the bureau staged a meeting in January, purportedly to discuss the company's plans in East Asia. Dr. Lee came back to the room after business hours and was caught by an FBI video camera, winter gloves and all, rifling the plans. Confronted by the evidence, Dr. Lee first denied, then confessed to the entire scheme and agreed to cooperate with the FBI.

In September 1997, Dr. Lee invited Mr. Yang and his daughter, Sally Yang, herself a chemical engineer and a Four Pillars executive, to a hotel room in Cleveland. There, an FBI camera recorded Mr. Yang snipping "confidential" stamps off of Avery documents Dr. Lee pretended to be delivering. The Yangs were arrested the same evening at Cleveland's international airport. In 1999, a federal court convicted Mr. Yang and his daughter in the first-ever trial under the Economic Espionage Act.

Source. Starkman, Dean. 1999, April 29. Two Taiwanese executives convicted for espionage in Avery Dennison case. *The Wall Street Journal,* p. B16; Starkman, Dean. 1997, October 23. Secrets and lies: The dual career of a corporate spy. *The Wall Street Journal,* pp. B1, B4.

PREPARING FOR ETHICAL AND SOCIALLY RESPONSIBLE CONDUCT

A leading U.S. investor, Warren Buffet, is supposed to have said, *"Our reputation is our only asset. Without it, we are worthless."* International firms have begun to heed this advice in large measure because of a growing backlash against globalization and heightened activism on the part of advocacy groups. International firms are being forced to respond to public concerns and expectations. In 1999, Monsanto had to abandon research and production of genetically modified (GM) foods in the face of protests against such foods in Europe. As the opening vignette showed, Shell, despite working with independent agencies and the government to dispose of the *Brent Spar,* had to contend with opposition from other advocacy groups.

How can firms prepare themselves and their managers to handle ethical dilemmas and to conduct themselves in a socially responsible manner? As businesses have developed various ways to do this, managers should bear in mind five key principles, which are presented in Table 12-3.

CORPORATE CODES OF CONDUCT

Ninety percent of Fortune 500 firms have a **corporate code of conduct.** A code of conduct attempts to articulate the organization's values and culture and creates a set of guidelines for managers to work by. Codes are effective if they specify the organization's

---

Table 12-3   Managing Corporate Reputation

1. Protect the interests of the host community

E.g., A global consumer beverage company that takes over smaller local brands should demonstrate that it brings more than another cola to the host country. It should bring in new distribution technology, leading edge marketing methods, and innovative management.

2. Treat customers as intelligent buyers

E.g., Misleading consumers does not work over the long haul because buyers invariably find out that they have been cheated. Monsanto was slow to recognize that European consumers wanted a choice between GM and non-GM foods. By insisting that GM foods were superior, Monsanto came to be seen as arrogant.

3. Recognize that customers are becoming better informed

E.g., Advocacy groups watch closely how firms treat their stakeholders, and then use the Internet and the mass media extensively to report their findings and views. An informed public requires convincing answers from the firm and is a force that is nearly impossible to ignore.

4. Develop a code of conduct

E.g., Just because certain behaviors are possible in a setting due to absence of local legislation does not mean that the firm should engage in them. A code of conduct that is applied rigorously and consistently throughout its operations will enhance the firm's reputation.

5. Listen to the advocacy groups

E.g., A company that listens is likely to be in tune with the wide variety of views that exists in contemporary societies. BPAmoco, the oil company, consults with advocacy groups, governments, employees, and trading partners as part of its business activities.

Source: Glen Peters. 1999, December 7. Why nice guys finish first. *Financial Times Survey,* p. VII.

position and operating practices on particular issues (such as bribery) and if they are enforced by top management. Clear directions on what to do under specific circumstances provide unambiguous guidelines to managers. A pronouncement that use of child labor in the production process is unacceptable to the firm should be backed up by guidelines on what constitutes child labor and what the action of the firm should be. Such a code must be communicated to all employees and obvious deviations from its application swiftly and effectively corrected. Firms must reassess performance and reward schemes so that ethical behavior is rewarded and unethical conduct is proscribed. It also means that a process must exist to assist employees to identify and separate the various dimensions of an ethical issue.

While many companies do nothing with their code except to have it posted on the office lobby walls, others strive to live by it. Lockheed Martin, for instance, has a Web site that gives employees, customers, and suppliers access to the company's code and the opportunity to express complaints. The Canadian telecommunications company, Nortel, provides its employees clear guidelines for ethical decision making with regard to relationships with other firms, for offering and accepting gifts and entertainment or bribes and kickbacks, for investments and securities trading, and the position or actions of family and friends. For instance, the guidelines state that if an employee has difficulty determining whether a specific gift or entertainment offer lies within the bounds of acceptable business practice, the employee should ask these guiding questions:

- Is it clearly related to the conduct of business?
- Is it moderate, reasonable, and in good taste?
- Would I feel comfortable owning up to the giving or receipt of this gift in front of other customers and suppliers? Other employees? My manager? My family? The media?
- Do I feel any pressure to reciprocate or grant special favors as a result of this gift?
- Am I certain the gift does not violate any law or business regulations?

Employees are asked to contact their manager or the company's business ethics department should concerns or uncertainties persist.[17]

Table 12-4 provides the code of conduct adopted by Reebok, a footwear products company, regarding production standards it expects its contractors to follow.

Even though codes of conduct need to be explicit to be useful, they should also be flexible enough so that managers can use their own judgment in specific contexts or settings. It is difficult to imagine how a home country-based code can be fully applied in every situation in every country. Giving discretion to the manager does not mean that the application of the code is being relaxed. Instead, it acknowledges acceptance of host country practices and an appreciation of the context in which these practices occur. Some companies, such as Rhone-Poulenc Rorer, a French pharmaceutical firm, seek input from their foreign subsidiaries to establish ethical standards and interpret ethical issues. Recognizing that small and medium-sized companies and those new to international business may be less prepared for coping with the ethical issues and social

---

[17]Living the commitments: Guidelines for ethical decision making (*www.nortel.com/cool/ethics/decision7.html*), p. 5.

Table 12-4	Production Standards at Reebok

- **Nondiscrimination**

  Reebok will seek business partners that do not discriminate in hiring and employment practices on grounds of race, color, national origin, gender, religion, or political or other opinion.

- **Working Hours/Overtime**

  Reebok will seek business partners who do not require more than 60-hour work weeks on a regularly scheduled basis, except for appropriately compensated overtime in compliance with local laws, and we will favor business partners who use 48-hour work weeks as their maximum normal requirement.

- **Forced or Compulsory Labor**

  Reebok will not work with business partners that use forced or other compulsory labor, including labor that is required as a means of political coercion or as punishment for holding or for peacefully expressing political views, in the manufacture of its products. Reebok will not purchase materials that were produced by forced prison or other compulsory labor and will terminate business relationships with any sources found to utilize such labor.

- **Fair Wages**

  Reebok will seek business partners who share our commitment to the betterment of wage and benefit levels that address the basic needs of workers and their families so far as possible and appropriate in light of national practices and conditions. Reebok will not select business partners that pay less than the minimum wage required by local law or that pay less than prevailing local industry practices (whichever is higher).

- **Child Labor**

  Reebok will not work with business partners that use child labor. The term *child labor* generally refers to a person who is less than 14 years of age, or younger than the age for completing compulsory education if that age is higher than 14. In countries where the law defines *child* to include individuals who are older than 14, Reebok will apply that definition.

- **Freedom of Association**

  Reebok will seek business partners that share its commitment to the right of employees to establish and join organizations of their own choosing. Reebok will seek to assure that no employee is penalized because of his or her nonviolent exercise of this right. Reebok recognizes and respects the right of all employees to organize and bargain collectively.

- **Safe and Healthy Work Environment**

  Reebok will seek business partners that strive to assure employees a safe and healthy workplace and that do not expose workers to hazardous conditions.

- **Application of Standards**

  Reebok will apply the Reebok Human Rights Production Standards in our selection of business partners. Reebok will seek compliance with these standards by our contractors, subcontractors, suppliers, and other business partners. To assure proper implementation of this policy, Reebok will seek business partners that allow Reebok full knowledge of the production facilities used and will undertake affirmative measures, such as on-site inspection of production facilities, to implement and monitor these standards. Reebok takes strong exception to the use of force to suppress any of these standards and will take any such actions into account when evaluating facility compliance with these standards.

Source: www. reebok.com/humanrights/product.html

responsibility roles, the foreign office of the British government has produced a manual, made available to firms and British embassies and consulates abroad. The manual provides practical advice on issues such as environmental protection and bribery.[18]

A study by the International Labor Organization (ILO) found that many corporate codes of conduct, social labeling, and ethical investment initiatives had not helped those parties the codes were supposed to benefit. Many of these initiatives are highly selective. Some, for instance, target only child labor. Few corporate codes, however, are based on accepted international standards and most are drawn up without consulting workers in less-developed countries, usually the intended beneficiaries. The ILO's analysis of 215 codes of conduct found that three-quarters contained provisions on occupational safety and health, two-thirds addressed discrimination in employment, slightly less than half concerned child labor, and about one-quarter prohibited forced labor. Though 40 percent referred to wage levels, often rather vaguely, only 15 percent made any references to freedom to join a labor union and bargain collectively. Furthermore, the codes were often not known or available or translated in the foreign locations. Monitoring varied from simple self-assessment to external audits.[19] Credibility about the code and its application invariably rises when monitoring is performed by an external independent agency.

ETHICS TRAINING

Firms train their managers by anticipating and recognizing morally ambiguous situations. A Dutch financial group, ING, trains its 83,000-strong worldwide staff in ethics using an interactive CD-ROM linked to the Internet. Employees around the world watch the same ethical dilemmas being played out on screen and discuss with their local managers how best to handle them.[20] Ethics training exercises are used to sensitize employees to potential ethical problems and to prepare them to handle the issues properly. Some firms have established ethical ombudsmen or committees to evaluate morally ambiguous situations. Executive training programs at universities as well as in-house workshop programs increasingly focus on exposing managers to ethical dilemmas and how to address them. Managers are trained so that they can ask two questions: (1) Is it possible to conduct business successfully in the host country without undertaking a questionable practice? and (2) Is the practice a violation of a core human value? If the answer to both questions is negative, then the manager should consider a practice to be permissible.

WHISTLE BLOWING

Another way to ensure ethical conduct is to encourage **whistle blowing.** Here, an employee reports unethical behavior on the part of the organization or specific individuals to an outside entity such as the media, government bodies, or special interest groups. Whistle blowing is resorted to when the employee is unable to resolve the matter within the organization. In the United States, laws usually forbid employers to discriminate against or discipline whistleblowers. In 1996, Mitsubishi Motor Manufacturing Company was faced with a lawsuit by the U.S. Equal Employment Opportunity Commission

---

[18]Parker, Andrew. 1999, January 2–3. Companies to receive guide on ethics. *Financial Times,* p. 5.
[19]Williams, Frances. 1998, November 10. Company conduct codes "fail to hit target." *Financial Times,* p. 4.
[20]Maitland, Alison. 1999, August 26. Common principles in a diverse world. *Financial Times,* p. 8.

(EEOC) after it received complaints from women employees at the Japanese firm's factory in Illinois about widespread sexual harassment. The aggrieved women complained to the government because, despite the company's sexual harassment policies, coworkers and managers allegedly engaged in improper behavior, leaving no one to whom to complain. The case of Mitsubishi is discussed in Management Focus 12-3.

RELATIONSHIP ANALYSIS

Because managers perform multiple roles (employee, manager, citizen, expatriate, and parent) and are responsible to multiple stakeholders (the firm, shareholders, host government, home government, and professional bodies), one approach is to conduct a **relationship analysis.** Such an analysis would include the following:

- Identifying the stakeholders that will be affected by a decision and the nature of their interests
- Evaluating the level of responsibilities and obligations to each of these stakeholders
- Relying on facts and information as much as possible
- Evaluating all options
- Considering ethical issues in addition to economic, political, managerial, and legal consequences
- Distinguishing clearly between culturally determined behaviors and an individual's personality and behavior
- Evaluating the impact of a decision on an individual manager's personal value system

KYOSEI

A philosophy of corporate social responsibility with origins in Japan is known as **kyosei.** Defined as a spirit of cooperation, kyosei calls for individuals and corporations to live and work for the common good. A firm that practices kyosei establishes harmonious relationships with its customers, suppliers, competitors, the governments with which it interacts, and the natural environment. The ability to pursue kyosei is based on a sound economic performance of the firm.

The five stages of corporate kyosei are presented in Table 12-5. The foundation and the first stage of kyosei is to ensure that the firm is profitable. This stage comes in the form of steady streams of cash flow, strong market share, and needed products, which are made by workers using local raw materials. This profit enables the firm to play a larger role in society. In the second stage, managers and workers cooperate with each other for the success of the firm. The interests of both parties are similar. In stage three, the firm moves its focus away from within to without and develops cooperative ties with customers, suppliers, and competitors. Customer satisfaction is deemed important to win customer loyalty. The firm works closely with suppliers to obtain high-quality inputs on time. Joint ventures and strategic alliances are sought with competitors to increase overall profits. Stage four is characterized by expansion of the firm into foreign countries not only to increase profits but also to reduce trade friction, create employment, train host country employees in advanced competencies, and introduce new technologies. After this point, the firm is ready to move into the fifth and final stage. Few companies are in this stage where the

> ### MANAGEMENT FOCUS 12-3
>
> ## SEXUAL HARASSMENT AT MITSUBISHI MOTORS
>
> In the spring of 1996, the EEOC began investigating charges of sexual harassment at the plant of auto-maker Mitsubishi Motor Manufacturing of America, Inc., a member of the largest Japanese industrial group, Mitsubishi. The automaker was charged with countenancing physical abuse of female workers, sexual graffiti, and abusive comments while management took little or no disciplinary action. Some of the women who complained and were still working at the plant complained of threats by coworkers. As one woman left a gathering of employees, another worker snapped, "Watch your back, bitch." In the class action suit filed by the EEOC, it was stated that at least 300 women who worked on the assembly line and elsewhere in the big plant had been subjected to insulting sexual innuendo and "unwanted grabbing, groping, and touching."
>
> How did the company react? It adopted a hard-line posture toward the allegations. The company denied that it permitted sexual harassment to occur on its premises. On the contrary, the company had disciplined workers in the past for harassment and regarded any such behavior as grounds for firing. Their attorney claimed, "Our policy with respect to sexual harassment is zero tolerance." It attacked the EEOC's actions as politically motivated. At the same time, the company paid 3,000 workers a day's wages to travel to Chicago to picket the EEOC office there. It also installed phone lines at the plant so employees could lobby politicians about the case. It held meetings with all the work-ers where it was noted that jobs may be lost if the company lost the case.
>
> Such tactics exposed the company to charges of intimidation, not only against the complaining employees (which is illegal), but also against a federal government agency. The negative fallout affected the more than 100 other companies that bear the Mitsubishi name in the form of hurt image. Advocacy groups such as the National Organization of Women and civil rights activist Jesse Jackson's People United to Save Humanity (PUSH) began demonstration against Mitsubishi facilities and boycotting Mitsubishi products.
>
> The company's Japanese parent did not intervene in the dispute affecting its U.S. subsidiary. However, as the backlash built, efforts began to reach a negotiated settlement. The company hired Lynn M. Martin, a former labor secretary under President George Bush, to conduct a review of its employment practices. In 1998, the company settled, without acknowledging any wrongdoing. It agreed to pay $34 million into a fund to compensate the aggrieved women and set up a number of programs aimed at preventing harassment in the future, including sensitivity training programs. At the settlement, Kohei Ikuta, an executive vice president of the U.S. subsidiary, said, "There have been problems involving sexual harassment in our plant, which required correction. We again extend our sincere regret to any woman who has been harmed."
>
> *Source:* Fear and loathing at Mitsubishi. *Business Week.* May 6, 1996, p. 35; Mitsubishi's morass, *Business Week.* June 3, 1996, p. 35; Miller, James P. 1998, June 12. Mitsubishi will pay $34 million in sexual-harassment settlement. *The Wall Street Journal,* p. B4.

firm leverages its resources and power to influence national governments to address global issues such as environmental pollution, barriers to trade, and economic poverty.

Individual managers on the front line are often faced with choosing between difficult options—the need to balance the manager's own self-interest (in terms of promotion, pay, bonuses, and workplace success) with the employer's interests (profit-making, return on investment, and market share) and societal expectations (social responsibility and ethical conduct). Figure 12-2 provides a useful framework for managers to live by.

Table 12-5   The Five Stages of Kyosei

Stage 1	Economic Survival	Focus on the firm's growth and profitability
Stage 2	Cooperating With Labor	Close relationship between employees and management
Stage 3	Cooperating Outside the Company	Close relationship with customers, suppliers, and rivals
Stage 4	Global Activism	Establish operations in foreign countries
Stage 5	Partnership With the Government	Influence governments to make societal changes

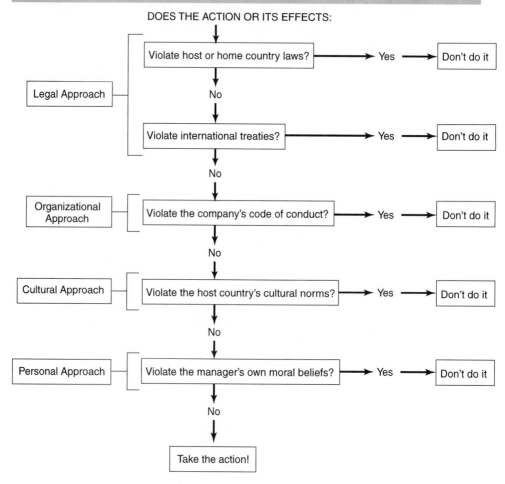

FIGURE 12-2   A Road Map for Ethical Decision Making

DOES THE ACTION OR ITS EFFECTS:

Legal Approach

Violate host or home country laws? → Yes → Don't do it

No

Violate international treaties? → Yes → Don't do it

No

Organizational Approach

Violate the company's code of conduct? → Yes → Don't do it

No

Cultural Approach

Violate the host country's cultural norms? → Yes → Don't do it

No

Personal Approach

Violate the manager's own moral beliefs? → Yes → Don't do it

No

Take the action!

CRISIS MANAGEMENT

One area where the firm's sense of social responsibility comes under severe scrutiny is when the firm is confronted with a crisis. A crisis may be caused by an occurrence in the external business environment (e.g., opposition to the sinking of the Brent Spar rig) or by failures inside the organization (e.g., allegations of sexual harassment at Mitsubishi discussed previously). The nature of the crisis may be technical, economic, people-oriented, social, or even organizational.

How does the firm respond to a crisis? In terms of social responsibility, the firm can choose strategies on a continuum, from denial at one end to responsibility at the other. In this **Crisis Response Option Model,** the four strategies in this continuum are reaction, defense, accommodation, and proaction.

- In *reaction,* the firm denies that the problem exists, or if it does, it is not the organization's fault. When Perrier water was found to contain impurities, the French firm flatly denied that anything was wrong in the production process.
- In *defense,* the firm seeks to explain the problem in legalistic terms and usually mounts a vigorous public relations campaign to project its story. In the Perrier case, the firm pointed out that the level of impurities was far below the established standards for such a product.
- In *accommodation,* the firm is compelled to assume some responsibilities, usually by various interest groups or the government. In the Perrier case, because of mounting pressure the firm agreed to buy back bottles of its water already sold.
- In *proaction,* the firm on its own takes initiative to resolve the problem. With such a strategy, the firm acknowledges the problem and goes about correcting it without delay and without prodding from various stakeholders. If Perrier had used a proactive strategy, it would have immediately accepted the test results and announced an honest investigation. In retrospect, it was apparent why the firm did not do that. Claiming that its product was "pure" meant it did not go through any chemical treatment, making it hard to explain how chemicals, however minute, got into the product. Perrier had to admit that its product was not "pure" in the first place, meaning that the water was indeed treated before being bottled.

Ideally, the socially responsible firm would pursue the proactive strategy. Many firms move along the continuum from an initial reactive strategy as the crisis unfolds. Smart managers should look beyond the immediate crisis to the longer-term effects of its current posture. In most cases, a proactive strategy is the best way to secure the future for the firm and the product.

SOFT LAWS

Several attempts have been made to create guidelines that would both regulate the conduct of multinational firms and also provide a set of pointers to help them navigate through the global ethical maze. Known as **soft laws,** these guidelines and codes are voluntary in nature and have been developed by intergovernmental bodies (e.g., Organization for Economic Cooperation and Development), national governments, and advocacy groups. While some codes have been adopted, their voluntary nature precludes adherence to them, and the enforcement of sanctions have been spotty and undocumented. The major areas these codes tend to cover are relationship between national governments, the public, and the foreign firm; environmental protection; consumer protection; employment practices; and human rights.

In 1997, the U.S. government created a voluntary, general code for U.S. companies operating abroad. Under the code, companies operating overseas would pledge to provide a safe workplace, to recognize the rights of workers to organize, and to not use either forced labor or child labor in the production of their products. The code asks the companies to report on their activities abroad.[21]

One of the most well-known voluntary codes of conduct is the **Statement of Principles** (formerly the Sullivan Principles). In 1977, Leon Sullivan, a minister who served on the board of General Motors, created a list of permissible behaviors for U.S. firms operating in South Africa during the years when the white supremacist government pursued the policy of apartheid or racial separation. The activities of U.S. firms in South Africa were tracked, recorded, and reported annually by Arthur D. Little Inc., a consulting firm, on behalf of a group of corporate executives representing the Sullivan signatory companies. Adherence to the principles was voluntary. In time, these principles acquired the stature of a moral prescription and various advocacy groups used the annual reports on compliance to put pressure on firms, on the government, and on the public. Protests in the United States forced most U.S. firms to either cease operations in South Africa or sell off their holdings to local and foreign companies. In due course, the U.S. government passed legislation making it unlawful for U.S. firms to do business in South Africa. Table 12-6 lists the seven major clauses of the principles.

The Statement of Principles encouraged other countries to develop similar guidelines for their firms doing business in South Africa. Australia, Canada, and the European Community instituted such voluntary codes. The principles were widely credited with creating international awareness about apartheid, forcing multinational firms to cease operations in South Africa, and that, in turn, served as a catalyst for the subsequent collapse of that race-based system.

SOCIAL CLAUSE IN TRADE TREATIES

Advocacy groups, particularly labor unions, have complained that multinational firms locate operations in less-developed countries to exploit low-wage workers, take advantage of poor working conditions, and ignore environmental concerns. These groups want to include a **social clause** in bilateral and multilateral trade treaties that would link labor standards to liberalization of trade. Less-developed countries would be expected to abide by internationally agreed upon standards and in return would gain trading access to the markets of developed nations. The key element of the social clause is **core labor standards**—freedom of association (right to form labor unions), prevention of child labor, prevention of forced labor, and nondiscrimination in employment. Failure to abide by such labor standards would result in trade sanctions. Including a social clause, its advocates believe, would eliminate the most egregious forms of workplace degradation and eliminate a source of what is seen as unfair competition from countries where lower production cost can be traced to the denial of elementary workplace standards and basic worker rights.

---

[21]Greenberger, Robert. 1995, March 24. Code for firms selling abroad arrives soon. *The Wall Street Journal,* p. A16.

Table 12-6	The Statement of Principles (formerly the Sullivan Principles)
Principle 1.	Nonsegregation of the races in all eating, comfort, and work facilities.
Principle 2.	Equal and fair employment practices for all employees.
Principle 3.	Equal pay for all employees doing equal or comparable work for the same period.
Principle 4.	Initiation and development of training programs that will prepare, in substantial numbers, blacks and other nonwhites for supervisory, administrative, clerical and technical jobs.
Principle 5.	Increasing the number of blacks and other nonwhites in management and supervisory positions.
Principle 6.	Improving the quality of employees' lives outside the work environment in such areas as housing, transportation, schooling, recreation, and health facilities.
Principle 7.	Working to eliminate laws and customs, which impede social, economic, and political justice.

The social clause is opposed by international firms and the governments of developing countries. The firms believe such a clause would interfere with free trade and hurt operations, which need to be flexible to remain competitive. Developing countries argue that their low costs are a source of competitive advantage, that their labor standards reflect a low level of economic development, and that the social clause is a disguised form of protectionism—to keep cheap imports from entering developed markets and to protect domestic firms. However, because of intense pressure from U.S. unions and environmentalists, the NAFTA includes side protocols covering labor and environmental issues and allow for parties to bring complaints about violating environmental and labor laws before specially designated bodies. However, these bodies do not have any enforcement powers. Efforts to include the social clause in trade agreements under the World Trade Organization have not succeeded.

RESPONSE TO SOFT LAWS

How do firms react to voluntary codes of conduct? The voluntary character of a code does not entail any kind of enforcement of its provisions. However, businesses would prefer that these codes did not exist because first, they restrict the firm's ability to fashion responses to their unique situations; second, codes imply that businesses on their own are unethical and need guidance; and third, the apprehension is that a voluntary code is a precursor to a mandatory requirement.

With no legal cost, should the firm not sign such a code and ignore it? As the experience with the Sullivan Principles showed, as the general public articulated its opposition to apartheid in South Africa, U.S. firms operating there came under mounting pressure to first sign the principles, and then to report progress under the seven clauses, and finally to stop operating there. Firms must consider carefully the implications of alternatives available to it. Essentially, a firm has three alternatives:

- Sign the code and abide by it.
- Do not sign the code and yet abide by it.
- Do not sign the code and do not abide by it.

The first option opens the firm to the scrutiny of external auditors. However, a signatory firm would have an inside role in the application of these codes and in the development of future standards. Thus, the firm would be in a position to moderate any extremist demands from the external evaluators. Additionally, being a signatory would bring the firm a positive public relations dividend.

The second option has the advantage of enabling the firm to retain its independence and be free of external audit and scrutiny. Additionally, because it is implicitly abiding by the standards, it need not fear receiving a failing grade from external sources, such as the press or the general public. However, a firm may not be able to have a forceful say if stricter rules are devised by the signatory group.

The third option is potentially harmful. The firm can be easily targeted and its activities publicized. It would be vulnerable to various forms of pressure to sign the code. Lawsuits would be harder to defend against and may trigger the government to consider more stringent rules than the existing code.

To whom do these options and codes apply? U.S.-based codes have the maximum impact on U.S. firms operating in the United States and abroad, and on foreign firms operating in the United States. They also affect the behavior of foreign firms in their home country or third countries if their business operations are substantial in the United States. A foreign firm with minimal or no U.S. presence might be able to escape the reach of these codes.

Ignoring or violating voluntary codes may trigger a wide variety of actions that could be injurious to the firm, such as the following:

1. Divestment of investment holdings by interested groups
2. Boycott of products/services
3. Demonstrations in front of the firm's offices and facilities
4. Negative coverage in the media
5. Pressure on political representatives to, in turn, pressure the firm
6. Whistle blowing by unhappy employees
7. Lawsuits

In an increasingly litigious world, a firm would be wise to develop and communicate to all concerned parties its policies on the topics the codes seek to cover. These actions might reduce the fines and costs the firm would face.

What Are International Firms Doing?   Concerned over adverse public opinion, negative portrayal in the media, and strong criticisms from advocacy groups, multinational firms have adopted a variety of measures to improve the working conditions in their operations in poor countries. Examples of these efforts by international firms are provided here:

- *Improving working conditions.* Nike, Inc., responding to criticisms, agreed to stop its contractors from employing underage workers and ensure air quality controls that match standards set in the United States. The company pledged to allow outsiders from labor and human rights groups to join independent auditors to inspect the foreign factories, interview workers and assess working conditions. Independent monitoring is deemed essential if the company's claims that it buys products made in humane conditions is to have any credibility.[22]

---

[22]Study: Nike more than adequate. *The Oregonian.* October 17, 1997, pp. C1, C3; Cushman, John. 1998, May 13. Nike pledges to end child labor and apply U.S. rules abroad. *The New York Times,* pp. D1, D5.

- *Ceasing operations.* Reebok, for instance, ceased operations in South Africa in 1986 to protest apartheid in that country. Levi-Strauss and Company, an apparel manufacturer, withdrew its contracts from suppliers in China and Myanmar in protest against human rights abuses in those countries. In 1997, Nike severed contracts with four factories in Indonesia where workers were paid below the government-set minimum wage.[23]
- *Establishing social welfare projects.* Garment exporters and advocacy groups in Bangladesh have arranged for schooling for children as an alternative to them being employed in the factories. Minimum age requirements for employment have been agreed upon.[24]
- *Working with advocacy groups.* The World Soccer Federation (FIFA) has signed a Code of Labour Practice with advocacy groups, which promises that goods endorsed by FIFA are produced without the use of child labor in a workplace where all workers are treated equally regardless of sex, race, color, religion, political opinion, nationality, or social origin, and where workers are given secure employment and afforded decent wages and conditions and have the right to be represented by a trade union of their choice. In Canada and the United States, the Chicago-based Labor Education Project influenced the Starbucks coffeehouse chain to adopt a code of conduct setting minimum working, health, and safety standards for its supplier companies. Initially focusing on coffee suppliers in Guatemala, the campaign has spread throughout Central America. Dave Olsen, Starbucks' executive, said that the company was sponsoring community development projects *"improving the lives of millions of people living in coffee producing regions."*[25]
- *Labeling products.* A label is information that the manufacturer or marketer of a product provides to consumers at the point of sale. Social labels inform the consumers about the equitable working conditions in which the product was made. An example of such labeling is Rugmark, which guarantees that hand-knotted oriental carpets are created without the use of child workers. Consumer, religious, and humanitarian groups collaborate to inspect carpet production in the Indian subcontinent and assign the Rugmark label, which is now registered as an international trademark.[26]
- *Obtaining certification of proper conduct.* In 1997, a plant of Avon Products in New York became the first factory certified as meeting standards on social accountability. The Social Accountability 8000 or **SA 8000** standard, patterned after the manufacturing quality system ISO 9000, takes into account the core labor standard principles set by the International Labor Organization. To be awarded the SA 8000 certification, a plant must pass verifiable tests on child labor, forced labor, health and safety, freedom of association, discrimination, disciplinary practices, working hours, compensation, and

---

[23]Nike cancels pacts with Indonesia plants over wage policies. *The Wall Street Journal.* September 23, 1997, p. A6.

[24]Williams, Frances. 1998, October 23. Carpetmakers agree to end child labor. *Financial Times,* p. 4.

[25]Buycott, not boycott. *World Press Review,* December 1992, p. 32.

[26]Hilowitz, Janet. 1997. Social labeling to combat child labor. *International Labour Review* 136(2), pp. 215–232.

management systems. The standards on social accountability have been developed by the Council of Economic Priorities Accreditation Agency in New York, a public interest group.[27]

An integrated approach that incorporates a variety of responses is necessary to ensure that the firm enjoys the confidence of the stakeholders. International firms have found that making piecemeal changes does not bring about systemic change in the working environment nor does it gain the approval of the advocacy groups as Management Focus 12-4 shows.

The opening vignette of this chapter sharply illustrated the limits of a "decide-announce-defend" approach on the part of Shell Expro. Although the company had complied with the laws, had the backing of the government, and had a policy based on extensive scientific and technical research and data, it had failed to anticipate the potential for emotion-driven public outrage. Indeed, the company was surprised that large segments of the population were willing to believe that the company was irresponsible enough to be destroying the seas. By focusing on technical risk and regulatory compliance, the company had not considered the effects of its decision on individuals in foreign countries and how it would be perceived by the general public. The appropriate approach should have been "dialog-decide-deliver."

PUBLIC AFFAIRS STRATEGY

Large multinational firms establish a department of public and governmental affairs to handle the tasks associated with external interface and liaison. Smaller firms assign the responsibility to specific managers. The legal department or the public relations department is often the obvious place to go for explanations and obtaining information. The public affairs office in a firm is typically a staff function and is often attached to the chief executive's office.

Given the high profile of many international firms and the close monitoring by various advocacy groups, the staffing of such departments has assumed greater importance than ever before. Managers have to keep close ties with home and host governments, with advocacy groups, customers, suppliers, and other firms. They have to respond to crises, explain the firm's conduct, and work to deflect negative publicity. To do these tasks, they develop lines of communication with various groups such as the government and political establishment, well-regarded individuals and institutions, various interest groups, the news media, the general public, and the firm's employees and stockholders.

The skills required for an effective public affairs function include the ability to scan the environment so as to understand the issues that engage the advocacy groups, the politicians, and the public. Ability to do this depends on the reliability of an extensive information-gathering system. Analysis of information is no longer limited to economists. Increasingly, they are assisted by psychologists, pollsters, advertising mavens, sociologists, and political scientists. Other important qualifications include the ability to perform a cost-benefit analysis of a public affairs effort, a high level of communication skills, and a capacity to negotiate with advocacy groups and public authorities so as to

---

[27]Bernstein, Aaron. 1997, October 20. Sweatshop police. *Business Week*, p. 39; A workplace code gains ground among multinational companies. *The Wall Street Journal*. July 16, 1998, p. 1.

GENERAL MOTOR'S
HOUSING PROGRAM IN MEXICO

Sister Susan Mika is a Roman Catholic nun who leads the Coalition for Justice in the maquiladoras. She wants higher wages and better working conditions for Mexican workers employed in U.S. businesses on the Mexican side of the border. Financed by the church as well as U.S. labor unions, Sister Susan and her supporters provide a religious cloak to their social activism.

Sister Susan and a shareholders' group persuaded General Motors (GM), the largest private sector employer in Mexico with more than 70,000 employees, to send a delegation of executives to visit the homes of workers who assemble automobile frames in the town of Ciudad Juarez, across the border from El Paso. Many lived in wooden or cardboard shacks with no plumbing or running water.

After the report was submitted, GM's chairman, John Smith, Jr., announced a program to build and sell at a subsidized price, homes to its Mexican workers. In the first phase, the company planned to build 7,000 homes. The typical house price is $13,000 with each worker needing to provide about $1,500 as down payment. GM would match the down payment and monthly payments, not to exceed 25 percent of the worker's salary, would be subtracted to pay for the 30-year mortgage. The typical house is 400 square feet, and includes one bedroom, a living room, a toilet, shower, and tile floors. The houses are built in a way that would allow additional rooms to be constructed easily. At a time when many multinational firms were attacked for running sweatshops in developing countries, GM was proud of its project. "We do care. We

have worked very hard to establish a major housing program in Mexico that no other company has done," said Mr. Smith.

This apparent act of good citizenship, however, did not win praise for the company from advocacy groups. Instead the company was criticized for not raising the wages of its workers in Mexico. For its starting or basic line workers it paid about $1.33 an hour, including benefits, compared with the average $44 an hour that union workers in the United States made. According to Mexican government labor statistics, GM's wages were about in line with average manufacturing pay. But advocates charged that the wage of about 90 cents an hour (not including benefits) left workers struggling to put food on the table. The church group complained that the housing program was still unaffordable to most workers and benefits were too few. Another nun observed, "As long as the workers are not receiving a living wage, GM still has an obligation to look at increasing the wage base."

GM responded that it cannot pay more than the prevailing wage in Mexico because doing so would damage its own competitiveness in the cutthroat global economy and hurt Mexican-owned companies compelled to respond by matching the higher wages.

Those employees who can afford them, though, welcomed the houses. GM also hoped that the housing program would boost morale and reduce turnover. The company required that the workers buying houses remain in its employment for five years, or repay the down payment.

Source: Aguayo, Jose. 1998, February 9. Saint Benedict and the labor unions. *Fortune*, p. 64; Blumenstein, Rebecca, and Dianne Solis. 1997, June 20. GM's Mexican houses on shaky ground. *The Wall Street Journal*, p. A15.

match corporate goals with the public interest in a framework of ethical and socially responsible conduct.

CONCLUSIONS

Cultural differences, intensive competitive pressures, new technologies, and variations in economic and political conditions have placed on international business managers a moral challenge of reconciling conflicting and competing interests. Ethical conduct with a proactive sense of social responsibility has now come to be the expectation of businesses. The reputation and effective functioning of firms is often determined by the ability of the managers to anticipate and make decisions that are seen to have the best interests of the society in mind. This chapter has examined the difficult choices that managers face in today's international environment and the types of strategies international firms have adopted to instill ethics and social responsibility in their conduct and policies. Often times, managers do not have any guideposts to determine the appropriate course of conduct; the law is often slow to keep pace with global changes. Consequently, the international manager, at the front line, is forced to devise suitable codes of conduct that meet both societal expectations as well as corporate goals. Employers assist by training their employees appropriately and by establishing and enforcing rules

---

OPENING VIGNETTE EPILOGUE

On June 20, 1995, citing mounting opposition by European governments, increasing protests against Shell installations in Europe, and continued interference by Greenpeace activists with the disposal operation, Shell U.K. announced that it was scrapping plans to sink the Brent Spar. The company would explore alternative ways of disposal. The British government, which had approved the deepsea disposal and had defended Shell's actions in Parliament only hours earlier, was completely taken aback by this about-face on the part of Shell. It called the company's top management "a bunch of wimps." The company's CEO apologized to the British prime minister for the embarrassment.

The *Brent Spar* was towed to a sheltered fjord, Ertfjord, Norway—one of the few sheltered anchorages in Europe deep enough to take it—and moored while new disposal options were considered. Chris Fay, chairman and chief executive of Shell U.K., commented after the episode, "The world has changed. The days when companies were judged solely in terms of economic performance and wealth creation have long disappeared. Today, companies have far wider responsibilities to the environment, to local communities and to broader society. These are not optional extras or 'icing on the cake.' Our wider social responsibilities form a fundamental and integral part of the way in which we do business, and are vital to our long-term economic performance."[28]

[28]*www.shellexpro. brentspar.com/shell/brentspar/news*

and codes. Employers also need to study a society's structure and functioning and form alliances with other firms and advocacy groups. By evaluating the short- and long-term consequences of its actions, a firm is better able to make difficult decisions. The strategic management of ethical issues is crucial, for those issues represent, in many cases, the external interface with both host and home communities, and reputations and profits can be easily lost through a failure to make the right choices.

Key Terms

- ethics
- individual relativism
- cultural relativism
- ethical imperialism
- universalism
- corporate social responsibility
- bribery
- Foreign Corrupt Practices Act

- economic espionage
- Economic Espionage Act
- competitive intelligence
- corporate code of conduct
- whistle blowing
- relationship analysis
- kyosei
- crisis response option model

- soft law
- Statement of Principles (The Sullivan Principles)
- social clause
- core labor standards
- Social Accountability 8000 or SA 8000

Discussion Questions

1. What are the main features of the Foreign Corrupt Practices Act? How can a firm prepare its managers to abide by the terms of the act?

2. Assume that a distinguished panel of internationally recognized jurists has drawn up a voluntary code of conduct requiring firms to cease doing business with or in countries that allow capital punishment of criminals. Your business comes within the ambit of this code. What would your firm's position be with regard to this code? Explain fully.

3. A French firm has established a marketing office in Warsaw, Poland, to sell computer software. The Warsaw office is able to sell only to western multinational firms in Poland. Polish firms and private individuals do not buy the firm's software but a survey indicates that they own and use the software. While usage of software is increasing, sales are not. Speculate on what is going on. What steps can the firm take to increase the sales of its products in Poland? Be specific in your answers.

4. The British beef industry has learned that because of changes in the diet of cattle, a disease could be transmitted to human consumers of beef that is sometimes fatal. It has now been reported in Spain that two persons have fallen ill and died from consuming British beef. What should be the response of the British beef industry, which depends on overseas markets for much of its profits? Apply the crisis response option model and explain the pros and cons of each of the strategy options.

5. A U.S. tobacco company with rising sales and lucrative profits in Thailand has noticed an emerging grassroots movement in that country that opposes smoking. This movement is being financed by antitobacco activists in the United States. Describe a public affairs strategy the firm should adopt in Thailand to safeguard its economic interests. Be as specific as possible.

Writing Assignment

Your company can produce a chemical that is highly effective against a pest that afflicts banana plants. The product is not approved for use in the United States because of its negative side effects on other plants. A banana company in Honduras has asked to buy a quantity of this chemical to use against a serious attack by pests to its banana plantations there. Bananas are the single largest export item of Honduras, and the industry employs thousands of workers. The Honduras government is not familiar with the product. The effect of the product in a tropical country such as Honduras is unknown. Prepare a two-page report that would ethically justify why your company should make and sell the product to the Honduran company.

Internet Exercise

Access the Web sites of three different firms in different industries and obtain their corporate codes of conduct. Compare the three codes and evaluate them. Based on information on the Web, determine the comprehensiveness of the codes, the manner in which they are communicated, how they are translated into actual practice, and their effectiveness.

Internet Resources

A wide range of information and resources on business ethics and social responsibility is available on the Internet. Accessing a site such as *www.ethics.ubc.ca/resources/ business* operated by the Centre for Applied Ethics at the University of British Columbia will introduce the reader to an extensive list of materials on ethics including the codes of conduct of many firms. Another excellent central source is the site of the Center for Business Ethics of Bentley College at *http://bnet.bentley.edu/dept/cbe/*. DePaul University also maintains a Web site that is hotlinked to numerous other sites. The address is *www.depaul.edu/ethics/newspaper.html*. The International Business Ethics Institute at *www.business-ethics.org* is yet another source. For updates on corruption around the world, the Web site of Transparency International—*www. transparency.de*—is excellent. Numerous sites on counterfeiting and piracy are available. Microsoft maintains one about software piracy at *http://microsoft.com/europe/ antipiracy.htm*. As always, use a search engine such as Alta Vista or Yahoo! to locate materials about a particular term or event.

Experiential Exercise

BUSINESS SCRUPLES

Aim: This game presents a variety of international business ethical dilemmas and forces the participants to address the problems from the perspective of an employer, employee, and member of the general public. This game is played in groups, and scorekeeping allows for identifying "winners" and "losers."

Format of the exercise: The class is divided into groups, each with an odd number of members, preferably seven. Every group gathers in a circle and every player should have a pencil and paper. The instructor will place two sets of cards describing well-defined business dilemmas in front of each group. One set contains dilemmas presented from the view of the employer, the other presents the same issues from the perspective of the employee. The same dilemma from the society's perspective is presented on an overhead screen by the instructor. A score calculation and recording chart is provided by the instructor to every group.

The play of the exercise: Each participant in a group takes a turn in playing each of the three roles: employer, employee, or member of society at large. The first player assumes the role of the employer and picks a card and reads the dilemma stated. A Yes or No decision response is required, and the player records that response in confidence. At the same time, the next person, in the role of the employee, picks a card from the set of employee dilemmas. This player too records a response without letting anyone see. The instructor presents the dilemma from the societal point of view to the entire group. The group debates the issue with the majority deciding the "right" answer to the dilemma, reflecting the general opinion of society. The employer and employee now reveal their respective responses. The views of the three groups are compared and recorded in the recording chart.

After the first dilemma is played, the game continues with the players assuming new roles. Ideally, every player should have gone through the exercise having played the roles of the employer, employee, and a member of the society. "Winners" and "losers" are determined by the scores obtained by the players as employees and employers.

The instructor determines how many dilemmas will be played.

Time: One hour; no background preparation needed.

Note: The instructor will provide several ethical dilemmas as well as the scoring chart.

Case 12–1   THE LOPEZ AFFAIR

On September 22, 1998, prosecutors in Germany announced that they had dropped their criminal case against Jose Ignacio Lopez de Arriortua stating that the matter was too complicated to sort out. Mr. Lopez was fined $225,000 with no admission of wrongdoing. A team of federal prosecutors in the United States, though, remained on the job pursuing a case that saw Mr. Lopez leave General Motors (GM) with boxes of trade secrets and go to work for the German automobile giant, Volkswagen (VW). After five years of a bruising media and legal battle, GM was now ready to close the chapter on this extraordinary incident.

THE MAN

While working at GM's European subsidiary, Adam Opel, Mr. Lopez had acquired a formidable reputation as a cost-cutter. In an industry marked by overcapacity and intense competition, GM and its rivals were actively engaged in increasing productivity, cutting costs, reducing waste, and streamlining production. In 1992, Jack Smith, GM's chief executive officer, impressed with Mr. Lopez's achievements in Europe as head of purchasing, brought him to the United States to reduce the cost of building automobiles in North America.

The contractors who supplied GM with hundreds and thousands of components feared Mr. Lopez. Compared to other automobile manufacturers, GM's costs were higher and it was feeling great pressure to cut costs. Mr. Lopez approached his job with a ruthlessness that alienated the suppliers, many of whom had relations with GM going back decades and in some case were subsidiaries of GM itself. He did not care about these relationships. He put those wanting to do business with GM through relentless rounds of bidding, then demanded that the survivors hit even lower prices. When they protested that they could not meet his impossible targets, Mr. Lopez sent teams of efficiency experts to their factories to teach them how to improve the manufacturing process. Critics said that by forcing prices down, he sent many small-scale suppliers out of business. Others credited him for making the auto industry leaner and more competitive.

With a track record of slashing costs, Mr. Lopez developed a sort of cult following among his subordinates. He called his three dozen or so top aides "warriors"; they ate a "warrior diet" (fresh fruits, no meats or coffee) and had their own rituals. For instance, whenever a bid met their pricing target, the warriors would loudly pound their fists on the table. It almost seemed that the loyalty of these managers were not to GM but to Mr. Lopez.

"Inaki" to friends, he was a physically trim, balding man, with brooding eyes, a stiff, almost formal bearing, and a melodramatic speaking style. Everyone acknowledged that he was highly charismatic and prone to dramatic gestures. For example, during a dinner at Mr. Smith's house, he grandly took his watch off his left wrist and strapped it to his right, announcing that he would keep it there until GM made record profits in North America. Mr. Smith instantly followed suit and so did the warriors—all switching to wearing watches on their right wrist.

LOPEZ'S LOVE

Lopez, born in 1941 in Amorebieta in the Basque region of Spain, retained an almost fanatical love for his homeland. He would often tell interviewers, "You need to understand the Basque," his eyes glowing. "Nobody loves their country like a Basque! The love of country for a Basque is fantastic! You will give everything for your country."

This love for his homeland led an overarching ambition to build a state-of-the-art automobile factory in Amorebieta. From the moment he arrived in Detroit, he began lobbying for "Plant X," as GM labeled it. He even assembled a consortium of banks and businesses in Basque that would help underwrite such a project.

VW WOOS LOPEZ

GM did not share Mr. Lopez's enthusiasm for a new factory in Basque country. The chairman of Adam Opel, Lou Hughes, noted that the European automobile market was in recession and could not support a new plant. Fearing that an outright rejection of Plant X would turn off Mr. Lopez, a compromise was reached under which Mr. Lopez wrote a letter to his Basque consortium stating that the project was "frozen"—on hold, but not canceled.

A few weeks later, GM's board reviewed the proposal to build Plant X in the Basque region of Spain, and rejected it. To mollify Mr. Lopez, the board promoted him to group vice president and boosted his stock options. However, to Mr. Lopez, these rewards mattered much less than getting the automobile plant for his homeland.

About this time, Mr. Lopez came into contact with Ferdinand Piech, the newly appointed chief executive officer of Volkswagen (VW). VW, although the largest automobile company in Europe, suffered from low levels of efficiency, paper-thin profit margins, and a U.S. market share of less than 1 percent. Mr. Piech needed to turn VW around quickly, and this need forced him to consider recruiting Mr. Lopez.

Secretly, in January 1993, Mr. Piech and Mr. Lopez met over two days. Mr. Lopez was given a private tour of the company's plants in Wolfsburg, Germany, and shown how inefficient the operations were. He was offered power—a promise to make him a member of the company's *Vorstand* (the management inner circle). He was offered money—a quadrupling of his annual salary to $1.6 million from the current $400,000. And Mr. Piech offered Lopez the hope that, under VW, Plant X would become a reality.

On February 15, a top VW executive faxed to Mr. Lopez, at a secure location, a proposed employment contract. On March 9, despite many public statements by him that he would remain with GM, Mr. Lopez signed the contract to join VW. The next day, he presented Mr. Smith a hand-scrawled resignation letter. He wrote: "Jack, you are the most wonderful person . . . I ever worked for. You know how much I admire you and love you." And he continued, "I must materialize this dream of building this plant . . . because it is critical for my country. They need me."

GM tried its best to keep Mr. Lopez. It offered him more money than what VW had said they would give, and a promotion to the position of president of the entire North American operations. GM also promised to build Plant X in Amorebieta. Mr. Lopez agreed to remain. But on March 15, claiming that GM's general counsel had tried to make him sign a five-year employment contract and that he no longer trusted the company, Mr. Lopez flew with his family to Frankfurt, Germany. Ultimately, Mr. Lopez was followed by seven of his warriors.

THE THEFT

GM began its detective work on March 16, 1993, the day after Mr. Lopez resigned from the company. The company's lawyers poured over phone bills, expense accounts, and freight records. They debriefed just about anyone who had ever worked for Mr. Lopez. Executives from GM's worldwide purchasing group took an inventory of Mr. Lopez's office and quickly found that a large number of valuable documents had disappeared. The documents that were missing, and according to GM, taken by Mr. Lopez in 20 cartons fell into four categories:

- A set of documents about the "Plant X" studies that aimed to cut production costs by having large portions of a vehicle assembled by suppliers—not the manufacturer—under one roof.
- Supplier information—thousands of documents and computer disks containing information on the price and sources for 60,000 automobile parts. The database on automobile parts, which ran into 4,000 pages, provided the key to buying parts at the lowest possible prices. Known as the European Purchasing Optimization System, the database had been compiled over many years and, GM claimed, would have been difficult to duplicate.
- Pictures and information on future GM cars.
- Presentation materials—slides, charts, graphs—about Mr. Lopez's program for reducing supplier costs.

GM suspected that Mr. Lopez and some of his warriors had secretly compiled materials for months, then shipped them in boxes to Mr. Lopez's brother-in-law in Spain for safekeeping. His actions would imply that Mr. Lopez had long ago planned to quit GM and that his vacillation was merely a pretext to gain time to ship out the documents.

THE LEGAL MANEUVERING

Believing that it had been betrayed, GM assembled a team to counter the damage. Two forces emerged to lead the project. One was Lou Hughes, whose passionate approach to projects had earned him the nickname "Mad Dog." As head of GM's European subsidiary, Mr. Hughes had the task of competing with VW throughout Europe. He had the most to lose from Mr. Lopez's move to VW especially if Mr. Lopez's cost-cutting methods bore fruit. He was also the executive closest to Mr. Smith and appeared to be the most personally offended by Mr. Lopez's departure. Mr. Hughes was determined to make Mr. Lopez pay. He adopted an aggressive stand and opposed any settlement unless VW got rid of Mr. Lopez.

The other force was GM's own legal department. Harry Pearce, the general counsel for the company for many years, now sat on its board of directors. The legal department had become confident and assertive following its success in defending the company against a television report that alleged that some GM pickup trucks had defective gas tanks. Mr. Pearce, a soft-spoken and supreme strategist, pushed top GM management to press a legal case against Mr. Lopez.

GM hired private investigators to uncover the extent of Mr. Lopez's deception and gather incriminating evidence. One effort focused on using an attractive young woman to ride on a bike into the path of a car driven by two of Mr. Lopez's warriors—Rosario Piazza and Jorge Alvarez—and then pretend to be hurt. The warriors came to her aid, and she eventually wheedled her way into the house but she could not uncover anything damaging.

GM also began filing lawsuits, starting with a "poaching" suit aimed to prevent other warriors of Mr. Lopez from moving to VW. A criminal complaint was filed in Germany against Mr. Lopez. Information was also leaked to newspapers, especially *Der Speigel*.

On June 22, 1993, police in Wiesbaden, near Frankfurt, seized four boxes containing documents in the apartment of none other than Mr. Piazza and Mr. Alvarez. It was learned that at Mr. Lopez's direction, the two warriors had run a huge copy-and-shred operation over several days at several secured locations. VW acknowledged that GM documents had turned up, but that Mr. Lopez had ordered them to be shredded to keep anyone at VW from using them. Until now, VW and Mr. Lopez had adamantly denied that they had done anything wrong. A VW board member even accused GM of seeking to "break VW" and of attacking "Germany as an industrial location." The language was becoming inflammatory.

At a press conference, Mr. Piech was combative. "We are in an economic war," he asserted. "We will avail ourselves of all means to emerge from this battle as the victor." He went on to suggest that the GM might have planted the papers to frame Mr. Lopez. This accusation infuriated GM, and an apology from Mr. Piech became a nonnegotiable demand.

Attempts to reach an out-of-court settlement between GM and VW failed. Mr. Hughes would weigh in saying no settlement was possible as long as Mr. Lopez remained with VW. Mr. Hughes said, "Look, this is not a question of business. This is a question of ethics."

PIECH AND VW

Ferdinand Piech was a brilliant automotive engineer with a strong streak of toughness and attention to detail. He was the wealthy grandson of Ferdinand Porsche—who founded not only the sports car company but also VW. He was described by an associate as someone who "communicates better with a car than he communicates with you and me."

Throughout the dispute with GM, Mr. Piech gave Mr. Lopez his unconditional support. He told one magazine, "I would lay my hand in the fire for him." He accompanied Mr. Lopez to a meeting with the same Basque consortium that had been assembled when Mr. Lopez was at GM. Mr. Piech was able to come up with a good reason not to proceed with building a new plant in Amorebieta. VW's Spanish operation, SEAT, had announced a huge loss of nearly a billion dollars for the year and was laying off thousands of workers. He offered Mr. Lopez the opportunity to build his super-efficient factory in Brazil where VW was doing well. The factory was completed in 1996 using the secret Plant X documents.

VW'S STRATEGY

VW was unable to counter GM's legal strategy. It went to court to stop *Der Spiegel* from publishing materials leaked to it by GM. The effort failed and alienated the German press. A subsequent defamation suit against GM was rejected by a Frankfurt court.

The company hired U.S.-based crisis management consultants who advised Mr. Piech to avoid the press and instead focus on the company's success in the marketplace. They also persuaded Mr. Piech to stop giving unflinching support to Mr. Lopez especially since new GM material had been unearthed by the police from the homes of Mr. Lopez and his warriors.

VW also hired KPMG Peat Marwick to conduct an independent investigation and who, in a report in late 1993, declared the company clean on the claims of industrial espionage. In 1994, a German TV program exposed GM's use of private detectives. In defensive reaction, GM sent rebuttal materials to every member of the German Parliament, and fired the detectives.

VW also hired Robert Strauss, a well-connected Washington lawyer. He initiated efforts to resolve the dispute and opened a secret back door communication link to GM. These efforts made little headway. Mr. Strauss was presented with a list of demands by GM: Mr. Lopez and his associates had to be fired; VW had to admit secret documents were entered into its computers; and VW had to apologize. The demands were rejected.

The delays did not appear to unduly concern VW. The KPMG Peat Marwick report had given the company a reasonable line of defense, the criminal trials were not progressing, and the media had dropped the subject. The company figured that as long as the dispute was contained in Germany, it was on strong grounds. VW was a national icon—virtually untouchable. In contrast, if the issue escalated, GM would be hurt with German consumers turning against it. GM manufactured 700,000 automobiles in Germany and fiercely competed with VW for market dominance in Europe. For the past six years, GM brand cars and trucks had been the market leaders in Europe, with 11.8 percent of the market, compared to 11 percent for VW. See Table 1 for a list of GM's important markets. More importantly, Mr. Lopez and his warriors could continue implementing their cost-saving strategies.

LEGAL COMPLAINTS IN THE UNITED STATES

By the end of 1994, GM had assembled the documents in support of its case of corporate espionage. Although criminal cases were proceeding in Germany and the U.S. Department of Justice had opened a grand jury probe in Detroit, GM decided to ratchet up its aggressive pursuit of VW. It decided to file a charge in U.S. federal court accusing Mr. Lopez and VW with collaborating in an "ongoing criminal enterprise." By invoking the Racketeering Influenced and Corrupt Organizations Act (RICCO), GM left VW open to triple damages if the charges held up in court. For the next 14 months, GM tried to club VW into submission by threatening to file the suit. It shared the draft with VW.

Negotiations on a settlement continued but on March 7, 1996, GM filed its racketeering charges. It listed Mr. Piech, Hens Neumann, the chief lawyer for VW, Mr. Lopez, and all seven defecting warriors among the defendants. In a series of decisions, the federal judge rejected VW's efforts to dismiss the case and set the stage for a trial. In retaliation, VW sued GM for defamation in Germany. However, the RICCO suit made VW realize the enormity of the consequences should it lose the case, a likelihood since it would be fought on GM's turf. The prospect of a huge triple-damage racketeering judgement—while still a long shot—created a panic. The price of VW shares plunged.

Table 1	GM/Opel's Major Markets	
Major Market	*Number of Cars Sold (in thousands)*	*Share of Total Sales (in %)*
United States	4,895	57.2
Germany	581	6.8
Canada	385	4.5
Brazil	348	4.1
Britain	335	3.9

Source: The New York Times. 1997, January 11, pp. 37, 39.

The suit in the United States also galvanized the German prosecutors. After mulling over the evidence for nearly three years, the prosecutors let it be known in October 1994 that they would probably file charges against Mr. Lopez and several of his associates.

Negotiations between GM and VW took on a new urgency. On November 29, 1996, Mr. Lopez resigned from Volkswagen. GM commented on the resignation as follows: "The resignation of VW management board member Jose Ignacio Lopez de Arriortua is a long-overdue step that has been needlessly delayed for more than three years. The harm caused to GM by the wrongful conduct of Lopez and his collaborators remains to be remedied. It is now time for Volkswagen management to address the real issues in this matter in a responsible manner rather than continue to create irrelevant side issues." VW noted that Mr. Lopez had "made excellent contributions" and "achieved much success for the company through his high qualifications as an engineer and the charisma of his personality." On December 13, 1996, Mr. Lopez and three of his warriors were indicted by the German courts for industrial espionage. In Mr. Strauss's office, a deal was struck.

THE SETTLEMENT

By the time he walked into Mr. Strauss's Washington law office, Mr. Neumann, the chief lawyer for VW, knew that GM was holding the cards. On January 9, 1997, both sides announced an out-of-court settlement of their four-year-old dispute. Under the settlement, VW agreed in principle to pay GM $100 million, to buy at least $1 billion worth of GM parts over the next seven years, and to issue a statement that acknowledged GM's "concerns with respect to possible wrongdoing"—a sort of apology. The statement in the

form of letters was exchanged between Mr. Piech and Mr. Smith. The body of the two letters are presented in Exhibits 1 and 2.

The news of the settlement was received with relief at VW's headquarters in Wolfsburg. Initially fearing a payment of $3 billion to $4 billion to GM, the amount of $100 million was seen as a small price. VW's stocks, which had slipped when Mr. Lopez was indicted in December 1996, rose at the news of the settlement to $61.025—the highest in years. VW, which had all along insisted that it had never received any documents, agreed to send GM back whatever was left from Mr. Lopez's hoard. In early March, VW returned to GM four binders of GM documents. When Mr. Lopez came to VW in 1993, the company was losing $1.045 billion. His cost-cutting methods and efforts to improve productivity had contributed to VW making a profit of $304 million in the first nine months of 1996.

For GM, the battle was over more than money. The company had felt betrayed by Mr. Lopez, especially because he had at various times insisted he had no intention of quitting. It wanted an apology of some sort and an acknowledgment by VW that it had wronged GM. GM said it had spent about $7.5 million on the entire Lopez affair. The company also spent enormous personal energy in terms of both detectives and lawyers.

After resigning from VW, Mr. Lopez returned to Bilbao, Spain, a short drive from his hometown of Amorebieta. He opened a consulting firm and waited for his trial in Germany. He had yet to accomplish his dream of having an automobile factory in his hometown. But he still wore his watch on the right wrist. "I still have a mission to accomplish," he observed. "I wear this until I have my plant. I am going to have this until I have one plant in Amorebieta."

Exhibit 1	The Letter from VW to GM

. . . This letter is part of our agreement to settle the civil disputes between Volkswagen AG on one side and General Motors Corporation and Adam Opel AG on the other side.

We confirm that Volkswagen has accepted the resignation of Messrs Lopez and Gutierrez as of November 29, 1996. Messrs Alvarez and Piazza will resign or take administrative leave no later than by the end of January 1997.

The indictment of Messrs Lopez, Gutierrez, Alvarez and Piazza brought by the Darmstadt prosecutor in December 1996 alleges illegal activities which are presently in front of a German court. Therefore, Volkswagen acknowledges the possibility that illegal activities by the individuals may have occurred. These allegations remain to be proven or disproven.

Volkswagen understands GM/Opel's concerns with respect to possible wrongdoing by the indicted individuals. Volkswagen also respects, however, the constitutional right of these individuals to be considered innocent until proven guilty.

You have informed us that GM/Opel's commencement of legal actions or public statements were not designed to harm Volkswagen's image or to defame Volkswagen or its executives. We accept this clarification and rescind any statements we have made to the contrary.

Volkswagen regrets any statements that have been interpreted to suggest that GM/Opel had planted or fabricated evidence. We do not believe that GM/Opel's actions constituted an attack on Germany as an industrial location.

Volkswagen is pleased that this letter and the actions taken allow us to bring the civil disputes to an end. We regret, as we understand GM does, that there has been such a public escalation of our disputes. The agreement reached between GM/Opel and Volkswagen creates future business opportunities for both sides, while remaining competitors in the automotive industry. . . .

Source: Reprinted from "News: Europe: Letters Exchanged in Settlement of GM-VW Dispute," p. 2, *Financial Times,* January 10, 1997, with permission.

Exhibit 2	The Letter from GM to VW

. . . This letter responds to the letter you have sent us as part of our agreement to settle and resolve the civil disputes which our management has had with Volkswagen's management over the Lopez matter.

It is regrettable, as you indicate, that this dispute between our companies escalated to such a great degree. Circumstances required that we avail ourselves of the United States civil law causes of action. We have directed our counsel to dismiss the charges made against Dr. Piech and Dr. Neumann and, pursuant to the terms of our agreement, to dismiss our complaint against the rest of the defendants as well.

Our civil complaint against Volkswagen and some of your executives did not constitute criminal charges. We will continue to cooperate fully with the public prosecutors as requested by them. General Motors and Opel necessarily will abide by and respect the judgments of the prosecutors and the outcome of their investigations and proceedings.

We are pleased that Volkswagen has acknowledged the legitimacy of our concerns and that our companies have found a satisfactory basis for the resolution of our outstanding civil disputes. We look forward to a future unencumbered by the legacy of this matter. . . .

Source: Reprinted from "News: Europe: Letters Exchanged in Settlement of GM-VW Dispute," p. 2, *Financial Times,* January 10, 1997, with permission.

QUESTIONS

1. As with trade secrets, so with highly talented managers—employers are understandably keen to hold on to such precious assets. What can firms do to stop managers from resigning to accept positions with a rival organization?

2. Was Volkswagen being ethical when it wooed Jose Ignacio Lopez with an attractive offer to make him leave General Motors?

3. Was Jose Ignacio Lopez wrong in leaving his employer, General Motors, with documents and plans, of which he was the architect?

4. In retrospect, would it have been better for General Motors to pursue a different approach to handling the departure of Jose Ignacio Lopez?

5. Given the terms of the settlement of the dispute, who won—General Motors or Volkswagen? Explain your answer.

References

Andelman, David A. 1998. Bribery: The new global outlaw. *Management Review.* April, pp. 49–51.

Calof, Jonathan. 1997. For king and country and company. *Business Quarterly* 61(3), pp. 32–39.

Chaudhry, Peggy, and Michael Walsh. 1995. Intellectual property rights: Changing levels of protection under GATT, NAFTA, and the EU. *Columbia Journal of World Business* 30(2), pp. 80–92.

Harvey, Michael, and Ilka Ronkainen. 1985. International counterfeiters: Marketing success without the cost and the risk. *Columbia Journal of World Business.* Fall.

International Business in South Africa 1995. 1995. Washington, DC: Investor Responsibility Research Center.

Kaku, Ryuzaburo, 1997. The path of *kyosei. Harvard Business Review.* July–August, pp. 55–63.

Lee, Eddy. 1997. Globalization and labour standards. A review of issues. *International Labour Review* 136(2), pp. 173–189.

OECD. 1992. *The OECD Declaration and Decisions on International Investment and Multinational Enterprises: 1991 review.* Paris: OECD, pp. 101–120.

Phatak, Arvind, and Mohammed Habib. 1998. How should managers treat ethics in international business? *Thunderbird International Business Review* 40(2). March–April, pp. 101–117.

Pitman, Glenn A., and James P. Stanford. 1994. The Foreign Corrupt Practices Act revisited: Attempting to regulate "ethical bribes" in global businesses. *International Journal of Purchasing and Materials Management.* Summer, pp. 15–20.

Stipp, David. 1996, May 27. Farewell, my logo. *Fortune,* pp. 128–140.

World Bank. 1992. *Legal framework for the treatment of foreign investment,* vol. II. Report to the Development Committee and Guidelines on the Treatment of Foreign Direct Investment. The World Bank Group, pp. 1–7.

Part I THE SETTING OF INTERNATIONAL MANAGEMENT—*MTV EUROPE AND YAHOO!*

MTV Europe and Yahoo! have taken into consideration both sociocultural and political factors when penetrating new markets abroad. In essence, the message from both companies is, "When in Rome, do as the Romans do." Both have been very sensitive to the culture, social structure, and political climate of other countries to which they have expanded, and they have customized their products and services to satisfy local demands. MTV Europe and Yahoo! have also looked at the traditions and histories of the countries in which they want to do business—China, France, Denmark, Sweden, and Mexico.

Since it was launched in 1981, MTV has become an international player, especially in Europe, by "thinking globally and acting locally." Peter Einstein, president of MTV Europe, led the charge when he said, "Be there, giving them what they want, in whatever form." MTV Europe currently reaches 77 million homes and has adopted a European strategy; It offers local versions of its satellite/cable TV network programming to compete in individual European countries. These more tightly focused offerings have gradually replaced MTV Europe's wider regional programming, and versions for the Netherlands, Spain, and Eastern Europe are now being considered.

When the network launched MTV Central Germany, it added 11.2 million homes to its customer base.

Wider regional advertisers still make up the largest share of the network's ad revenues, but the number of advertisers has tripled overall and now includes many more local advertisers.

Yahoo! is an Internet search engine with corporate offices headquartered in Santa Clara, California. Its principal product is an ad-supported Internet directory that links users to millions of Web pages on demand. The site leads the field in volume of traffic (over 95 million pages viewed each day) and is second only to Netscape in on-line advertising revenues. Yahoo! has targeted guides for geographic audiences (Yahoo! Finance and Yahoo! News), demographic audiences (Yahooligans! a Web guide for children), special-interest audiences (Yahoo! Finance and Yahoo! News), and community services (Yahoo! Chat).

The company is moving into the Internet access market through an alliance with AT&T and has agreed to acquire fellow Internet player GeoCities. Japan's SOFTBANK, the largest shareholder in Yahoo!, has 15 international Web properties outside the United States. Yahoo! now has offices in Europe, Asia, and Canada and a global network of 22 world properties. Net revenues for the first quarter of 2000 were over $228 million, a big increase over revenues for all of 1998, which were $25.6 million.

QUESTIONS

1. What do you think would have happened had MTV Europe not localized its content in each foreign market? How would that have helped MTV Europe? How would it have hurt MTV Europe?
2. How did MTV Europe approach penetrating the cultures of the various countries with which it had dealings? Give details. What approach did Yahoo! take? Give details.
3. To what extent do you think Yahoo! and MTV are exporting U.S. culture along with their products and services? How much can, or should, other companies tailor their offerings, and how much should they use their U.S. origin as an asset?
4. As a global medium, the Internet may both affect and be affected by the political environment of countries around the world. How might an Internet company such as Yahoo!, for example, undermine a country's authoritarian regime?

EXERCISES

1. Break into groups of two to three people and prepare analyses of the domestic and international environments for Yahoo! and MTV Europe. Be prepared to present your analysis to the rest of the class.

2. Use the Internet to research the problems McDonald's faces as it expands into France. Prepare a report on the cultural issues raised and decide whether you agree with McDonald's or with those who protest the "Americanization" of French culture. Give reasons for your decision.

3. Divide into small teams and assume you are the management group of a small company hoping to expand into China. Identify the political risks you face and prepare a plan for helping to minimize them.

Part II MANAGING UNDER DIFFERENT ENTRY METHODS—*LANDS' END AND YAHOO!*

This video segment shows how two very different companies, Lands' End and Yahoo!, approached the same goal—expansion into international markets. Lands' End is a retail business that sells its products through its print and on-line catalogs. Yahoo! is an Internet search engine that supplies its service to Web surfers worldwide.

A firm may decide to expand internationally for any number of reasons, including the drive to increase sales volume and the desire to access resources in other national markets. Lands' End wanted to increase sales volume in markets such as Japan, Germany, and the United Kingdom. Yahoo! wanted to dominate the global Internet industry by penetrating markets such as China, Japan, Sweden, Norway, and France.

Lands' End began in 1963 by selling sailing equipment by catalog. By the late 1970s, the focus had shifted to clothing. In 1980, the company established a toll-free phone service that operated 24 hours a day, and by 1984, the Lands' End catalog began to appear monthly. For fiscal 1999, the publicly owned firm boasted sales of $1.37 billion and currently is one of the largest apparel brands in the United States, with many specialty catalogs and a growing international reputation.

In 1991, Lands' End sent catalogs to customers in the United Kingdom for the first time, and in 1993, it opened a warehouse and phone center there. The following year, Lands' End opened operations in Japan, and in 1995, it launched its interactive retail Web site. Still building its overseas presence, Lands' End opened a phone center in Germany in 1996.

For information about Yahoo!, please refer to the video case for Part I on page 490.

QUESTIONS

1. Compare the different reasons why Lands' End and Yahoo! decided to expand internationally.
2. How did Lands' End succeed in establishing itself in the United Kingdom and Japan?
3. How did Yahoo! succeed in France and China?
4. What international issues have challenged the two companies?
5. How did Yahoo! customize its global products and services to local markets?

EXERCISES

1. Break into small groups and discuss other expansion options that Lands' End could consider, such as licensing and forming strategic alliances. Prepare a report, as if for Lands' End's top managers, on the pros and cons of each option.
2. Use the Internet to research ways in which service firms like Yahoo! are protecting their intellectual property. What copyright issues do you think might apply to a firm like Yahoo!, and what protections are available? What legal questions remain unresolved?
3. Assume you are a small manufacturer of children's clothing and are about to begin exporting abroad. What can you do to prevent counterfeiting of your designs? Prepare an action plan listing the steps you would take and why.

Part III   ORGANIZING THE FIRM'S ACTIVITIES—*TEVA AND DECKERS*

While spending his college summers in the 1980s as a boatman working on the Colorado River, Mark Thatcher fell in love with river running. Determined to avoid a 9-to-5 job, he soon saw an opportunity to fill the need for a well-made water sandal that would appeal to fellow boatmen and water sports enthusiasts. Thus, the innovative Teva sandal was born, and Mr. Thatcher literally took his first samples on the road, working out of an old pickup truck to market them to outfitters along the rivers of Arizona, New Mexico, Utah, and Wyoming. Success was almost instantaneous.

Today, there are over 60 Teva styles, in categories like casual, precision sport, wilderness, and utility. With their famous patented-strapping system, they are designed for men, women, and children, and they are just as popular for their comfort and style as they are for their hardiness in adventurous outdoor uses like kayaking and sailing. Now based in Flagstaff, Arizona, Teva (the name means "nature" in Hebrew) is still a privately owned firm with which Thatcher is closely associated. Its products are made in Costa Rica, Mexico, China, and the United States under exclusive license to Deckers Outdoor Corp. and are available, through Deckers wholesale and distribution arm, at most sporting good and specialty outdoor gear shops.

In 1996, Teva realized the great potential of the Internet in both building the brand and serving customer needs. A Teva Web site was launched, and although the company doesn't give out any figures, it's safe to say that the venture has been a great success. Danielle Schoeb, Teva's vice president of operations, feels the on-line store "has done a great deal for brand recogni-

tion." Customers from all over the world can browse, check product information, or purchase products directly from the company in the size and color they want. In fact, the ability to make the full range of products available has been one of the biggest advantages the company has gained from its Internet presence.

Still a big factor in the worldwide popularity of Teva sandals, however, is the international production and marketing savvy of Deckers, which has exclusive rights to manufacture and distribute Teva products. Deckers is based in Goleta, California, and its relationship with Teva is of long standing.

Deckers handles all the domestic and international negotiations, contracts, and agreements concerning new plant locations, raw materials purchasing, and sales to distributors at home and abroad. If a new manufacturing plant is needed overseas to increase capacity, Deckers will research sites, select a location, and negotiate all the relevant government regulations, laws, restrictions, and customs until an agreement satisfactory to all parties can be reached. If new raw materials sources are needed, Deckers investigates suppliers' ability to deliver high-quality materials on time at reasonable cost and negotiates the best possible contract. When wholesalers are ready to place their orders, Deckers assures them of receiving the styles and quantities they want, when they want them.

In all these tasks, Deckers must work with myriad government regulations and cultural norms in each of the countries in which it operates. Language differences, exchange rate fluctuations, and even ethical issues can all come into play.

QUESTIONS

1. If Deckers outsources its manufacturing to other companies overseas, what are some of the challenges it might face in ensuring that these companies adhere to high standards in their employment practices?

Sources: Scott Walters, "Taking the Trade Online," *Arizona Daily Sun*, September 26, 1999, p. 19; "Mark Thatcher," *The Pine* (NAU alumni magazine), Winter 1999, p. 9; Teva Sports Sandals; Deckers Outdoor Corp.

Does Teva have any responsibility for Decker's decisions on plant locations and labor practices, or is that Deckers' sole responsibility?

2. What are the major challenges Deckers is likely to face in interacting with different governments abroad? As Teva's strategic partner, how can Deckers develop the expertise it needs to be successful in widely differing manufacturing environments overseas?

3. Should Teva continue to let Deckers take care of all its global efforts? What are the pros and cons of letting Deckers do so much?

4. How can international firms acquire expertise in their dealings with the governments of foreign nations? Do you think Deckers faces any handicaps in building its international relationships, and if so, what are they and how can they be overcome?

EXERCISES

1. Assume that Deckers and Teva function like two divisions of the same company. Draw an organization chart that shows them in this relationship; include as many details as you can.

2. Imagine that you are the president of a growing information systems company and that you would like to win Teva as a client. Prepare a presentation for Teva's management team and outline the business functions you think your company could fulfill for Teva. Include a plan for interacting with Deckers.

3. Divide into teams of two and take the roles of a manager from the home country of an international consumer products firm and a subordinate based in a European capital city. Work together to devise a script for your monthly status meeting, making sure you include all relevant control issues you would discuss. Now work separately to determine how your meeting would be different if it took place via teleconference instead of in person. When you are finished, compare notes. Repeat the exercise with roles reversed if you like.

Part IV   MANAGING EMPLOYEES AND SOCIAL RESPONSIBILITY— *WATERFORD CRYSTAL*

While the history of glass-making in Ireland is lost in the mists of time, Waterford Crystal as it exists today began in Ireland amid the ruins of World War II, not far from the site of an eighteenth century glass factory that was the first establishment to carry the Waterford name. Begun on a small scale with workers trained by Eastern European craftsman, today's firm now dwarfs its original premises and stands for the highest quality and standards in luxury crystal products worldwide. Computer technology has been added to master craftsmanship on the factory floor, and over the last five years, the company's sales, mostly to Waterford's largest customer, the United States, have more than doubled.

According to Diarmuid Ryan, Waterford's director of human resources, today's Waterford reaches back to a long tradition of quality shared with the original, short-lived, glass-making firm. The Waterford of 1799 sought to "merit the approbation of their customers," and today the firm's mission is "to delight the world with beautiful gifts."

You might expect that a company whose traditions go back so far would experience little change. In fact, not only has Waterford survived a bitter strike and a major downsizing effort, but it has also cherished and nurtured a spirit of innovation and acceptance of change. Change has come not just in terms of bringing computer technology into its factory techniques and adding outsourcing to its manufacturing strategy, but also in the company's structure and its product lines. Indeed, new products like the millennium line account for most of Waterford's incremental sales.

When it comes to change and innovation at Waterford, Diarmuid Ryan foresees even more to come. Based on recent successes in collaborating with contemporary fashion designers to develop new products, Waterford expects its own future designers may come from the world of fashion rather than from the traditional source, the factory floor. After all, what Mr. Ryan looks for in Waterford's creative employees is an innate ability to change or, as he puts it, to "*see* the wind blow."

QUESTIONS

1. Waterford is the major employer in the small community in which it is located and often hires several members of the same family. When a firm has this kind of economic impact in its community, what do you think it should do before it undertakes any major changes in its workforce such as downsizing, outsourcing, or relocating?

2. Are human resources decisions easier for a firm when its survival is on the line? Why or why not? Do international firms face different issues when it comes to downsizing and reorganizing?

3. Waterford seeks to hire people with the innate ability to change and create innovation on their own. What special issues do international firms face in trying to hire people with particular characteristics? How can human resource managers deal with these issues?

4. One particular change that has been taking place at Waterford is the education of the employees in the workings of the business. Which employees do you think would benefit from knowing more about the financial health of the firm—all, or only those in the home country, or none? Why?

EXERCISES

1. Assume you are moving from the United States to Waterford, Ireland, to manage a new marketing initiative for the U.S. market. You are taking your spouse

and your two teenagers with you. What would you want to know about Waterford and about Ireland to prepare you for the move? Prepare a list of questions that you and your family want answered, and indicate for each where you would go to find the answers. Use as many sources as you can.

2. Suppose you have just been placed in charge of overseeing the return of expatriates, and a top executive in your firm is returning tomorrow from a year in Japan. Draft a list of tasks you will need to accomplish in order to ease her transition back to the home office.

3. Do you think international firms should adopt the ethical standards of the countries in which they operate? Select three possible ethical conflicts that can occur in international management, describe the course of action you would chose in each case, and state your reasons.

INDEX

- **The Top Rated Graduate Programs in International Business, 2000**

  1. Thunderbird Graduate School, Phoenix, AZ
  2. University of South Carolina, Columbia, SC
  3. University of Pennsylvania, Philadelphia, PA
  4. Columbia University, New York, NY
  5. Harvard University, Cambridge, MA
  6. New York University, New York, NY
  7. University of Michigan, Ann Arbor, MI
  8. Stanford University, Stanford, CA
  9. University of California, Los Angeles, CA
  10. University of California, Berkeley, CA
  11. Duke University, Durham, NC
  12. Georgetown University, Washington, DC
  13. University of Southern California, San Diego, CA
  14. Northwestern University, Evanston, IL
  15. University of Chicago, Chicago, IL
  16. Massachusetts Institute of Technology, Cambridge, MA
  17. Indiana University, Bloomington, IN
  18. University of Washington, Seattle, WA
  19. Cornell University, Ithaca, NY
  20. Dartmouth College, Hanover, NH
  21. University of Hawaii, Manoa, HI
  22. Michigan State University, East Lansing, MI

  Source: U.S. News (www.usnews.com)

- **The 25 Best Employers in the United States (Firms with over 10,000 workers and with operations abroad), 2000**

  1. CISCO, San Jose, CA, computer networking, www.cisco.com
  2. Edward Jones, St. Louis, MO, brokerage, www.edwardjones.com
  3. Charles Schwab, San Francisco, CA, brokerage, www.schwab.com
  4. MBNA, Wilmington, DE, banking. www.mbnainternational.com
  5. Pfizer, New York, NY, pharmaceutical. www.pfizer.com
  6. Microsoft, Redmond, WA, computer software, www.microsoft.com
  7. Continental Airlines, Houston, TX, airlines, www.continental.com
  8. Enron, Houston, TX, energy, www.enron.com
  9. Deloitte & Touche, Wilton, CT, consulting, www.us.deloitte.com
  10. Merck, Whitehouse Station, NJ, pharmaceutical, www.merck.com
  11. Hewlett Packard, Palo Alto, CA, computer, www.hp.com
  12. Lucent Technologies, Murray Hill, NJ, networking equipment, www.lucent.com
  13. America On-Line, Dulles, TX, Internet communication, www.aol.com
  14. Eli Lilly, Indianapolis, IN, pharmaceutical, www.lilly.com
  15. Federal Express, Memphis, TX, package delivery, www.fedex.com
  16. Capital One Financial, Falls Church, VA, finance, www.capitalone.com
  17. Intel, Santa Clara, CA, computer chips, www.intel.com
  18. Johnson & Johnson, New Brunswick, NJ, pharmaceutical, www.jnj.com
  19. Marriott International, Washington, DC, hospitality, www.marriott.com
  20. American Express, New York, NY, finance, www.americanexpress.com
  21. Dell Computer, Round Texas, TX, computer, www.dell.com
  22. Lenscrafters, Cincinnati, OH, eye glass, www.lenscrafters.com
  23. Sun Microsystems, Palo Alto, CA, computer systems, www.sun.com
  24. Ernst & Young, New York, NY, consulting, www.ey.com
  25. Starbucks, Seattle, WA, coffee shop, www.starbucks.com

  Source: Fortune (www.fortune.com)